"Raising our Sons *and* Raising our Daughters Parenting Guides *offer a wealth of resources, information, tips, and an excellent format for supporting each other as parents. I have seen a lot written in the many years I have been teaching parenting and rarely have seen a resource with such depth and breadth as this work. What I really appreciate is the power of these guidebooks to bring parents together, to connect honestly about their concerns and focus on sharing solutions ideas. It is the "village" approach to raising kids, which is more effective in the complex world we all live in today. Great job Kathy and team!*

> **Jane Nelsen, EdD, MFT** author of *Positive Discipline, Positive Discipline for Teens* and many more books on parenting

"I have not seen a more comprehensive guide for raising boys and girls than these discussion manuals. With so many down-to-earth topics and so many experts writing about what they know well, these guides are treasure troves for parents seeking reliable help for raising children in today's challenging world."

> **William Doherty, PhD**, author of *Intentional Family, Putting Family First*, many books on supporting healthy marriages and founder of *Putting Family First* at puttingfamilyfirst.org

"It is so difficult to maintain perspective when parenting. What impresses me most about Raising Our Sons *is the opportunity it creates for parents to come together and have productive conversations about the issues they are facing. Through these conversations parents are empowered to be less reactive and more intentional in their parenting. Thank you for this great resource."*

> **Howard Hiton, LPC**, author of *BAM! Boys Advocacy and Mentoring*

"What I love the most about Raising Our Sons *and* Daughters *is that they are comprehensive. It is wonderful to have great ideas from so many people. I feel empowered by just having so many resources all in one place."*

> **Sue Wellman**, founder of *The Ophelia Project*, Erie, PA, author of CASS program

"Thanks for sending Raising our Sons *my way. The collection of materials is impressive and sure to give parents a wealth of information to help them do a great job raising their children."*

> **Lynn Lott, MA, MFT**, author of *Positive Discipline for Teens* and 22 other books at empoweringpeople.com

*"Raising Our Sons *and* Daughters *are comprehensive and thoroughly produced guidebooks for parents and caregivers who are looking for the road map to raising healthy children. Kathy, you and your team have put your life's work into this very generous resource. Thank you!"*

> **Diana Sterling**, CEO, New Generations International, author of *The Parent as Coach Approach*

Raising Our Sons Parenting Guide
...a new, unique way to support you,
as a parent or caring adult, to:

- Create a thriving family now and prepare for the teen and tween years.
- Learn from the perspective of many different voices from over 100 authors.
- Get a broad exposure to many parenting books, DVDs and other resources.
- Gain clarity on parenting by reading, discussing and exploring what works.
- Discover which of these parenting resources are the "best fit" for you.
- Learn the power of focusing early on preventive, proactive parenting.
- Connect to your own "inner wisdom."
- Be empowered to be the best mom, best dad, or best caring adult with your unique approach.
- Understand the incredible power you have as an adult who reaches out to connect with kids.
- Learn many ways to weave a network of support for your son and other children you care about.
- Be empowered to contribute to a community that takes action to show they care about children.

Form a discussion group with these *Parenting Guides*, and you will:

- Have a format to share honestly, create connections with other concerned parents, and find allies on your parenting path.
- Discover you are not alone, as you learn about other family's struggles and issues.
- Gain wisdom from other parents.
- Support each other and be encouraged to focus on long-term parenting.
- Create the life, the family, and the community you want to see in the world.
- Enjoy your family and have fun.

The magic that can happen when using Raising Our Sons Parenting Guide *with a group
is that you create a support network of people who not only care about you,
but also care about your children. In essence, you can create a group of "aunties" and "uncles"
who look out for all the children in your everyday life.*

—Kathy Masarie, MD

RAISING OUR SONS

The Ultimate Parenting Guide
For Healthy Boys and Strong Families

Kathy Masarie, MD
with
Jody Bellant Scheer, MD
Kathy Keller Jones, MA

Family
Empowerment
Network

Jody Bellant Scheer, MD, Kathy Masarie, MD, and Kathy Keller Jones, MA (pictured left to right), created *Raising our Sons, Raising our Daughters* and *Kids Social Lives* with a diverse, insightful group of volunteers and co-authors.

We would like to thank the many writers, contributors, family photographers, organizations, and our own families for their contribution and support on this ten-year project.

Binoy Bahuleyan	Claire Ersan	Kaitlin Masarie	Leann Scotch
Michelle Bailey	Adrienne Greene	Ruthie Matinko-Wald	Peter Serrell
Harmony Barrett	Chris Harrington	Ann Matschiner	Lisa Sloan
Ann Baumgartner	Sally Hersh	Glenda Montgomery	Madelyn Stasko
Chithra Binoy	Nancy Huppertz	Christine Nelson	Elizabeth Stevens
Cindy Broder	Annette Kleinfelter	Nelle Nix	Cynthia Thomas
Francis Bubalo	Dana Lodhie	Michelle Roehm	Susan Thomson
Kathy Bunn	Lindsey Lodhie	Alice Rose	Debra Tomsen
Ann Cleveland	Trudy Ludwig	Carol Sherman Rogers	June Tremain
Karen Costello	Chip Masarie	Karen St. Clair	Tim Turner
Mary d'Autremont	Jon Masarie	Eileen Schmidt	

Graphic design	Anita Jones at www.anotherjones.com
Cover design	Machele Brass at www.brassdesign.net
Proof Editors	Bridget Weber, Leslie O'Neill and Glenda Montgomery
Marketing Consultant	Michael Kosmala, The Canoe Group at www.thecanoegroup.com
Published by	Kathy Masarie at www.family-empower.com

We thank the 2001 7th and 8th grade art students of the West Linn-Wilsonville School Districts who contributed their drawings from Charcoal Challenge Art Class, taught by Sally Nelson: Brittany Baartlein, Drew Bardana, Caelen Bensen, Sarah Bernert, Matt Boggess, Katie Bonham, Kamon Bryck, Tom Flannery, Stephani Graap, Liana Hochhalter, Shelby Lindstedt, Andrea Millen, McKenna Miller, Carley Nelson, Lindsay Nelson, Lee Ogle, Eric Ramfjord, Thomas Ramfjord, Amanda Russel, Kara Tucker, and Danny Walinsky.

Finally, we would like to acknowledge Northwest Earth Institute, founded by Dick and Jeanne Roy, whose own courses were the model for this discussion guide.

Family Empowerment Network

Please contact us at:
Family Empowerment Network™
6663 SW Beaverton Hillsdale Highway PMB 158, Portland, OR 97225
coach@kathymasarie.com   www.family-empower.com

Preface

You are on a parenting journey, one that can bring more joy, more worry and occasionally more despair than you probably ever imagined. How can you both enjoy yourself and be your best, while maximizing precious moments with your children and nurturing them to discover their best selves and unique talents? As parents, we feel stretched in many directions with higher expectations than previous generations. We are constantly bombarded by cultural messages to buy more and be more while receiving little support in exchange.

Mary Pipher, author of *Reviving Ophelia,* says, "Raising your family in isolation is like buying a first class ticket on the Titanic." In today's culture, it is easy to feel alone. In her pediatric practice, Dr. Kathy Masarie saw parents of teens struggling in isolation with big problems: pregnancy, depression, risky drinking and drug use. With her own teens, she experienced how hard and sometimes embarrassing it was to share her struggles with others. Dr. Masarie wanted to encourage the networking she saw among parents of young kids and to provide a continuum of support as families evolved. In 1996, she founded the non-profit, *Full Esteem Ahead,* to "support parents to support kids and one another" and created these parenting guides in the process.

Since then, *Raising Our Daughters* and *Raising Our Sons* have provided parents, schools and caring adults with powerful vehicles for learning, self-discovery, networking, and the importance of connecting with all kids. These guides respond to parents' crucial needs: to talk to each other honestly and authentically, to support each other's families, and to collaborate in building family-friendly communities. Initially created by a team of volunteers who gathered the best information from over 200 new and timeless resources, Kathy and her co-writers, Jody Bellant Scheer, a pediatrician, and Kathy Keller Jones, a school counselor, have updated and expanded *Raising Our Sons* and *Raising Our Daughters.*

Busy parents and other caring adults often look for quick, easy answers from the "experts." At *Family Empowerment Network,* we believe that you have the best answers. You know yourself and your children better than anyone. When you take the time to read and discuss common concerns with other parents, your mind opens to new ideas. You recognize which of many effective solutions are a "good fit" and then you become the expert in your own life. You have the power to come together as parents, school communities, and neighborhoods to create alliances and communities that nurture thriving, healthy children. **And most importantly, you connect with young people so they know they matter.**

Thank you for your participation from all of us at Family Empowerment Network.

Kathy Masarie, MD	Kathy Keller Jones, MA	Jody Bellant Scheer, MD
Pediatrician	School Counselor	Pediatrician
Parent/Life Coach	Parent Coach	Compassionate Communication

Contents

Introduction

Discover the overall purpose of *Raising our Sons Parenting Guide,* an overview of topics and articles covered in each session, and how to run your own discussion group.

In spite of the challenges they face today, parents have the power to make a positive difference in their son's lives and the lives of other children. Learn how the 40 Developmental Assets can guide you.

Become familiar with the powerful media influence in your son's world, as well as the ways commercialism creates his culture. In becoming more media literate, parents can reduce the harm of the media and guide their families in making wise decisions about what to watch, play and purchase.

Explore parenting strategies that help avoid sabotages and encourage compassionate communication. Learn about the importance of family rituals, character development, and teaching financial responsibility.

Learn about your son's transition into manhood, including understanding puberty, cultural pressures, and how to share this with him. Explore how to support your son in his friendships.

Learn about the cultural pressures boys feel to be "stoic, tough guys." Recognize ways boys can connect to their own feelings, control anger, and develop emotional intelligence. Empower our boys with resiliency. .

Recognize the value of partnership between families and schools in preparing children for the future. Raise your awareness about how boys learn, boy-friendly teaching styles, and relational aggression in schools.

Explore your priorities in life and become more aware of the choices you are making regarding work, busyness, and stress. Realign your time with your true priorities and have more quality time with loved ones.

Understand that a goal of adolescence is to form one's own identity and that this often involves experimentation and risk-taking. Know that, as a parent, you are the first line of defense between your son and common health and safety risks. Establish support structures that help keep him safe.

Develop "safe havens" where your son can be himself and develop relationships with other caring adults. Design a rite of passage. Understand the importance of fitness to mental and emotional well-being.

Solidify your vision and plan to create a nurturing, supportive, and connected family and community using the 40 Developmental Assets. Include volunteering. Stay connected to other families.

The permission's list acknowledges the wonderful authors and organizations who contributed to this project, along with sharing contact and reprint information.

Contents: Articles

GUIDELINES FOR DISCUSSION GROUPS

These guidelines will help you create a supportive parent discussion group and effectively share this *Parenting Guide*. Parent groups most often meet once or twice a month to discuss a chapter of the *Parenting Guide*. Group leadership rotates—then each participant is empowered to have an equal voice and the group's shared wisdom can be maximized.

HOW TO START YOUR OWN PARENTING DISCUSSION GROUP
- Talk to your friends, parents of your child's friends, scout or soccer team parents … Find a co-leader.
- Share the *Parenting Guide* with your school counselor and ask if s/he would like to get involved.
- Talk to the principal about putting an ad in your school newsletter to announce an "info meeting."
- Host a parenting seminar with a local speaker. Send around a sign-up sheet to tap interest in a class.

OPENER GUIDELINES
- The role of **opener** rotates each session among participants.
- The purpose of the opening is to transition from the outside distractions of daily life to the discussion group.
- Start on time. Late members can join in as they arrive. Groups committed to starting on time may add fifteen minutes to the beginning of the meeting for greetings and snacks.
- The opening is an opportunity for the opener to express appreciation of parenting or their child(ren). This may be done by relating a personal experience, sharing a family ritual, reading a poem or a passage from a favorite book, doing a short activity with the group, singing a song or doing a dance or a meditation.

FACILITATOR GUIDELINES
- The role of **facilitator** rotates each session among participants. Facilitators generally take time to read all of the materials of the chapter. They are not expected to be experts on the topic.
- Start on time with the opening. End on time with the action steps. Groups generally meet for one-and-a-half hours.
- The session starts off with the **Circle Question.** Each participant takes a turn so everyone's voice is heard over about 20 minutes. The group then chooses the most relevant **Discussion Questions** and the facilitator guides the discussion for about 30 minutes, leaving time for solutions and action steps.
- The facilitator's principal role is to keep the focus on the topic and to foster a comfortable environment for everyone to share ideas fairly and respectfully. The articles and the discussion questions are only a guide to the topic. Add in your own, and if the group discussion is branching off in a relevant, fruitful direction, follow it. Conversation that drifts off topic too far can be gently brought in with a comment such as, "I noticed we are talking about … rather than …"
- When a participant or two dominates discussion, thank them for their opinions. Then ask someone else for their opinion. If it continues, share your experience with that person privately later.
- Listen carefully and talk less to help guide the discussion effectively. Keep in mind:
  › Consensus is not the goal of the group. Disagreements should be expected and welcomed.
  › Interrupt any discussions where respect is being jeopardized or one person is monopolizing.
  › Agree ahead of time how you are going to handle one or two people dominating discussions.
  › Consider having a visible clock, using a sand timer or a talking stick to foster fair sharing.
  › Keep the discussions moving along, so there is time to discuss the **Putting It Together** action steps and solution ideas.
- This course is for personal exploration and to discover how the participants can make a difference in their own lives in connection with their families, communities, and schools. Write down your personal ideas you want to implement in **Putting it Together—Your Version.**

CLASS SCHEDULE AND SIGN-UP

All participants fill out this sheet at the first session. Two volunteers are needed for each session: someone to provide an Opening and someone to serve as Facilitator. Snacks are provided by the hosting member.

	SESSIONS	DATE	OPENER	FACILITATOR	LOCATION
1	What is Happening to Him?				
2	What Influences Him?				
3	Parenting Him				
4	Nourishing Healthy Masculinity				
5	Nourishing Emotions and Compassion				
6	Teaching Him				
7	Making Time for Him				
8	Keeping Him Safe				
9	Supporting Him				
10	Creating Community				
	Gathering to Celebrate				

TIPS FOR A MEANINGFUL, CONNECTED, SUPPORTIVE DISCUSSION GROUP

- Bring an open mind and acceptance to each meeting. Share honestly.
- Attend every meeting, and show up on time for the opening.
- Prepare for each session by doing as much reading as you can. At least, try to read the overview.
- List one or more goals for what you want to create in your life during this discussion group time.
- Take your turn with the co-leader roles: **opener and facilitator.**
- Ideally everyone monitors his/her own talking and makes sure it is a "fair amount of time." This is critical. Putting structures in place to support equal sharing can be helpful.
- Allow time for discussion of solutions and action steps in each session.
- Take ownership of solutions. Focus your energy on what you can change personally or contribute as a group. Avoid "should" as in: "my child, partner, the media, school, counselor ... should ..."
- **Set ground rules for the group** at the first meeting and share how you are best supported by others:
  › Observe confidentiality of personal stories.
  › Seek clarity, not consensus. Maintain respect for everyone's opinions.
  › Avoid finger pointing, blaming others or ganging up on someone with a differing opinion.
- Handle conflict directly and early, such as one or two people dominating the discussions
  › Avoid third party talk.
  › If you have a problem with a fellow participant, talk with them directly and when the problem is small and easier to resolve. Everyone matters and the group success depends on honest interactions.
  › If the problem continues, or a group problem arises bring it up at the next meeting to discuss together.
- Participants with serious problems with their adolescent or with themselves will find more effective support from outside, for example, from professional counseling.

What's Happening to My Son?

1

2

3

4

5

6

7

8

9

10

What's Happening to My Son?

"What we are teaches the child far more than what we say, so we must be what we want our children to become." —Joseph Chilton Pearce

"A hundred years from now, it will not matter what my bank account was, the sort of house I lived in, or the make of car I drove. But the world may be different, because I was important in the life of a child." —Anon

"There is a story about a town where people were falling off its cliffs. The city elders met to debate whether to build a fence at the top of the cliff or put an ambulance down in the valley. This story summarizes the essential differences between treatment and prevention." —Mary Pipher

"Nothing in life is to be feared, it is only to be understood. When you dare to face the things that scare you, you open the door to freedom." —Anon

GOALS

- To understand the power parents have to make a positive difference in their children's lives and in the lives of other people's children
- To understand the 40 Developmental Assets that help every child navigate childhood and adolescence in a positive and healthy manner
- To empower parents to make more connections with the children in their lives
- To acknowledge the difficult challenges that boys and parents are facing today
- To get acquainted with the other parents in your parenting group

OVERVIEW

You are on an exciting, wonderful journey called parenting. We are honored you chose this parenting guide to support you. We believe that through the voices of more than 100 authors you will find your own voice, your inner wisdom. No one knows your deepest values as well as you do. No one cares for and is as invested in the well-being of your son as you are. By reading these different perspectives and having discussions with other dedicated parents, you can discover a renewed confidence in yourself and your ability to support your child as they discover who they are.

One of the best activities to start you on this journey is to take a moment and think about what inspired you to make the commitment to read this parenting guide. What would you most like to gain from this activity? What is it that you most want for your son? Taking the time to make a list of the positive visions and wishes that you have for your son will help support you in your parenting journey. It is a lot easier to be an empowered and effective parent when you are in touch with these long-term goals. Focusing on what you don't want to happen and what you fear is a common parenting pitfall, especially as children approach their teens. Unfortunately, this encourages a high state of parental anxiety and hopelessness, with feelings of impotence towards protecting your son from the dangers of adolescence. Actually, there are many things you can do to help your son grow up safely and successfully. That is what *Raising Our Sons* is all about: working with other involved parents to create a positive vision for your sons' futures and looking at preventive strategies that will strengthen our boys and ensure their success in the long run. Mark Amendola shares his parenting goals in the first article of this chapter, **"What I Want for my Sons"** (p. 1:10).

Family Empowerment Network™ (FEN) offers this parenting guide to acquaint parents with a variety of preventive parenting strategies that instituted now, will help your children navigate through adolescence with safer and better decision-making skills. Furthermore, we would like to introduce you to a variety of issues that affect the mental, social and emotional health of boys

as they grow up in contemporary American society. We would like to empower parents to support each other and to network within their community to create a nurturing and healthy environment for all youth. Finally, we would like to support parents in their parenting struggles. Although parents may at times feel inadequate or overwhelmed, FEN believes that parents are the very best resource around for helping their kids survive the transition from childhood to adulthood, and for creating an environment that will support their children's emerging competence, caring, and responsibility. Parents, however, may need to get some help along the way, as this is a difficult if not impossible task to do all alone. Children are social creatures and require relationships with adults and children outside of their own homes to ensure their full and healthy development. The African wisdom that "it takes a village to raise a child" is truly applicable in our modern lives as well. It is also true that adults can create healthy contemporary "villages" that will support and nurture our children, if they so choose. FEN is making the assumption that you are one of the parents who chooses to make a difference.

Our introductory chapter addresses the power parents have to make a positive difference in the lives of their own children and in the lives of other youth. Family Empowerment Network is excited to introduce you to a grassroots movement called "asset building" that is based on the Search Institute's twenty-five years of research on resiliency and protective factors for children. The Search Institute, a nonprofit organization based in Minneapolis, Minnesota, began their project by asking, "Why do some kids from an incredibly impoverished neighborhood do well, while others who have plenty of advantages do poorly? What internal resources and external supports are necessary for a child from any background to become successful, resilient and healthy?"

By researching scientific literature, conferring with child health and educational professionals, and by talking extensively with children and families themselves, the Search Institute found that there are 40 building blocks or assets that all kids need in their lives to succeed. These Developmental Assets represent 40 essential socialization experiences that have been shown in extensive testing to support health-promoting behaviors and to decrease risky behaviors in all youth, consistent across gender, racial, economic and cultural lines. These assets entail actions which a family can readily promote and over which a family and community of people can exert considerable influence.

The list of **"40 Developmental Assets"** is the second handout in your parenting guide (p. 1:11). Please copy this list and POST IT ON YOUR REFRIGERATOR! These assets are grouped into 20 external assets (including the categories of support, empowerment, boundaries and expectations, and constructive use of time) and 20 internal assets (with the categories of commitment to learning, positive values, social competencies, and positive self-identity). Assets have been shown to be cumulative; the more kids possess, the better off they are. As the number of assets in a child's life increases, so does that child's well-being, as assets help inoculate youth against high-risk behaviors. Having 30 of 40 assets is protective against high-risk behaviors. Sadly enough, even though most people will recognize the importance of these 40 assets, the vast majority of our nation's youth possess less than one half of them in their lives. Only 8% have 30 or more assets. What may sound like good common sense is not yet common practice for most of our youth.

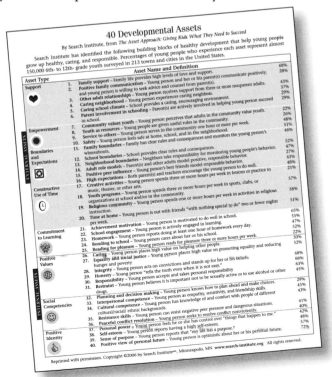

Using the assets as a guide, parents can find ways to strengthen their own child's potential to do well in life, as well as to positively impact the lives of other children. Time and again during the Search Institute's research, it was impressive to see the positive power of growing up in a neighborhood where multiple adults took an interest in the well-being of children, and where these adults also helped set boundaries and monitor out-of-bounds behaviors. Taking an active interest in the children and adolescents in your own community can be a huge step toward improving the lives and Developmental Assets of all of your community's children. It is interesting to note that only nine of the 40 Developmental Assets are built within the family. This helps explain why parents so desperately need the help and support of others—adults, schools, neighborhoods and communities—to ensure the success and healthy development of their sons.

Asset building within your community can be as simple as showing up at your son's school and greeting all the children there by name, volunteering as a sports coach, arranging constructive after-school activities for kids on your block or in your community, or encouraging your local newspaper to run more articles with positive stories about local youth and families. The assets framework can be a great tool for increasing the impact and interactions of adults in the lives of a community's children, which exactly complements the goals and work of Family Empowerment Network. Of course, we hold high hopes that you will make good use of this helpful tool. Our hope is to see parents, families, organizations and neighborhoods pitching in to reclaim their own personal capabilities and responsibilities for raising a community of healthy and resilient youth.

What we find most attractive about asset building is that it is a positive, proactive approach that builds on what's right in a community, and creates changes that become a part of the ongoing infrastructure of schools, homes and neighborhoods. This approach empowers parents and communities by looking at youth as resources, by involving everyone (including kids) in creating a healthy, cooperative and hopeful community, and by paying attention to all children, not just the troublemakers. Family Empowerment Network bases much of its philosophy on these assets. We are not alone. Over a thousand communities have adopted these assets around the nation, including the entire State of Colorado. You will be introduced to the key aspects of asset building in this chapter. In subsequent chapters, the assets relevant to that chapter will be listed and related asset-building articles will be included.

There are five articles from the Search Institute on Developmental Assets that are included in your syllabus. These are: **"Fast Facts about Developmental Assets," "The Power of Assets: Protecting Youth from High-Risk Behaviors and Promoting Positive Attitudes and Behaviors," "The Challenge Facing Communities," "How You Can Build Assets,"** and **"The Asset-Building Difference"** (pp. 1:12 - 1:16). **"Tips for Adults to Connect with Children"** (p. 1:17), discusses the essential need for meaningful relationships between adults and teenagers and includes suggestions on how to create them. The next article, **"Are Americans Afraid of Teens?"** (p. 1:18) discusses the fears adults have of teens, which are largely due to the influences of negative media messages, derogatory stereotypes, unrecognized racism and lack of opportunities to interact with teenagers. The article includes tips for connecting with teens, including increasing opportunities for positive interactions and taking the time to listen to teens' stories and concerns.

In fact, children born in the last two decades of the 20th century (1981–1999), "The Millennials," also known as "Generation Y," may be the key to a more peaceful future, according to Life Coach Sally Gardiner who wrote **"The Millennials—Our Future Hope?"** (p. 1:21). Millennials, the most technologically advanced generation ever, are global citizens who are tolerant and value diversity. They love working collaboratively since they have been involved in family decision-making throughout their lives by child-focused parents. As parents, we may need to help Millennials find a balance between the attitude that they can have, be, or do anything they want, and the reality that success takes hard work and determination.

Using the asset model as a guide, what can be learned about what's up with boys? Boys, on average, report having fewer Developmental Assets than girls at every age. Boys also have fewer internal assets, on average, than girls. The article, **"Connecting with Boys: Closing the Asset Gap"** (p. 1:22) discusses how and why boys have fewer building blocks for success in their lives. It then makes six suggestions for strategies to use for asset builders who want to support and celebrate our boys, to set appropriate limits, and to channel boys' energy into productive outlets.

There are indicators other than assets research that highlight the degree to which our boys need our attention. Indeed, boys perpetrate over 90% of youthful violent crimes and are also overwhelmingly the victims of this violence. More boys than girls experience suicide, homicide, bullying, arrests for violent behavior, referrals for conduct disorders, attention deficit disorders and special education. Fewer boys than girls worldwide are now graduating from high school, going to college and graduate school, and earning graduate degrees. One of the most powerful messages from boys in recent years has been from several of them who decided to solve their problems by shooting their classmates and teachers. This finally captured the attention of our nation. Since the mid-1990's, an international movement has been created to examine how to improve the lives of boys. Studies have been undertaken, books have been written and men as well as women are now more aware of the need to become involved in raising boys to be more happy, successful, and emotionally connected.

Family Empowerment Network agrees that boys are in need of support. What this curriculum won't do is to compare who has it worse—boys or girls. All of our children face risk factors in being raised in our complex, modern society and they all need our support. Rather than pitting the needs of boys against those of girls, it is better to commit ourselves to raising boys and girls who respect themselves and each other, and who are willing to work together to make the world a more humane place for all. Supporting boys *more* does not mean we have to support girls *less*, or vice versa.

The last two articles in this chapter, **"Raising Better Boys"** and **"Listening to Our Sons"** (pp.1:26-1:30) discuss how boys are at special risk in our culture due to their masculine upbringing and what we can do about it. Dr. William Pollack's book *Real Boys' Voices* teaches us the importance of listening deeply to our sons. He reminds us that if we want our sons to speak openly to us we need to create a "shame-free zone" where they feel safe. Furthermore, our sons may need some time to think things through on their own before they are ready to talk, i.e., "timed silence." Many boys are more comfortable talking while they are doing an activity, like shooting baskets, building something, going for a drive, or hiking. Pollack calls this "action talk." Above all, we want to let our sons of all ages know how much we love them, that we are always available to listen and will never shame them. To help parents understand the cultural dictates of masculinity, an exercise called the **"Boy in the Box"** (p. 1:31) is included at the end of this chapter for use at your first Raising Our Son's meeting. This explores the "boy box," which is a strict code of masculine behavior promoted by our media and culture that causes boys to hide their emotions and vulnerability and to act with bravado and insensitivity, "just like a man." Teaching our boys a newer, more compassionate model of masculinity will go a long way towards lessening the risks for high-risk behaviors in our sons as they grow up. This will take the combined efforts of both the men and women in your son's life.

Also included at the end of this chapter is **"An Asset Checklist"** (p. 1:32). This simple checklist can give you an opportunity to see how many Developmental Assets you feel your son currently has. It would be an interesting exercise to also have your son fill this form out from his own perspective. An active discussion about your son's Developmental Assets would be a great starting point towards understanding your son's current world and his own special point of view.

To sum up, all of our kids need the active support of the adults in their communities. This support will come from people like you, the involved parents who care a lot and who are not willing to be discouraged. We are the ones who can turn this culture around by taking action to support all kids—not just our own, but all of the kids in our neighborhoods, schools, and places of worship. By working together to create resources and support systems that truly encourage all children to develop into competent and caring adults, and by focusing on strengths, we parents can truly create a more hopeful world for ourselves and for our children—if we will only choose to take the time.

ACTIVITIES TO DO BEFORE YOU MEET WITH YOUR GROUP

Imagine you were raising your son in a perfect environment. What would this vision look like? What support would be there for him from his family, community, government and school? Write these down and refer back to them as you read this book.

Fill out the "Asset Checklist" at the end of this chapter for every child in your family and for the adults in the family when they were children. What are your family's strengths? Name the area you would most like to improve.

CIRCLE QUESTION

Take some time to do the "Boy in the Box" activity together as a group. Then, have each of you share something that you learned from doing this activity. Did this activity bring up something about growing up male that you hadn't thought about before? Compare life for your son to your own experience growing up.

POSSIBLE DISCUSSION QUESTIONS

1. What does your vision for your son look like? What kinds of support would you like there to be for him?
2. Draw a family tree. Who were the powerful influences in the family both male and female? Keep this in your book.
3. What are the differences in expectations between the boys (men) and girls (women) in your family? In your family of origin?
4. Review the protective power of assets against drugs, alcohol, sexual activity and violence. Why do you think that having more than 30 assets has such power and protects children?
5. Look over the asset checklist and discuss how you can build and maintain assets.
6. How many adults, other than parents, does your child have involved in his life? How could you get more adults involved in his life? How many children are there in your life, other than your own, whose lives you influence?
7. What top 3 activities does your boy do with his time? What would you like to see less of? More of?
8. Describe 3 top issues your son struggles with now or you worry he will struggle with in the near future.
9. List the traits you would like to see in an ideal role model in your son's life. What qualities do they have? What are their interests? How do they relate to women? To men?
10. How aware are you of the culture your child lives in?
11. Have you had an experience of being "pleasantly surprised" by connecting with teens, finding they weren't as frightening as you thought?

PUTTING IT INTO PRACTICE:

- Get all adults who live in the household involved in this curriculum, either by attending the class together or reading this book alongside you and discussing it. For single parent households, get your support adults involved too.
- Honor your sons need for "timed silence," "shame-free zones" and "action talk."
- Examine carefully how your expectations of boys and girls differ.
- Do the "Boy in the Box" exercise with your son (and his friends) to learn what he thinks about the cultural expectations of boys.
- Ask your son who his role models are.
- Ask your son who he would feel comfortable talking with if he were having problems.
- Ask your son what he is most worried about when he grows up.
- Use the asset checklist to assess your family's strengths. What areas could be actively worked on?
- Post the assets on your refrigerator and look at them a few times every week.
- Encourage your son to get involved with a group whose activities he enjoys.

PUTTING IT TOGETHER—YOUR VERSION

Write down three or four ideas you have been inspired to implement after reading and discussing this chapter.

1. _____

2. _____

3. _____

4. _____

TOP RESOURCES FOR RAISING OUR SONS:

1. *Real Boys: Rescuing our Sons from the Myth of Boyhood* and *Real Boys Voices* by William Pollack, PhD

2. *It's a Boy!: Understanding Your Son's Development From Birth to Age 18* by Michael Thompson, PhD

3. *The Men They Will Become: The Nature and Nurture of Boys* by Eli Newberger, MD

4. *The Courage to Raise Good Men* by Olga Silverstein and Beth Rashbaum

5. *Raising Boys: Why Boys are Different and How to Help Them Become Happy and Well-Balanced Men* by Steve Biddulph

TOP RESOURCES FOR RAISING OUR CHILDREN

1. *Parenting From the Inside Out: How a Deeper Self-Understanding Can Help You Raise Children Who Thrive* by Daniel Siegel, MD and Mary Hartzell, MEd

2. *How to Talk So Your Kids Will Listen, and How to Listen So Your Kids Will Talk,* by Adele Faber and Elaine Mazlish

3. *Positive Discipline: A Classic Guide for Parents and Teachers to Help Children Develop Self-Discipline, Responsibility, Cooperation, and Problem-Solving,* by Jane Nelsen EdD and *Positive Discipline for Teenagers: Empowering Your Teen and Yourself Through Kind and Firm Parenting* by Jane Nelsen, EdD, MFT and Lynn Lott, MA, MFT

4. *Uncommon Sense for Parents of Teenagers* by Michael Riera, PhD

5. *The Parent as Coach Approach: The Seven Ways to Coach Your Teen in the Game of Life* by Diana Sterling

6. *The Good Father: On Men, Masculinity, and Life in the Family* by Mark O'Connell

7. *Parenting From Your Heart: Sharing the Gifts of Compassion, Connection, and Choice* by Inbal Kashtan

8. *Respectful Parents, Respectful Kids: Seven Keys to Turn Family Conflict into Cooperation* by Sura Hart and Victoria Kindle Hodson

9. *Putting Family First: Strategies for Reclaiming Family Life in a Hurry-Up World* by William Doherty, PhD and Barbara Carlson

10. *Best Friends, Worst Enemies: Understanding the Social Lives of Children* by Michael Thompson, PhD

TOP RESOURCES FOR TEENS

1. *Six Most Important Decisions You'll Ever Make* by Sean Covey

2. *Seven Habits of Highly Effective Teens* by Sean Covey

3. *Perfectionism: What is Bad about Being Too Good* by Mariam Adderholdt and Jan Goldberg

4. *Fighting Invisible Tigers: A Stress Management Guide for Teens* by Earl Hipp

Ophelia Project
What I Want For My Sons

By Mark Amendola

I LOOK AT MY TWO sons and know they are full of promise and possibilities. Still at an impressionable age, they are growing up in a culture with messages that may cloud how they view relationships: how they shape their personal interactions. I will not let that happen. My sons will mature into healthy young men, understanding of their environment and of the world in which they live.

I want my sons to be honest and trustworthy—true to themselves, while treating others as they want to be treated. I want them to understand that the true elevation of "self" takes place only through the practice of positive social attitudes toward others.

I want my sons to respect life and be compassionate toward others. My own father taught me one of the greatest lessons I ever learned: that "all people are people." Despite our differences we are all human beings, each with a heart, a soul and a need to be treated with respect and dignity. I want my sons to understand the meaning of work and the value of giving to someone who would not necessarily ask for help but is truly in need.

I want my sons to live in a world free of violence and aggression, understanding that what makes the world a special place is how different we are from one another. I want them to know that men can be men and still show emotion and feelings without fear of ridicule or embarrassment; and that the outward expression of emotion is healthy and preferred. It IS okay to cry.

I want my sons to be prepared to face all of life's challenges with courage, hope and faith. I want them to live their lives sharing triumphs and struggles with those close to them. I want my sons to treat all who cross their paths with love in their hearts and spirit in their souls. I know their relationships with others will have a huge impact on their lives and I want them to be able to manage and fully participate in them. These are the things I want for my sons and your sons too.

Mark is the father of two sons, aged 9 and 11, and is the Executive Director of Perseus House in Erie, Pennsylvania.

40 Developmental Assets
By Search Institute

Search Institute has identified the following building blocks of healthy development that help young people grow up healthy, caring, and responsible. Percentages of young people who experience each asset represent almost 150,000 6th- to 12th-grade youth surveyed in 213 towns and cities in the United States.

Asset Type		Asset Name and Definition	
Support	1.	**Family support** – Family life provides high levels of love and support.	68%
	2.	**Positive family communication** – Young person and her or his parent(s) communicate positively, and young person is willing to seek advice and counsel from parent(s).	28%
	3.	**Other adult relationships** – Young person receives support from three or more nonparent adults.	43%
	4.	**Caring neighborhood** – Young person experiences caring neighbors.	37%
	5.	**Caring school climate** – School provides a caring, encouraging environment.	29%
	6.	**Parent involvement in schooling** – Parent(s) are actively involved in helping young person succeed in school.	29%
Empowerment	7.	**Community values youth** – Young person perceives that adults in the community value youth.	22%
	8.	**Youth as resources** – Young people are given useful roles in the community.	26%
	9.	**Service to others** – Young person serves in the community one hour or more per week.	48%
	10.	**Safety** – Young person feels safe at home, school, and in the neighborhood.	51%
Boundaries and Expectations	11.	**Family boundaries** – Family has clear rules and consequences and monitors the young person's whereabouts.	46%
	12.	**School boundaries** – School provides clear rules and consequences.	52%
	13.	**Neighborhood boundaries** – Neighbors take responsibility for monitoring young people's behavior.	47%
	14.	**Adult role models** – Parent(s) and other adults model positive, responsible behavior.	27%
	15.	**Positive peer influence** – Young person's best friends model responsible behavior.	63%
	16.	**High expectations** – Both parent(s) and teachers encourage the young person to do well.	48%
Constructive Use of Time	17.	**Creative activities** – Young person spends three or more hours per week in lessons or practice in music, theater, or other arts.	21%
	18.	**Youth programs** – Young person spends three or more hours per week in sports, clubs, or organizations at school and/or in the community.	57%
	19.	**Religious community** – Young person spends one or more hours per week in activities in religious instruction.	58%
	20.	**Time at home** – Young person is out with friends "with nothing special to do" two or fewer nights per week.	51%
Commitment to Learning	21.	**Achievement motivation** – Young person is motivated to do well in school.	65%
	22.	**School engagement** – Young person is actively engaged in learning.	55%
	23.	**Homework** – Young person reports doing at least one hour of homework every day.	47%
	24.	**Bonding to school** – Young person cares about her or his school.	52%
	25.	**Reading for pleasure** – Young person reads for pleasure three or more hours per week.	22%
Positive Values	26.	**Caring** – Young person places high value on helping other people.	50%
	27.	**Equality and social justice** – Young person places high value on promoting equality and reducing hunger and poverty.	52%
	28.	**Integrity** – Young person acts on convictions and stands up for her or his beliefs.	68%
	29.	**Honesty** – Young person "tells the truth even when it is not easy."	66%
	30.	**Responsibility** – Young person accepts and takes personal responsibility.	63%
	31.	**Restraint** – Young person believes it is important not to be sexually active or to use alcohol or other drugs.	45%
Social Competencies	32.	**Planning and decision making** – Young person knows how to plan ahead and make choices.	29%
	33.	**Interpersonal competence** – Young person has empathy, sensitivity, and friendship skills.	45%
	34.	**Cultural competence** – Young person has knowledge of and comfort with people of different cultural/racial/ ethnic backgrounds.	43%
	35.	**Resistance skills** – Young person can resist negative peer pressure and dangerous situations.	41%
	36.	**Peaceful conflict resolution** – Young person seeks to resolve conflict nonviolently.	40%
Positive Identity	37.	**Personal power** – Young person feels he or she has control over "things that happen to me."	42%
	38.	**Self-esteem** – Young person reports having high self-esteem.	48%
	39.	**Sense of purpose** – Young person reports that "my life has a purpose."	57%
	40.	**Positive view of personal future** – Young person is optimistic about her or his personal future.	72%

EXTERNAL ASSETS

INTERNAL ASSETS

Fast Facts
About Developmental Assets for Youth
By Search Institute from *Pass It On! Ready-to-Use Handouts for Asset Builders*

IMMUNIZATIONS KEEP YOUNG children healthy and protect them from disease. Similarly, Developmental Assets help kids make healthy choices and inoculate them against a wide range of risk-taking behaviors, including substance abuse, violence, and school failure. The more assets young people have, the more likely they are to be healthy.

Other Facts About Developmental Assets:

- **Young people with more assets are less likely to engage in risk-taking behaviors.** Young people with 10 or fewer assets say they are involved in an average of about 4.5 high-risk behaviors. Young people with 31 assets or more report an average of less than one high-risk behavior.

- **As young people's assets increase, their positive behaviors also increase.** While young people with 10 or fewer assets report an average of fewer

than 3 positive behaviors, those with 31 assets or more average 6 positive behaviors. This includes school success, informal helping, valuing diversity, and exhibiting leadership.

- **The average young person surveyed has 18.0 of the 40 assets.** But levels of assets decrease for older youth. While the average sixth grader surveyed has 21.5 assets, the average 12th grader surveyed has 17.2 assets.

- **The most common asset is #40: positive view of personal future.** Seventy percent of young people surveyed report having this asset.

- **The least common asset is #17: creative activities.** Only 19 percent of young people report having this asset.

- **Girls typically have more Developmental Assets than boys.** However, boys are more likely to have #10: safety; #18: youth programs; #38: self-esteem; and #39: sense of purpose.

- **Assets that decrease in frequency between 6th and 12th grades are** #31: restraint (71 percent of 6th graders vs. 21 percent of 12th graders); #12: school boundaries (70 percent vs. 34 percent); and #15: positive peer influence (82 percent vs. 49 percent).

- **Assets that increase in frequency between 6th and 12th grades are** #10: safety (45 percent vs. 68 percent); #37: personal power (40 percent vs. 55 percent); and #28: integrity (63 percent vs. 75 percent).

The Developmental Assets are 40 opportunities, skills, relationships, values, and self-perceptions that all young people need to succeed.

The Challenge Facing Communities

By Search Institute, from *The Asset Approach: Giving Kids What They Need to Succeed*

While the assets are powerful shapers of young people's lives and choices, too few young people experience many of these assets. Twenty-five of the 40 Assets are experienced by less than half of the young people surveyed.

Average Number of Assets by Grade and Gender

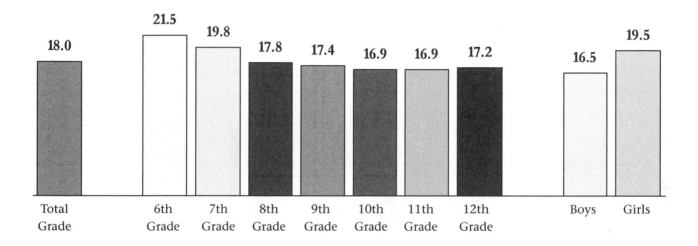

Youth with Different Levels of Assets

Ideally, all youth would experience at least 31 of these assets. Yet, as this chart shows, only 8 percent of youth experience this level of assets. Sixty-two percent experience fewer than 20 of the assets.

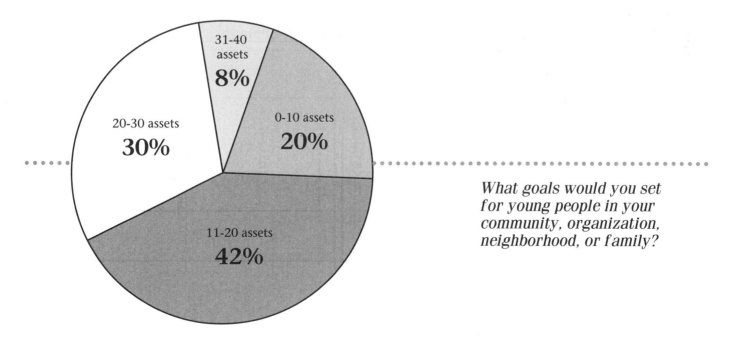

What goals would you set for young people in your community, organization, neighborhood, or family?

The Power of Assets

By Search Institute, from *The Asset Approach: Giving Kids What They Need to Succeed*

On one level, the 40 Developmental Assets represent common wisdom about the kinds of positive experiences and characteristics that young people need and deserve. But their value extends further. Surveys of almost 150,000 students in grades 6–12 (ages appoximately 11–18 years) reveal that assets are powerful influences on adolescent behavior. Regardless of gender, ethnic heritage, economic situation, or geographic location, these assets both promote positive behaviors and attitudes and help protect young people from many different problem behaviors.

0–10 assets   11–20 assets   21–30 assets   31–40 assets

Promoting Positive Attitudes and Behaviors

Our research shows that the more assets students report having, the more likely they are to also report the following patterns of thriving behavior.

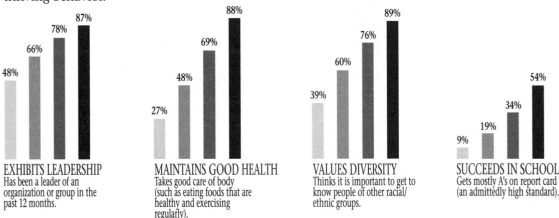

EXHIBITS LEADERSHIP
Has been a leader of an organization or group in the past 12 months.
48% 66% 78% 87%

MAINTAINS GOOD HEALTH
Takes good care of body (such as eating foods that are healthy and exercising regularly).
27% 48% 69% 88%

VALUES DIVERSITY
Thinks it is important to get to know people of other racial/ethnic groups.
39% 60% 76% 89%

SUCCEEDS IN SCHOOL
Gets mostly A's on report card (an admittedly high standard).
9% 19% 34% 54%

Protecting Youth from High-Risk Behaviors

Assets not only promote positive behaviors, they also protect young people: The more assets a young person reports having, the less likely he or she is to make harmful or unhealthy choices. (Note that these definitions are set rather high, suggesting ongoing problems, not experimentation.)

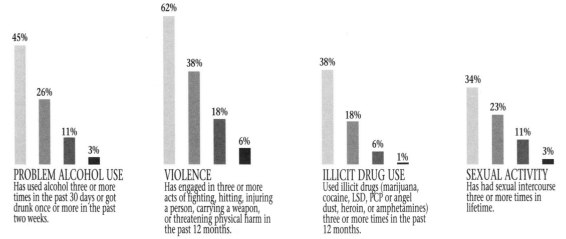

PROBLEM ALCOHOL USE
Has used alcohol three or more times in the past 30 days or got drunk once or more in the past two weeks.
45% 26% 11% 3%

VIOLENCE
Has engaged in three or more acts of fighting, hitting, injuring a person, carrying a weapon, or threatening physical harm in the past 12 months.
62% 38% 18% 6%

ILLICIT DRUG USE
Used illicit drugs (marijuana, cocaine, LSD, PCP or angel dust, heroin, or amphetamines) three or more times in the past 12 months.
38% 18% 6% 1%

SEXUAL ACTIVITY
Has had sexual intercourse three or more times in lifetime.
34% 23% 11% 3%

How You Can Build Assets

By Search Institute, from *The Asset Approach: Giving Kids What They Need to Succeed*

...On Your Own

Everyone—parents and guardians, grandparents, teachers, coaches, friends, youth workers, employers, youths, and others—can build assets. It doesn't necessarily take a lot of money. But it can make a tremendous difference in raising confident, caring young people. What it takes is building relationships, spending time together, and being intentional about nurturing positive values and commitments. Some things you can do:

- Get to know the names of kids who live around you. Find out what interests them,
- Get to know what young people around you are really like, not just how they are portrayed in the media,
- Eat at least one meal together every day as a family. Take time to talk about what's going on in each other's lives,
- Volunteer as a tutor, mentor, or youth leader in a youth-serving program.

...In Your Organization

If you're involved in an organization such as a school, youth organization, family service agency, health-care provider, or business—either as an employee or volunteer—you can encourage asset-building action within that organization. Some possibilities:

- Educate your constituency, employees, or customers about their potential as asset builders,
- Develop policies that allow parents to be involved in their children's lives and that encourage all employees to get involved with kids in the community,
- Contribute time, talent, or resources to support community asset-building efforts,
- Develop or strengthen programs and activities that build assets, such as mentoring, service-learning activities, peer helping, and recreation.

...In Your Community

Hundreds of communities across the Unites States are discovering the power and potential of uniting efforts for asset building. They involve people from all parts of the community in shaping and coordinating strategies that will help all young people be more likely to succeed. You can use your influence in the community to:

- Talk about asset building with formal and informal leaders and other influential people you know. Get their support for asset building,
- Conduct a survey to measure the asset levels of young people in your community. (Call Search Institute for information.),
- Develop opportunities for youth to contribute to the community through sharing their perspectives and taking action and leadership,
- Celebrate and honor the commitments of people who dedicate their lives and time to children and youth.

Six Keys to Asset Building

It doesn't cost a lot of money or require special training to build Developmental Assets. Here are six key ways to guide asset-building action.

1. Everyone can build assets. Building assets requires consistent messages across a community. All adults, youth, and children play a role.

2. All young people need assets. While it is crucial to pay special attention to those youth who have the least (economically or emotionally), nearly all young people need more assets than they have.

3. Relationships are key. Strong relationships between adults and young people, young people and their peers, and teenagers and children are central to asset building.

4. Asset building is an ongoing process. Building assets starts when a child is born and continues through high school and beyond.

5. Consistent messages are important. Young people need to receive consistent messages about what's important and what's expected from their families, school, communities, the media, and other sources.

Intentional redundancy is important. Assets must be continually reinforced across the years and in all areas of a young person's life.

The Asset-Building Difference
By Search Institute, from Pass It On! Ready-to-Use Handouts for Asset Builders

For healthy community development to occur for all children and youth, we need to rebuild communities where young people and organizations feel connected, engaged, responsible, and committed to young people. In order to do this, some essential shifts in thinking need to happen.

Moving From...

- Talking about problems
- Focusing on troubled and troubling youth
- Focusing primarily on ages 0 to 5
- Age segregation
- Viewing young people as problems
- Reacting to problems
- Blaming others
- Treating youth as objects of programs
- Relying on professionals
- Competing priorities
- Conflicting signals about values and priorities
- Managing crises
- Despair

To...

- Talking about positives and possibilities
- Focusing on all children and adolescents
- Focusing on all young people, ages 0 to 18
- Intergenerational community
- Seeing youth as resources
- Being proactive about building strengths
- Claiming personal responsibility
- Respecting youth as actors in their own development
- Involving everyone in the lives of young people
- Cooperative efforts
- Consistent messages about what is important
- Building a shared vision
- Hope

The Developmental Assets are 40 opportunities, skills, relationships, values, and self-perceptions that all young people need to succeed.

Reprinted with permission from *Pass It On! Ready to Use Handouts for Asset Builders* Handout [#6]. Copyright ©1999, 2006 Search Institute®, Minneapolis, MN 55413; www.search-institute.org. All rights reserved.

Tips for Adults to Connect with Children: What Can We Do???

By Kathy Masarie, MD

Mary Pipher, author of *Reviving Ophelia: Saving the Selves of our Adolescent Girls* and *The Shelter of Each Other, Rebuilding our Families,* gets to the heart of what parents can do to help their children. Here are some of her ideas from a talk given in Portland, Oregon.

- **Take It Easy On Ourselves.** The role of parenting today is more complicated than ever. Instead of having community support to gently introduce our children to our culture, we have little support and want to hide them from our culture. Troubled kids often have pretty balanced families, but we all need to slow down.

- **Form Support Groups.** Everyone's as dysfunctional as you are. Sharing problems and solutions helps.

- **Learn About The World Your Children Are Living In.** Check out the malls, movies, and video arcades. Know their friends. The author's family had a rule that any kid could come over to the house for the evening, but their kids were not allowed to go out with anyone the parents didn't know.

- **Share Your Values With Your Kids.** One of the best times to talk to your kids is over dinner. Only 7% of families in America eat their meals together. Go over what happened in the world, as well as what happened in their and your day.

- **Teach Kids Resistance Training.** Saying "No" to a good friend or a popular kid can be very difficult for our peer-pressure-driven teens. The D.A.R.E. (Drug Awareness Resistance Effort) and the Drug Free Years (for parents) courses help with this.

- **Choose Your Media As Carefully As Your Friends.** They are living in your home and influencing your kids as powerfully as any live friends. Fund PBS. Control bad TV with letters of protest.

- **Satisfy Their Needs For:**
  - **Meaningful Work** - There is no more important work for a child than school. Put in effort to help.
  - **Challenging Talents And Interest** - Sports, music, collections, languages, Scouts....
  - **Learning Skills To Cope With Stress** - Exercise is a healthy outlet for stress for everyone.
  - **Sense Of Purpose** - This comes from a combination of all the things we have talked about.

- **Provide The Opportunity For Volunteer Work.** The author's daughter wanted to help the homeless and volunteered at a shelter. It got her away from her peers and got her around people whose smoking and drinking didn't look so glamorous. Homeless people have plenty of time and could talk with her as long as she wanted—not an option with most adults who are "too busy." She also learned she could help and that her actions could make a difference!

- **Have Them Read Books About Competent Girls And Women.** Have your daughters read the magazine "New Moon, A Magazine For Girls And Their Dreams," P.O. Box 3587, Duluth, MN 55803 or *Great Books for Girls* by Kathleen Odean summarizing 600 books to inspire girls.

- **Form Alliances / Support Groups For Kids.** Ideally groups start as young as 8 (12 at the latest) and last until 18, with 2 adult facilitators of different ages, who shouldn't be one of the kids' parents. It may take a year of activities and outings before the kids will start talking about issues you feel are important.

- **Get To Know Other People's Children.** Bring back that community spirit and be an available caring adult. Sometimes kids can't talk to their own parents and you, as their "mentor," may literally save them. The children of America are all "our children."

- **Celebrate Adolescence With Coming Of Age Ceremonies.** One family had all the women involved in the girl's life, draw or sew quilt pieces that represented their relationship with her. Then, they all got together and promised one thing they would each do to help her become an adult.

- **Encourage Situations Where Your Child Can Have Friends Of All Ages.** Being influenced by only single age peers can be very dangerous. Scouts or church groups are excellent opportunities for 17-year-olds to talk to struggling 13-year-olds. Single gender experiences are very important.

- **Encourage Your Child To Keep A Journal.** Teens could write down things they like about themselves and are proud of. It is very therapeutic to write down your thoughts when you are angry. It helps take it out of your head where it spins around in a vicious circle and place it on the paper in an organized way. A child may prefer taping his or her thoughts, rather than writing them.

Are Americans Afraid

Assets Magazine, Summer 1998

'Teens these days'

Like millions of American adults, they perceive that teens today are unruly, rude, lacking in basic civility, and oftentimes, downright dangerous. Are they right?

If one relies on mass media for an image of teenhood today, the answer would be certain. Consider the grizzly scenes of the school killings in Jonesboro, Ark., at the hands of youth ages 11 and 13; the shootings in Springfield, Ore., the work of a troubled teen; or the gritty photos of streetwise teens, pierced, tattooed, and gun-toting, as portrayed in *George* magazine in its feature, "Why Kids Are Ruining America."

But what do the statistics say? The Federal Bureau of Investigation (FBI) reported in 1995 that only 6.2% of all people arrested in the nation were under the age of 15. Only one-half of 1% of teens are arrested for a violent crime in any given year, says the FBI.

Still, this is not to say that teens never commit crimes. And it's not to say that violence by teens should be glossed over or dismissed. The point is that the vast majority of teens are not hoodlums or dangerous and don't aspire to be. So why is fear that should be reserved for genuinely dangerous teens often overlaid on virtually all teens?

In a middle-income neighborhood in a Midwest community known for its nice homes, clean environment, safe streets, and good schools, a shy 15-year-old girl rose nervously from her chair during a heated neighborhood hearing on how to spend a government grant.

Face flushed, voice shaking, she made her case: "Please, won't you think about us teens? We don't have anywhere to go, especially in the winter. We really need something to do in our neighborhood. We could really use a community center."

Her poignant plea notwithstanding, the neighborhood council decided to use the money to refurbish a school playground. The rationale? One argument raised was that building facilities that encouraged teens to "hang out" could create an intimidating environment for toddlers and preschoolers.

No one raised the obvious question: Just what would these younger kids do and where would they go 10 years from now when they come of age in a community that clearly values childhood innocence over adolescent awakenings?

And how is it that these well-educated, typically well-meaning adults could leapfrog logic, ignoring the fact that these teens were the same ones they depend on to babysit their toddlers, mow their lawns, and shovel their sidewalks?

In a word, fear.

Out of the **mouth of teens...**

The Mall of America in Bloomington, Minn., is a favorite gathering place for hundreds of teens and a destination for thousands of shoppers worldwide. *Assets* Editor Kathleen Kimball-Baker spent a recent afternoon at the mall interviewing teens. Here's what she heard:

Hector,* 17, is a tall lanky Latino youth who dressed in baggy black pants, a black shirt, a backwards baseball cap. He was walking the mall.

KKB: *Do you think Americans are afraid of teens?*

H: Yeah. They're scared when someone like me walks by–scared something will happen to them. But I give no one reason to be afraid.

KKB: *How do you know they're afraid of you?*

H: (Grins) When I pass by they lock their doors or walk on the other side of the street

KKB: *Why do you think they're afraid?*

H: The movies they see about wild teenagers. My town has a lot of old people in it. They shouldn't be scared. They should understand us, get to know us, pay attention to us to see how we are.

# of Teens?

Appearances can be deceiving

The problem is perceptual, often confounded by racism, classism, and stereotypes. Can the average adult, for example, tell the difference between a kid in sagging, baggy pants who's only trying to "fit in" from one who's armed for a fight? Not always. Maybe never.

And then there are the facial expressions. Can adults tell if the teen with the angry look is ready to lash out violently, or is she simply trying to process a perceived slight by her best friend? And what about those loud teens sitting on the sidewalk in front of the dollar cinema: Are they about to accost and embarrass the moviegoers in line–or are they just trying to figure out if they have enough change to buy a ticket?

Without knowing, many adults may simply be taking caution too far. If so, the result is ever-growing alienation and misunderstanding. And worse, such perceptions may be chipping away at a fundamental faith that teens will grow into adults who may actually make the world a better place some day.

A Princeton survey sponsored by Newsweek and NBC News in April found that three-quarters of American adults held the belief that teens with poor education, dim job prospects, and worrisome values pose a greater danger to this country than any foreign threat.

A recent poll of Colorado adults, conducted by Search Institute, together with Norwest Public Policy Research Program at the University of Colorado – Denver, found that two-thirds of the 934 adults polled think youth don't respect adults and that teens get into more trouble today than youth did years ago.

The 'enemy' within: youth or fear?

According to Kids These Days: What Americans Really Think About the Next Generation, a report published by Public Agenda, a nonprofit research organization based in New York: "Americans are convinced that today's adolescents face a crisis – not in their economic or physical well-being but in their values and morals. Most Americans look at today's teenagers with misgiving and trepidation, viewing them as undisciplined, disrespectful, and unfriendly." Public Agenda based its findings on telephone surveys of 2,000 adults and 600 young teens, focus groups, and follow-up interviews.

But, at the same time that Americans are extremely critical of teens, they also refuse to give up on them.

Shireen,* 17, is a young woman of Middle-Eastern descent. She was wearing jeans, a t-shirt, and a black head covering. She was sitting on a bench, talking with her friend, Ali.

KKB: *Do you think Americans are afraid of teens?*

S: Actually, I don't think people are really afraid of teens. I just think they think there's no use trying to do anything about them, that they're just going through a phase.

Mara,* 16, a white youth, hangs out regularly at the mall. Heavily made up and chain-smoking, she sat with a group of friends just outside the mall.

KKB: *Do you think Americans are afraid of teens?*

M: I used to dress better than I dress now…but I don't see why people should be afraid of me.

KKB: *How long have you been smoking?*

M: (Counts on her fingers.) Four years.

KKB: *Don't you think that the fact that you smoke and are so young may intimidate some adults?*

M: That shouldn't intimidate you.

KKB: *What do you want adults to know about you?*

M: We're not bad kids. They shouldn't judge us by our appearance. Our

group here is the nicest little group of people you could ever meet, aren't we? (Chuckles among group follow.) I want them to make an effort to get to know us.

KKB: *Some adults think teens today don't have good values. Do you have values?*

M: What are values?

KKB: *Well, things like honesty, respect, responsibility.*

(No response)

KKB: *Good-heartedness…*

M: Yeah, I've got a good heart! (Laughter follows.) I'm honest to an extent, but you can't trust that many people.

KKB: *What about drugs? Do you think drugs can make kids violent?*

M: Drugs don't make you violent if you're not violent to begin with. I'll tell you a violent drug, though: alcohol.

*Names have been changed.

According to the report, adults "care deeply" about young people and "are stubbornly optimistic about the chances of reclaiming the lives of even the most troubled teens." Respondents were unified in their belief that solutions center on building character. Parents, they said, need to spend more time with their kids, schools need to do a better job of teaching kids "discipline, honesty, and respectfulness towards themselves and others," teens need to be involved in more constructive activities, and such boundaries as curfews and sanctions for wrongdoings must be firm.

Helping Adults Overcome Their **Fear of Teens**

How do we address the fears and negative attitudes people have about teens? The perceptions are complex and deeply embedded in our society and culture. However, here are ways asset-building communities can begin helping people shift from fearing to valuing youth:

- **Name the issue**—Negative stereotypes of teenagers are so much a part of the culture that many people don't even notice them...until you point them out. Naming the assumptions begins to disarm them.
- **Listen to young people**—Having young people tell their own stories and experiences personalizes the issue and brings it close to home. Just asking teenagers in your community how adults treat them in stores, on street corners, in parks, and other public places can start powerful conversations.
- **Provide opportunities for interaction**—One of the best ways to overcome stereotypes is to provide safe, comfortable places for interaction across generations.
- **Highlight the positives**—Go out of your way to recognize, affirm, and tell about ways young people (particularly those who defy the stereotypes) contribute to the community.
- **Challenge negative stereotypes**—When you see or hear blanket negative statements about teenagers in public settings, the media, or your own social network, find ways to challenge them—or at least offer balance. (This response may be as simple as offering an alternative perspective in a conversation.)
- **Put crises into perspective**—Too often, major crises involving youth (such as the recent school shootings) only confirm people's negative stereotypes of all youth. It's important to remember that the perpetrators of these tragedies are seriously disturbed teenagers–just as adult murderers are seriously disturbed adults. We must find ways as a society to prevent these kinds of tragedies–not use them to reinforce our stereotypes.
- **Recognize the influence of racism**—Complicating adult fears of youth is racism. Many men of color, for example, can easily recount episodes of being regarded with suspicion and fear by white persons. Being intentional about addressing this issue adds a particular focus to the strategies suggested above.

Moving through fear and discomfort

If Americans agree on solutions when it comes to teens, can they actually enact them? If so, first they must come to terms with their fear and next with their discomfort.

One of the sponsors of the Public Agenda report is the Advertising Council, based in New York, which plans to launch a decade-long effort to mobilize citizens to volunteer in their own communities on behalf of children and teens. Ruth Wooden, executive director of the Ad Council, believes important messages emerged from the study that can guide how her organization approaches its efforts.

Of great importance, says Wooden, is "humanizing the struggle of parents to raise their children" and emphasizing their need for help from the community. Surveys and interviews showed that many people know they need to pitch in, but they fear embarrassing those who they are trying to help. To change perceptions, says Wooden, a television spot could, for example, show a struggling single mom working several jobs and expressing appreciation for help from neighbors or community organizations.

One-on-one works, too

While the Ad Council works on a national scale, a good deal can happen locally. In Hardwick, Vt., for example, students stunned a group of adults in one day-long workshop by repeating back the frighteningly negative messages they have gotten from adults. The alternative list of how young people wished to be perceived led to a community education project called "Flip the Page."

On an individual level, many adults have to overcome a very basic fear–that of the unknown. But adults who've pushed past their discomfort with teens are often startled at how rewarding interactions with them can actually be, even very simple ones like greeting a teen neighbor by name or smiling at a young person cruising the shopping mall.

A security guard named Carol, who works at one of Minnesota's favorite teen hang-outs, the Mall of America, offered the following observation: "Most of the kids, even the regulars, the ones who dress up like vampires, are good kids. Yeah, they may walk around with what looks like an attitude. But adults are always downing them. It's not an attitude–it's a shield. I'd be doing that too if I was treated that way."

Kathleen Kimball-Baker is Editorial Director and Eugene C. Roelkepartain is Director of the Publishing & Communications Division at Search Institute in Minneapolis, Minnesota

The Millennials—Our Future Hope?

By Sally Gardiner

WILL THIS GENERATION (born 1981-1999) be the greatest generation? Some think so. Others are worried they will never be able to lead the world of tomorrow or even care to. Why such opposite views? Those who have studied the generations have high expectations. Those who only pay attention to the media hype and tragic events involving teens believe the worst. What's real?

The Millennials have some of the best characteristics of all who have come before. They show up as loyal, much like their traditionalist grandparents, optimistic like their boomer parents tempered with caution from their Gen X older siblings. In a word, they are realists.

They are the most technically advanced generation of all time, born with cell phones stitched into their onesies. They are true "Global Citizens" as the world has always been available to them with the click of a mouse or a remote. They assimilate information at a rapid pace from multiple sources at the same time and make decisions quickly. Thus they may appear cocky or less than thorough. Growing up with constant and immediate information, is it any wonder that they can move quickly when problem solving?

Their parents have involved them in family decision making. Being part of the solution is what they understand. They book vacations online for the family and do comparison shopping over the Internet. They expect to "play" as soon as they hit the job market and are not interested in and don't understand why "paying dues" is relevant with today's rate of change. They are communicative and tough to bully and can fend for themselves, yet they love being part of a team and collaboration is their middle name.

This generation has been raised by child-focused parents, overprotective and involved. The overprotection comes from fear of child abduction, molestation, AIDS and terrorism. This generation lives with fear for their personal safety COUNTERED with the support of involved parents. This balance was lacking for Gen Xers (whose parents both worked or who came from single parent families due to a 50% divorce rate), so the Millennials are emerging as cautious but confident team players.

This confidence is showing up in other ways as well. This generation has been raised to believe that they are "special." They have been told by their parents and teachers that they can have, be and do anything they choose. Many expect to be "famous & rich." Take for example the hit TV reality show "American Idol." In the early auditions, young people with virtually NO SINGING talent whatsoever, audition to be the next Idol! Do they do it for their "15 minutes of fame" (often the "really bad" auditions are shown on TV) or do they do it because of this belief that they can be, do and have whatever they want? As adults, have we inadvertently taught them that "believing" is all that is required for success? Have we stopped stressing hard work, determination, ability and talent? Is this specialness evolving into "entitlement"? As parents we need to help Millenials find the balance between being special (because they certainly are) and the reality of the attributes they possess and can develop.

One attribute they truly possess is tolerance. Diversity isn't a goal; they live it every day. Allowing others to live life in their own way is part of their value system. This may cause some elders to believe this generation doesn't stand for anything and will not fight for what is right. Could it be that tolerance and acceptance is the true "right" for everyone and finally there is a generation who gets this?

The Millennials may be the key to a more peaceful future. Their confidence, team mentality, technological expertise and tolerance of others ensure their influence will be nothing short of remarkable!

Written for Family Empowerment Network by Sally Gardiner, Certified Professional Coach, Reality Therapy Certified © 2008. For reprint requests, contact www.family-empower.com.

Connecting with Boys
Closing the Gap
By Eugene C. Roehlkepartain

BY SOME MEASURES, boys and men in the USA have it made. On average, men make more money than women. They're more likely to attain positions of authority. They're less likely to be victims of violence or abuse. So what do we make of the following statistics?

- Boys are more likely than girls to be incarcerated, be violent or commit homicide, and be victims of serious violent crime.
- Boys are more likely than girls to have chronic conditions such as asthma, to be diagnosed with learning disabilities, and to drop out of school.
- Boys and young men are less likely than girls and young women to volunteer and to be spiritually grounded.

In the recent flurry of media attention on the topic, explanations are varied and sometimes contradictory. Some people worry that paying attention to boys will undermine the important gains girls have made in recent decades. To establish that girls and women still draw the short end of the stick, they point to the statistics documenting the number of women who live in poverty or their unequal salary levels. Others counter that feminists have demonized masculinity; they suggest that boys need to harden up, not open up.

That's how the pundits have framed the issues. But how do we as asset builders respond? The values our 40 assets measure are often at odds with the societal measures of success and status in which men have traditionally excelled. Our goal as asset builders is to help our children grow up to be healthy, well-rounded individuals. But from an assets perspective, our boys are struggling, reporting fewer assets on average than do girls. How do we build strengths in boys without taking away from the gains of girls?

An Asset Snapshot

Taking a closer look at the Search Institute Profiles of Student Life: Attitudes and Behaviors survey data provides an overview of the issues facing boys. Among almost 100,000 6th- to 12th-grade students surveyed in 1996-1997, we found:

- Boys, on average, report having three fewer of the 40 Developmental Assets—16.5 vs. 19.5 for girls.
- There are 18 assets that girls are more likely to report having than are boys, but only 3 assets that boys are more likely to report having. (See chart on p. 1:25)
- Fifteen of the assets more commonly reported by girls than boys are internal assets.

These data suggest that something troubling may, indeed, be going on with boys. After all, we know that both boys and girls who experience more of the Developmental Assets are more likely to make healthy choices. And those who report fewer are more likely to try high-risk behaviors and disengage from school.

Why the Gap?

It's tempting to avoid asking this question. No one wants an unproductive debate over who or what's to blame. Yet thoughtful reflection on possible factors can help shape our responses. Here are some possibilities:

Biological differences. Boys and girls have distinct developmental pathways through childhood and adolescence. They typically have different ways of learning and different interests. While these differences are shaped by culture, many are also grounded in biology.

Researchers are learning, for example, that boys tend to have their first developmental "crisis point" in the early elementary years, not in early adolescence, which is the case for girls. In addition, fine motor skills (needed to hold a pencil in school) and reading abilities tend to develop later in boys. Boys also tend to be more active than girls. Thus, a one-size-fits-all approach will serve neither gender well.

"Most schools do not recognize that boys and girls learn at different tempos and in different styles," says Harvard Medical School's William Pollack. "Children are still expected to sit quietly for long periods and learn visually. But boys do better if they can move around and handle things. In many schools that's considered bad behavior or a conduct disorder; so instead of learning, boys are sent to the principal's office."

Social pressure. Though society is showing some signs of change, the dominant messages boys receive reinforce stereotypical masculinity. For example, a 1999 study of the influence of the media on boys by Oakland, California-based Children Now (www.childrennow.org) found that "In spite of the complex and changing work and family experiences of real-life men, media portrayals do not reflect this complexity. Rather, messages and images remain strongly stereotypical."

In *Real Boys*, Pollack argues that males are pressured to follow what he calls "the boys code," which involves "living behind a mask of masculine bravado that hides the genuine self." One upshot of this enforced bravado is that we too often dismiss aggression and insensitivity with the platitude that "boys will be boys." While we have expanded "acceptable" options for girls and women in such spheres as sports and business, we haven't done as well at inviting boys and men to explore personal interests that emphasize relationships, caring, and creative expression. Cultural norms tell boys that such interests aren't "masculine."

Ironically, as society has learned to value more nurturing qualities (traditionally associated with femininity), it may also have become less tolerant of "normal" behavior in boys. A high level of physical energy and an urge to conquer were, in an earlier age, essential to survival. As Michael Gurian, author of *Boys and Girls Learn Differently*, pleads: "We need to love boys for who they are. Let's not try to rewire them."

A different measure of success.

By and large, male success in this culture is weighed in

Photo by Hoby Finn

economic and political terms. By these measures, US culture is clearly biased against girls. The cultural role assigned women is preserving relational and emotional health—an important job that doesn't earn money and so is undervalued. Thus attention in recent decades has appropriately focused on addressing such issues as inequities in income for women, glass ceilings that limit their power and influence, and how girls can be hurt by a society that too often objectifies and undervalues them.

However, if the measure of success is a well-adjusted human being, as we at Search Institute believe, then we also need to ask whether and how US culture is problematic for boys. The asset framework attempts a holistic approach to identifying what young people need to grow up healthy, caring, and responsible. That boys lag behind girls most dramatically on the internal assets suggests that cultivating relationships and a rich inner life is particularly challenging for them. It is also revealing that the asset with the greatest gap between girls and boys is interpersonal competence.

Strategies for Asset Builders

So, as asset builders, how do we respond? We want to celebrate boys' innate qualities, while also setting appropriate limits and channeling their energy into productive outlets. This means finding ways to connect more effectively with individual boys, as well as entering the public dialogue about how society can better address gender issues.

Here are some approaches to consider:

Avoid sensationalizing boys' problems. Intensive scrutiny of a few dreadful incidents can lead to a crisis mentality that demonizes all boys. Tragically, a few boys have opened fire on their fellow students. However, the vast majority of boys are following a relatively innocuous pathway toward adulthood.

Yes, there's work to be done. Yes, there are areas of serious concern. But sensationalizing the issue sends boys the message that they are problems, rather than resources and gifts. It also makes adults feel powerless to make a difference—when their active engagement with boys is precisely what's needed.

Don't put boys against girls. When looking at typical differences between genders, the temptation to pull out a scorecard to mark who's ahead and who's behind is tempting. But boys aren't in their current situation because we've been paying too much attention to girls. Indeed, one can argue that we haven't paid enough attention to either boys or girls.

Despite the tremendous emphasis on opportunities for girls in recent decades, there is still much work to be done. A 2000 study of youth development organizations by the Washington, D.C.–based Public Education Network (www. PublicEducation.org) found a "dearth of opportunities for young women… We found both an absolute level of under service to girls overall in communities, and too many instances of girls being treated as second-class citizens in coeducational programs."

Offer alternatives to common stereotypes. If the dominant male images are one-dimensional, stereotypical snapshots, then we need to reframe what success and wholeness can mean. Seeing men in their own lives and in the media acting in ways that are both strong and emotional, driven and contemplative, will encourage boys to explore more dimensions of themselves.

Move beyond one-size-fits-all thinking. If nothing else, the differences between boys and girls remind us that young people are diverse in every aspect of their lives. Tailoring our interactions to the individual needs of each young person will better help each learn and grow. Focusing separately on the developmental needs of boys and girls may sometimes also be appropriate. Michelee Curtze of Edinboro, Pa., offers separate classes for seventh- and eighth-grade boys and girls in her school district. The young people work in small groups with volunteer community mentors to identify issues they have growing up male or female and to find ways to address them. Not only do the boys and girls have a chance to talk about

their lives, but they also build an important connection with a caring adult and positive role model.

Tap boys' interests. A basic tenet of asset building is to connect with young people around their strengths and interests. While boys can get fired up about everything from rock guitar to football to debate team, they often seem drawn to activities that emphasize physical or intellectual challenge or competition, not the relationship building or inward reflection that is so central to asset building.

Still, a creative approach on the part of asset builders can yield results. If a boy is interested in computers, for example, consider tapping him to work on your initiative's Web site. If sports are his passion, emphasize teambuilding over winning at all costs. If he enjoys working with his hands, then work alongside him and talk while you work. If he's a video game aficionado, consider asking him how video games help him build assets (see "First-Person Perspective" on page 15).

Challenge boys to stretch themselves. Targeted efforts to address those areas where many boys struggle also seem warranted. The Developmental Assets data suggest that boys may need to be challenged with opportunities that help them develop relationship skills, nurture their inner life of values, and foster a sense of caring and service to others.

Lee Manogg of Newark, Ohio, says that she wishes she had been more intentional in encouraging her son, who was not a "joiner," to participate in after-school activities. "I let him convince me that he didn't need to be involved in structured activities," she says, "and I believe he still struggles to know how to approach a group and find his own way within it."

Celebrating Boys
The challenge we face as asset builders, then, is to celebrate boys' innate qualities, while also setting appropriate limits and channeling their sometimes abundant energy into productive outlets. Cultivating internal and relational strengths such as caring, interpersonal skills, restraint, and positive values will be crucial. Those same qualities offer a necessary foundation for deep relationships, civic engagement, and active parenting in a time when men and women are renegotiating roles and responsibilities in a changing world.

Books for Boys

Here are recent books on raising boys. Reader alert: These folks definitely don't all agree!

- Geoffrey Canada: *Reaching Up for Manhood: Transforming the Lives of Boys in America.* Boston: Beacon Press, 1998.
- Michael Gurian and Patricia Henley with Terry Trueman: *Boys and Girls Learn Differently: A Guide for Teachers and Parents.* San Francisco: Jossey-Bass, 2001.

- Christina Hoff Sommers: *The War Against Boys: How Misguided Feminism Is Harming Our Young Men.* New York: Simon & Schuster, 2000.
- Dan Kindlon and Michael Thomspon: *Raising Cain: Protecting the Emotional Life of Boys.* New York: Balantine, 1999.
- William Pollack: *Real Boys: Rescuing Our Sons from the Myths of Boyhood.* New York: Holt, 1998.

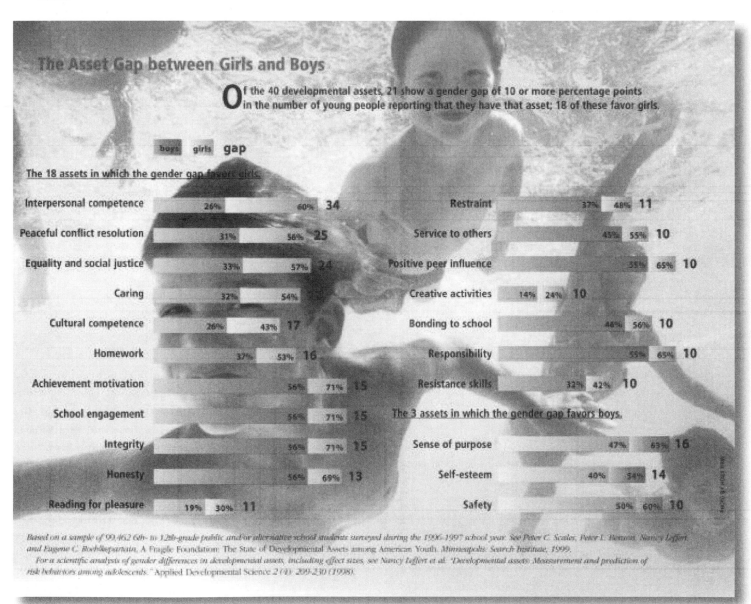

The Asset Gap between Girls and Boys

Of the 40 developmental assets, 21 show a gender gap of 10 or more percentage points in the number of young people reporting that they have that asset; 18 of these favor girls.

boys   girls   gap

The 18 assets in which the gender gap favors girls:

	boys	girls	gap
Interpersonal competence	26%	60%	34
Peaceful conflict resolution	31%	56%	25
Equality and social justice	33%	57%	24
Caring	32%	54%	
Cultural competence	26%	43%	17
Homework	37%	53%	16
Achievement motivation	56%	71%	15
School engagement	56%	71%	15
Integrity	56%	71%	15
Honesty	56%	69%	13
Reading for pleasure	19%	30%	11

	boys	girls	gap
Restraint	37%	48%	11
Service to others	45%	55%	10
Positive peer influence	55%	65%	10
Creative activities	14%	24%	10
Bonding to school	46%	56%	10
Responsibility	55%	65%	10
Resistance skills	32%	42%	10

The 3 assets in which the gender gap favors boys:

	boys	girls	gap
Sense of purpose	47%	63%	16
Self-esteem	40%	34%	14
Safety	50%	60%	10

Based on a sample of 99,462 6th- to 12th-grade public and/or alternative school students surveyed during the 1996-1997 school year. See Peter C. Scales, Peter L. Benson, Nancy Leffert and Eugene C. Roehlkepartain, A Fragile Foundation: The State of Developmental Assets among American Youth. Minneapolis: Search Institute, 1999.

For a scientific analysis of gender differences in developmental assets, including effect sizes, see Nancy Leffert et al. "Developmental assets: Measurement and prediction of risk behaviors among adolescents." Applied Developmental Science 2 (4): 209-230 (1998).

Raising Better Boys

By Geoffrey Canada, author of *Reaching Up for Manhood*

BOYS TODAY FACE **overwhelming challenges—from negative media images to epidemics of violence. But with family and community support, our boys can learn about responsibility, healing, and self-respect.**

I had just come back to my office from a meeting when I was told that a reporter was on the phone. When I answered the call, the reporter asked what by now has become a familiar question: "Did you hear about the shooting?"

Because the reporter called me, I knew several things right away. First, whoever was shot was a child. Second, the victim was not a child with whom I work. When one of my children from Harlem is shot and killed, nobody calls; death by handgun is so common that it is no longer considered news. This shooting must have taken place in a nice, middle-class suburban or rural community. Third, I knew that more than one child was shot. Today in the United States, the shooting of one child, even in affluent communities, is not considered newsworthy. And fourth, I knew that the shooter was a boy. In this country, our girls surely have their problems, but our boys are the ones who kill.

Boys in Trouble

At a time when we have made incredible advances in technology and medicine, we have managed to create a generation of boys who are more in trouble than ever before. The signs ought to be clear, but we are not heeding the warnings. The shootings in Paducah, Jonesboro, and Littleton might seem, by themselves, like isolated tragic incidents, but collectively they form a familiar pattern.

I saw a similar pattern begin in 1985, although I must admit that with all my years of working with children, I didn't have a clue about what I was witnessing. In 1985, one boy with whom I worked at the Rheedlen Centers for Children and Families was shot and killed. In 1986, two more of our boys were shot and killed. In 1987, four of our boys were shot and killed. This pattern continued until, in 1989, seven boys were shot and killed. Even then I didn't recognize the killings for what they were. I tried to understand each killing as the separate act of a violent perpetrator against an innocent (and sometimes not so innocent) victim. Not until 1990 did I realize what was happening in my New York City community, Harlem, was happening in communities in Chicago, Detroit, Kansas City, Los Angeles, Boston—indeed, in cities and towns across the United States. We had not a series of individual violent acts, but evidence of a full-scale epidemic of violence.

In my first book, *Fist Stick Knife Gun, A Personal History of Violence in America* (1994), I wrote about the escalating violence in poor communities. By then, we had lost more than 60,000 children to handgun violence in less than 10 years. My purpose for the book was not just to recite the facts and horrors about poor children who grow up in war-like conditions, but also to serve as a warning. This epidemic would spread out of the ghettos and into our middle-class enclaves if we didn't do something about it.

We haven't done much, and the killings have not been abated. The Children's Defense Fund reports that between 1979 and 1996, more than 75,000 US children and teens were killed by firearms and a staggering 375,000 were

> "During soccer season, some of my white friends and I went to 7-Eleven to buy soda. And as soon as I walked in with them, I was followed all the way around the store. Meanwhile, my white friends were stealing soda. People think that racism is gone, but it's still there"
> —10th grade boy

wounded. And we see the first signs of the same pattern of epidemic violence in communities that are not poor, not minority, not urban.

In 1996, after taking a closer look at children and violence, I realized that boys seem particularly susceptible to the most virulent form of the epidemic. The more research I did, the worse the news seemed—not just in terms of violence, but within a whole range of categories. I found a disturbing pattern among people ages 15 to 25. Three out of four deaths are of males. Males are five times more likely to die from homicide than females are. Six out of seven suicides in this age range are by males. Nine out of 10 arrests are of males. My research led to a shocking conclusion: Not just a small sample, but a huge number of boys are doing poorly.

My second book, *Reaching Up for Manhood* (1998), focused on the troubling social and environmental conditions that boys face today. On the basis of my research, I suggested what we can do to raise better boys.

Healing

Boys are in pain. Years of conditioning starting when boys are toddlers teach them to deny their pain, that "boys don't cry." But boys should cry. It is a natural reaction and a way to acknowledge and release pain, both physical and emotional. Denying emotions not only represses and stunts emotional growth, but it also masks our hurt from others so that they don't know that we need help.

We have to reach out to our boys early on and get them to talk about their feelings. This is easier when boys are young, but somewhere between 10 and 13, boys begin to resist talking. When they hit puberty, boys feel that it is taboo to talk about shame and inadequacy, especially with their parents. How do we get boys to remain in touch with their feelings? How can we ensure that adults in their lives are compassionate and skilled at talking with them and listening to them during this crucial period? For every boy we work with, we must ask, "With whom does he talk?" When the answer is no one, we must find the right people to fill that void.

Risk

Boys are encouraged to take risks very early in life. We think it natural for boys to jump off steps, climb trees, and jump puddles.

Adults, including parents, often consciously or unconsciously reinforce this risk-taking behavior, and boys confuse taking risks with being male and masculine. This prepares our boys for dangerous risk taking when they become adolescents. Boys often break the laws (both legal and parental) when peers challenge them. The words "I dare you" or "What's the matter, you scared?" have ruined the life of many a boy.

We must make sure that our boys can take risks in safe environments. There are plenty of risky things for boys to do that challenge them, but in a healthy and developmentally appropriate way. Some boys play sports, some dance, some ride bikes or horses. We must offer a full menu of choices. All boys don't like basketball; some get a thrill from facing an opponent one-on-one in a game of chess; others find that nothing short of jumping into the air on a skateboard and doing a 360-degree turn will do. But one thing is certain: If we don't provide safe risks for boys, they will engage in dangerous activities that can leave scars more damaging than scraped knees and wounded egos.

Self-Worth

Our boys are the target of successful sales and marketing strategies by large and sophisticated retailers. They connect our boys' sense of self-worth to how they look and what they wear, eat, or drink. Boys get the message that they are what they look like and what they consume. Vulnerable boys are taught to focus less on their internal development than the external world. Parents and teachers struggle to get boys to pay attention to such values as cooperation, kindness, and service. We think our boys are shallow and lack values, but we fail to realize that their minds are influenced by the smartest and most savvy advertisers in the world.

We must recognize that our boys are brainwashed by the sneaker companies, the fast food industry, the soft drink industry, and others too numerous to name. Remember Joe Camel? The cigarette company knew what would appeal to our children and launched a successful campaign. Our children are a market, and marketers understand our children's fears, aspirations, and fantasies—often better than we do. They use this understanding to shape our children's attitudes and beliefs.

> Boys struggle to understand the concept of manhood, and if they don't have positive role models, too many of them look to the streets, to television, or to the movies to understand what it takes to be a man.

We must pay attention to the values that these industries sell to our children and contrast them with the values that we talk to them about. Most teachers and parents do well to give their children five positive messages a day. In contrast, by the time that day is over, our children will have heard 50 negative messages from their music, television, video games, and radio. It's not that our children don't value our messages. Rather, we are drowned out by the number of negative messages that they hear from other sources.

We have to even out this equation by giving more positive messages of self-worth and by reducing the number of negative messages from others. We must talk with our boys about how they view themselves on the inside and encourage and reward them for focusing on both their internal and external selves.

Mentors

Too many boys lack positive male role models. The number of fathers who are not intimately involved in raising their sons because of separation, divorce, or abandonment has reached staggering proportions. Boys struggle to understand the concept of manhood, and if they don't have positive role models, too many of them look to the streets, to television, or to the movies to understand what it takes to be a man. In these places, they are liable to find manhood defined as a combination of toughness, promiscuity, hard drinking, and a willingness to solve every dispute with violence. Boys emulate those visions of manhood with the youthful exuberance with which teens embrace most things.

We must ensure that our boys have male role models who take a personal interest in their moral, intellectual, and emotional development. Where should we look for male mentors? At our institutions of faith, at our college fraternities, at our youth organizations. Boys need not one, but several male mentors in their lives.

What We Can All Do

Can we raise better boys? We can and we must. In one year alone, more than 1.3 million boys under 18 were arrested. One out of every four males in the United States has a record. Fully two-thirds of boys who reach the age of 15 in Harlem can expect to die in young or middle adulthood. If we raise our boys in the same way, we will continue to produce huge numbers of boys who are crippled emotionally and are unprepared to fulfill their roles as fathers, husbands, and productive members of our society. The following are some additional suggestions.

Monitor What They See and Hear

Our children watch too much television, and with the advent of cable, children at very young ages are exposed to violence and sex in a way that was unimaginable 20 years ago. Do you know the lyrics to the latest rap song? Do you watch MTV? Looked at Saturday morning cartoons lately? We should watch what our boys are watching. The mass media shape so much of a boy's sense of himself and his image of manhood. If we spend time watching and listening with them, we will find plenty of opportunities to engage boys in real conversations about real issues before someone else is allowed to shape their thinking.

Find a Place for Spiritual and Moral Education

Most people from my generation (I'm 47) were introduced to spiritual and moral development through a formal institution of faith. I'm a Christian, and my mother made me go to church every Sunday, even though I didn't want to until I was 12 years old. In church, I heard about good and evil and about the responsibility to give back, to help others, and to do unto others as you would have them do unto you. Too many of our boys receive scant, if any, education in these crucial areas. It doesn't matter what our particular faith is; we must encourage parents to expose their boys to their faith institutions. Too often, we don't think about the moral development of boys until they are in trouble. Everyone who is raising a boy should plan out his moral and spiritual development while he is still young.

Expose Boys to Different Cultures and Points of View

Boys tend to be intolerant of others. They can be racist, sexist, and cruel to other boys who don't conform to their ideas or standards. We give too little thought to broadening the experiences of boys so that early in their lives, they learn about many different cultures, attitudes, and beliefs. We wait until our boys have developed rigid prejudices before we talk with them about differences and tolerance. Our work should begin in elementary school and continue throughout their educational lives.

Know Their Friends

By the time most boys reach puberty, they do what their friends do. If you want to know what any one boy is doing, find out what his friends are doing. Sooner or later, he will do the same thing. This means that when we try to influence a boy, we should not work exclusively with that boy, but also with his friends. Too many times, we try to reach boys as individuals without acknowledging the power of the peer group.

Expose Boys to New Experiences

Take boys on nature walks. Start with frogs and turtles, but include plants and flowers. Teach them about the environment, sailing, singing, sewing, and dancing. By the time boys are 12, they usually say they don't want to try something new if we haven't made a habit of expanding their experiences when they were young. Very quickly, boys decide that some activities are for boys—riding a bike, playing sports—and some are not—smelling flowers, baking bread. Our job is to not allow hastily developed, arbitrary beliefs to deprive boys of a fuller set of experiences.

Have a Multilayered Support System

I have found (not surprisingly) that boys who have several strong support systems—parents, grandparents, uncles and aunts, cousins their own age, coaches, teachers, and caring adults who run after-school activities—do better than boys who don't. Boys with more support systems get into less trouble, and if they do get into trouble, they get out of it more quickly and are less likely to get back into it. Part of our responsibility in raising better boys is to expand the number of support systems that exist for them. The less influential their family support, the more they need community support.

Reconnecting with All Our Children

Our boys are in trouble, but all is not lost. We have the know-how and the resources in the United States to dramatically change boys' lives for the better. We must find ways to bring new attention and energy to boys—without ever losing our focus on girls. This calls for us to rededicate ourselves to ensuring that we give the best that we have to all our children.

From the Educational Leadership Journal; December 1999, January 2000 published by Association for Supervision and Curriculum Development, ©1999. Geoffrey Canada is President of the Rheedlen Centers for Children and Families, 2770 Broadway, New York, NY 10025.

Listening to Our Sons

By Kathy Keller Jones, MA

ONE OF THE MOST important things we can do for our sons is to listen deeply to their feelings, needs, and experiences. Of course, listening empathetically without interrupting, problem solving, or minimizing is a critical skill in all of our social interactions, so why is this particularly important in parenting our sons? As they grow, young males in our culture are very affected by "The Boy Box" which pushes them to act tough and hide their real feelings (except anger). Other boys and even adults reinforce this "box" by shaming boys who don't match these expectations, using put-downs and bullying. Fathers and mothers may also encourage toughness in their sons or prematurely push them to be independent, and feel worried if they see "sensitivity." Michael Thompson in *Speaking of Boys* speaks directly to this issue when he reminds us that our sons' "sensitivity" is really the beginnings of "emotional literacy" that will serve him well his whole life:

> *All you have to do is respect his need to appear strong at times, and make it safe for him to open up his heart to you. There is a huge body of research suggesting that sensitive boys, emotionally literate boys, are going to have a much larger repertoire with which to meet the many complex and challenging emotional experiences in life, of which teasing is just one. Congratulations on raising a sensitive son.*[1]

Our sons have an even greater need for additional support in the area of emotional literacy because their brains, which are so competent in other respects, have smaller communication and emotional memory centers, and there is less activity going on between the two sides of the brain.[2] This means that our sons will benefit from lots of direct experience talking about feelings, recognizing their own and other's emotions, and problem solving through quiet reflection.[3]

How, you may wonder, given the culture in which they grow up, can we get our boys to talk to us about what they are really feeling? Dr. William Pollack, author of *Real Boys' Voices*, is an expert on this topic. He reminds us that our boys need us to establish a confidential "shame-free zone"[4] where they can talk about their real thoughts and feelings while feeling safe from judgment and shame. Our son may need time to think things over before he talks, "timed silence,"[4] so we let him know we are available when he is ready. Boys are also most comfortable talking when they are doing some kind of activity, like shooting baskets, going for a drive, or a hike. Pollack calls this "action talk."[4] Even when our boys are in trouble we can provide empathy for their situation while also following through calmly with consequences. By giving our boys empathy, love, and regular periods of undivided attention and listening space, we are developing our sons' emotional literacy skills and aiding them in becoming their true selves.

[1] Thompson, M. *Speaking of Boys* (2000).
[2] Brizendine, L. *The Female Brain* (2006).
[3] Biddulph, S. *Raising Boys* (1998).
[4] Pollack, W. *Real Boys' Voices* (2000)

"Boy in the Box" Activity

Adapted from *Boys Will Be Men: Raising our Sons for Courage, Caring and Community* by Paul Kivel

This exercise can be used with adults and boys from 4th grade and up. It helps participants see the pressure on our boys and men to be "hyper-masculine."

THE ACTIVITY:
- Draw a box.
- Have the group brainstorm and list all of the messages from our culture and the media about how a young man should look or act. Write these words and phrases inside of the box.
- On the left side of the box, have the group list names and words that a boy is called if he is not behaving according to the words within the box, or is not behaving "like a man."
- On the right side of the box, have the group list all of the physical things that may happen to the boy if he is behaving contrary to the words within the box.

THE LESSON:
From a very early age, boys are taught to hide the majority of their normal human emotions, such as pain, confusion, sadness, love, excitement, curiosity, frustration, humiliation, shame, grief, self-doubt, loneliness and low self-worth (to name a few…). Instead, they are taught to appear tough and always in control, as well as aggressive, in charge, sexual, not making mistakes. Anger becomes the only acceptable feeling, and most importantly, boys are taught never to cry.

The Box represents everything that a "man" is supposed to be. Every time a boy tries to step outside of the box, he is pushed back inside with verbal assaults such as the ones written on the left side of the box that you as a group just listed, and by the physical abuse like those that you just listed on the right side of the box.

Boys are forced to fit themselves inside of this very limiting box in order to meet the widespread expectations that our society holds for them. They patrol themselves in order to avoid the verbal and physical abuse, while also patrolling each other by abusing others for not acting within the confines of the box. In addition, the feelings produced by the abuse, training and pressure each time a boy tries to step outside of the box are only met with more criticism, forcing the boy even deeper inside the box.

Every single young man needs respectful, physical affection from the adults around him. However, our desire for closeness is often at odds with our desire to toughen up our boys so they will not be vulnerable in a world that expects men to be tough. Instead of giving in to the belief that "boys will be boys," we need to remind ourselves that "boys will be men" and they need our support in figuring out how to be men who are not trapped inside of the box.

Example: "Boy in the Box"

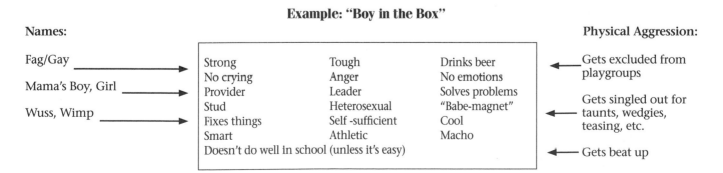

Names:				Physical Aggression:
Fag/Gay	Strong	Tough	Drinks beer	Gets excluded from playgroups
Mama's Boy, Girl	No crying	Anger	No emotions	
	Provider	Leader	Solves problems	Gets singled out for taunts, wedgies, teasing, etc.
Wuss, Wimp	Stud	Heterosexual	"Babe-magnet"	
	Fixes things	Self-sufficient	Cool	
	Smart	Athletic	Macho	
	Doesn't do well in school (unless it's easy)			Gets beat up

An Asset Checklist

By Search Institute, from *The Asset Approach: Giving Kids What They Need to Succeed*

Many people find it helpful to use a simple checklist to reflect on the assets young people experience. This checklist simplifies the asset list to help prompt conversation in families, organization, and communities. ***Note:*** *This checklist is not intended nor appropriate as a scientific or accurate measurement of Developmental Assets.*

☐ 1. I receive high levels of love and support from family members.

☐ 2. I can go to my parent(s) for advice and support and have frequent, in-depth conversations with them.

☐ 3. I know some nonparent adults I can go to for advice and support.

☐ 4. My neighbors encourage and support me.

☐ 5. My school provides a caring, encouraging environment.

☐ 6. My parent(s) or guardian(s) help me succeed in school.

☐ 7. I feel valued by adults in my community.

☐ 8. I am given useful roles in my community.

☐ 9. I serve in the community one hour or more each week.

☐ 10. I feel safe at home, at school, and in the neighborhood.

☐ 11. My family sets standards for appropriate conduct and monitors my whereabouts.

☐ 12. My school has clear rules and consequences for behavior.

☐ 13. Neighbors take responsibility for monitoring my behavior.

☐ 14. Parent(s) and other adults model positive, responsible behavior.

☐ 16. My parent(s)/guardian(s) and teachers encourage me to do well.

☐ 17. I spend three hours or more each week in lessons or practice in music, theater, or other arts.

☐ 18. I spend three hours or more each week in school or community sports, clubs, or organizations.

☐ 19. I spend one hour or more each week in religious services or participating in spiritual activities.

☐ 20. I go out with friends "with nothing special to do" two or fewer nights each week.

☐ 21. I want to do well in school.

☐ 22. I am actively engaged in learning.

☐ 23. I do an hour or more of homework each day.

☐ 24. I care about my school.

☐ 25. I read for pleasure three or more hours each week.

☐ 26. I believe it is really important to help other people.

☐ 27. I want to promote equality and reduce world poverty and hunger.

☐ 28. I can stand up for what I believe.

☐ 29. I tell the truth even when it's not easy.

☐ 30. I can accept and take personal responsibility.

☐ 31. I believe it is important not to be sexually active or to use alcohol or other drugs.

☐ 32. I am good at planning ahead and making decisions.

☐ 33. I am good at making and keeping friends.

☐ 34. I know and am comfortable with people of different cultural/racial/ethnic backgrounds.

☐ 35. I can resist negative peer pressure and dangerous situations.

☐ 36. I try to resolve conflict nonviolently.

☐ 37. I believe that I have control over many things that happen to me.

☐ 38. I feel good about myself.

☐ 39. I believe my life has a purpose.

☐ 40. I am optimistic about my future.

What Influences Him? 2

Kara Tucker, 8th Grade, Rosemont Ridge Middle School

What Influences Him?

> *"Average six-year-old children have spent more time watching TV than they will spend talking to their fathers in their lifetimes."*
> *Television, Violence, and Children* —U of O Thesis Paper, by Carla Kalin (1997)
>
> *"Advertising has a thousand principles, one purpose, and no morals."* —Humorist Finley Peter Dunne, 1909
>
> *"Kids are the epicenter, the top agents in decisions about what the family buys."*
> —Juliet Schor, author of *Born to Buy*
>
> *"Marketing to teens is like untapped Africa—a market segment worth $150 billion."* —*Merchants of Cool* video
>
> *"Three minutes spent looking at models in a fashion magazine caused 70% of women to feel depressed, guilty and shameful."* —1995 psychological study
>
> *"The best screening device is between the ears of your child."*
> —Nancy Willard, author of *Cyber-Safe Kids*

GOALS

- To become familiar with the research establishing a link between violence in our society and violent TV shows, movies, and video games

- To become familiar with the research about the media culture our boys are growing up in today and how powerfully the media influences them

- To explore the power of advertising and marketing not only on our sons directly, but also the ways in which commercialism creates their culture

- To become more media literate so that we can guide our families in making wise decisions about what to watch, play and purchase

OVERVIEW

Media as Teacher

Where do children learn their values and develop a vision of their future? That can depend upon where you live, according to Dr. Bill Daggett of the International Leadership Institute. Children in Europe learn from family, religion and national leaders. Media is a distant fourth. Children in Japan learn from leaders and family (a close tie) with religion a distant third and media fourth. However, children in America learn from TV first, then leaders (these being leaders in entertainment and sports, such as Bart Simpson, sports and reality stars). Family is a distant third and religion is fourth. What values are American children learning? What is the "vision of the future" that our children hold?

Viewed from this standpoint, parents can see how important it is to become empowered to lessen the grip that the media has over their own kids' lives and to teach their children critical media viewing skills. Becoming an educated, conscientious, media-literate parent goes a long way towards putting your own family values first in your child's life. The purpose of this media chapter is to give parents a better understanding of the ways in which the media bombards children with messages, and to learn how to mitigate the negative effects that the media has on our children's lives. Our hope is that parents will become more conscious "consumers" of the media, will buffer their children from the negative effects of media violence and consumerism, and will start taking an active role in holding corporations accountable for their children's programming and entertainment.

The Research

Look around you. **"Some Media Facts to Get Us Started"** (p. 2:17) explores how children in the United States are surrounded by influences from the media, from intense advertising, exposure to violence, and loss of time that could have been spent on reading, homework, using their imagination, getting outside, exercising or interacting with friends and family. And our children start young with their screen time, with babies less than 18 months old spending, on average, two hours per day in front of the TV, in spite of the

strong recommendation of the Academy of Pediatrics that children under two should not watch television at all.

A 2005 Kaiser Family Foundation study called "Generation M: Media in the Lives of 8-18 Year Olds" looked at screen time. The average American child spends almost 4 hours a day watching TV/movies, 1 hour on the computer outside of school work (internet and instant messaging) and just under 50 minutes a day playing videogames. Over the last five years the total amount of media content children consume has increased one hour per day, but because kids multitask their media, the total number of hours has stayed the same. **"Summary of Generation M"** (p. 2:19) shares more details on this study. Today's teens experience the world as a multi-media network of instant connections.

Consumerism and Cool Hunting

The media certainly has also latched on to our kids as consumers. **"Our Children and Consumerism"** (p. 2:20) discusses the moral cost of advertisers preying on the vulnerabilities of our children and using them to the marketer's advantage. Juliet Schor's book *Born to Buy*, as summarized in **"The Silver Bullet"** (p. 2:21), shares how deeply consumerism affects our families. Two-year-olds know brand names. Consider the impact of the "Nag Factor" in your life? Do you work longer hours for the stuff your children say they need?

The video *Merchants of Cool* (PBS Frontline) talks about the teen market in 2002 which was 32 million strong—the largest generation ever, even bigger than the baby boomers. Teens spent $100 billion a year on themselves and they influenced their parents to spend another $50 billion yearly. Retailers have taken note. Everywhere our teens look, they are bombarded with marketing messages—over 3000 per day!

Teens do not respond to traditional marketing, but they do respond to "cool." Major media outlets (like Rupert Murdock's NewsCorp, Disney, Viacom, AOL/Time Warner and Universal/Vivendi) are always looking for "cool." They employ "cool hunters," or culture spies, to study our teenagers. Cool hunters look for the 20% of kids who are trend-setters or early adopters. They pick up their ideas and styles and then sell them back to the masses. Ironically, as soon as something is successfully marketed to teens as "cool," it is no longer "cool." "Cool" has a very short shelf life thus the frenzy to keep it all going.

If your son is older than 12, consider watching the "Merchants of Cool" together. Discuss how corporations use the media to sell to kids for their own profit and with no thought about how it affects the children to whom they sell. When watching this show with your son, it helps to remember that it is more important to share and respect each other's opinions and interpretations than to agree on everything.

Media and Health

"Impact of Media on our Children's Health" (p. 2:20) presents some of the positive and negative impacts the media can have on our kids. The first section of the article, "When Children Walked the Earth: Is the Active Child Becoming Extinct" is a sad commentary on the state of affairs of our children's physical health. There is a clear link between screen time, overeating and lack of activity. This contributes to the epidemic of obesity and diabetes. Some believe that the lack of time spent playing and interacting with other kids and adults has even led to decreased social skills and problem-solving ability. In addition, other problems for avid media consumers

can include depression, low self-esteem, and addiction to cigarettes, alcohol and drugs. Alcohol is heavily marketed to our children. Beer ads in sports games equate drinking beer with popularity, being "cool" and success with women. Magazines with high youth readership,

advertise beer and hard liquor so heavily that youth actually see MORE alcohol advertising than adults according to The Center on Alcohol, Marketing and Youth.

Of course, media can also be used for good purposes. For example, the "Elmo Broccoli Study" found that broccoli with an Elmo sticker was preferred over a chocolate bar with an unknown character. Other studies show that just a "little bit" of media literacy education can reduce teen smoking choices.

"Fear Sells: Is No News Good News?" (p. 2:23) reminds us that children don't see the media with the same screening lens that we do. The evening news can promote the "mean world syndrome" in our children, as well as in ourselves. The more bad news we watch, the more we think the world is a bad place. Children need to develop a joyful, hopeful sense of place, before they face the distorted perspective of bad news. Our own fears can interfere with thinking clearly about how to parent wisely. Today, many parents imagine that their kids are safer watching screens full of strangers than playing in their own neighborhood.

Lookism

Lookism is "discrimination against or prejudice towards others based on their appearance." The sad thing about "cool" is that it really hits our teenagers' insecurity hot button. "Cool" implies that without a certain product or look, you will never be popular, independent, masculine/feminine, successful, or good-looking enough. Our teens are encouraged to become obsessed with their appearance.

For boys, there are also various popular looks or images. In an effort to be "buff" enough, some boys become obsessed with working out and taking steroids to improve their appearance and performance. Another image marketed to our sons is called, in the media industry, the "mook." A mook is crude, loud, obnoxious and in your face. He thinks that sexual harassment is entertaining. He does not care what other people think. (Think of Howard Stern or the stars of *Jackass*.) One female look being marketed is called, in the corporate media world, a "midriff." (Think Britney Spears.) A midriff is a premature adult, consumed by appearance, seeing herself primarily as a sexual object and proud of it. Sexuality is equated with power and liberation. And, she had better be skinny! Teen girls particularly fall victim to "lookism" which can drive them to eating disorders and death.

A mook and a midriff may not be true to life, but these are the images being marketed to our children, along with the unprecedented sexual sophistication of many shows on MTV, sitcoms and in the movies. And, sadly enough, because the major media outlets go out of their way to "understand" teens and their culture and deliver what teens "want," our teens tend to view their parents and teachers as nerds and geeks who simply don't understand them. Corporate sponsors can become the superheroes who do understand.

Sexuality

As our boys transition from childhood to adolescence, messages in the media pressure boys to act macho, aggressive, and insensitive to feelings (see "Boy in the Box," Chapter 1). They may also feel pressured to view girls as sex objects since this is how girls typically appear in video games, MTV and some movies. Boys are pressured to prove their manhood by "scoring." When alcohol enters a boy's world he can be at even greater risk, both for unplanned and sometimes unwanted sexual behavior, as well as for alcohol abuse. Our commercial culture actually uses the concept that beer will encourage popularity and sexual behavior in order to sell more beer. Teen boys can support each other in being themselves in spite of the media messages, and stick together to make sure they and their friends who are girls are all safe in teen social situations. As with all negative media messages, communicative parents and a warm stable home provide a critical counterpoint to the stresses of the teen world. Boys and girls need to be·encouraged to "lead" with their personalities, intelligence, and talents rather than their sexuality.

Media and Violence

Look around you. Children in the United States are surrounded by influences from the media. If the average American child spends four hours a day watching television, that adds up to 25,000 hours by the time

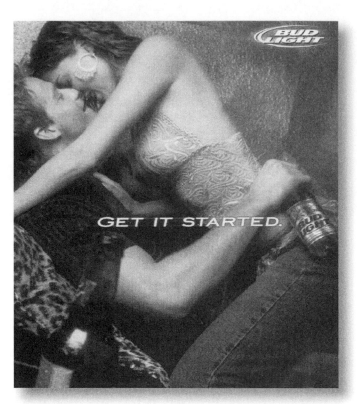

they graduate from high school, which means that they spend almost twice as much time in front of the TV as they do in school.[1] What are children watching? Even animated films with a 'G' rating contain "a significant amount of violence" that may not be acceptable for young viewers.[2] And prime-time TV, as well as network news programming, brings a violent world right into our living rooms. According to The National Center for Violence Prevention, by the age of 18, the average teenager has seen 16,000 murders and 200,000 acts of violence on television.

Since 1950 there have been more than 3,500 research studies about the negative effects of media violence on the general population, and on children in particular.[3] Unfortunately, many of these studies are in professional journals and are not readily available to the general public. The media have tried to denigrate these studies, just as the tobacco industry executives have tried to deny a link between smoking and cancer. In the case of tobacco, however, the public could rely on the media to keep them informed of the issues. With media violence, the same level of information is not available due to the economic conflict of interest in the news and entertainment industry.

The violence that surrounds us in this country increasingly involves young men and boys. Boys have committed all of the school shootings. What would the public reaction be if two girls entered a school and gunned down fellow classmates? Has our society grown to expect boys to be violent? Part of the problem may be the assumption that boys and men normally resolve problems with violence. The media contributes to this problem by regularly depicting males as violent, powerful, intimidating, controlling, and non-empathetic.

Movies and TV shows are increasingly violent. The whole genre of "slasher films" is aimed at the teenage market. Shockingly, in a TV Guide poll, 89% of eleven-year-olds and 20% of children under the age of five have seen the R-rated movie *Nightmare on Elm Street,* which stars the disfigured and cruel child molester and murderer, Freddy Krueger.[4] In the 1990's, the PG-rated film *Dick Tracy* had "only" 14 killings. This was a higher number than the 1974 *Death Wish,* which many people then considered to be a very violent film. The widespread availability of cable television also tremendously increases the amount of violence that viewers can watch, and the TV shows in the United States are more violent than those in any other country. A 1996 study by the National Cable Television Association found that there was violence in 85% of shows on premium cable stations compared with 44% of network shows and 15% of PBS shows. Much of the increase in violent programming is due to desensitization; in other words, viewers require higher levels of violent stimulation over time to maintain interest and excitement. To maintain viewer habits, the media industry has increased the intensity, realism and prevalence of violence in the media, with apparent public acceptance. Concerned parents are now wondering how much *more* violence the public will accept and expect. What will it take to make the public and the media provide more responsible programming for our children?

Video Games and Violence

Video games add a new and horrifying dimension because our kids can now participate personally in media violence. In many of these games, which often are racist and sexist[5] along with being blatantly violent,

the players are rewarded for killing and destroying. Lt. Col. Dave Grossman, author of *Stop Teaching Our Kids to Kill,* sounds a loud alarm about these games, which he calls "murder simulators." In fact, the military marksmanship-training device used by the United States Army is basically a modified Super Nintendo game. The firearms training simulator used by most law enforcement agencies is practically identical to an ultra-violent video game found in many arcades. These training devices and video games have three things in common: they teach the user to shoot at a target; they allow the user to practice killing; and they use guns that have recoil, meaning that the slide slams back when the trigger is pulled.

According to Lt. Col. Dave Grossman, humans have a natural resistance to killing, and would need to be conditioned in order to overcome it. Kids today amuse themselves by shooting and killing on video games, which now use realistic human figures for targets. In video games, unlike in real life, there is always an incentive and the intention is to shoot and kill. The player is rewarded with points for killing—the more hits, the more points. Grossman says, this "teaches children to associate pleasure with human death and suffering." One consistent factor with all of the boys who committed recent school shootings is that each one of them regularly played violent video games. In Paducah, Kentucky, for example, a 14-year-old boy who had never fired a real gun before fired eight shots and hit eight students, better than the average law enforcement officer in a similar situation. How did this child acquire such killing ability? He practiced on video games.

Video game technology has changed so rapidly that it is hard for many parents to understand how the new games differ from those of just a few years ago. Therefore, many parents fail to pay attention to the content or ratings of these games. One aspect that has advanced is the accuracy of depiction, including blood, guts, and gore. In the Duke Nukem series, for example, players move through the world behind a weapon and destroy people, monsters, tanks, and aircraft. In one game, Duke moves through pornography stores and strip clubs, and is encouraged to kill defenseless, bound women. After that, he blows up church windows. In the game Doom, which the Columbine killers played obsessively, players are engaged in a killing spree, moving from place to place and shooting everyone in their path. To make things even more realistic, some of these games allow the player to scan in photographs of their fellow students and teachers and practice shooting at them. Some games associate dark-skinned people with evil. Furthermore, some games use visual and musical effects that stimulate sexual arousal just before finding sexy, partially clothed "prostitutes" to kill. There is a serious impact on our psyches when any of us see or participate in media where sexuality and violence are combined. In males, this can lead to a feeling of sexual entitlement, increasing the possibility of acquaintance rape or assault. Parents who care about the values their kids are exposed to will need to be especially aware of the content and hidden messages embedded within the video games that are marketed as mere entertainment to their kids.

According to "Generation M," a 2005 Kaiser Family Foundation study of media in the lives of over two thousand 8- to 18-year-olds, surprisingly few parents are actually limiting the time spent and content of their children's video gaming. In this study 63% of boys (33% of girls) have a video game console in their bedroom and 83% of households have a console in their home. Children with video games in their bedroom spend 3 times as much time playing video games as those who do not. Averaging boys and girls together, young people spend about an hour a day playing video games and 15- to 18-year-olds spend a half an hour a day. Only 17% of parents in this study restricted the amount of time their kids could play video games and only 10% check the advisories on video game content. Parents are more likely to restrict TV and computer use than video game use. The children of parents (20% to 46%) setting limits, however, have almost 2 hours less daily media exposure. Clearly parents as a whole are not getting the message about the damaging effects of gaming, particularly violent gaming, on their children's development. No parent intends to raise children who are desensitized to violence, lacking in empathy, isolated, and obsessed with another reality, yet this is a real possibility if boys are left to their own devices when it comes to video games.

Video games are cleverly made to appeal to the systemizing abilities of the male brain and the time spent playing them can interfere with social, physical and intellectual experiences that are critical to successful male development. Furthermore, the addictive quality of video gaming, especially group games, is becoming more and more apparent. Dr. Maressa Orzack from McLean Hospital in Belmont, Massachusetts, estimates that 40% of the people playing the World of Warcroft are addicted. The addictive rush one gets from playing video games (or gambling or using meth) is all about dopamine, the hormone in the brain that regulates feelings of anticipation, motivation, reward and pleasure. Our children need to experience dopamine in healthy, real life excitement, not in the online excitement which gamers often use to escape from real life problems. Let's take video game use and content seriously and make sure our children are leading balanced healthy lives.

Toys and Violence

Young children can also be introduced to violence and sex through toys. Traditionally, one might not consider

a toy part of "the media," but we now have media-linked toys. We've all seen them—characters from recent TV shows, movies, video games (many with PG-13 and Teen ratings)—all marketed to children as young as 4 years old. Products run the gamut from fast food toys, clothes, lunchboxes, bed sheets, soda, and candy. Consider the World Wide Wrestling Federation action figure toy "Sable," recommended for children aged 4 and up. Based on the real-life female wrestler of the same name, Sable comes complete with an angry face, a whip and chair, minimal black leather

clothing and spiked red high heels. Her breasts are enormous and her leather bra is unzipped in front. The box shows other WWF wrestlers—all males. One, Al Snow, is holding the severed head of a woman. A toy like this, especially because it is connected to "real" people children see on the weekly TV show, cannot help but contribute to increasing confusion for children about gender roles, sexuality, violence, and relationships between males and females.

Why are manufacturers making media-linked toys for such young children and trying to lure children into media rated for older children? It is very hard to argue that there is positive value for children in these toys. Obviously, these toys are made to make money. The media targets even our youngest children as consumers.

Effects of Violent Media

The reality is that the current childhood media culture, described above, is a relatively recent development. It only became possible in 1984 when children's television was deregulated in the United States. Prior to 1984, FCC regulations limited the number of advertising minutes per hour allowed on children's television. The FCC also had a rule which stated that marketing toys with a TV show constituted a program-linked commercial, and therefore violated the limit on the number of advertising minutes per hour. Deregulation has led to dramatic changes in children's media, children's toys and children's play.

How much is media/screen violence contributing to the violence in our society? The answer is clear. Voluminous research shows that media/screen violence affects our children and contributes to violence in our society. The effects are summarized in **"Media Violence: What Is It Doing to our Kids and What Can We Do About It"** (p. 2:24):

- Media violence encourages children to act more aggressively.
- Media violence encourages attitudes that are distorted, fearful, and pessimistic.
- Media violence desensitizes children to real-life violence.

- Desensitized children are more likely to be aggressive than children who are not desensitized.
- Desensitization interferes with a child's capacity for empathy.

Violence continues to take an unnecessary toll in our children's lives. The major causes of mortality and morbidity among teenagers have shifted from infectious to behavioral etiologies, with violence having an increasing impact. Young people now have more to fear from their own behavior than they do from disease. In this country, every five minutes a child is arrested for committing a violent crime and gun-related violence takes the life of a child every three hours. Parents can have a huge impact on the role that violence plays in the lives of their own children by monitoring how much and what media and screen time their children are exposed to at home. "Reviewing my Movie Choices" (p. 2:29) reminds us that it is never too late to reevaluate the media to which we are exposing our kids.

Music

Music can be another media quagmire for parents. For many boys music will be the medium they use to express their emerging sense of self. Music can really help kids to connect to their feelings and emotions, which may otherwise be hard to name or express. But it is easy to worry about our kids when they only want to listen to depressing or angry music. Is this a cry for help? Not necessarily.

The article **"Music in the Millennium"** (p. 2:30) discusses tips on how to evaluate the influence of music in your own son's life. Remember that our kids may just be trying to exert their independence by being a little rebellious, or fit in with the crowd, or may just like the way something sounds without even paying attention to the lyrics. Think back to the way your own parents reacted to your music choices. If the lyrics to a song really offend you, then it is time to start a dialogue with your son. Talk about what he believes, what he likes and who he is. This conversation could be a window to your son's life and emotions. If you come down on him hard and try to forbid his listening to a particular song or group, you may miss the opportunity to learn more about him.

As William Pollack, author of *Real Boys*, says

> *Music provides an important way for a boy to connect with and release his emotions, evolve an aesthetic sense, and act as a creative person. It's also a way for him to practice his developing critical intelligence, if adults will pay respectful attention to his choices and tastes. If a parent can possibly stand not to set limits on a boy's musical choices, it's an especially good place to back off and let him be himself.*

Music videos, however, as opposed to listening to music, introduce a whole new often troubling dimension to today's popular music, and require limits and supervision for our younger teens. Some families avoid MTV altogether by not paying for extended cable since they do not want their children to conclude that the most important aspect of a woman is her sexuality.

The Internet

Several years ago, if our sons spent a lot of time on their computers we probably wouldn't have been alarmed. After all, computers are educational. But with the advent of the Internet and all that it exposes our kids to, parents are now worried about their sons' computer use. For example, how can we monitor what our sons find on the Internet? How can we protect our boys from harm resulting from his Internet use? How can we prevent Internet use and instant messaging from dominating our son's time, even if they are an important part of his social life? Is text messaging interfering with learning at school? To learn more on this important topic see the PBS Frontline *Growing up Online* (2008) and the related discussion at www.pbs.org/frontline.

In working hand-in-hand with our sons, parents can come up with guidelines that make sense for their own situation. We must be sure that our younger sons know that they can't believe everything they read. Parents need to also be aware that even child-centered chat rooms, like a children's author's site, can expose children to relationships and conversations that are confusing and can draw them out of their own reality. Just as we warned our sons about personal safety in the neighborhood, they likewise must be warned that there are people who prey on innocent children on the Internet. We need to be assured that at each stage of use our children know the ground rules of being safe on the Internet, e.g., never give any personal information to anyone they do not know in person. Our sons also need to know not to post anything on the Internet in writing or photos that they would not want a future college or employer to see. Older teens may also have to search to make sure no one else has posted information which includes their name. Tips on Internet and chat room use by your son are included in the article, **"Internet Literacy"** (p. 2:32).

Basic Internet Use Guidelines

- Set limits on the amount of time a child spends online each day or week.
- Do not let the Internet take the place of homework, dinner time, playing outside or with friends or pursuing other interests.
- Never use bad language or send mean messages online.

Basic Internet Safety Rules (Net Smart Rules)

- Do not give out any personal information or fill out details to "win" a prize.
- Never share passwords—even with friends.
- Never arrange a face-to-face meeting with someone online, unless your parent approves the meeting and is with you to meet him or her.
- Make sure you are aware that people online are not always who they say they are and that online information is not private.
- Be careful of any advice given to you on a website, especially if you are advised to not "tell anyone" or keep it a secret.

The Internet is unfortunately an excellent medium for social aggression among our teens. Therefore your son needs to be aware of his responsibility to use kindness, restraint, respect and the Golden Rule in his written communications as well as in his face-to-face communications. He may also need a plan and a listening ear if he discovers that his peers are using the Internet in mean ways, i.e., cyberbullying. The article **"CyberbullyingNOT: Stopping Online Social Aggression"** (p. 2:33) explains the definition of cyberbullying, the harm it causes, how your child can avoid being a target or aggressor, and what to do when it happens. Boys need to know that it is important to report cyberbullying just like one would any other type of bullying.

Social networking sites frequently play a powerful role, for better and for worse, in the social lives of teens. Parents have a responsibility to become familiar with the power of these sites while modeling appropriate computer-use behavior them selves, so that they can design boundaries for their teens. Adults use the term "social networking sites" but teens refer to these sites by their names such as MySpace, Facebook, Stickam (web-cam), or YouTube (video sharing). Candice M. Kelsey, is the author of a great resource for parents called *Generation MySpace – Helping Your Teen Survive Online Adolescence: How Social Networking is Changing Everything About Friendship, Gossip, Sex Drugs, and Our Kids' Values.* She reminds us that social networking sites teach our teens that they deserve to be entertained at all times, that voyeurism, exhibitionism, and even narcissism are normal and expected, and that success means having the "right" image. As a high school teacher, Kelsey has seen how easily kids get addicted to these sites and exposed to the prevalent message about sexuality, drug use, and consumerism. The book describes how to set age-appropriate limits such as turning off (collecting, securing) electronics at 9 PM, keeping computers out of bedrooms, setting profiles to "Private" (while knowing they may not be), supervising profile settings, setting time limits, and creating an Internet contract.

Media Literacy

Who wants an hour of meaningful conversations with your family members each day or a kid who rarely pressures you to buy brand names and popular toys? Need inspiration to unplug? Read **"TV- Free Families"** (p. 2:34). Maybe you are not ready to totally get rid of the TV, but reducing exposure can reduce the harm. **"12 Tips to Tame the Tube: Ideas to Give You Control over Television"** (p. 2:37) has excellent tips to get you started. Taking the TV out of the children's bedroom alone, reduces their TV viewing, on average, by 1 ½ hours per day, reduces video game playing by 30 minutes per day and increases reading time. TiVo (www.

Tivo.com), which pre-tapes shows, is an excellent way to fast forward through commercials and manage TV time wisely. Parents need to think carefully about the location of computers as well. No one wants their child online or text messaging at 2 AM.

In our homes we can set up screen standards which reflect our family values. However, what are we to do when our children are watching DVDs, playing games or watching TV in their friend's homes? By adolescence, we trust our children to handle themselves away from home and to feel relaxed about discussing any confusion they may have about what they see. Before then, it pays to be in close communication with other parents and set limits as needed. We can also let our children know that they always have the option of taking a book along and not watching the movie being shown even if it does have appropriate ratings.

Your family may also benefit from one of the excellent blocking devices for both TV and computers that can be found on www.familysafemedia.com, such as BOB:

> *BOB helps parents monitor and manage the time their children spend using in-home media. BOB is an easy-to-use, small device that sits next to a TV, video-game system or computer. The power cord from one of these devices plugs into the back of BOB and is locked in place. Then, BOB plugs into an electrical outlet. After set up—a process that takes about three minutes—the machine monitors the amount of time a child spends using that media device. Parents decide an acceptable amount of viewing time for each child per day or per week. Specific time periods can be blocked entirely for studying, chores, family time, or sleeping. Each child in the house (up to 6 users) has a four-digit PIN that they enter before they can turn on the attached device. BOB tracks the time used. A "master pin" allows a parent to turn on the connected device at any time.*

Media literacy is a key skill that will help parents and families analyze, understand and mitigate the effects of the media on their lives. Media literacy is about understanding the workings of the media and having the ability to analyze, investigate, evaluate, and create one's own media interpretation. Being media literate requires critical thinking. Some people may think they are immune to advertising or the mass media, but in reality, no one is unaffected. Other than our own immediate experience, our perception of the rest of the world is filtered for us directly via the media. An excellent review of media literacy is in **"Media Literacy in Action"** (p. 2:38). Parents who educate themselves and their children in the skills of media literacy can greatly diminish the negative effects the media has on their lives.

Media Activism and Advocacy

It is the hope of Family Empowerment Network that parents will use the information in this chapter to consider the role that media plays in their own families and take positive action to mitigate any untoward effects they might see on their children. **"Examples of Media Activism Successes"** (p. 2:40) share a few of the inspiring stories of success that we have heard. Some of you may want to take a more active role in holding the creators of media programming and entertainment accountable for their products.

Resources

1 Kalin, C., *Television, Violence, and Children*, University of Oregon College of Education Synthesis Paper.
2 "Violence in G-Rated Animated Films," Journal of the AMA, May 2000.
3 Grossman, D. & DeGaetano, G. *Stop Teaching Our Kids to Kill*, p. 24.
4 Levine, M. *See No Evil*, p. 131.
5 One study of 100 arcade games found that 92% had no female role; in the other 8%, 6% had damsels in distress and 2% had non-human females. J. Cassell & H. Jenkins, *From Barbie to Mortal Kombat: Gender and Computer Games* (MIT Press) 1998.

THE 40 DEVELOPMENTAL ASSETS Essential to Every Young Person's Success

Those families practicing media literacy and decreasing screen time will suffer less from the effects of media and will have more time to foster healthy behaviors. If you know you've made bad media choices in the past, don't worry; it is never too late to change. Screens steal time from our families that could be spent conversing, playing, reading, drawing, or helping out with a chore. At Family Empowerment Network, we would say time spent in front of a screen is time a child is not building assets. Asset building for this chapter focuses on replacing screen time with activities that build assets instead.

- **Asset #2 Positive Family Communication:** Young person and his/her parent(s) communicate positively, and young person is willing to seek advice and counsel from parent(s).
- **Asset #9 Service to Others:** Young people volunteer one hour or more per week to help others.
- **Asset #17 Creative Activities:** Young people are involved in music, theater or other arts three hours per week.
- **Asset #18 Youth Programs:** Young people are involved in sports, clubs or organizations at least three hours per week.
- **Asset #25 Reading for Pleasure:** Young people enjoy reading on their own for at least three hours per week.
- **Asset #33 Interpersonal Competence:** Young person has empathy, sensitivity, and friendship skills.

CIRCLE QUESTION

What are the primary ways in which you and your son are affected by the media and what are you doing to counter the negative effects?

POSSIBLE DISCUSSION QUESTIONS

1. What screen time monitoring systems work and don't work for you?
2. Would your family consider giving up TV for a short or long period of time? What are the pros and cons?
3. How does the "mean world syndrome" influence the extent to which your kids have freedom in their neighborhood and their community?
4. How involved do you get in your son's screen time at friend's homes?
5. How did your parents feel about the music you listened to? How do you feel about your kid's music?
6. Is your son more Internet and computer savvy than you are? What are the challenges you've experienced in monitoring his computer time?
7. Do you see the cultural diversity you'd like to see in mass media?
8. How do you feel about the concept of "cool hunting" by corporate interests?
9. Large corporations market to kids because they know kids have buying power. Can parents increase, moderate or limit their kids' buying power? And, would it have any effect on how corporations market to kids?
10. What can we do to influence the media to stop producing violent movies, TV shows, and video games?

PUTTING IT INTO PRACTICE

- Avoid television for children less than two years of age per advice of American Academy of Pediatrics.
- Provide young children with toys that encourage creative play.
- Keep all TVs, video game consoles, computers and cell phones (after 9 pm) used by kids in the shared spaces of your home (at least until later in adolescence when your emerging independent young person benefits from having privacy and experiencing choice).
- Teach children to watch TV with a purpose. No channel surfing!
- Limit your own TV viewing—model the behavior you'd like from him.
- Agree on a set number of hours of screen time and turn them off when the limit is reached.
- Include your son in the decision making of screen time rules in your home.
- Use blocking devices, such as BOB at http://hopscotchtechnology.com/products.html to help you enforce your rules.
- Don't have extended cable at your home.
- Watch TV/movies with your kids and ask questions about the program and commercials.
- Preview TV shows, video games, music CDs, movies for violence and harmful content.
- Read reviews at www.gradingthemovies.com and www.teachwithmovies.org.
- Tape the kids' favorite TV shows and watch them later without the commercials.
- Use TIVO at www.TiVo.com to help plan viewing and fast forward through commercials.

- Watch PBS Frontline's "Merchants of Cool" and "Growing up Online" with your adolescent son (or on your own).
- Try his video and computer games with him. It will show him you are trying to relate to him on his level and you will see first hand what he is playing.
- Let your voice be heard! Speak out when you see programming or ads that offend you.
- Encourage your schools to offer classes on media literacy and do a yearly school-wide TV Turnoff Week.
- Encourage the PTA to buy videos for your school library from the Media Education Foundation (see below), who make documentary films to inspire critical reflection on the social, political and cultural impact of American mass media. Host a parent educational evening using them.
- Stay informed and connected to media activism. Pick a favorite media website or subscribe to it. We recommend: National Institute on Media and the Family and Campaign for a Commercial Free Childhood.

PUTTING IT TOGETHER—YOUR VERSION

Write down three or four ideas you have been inspired to implement in your own life after reading and discussing this chapter.

1. _____

2. _____

3. _____

4. _____

FURTHER READING

Websites

National Institute on Media and the Family: www.mediafamily.org; www.mediafamily.org/research
   FREE parent guides on online social networking at www.mediafamily.org/network_pdf/Social_Networking_2008.pdf

Center for Media Literacy: excellent all around source at www.medialit.org/focus/par_home.html

Campaign for a Commercial Free Childhood: fantastic advocacy for children at www.commercialfreechildhood.org

Media Literacy: resources for advancing media education at www.medialiteracy.com

Media Matters by American Academy of Pediatrics: www.aap.org/advocacy/mediamatters.htm

Media Education Foundation: fantastic source of educational videos (see below) at www.mediaed.org

Center for Safe and Responsible Internet Use: wonderful source by Nancy Willard at www.csriu.org

American Library Association: promotes healthy reading habits at www.ala.org

Media Awareness Network: www.media-awareness.ca/english/index.cfm. Resources and support for everyone interested in media and information literacy for young people.

Media Literacy Clearinghouse: a website designed for K-12 educators at www.frankwbaker.com

ESRB Entertainment Software Rating Board: www.esrb.org

PBS Teacher Source: multimedia resources and professional development for America's pre K through12 educators at www.pbs.org/teachers/, search for Media Literacy

New Mexico Media Literacy Program: fantastic resources on media literacy programs at www.nmmlp.org

Media Watch: challenging racism, sexism and violence in the media through education and action at www.mediawatch.com

Center for Screen Time Awareness: sponsors Turn Off TV Week at www.tvturnoff.org, www.screentime.org.
Media Think: media literacy courses and resources, located in Portland, Oregon at www.mediathink.org
Parent Books: Media and Children: up-to-date list of books at www.parentbooks.ca/Media_&_Children.html

Books

The Other Parent: the Inside Story of the Media's Effect on our Children by James Steyer
Remote Control Childhood? Combating the Hazards of Media Culture by Diane E Levin
The Children are Watching: How the Media Teach About Diversity by Carlos E. Cortes
    Looks at how TV and other media influence how children think about race, ethnicity and gender.

Television and Movies

The Big Turnoff: Confessions of a TV-Addicted Mom Trying to Raise a TV-Free Kid by Ellen Curry Wilson,
    a fun book which is thought provoking
Mommy I'm Scared: How TV and Movies Frighten Children and What We Can Do to Protect Them by Joanne Cantor
    This book for parents discusses how TV viewing may be influencing children's sense of fear.
Talking Pictures: A Parent's Guide to Using Movies to Discuss Ethics, Values, and Everyday Problems with Children by
    Ronald J. Madison. This book offers parents suggestions for using films to talk about ideas and issues
TV-Proof Your Kids, A Parent's Guide to Safe and Healthy Viewing by Lauryn Axelrod
The Smart Parent's Guide to KID'S TV by Milton Chen

Computers and the Internet

E-Parenting: Keeping up with Your Tech-Savvy Kids by Sharon Miller. Learn how to make the most of what
    the internet, your computer and other technologies have to offer your family.
Imagination and Play in the Electronic Age by Dorothy and Jerome Singer. With guidance from parents and
    teachers, empathy, creativity and imagination can expand and intensify in the electronic age.
Cyber-Safe Kids, Cyber Savvy Teens by Nancy Willard, supporting kids to use the Internet safely at
    www.cyber-safe-kids.com
Cyberbullying and Cyberthreats: Responding to the Challenge of Online Social Aggression, Threats, and Distress by
    Nancy Willard at www.csriu.org
Generation MySpace – Helping Your Teen Survive Online Adolescence: How Social Networking is Changing Everything
    About Friendship, Gossip, Sex Drugs, and Our Kids' Values by Candice M. Kelsey
Youth Risk Online: A Guide for Adults Who Work with Children and Teens by Nancy Willard

Consumerism

Born to Buy: The Commercialized Child and the New Consumer Culture by Juliet Schor
Consuming Kids: Protecting our Children from the Onslaught of Marketing and Advertising by Susan Linn

Violence

Stop Teaching Our Kids to Kill by Lt. Col. Dave Grossman and Gloria DeGaetano
Kid Stuff: Marketing Sex and Violence to America's Children by Diane Ravitch and Joseph Viteritti
See No Evil: A Guide to Protecting our Children from Media Violence by M. Levine PhD

Articles

Cyberbullying: 8-page summary of information and resources at www.kathymasarie.com under
    Resources/ Addressing Relational Aggression and Bullying
Generation M: Media in the Lives of 8-18 Year Olds: 2005 Survey by Kaiser Family Foundation at
    www.kff.org/entmedia/entmedia030905pkg.cfm

TV Violence: It's Time to Break the Circle of Blame: summary of testimony to the United States Senate
Commerce Committee, July 12, 1995", by Elizabeth Thoman, Center for Media Literacy, Los Angeles at
www.medialit.org.

Television Violence: A Review of the Effects on Children of Different Ages by Wendy L. Josephson, PhD
Department of Canadian Heritage, February 1995. Child and Family Canada Media Awareness Network.
www.cfc-efc.ca.

Magazines & Journals

Adbusters Magazine: an ad-free critique of consumer culture and the machine that drives it at www.adbusters.org

Products to Support Healthy Viewing

BOB at www.hopscotchtechnology.com/products.html, can set limit to #/hours of TV viewing

Media Literacy Toolbox-$79; Teaches basic media literacy concepts like "language of persuasion" and how to
Deconstruct a media message. Examine media messages about body image, alcohol, tobacco, race, class,
aging, and other topics, and explore new marketing techniques, like stealth marketing and viral marketing.
New Mexico Media Literacy Project at www.nmmlp.org

TIVO at www.tivo.com, tapes TV programs so you can watch them later and fast forward commercials

Videos from PBS (1-877-PBS-SHOP for $19.99 apiece, fantastic educational investment)

Growing up Online: PBS Frontline examines the ways online activities have taken over teen life and the Struggles
of parents to handle various situations at www.pbs.org/wgbh/pages/frontline/kidsonline.

Merchants of Cool: PBS Frontline examines the energy spent to market cool to our teens who have $150
billion in expendable income at www.pbs.org/wgbh/pages/frontline/shows/cool/view.

Videos from Media Education Foundation: Challenging media at www.mediaed.org

*Spin the Bottle: Sex, Lies and Alcohol with Jean Kilbourne and Jackson Katz. Focuses on the normalization of
alcohol abuse despite the fact that use leads to deaths, sexual assaults, violence among our youth

Deadly Persuasion: The Advertising of Alcohol and Tobacco with Jean Kilbourne

*Tough Guise: Violence, Media and the Crisis in Masculinity with Jackson Katz

Game Over: Gender, Race and Violence in Video Games

*Dream Worlds 2: Desire, Sex and Power in the Music Industry

Teen Sexuality in an Age of Confusion

Date Rape Backlash: Media and the Denial of Rape

Beyond Good and Evil: Children, Media and Violent Time

Advertising and the End of the World

Captive Audience: Advertising Invades the Classroom - exposé of schools becoming advertising vehicles

Money for Nothing: The Political Economy of Pop Music

No Logo: Brand Globalization Resistance, Naomi Klein addresses the dynamics of corporate globalization

Mickey Mouse Monopoly: Disney, Childhood and Corporate Power, Disney gender, race, commercialization

Behind the Scenes: Hollywood Goes Hypercommercial, product placement, toy and fast food promotion

*Reviving Ophelia: Saving the Selves of Adolescent Girls with Mary Pipher

Slim Hopes: Advertising and our Obsession with Thinness with Jean Kilbourne

Killing Us Softly 3: Advertising's Image of Women with Jean Kilbourne

Off the Straight and Narrow: Lesbians, Gays, Bisexuals and Television

Playing Unfair: The Media Image of the Female Athlete, journalism is lagging far behind Title IX

The Military in the Movies

Getting the Message Across: A Video About Making Videos

Some Media Facts to Get Us Started

By Carol Ann McKay and Dr. Riva Sharples

As DIFFERENT AS WE ALL ARE from each other, most parents seem to have similar hopes and dreams for their children. We want children to be strong and healthy, successful in school, to have good interpersonal skills, and be proud of who they are. While there are wonderful television programs available for children, too much television and specifically too much of the "wrong" television can infringe on each of these goals. Television isn't the only culprit, as parents must also consider the lyrics of music, the images in video games, and the subject matter of e-mail chat rooms.

What Is All of This Costing Us?

- An hour spent being passively entertained is time that could be spent reading, doing homework, interacting with friends and family members, or getting fresh air and exercise.
- Many advertisements for children's shows are for foods with high sugar and fat content, encouraging poor dietary habits.

Consider These Statistics:

- By the time the average American child turns 5, he or she has spent the equivalent of 8 months, 24 hours a day, in front of the television. By age 18, he or she will have watched an average of 18,000 hours of television and videos. Meanwhile, that child will have averaged a whopping 15 minutes each day of real interaction with his or her parents while spending approximately 3.9 hours each day in front of the television.
- More children can identify and name the main characters in a popular video game than they can their real life neighbors. As people move farther away from their extended families, the imaginary relationships with characters on television become more important than real relationships with people. A majority of US children know more about the history of fictional television families than they do about their own.

Are We Selling Out Our Children?

Children's television exists to sell products. Children are exposed to a barrage of advertisements telling them they need to buy certain toys, eat a specific brand of cereal or buy the right brand name of clothes so that they can look a certain way. Advertisers work by making us dissatisfied with the lives we have. They know that this effect is enhanced with children who often can't distinguish between a television program and its advertisements. It is sobering to consider that every five hours of television watched contains one full hour of advertisements.

Loss of Creativity and Imagination

One of the biggest problems with children and television, movies, and video games is the loss of creativity and imagination that occurs. Studies show that young children (particularly those under the age of 5) exposed to TV, movies, and video games never fully develop the ability to imagine, dream and entertain themselves. Television, movies and video games provide visuals and a story line for a child so there is nothing left for the child to do but sit and stare, and perhaps (with a video game) follow a mostly pre-ordained path. In a study of six-year-olds in California, those children who watched a lot of television, movies, and video games often recreated scenes from movies or video games while the children with limited television and game time (or no TV or game time at all) created plots and ideas from their own surroundings and experiences that were unique and individual.

How Far Will It Go?

Television shows keep "upping the ante" as violence, conflict and shock value can grab the audience's attention. Even "wholesome" shows like "Malcolm in the Middle" (praised because it is "realistic") contains more drama, violence, and conflict in one episode than most families see in 6 months. Television, movies and video games are visual mediums, fulfilling our growing need to be constantly entertained and meeting the stations' demands for higher ratings. It's understandable why most television shows are "must see" shows with amazing twists every week.

Effect on Education

Consider that not only does all this exposure take up precious time that can be spent reading or doing homework, it creates difficulties for educators. Our children, with their fleeting attention spans, expect to be entertained. Educators are not entertainers and must try to impart knowledge to children who are used to slick presentations, flashing images and surround sound. Is it realistic to expect these same children to focus on a calculus problem or ponder the meaning of Tennyson's "Crossing the Bar"?

Desensitization to Violence

Studies have shown that not only does violence on television lead to more aggressive behavior in children, it may make them more fearful as they come to believe that violence is as common in the real world as it is on television. Children blur the lines between reality and fantasy all the time. Television, in particular, makes this confusion worse for children because the news is real, and some shows are real, but others are not.

Where Can We Start?

There are some wonderful programs out there but parents must guide their children toward them. PBS channels have no advertisements and programmers take into consideration the wishes of the viewing public who contribute to the station. There are programs that teach about science and offer positive role models for conflict resolution and moral dilemmas. Most parents know instinctively what is a positive message for children and what is a negative message. Parents

can steer children toward programming and images to enable them to grow into strong healthy adults. All messages are "educational" to children. Parents must decide what sort of an education they want their children to have.

Carol Ann McKay has worked as a nurse and an attorney and cuurently teaches law in upstate New York. Dr. Riva Sharples is an Associate Professor of Contemporary Media and Journalism Department at University of South Dakota. She has studied the effect of television on children extensively.

Reprinted with permission from Carol Ann McKay and Dr. Riva Sharples. From The Ophelia Project® Newsletter, August, 2003

Summary of Generation M: Media in the Lives of 8- to 18 Year-Olds

THE KAISER FAMILY FOUNDATION released its first major study of children's media use in 1999. In 2005 they published their follow-up survey documenting the dramatic changes taking place in family media use in our country. The report is based on a large national sample (2,032 anonymous questionnaires) of 8- to 18-years-olds and their families. The study also included nearly 700 young people who completed a detailed 7-day diary of their media use. Over the last 5 years there has been almost no change in the amount of time young people spend watching or listening to some kind of media (6+ hours per day). This includes watching TV (3 hours per day or almost 4 hours including DVDs/videos), 1 hour per day on the computer outside of school work, up to 50 minutes per day on video games and 1.75 hours per day listening to music. However, the presence of media has substantially expanded. A higher percentage of families have cable or satellite TV and premium TV channels, 3 or more VCR or DVD players, and multiple video game consoles. And more of these media have migrated to kids' bedrooms. Children have increased the amount of time they spend consuming more than one type of media at a time, i.e., multitasking - instant messaging while doing homework and watching TV, so they are actually exposed to 8 hours of media total. Home Internet access rocketed from 47% to 74%. In a typical day 62% of 8- to 18-year-olds used a computer. Important findings for parents trying to parent wisely in today's times are listed below:

- In a typical day, 81% of children watch TV, 47% go online, 46% read a book, 41% play console and 35% play hand-held video games, and 34% read a newspaper,
- For many young people, TV is a constant companion. Two-thirds live in homes where the TV is usually on during meals, and half live in homes where the TV is on most of the time whether anyone is watching it or not,
- Children's bedrooms: 68% have TV in their bedrooms, 54% have a VCR/DVD and a video game console (49%) and nearly one-third have a computer in their bedroom. The percentages for boys are even larger than for girls,
- Children with TVs in their rooms spend almost 1.5 hours more per day watching TV than those without a set in their room and read less than other kids,
- Children from homes where the TV is on most of the time watch an hour more of TV per day and read less than children from homes where the TV is on less often,
- Young people who live in homes where the TV is usually on during meals or is simply left on most of the time are less likely to talk their problems out with parents,
- Children who are heavy TV users spend less time engaged in homework,
- Boys spend more than twice as much time playing video games as girls do. Sixty-five percent of 7th to 12th graders have played the violent video game Grand Theft Auto,
- African-American youth spend far more time watching TV, going to movies, and playing video games than do white youth,
- Over half of 8- to 18-year-olds say their families have no rules about TV. Of the 46% who have rules, only 20% say that their rules are enforced most of the time. Even among the youngest children, 55% say they have no TV rules in their home. Parents are more likely to restrict the amount of time on the computer (23%) than video games (17% have rules),
- Those children who are the least content or get the poorest grades spend more time with video games and less time reading than their peers.

For the full Generation M report, researched by the Kaiser Family Foundation, check out: www.kff.org/entmedia/entmedia030905pkg.cfm.

Our Children and Consumerism

By Carol Ann McKay and Dr. Riva Sharples

THE REACH OF THE MEDIA, including television, magazines, video games, music and the Internet, is profound. Imagine our children living in a culture that inundates them with negative messages. We as parents and teachers may think our positive messages supersede the culture, but they often don't. They are often diluted by powerful external messages from the media. On a macro level all of us need to work to change the culture, but on a micro level—right now, in our homes—we have to change the environment. The culture is sending our children messages through our televisions, radios, CD's, video games and newspapers. We have to look at the media presences in our homes and take action to protect our children.

The Media Is Selling a Lie: How Bad Is It?

The primary concern of advertisers is not the wellbeing of our children. To the market, children are simply consumers in training. Our children are rushed along through those golden, once-in-a-lifetime years of childhood in the push to turn them into mini- adults. The buying habits of the young are the "cash crop" for advertisers as they hope to develop brand loyalty early. The messages of greed and consumerism are everywhere, preying on the vulnerabilities of children and using them to the marketer's advantage.

Advertising, in general, is geared to make us dissatisfied with the life that we have, convincing us that buying is good and will make us happy. Children and teens are the most naïve consumers and are very sensitive to these tactics—being led to believe that they are not cool enough unless they have the right product, look or attitude.

The Moral Cost Is High

The research has not supported the assumption that an environment teeming in consumerism is a happy one—especially for children. It's not an environment rooted in principle, faith or community. The moral cost is high as it promotes the sort of world where you don't think anything matters unless it serves your material gain. Why

be honest? Why have integrity? Why care about other people? No matter how many times we tell our children that happiness and self-esteem comes from within, the culture is saying that happiness is found in having things. We try to raise our children to be altruistic, kind and generous while the culture says "get all you can for yourself" and "the one with the most toys wins."

The frenzy of buying exaggerates the economic inequalities in our society and has families staggering under loads of debt. A broader environmental consequence of our uncontrolled buying is even more sobering. As we throw away still usable items to get the latest gadgets and material trappings, we are placing enormous strain on the world's resources.

Imagine Fish Swimming in a Fish Bowl

When we bring them home they are bright-eyed and energetic. They swim around like happy little fishes do. After a while we notice their fins starting to flop, their eyes clouding up, their swimming slowing down. They are ill. We try to make them well by adding some additional ingredients to their water. We add medicine to the water, but the medicine dilutes. But we don't check the quality of the water. It's impure. Fish absorb everything in their water, it is their very existence and if the water is impure and we don't change the water, the fish will continue being ill.

Now imagine our children living in a culture that inundates them with negative messages. Like a fish does water, they depend on the culture for survival. We may think our positive messages supersede the culture, but they often don't. They are often diluted by powerful external messages from the media.

Think of your children as the fish swimming in the fish bowl with tainted water. Children absorb everything in their environment. The culture is sending your children impure messages and they're gobbling up these messages. This is the water your children "swim in." We need to change the water.

Reprinted with permission from Carol Ann McKay and Dr. Riva Sharples. From The Ophelia Project® Newslatter, August, 2003

The Silver Bullet
Summary of Juliet Schor's talk, author of *Born to Buy*

NEW YORK TIMES best-selling author Juliet Schor strikes at the core of one of most insidious, powerful influences in our children's lives: advertising. Ads aimed at kids are virtually everywhere— in classrooms and textbooks, on the Internet, even at slumber parties and the playground. Product placement and other innovations have introduced more subtle advertising to movies and television. Companies are enlisting children as guerrilla marketers, targeting their friends and families. Even trusted social institutions such as the Girl Scouts are teaming up with marketers. Drawing on her own survey research and unprecedented access to the advertising industry, Juliet Schor, author of *The Overworked American* and *The Overspent American*, examines how a marketing effort of vast size, scope, and effectiveness has created "commercialized children."

Consider the impact of the "Nag Factor" in your life. When parents were asked, "Are you working longer hours for stuff your children say they need?" 30% said YES. Kids, 0-12 years, spend $30 billion of their own money and influence $670 billion spent on them by parents. Kids influence not only toy and clothes purchases, but also groceries, junk food, cars, hotels, and tourist destinations. Kids are now the "epicenter," the top agents in decisions about what the family buys.

What Schor's Research Shows Is That:
- As marketing has gotten more sophisticated, it has infiltrated every aspect of their lives. For example, the combination of "money-starved schools" and the appeal of a "captive audience" has led to the adoption of Channel 1 in 40% of our middle and high schools. This gives youth a daily mandatory infusion of ads, which include a strong push of junk food,
- Curriculums are being developed by corporations with propaganda (i.e. the logging and energy industry says clear-cutting is good and the ozone layer isn't a problem) to counter environmental information in the schools,
- In 1970's kids saw 20,000 TV commercials per day; they now see 40,000 per day,

- Kids watch TV an average of 5.5 hours/day,
- 20% of preschoolers have TVs in their rooms,
- 2-year-olds are asking for brand names,
- 3-year-olds identify their personalities with brand (I'm cool if I use…),
- For many years, the favorite commercial for 8-year-old boys has been Budweiser ads.

Why is advertising so successful? Over the last 10-15 years, advertisers have committed lots of money to researching kids to find strategies that work. There are 1000s of studies to show how to do it best (Nickelodeon alone has 100s of studies). Word of mouth remains the most powerful way to market kid-to-kid. An example is the *Girls Intelligence Agency,* which helps girls organize slumber parties to help with marketing research. Girls get money and/or prizes to sell out their friends.

What is the impact on advertising on kids? Studies have shown that the effects include depression, anxiety, low self-esteem, and obesity. The more kids watch TV, the more they:

- are depressed, anxious, and have headaches, low self-esteem and stomach aches,
- think their parents aren't cool,
- fight with parents,
- feel like their parents don't understand them,
- are vulnerable to peer pressure.

A silver bullet to reduce these problems is to **TURN OFF THE TV** or, at least, reduce it significantly. Blocking devices, such as BOB, can be incredibly helpful tools to help keep the TV limited. Adults must break through the "cycle of denial" that there is a problem. Media literacy is good too, but not enough. Kids will still buy products, even after being educated about how they are influenced.

Check out Parents' Bill of Rights, a legislative agenda created by Commercial Alert *(www.commercialalert.org) to "keep corporations from meddling in the relationship between parents and children."*

Impact of Media On Our Children's Health:
How Much Proof Do We Need?

This is the first generation that may actually live shorter lives than their parents—they are unhealthier, more overweight, and more sedentary with all the attendant complications these conditions create

When Children Walked the Earth: Is the Active Child Becoming Extinct?©

By Carol Ann McKay and Dr. Riva Sharples

Childhood obesity has hit epidemic proportions in this country with greater than 30% of children categorized as overweight. Besides low self-esteem issues, these children also face a higher incidence of asthma and hormone disturbances. A disturbing trend, noticed by pediatricians, is the emergence of diseases in children that were previously reserved for adults. These include type II diabetes, high blood pressure, and joint damage.

The sedentary lifestyle many children now have is one of the greatest contributors to this problem. Physical education programs have been decreased in many schools and much more of a child's leisure time is likely to be spent watching television, playing video games and working or playing on the computer. The American Academy of Pediatrics has suggested that obesity is greater among children and adolescents who frequently watch television not only because less energy is expended while viewing but also because of the concurrent consumption of high calorie snacks.

It is no surprise that we see such a dramatic increase in the media's influence on our children—junk values and consumerism are absorbed during those long hours in front of the tube or computer. And not only is the moral cost high, the future health of American children is at stake.[1] **Editors Note:** According to an International Journal of Pediatric Obesity report, researchers predict that nearly half of the children in North and South America will be overweight by 2010. Europe will go from 25% to 38% and even China will start seeing a problem.

Consumerism Leads to Poor Health

Juliet Schor, author of *Born to Buy*, found youth consumerism correlates strongly with alcohol, drug and cigarette consumption, emotional and mental health problems, poor nutrition and obesity. She studied 300 5th/6th graders and found that those who were more materialistic and consumer-oriented develop higher levels of depression, low self-esteem, headaches and poor relationships with parents. Being depressed did not lead to more consumerism but consumerism did lead to depression.

Marketing: Junk Food vs. "Elmo/Broccoli" Study

Addictions often begin during youth and some researchers suspect changes in brain chemistry occur that make early dependence difficult to break. Fast food marketers are taking advantage of the fact that in many households parents don't have a lot of time. They think that junk food saves time and money.

Food companies spend $11 billion per year marketing to kids. They often use popular characters to influence food choices, and kids go for it. What is very inspiring is that this can positively influence food choices, too. The Sesame Workshop's recent "Elmo/Broccoli" Study, supported by the Dr. Robert C. Atkins Foundation, concluded that children would choose broccoli over chocolate when the vegetable was labeled with an Elmo sticker, and an unknown character was placed on a chocolate bar. Yea!

More recently, another study conducted by the Institute of Medicine reinforced this concept and went on to recommend that licensed TV characters should only promote healthy foods. Now if we can just get lawmakers to value the health of our children over the corporations that produce junk food.
—Health and Wellness Directory, Lake Tahoe

Proof: Media Literacy Can Improve Teens' Health

One study found that if teens increase their "Smoking Media Literacy Scale" by only <u>one</u> point using basic media literacy education addressing (1) authors and audiences, (2) messages and meanings, and (3) reality and representation, they significantly reduced current smoking and susceptibility to future smoking. It is amazing that even a "little bit" of information can go a long way for schools daunted by adding yet another comprehensive program.[2]

Another study, has shown that even one media literacy training session can increase early adolescents' skepticism toward advertising, and that taking a more emotional rather than only fact-based approach may be most effective with middle-schoolers.[3]

[1]Reprinted with permission from Carol Ann McKay / Dr. Riva Sharples.
[2]Primack et al., "Association of cigarette smoking and media literacy about smoking among adolescents," *J Adolesc Health*. 2006; 4(39):465–472.
[3]Austin et al. "Benefits and costs of Channel One in a middle school setting and the role of media-literacy training," *Pediatrics*. 2006; 117: 423–433

Fear Sells
Is No News Good News?
By Carol Ann McKay

What Kids See...	The Message They Get...
• Horrible plane and car crashes	• It is not safe to travel
• Child abductions, Amber Alerts	• Children aren't safe, not even in their own homes
• Replays of events such as the World Trade Center bombings	• Terrorist attacks happen frequently
• SARS, West Nile Virus, Mad Cow Disease coverage	• Children will get these diseases; it is not safe to go outside
• Certain foods may cause cancer	• Not even our food is safe to eat
• Celebrity scandals	• Divorce, drug addiction, sex scandals, and adultery are common, even "cool."
• Bloody dead bodies as a result of war	• Violence and death are the inevitable result of conflict

THE STYLE OF NEWS REPORTING has raised attention grabbing to an art form. The problem is that it is the extraordinary that gets our attention and that is what is reported. War, the attacks on the World Trade Center, and the frightening string of child abductions in the summer of 2002 all have horrific images that grab our attention and keep us glued to the set. Even our weather has become attention grabbing with our storm Doppler and the flashes of warnings that run across our set in bright colors. Tornadoes and hurricanes provide lots of footage from the tedious preparations to their tragic aftermath.

The problem children have when they are confronted with these messages is that they don't have the life experience to put them into perspective. There is even a name for it—"mean world syndrome." They don't understand that the news stories are about things that DON'T happen every day. They are unable to understand that these images are happening, often, half a world away and not on the next street over. Even though the news is real it doesn't mean it is going to happen to them.

Tips for Newsworthy Parents
• Watch or read the news with your child so that you can fill in the facts and answer the questions on issues they don't understand. Remember that TV news is usually not appropriate for younger children.
• Share your feelings about the news, expressing your own morals or values concerning the subject matter
• Select "kid-friendly" news sources for your child where children are more likely to understand and less likely to be frightened.
• Explain that even though the news is real, you are hearing only a portion of the facts.
• Try getting your own news from sources such as public television or radio. These sources answer to the public, not to advertisers interested only in ratings.

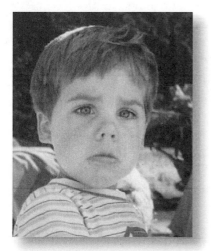

Carol Anne McKay has worked as a nurse and an attorney and is currently teaching law in upstate New York.

Reprinted with permission from Carol Ann McKay. From The Ophelia Project® Newsletter, August, 2003

Media Violence: What it Does To Our Kids & What We Can Do About It

By Jody Bellant Scheer, MD

TODAY'S CHILDREN GROW UP in a world of screen technologies, where powerful visual and auditory images create a filter through which adults and children perceive their world. TVs, computers, videos, and movies offer myriads of opportunities for entertainment, education, indoctrination, proselytization, and consumerism. One area of particular concern to parents, doctors, and educators is the level of media violence that permeates screen technologies, which is psychologically damaging to children and portrays a world that is much more violent and fearful than actual reality. It is now well known that there are negative long-term effects of exposure to widespread media violence, especially for young children. This leaves parents with the onerous task of trying to protect their children from the effects of media violence and wondering how to do this. Few families are willing to forgo screen technologies altogether, and even if they do, our culture is so media saturated that their children will be subjected to considerable media exposure outside the home. Developing family media literacy skills and conscious viewing habits helps to educate and protect children from the untoward effects of media violence, but parents need the support of other sectors of society as well. Elizabeth Thoman, of the Center for Media Literacy, summarized the need to move from blame to action in all sectors of society in her testimony to the US Senate Commerce Committee:

For 40 years, the American people have been engaged in a circle of blame about media violence: viewers blaming writers, writers blaming producers, producers blaming the networks, the networks blaming the advertisers. And advertisers blaming the public for watching! It's time to stop the circle of blame and recognize that we all share responsibility for the culture we are creating and passing on to our children.

The media industry must also accept responsibility for what they put into public space and time. Leaving this issue only up to parents is like asking parents to be responsible for the air their children breathe. That's impossible! Parents must be supported in their parenting task by the other sectors of society that also have everything to gain from the raising of healthy and well-adjusted kids.

According to the American Psychological Association's 1993 report, 'Violence and Youth: Psychology's Response,' there are not just one but four long-term effects of viewing violence: increased aggressiveness and antisocial behavior, increased fear of being or becoming a victim, increased desensitization to violence and victims of violence, and increased appetite for more and more violence in entertainment and real life.

The real question should be: *'What is the long-term impact on our national psyche when millions of children, in their formative years, grow up decade after decade bombarded with very powerful visual and verbal messages demonstrating violence as the preferred way to solve problems and normalizing fear and violence as the way things are?'* [1]

The concern about media violence is no trivial concern. The average American infant (0-18 months of age) spends

2 hours in front of a television each day.[2] The average American child spends more time watching screens than any other activity of their waking lives, at least 5 hours per day in recent studies.[4] The average child entering kindergarten has already seen approximately 8,000 murders and 100,000 assorted other acts of violence and destruction on television.[2] The American Academy of Pediatrics Committee Position Paper on Media Violence concludes from over 1000 studies that the link between media violence and increased aggressive behaviors in children is confirmed.[3] As stated by Nicholas Johnson, former FCC chairman, "All television is educational. The question is, what does it teach?" [4] Psychological research has found that media violence teaches a lot. Wendy Josephson, PhD summarizes the findings of contemporary research studies as follows:

> *Televised violence has numerous effects on the behavior of children of different ages. These include the imitation of violence and crime seen on television (copycat violence), reduced inhibitions against behaving aggressively, the 'triggering' of impulsive acts of aggression (priming), and the displacing of activities, such as socializing with other children and interacting with adults, that would teach children non-violent ways to solve conflicts. Television violence has also been found to have emotional effects on children. Children may become desensitized to real-life violence, they may come to see the world as a mean and scary place or they may come to expect others to resort to physical violence to resolve conflicts.[2]*

While most research and social concern has focused on children, virtually all of these effects have been found in older adolescents and adults as well. None of these effects appear to be specific to any certain age.[2] However, research tends to demonstrate that there are some behavioral differences in children's responses to media violence by age. "Preschoolers tend to demonstrate more physical aggression and other anti-social behaviors as a result of watching violence on TV than do older children up to about 9 or 10 years old. During adolescence, the effect of violent television (especially physical aggression) increases in boys and decreases quite dramatically for girls."[2]

Another area of great concern is the marked increase in the level of violence, as well as the graphic and realistic nature of the brutality that is portrayed in today's media. This phenomenon is related to desensitization: our nation's people have become so used to viewing violence in the media that it takes more graphic and more realistic levels of violent images to maintain viewer habits. This desensitization trickles down to affect what society deems appropriate viewing for even our youngest children. For example, two-thirds of Hollywood's movies released in 2001 were rated "R," and 80% of these were actively marketed to children under 17.[7] As well, prime time adult broadcasting now averages 3-5 violent acts per hour, while Saturday morning cartoons contain 20-25 violent acts per hour,[7] and the popular cartoon geared for toddlers and preschoolers, "Power Rangers," averages an astonishing 200 violent acts per hour.[6] Parents are rightly concerned about the long-term effects of exposing their children's young and vulnerable minds to such acts of media violence, which are portrayed as normal and acceptable forms of fun and entertainment.

The video gaming world uses multiple psychological reinforcements to encourage the habitual and addictive use of their games for entertainment and to link violence with feelings of excitement. Home and arcade games are designed with the following addictive elements: players experience feelings of mastery and control while playing the game; levels of play are exactly calibrated to the player's ability level, thereby ensuring feelings of success; immediate and continual reinforcements are used to encourage habitual play; and players experience gaming as a way to escape life and to be immersed in a constructed reality under their own complete control.[6] These elements might not be so concerning if it weren't for the widespread pattern these games have of linking personal experiences of fun and excitement to acts of graphic and realistic murder, violence, misogyny and racism.

The recent development of "first-person shooter" games allows players, with keyboard, joystick or laser activated guns, to participate more realistically in computer or video fantasy games, and in many cases, to simulate killing for pleasure. Lt. Col. David Grossman, a West Point psychology and military science professor outlines in his book, *Stop Teaching Our Kids to Kill*, that the current "first-person shooter" video games that are so popular with kids are actually the very same tools used by the military to teach soldiers to kill.[6] These games use a powerful form of stimulus-response training (called operant conditioning) to train users to perform under stressful conditions. Flight simulators use such measures to train pilots to respond reflexively to disasters during flight, while military and law enforcement agencies use video games only slightly different from popular arcade and home video games to train their recruits to kill.[6] The result of putting these games into the hands of children, without any complementary disciplinary training such as soldiers and law enforcement officers receive, is that our children are being trained to use guns to reflexively kill with uncanny accuracy, little cognitive involvement and minimal remorse.[6] A Paducah, Kentucky 14-year-old boy who had never held a handgun before in his life was able to shoot 8 of his classmates in a prayer group at school using 8 bullets, making 5 head shots and 3 torso shots. He was trained to do so vicariously by video games. By comparison, an average well-trained law enforcement officer would hit less than one bullet in five in a similar shootout at 7 yards.[6] The two teenage killers in the Columbine High School shootings

in Littletown, Colorado were likewise addicted to the popular, violent, "first-person shooter" game Doom. They able to reprogram the game to look like their own neighborhood, including the streets, the houses, and the people they supposedly hated.[6]

Other common and popular video games create fantasy environments that help foster sexism and racism. Some use images and music to intensify sexual arousal just before the finding and killing of scantily clad, busty, over-sexualized women (justified because these women are prostitutes).[8] Likewise, many of these games link inner cities, dark colors and dark-skinned human targets with evil.[8] The fact that these games are interactive, elevating children from passive viewers of media violence into the position of active participants, should send shock waves of concern through our nation. Unfortunately, these games are highly addictive, readily available, and enormously profitable. It is currently the arduous job of parents alone to monitor the content and underlying messages of their children's video games, as the gaming industry has not done so at all.

Parents: It's Time To Take Action!

The good news is that in a world in which violent media content is pervasive and children are susceptible to its effects, parents are the best mediators of their children's viewing and can very effectively limit their child's exposure to violence.

Take an active role in reducing the amount of violent media watched as a family

Children are exacting imitators; one of the best ways to influence their behavior is to model the kinds of conscious media-viewing habits that you want to see in your children. The television viewing patterns that children establish as toddlers are highly associated with their viewing habits throughout the rest of their lives.[2] This is good news, as it is relatively easy for parents to control the media habits practiced by their children in this age group. Limiting children's exposure to screen time and to violent media images are simple ways to mitigate the negative side effects of media violence, according to the American Academy of Pediatrics. The Academy's recommendation is to limit the total amount of television children watch to a maximum of 1 to 2 hours a day and to monitor the programs, music videos, games and films that children watch for violent themes and content.[3] The strategic location of televisions within the home can help to modulate the viewing habits of their users. Removing the television from prime social gathering places (living room, dining room) within the home and from children's bedrooms are effective tools to diminish TV's impact on and use by the entire family. Monitoring is also more easily done if televisions and computers are placed in public areas of the home commonly frequented by family members.

Learn skills to mitigate the impact of violent images that are seen or heard

The skills of communication and critical thinking can help mitigate the untoward effects of violence in media-literate families.[5] Family discussions about TV or video programs watched helps kids to put violence in a more realistic perspective, and can diminish fear and/or aggressiveness in children.[2] Parents who watch programs with their kids or play video games with their kids not only can monitor content, but can engage their children by asking probing and challenging questions about what they have viewed, sharpening essential critical thinking skills.[5] Helping children to understand and evaluate the content of what they are watching is probably the most helpful tool for helping mitigate untoward effects of media violence in older children and adolescents.[2] It is helpful for young children as well, as they have difficulties distinguishing between fantasy and reality,[3] program content and commercials,[5] and real and imagined scenarios.

Locate and appreciate alternative entertainment that is not violent

Parents can take an active role in screening what their children are watching or playing in order to minimize exposure to violence. Adults often think that television and video games are the only form of entertainment that can hold a child's attention, but this is far from true.[5] When offered an alternative activity or one that involves interacting in a meaningful way with an adult (especially one as special as a mother or father), most children are very likely to prefer it. It is important to note that constructive learning and play will not necessarily just happen when the television or computer is turned off. However, in one study, first graders who had their television viewing time decreased and replaced by more time with their parents showed improvements in their reading and cognitive skills.[2] Parents and children have a lot to gain by taking the effort to find and utilize alternative non-violent entertainment.

Express informed opinions to policy makers, the media industry, and to one another in public forums

Consumers can have a huge impact on media issues, including violence, if they exercise their voices and opinions. Consumer spending habits are another arena where parents can make conscious choices that send both a strong message to the media industry, as well as support their own family values and beliefs. Putting family media literacy into action is a challenge that faces all modern parents. "Armed with media literacy skills, children and teenagers will reflect upon visual technology's role in their lives, they will understand its power, analyze its messages and learn to use it wisely."[5] Developing family media literacy skills will be a project that takes time, energy, knowledge and conscious intention. Moving from blame into action, however, can be a very effective way to diminish the harmful effects of media violence on your own family.

Parents have a lot of power to protect their children from the deleterious effects of media violence. It is up to concerned parents like yourselves to help your family become media literate, and to hold our country's entertainment industry accountable for their children's programming. In this way, parents can help mitigate the heavy toll media violence takes on their own family, as well as others.

References:
1. "TV Violence: It's Time to Break the Circle of Blame, Summary of testimony to the United States Senate Commerce Committee, July 12, 1995", by Elizabeth Thoman, Center for Media Literacy, www.medialit.org.
2. "Television Violence: A Review of the Effects on Children of Different Ages", by Wendy Josephson PhD Dept. of Canadian Heritage, February 1995. Child Family Canada Media Awareness Network. www.cfc-efc.ca.
3. "Some Things You Should Know About Media Violence and Media Literacy." American Academy of Pediatrics Committee on Communications. www.aap.org.
4. National Institute on Media and the Family. www.mediafamily.org.
5. *Screen Smarts, A Family Guide to Media Literacy*, by G. DeGaetano and K. Bander. (1996) Ch 2: pg 27-53.
6. *Stop Teaching Our Kids To Kill*, by Lt. Col. David Grossman and Gloria DeGaetano (1999).
7. Media Education Foundation: www.mediaed.org
8. "Game Over: Gender, Race and Violence in Video Games" 2000, video exposé by www.mediaed.org.

Reviewing My Movie Choices

By Holly H. Nishimura

I AM A CHILD OF THE 50's, flower child of the 70's and parent of the 90's—maybe you can identify. Every 20 years I boldly move into a new mode and only realize it when a landmark movie tells me so. *Forrest Gump* gave me a sweeping summary of my life and *The Big Chill* reminded me of earlier idealism. *Then and Now* brought back girlhood where friendships were everything and so very fragile all at once. As a child, I spent Saturday afternoons at the local theater where 35 cents bought a double feature with great cartoons in the beginning. We lined up with our tickets and nickel candy bars that were as big as the 50 cent ones of today.

I introduced a love of movies to my daughter and we've been watching since she was 2 when I'd lug a booster seat to the theater [yes, Virginia, there were movies before Tinsel Town]. But when I consider what she's been exposed to, I'm not proud. We are now well versed on the plastic explosive C4, could easily spot a bomb wired to the ignition of the car, know to swim under and away from a burning oil slick, and could land a 747 with only minor coaching from the tower. We could find the safety on most handguns, change Uzi clips as quickly as we change earrings, and know never to enter a darkened room because that's ALWAYS where the bad guy is waiting [duh!]. Together we have witnessed buildings blown up, countless train wrecks and derailments, murders, rapes, stabbings, robberies, torture, alien beings bursting out of unsuspecting co-stars' chests, flesh-eating monsters, mutant human-like life forms who swim in sewers, and so much more. We've witnessed kidnappings, hostage meltdowns, enough births to populate New Hampshire, drownings, every form of drug paraphernalia being used, more surgical procedures than any 6 months in a trauma unit, drunken spectacles and heroic acts of courage and death. We know for a fact—because these were BASED on fact—that parents can and will sell, kill, torture, rape and desert their children, adults will do the same to their parents, and kids will do the same to their friends and parents. But we don't live in Sarajevo or Nairobi where acts of terror and war are routine, and humanity is lost among political issues, hateful factions and everyday survival. No, we buy tickets to see this for fun!! We call this "Entertainment" and sit in quiet anticipation with our popcorn while the multiple

> After seeing all those cut-kill-destroy-explode movies with my daughter, how can I suddenly decide they are not okay?

speaker system brings us every blood-curdling scream and the special effects-laden images flash the brightest of reds and pyrotechnics. This is what I passed on to my child. Sound familiar?

I'm not here to pass judgment or justify my earlier choices. Those choices seemed sound at the time [what WAS I thinking??] and passed for mother-daughter activities. After seeing all those cut-kill-destroy-explode movies with my daughter, how can I suddenly decide they're not okay? [I'd bought the tickets after all!!] Like this: I changed my mind. Those violent, sexual, exploitive movies had changed my mind over time and I chose to change it back. It's mine again! As a swan song we rented *Aliens: The Resurrection* for our last gross-me-out-athon that I first refused to watch. But the ritual had meaning so I sat and squirmed and looked away and wondered how they made that slimy thing look so disgustingly real. Then it was over and we were done. We'll still see an occasional action movie but will be much more selective about the amount of violence, sex, pain and harm I'll pay to witness.

Not everyone can or will make a change after so long —it's a big move. But if you're wondering whether you can change your vote, take back your acceptance and again define what you consider acceptable, the answer is only two words: YOU CAN. You'll save the time previously spent 'explaining' that the vile language, sexual activity, violent outbursts and acts of torture in the movie are not real AND not allowed in your house. You can spend that time watching movies about all the other topics that don't involve horrific and negative themes. Or not. You could spend that time NOT doing movies and witnessing someone else's vision of a story and plot, of character development and human emotion. Maybe you will read about or live or share your vision of those same things with your child, and listen to hers. The initial silence could be filled with ideas and ideals and experiences you'd otherwise have missed while watching a movie.

Holly Nishimura was a board member and active volunteer with the Ophelia Project, of Erie, PA, dedicated to saving the selves of girls by protecting and reconnecting families.

Reprinted with permission from Full Esteem Ahead, *Wings* Newsletter, Fall 1999

Music in the Millennium: An Interview with Peter Christenson

By Julie Salmon

PICTURE THIS SCENE: Your fifteen-year-old daughter, formerly of the khaki pants and t-shirt set, starts showing up in combat boots and black lucre. Earrings, which once graced her lobes, now start appearing in even stranger places—her nose, her navel, the center of her tongue. And her music—forget about it! The slightly tinny strains of Spice Girls and Britney Spears have given way to another sound altogether, one in which young girls like your daughter are not held in high esteem. Do you panic? Ship her off to boot camp? Is this daughter of yours irretrievably lost?

Not necessarily, according to Peter G. Christenson, professor of Communications at Lewis and Clark College. Christenson, co-author of *It's Not Only Rock & Roll, Popular Music in the Lives of Adolescents* (Hampton Press, 1997) believes you need to examine all areas of the child's life in order to determine if that child is heading for trouble. "I would tell parents, with music or video games, that the way to find out if there's a problem is not so much to pay attention to that behavior but to pay attention to the rest of the kid's life," says Christenson. "If the kid doesn't have friends or doesn't interact when interaction is what to do, that's when you should worry."

Christenson does not deny the power of music to influence kids, however. In fact, he believes it is the single most important medium in an adolescent's life. He cites a study in which researchers asked adolescents to choose what mass media they would take with them if stranded on a desert island. Most of the teens picked music over television, newspapers, magazines and books. "It's not that they watch less television and listen to more music," he explains, "it's just that the most important moments of their lives, the times they're with friends, having a great time, or the times they're depressed or they're searching for something of meaning in the media, it's music they turn to. Television is kind of vegetation time."

Since music clearly has the power to influence our kids, should parents monitor the lyrics, even censor some songs? "There's a lot of argument about whether kids pay attention to lyrics. Sometimes they do, and sometimes they don't," says Christenson. Kids process lyrics in different ways. When listening to songs on the radio, kids may be completely unaware of the significance of the words. Other times they may write the lyrics down and pour over them, just as their parents did before them.

Communication, rather than censorship, is the key to influencing your child's attitude towards any medium. "I think people should talk to their children about the values that are imbedded in the music," says Christenson. Tell kids what you like and don't like in music, television and on the Internet. Help them understand your values and discuss their own. Then set guidelines. "You can say, 'I know enough about that music to know that some of the things in it are personally offensive to me,' and, frankly, the kid probably knows that too," says Christenson.

It is much easier for parents to evaluate the television shows or movies their children will watch than to review their music, their video games, or their Internet activity. Christenson makes a distinction between "visible" and "invisible" media as a way of understanding the difficulty a parent faces in monitoring the media. "Television and movies are very visible," he explains, but when it comes to music and video games, and certainly the Internet, parents are less likely to encounter them. These activities are easier to ignore because they usually happen in the bedroom. They're alien and a little bit frightening. As a result, many parents may want to simply forbid some of the "invisible" activities outright, particularly in regard to Internet use. But Christenson points out that these new technologies can have a positive effect on our kids as well as a negative one. Any kid entering the 21st century will certainly have to know his or her way around a computer. "Forbidding [computer use] entirely is a projection of our values onto a technology which may be rather neutral," says Christenson. Better to promote the wise use of technology than to ban it.

When your children are young, you should make a concerted effort to monitor their use of any media. As Christenson points out, it's easy to guide kids up to the ages of five and six towards, for example, TV shows on PBS or educational software. "When it's appropriate to control the child, then steer them to good stuff and away from bad stuff. Steer them away from the media to the extent you can without alienating them totally and steer them towards the good stuff by example, if possible." In other words, don't let them catch you sitting around watching *Terminator II* or listening to Snoop Doggy Dog. Let them find you reading a good book instead. Better yet, read a good book with them and talk about it. As your child matures, continue setting an example and keep the lines of communication open. "By the time your kid's a teenager," says Christenson, "you have to accord them a certain amount of freedom to make their own cultural choices and the best you can hope for is that those [choices] will reflect the good values of your family."

Parental Advisory

The parental warning "explicit lyrics" labels put on CD's are at the discretion of the music industry; there are no formal rules or regulation. The recognizable black and white "Parental Advisory Explicit Lyrics" label is the most commonly used. Another common one is "Parental Advisory-Explicit Content."

Can the music rating system help parents monitor what comes into their homes? Yes and no. These labels are used by three groups—music stores, parents, and the kids themselves. Music stores occasionally use them to restrict sales to those less than 18 years of age. "These ratings are good as long as it's parents who use them."

On the other hand, if they are not used by the parents, the kids may actually gravitate towards the higher ratings simply as a way of testing their limits or showing their sophistication—the 'forbidden fruit' theory. This may be why the record companies are "cooperating" so well with the voluntary system. One study in Portland showed that out of a random sampling of 1000 records the following had the parent warning label: Rap 59%, Heavy metal 13%, Alternative 8%, Pop 1%, and Misc 8%.

If parents use them, ratings can give a logical standard to apply to this vast array of material. Still a parent's best defense is familiarizing yourself with the music and the lyrics and setting your own standards.

Julia Salmon is a freelance writer/editor and mother of three children.

Reprinted with permission from Full Esteem Ahead, *Wings* News-letter, Fall 1999

Internet Literacy: Safe Surfing in the Online World

THE INTERNET IS NOW A major part of the media mix that surrounds us, and an important component of media literacy—especially for young people. The under-18 demographic comprises over 20% of the US online population, and nearly one-half of all kids and teens are online. The average teenager spends about 9 ½ hours a week online (and another 18 hours a week watching TV), with an even 50/50 split of male and female online teens, doing different activities. Their online time is typically spent on email, instant messaging, doing homework, and playing games.

With so many young people spending so much time online, this market has become a focus for advertisers. According to eMarketer, a leading advertising publication, "marketers all across the Web are working overtime to win over kids and teens." In addition, the internet presents new risks around privacy, safety and the manipulation of facts.

Fortunately, there is also a growing base of online resources to help with the challenges of building "Internet literacy." Individuals should determine their own comfort level with limit-setting, filtering software, online safety rules and other available techniques, but it is essential to make the Internet a significant part of any media literacy effort. The annotated list (at right) provides selected sites that offer research, suggestions, tools, and further links.

5 Things You Can Do Today

1. Start a conversation about Internet usage—make sure you know what sites your kids are using, with whom they are using chat rooms, and the importance of protecting their personal information.
2. Share some Internet time with your kids. By using the Internet together you can learn a lot about their familiarity and level of online sophistication, and also help to set age-appropriate limits.
3. Help them understand authenticity issues by using the Internet to verify information as fact or fiction.
4. Become familiar with your computer's "history" and "cookies" folder, and explore software that can limit or monitor online usage.
5. Become aware of online commercial messages in all their guises, and help your kids to identify which parts of a website are sponsored for advertisements.

RESOURCES FOR PARENTS:
www.getnetwise.org/
A public service website providing extensive resources about online child safety, privacy, security, and email issues. Includes lists of relevant computer software.

www.media-awareness.ca/english/special_initiatives/web_awareness/
A comprehensive educational resource from Web Awareness Canada. This site is designed to offer parents and teachers with "practical information and hands-on activities to help give kids the cyber smarts they need to make wise, safe, and responsible online decisions."

www.familyinternet.about.com/
Extensive list of articles about making your Internet experience more "family friendly." Be sure to see the list of "Articles and Resources" that deal specifically with kids and online safety.

www.nsbf.org/safe-smart/
Research and guidelines for children's use of the Internet (based on a national survey of parents and children by the National School Boards Foundation).

RESOURCES FOR KIDS
www.pbskids.org/license/
An interactive test that challenges kids to understand Internet protocol and safety practices for online surfing.

www.safekids.com and www.safeteens.com/
Good general resource sites – created by syndicated technology columnist, Larry Magid (author of "Child Safety on the Information Highway" and "Teen Safety on the Information Highway" from The National Center for Missing and Exploited Children.)

CyberbullyNOT: Stopping Online Social Aggression

Cyberbullies use the Internet or cell phones to send hurtful messages or post
information to damage the reputation and friendships of others.

Types of Cyberbullying

- Flaming. Angry, rude arguments.
- Harassment. Repeatedly sending offensive messages.
- Denigration. "Dissing" someone online by spreading rumors or posting false information.
- Outing and trickery. Disseminating intimate private information or tricking someone into disclosing private information, which is then disseminated.
- Impersonation. Pretending to be someone else and posting material to damage that person's reputation.
- Exclusion. Intentionally excluding someone from an online group.
- Cyberstalking. Creating fear by sending offensive messages and engaging in threatening activity.

How, Who, and Why

- Cyberbullying occurs via personal Web sites, blogs, e-mail, discussion groups, message boards, chat, instant messaging, or voice, text, or image cell phones.
- A cyberbully may be a person whom the target knows or an online stranger. A cyberbully may be anonymous and enlist the aid of others, including online "friends."
- Cyberbullying may be a continuation of, or in retaliation for, in-school bullying. It may be related to fights about relationships or be based on hate or bias. Some teens think cyberbullying is a fun game.
- Teens might think…
  - o They are invisible, so they think they can't be punished.
  - o No real harm has been caused online
  - o They should have a free speech right to post whatever they want, regardless of the harm

The Harm

Cyberbullying can cause great emotional harm. The communications can be vicious and occur 24/7. Damaging material can be widely disseminated and impossible to fully remove. Teens are reluctant to tell adults for fear they will be restricted from online activities or the cyberbully will retaliate. Cyberbullying can lead to youth suicide and violence.

Responsible Management of Internet Use

- Keep the computer in a public place and supervise.
- Find out what public online sites and communities your child uses and review what your child is posting. Emphasize that these are public places!

Prevent Your Child from Being a Cyberbully

- Make it clear that all Internet use must be in accord with family values of kindness and respect for others.
- Recognize that you can be held financially liable for harm your child causes to another through cyberbullying.
- If your child is being bullied at school, work with the school to stop the bullying and make sure your child knows not to retaliate online.
- If you know your child has cyberbullied others, be very proactive in preventing any continuation.

Prevent Your Child from Becoming a Target

- Make sure your child knows not to post information that could be used maliciously.
- Visit your child's online communities and discuss the values demonstrated by those who participate.
- Bully-proof your child by reinforcing your child's individual strengths and fostering healthy friendships.

Warning Signs

- Sadness or anger during or after Internet use
- Withdrawal from friends and activities, school avoidance, decline of grades, and depression
- Indications that your child is being bullied at school

Action Steps and Options

- Make sure your child knows not to retaliate, to save the evidence, and to ask for help if he/she is having difficulties.
- Identify the cyberbully or bully group. Ask your Internet service provider for help.
  There are different ways that your child or you can respond to cyberbullying:
  - Calmly and strongly tell the cyberbully to stop and to remove any harmful material.
  - Ignore the cyberbully by leaving the online environment, blocking communications, or both.
  - File a complaint with the Internet or cell phone company.
  - Send the cyberbully's parents a letter that includes the evidence of cyberbullying. Demand that the actions stop and harmful material be removed
  - Seek assistance from the school.
  - Contact an attorney to send a letter or file a lawsuit against the cyberbully's parents.
  - Contact the police if the cyberbullying involves threats of violence, coercion, intimidation based on hate or bias, or any form of sexual exploitation.

Reprinted with permission from Nancy Willard, author of *Cyber-Safe Kids and Cyber-Savvy Teens* at www.cyberbully.org. All rights reserved.

TV-Free Families: Why—and How—They Unplug

By Nelle Nix

"We were afraid that it could foster a short attention span. It was so fast-paced, so loud, so frenetic that we became concerned that it was a negative influence. And with that, we just quit watching TV." —Steve Cook

TELEVISION NEVER HELD much charm for Jody Bellant Scheer. So when the part-time pediatrician had children of her own, it seemed quite natural to declare her family's home a TV-free-zone.

"We made the choice that it wasn't worth the negatives," she says of the decision she and her husband, Stephen Scheer, made. "It wasn't a forbidden fruit. They had access to television—at friends' houses and at their grandparents'—and it wasn't like they never watched it. But it wasn't something they were focused on."

Instead, Gabe and Maya Scheer, about two years apart in age, developed a talent for entertaining themselves. When they were little, their mom says, she did spend perhaps more time than some parents do reading books to them and playing with them outside. But Gabe and Maya could also spend hours amusing themselves with imaginative play, and when they were older, they spent lots of time playing outdoors with the many kids who lived in the neighborhood.

Occasionally a friend would come over for a play date and immediately ask where the television was. "We say, 'We don't have one,'" Scheer recalls. "It would take them about 40 minutes then to figure out how to play, but they would figure it out. Some kids really had forgotten how to play. That's one of the things that motivated me to stick with the no-TV resolve," says Scheer.

That resolve made the Scheer family a rarity. Just two percent of America's families forgo having a television in the house, according to a Nielsen Media Research study published in 2000. That same study found that the average American child, ages 2 to 19, spends 19 hours and 40 minutes each week watching TV.

The idea of families going without television intrigued Eastern Washington University professor Barbara Brock. Four years ago, she placed ads searching for some of these families in Parents magazine, the Chinaberry Book catalog and the TV-Free America newsletter. The response overwhelmed her. She signed up 385 families from 43 states for the 22-page, 100-question survey. In the end, 280 families responded.

Some of Brock's findings, which she titled "TV Free Families: Are They Lola Granolas, Normal Joes or High and Holy Snots?" include the following:

- **TV-free families have an hour of meaningful conversation each day with their children (compared to the national average of 38 minutes per week).**
- **While they come from all walks of life, income brackets, levels of education, races, etc., most are in their 30's, married with two children, have college degrees, earn $60,000 to $80,000 per year, and have religious affiliations.**
- **41 percent send their kids to public schools, with private and home school equally dividing the rest.**
- **92 percent of parents say their children "never or rarely" complain about the lack of TV or pressure them to buy brand names and popular toys.**
- **51 percent of the children receive mostly or all A's in school.**
- **81 percent of the families responded that they were "very satisfied with life."**

BROCK SAYS THAT WITH a growing body of research indicating a relationship between sedentary watching of media and obesity, lack of physical activity and aggression, more and more families are choosing to shelve their TVs.

"They were NOT Lola Granolas or High and Holy Snots!" says the recreation management professor, whose tentatively titled book *"No TV? No Big Deal! (How Hundreds of Americans are Living Outside of the Box),"* will be published in the spring of 2005 by the Eastern Washington University Press. "They were Normal Joes who found a ton of benefits attached to the TV-free lifestyle."

"I truly feel the trend is upon us and that more families are choosing to go TV-free," Brock says. "Lots of studies (over 4,000) have already been done of the negative effects [of television viewing]. My research was the first to point out that hundreds of families have made the choice and are not only surviving, but thriving!"

At the home of Steve Cook and Marianne Parshley, the television exists but it's mostly a silent guest instead of a constant companion.

"With [oldest daughter] Mimi, we were careful from the start," says Cook, an attorney. "When she was like 3, we did let her watch 'Sesame Street.' Initially we thought it was a great show. But one of the things we began to notice is that she would just sit there and stare."

"The second thing we noticed is that 'Sesame Street' is boom, boom, boom—sort of like music videos. We were afraid that it could foster a short attention span. It was so fast-paced, so loud, so frenetic that we became concerned that it was a negative influence. And with that, we just quit watching TV."

Now, with Mimi at 16, Gwen, 13, and Kathleen, 8, the family is far too busy pursuing their various interests including drama, soccer, basketball, and reading—not to

Teaching Your Child to Be Media Literate

The average American child sees some 20,000 TV commercials each year, according to the American Academy of Pediatrics.

But even if you decide to turn off your own TV – for good – the influence of the media is inescapable, according to Peter Christenson, professor of communication at Lewis and Clark College.

"The impact spreads way beyond the actual viewing," Christenson says. "The extent to which kids are bombarded with commercial messages is amazing. They're on every surface."

That's why, Christenson says, it's critical for parents not to ignore the television entirely, but to talk about it. In fact, Vanessa Hughes of the Northwest Media Literacy Center says that while participating in events such as TV-Turn-off Week, April 19-25, is important as a way of heightening awareness of the media's influence, she does not like to see people tune out entirely.

"Opting out is not really the solution," says Hughes, an artist, filmmaker, and educator. "To be truly media literate," Hughes says, "we need to turn the tables on the passive relationship most of us have and start being much more intentional." The goal, according to experts, is for both parents and kids to be able to critically analyze the media that they're consuming.

So how can parents help their children become more media literate? Here are some tips:
Talk about what you see in the media, whether it's television, magazines, billboards or Internet sites. Media literacy experts call this "deconstructing"—essentially taking apart the media in question and analyzing it. By doing so, you can help your kids to fully understand media's role and impact. Hughes suggests some questions you might ask your children (depending on their age):

- Who created this message? Or if it's a commercial, what product are they selling and what audience are they selling to?
- What techniques did they use to get their message across—humor, sex, science …? (Be sure to point out that the famous people kids may see in commercials—like basketball and rock stars—are paid big bucks to endorse products.)
- How might different people understand this information differently?
- What are the lifestyles, values and points of view represented in this message?
- What's left out of this message?
- How does it make you feel?

Be intentional about what you watch. With all its promotional spots for future programming and sometimes seamless transitions from one show to the next, it's easy to get pulled along and find yourself spending far more time in front of the television than you'd intended. Hughes suggests looking at the TV schedule with children, deciding which programs are important, and then sticking to that plan.

Interact with the media. Complain when it's bad, but be willing to offer praise when it's good, too, Hughes says. "I believe there are a lot of talented people in the industry, and if consumers demand high-quality media, they'll start producing it," she says. —Nelle Nix mention homework—to worry about what they're missing on television.

Everyone in the family reads voraciously, and the family typically starts its day with the newspaper at the breakfast table. In recognition of the kids' need to participate at least to a degree in pop culture, the family does rent occasional movies and enjoys debating their merits.

But for the most part, the kids don't seem to feel like they're missing out by not being up-to-date on the latest round of "Survivor" or the final episode of "Friends." "I expected more of a battle," Cook says, "but it really is not an issue."

Like the Cooks, the Scheer family also has a TV now, though it spends weeks at a time tucked away in a cabinet. "We got it when the kids were in high school," Scheer says. "They didn't ask for it, but we wanted them and their friends to come around more. And we noticed that TV was a help ... it was an icebreaker."

Now, with Maya at 21 years old and Gabe at 19, the television is pulled out only occasionally. Certainly, Gabe says, when he was younger, there were times he felt ever-so-slightly isolated as his friends talked about their favorite shows.

"It was just stupid stuff, like 'Did you see the new episode of 'The Simpsons,'" he says. "I kind of felt left out then. But in retrospect, it was so much better, not having a TV. Instead of coming home from school, sitting and watching TV, we'd come home and go out and build forts in the woods or go fishing. It was definitely way better."

And, in perhaps the ultimate testament to the advantages of a TV-free lifestyle, Gabe adds, "I think I would even go so far as to raise my kids with less TV than I got if possible."

Nelle Nix is a Portland freelance writer and mother of two.

Ideas for unplugging

How can you move toward less—instead of more—TV viewing in your house? Parents Jody Bellant Scheer and Steve Cook offer the following advice:

- **Be vigilant about your own television viewing because kids do tend to imitate what their parents do.**
- **Avoid making TV the focus of any room. "Have it be something that may be watched, but don't make it have to be watched," Cook says. One**

solution is to make TV viewing inconvenient by, for example, relegating your television to a basement room or closing it off in a cabinet, as the Scheers have done.

- **Set viewing limits and stick with them. This means turning off the television after a favorite program rather than sitting through the next not-so-great program just because the TV is still on.**
- **Avoid making TV a "forbidden fruit," Scheer says. Instead, when kids watch a program, talk about what you've seen.**
- **Intervene early. It's much easier to control what a toddler watches than what a 12-year-old watches, Cook says, and a child's viewing pattern as a toddler is predictive of what the pattern will be when they're older.**

Resources

Turnoff Week, encourages children and adults to decrease screen time in order to promote healthier lives and communities. See "Take Action Programs" and "Turnoff Week" at http://www.screentime.org. Barbara Brock shares more in *Living Outside the Box: TV-Free Families Share Their Secrets.*

"It was so much better, not having a TV. Instead of coming home from school, sitting and watching TV, we'd come home and go out and build forts in the woods or go fishing. It was definitely way better."
— Gabe Scheer

12 Tips to Tame the Tube: Ideas to Give You Control Over Television
National Institute on Media and the Family

Avoid Using TV/Computer as a Babysitter: Think of how careful you are about choosing a baby-sitter and day care. Try to be just as careful about what your children watch on TV every day.

Know What Your Kids Are Watching: It is important to be aware of program content as well as the content of the daily news. The younger the child, the more impressionable he or she is, and the less experienced in evaluating content against the values of family and community. Additionally, emotional images may intrude upon and interrupt sleep.

Keep TV's and Computers Out of Kids' Bedrooms: It is difficult to monitor what your children are watching when they are watching TV in their own room. Having a TV in a child's room discourages participation in family activities and encourages them to watch TV when they could be studying, reading, or sleeping.

Set Some Guidelines About When and What Children Watch: This can be done in conversation with your children, but the final call belongs to the adults. The clearer the rules (i.e., no TV before school, or until homework is completed, etc.), the better. Setting new limits may be upsetting to your children at first, but consistency is very important.

Practice "Appointment" TV. Decide in Advance What's Good and Watch it as a Family: Go through the TV guide in the paper on Sunday and make family decisions on shows to watch for the week. Discuss reasons for the decisions with your children. If in doubt, get more information. In choosing TV shows or videos, make use of independent evaluations, like **KidScore®**, TV and movie guides, articles in magazines, etc. Discuss issues and ideas with other adults, friends, and parents of your children's playmates.

Talk to Your Child About What He or She is Watching: Discuss what you are watching and ask specific questions. Ask what they see, as it may be very different from what you see. Ask them to tell you what things mean to them. Ask them why they watch specific shows, what characters they like and don't like. Discuss the commercials and their perception of toys, cereals, etc. and the people who sell them.

Turn TV Off During Meals: Catch up with one another. Focus on each other. Share stories and activities from each family member's day.

Use the VCR to Your Advantage: Tape a good show and schedule a special family viewing—complete with popcorn. If a show is on at an inconvenient time such as meal time, homework time, or family time, tape it to watch later.

Put the Family on a TV Diet: Schedule some fun alternative activities. When you do watch television, watch it with your children.

Create a TV Coupon System: Kids get coupons and turn them in when they watch a program. Unused coupons can be "cashed in" for a special family activity.

Don't Make TV the Focal Point of the Room: Make your children the focus of your attention, not the TV. Research shows that people watch less TV if it is not in the most prominent location in the room.

Patronize Good Programs & Games and Demand More of Them: Express your opinions to TV and radio stations, network executives, and advertisers. Tell them not only what you do not like, but also what you like. Addresses for networks and local stations are in your TV guide. Also, remember that your money has its own voice.

Check out National Institute on Media and the Family: Building Healthy Families through the Wise Use of the Media at www.mediafamily.org. They have many reports on the latest in recommendations for games, TV, and movies that are healthy and are unhealthy, research on impact of the media on children's health, learning, social skills and general well-being and tips on how to reduce the harm of media in your child's life.

Media Literacy in Action

Since the year 2000, the organization Media Think has given many presentations to groups throughout the area. As a result of hearing and answering concerns about the media, Media Think has compiled a list of actions to improve media and our relationship to them.

Here are some major points we make to groups and individuals.

1. Start With Yourself

Ask yourself how much you spend on media...in both time and money. If you are like the others, you will be surprised on both counts.

We are both active and passive media consumers. When active, we sometimes binge without paying attention to the consequences. We fill each waking moment with media, whether it be the radio in the background or the television during dinner. Many of us screen out the sounds of the natural environment with portable audio players.

When we are passive consumers, we don't realize how much media we are exposed to. While reading the newspaper, we are exposed to dozens of ads; while driving down a major street, we scan hundreds of signs; and while strolling a supermarket aisle, we face thousands of alluring labels.

Whether active or passive consumers, we need to be media aware.

Accounting for the money we spend on media is another form of awareness. Add up the monthly costs of your magazine or newspaper subscriptions, of the Internet service, the cable bill, movie tickets, the telephone and the cost of newsstand purchases or CDs. Your monthly media bill can easily run to $200 a month.

Realize that the choices you make become part of the economics of the multi-billion dollar media business. One of the five main principles of media literacy is that all media messages have an economic underpinning— starting with your dollars.

Finally, think about how your media consumption habits set examples for other family members—particularly children. The media habits of friends can also influence you and vice versa. Whether you go on a walk together or watch a sitcom is determined by your habits.

2. Communicate

When you watch TV (or read a book or magazine for that matter), talk about it. Experience media together. One of the enjoyments about going to a movie with a friend is sharing perceptions about it afterwards. What is the first thing we do when we walk out of a theater? We ask the other person what he or she thought.

Another of the principles of media literacy is that no two people "read" a media message in the same way.

Without such sharing, media can be isolating. We become lone, unprotected "targets" of messages. But if we engage in the media together and discuss its content, it can bring us together. Ask this: If a program isn't worth talking about, is it worth watching?

3. Change Behavior

To discover more about your relationship with media, try going without it for a set period.

Every third week in April, thousands of families across the country parti-cipate in "TV Turn-off Week." The experience of removing television from our daily lives often reminds us of constructive activi-ties we have lost and how little time many of us have been spending together. Without television on, we actually talk at the dinner table. Without television, we become acquain-ted with the fun of games and the joy of reading to each joy of reading to each

other. And without TV, we also learn what programs we truly miss and which ones we literally can do without.

Of course, many people go on "media fasts" on their own and under their own terms. Computer games, the daily newspaper, magazines—all can be subjected to "fasts."

4. Know The Effects Of Media

Very often changing our relationship with media will tell us what its effects have been on us. In spite of that, we often are unaware of how media affects us and others around us. We need to stay informed of what researchers are learning. For example, recently links between attention deficit disorder and television viewing have been found. Low self-esteem among adolescent girls, obesity, low grades and heightened fear has also been linked to certain habits of media consumption. There are hundreds of studies about such media effects.

Numerous media literacy websites will keep you informed of the latest findings. You can find a list of resource links at Media Thinks' web site: www.mediathink.org. Remember that media literacy is an on-going process, not a goal, so return to these sites routinely.

Excellent books have also been written alerting the public to harmful effects of the misuse of media. "Screen Smarts" by Gloria DeGaetano and Kathleen Bander and "The Other Parent" by James Steyer are just two among many.

5. Work To Change The Media

We often complain about the media, but how often do we complain to those who are responsible for media decisions? We become part of the problem if we don't. Phone a television station to complain about gratuitous violence or demeaning stereotypes. Write sponsors of programs that you disagree with. Letters to the editor are among the most read parts of newspapers—use the newspaper as a forum for your criticism.

Just as important as complaining is complimenting when you see something you like. Media can seem impersonal and distant, but it is run by real people who want to know what others think of their work. Tell them.

> ### MEDIA ACTIVISM
> ### A RECAP IN BRIEF
> 1. **Start with yourself**
> 2. **Communicate**
> 3. **Change behavior**
> 4. **Know the effects of media**
> 5. **Work to change the media**
> 6. **Don't media bash**

6. Don't Media Bash

Likewise, remember the problem isn't the media themselves; it is how media are used. Nicolas Johnson, one of the most critical commissioners ever to serve on Federal Communications Commission, once said, "All television is educational television. The only question is: what is it teaching?"

By educating ourselves, by being selective, by speaking out, we can shape media to be a positive force in society and in our lives. Media Think was founded on the premise that a public that is knowledgeable about the media and acts on that knowledge will ultimately change the media for the better.

Reprinted with permission from Media Think. Media Think (formerly the Northwest Media Literacy Center) is a group of volunteers committed to strengthening critical thinking skills for understanding media, and empowering people to shape media that better serve the needs of individuals and communities. www. MediaThink.org

Examples of Media Activism Successes

Never Underestimate the Power of Angry, Intelligent Girls: A boycott of Abercrombie & Fitch by a group of 23 Pennsylvania girls gained national attention and ended when the retailer agreed to stop selling two controversial T-shirts: "Who Needs Brains When You Have These?" and "All Men Like Tig Old Bitties." (Other A&F shirts say. "Muck Fe" and "You Blow I'll Pop"). The girls dubbed their action a "girlcott." This inspired Women and Girl Foundation to submit their own T-shirt ideas to A&F. (Story from *Chicago Tribune's* "Red Eye," 11/7/05.)

Stand for Children Supports Families by Helping to Get Rid of Junk Food in Oregon Schools: Junk food got into our schools under the guise of "helping" by bringing in money, but research

shows that schools can actually make more money selling healthy food than junk food. Although revenues drop at first, they increase as more parents give their kids money to eat in the cafeteria and more teachers and staff buy meals at the school. Furthermore, the schools tend to discover they have fewer behavior problems when kids are not hopped up on sugar and empty calories. When you add in the savings in future health care costs as kids develop healthy eating habits, getting rid of junk food makes financial sense. California became the first state to ban soft drinks in 2003 and then junk food in 2005. Stand for Children (www.stand.org). addressed this problem in Oregon in 2007 by helping craft and win passage of statewide legislation requiring the replacement of high-sugar, high-fat junk food and soda with healthier snacks in school vending machines, student stores, and à la carte bars.

Bringing Media Literacy to Hollywood: Where better to introduce media literacy than in a community situated near Hollywood, "the entertainment capital of the world." Father Bill Kerze at Our Lady of Malibu Parish and School in Malibu, California says, "The world we live in is clearly permeated with media. We teach our kids how to read and write, yet we're not really cognizant of the language of media and its powerful effect. My goal is to help people become better aware so they can make more informed choices." Components included: grade-specific lesson plans in consumerism and violence prevention, a 7th-grade video project, newspaper article production and an animation workshop for 5th- to 8th-grade students. The Center for Media Literacy (www. medialit.org) helped develop the curriculum.

Although media literacy education has been practiced in Canada, Great Britain, and Australia for three decades or more, it is just now gaining a foothold in the US. The movement has spawned two national organizations that advance media education training, networking, and information exchange through professional conferences and media list-serves: Alliance for a Media Literate America (AMLA) and Action Coalition for Media Education (ACME).

Celebrating "Beauty on the Inside": To counter *People Magazine's* yearly report of the 25 most beautiful women, *New Moon Magazine for Girls and Their Dreams* publishes "25 Beautiful Girls" every June which celebrates inner beauty—the beauty of conviction, caring, and action. All New Moon content is geared for girls age 8-15. It is for girls, written by girls, and is about girls and their interests. They remain free of advertising and external media influences in order to avoid "perfect girl" stereotyping, and to remain accountable only to girls and their needs.

***Girls Get the Message* from Girls Inc.:** Girls Incorporated (www.girlsinc.org) has a unique program to help girls develop the skills to wade through the media messages that bombard them. Girls Get the Message® is a national program that encourages girls and other media consumers to evaluate the messages in media such as television shows, films, CDs, newspapers, websites, music videos, magazines and video games. The program helps girls recognize stereotypes in media and differentiate between those stereotypes and their own lives. Girls learn to "read" media messages with a critical eye as they consider issues of ownership, media business and the roles of women and minorities "behind the scenes" in media careers. In Girls Get the Message, girls learn how to directly communicate with media industry professionals to make their voices heard. Girls Inc. continues this dialogue by hosting events that bring girls and media industry leaders together. At these events girls express their views on how to create more positive and realistic portrayals of girls and women in media.

McDonalds Gets Out of Report Cards: McDonald's has ended its controversial report card advertising in Seminole County, Florida. Children in kindergarten through fifth grade had been receiving their report cards in envelopes adorned with Ronald McDonald promising a free Happy Meal to students with good grades, behavior, or attendance. The Campaign for a Commercial-Free Childhood (CCFC) at www.commercialfreechildhood.org, was alerted to the advertising by Seminole County parent Susan Pagan and launched a campaign which resulted in nearly 2,000 letters to McDonalds and plenty of bad publicity for the fast food giant. The following is CCFC's statement on McDonald's decision to end the program. *In the absence of needed government regulation to protect school children from predatory companies like McDonalds, the burden is on parents to be vigilant about exploitative marketing aimed at children. One parent can make a difference. There is no doubt that the Seminole County ads would have continued—and violated McDonald's pledge to stop advertising in elementary schools—had one parent not called attention to the problem. And when that parent was joined by other parents and CCFC members, one of our nation's largest corporations was forced to back down. What we accomplished in Seminole County should put all marketers on notice: advertising has no place in our nation's schools. Working together, we can reclaim childhood from corporate marketers.*

You can keep updated and get involved by simply signing up for the CCFC newsletter.

Media Literacy Resources to Combat Sexualization of our Girls: Girls get one message repeatedly: What matters is how "hot" they look. It plays on TV and across the Internet. You hear it in song lyrics and music videos. You see it in movies, electronic games, and clothing stores. It's a powerful message which harms girls. Sexualization occurs when:

- a person's value comes only from his or her sexual appeal or behavior, to the exclusion of other characteristics;
- a person is held to a standard that equates physical attractiveness (narrowly defined) with being sexy;
- a person is sexually objectified—that is, made into a thing for others' sexual use, rather than seen as a person with the capacity for independent action and decision making; and/or
- sexuality is inappropriately imposed upon a person

All four conditions need not be present; any one is an indication of sexualization. As parents, you are powerful, too. You can teach girls to value themselves for who they are, rather than how they look. You can teach boys to value girls as friends, sisters, and girlfriends, rather than as sexual objects. You can advocate for change with manufacturers and media producers. Check out: www.apa.org/pi/wpo/sexualizationres.html

Parenting Him

1

2

3

4

5

6

7

8

9

10

Liana Hochhalter, 8th Grade, Rosemont Ridge Middle School

Parenting Him

> *"Effectiveness as a parent is much more from what you hear than from what you say."*
> —Mira Kirshenbaum, author of *Parent Teen Breakthrough*
>
> *"Parents have become so convinced that educators know what is best for children that they forgot that they themselves are really experts."*
> —Marian Wright Edelman, Children's Defense Fund
>
> *"Motherhood: 24/7 on the frontlines of humanity. Are you man enough to try it?"*
> —Maria Shriver
>
> *"The most important thing she had learned over the years was that there was no way to be a perfect mother and a million ways to be a good one."*
> —Jill Churchill

GOALS

- To explore and implement positive parenting strategies for today's world and avoid common sabotages

- To provide support for each other in our struggles, recognizing that there are often no easy answers and many possible solutions

- To develop strategies for encouraging open and compassionate communication, including family rituals, family meetings and meals together

- To explore the impact your own childhood has on the way you parent your children

- To recognize and embrace the important role of a father, as well as a mother, in raising a son

OVERVIEW

Modern parenting is a complicated business. When we "signed-up" for parenting and were holding that darling little baby—we thought THAT was complicated. Little did we know what was to come. The poem, **"Letting Go,"** (p. 3:14) reminds us that in the process of supporting our children as they grow, we develop right along beside them, and expand our capacity and flexibility in ways we could never have imagined before we had children. Through all of the difficulties of maintaining family relationships, there is one thing that is clear: when times get tough, it is our families that we turn to, and our families that help pull us through. Our first article in this section, **"Family Comes First"** (p. 3:15), reminds us of this fact. Our busy lives often distract us as parents from what is most important in our lives: the lifelong relationships we are building with our children.

Connected Parenting

There is simply no easy rulebook for parenting. Parenting strategies and advice abound and there are thousands of books written on the subject. You will find that no one technique works for any single child in all situations. As our kids grow and develop, the strategies we use with them must also change, so as they grow, we grow. However, we would like to acquaint you with one overall parenting approach, which we call **"Connected Parenting"** (p.3:17). Connected parenting helps children of all ages develop into happy, self-reliant and capable individuals, and respects the dignity and wholeness of both parents *and* child. Jane Nelsen, author of *Positive Discipline* is one of a number of experts who encourage connected parenting, which:

1. Helps children feel a sense of connection (belonging and significance),
2. Is mutually respectful and encouraging (kind and firm at the same time),
3. Is effective long-term (gets inside the kid's head about what she is thinking, feeling, learning and deciding about her world),
4. Teaches important social and life skills (respect, concern for others, problem solving, and cooperation, as well as the skill to contribute to the home, school, and community).

In **"Comparison of Common Parenting Styles"** (p. 3:18) you can get a feel for three parenting styles:

1. Permissive child-centered
2. Connected, authoritative, Adlerian
3. Strict, authoritarian, parent-centered.

A common scenario is "yo-yo" parenting when we go from overly permissive (because it's easier, fun and child-centered) to overly strict (because the kids "crossed the line" and we are exhausted and angry). This is why it can benefit everyone to strive for the middle-ground where everyone's needs for respect are met. Jane Nelsen's positive discipline is an excellent model. Positive discipline, as described in **"Positive Discipline Guidelines"** (p. 3:16), is based on understanding the underlying positive intentions that hide behind a child's mis-behaviors. Parents can then create a response which supports the self-esteem, growth and self-discipline of the child that is also respectful, loving and non-punitive. Parents and kids both feel better with this approach.

Connected parenting acknowledges that children make decisions about their lives every day. Parenting is focused on helping children to develop good decision-making skills by letting them practice making choices and learning from the natural and logical consequences of those choices. Children who are allowed to learn from their mistakes when they are young are less likely to act out in dangerous ways as teenagers. They understand that there are personal consequences for the choices that they make that are a direct result of their actions. Connected parenting encourages parents to see mistakes as wonderful opportunities to learn. Setting clear and appropriate boundaries that are wide enough to allow children plenty of room to make lots of choices and mistakes is the hallmark of positive, compassionate parenting.

An important element to parenting is a deep regard for preserving the humanity and dignity of the child and the parents. Learning to discipline with compassion, kindness and firmness, instead of guilt, shame, or coercion, is a skill any parent can learn. Few of us, however, were raised with this model ourselves. The articles **"Connected Parenting"** (p.3:17) and **"Taking Charge: Basic Concepts of JoAnne Nordling's Caring Discipline"** (p. 3:20) will help you to gain your child's cooperation and enhance their mastery of important life skills. The other payoff to parenting with humanity and respect is that a parent usually feels better about him or herself.

Spanking is a common parenting tool used in our culture that carries a number of negative long-term side effects, as outlined in **"Spanking: A Slap at Thoughtful Parenting"** (p. 3:21) originally written by developmental-behavioral pediatrician, Dr. Barbara Howard. Spanking can lead to a belief that those who are the strongest have "power over" those who are weaker. Learning to use positive parenting techniques rather than spanking respects the dignity and humanity of the child and teaches children that there are ways other than hitting to resolve disputes.

"Your Emotions as Tools" (p. 3:22) and the **"The Mistaken Goal Chart"** (p. 3:24) reminds us how difficult it can be dealing when our own feelings when we are addressing children's misbehavior and how to use our emotions to inform our parenting. Lionel Fisher's article, **"Parent's Job: Step aside, Let Kids Become Heroes"** (p. 3:26), encourages us to guide children in finding their own path based on their own inner compass.

Parenting Teens

Parenting teenagers can be a challenge for any parent, and due to the developmental changes in adolescence, your effectiveness as a parent will greatly increase if you change too. The article, **"Overview of One of Our Favorites: *Positive Discipline for Teenagers*"** (p. 3:26) highlights key points from the excellent book, *Positive Discipline for Teenagers: Resolving Conflict with Your Teenage Son or Daughter,* by Jane Nelsen and Lynn Lott. This book is especially useful for helping parents to understand that teenagers, more than ever, need opportunities in their lives for decision-making. By age 18, teenagers are expected to be fully functioning within adult society. Learning to respectfully guide and trust our teenagers through adolescence, while allowing teens to learn from their own experiences and mistakes, is truly one of the most difficult tasks that any parent faces. This book is a blessing for anyone wanting to learn how to parent their teenagers effectively, in a way that preserves everyone's dignity, respect, sanity and safety.

Effective communication and connection with your child continues to be the most powerful protection against future risky behaviors. A US study, titled "Protecting Adolescents from Harm" published in the Journal of the American Medical Association (9/10/97, Vol. 278, pp. 823-32) surveyed 12,000 youth and showed that the single most protective factor against risky behaviors was good connection with parents. A great way to seek more connection and fulfillment as a parent is to simply become curious about who our sons are and what they think.

Listening to our sons' stories, as well as to their nonverbal behaviors, can be immensely helpful for understanding our boys. It also sends them a loud and clear message that they are valued, loved and cared about. Listening is a skill that can be learned, and parents who make a point to listen more and lecture less will be rewarded with more intimacy and connection with their child. We can use curiosity and observation to hone our listening skills. **"Curiosity Kills the Cat but Connects the Family"** (p. 3:27) speaks to the power of curiosity—just wondering what is going on inside the head of your child. It can help to let go of your agenda and focus on what is important to your child; what are the needs behind his actions? Your child will then be in a more receptive state to listen to what is important to you.

Compassionate Communication

"Peaceful Parenting" (p. 3:28) by Sura Hart and Victoria Kindle Hodson, introduces a powerful communication approach called nonviolent or compassionate communication. It is based on the idea that every action we do is motivated by attempts to meet needs or values and that trusting relationships are built through attentiveness to those needs. When a child says "no" to your request (or demand), to what underlying need may she be saying "yes"? The **"Feelings and Needs Inventories"** can support you in exploring the values that are behind the behavior. When both sides get clarity on their underlying needs, new solutions can arise that meet everyone's desires.

Character Development

Eli H. Newberger MD, pediatrician and author of *The Men They Will Become* has some insightful ideas in **"Your Son's Character Development."** (p. 3:31). In his model, character development starts in the cradle, and is nurtured by the child's relationship with his parents. Parents are a boy's first role models. As parents, our actions speak louder than our words, and as parents of teenagers, we will be held strictly accountable for what we think, say, and do. It is easy to define a set of values and morals that we want our sons to incorporate. But if those values and morals are not present in and modeled by us, it will be extremely difficult for them to grow in our sons. Whether or not we actually practice the values we claim to uphold dramatically affects our credibility and any influence we hope to have on the opinions, beliefs, and choices of our boys.

Single Parenting

Single mothers often find themselves wondering if they can raise their sons alone. Numerous child development authorities agree that single mothers can be excellent role models for their sons, though they may be faced with extra parenting challenges. In her book, *Between Mothers and Sons, The Making of Vital and Loving Men,* Evelyn S. Bassoff, PhD, suggests that, in the absence of a biological father, a mother can lead her son to other male role models—men who are invested in the child and who can be consistently there for him. Furthermore, she suggests that while a son's relationship with a reliable male role model is important, the relationship he has with his mother is of even greater significance, especially when she is the person on whom he primarily depends. Single mothers must put aside their anxieties, reassure themselves that they are capable parents, and call on all available resources for support. When a mother, either single or married, finds fulfillment in her work, in her creative activities, in her relationships with family and friends, and in her aspirations to continually learn and grow, she releases her son from the task of "making her happy." Olga Silverstein and Beth Rashbaum dispute the myth that every young boy needs a male role model in their book *The Courage to Raise Good Men,* which is included in your Further Reading list. Women are capable of "nurturing and leading; they can be loving

and competent; they can be figures of authority and compassionate."

Fathers can play a tremendous role in raising capable, loving and responsible sons. Fathers who define for themselves a clear parenting role, and who create a comfortable balance between home and job obligations, will find more joy and fulfillment in parenting, as described in Howard Hiton's article **"Healthy Men, Strong Families"** (p. 3:33). One of the ways fathers can help their sons grow up is to look closely at how they define and model masculinity. Boys desperately need to have close, loving connections with their fathers, mothers and family, and to be able to express a full range of emotions without being shamed or ridiculed about their masculinity. This is such an important issue in the lives of our boys that the *Raising Our Sons Parenting Guide* has dedicated two whole chapters to masculinity and emotions. You may find that, as a father, you can do a lot to help your son counteract the negative images of being masculine that he is likely to face in our larger society.

Family Rituals

"Family Rituals: The Ties that Bind" (p. 3:34) is written by William Doherty, author of *Putting Family First.* We live in a culture that tears the family in many different directions: work, school, sports, and lessons. Rituals can create a "gravitational field" that connects the family. When adults are asked what they remember about their childhood, they remember three things, all of which are rituals: meals, vacations and holidays (many add getting tucked into bed). You could start with meals; set out candles, and turn off the phone, the TV and the scolding. This keeps dinner time "safe." If each family member tells about the best and worst thing that happened that day you will learn a lot about each other. **"At the Heart of Parenting: Eating Together"** (p. 3:36) describes why family meals are incredibly powerful protective factors. Research shows that family meals are correlated with school success and reduction of risky behavior. Meals together is one of the most important ways to strengthen your family. One-on-one dates and vacations are powerful rituals, too. Dad might go on a regular ice cream run once a week with one kid, and play golf every other week with the other. Mom might go camping with one of the kids.

Family Meetings

Regular family meetings are a fabulous "ritual" that sets up open communication between family members. Little things that are bothering a family member can get addressed in these regular meetings and prevent a big "blow-out" later. Meetings that are friendly and comfortable, including some favorite treats, put everyone at ease. All family members add to the agenda, participate in problem solving and voice their opinions so that they feel empowered. This simple tool is reviewed in the article **"Tips on Running a Successful Family Meeting"** (p. 3:39). The following example uses a family meeting to lessen a family conflict over chores. At a family meeting, in response to nagging and pleading to get the kids to routinely finish their chores on time, the family established a set of agreements and consequences around chores. Because the kids were involved in setting up the agreements as well as the consequences for chores that were not done, they became more invested in carrying through on their agreements. The entire family benefited as chores got done without conflict, and the kids learned accountability and felt good about their contribution to the family's welfare.

Financial Responsibility

An enormous avenue of empowerment for our sons is to teach them financial responsibility through practical experience. Giving them an allowance not only shares the financial resources of the family, but it more importantly teaches boys to spend and save money by the direct experience of doing so. This means that parents will need to make agreements with their sons over what purchases they are to cover with their allowance, what percentage to save for college or give to charity organizations. Our job is to also allow logical consequences to work when they overspend and run out of money for that lunch or pair of jeans that they really want. Kids will never learn to save until they first experience the sorrows of being broke! And, the repercussions of being broke at age 8 are much less serious than those that can occur at age 21!

Good money management and business skills are best taught to boys from an early age, as outlined in **"Nine Steps to Raising Money-Smart Kids"** (p. 3:41). Whether they are aware of it or not, parents will be their child's primary financial teacher, guide and resource through their own daily examples of money management and fiscal responsibility. In today's times the wise use of debit cards and credit cards is an essential skill. It is helpful to become aware of your own spoken and unspoken values around money, so that you can share them directly with your son. This helps you to align your values with your actions, and ensures that you will pass on to your son the financial habits and experiences that you most value. Bankers are also often willing to talk to teens about money management.

In summary, parenting is not a perfect science, but more of an art. With the myriad of influences that our sons are exposed to on a daily basis through peers, media, institutions, and the ever-increasing pace of life in our society, we parents can provide a "haven" where our children and teens can feel at rest, safe, accepted and understood. Our sons deserve our love and support, so they can experiment and experience who they are without fear of harsh judgment. In this way, they can truly discover and grow into the persons they are meant to be.

Parenting for mothers and fathers of sons is not easy. It requires endless patience, tenacity, energy, and attentiveness combined with unconditional love. It requires believing in, protecting, and celebrating your son's inner sense of worth. Although the responsibility of raising a son can be daunting, the journey can be filled with joy and love. Our goals as parents were aptly summed up by Hodding Carter, Jr., when he said,

> *There are only two lasting bequests we can hope to give to our children … one of these is roots, the other, wings.*

---

[1] "Protecting Adolescents from Harm," Journal of the American Medical Association, 9/10/97, Vol. 278, pp. 823-32.

THE 40 DEVELOPMENTAL ASSETS Essential to Every Young Person's Success

The 40 Developmental Assets are research-proven building blocks that support the healthy development of our youth and help them to grow up to be caring and responsible. The following assets relate directly to a child's experiences with his parents and within the home:

- **Asset #1   Family Support:** Family life provides high levels of love and support.
- **Asset #2   Positive Family Communication:** Young person and his parents communicate positively and young person is willing to seek advice and counsel from parents.
- **Asset #6   Parent Involvement in Schooling:** Parents are involved in helping young people succeed in school.
- **Asset #11   Family Boundaries:** Family has clear rules and consequences and monitors the young person's whereabouts.
- **Asset #14   Adult Role Models:** Parents and other adults model positive, responsible behaviors.
- **Asset #16   High Expectations:** Both parents and teachers encourage the young person to do well.

CIRCLE QUESTION

What were the advantages and disadvantages of the parenting style your parents used raising you? Specifically, what contributed to your well-being and health that you would like to include in your parenting? Name one thing you are doing differently.

POSSIBLE DISCUSSION QUESTIONS

1. What do you love about your son? What is special and unique about him?
2. What positive qualities does he bring out in you? How does he challenge you to grow?
3. Share a successful parenting story. How did some of the most rewarding moments with your son come about? What is your biggest parenting struggle right now?
4. What other adults are involved in your child's life and how did these relationships evolve? How do you seek out support for your parenting from other adults? Who are they? How do they help?
5. What are effective alternatives to nagging?
6. Have you found rewards to be useful in parenting? In what situations? Do you think they might be potentially damaging?
7. How do you and your child "match" in terms of temperament?

Connection/Listening

8. Where does your parenting style fall along the spectrum of strict versus permissive?
9. How do you as a parent balance/assert your own needs with those of your children?
10. How do you express anger constructively in your family? What constitutes "confrontation" in your house?
11. Describe an instance where you allowed your son to experience some difficult consequences of a mistake, without rescuing or buffering him. How did this work?
12. How difficult would it be for you to start allowing your son to make more choices and mistakes in his life? In what areas of his life would it be easiest for you to start this new tactic?
13. What is the difference between punishment and positive discipline?
14. How do you react when your son makes a mistake, acts out in front of others, or expresses his outrageous individuality? Now, pretend you are your son. How might he interpret this response and how might he feel?
15. Go over the needs list and decide what your biggest unmet needs are, as a parent. Imagine your life if these needs were met and describe it to each other.

Rituals

16. What are the rituals in your home that increase connection/communication?
17. What do you like/dislike about family meals in your home?
18. Describe the one-on-one activities you do with each of your kids.

Teens

20. How is your teen different from you when you were a teen?
21. How do parents balance setting limits with allowing independence?
19. Did you learn some of your most important life lessons from your own experiences or other's advice?
20. What preconceived ideas do you have of the type of person your child will become as a grown-up? Has that idea changed over time? How realistic is it?
21. What type of relationship do you imagine having with your child when he is an adult?
22. What boundaries are the most important for your teen?
23. How are you teaching financial responsibility to your son?

Fathers/Mothers

24. Whether you are a mom or a dad taking this course, how can you share what you are learning with your spouse?
25. How involved are male relatives—father, grandfather, uncles—and close family friends in your son's life? If you feel your son would benefit from more time with them, how can you foster that?

PUTTING IT INTO PRACTICE

*   Shift parenting style to a more positive approach that supports relationships, teaches responsibility, sets reasonable boundaries and respects the dignity of the child and integrity of the parent.
*   Encourage independence and interdependence.
*   Respect your adolescent's privacy.
*   Accept your teen's grumblings as normal and natural—don't take it personally
*   Develop family rituals aimed at strengthening your family structure and relationships.
*   Consider establishing a family mission statement and having regular family meetings.
*   Include your son more and more in the decision-making processes that affect him.
*   Maintain your balance and assert your own needs, especially for stress reduction and self-care.
*   Seek out a support system for you and a mentoring system for him.
*   Spend more one-on-one time with your son.
*   When in conflict with your son, re-examine the content when calm, connect with your underlying need or value behind what you want, and consider your son's point of view.

PUTTING IT TOGETHER—YOUR VERSION

Write down three or four ideas you have been inspired to implement in your own life after reading and discussing this chapter.

1. _____

2. _____

3. _____

4. _____

FAVORITE PARENTING RESOURCES

Connection and Empathy

Nonviolent Communication (NVC), by Marshall Rosenberg, introduces the basic concepts of the compassionate communication approach to interacting with others, leading to a deep connection both to ourselves as well as the other person. It is based on the premise that we are motivated by attempts to meet needs, and trusting relationships are built through attentiveness to those needs. Sura Hart and Victoria Kindle, authors of *Respectful Parents, Respectful Kids: 7 Keys to Turn Family Conflict Into Cooperation*, get to the heart of family conflict with powerful insights. In her book *Parenting from Your Heart: Sharing the Gifts of Compassion, Connection, and Choice*, Inbal Kashtan applies these NVC principles to parenting. Instead of focusing on authority and discipline, attachment parenting and NVC provide theoretical and practical grounds for nurturing compassionate, powerful, and creative children who will have resources to contribute to a peaceful society.

Understanding Temperament

Raising Your Spirited Child by Mary Sheedy Kurchinka is an important resource for understanding the effects of temperament. As you know, there is no one simple answer for what to do in any given situation. Each of our own children may need different approaches. Parents have different personalities, and so do kids. Sometimes the problem is simply that the two sets of personalities are just not matching up well. There are nine temperament traits we are born with that remain fairly consistent our entire lives. They are: activity level, intensity, persistence, distractibility, regularity, approach-withdrawal, adaptability, mood and sensory threshold. The better we understand temperament, the more we can match our parenting to these differences and help children value and understand themselves.

Teens

Parenting a teenage boy is an especially difficult task for most parents, who may be frightened not only by the growing autonomy of their son, but also by the myriad of toxic influences in our modern culture. Parents are also influenced by their own experiences as teenagers, when they likely rebelled against their own parents and culture. The following parenting resources can help parents to support their teens with love, connection, and respect during the turbulent teen years. The bonus is that you can be closely connected with your son and actually enjoy yourself, too.

Positive Discipline for Teenagers by Jane Nelsen and Lynn Lott provides one of the best all-round approaches to parenting teens. When our children are struggling and we jump in and "solve" it for them, it turns the situation into "our problem." When we can let go enough to hold our tongue and help them think through their own solutions, children learn about responsibility and how to cope with their own problems.

Parent as Coach by Diana Haskins is an east-to-read book that is just packed with powerful, new ideas encouraging parents to switch from administrating to coaching their teen. It is based on a poem, titled "Message to Parents," written by teens who had received coaching. By focusing on respect, listening, understanding, appreciation, and support, our teen will have the resources to become responsible and independent.

If you Respect me,
I will hear you.
If you Listen to me,
I will feel understood.
If you Understand me,
I will feel appreciated.
If you Appreciate me,
I will know your support.
If you Support me as I try new things,
I will become responsible.
When I am Responsible,
I will grow to be independent.
In my Independence,
I will respect you and love you all of my life.

Mira Kirshenbaum and Charles Foster, PhD, authors of *Parent/Teen Breakthrough: The Relationship Approach,* help parents to switch from control to connection. Children are already making hundreds of decisions in their daily lives independent of parental control. Parents who connect with their budding teen rather than attempting to control him, will have a far greater chance of supporting him through the "rocky roads" of adolescence towards adulthood.

The Romance of Risk: Why Teenagers Do The Things They Do, by Dr. Lynn Ponton, helps parents to recognize that risk-taking in teenagers is a normal and developmentally-appropriate behavior. Helping your teenage son to find positive challenges and risks and steer clear of dangerous behaviors is a special parenting skill that will help your teenager immensely. Current thinking is beginning to acknowledge that adolescence is a time of risk-taking, that is not solely harmful. On the contrary, risk-taking is a normal, healthy behavior for adolescents. It is during adolescence that young people experiment with many aspects of life, taking on new challenges, testing out how things fit together, and using this process to define and shape both their identities and their knowledge of the world.

Rituals

Bill Doherty, author of *The Intentional Family* and *Putting Family First,* believes in increasing family connection through the use of rituals. He has an entire chapter on how to create a rich bonding and social time around family mealtimes. In the face of the complex obstacles and distractions of our busy society, families breaking bread together can enrich themselves body and soul.

Seven Habits of Highly Effective Families by Stephen Covey and *Seven Habits for Highly Effective Teens* by his son, Sean Covey, outline a list of habits that can be practiced by any family to strengthen their relationships: Be Proactive, Begin with the End in Mind, Put First Things First, Think "Win-Win," Seek First To Understand … Then to Be Understood, Synergize and Sharpen the Saw. Sean also wrote a wonderful book for teens, called *The Six Most Important Decisions You'll Ever Make,* asking teens what they are going to decide about: school, friends, parents, dating and sex, addictions and self-worth.

Fatherhood

Fatherneed by Kyle Pruett, shares research on the importance of fathers in the lives of our children.
The Good Father by Mark O'Connell looks at masculinity, the role dads play, and how dads parent differently
   from mothers.
Father Courage: What Happens When Men Put Family First by Suzanne Braun Levine
The Season of Life: a Football Star, a Boy, a Journey to Manhood by Jeffrey Marx
Covering Home: Lessons on the Art of Fatherhood, from the Game of Baseball by Jack Petrash
What's Up With Middle School Boys? by Cesa Newist, Northeastern Wisconsin In-School Telecommunications,
   2420 Nicolet Drive, Green Bay, WI 54311, (920) 465-2599

FURTHER READING

General

How to Talk So Kids Will Listen and Listen So Kids Will Talk by Adele Faber and Elaine Mazlish, a mainstay for
   those raising school-aged children
Liberated Parents, Liberated Children: Your Guide to a Happier Family by Adele Faber and Elaine Mazlish,
   ways to use language to build self-worth, and encourage responsibility in children of all ages

Growing Up Again: Parenting Ourselves, Parenting our Children by Jean Illsley Clarke and Connie Dawson
Taking Charge: Caring Discipline That Works, at Home and at School, 4th edition by JoAnne Nordling, MS, MEd
Positive Discipline, by Jane Nelsen, EdD, MFT, an approach that leaves your child feeling respected and valued
Parenting with Love and Logic: Teaching Kids Responsibility by Foster Cline, MD and Jim Fay
Parenting Teens with Love and Logic: Preparing Adolescents for a Responsible Adulthood by Foster Cline MD and Jim Fay
Whole Parenting Guide: Strategies, Resources and Inspiring Stories for Holistic Parenting and Family Living
    by Alan Reder, Phil Catalfo, and Stephanie Renfrow Hamilton

Compassionate Communication

Raising Children Compassionately: Parenting the Nonviolent Communication Way by Marshall Rosenberg
Empathy Magic website of Holley Humphrey: videos and books to use with kids at www.empathymagic.com

Mothers

The Courage to Raise Good Men by Olga Silverstein and Beth Rashbaum

---

HOW IS THE DISCUSSION GROUP WORKING FOR YOU?
If you are part of a parenting group, this is a great time to talk with each other about how things are going. What's working, not working? Is everyone getting a fair chance to talk? Are you getting a fair chance to talk? Do you feel safe in the group so that there is comfort in sharing deeply and honestly? Brainstorm solution ideas. Make a commitment to each other to share when your needs, such as fairness, honesty, consideration, acceptance, support, appreciation, or openness,are not being met.

Letting Go

To "let go" does not mean to stop caring;

it means I can't do it for someone else.

To "let go" is not to cut myself off;

it's the realization I can't control another.

To "let go" is not to enable,

but to allow learning from natural consequences.

To "let go" is to admit powerlessness,

which means that the outcome is not always in our hands.

To "let go" is not to try to change or blame another;

it's to make the most of myself.

To "let go" is not to "care for,"

but to "care about."

To "let go" is not to "fix,"

but to support.

To "let go" is not to judge,

but to allow another to be a human being.

To "let go" is not to be in the middle arranging outcomes, but to

allow others to affect their destinies.

To "let go" is not to be protective;

it's to permit another to face reality.

To "let go" is not to deny, but to accept.

To "let go" is not to nag, scold, or argue,

but instead to search out my own shortcomings and correct them.

To "let go" is not to adjust everything to my desires,

but to take each day as it comes.

To "let go" is not to criticize and regulate anybody,

but to try to become what I can be.

To "let go" is not to regret the past,

but to grow and live for the future.

To "let go" is to fear less . . . and love more.

—Unknown

Family Comes First

By William J. Doherty, author of *Putting Family First*

ON SEPTEMBER 11, 2001 our nation's boundaries were violently breached and our sense of invulnerability shattered. After the initial shock, the reaction most people had was to contact loved ones. When hijacked airline passengers found telephones, they called their spouses or parents to say, "I love you" and "goodbye." When office workers in the World Trade Center felt the shock of the airplane collisions and saw the smoke, they called a family member to offer reassurance that they would get out safely. When the rest of us heard the news of the attacks, we called our spouses, children, parents, or siblings. Parents everywhere gathered their children around them.

We know that not all families are connected enough to be helpful in such a crisis. A mental health worker in New York recounted that the most distressed survivors he encountered during the aftermath of the attacks were people who were cut off from family members and uncertain if they could contact them.

The message could not be clearer: family relationships are the irreplaceable core of a full human life. However, a rich family life alone is not enough because we also need strong neighborhoods, schools, communities, governments, nations, and a cooperative international community. But none of these, alone or together, can substitute for family life.

The frantic pace of contemporary American family life is eroding family closeness and depriving our children of their childhood. Today's families are sorely lacking time for spontaneous fun and enjoyment, for talking over the day's events and experiences, for unhurried meals, for quiet bedtime talks, for working together on projects, for teaching and learning life skills such as cooking and gardening, for visiting extended family and friends, for attending religious services together, for participating together in community projects, and for exploring the beauty of nature. Not enough time, that is, to be a family with a rich internal and external life.

There are many contributors to the "time famine" experienced by many families, including parents' work commitments, employers' expectations for increased work hours, and larger economic forces. Some of these forces can be controlled by individual families, and others cannot. One thing that parents can control is the problem of over-scheduling children in a competitive culture; maybe your child doesn't have to take up a

second musical instrument or join a traveling sports team. You might not have control over whether you can be home for dinner reliably at six o'clock, but your family can decide to snack early and then eat later in the evening when you can all be together. When you are scheduling your summer, you might not be able to claim the exact weeks for vacation that you would prefer, but you can hold sacred the vacation time you do have— and not surrender it to the vagaries of children's baseball schedules or French lessons.

You may feel regret or guilt at times as you read along. You may have surrendered your family dinners to over-scheduling and television watching. You may not have created bedtime rituals for your children because you don't need the hassle of getting them to bed. A certain amount of regret and guilt comes with the territory of being a caring parent, because it is a big job and we all make mistakes. But two ideas can help to offset the guilt and turn it into constructive action. First, the problems we are talking about are rooted in the broader culture we have created together; they are not primarily the fault of individual parents. Second, the solutions, both personal and communal, are within our grasp if we reach for them. We are not talking about solving an intractable social problem such as world poverty or ethnic hatred. We can do something right now, in our own lives and with our neighbors, about the problem of overscheduled kids and under-connected families. We can take back our kids and renew our family time.

Along with our fellow citizens, we will be processing for many years the meaning of the events of September 11, 2001. But our first conclusion is this: that everything has changed and nothing has changed. We have awakened as from a slumber to the sobering new world of the twenty-first century, where the risks and the rules are different. But we have also realized anew something we have known all along, something we lose sight of in our high speed, consumerist culture: that close families, immersed in vibrant democratic communities, have always been the source of our strength as a people.

Written for Family Empowerment Network by William J. Doherty, PhD, co-author of Putting Family First, *(Henry Holt, August, 2002) about reclaiming family time in a frantic world, and has a nonprofit for families at www.puttingfamilyfirst. For reprint requests, contact www.family-empower.com.*

Positive Discipline Guidelines

From the book *Positive Discipline* by Jane Nelsen, EdD, MFT

1. **Misbehaving children are "discouraged children"** who have mistaken ideas on how to achieve their primary goal—to belong. Their mistaken ideas lead them to misbehavior. We cannot be effective unless we address the mistaken beliefs rather than just the misbehavior.

2. **Use encouragement to help children feel "belonging"** so the motivation for misbehaving will be eliminated. Celebrate each step in the direction of improvement rather than focusing on mistakes.

3. A great way to help children feel encouraged is to **spend special time** "being with them." Many teachers have noticed a dramatic change in a "problem child" after spending five minutes simply sharing what they both like to do for fun.

4. When tucking children into bed, ask them to **share with you** their "saddest time" during the day and their "happiest time" during the day. Then **you share with them.** You will be surprised what you learn.

5. Have **family meetings** or **class meetings** to solve problems with cooperation and mutual respect. This is the key to creating a loving, respectful atmosphere while helping children develop self-discipline, responsibility, cooperation, and problem-solving skills.

6. Give children **meaningful jobs.** In the name of expediency, many parents and teachers do things that children could do for themselves and one another. **Children feel belonging when they know they can make a real contribution.**

7. **Decide together** what jobs need to be done. Put them all in a jar and let each child draw out a few each week; that way no one is stuck with the same jobs all the time. Teachers can invite children to help make class rules and list them on a chart titled, "We Decided:" Children have ownership, motivation, and enthusiasm when they are included in the decisions.

8. **Take time for training.** Make sure children understand what "clean the kitchen" means to you. To them it may mean simply putting the dishes in the sink. Parents and teachers may ask, "What is your understanding of what is expected?"

9. **Teach and model mutual respect.** One way is to **be kind and firm at the same time**—kind to show respect for the child, and firm to show respect for yourself and the "needs of the situation." This is difficult during conflict, so use the next guideline whenever you can.

10. Proper **timing** will improve your effectiveness tenfold. It does not "work" to deal with a problem at the time of conflict—emotions get in the way. Teach children about cooling-off periods. You (or the children) can go to a separate room and do something to make you feel better—and then work on the problem with mutual respect.

11. **Get rid of the crazy idea that in order to make children do better, first you have to make them feel worse.** Do you feel like doing better when you feel humiliated? This suggests a whole new look at "time out."

12. **Use Positive Time Out.** Let your children help you design a pleasant area (cushions, books, music, and stuffed animals) that will help them feel better. Remember that children do better when they feel better. Then you can ask your children, when they are upset, "Do you think it would help you to take some positive time out?"

13. Punishment may "work" if all you are interested in is stopping misbehavior for "the moment." Sometimes we must **beware of what works** when the long-range results are negative—resentment, rebellion, revenge, or retreat.

14. Teach children that **mistakes are wonderful opportunities to learn!** A great way to teach children that mistakes are wonderful opportunities to learn is to model this yourself by using the Three R's of Recovery after you have made a mistake:
    (1) **Recognize your mistake.**
    (2) **Reconcile: Be willing to say "I'm sorry, I didn't like the way I handled that."**
    (3) **Resolve: Focus on solutions rather than blame.** (#3 is only effective if you do #1 & #2 first.)

15. Focus on **solutions** instead of **consequences.** Many parents and teachers try to disguise punishment by calling it a logical consequence. Get children involved in finding solutions that are (1) **Related** (2) **Respectful** (3) **Reasonable** and (4) **Helpful.**

16. **Make sure the message of love and respect gets through.** Start with "I care about you. I am concerned about this situation. Will you work with me on a solution?"

17. **Have fun!** Bring joy into homes and classrooms.

Connected Parenting

By Jody Bellant Scheer, M.D and Glenda Montgomery

PSYCHOLOGISTS TEND TO divide parenting styles into three broad categories with varying levels of power and control. Although there are many different names for these three categories, they are generally referred to as:

- **Permissive:** low parent effectiveness, no limits, freedom without order
- **Connected or authoritative:** parenting based on relationships without need for punishment or humiliation, choices allowed within limits that respect all, freedom with order
- **Authoritarian or strict:** parent attempts to control child, few choices allowed, narrow limits, order without freedom.

Many parenting books offer strategies to produce happy, self-reliant and respectful children, and advocate a "connected" or authoritative approach to child-raising. This kind of approach is neither per-missive nor punitive and places a high value on fostering relationship connections while working toward long-term goals. Providing opportunities for children to develop a sense of belonging and a sense of themselves as competent and worthwhile human beings are key components. Underlying this approach is a high regard for the humanity of children, for treating all family members with equal dignity and respect, and for the parents' message of love and support to shine through as the primary message even when the child has made a mistake.

Connected parenting approaches are designed to address the underlying motivations of a child's mis- behavior instead of just reacting to their naughty deed. This is counterintuitive at times. A parent using a traditional approach may look at a child's annoying misbehavior and may either punish the child or say, "Oh, ignore him. He just wants attention." Whereas, a parent practicing a connecting approach may say, "Oh, it seems he really needs attention. I'll ignore this behavior and will ask for his help and get him involved in something useful so I can give him attention in a positive way."

This kind of parenting requires a long-term approach to parenting, and thoughtful reactions to misbehavior. Many parents lack experience with such approaches, having been raised for the most part in either permissive or over-controlling households themselves. It may take a bit of stretching and personal growth to understand how a connected parenting approach works, and to trust that learning these skills will improve all of your interpersonal relationships. But it makes sense that if we want our children to be in control of their emotions, to be patient and understanding, to be open to changing their behavior, and to take an active and respectful role in resolving

conflicts, we should expect only the very same behaviors of ourselves.

Sometimes, all that is needed for motivation is to step back and imagine how your child sees you when you are angry and upset. Somewhere in our culture, we have developed the crazy notion that kids will want to do better only if we first yell, lecture, or punish them. This does not meet the child's needs for empathy or compassion, and only fuels the fires of feeling worse! Certainly adults are not motivated by such techniques, and neither are our kids. In our guilt, we sometimes do "yo-yo parenting," going from overly permissive (because it is easier, fun and is child-centered) to overly strict (because the kids "crossed the line" and we are exhausted and angry).

Children, like adults, learn best when their needs for respect and understanding are met. Finding ways to support and guide our children, while building their sense of worthiness and competence, their self-esteem and self-discipline, their ability to make choices, and their capacity to learn from their experience is at the heart of connected parenting.

The following two pages contain an overview of strategies involved in all three of the primary styles of parenting. It is never too late to change your parenting approach and to transform your family relationships. Choosing to parent with a connected approach is a sure way to enrich your family's competence, warmth, and long-term success.

Comparison of Common Parenting Styles:

(Note: these styles are often practiced unconsciously, a legacy of our own upbringing)

	Permissive	Connected, Authoritative	Authoritarian, Strict
Beliefs about Misbehavior	A child misbehaves because the parent is not doing enough for the child. A child will be motivated to do better when parents coddle, cajole and plead with them.	A child's behavior is driven by his attempts to meet his needs, especially the need to belong and to be loved. Misbehavior is often a sign of a child's discouragement, thinking he is insignificant or doesn't belong. A child will do better when his underlying needs for love and understanding are met, so this becomes one of the primary intervention goals of connected discipline.	A child misbehaves because he is bad and needs to be "fixed." A child will be motivated to do better when he is humiliated, threatened, intimidated, lectured at, or made to feel guilty. If a kid doesn't improve, the punishment is made more severe, as this will surely teach him or her a lesson.
Power	Freedom without order. Ruled by the child, assumes parent has little or no control or influence over child's behaviors.	Freedom with limits. Shared power, assumes parents can guide and support a child's behavior without having to punish or control, trusts that child can learn from his own mistakes and can be an independent and competent thinker/doer.	Order without freedom. Ruled by the parent, who assumes the child cannot behave in an appropriate manner without oversight by a parent or other authority figure.
Control	Lack of parental control or limits, lots of rescuing and buffering children from consequences of their behaviors (overprotection), often overly solicitous.	Parent acknowledges that child operates with free will. Parent holds high degree of control & integrity over what *parent* will do, guides and supports children instead of trying to control, allows choices within broad but clear limits.	Parent is over-controlling, doesn't allow child to make choices, maintains tight control and narrow limits.
Responsibility	Few and inconsistent rules. Parents expect child to become responsible naturally without much parental effort due to the gratitude the kid will feel for the constant parental sacrifices made on their behalf. Bribery is also often used as a motivator for responsible behavior.	Fewer rules as kids age. Kids are taught responsibility through parents modeling the behaviors they wish to see in their children and by parents keeping their own agreements with their kids. Parents also take time to train, to gain co-operation, to make and follow through on mutual agreements, and to empathically hold their kids accountable for all the consequences (good and bad) of the choices and behaviors they choose.	Lots of rules. Parents assume kids are irresponsible and need to be shown who is the boss. Use of demands, lectures, intimidation, threats, humiliation, ultimatums and guilt to teach kids responsibility.
Approach to Adolescence	Supports individuation (creating unique self & interests) somewhat, but parents often are enmeshed with child, hindering differentiation (ability to separate from family & establish one's own values).	Allows child to test and learn life skills so that by age 18, child is making most of his/her own life decisions. Supports individuation and differentiation as normal and expected developmental goals during adolescence.	Protects adolescents by placing more rules on them than on younger children. Low tolerance for exploration, rebellion or differing values. Hinders normal adolescent processes of individuation and differentiation.
Warmth	Usually high degree of warmth, relationship may be close but tends to be enmeshed and/or disrespectful.	High degree of warmth & empathy, value is placed on creating respectful, long-term relationships where needs of parents and kids are equally valued.	Usually low warmth and empathy, long-term relationship is often strained.

continued

	Permissive	Connected, Authoritative	Authoritarian, Strict
Short-term Parenting Goal	Give child whatever s/he wants to avoid disappointment or conflict, be "friends" with the child, rescue and buffer child from the negative consequences of his/her mistakes. Avoid hard decisions because it takes too much time and energy to create & enforce clear boundaries. Often unclear on what to do- waits and hopes problem will either get better or go away on its own	Parent models dignity and respect of child and parent by being in control of his/her own behaviors & by using good conflict resolution skills. Gains cooperation, uses discipline techniques that support a child's self esteem and competence, & allows a child to make choices within safe limits. Supports the child while s/he learns from the natural and logical consequences of his/her successes and failures.	Stop any misbehavior immediately. Punish and humiliate the child for mistakes. Force the child to do what the parent wants or what the parent thinks is in the best interest of the child.
Long-term Parenting Goal (often unconscious)	Dependence on parents.	Independence, success, self-discipline. Child is able to make decisions that actually meet his/her own needs, which at the same time take into consideration the needs of others.	Dependence on outside authorities: child often substitutes other voices for parents' (peers, romantic partners, bosses, pop culture idols, etc) as s/he grows up.
Likely Long-term Outcome for Child	A child who may appear to be selfish, demanding, irresponsible, and not responsive to social cues. Often exhibits high self-regard, low self-esteem, and high sense of entitlement (expects others or parents to take care of him/her).	A child with high self-esteem, in control of his/her own behaviors and emotions, able to operate with personal power to create positive results in their lives, able to make decisions and learn from the consequences of those decisions.	Children tend to appear either rebellious or submissive, have low self-esteem and high self-doubt, and have few opportunities to learn life skills. Often unable to handle the responsibility of learning by trial and error, tend to blame the world for their problems, & tend to seek sources outside themselves for validation and direction. Tendency towards unhappiness and addictions.
Likely Feelings Kids Hold Towards Parents	Love, often lacking empathy or understanding of parents/others	Love, connection, respect	Feelings of rebellion, anger, hatred, intimidation, resentment, sneakiness, withdrawal

A List of Books about Parenting with Empathy and Connection:

Positive Disicpline by Jane Nelsen, EdD, MFT

Positive Discipline for Teenagers: Resolving Conflict with Your Teenage Son or Daughter by Jane Nelsen, EdD, MFT and Lynn Lott, MA, MFT

Parenting with Love and Logic: Teaching Kids Responsibility by Foster Cline, MD and Jim Fay

Parenting Teens With Love and Logic: Preparing Adolescents for Responsible Adulthood by Foster Cline, MD and Jim Fay

Seven Habits of Highly Effective Families by Stephen Covey

The Seven Year Stretch: How Families Work Together to Grow Through Adolescence by Laura S. Kastner, PhD and Jennifer Wyatt, PhD

Parent as Coach: Helping Your Teen Build a Life of Confidence, Courage, and Compassion by Diana Sterling

Parenting from your Heart: Sharing the Gifts of Compassion, Connection and Choice by Inbal Kashtan

Respectful Parents, Respectful Kids: 7 Keys to Turn Family Conflict into Cooperation by Sura Hart & Victoria Kindle Hudson

Nonviolent Communication by Marshall Rosenberg, PhD

Raising Children Compassionately: Parenting the Nonviolent Communication Way by Marshall Rosenberg PhD

Raising Self-Reliant Children in a Self-Indulgent World: Seven Building Blocks for Developing Capable Young People by H. Stephen Glenn and Jane Nelsen

How to Talk so Kids Will Listen and Listen so Kids Will Talk by Adele Faber and Elaine Mazlish

Liberated Parents, Liberated Children, Your Guide to a Happier Family by Adele Faber and Elaine Mazlish

Raising Your Spirited Child. A Guide for Parents Whose Child is More Intense, Sensitive, Perceptive, Persistent, and Energetic by Mary Sheedy Kurcinka

Temperament Tools: Working with your Child's Inborn Traits by Helen Nelville and Diane Clark Johnson

Parent/Teen Breakthrough: The Relationship Approach by Mira Kirshenbaum and Charles Foster

Taking Charge: Basic Concepts of JoAnne Nordling's *Caring Discipline*

Child's Staircase of Needs: This is based on Maslow's Heirachy of Needs. Lower needs need to be satisfied before higher needs can be met. We all regress during stressful times.

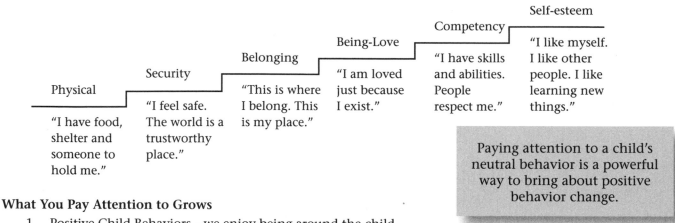

Paying attention to a child's neutral behavior is a powerful way to bring about positive behavior change.

What You Pay Attention to Grows
1. Positive Child Behaviors—we enjoy being around the child
2. Neutral Behaviors—child entertaining him/herself—no problem for parent
3. Negative Behaviors—child is angering or irritating us—parent's problem

Paying attention to a child's neutral behavior is a powerful way to bring about positive behavior change. Message to the child: "You are loved just because you exist." Paying undue attention to negative behaviors may cause them to misbehave to connect to you.

How Parents and Teachers Sabotage Their Discipline: There are five ways that even the best-intentioned parents get in the way of their own goals when they are teaching and disciplining.

1. **Procrastination**
    Act when you first see the misbehavior, and avoid the anger that arises when we repeat ourselves. Try not to give children the emotional energy they crave when they are misbehaving; you are encouraging the negative behavior.
2. **Talking and Talking about the Misbehavior**
    Rudolf Dreikurs said, "Act, don't talk." If possible carry out your discipline action calmly and do not mention it again. When negative emotions are present in the adult and/or the child, lecturing or verbally trying to teach in any way can cause the child to turn off their listening or even rebel in order to maintain their self integrity. Power struggles ensue. Teach and talk in neutral or positive situations.
3. **Forgetting to Pay Attention to the Child's Positive and Neutral Behaviors**
    Each child needs at least four positive attentions for every negative one for the child to feel and act well. Nonverbal attention is even more powerful than verbal.
4. **Negative Scripting**
    Children believe what they hear us say about them. Avoid negative scripts "He is just so unorganized!" and use positive scripting "Josh was so supportive of Jen!"
5. **Lack of Self-Care and Self-Love**
    Parents who take care of themselves and their unmet needs are much more able to be the kind of parent they want to be, even when the child is misbehaving.

Reprinted with permission from JoAnne Nordling, MS, MEd, author of *Taking Charge: Caring Discipline That Works at Home and at School*, and director of Parent Support Center at www.parentsupportcenter.org.

Spanking: A Slap at Thoughtful Parenting
Summarized from an article by behavioral pediatrician Dr. Barbara Howard

SPANKING IS A FORM OF discipline that is both common in America and associated with unintended negative side effects. One quarter of American parents spank infants only 1 to 6 months old and three-quarters of parents hit their one year olds, even though these infants are not old enough to understand the lesson the parent is trying to teach. Spanking gets worse as toddlers get older: by age 3, 90% of children are being spanked. Hitting doesn't stop as children grow older, even when parents think it should: 60% of children ages 10-12, 40% of those aged 14 years, and 25% of those aged 17 years are still being hit by their parents. These, in spite of the fact that one half of the time, parents concede that hitting was a knee-jerk reaction that was inappropriate in light of the offense for which it was given.

Spanking is associated with a number of negative side effects. Children who are spanked are four times as likely to be aggressive, are less attentive to social cues, and are more likely to have delinquent behaviors outside the home than their peers who are not spanked. Children who are spanked are also at higher risk to become adults who approve of spanking and who hit their own spouse and children. Additionally, painful punishments have been shown to make non-painful punishments less effective. Kids who are spanked by their parents think time-out at school is a joke they are therefore more difficult for teachers to manage and are at increased risk for behavior problems in school or day care. Lastly, in order to be effective, a painful stimulus must be increased over time to maintain its effectiveness. Since toddlers and preschoolers misbehave on average every 6-8 minutes, it's not surprising that there is going to be a lot of hitting, and it's likely to get more intense once spanking is embedded in a parent's disciplinary repertoire.

Research confirms that spanking is no more effective than non-painful forms of discipline, which are more effective and less harmful to the child in both the long- and short-term. Why then, do so many parents spank? Parents learn to hit because they were hit. Also, hitting is a short-term parenting strategy that looks like it works in the moment. A child who gets a swat is no longer participating in an undesired behavior because they are crying instead. The chance of the child going back to that behavior, however, is likely regardless of the consequence that is given, because that is how children learn: by repetition.

Parents may never have thought about the negative side effects of spanking. What can help many parents that were hit themselves as children is to look at the quality of their current relationships with their own parents. Close, warm, long-term relationships usually spring from parenting styles that include more positive strategies than negative. If spanking is one element of an otherwise overwhelmingly positive parenting strategy, that strategy may well work just as successfully without it. Parents would also do well to note if their own children are exhibiting negative side effects from spanking. Have their children started to hit them back? Are their children's relationships with other children going well?

What if a parent wants to change from spanking to alternative, non-painful forms of discipline? This can be a difficult, but successful task if parents are committed to long-term positive change. Non-punitive discipline alternatives, such as age-appropriate time-outs, natural and logical consequences and cooperative agreements, can take some time to establish. Parents need to think in terms of the long-term outcome: trying a new form of discipline may take 3-6 weeks of consistent use before changes in behavior are accomplished. It is helpful (but not necessary) for a parent to have the mutual support of their spouse during this transitional stage. In addition, ongoing professional or peer support can be beneficial. Parenting groups, pediatricians and school psychologists are good resources for parents to use if they need help. The benefits of establishing a positive disciplinary approach that uses respect and dignity, instead of pain and fear, to motivate desired behaviors include laying the foundation for your child to create warm, long-lasting, and secure connections with yourself and others.

> Kids who are spanked exhibit increased aggressive and delinquent behaviors and are at higher risk for behavior problems in school and daycare.
>
> Research confirms that non-painful forms of discipline are just as effective as spanking, and do not carry these negative side effects.

Complete original article first published in Pediatric News, July 2001.

Your Emotions as Tools:
Using the Positive Discipline Mistaken Goal Chart
By Glenda Montgomery

KA BAM! The door to my son's room slammed behind him as he bolted in to burrow under the sheets and blankets of his bed. I'd heard it was called "caving"—what some boys do when they are overwhelmed by emotion. I was left outside the closed door, exasperated. He'd lost his lunch box three times that week and I'd just discovered that he had, yet again, left his homework at school. Lately I'd been tearing my hair out over his behavior. He had me choosing his clothes in the morning, picking up after him, running his forgotten books to school and nagging him about chores that he'd been doing on his own for a couple of years. He was interrupting me when I was in a conversation with someone else, but wouldn't talk to me when I wanted to talk with him. Whenever he was criticized, which, I admit, was getting to be very regularly, he would run to his room and slam the door. I'd asked him what he thought was going on and what he was feeling, but he didn't seem to have a clue. I knew how I was feeling though: exasperated, irritated, annoyed, worried...and guilty that I wasn't handling it.

Parenting is a tough job. We didn't have to get a license to become a parent and no children that I know came with operating instructions. We tend to muddle through, using parenting strategies that come naturally to us, which of course are the strategies that our parents used on us. When things are going well, we feel blessed to have such wonderful kids and we believe that we are doing a pretty fine job of parenting. But, when things get difficult and the strategies our parents used aren't working, parenting can become a very emotional job. Our feelings can get the best of us: frustration, anger, worry, embarrassment, helplessness, hopelessness, fear. We can feel challenged, threatened, disappointed, disgusted, despairing and hurt. My kids haven't even hit the teen years and I think at some point or another I've felt every one of these emotions. Mostly, I am confused about why my child is 'misbehaving' and am desperate to try to find a solution.

Though I was brought up in a home where misbehavior was punished, through my learning and work as a teacher, I was able to see that we don't have to make children feel worse in order for them to do better. Think about it: if you've messed up at work do you feel inclined to do better if you've been shamed and punished? Or, are you more inclined to do better if someone supports you through figuring out what went wrong and why, and then is available to consult with you through the process of fixing the mistake? I know that in this way, children are no different. Children do best when they are *encouraged* ... not punished, not pampered. As a parent, I was solution focused but didn't know where to turn to figure out WHY my child was doing what he was doing, nor what I should try in order to help my son solve the problem and get the behavior to stop!

The most important piece of information I've received about parenting came from a parenting class based on Jane Nelsen's book, *Positive Discipline*. Now, when I am feeling completely perplexed and am in some kind of emotional chaos over the behavior of one of my children, I have a place to begin. It is called the Positive Discipline Mistaken Goal Chart.

Positive discipline is based on the work of famous psychiatrists, Alfred Adler and Rudolph Druikers, who proposed the idea that human beings are goal driven. As human beings, our top two goals are to feel significant (that we matter) and to feel a sense of belonging. We act in order to achieve our goals. In other words, much of our behavior is driven, often subconsciously of course, by the need to feel both important, and an integral part of something cohesive and larger than ourselves. Sometimes our kids have mistaken ideas about *how* to feel significant and *how* to get that sense of belonging, which leads them to do things that look like misbehavior to us. Our children's perplexing misbehavior truly does make sense when looked at with this understanding.

Rudolph Druikers saw *4 mistaken understandings* that children sometimes have about significance and belonging. Children may feel that:
1. They belong/are significant only if they are getting special service and special attention from others.

2. They belong or are important only if they are the boss and are running the show.
3. They are NOT feeling belonging/significance and as a result they feel angry and hurt so they're going to make everyone else feel as badly as they do.
4. They don't belong and are not significant, see no way to belong or become significant, and so they have given up.

Rudolph Druikers called these mistaken understandings, the mistaken goals of: *Undue Attention, Power, Revenge and Assumed Inadequacy*

My daughter is my first-born. When she was going through a difficult phase we would sit down and talk about it. She would explain how she was feeling and would be able to work on the "why" question as well. Together we would problem-solve and plan. I was feeling pretty smug. This was a piece of cake! Then my son hit school age. Talking to my friends with sons, I was able to understand that my son was not alone in having no idea what he was feeling, why he was feeling it and what to do about it. He was lost in the midst of the whirlpool of his behavior and emotion. The relief is, in order to successfully use the Mistaken Goal Chart, you don't have to know what your son is feeling, you only need to know how YOU'RE feeling! Using the Mistaken Goal Chart enables you to find out what mistaken belief is behind your child's misbehavior. Understanding your son's discouraged, mistaken thinking will help you to have more empathy and patience as you support his moving through this phase.

Back to standing outside my son's slammed door. AARRRGGH! Awash in my own chaos of emotions, I suddenly remember that instead of feeling overwhelmed and humiliated by this maternal storm of feeling, I could use it productively. Out came the Mistaken Goal Chart. I saw that what I was feeling and how I was reacting pointed toward my son having the mistaken goal of "Undue Attention." It let me know that my son had the mistaken belief that unless he was getting me to do things for him or was the center of my attention, he didn't think he belonged or was important. His message was, "Notice me! Involve me usefully!"

I started by looking at the calendar, and carved out some time in both of our days to spend time together. This would give him the message that he was significant enough to spend uninterrupted time with and that we belonged together. I wrote the time on the calendar for each week so it would be visibly posted. When he had calmed down and had come out of his room, my son sat down with me and we created a chart to help him get ready in the morning. I explained that it upset me a lot to nag, and so we would have to find other reminders other than my voice to do chores and piano practice. He suggested the timer on the stove and we figured out

specific times each day when chores and piano practice would be done. We also created some non-verbal signals I could use.

As the rest of the week progressed, I was careful to notice any time that he was successfully using his new strategies and doing things with no reminders at all. I shared these with him quietly at night when I tucked him in and was sure to ask him how HE felt about his successes and how he was doing keeping himself better organized. He was very excited about our "date" time and had a list of ideas for activities he wanted to do together. When we were both feeling closer and were cuddled up together one day that week, I shared with him how I felt when he ran off and slammed the door. We wrote down other ways that he could let me know that he was frustrated or angry or needed to have some time alone, so that he could come out and talk to me after he'd cooled down. He agreed that if I didn't follow him to his room, he would retreat without slamming the door. He also asked me to write down some phrases he could use to announce his need to be alone and we tacked them up on his bulletin board.

Knowing that my son needed to find other ways to see himself as significant, I gave him a choice of three new ways he could help our family (significance AND belonging). He chose mowing the lawn. My husband and I took time to train him how to safely use the mower and worked with him the first several times. He felt very good about this contribution he was now making. Finally, things began to turn around. He became more assured of the many ways in which he had significance and belonging. I was more patient and understanding when he slipped. He still forgets his lunch box at school occasionally, but he knows that when he does, he has to take his lunch in a paper bag until he brings home his lunch box and then must clean out the lunch box himself to prepare it for the next day's lunch. I don't nag about it, and he doesn't complain about it.

In the past, I used to feel overwrought and ashamed by the strength of the negative emotions I felt when confronted with my child's misbehavior. Now I tune into them and use them proactively. I am able to sit down with the Mistaken Goal Chart, find myself there and know that I will be able to see where my child is, too. My emotions steer me toward solutions that I would not have otherwise seen, giving me specific strategies to use and allowing me to better understand the world that my son is experiencing. The ironic thing is, now that I understand how important and useful these negative feelings are, they don't seem nearly as intense or as overwhelming! They are a new set of tools!

Reprinted with permission of Glenda Mongomery, parent coach and Certified Positive Discipline Instructor in Portland, Oregon at www.positiveparentingpdx.com.

Mistaken Goal Chart

The parent FEELS:	The child's mistaken goal is:	The parent reacts by:	The child's response is:	The BELIEF behind the child's behavior is:	What the child's message is, and what you can do to encourage your child to find a sense of significance and belonging:
EXASPERATED ANNOYED IRRITATED WORRIED GUILTY	UNDUE ATTENTION To be the center of attention and keep others busy giving special service	Reminding Coaxing Nagging Scolding Doing things for the child that the child can do by him/herself.	Stops temporarily but later resumes same or other disturbing behavior.	I count only when I'm being noticed or getting special service. I'm only important when I'm keeping you busy with me or doing things for me.	**NOTICE ME! INVOLVE ME!** Together, set up regular, scheduled one-on-one special time. Refrain from doing for your child. Involve your child in setting up routines. Create charts together and help her learn to use them. Retrain for tasks she can do herself and tell her you trust her ability to do them. Train child for new chore or family responsibility she thinks will be appealing. Notice her accomplishments and any tasks of self-reliance. Encourage them. Remind once then act kindly and firmly. No nagging. Together make up non-verbal reminders. Ask child to help problem solve. Find some tasks to do together. Say, "I love you and _____" Example: I love you and will spend time with you in half an hour. Right now I am busy."
ANGRY PROVOKED CHALLENGED THREATENED DEFEATED	POWER To be boss	Arguing Fighting Thinking, "You can't get away with it" or "I'll make you!" Wanting to be right and have the last word. Giving in	Intensifies behavior. Defiant compliance. Feels s/he's won if the parent is upset. Passive power	I count only when I'm boss or in control or proving that no one can boss me. "You can't make me!"	**LET ME HELP! GIVE ME CHOICES!** Choose to withdraw from power struggles. Acknowledge that you can't make her, and ask for her help. Try to offer limited choices or alternatives whenever possible. Redirect to positive power by asking for help in problem solving and planning. Let routines be boss. Decide what YOU will do. Act, rather than talking or yelling. Practice kind, firm follow through Find leadership opportunities for your child.
HURT DISAPPOINTED DIS-BELIEVING DISGUSTED	REVENGE To get even	Retaliating Getting even Thinking, "How could you do this to me?" Taking behavior personally	Retaliates Hurts others Damages property Gets even Escalates behavior	I don't think I belong. I'm not feeling important. I'll hurt others, as I feel hurt. I can't be liked or loved.	**I'M HURTING! VALIDATE MY FEELINGS!** Don't take the behavior personally. Don't retaliate. Spend time dealing with her feelings. Listen well. Use reflective listening so that you're sure to understand. Share your feelings. Apologize for your part. Show you care. Agree to start anew. Avoid punishment. Instead, allow her to find ways to make reparations. Make an effort to find, encourage and support her strengths. Focus on positive.
DESPAIR HOPELESS HELPLESS INADEQUATE	ASSUMED INADEQUACY To give up and be left alone	Giving up Showing utter discouragement Over-helping Doing for	Retreats further Remains passive. No improvement No response	I don't believe I can belong. I am helpless and unable. It's no use trying because I won't do it right.	**HAVE FAITH IN ME! DON'T GIVE UP ON ME!** Break things into tiny steps. Celebrate tiny accomplishments. Take time for training and retraining. Show faith. Refrain from doing things for your child that she can do. Encourage any positive attempt, no matter how small. Share personal stories of struggle. Spend regular one-on-one time to enjoy your child. Build on her interests. Focus on strength areas. Encourage, encourage, encourage. Stop all criticism. Don't give up!

Adapted by Glenda Montgomery from *Positive Discipline for Working Parents* by Jane Nelsen and Lisa Larson.

Parents' Job: Step Aside, Let Kids Become Heroes

By Lionel Fisher

"I've been poor and I've been rich," Sophie Tucker once said. "Rich is better."

My sentiments exactly, only in regard to parenting: I've been a father and I've been a grandfather. Grandfather is better.

I base my opinion, mind you, not on the relative importance of the two roles, but on their degree of difficulty. And their vastly different potential for pleasure.

> My problem, I've come to realize, is that I took fatherhood too seriously.
>
> I thought it was my job to make my children the best they could be. I know now this was their responsibility.
>
> Mine was to love them, shield them from harm, keep them from want. And try not to get in their way while they became the heroes they were meant to be.

Something each of us has to do for ourselves.

If someone else could do it for us, particularly our parents, what an amazing, if boring, world this would be.

There's something else I've come to realize.

As a grandparent, I'm much better equipped to be a parent than I ever was as a parent.

Back then, I viewed the job as an adult.

Today, I see it from a much different perspective: the viewpoint of a child.

Shakespeare understood. "An old man," he said, "is twice a child."

And Edith Wharton put it this way: "The life of a man is a circle from childhood to childhood."

I know this for a fact. Certainly, I've been told it enough times.

And what better mentor for a child to have than another child, one past meridian on the journey of life, greatly experienced in the ways of the world, yet still childlike in all things vital to happiness?

There's something else I've come to realize, sadly of late, that raising children imposes a stern obligation on parents to examine their own habits, scrutinize their own attitudes, question their own behavior, each day of their lives, for one critical reason.

Their children will surely absorb them.

Try or not—like it or not—we make chips off the old block. We can't help it. We do it by being ourselves, sometimes with enormous consequences.

Our "shadow side," psychologist Carl Jung called all the negative elements we see in ourselves but steadfastly deny. They are the demons we stuff in the closets of our psyche and rationalize away, thinking we've safely hidden them—while we pass them along to our children.

And what happens later? Heartache.

It's a universal truth, says U.S. Catholic magazine writer Dolores Curran, that parents have difficulty relating with the children most like themselves because they see in their offspring the things they dislike and repress in themselves.

From my perch as a grandparent, I now know: If I could be a parent once more, I would not try to make my children the best they can be.

It's what kept me from enjoying them.

I would relish and love them, marvel daily at their wonder and uniqueness, knowing the rest would take care of itself. That they would see to it themselves.

So easily said as a grandparent. So hard to do as a parent.

The young adult I was didn't understand this simple, marvelous truth.

The child I'm becoming again does.

Lionel Fisher is the author of several personal growth self-help books, including Celebrating Time Alone: Stories of Splendid Solitude *(Beyond Word Publishing, 2001).*

Reprinted with permission from Lionel Fisher, the author of several personal growth self-help books, including celebrating *Time Alone: Stories of Splendid Solitude* (Beyond Words Publishing, 2201). Originally published in the Oregonian, 9/25/03

Overview of One of Our Favorites: *Positive Discipline for Teenagers*

Authored by Jane Nelsen, EdD, MFT and Lynn Lott, MA, MFT

Brief Summary: *Positive Discipline for Teenagers* describes the normal developmental process of individuation during adolescence and how this affects parenting. Supporting a teen to explore their world, as well as to grow up into a self-reliant, resourceful and successful adult can be difficult, but will be infinitely more pleasant using positive parenting techniques. Nelsen and Lott support a positive parenting approach which educates, challenges and supports teenagers in an atmosphere of mutual respect, affirming the self-worth of both youth and parents. This is accomplished by using long-term parenting approaches as alternatives to punishments and control, the latter of which encourage long-term resistance, resentment and revenge. These rob teenagers of the opportunity to learn from their own experiences as they focus on their anger at adults. Parents are encouraged to support, empower and guide their teens to make as many decisions about their own lives as is reasonable. In this way, teens learn self-discipline and maturity by experiencing the consequences, both good and bad, of their own behaviors. A special section is included for differentiating normal from dysfunctional teen behavior and a study guide is included for further exploration and practice of positive discipline skills.

Issues Explored in Book:

The Individuation Process: Teenagers undergo individuation as a normal developmental process whereby they become their own unique selves. Knowing that adolescent experimentation is a normal and essential developmental task of adolescence can set many parents at ease. Teens learn best by making mistakes, by being held accountable for their own choices, and suffering (without parental rescuing or buffering) the consequences of all those choices. This section helps parents to understand their teen's world, to develop empathy and compassion for their teen's struggles, and to differentiate between long- and short-term parenting goals.

Nonpunitive Parenting: Alternatives to control and punishment are essential for developing mutual respect with teens. Alternatives include cooperative problem solving, setting and keeping agreements, family meetings, open communication and relationship building. Positive discipline does not advocate for the short-term parenting goal of controlling a teen's behavior (which is impossible), but rather for a long-term goal of supporting

teens to learn from their own choices, while holding them accountable for their agreements. This can be a scary new approach for many parents. This book also helps parents to explore their own rational and irrational fears and unresolved issues around adolescence that could be hindering their ability to foster the optimum development of their teen.

Normal and Dysfunctional Teen Behavior: This section deals with a myriad of risk-taking behaviors in teens and helps parents differentiate between exploratory and dysfunctional patterns of behavior. Tips on discussing and resolving these issues with your teen are included.

Key Points: Parenting teens requires a different approach from younger children, due to a teen's need for individuating and for gaining essential life skills such that she can be fully responsible for all of her life decisions by the time she reaches age 18. This requires parents to stretch and grow during their child's adolescence, as they must learn to trust their teenagers to make choices, to learn from their own experiences, and to be able to handle more and more freedom and autonomy as they grow older. "Positive discipline" involves offering adolescents guidance and support without trying to control or punish, setting clear parental boundaries that establish what *parents* (not kids) will do and institutes mutual dignity and respect as key ingredients of the parent-teen relationship. This model of parenting requires parents to place a high priority on the long-term goal of supporting adolescents in their developmental tasks of learning self-discipline and self-control. By putting teenagers in charge of their own growth, responsibilities and lives, parents are removed from power struggles and from the impossible task of controlling their teenagers' behaviors. When faced with primary responsibility for their own lives, teens tend to move from reacting and rebelling to authority towards making positive and more self-affirming decisions. Supporting and guiding adolescents, without rescuing or abandoning them, is a process that can be learned by any parent. This process respects that teens are operating with free will and are able to make their own decisions, but it also holds them fully accountable for all the consequences of their behaviors. This book helps parents to learn and implement such long-term parenting strategies, which result in enhancing a family's self-esteem, self-reliance, competency, and ability to communicate respectfully.

Curiosity Kills the Cat but Connects the Kid

By Kathy Masarie

OK, I AM THE FIRST TO ADMIT IT. I read over and over again the importance of listening to my children, especially my teens, and I said, "Of course, I listen to my kid. I am a good parent. All good parents listen."

But was I really listening? When my son was 16, he taught me to listen better than anyone else. That year, many of our interactions were struggling, yelling and arguing. It led to nowhere for either of us. I realized it had to be me that changed. When I stopped trying to control his behavior and focused my energy on understanding where he was coming from—that is when I actually started listening. We both calmed down. And, he started talking.

I was busily cooking dinner one night, trying to get it done "on time" when Jon started talking. As he talked, I realized how important and serious this was. I turned off the stove to give him my full attention. We talked for a solid half hour. Dinner was a little late, but I gained a new perspective on an issue he was struggling with that I didn't have before.

So what were the ingredients for this success?

First Step: Be Present

Would I have gotten the same information if I thought dinner had to be served at 6:00 instead of letting it go until 6:30? In *Putting Family First*, William Doherty talks about three kinds of parent/kid time: "being around" time, logistics time, and connecting time.

- "Being around" time is the building block of family time. As a preschooler my son would hang out wherever I went. As a teen, he still wants me to "be around" at four times during the day—morning, after school, at dinner and going to bed. We may or may not talk to each other, but I am there if needed.
- "Logistics-getting-things-done" time is what makes the "family business" run, where we talk about everyday routine and where most of us spend most of our talking time.
- "Connecting" talk is the most important! It's when you find out what really is going on with your child—what happened, how they're feeling, what they are worried about. It is the first to go when we are busy. It often happens when we are just "hanging out" with no agenda.

Stop Talking

With Jon, when I listened, he talked. Think about when you are with someone who talks too much and your energy drains just blocking their words from coming at you. **If you want your teen to talk, stop talking.** Imagine there are only a limited number of words that can be said between you and your child. If you say more, they say less, and now you know less. **"Effectiveness as a parent comes much more from what you hear than from what you say,"** says Mira Kirshenbaum in *Parent/Teen Breakthrough: The Relationship Approach*.

Be Curious and Actively Listen

I asked questions so I could really understand what he meant. This is not plying him for information with 20 questions. These are questions that keep teens talking and help them get clarity about their priorities and values. It also keeps me from jumping to conclusions, helps me see his point of view and have empathy for him. Questions like: How do you feel about that? Tell me more. What do you think about what happened? Just how important is this to you? Why is this so important to you? How do you think things will turn out if they go on as they are? What do you want to have happen? What are you going to do now? How can I be helpful? Is there anything else bothering you? Is there anything else I should know about this? What else could you tell me to help me better understand? What else?

> Effectiveness as a parent comes much more from what you hear than from what you say.

Be Honest

When I shared some of the things I did as a teen and why I did them, Jon was able to be more honest. This "honest talk" helped him be more open about his mistakes so we could deal with them together. It also helped to be honest and accountable for my mistakes, like when I lost my temper and yelled, I said, "Here is what I wish I would have done."

Keep It Simple: Brainstorm and Compromise

Jon had lots of ideas for solutions on his own. I didn't offer my ideas without asking permission. When I did, it was short, not a lecture. I didn't repeat myself later. After we brainstormed some solutions, we compromised and picked ones that worked for both of us. You know what? A lot of his ideas sounded like solutions I might have offered. What goes around comes around—and, in this case, I liked it.

Peaceful Parenting: How to Turn Parent-Child Conflict into Cooperation

By Sura Hart and Victoria Kindle Hodson

T'S NINE O'CLOCK ON a school night and 12-year-old Jesse is absorbed in his favorite video game until his mother comes into his bedroom and announces that it's bedtime.

Jesse: No, I don't want to go to bed!

Mom: But it's already past your bedtime, and you know you have to get your rest.

Jesse: But I'm not tired!

Mom: Well, you will be in the morning if you don't go to sleep soon.

Jesse: Shut up. Anyway, you can't make me go to sleep.

The conversation might go on this way until Mom, exhausted and angry, shouts something like, "I quit! Suit yourself!" Sound fam-iliar? It does to us. In our experiences leading parenting workshops in Non-violent Communi-cation—a way of communicating that facilitates honest, res-pectful, and compas-sionate connection between people— we've seen countless parents frustrated by the combative ex-changes they have with their children. Their conflicts are especially intense around daily activities such as going to sleep, waking up, and completing homework. Indeed many parents today find themselves engaged in what seems like a constant power struggle with their kids. As they engage in arguments like the one between Jesse and his mother, both sides stake out their territory and resist giving in to the other. Parents come away feeling worn out and irritated; children feel threatened and even more determined to resist their parents' demand.

Based on our years of observation, we believe the way through these conflicts lies in shifting the way parents use their power, from using power *over* kids to using power *with* them. In the example above, the mother's attempt to control her son, though well-intended, triggers resistance as will any attempt by one person to control another, no matter the age or relationship. As Christopher Boehm demonstrates in his essay in *Greater Good*, humans have been genetically predisposed to resent and resist being dominated for at least seven million years. While we may temporarily submit, we often do so with anger or resentment that will surface later. And when parents try to manage and control their children, everyone pays a high price especially in the loss of trust, goodwill, and willing cooperation among family members. This does not mean that parents should give up their power and permit their children to do whatever they want, whenever they please. Instead, what matters is *how* parents use their power. Parents who use their considerable power *over* children—by making demands and enforcing them with threats of punishment and promises of reward—often find themselves locked into bitter struggles. Fiercely protecting their autonomy, wary children test us to find out where they can get some power of their own. And, very early on, they take charge of two crucial realms of their lives: where and when they sleep; and what, where, and when they eat. Try as they might, parents can't make children eat, nor can they make them sleep. Their needs for power and autonomy are so strong that kids will sometimes deny themselves their basic needs for food and rest in order to assert control over their lives.

Even when children don't immediately or obviously resist parental demands, parents may still be creating an unhealthy environment for their family when they attempt to exert power over their kids. Marshall Rosenberg, the founder of Nonviolent Communication, makes this point when he asks parents two questions: *What do you want your children to do?* and *What do you want their reason to be for doing it?*

Many parents ask themselves only the first question and find they can, at times, get what they want by using threats, punishments, and rewards. However, when parents ask themselves the second question, *What do you want your child's reason to be?*, they realize why they feel so dissatisfied with their family's interactions. Their children are doing what they are told because they are afraid not to, not because they understand either what is important to their parents (and why), or what is important for themselves.

The parents we've met in our workshops say they want their children to develop strong inner characters and the skills to make the best choices for themselves, yet none of this can be developed when children act out of fear of blame or punishment. What's more, when parents use power-over tactics, anger and resentment often build up, even in children who seem to submit easily to parental control. Such anger and resentment may be expressed through self-destructive choices later in life, including extreme rebellion against authority or by relying excessively on the judgments of others.

Sometimes parents see only one alternative to the power-over strategy: to deny their own needs for rest, order, safety, and connection and give in to what their kids want.

What we advocate instead are ways parents can use power *with* their children. This third way is facilitated by the practice of Nonviolent Communication, which is based on equal concern and care for the needs of all. Parents, in daily interactions with their children, can model and teach their children how to take one's own needs and the needs of others into consideration. Let's revisit the scene between Jesse and his mother—but this time, with Mom taking a power-with approach.

Mom: It's time to get ready for bed.

Jesse: No, I don't want to go to bed

Mom: You're having a lot of fun playing now, huh?

Jesse: Yeah, and I'm not even tired.

Mom: So you just want to keep playing until you're tired?

Jesse: Yeah.

Mom: It must be frustrating to be asked to stop doing something that's so much fun when you don't feel tired.

Jesse: I never have time for what I want to do. I just have to come home and do homework.

Mom: Hmm. It sounds like this time between homework and bedtime is really important to you, and you wish it were longer?

Jesse: Yeah, Mom, I do.

Mom: Thanks for helping me understand that. You know, I'd like you to have as much time as you want

for the things that interest you. At the same time, I've also noticed that when you stay up after nine on school nights, you're tired the next morning. Do you hear?

Jesse: Yeah, you want me to get a good night's sleep.

Mom: Yes. Thanks for hearing that.

Jesse: I just need five more minutes to finish this game. Okay?

Mom: Okay. I'll get out your pajamas.

In this dialogue, Mom first chose to connect with her son's feelings and his needs for play and choice. When Jesse felt heard and realized that his needs mattered to his mom, he opened up to hearing her needs while also standing up for his own. Then he was willing to cooperate.

It's true that learning and implementing these communication skills, and reaching this kind of mutual understanding, can take time and effort. It is also true that children who are already accustomed to a power-over model often need time to develop trust that parents mean it when they say their child's needs matter. But these are skills we've seen many parents use and parents tell us they see more trust and cooperation within their family afterwards, which they say justifies all the early energy they invest.

Each time parents come to a workshop in Nonviolent Communication, we all ask ourselves, *What do we want for ourselves and for our children?* The answers we hear are always the same: kindness, respect, communication, cooperation, and responsibility. From the time they're young, we can prepare our children for a lifetime of power struggles, arguments, fights, and wars. Or we can help them learn skills to create a world that embraces cooperation and understanding as the only true ways to lasting peace and satisfying, sustainable relationships. When parents use their power *with* their children, they are subtly teaching them skills and strategies for practicing compassion and cooperation in all areas of their lives.

Reprinted with permission of Sura Hart and Victoria Kindle Hodson MA. Sura and Victoria are co-authors of three books: *The Compassionate Classroom: Relationship Based Teaching & Learning; Respectful Parents, Respectful Kids: 7 Keys to Turn Family Conflict into Cooperation;* and *The No-Fault Classroom: Tools to Resolve Conflict & Foster Relationship Intelligence (2008)*. They also offer consultation workshops, see website at www.k-communication.com. Originally published in *Greater Good Magazine*, Vol. 4, Issue 3, Winter 07-08.

Feelings and Needs Inventories

Needs Inventory:

"A need is life seeking expression within us." Marshall Rosenberg, PhD

Autonomy
- To choose one's dreams, goals, & values
- To choose one's plan for fulfilling one's dreams, goals, & values
- Freedom
- Choice
- Independence
- Space
- Spontaneity

Connection
- Acceptance
- Affection
- Appreciation
- Belonging
- Closeness
- Community
- Consideration
- Emotional Safety
- Inclusion
- Inspiration
- Interdependence
- Intimacy
- Love
- Reassurance
- Respect
- Self-love
- Support
- Sympathy
- Trust
- Understanding
- Warmth

Meaning
- Awareness
- Celebration of life
- Challenge
- Clarity
- Competence
- Consciousness
- Contribution
- Creativity
- Discovery
- Efficacy
- Effectiveness
- Growth
- Learning
- Making a contribution
- Making a difference
- Mourning
- Participation
- Purpose
- Self-expression
- Stimulation
- Understanding

Physical Nurturance
- Air
- Food
- Exercise
- Movement
- Physical Safety
- Rest/sleep
- Sexual expression
- Shelter
- Touch
- Water

Celebration
- Gratitude
- To celebrate the creation of life and dreams fulfilled.
- To celebrate losses: loved one, dreams, etc. (mourning)

Integrity/Honesty
- Authenticity
- Creativity
- Honesty
- Presence
- Self-worth

Play and Recreation
- Exercise
- Fun
- Humor
- Joy
- Laughter

Spiritual Communion
- Beauty
- Communion
- Ease
- Empathy
- Equality
- Harmony
- Inspiration
- Order
- Peace
- Unconditional Love

Adapted by Kathy Masarie and Jody Bellant Scheer from Nonviolent Communication by Marshall Rosenberg, PhD, the Center for Nonviolent Communication www.cnvc.org.

Feelings Inventory:
How We Are Likely to Feel When Our Needs ARE Being Met:

Adventurous, Affectionate, Alive, Amazed, Animated, Appreciated, Aroused, Astonished, Blissful, Calm, Carefree, Cheerful, Comfortable, Compassionate, Composed, Confident, Contented, Curious, Dazzled, Delighted, Eager, Ecstatic, Elated, Empowered, Encouraged, Energetic, Enthusiastic, Fascinated, Free, Friendly, Fulfilled, Glad, Glowing, Grateful, Gratified, Happy, Helpful, Hopeful, Inspired, Invigorated, Involved, Intrigued, Joyous, Lively, Loving, Moved, Optimistic, Overjoyed, Peaceful, Pleased, Proud, Radiant, Reassured, Rejuvenated, Relaxed, Satisfied, Secure, Serene, Stimulated, Tender, Tickled, Thankful, Upbeat, Wonderful, etc...

Feelings Inventory:
How We Are Likely to Feel When Our Needs AREN'T Being Met:

Afraid, Aggravated, Agitated, Alarmed, Alienated, Aloof, Ambivalent, Anguished, Angry, Annoyed, Anxious, Apathetic, Ashamed, Baffled, Bewildered, Bitter, Bored, Brokenhearted, Burned out, Concerned, Confused, Dazed, Dejected, Depleted, Depressed, Despairing, Detached, Devastated, Disappointed, Disconnected, Discouraged, Disengaged, Disgusted, Dismayed, Distaste, Distracted, Distressed, Disturbed, Downhearted, Dull, Edgy, Embarrassed, Embittered, Envious, Exasperated, Fatigued, Fearful, Fidgety, Flustered, Forlorn, Fragile, Frazzled, Frightened, Frustrated, Furious, Gloomy, Guilty, Harried, Heartbroken, Heavy, Helpless, Hopeless, Horrible, Hostile, Hurt, Impatient, Indifferent, Insecure, Irate, Irritated, Jealous, Lazy, Lethargic, Listless, Livid, Lonely, Mad, Mean, Miserable, Morose, Mortified, Mystified, Nervous, Nostalgic, Numb, Outraged, Overwhelmed, Pained, Panicky, Passive, Perplexed, Pessimistic, Puzzled, Rattled, Reluctant, Remorseful, Repulsed, Resentful, Sad, Scared, Self-conscious, Shocked, Sorrowful, Startled, Surprised, Suspicious, Tepid, Terrified, Torn, Troubled, Uncomfortable, Uneasy, Unhappy, Unsteady, Upset, Vulnerable, Wary, Weary, Worried, etc...

Your Son's Character Development

By Kathy Keller Jones, MA

NO CHAPTER ON parenting would be complete without a discussion of character and how we as parents can foster character traits in our children. "A baby boy," says Eli Newberger in *The Men They Will Become – The Nature and Nurture of Male Character,* "has traits but no character. As he grows, particular characteristics—attachment, honesty, self control, sportsmanship, generosity, courage—are either nurtured or thwarted."[1]

A parent may wonder how much of a son's personality is what he was born to be and what part can be influenced? Although the child arrives with a specific set of temperament traits, it is matching our parenting to those traits that begins to develop the character of our children. The capacity to love, be empathetic, confident and assertive are the complex products of our traits as well as the result of our relationships and experiences over the years. A child's personality is a unique and ongoing relationship between nature and nurture – each constantly affecting the other.

So how can we as parents nurture character? Relationships with parents and other adults are essential to building character. Family Empowerment Network and

the Search Institute both emphaze the central importance of quality relationships in building character and success through the 40 Developmental Assets.

A key for parents is to be aware of the nature of our relationships with our own children and to treat them with deep respect. Our ability to parent evolves as we evolve as individuals. Do we simply view our child through the lens of our own adult needs? Do we follow a list of predetermined rules that tell us what makes a good parent and a good child? Or do we view our sons and ourselves as unique individuals with unique needs and potential? How aware are we that our relationship with our sons is always growing and changing? It isn't necessarily easy or natural to be aware of the relationship you have with your child. The value of individuality and mutuality must be learned by both parent and child. Whatever our sons learn about relationships while they are growing up will be what they offer to their own child. As Harvard psychologist Howard Gardner says, "Parental attitudes and efforts will determine to a significant extent how a child resolves the conflicting messages of the home and wider community as well as the kind of parent the child will one day become."[2]

Parenting groups are a great way for parents to broaden their perspective and awareness. Hearing about how other parents deal with common problems can help parents see their own strengths and weaknesses. It can also help them consider new ways of parenting and relating. A *Raising Our Sons* group is a great basis for forming a parent support group.

Newberger points out that boys of good character

are not only raised in families with two biological parents. "Boys of good character are being raised by single mothers (unwed or divorced), single fathers, lesbian mothers and their partners, gay men and their partners, grandparents, other relatives, guardians and foster parents."[1] Nevertheless, Newberger feels that women in our culture have some advantages over men when it comes to parenting, since our culture expects females to be enthusiastic about parenting. Women find it easier to share their problems, including parenting problems, with each other than men do. Many women are also more likely to read books and seek parenting advice when they are stressed. And women are often more comfortable with the language of feelings and relationships.

Men have the ability and motivation to be good fathers, however, and mothers may need to back off at times so that men in their children's lives have a chance to develop skills and comfort level with parenting. Newberger strongly encourages a father's involvement in parenting. "The kinds of adjustments that need to be made in the lives of boys to nurture them toward good character in their adult life are coherent with — sometimes identical with—the adjustments that will make men more highly aware and nurturing fathers and role models. Boys need to become familiar with feelings and with the vocabulary of feelings, if only to be men of excellent character. This 'emotional literacy' will make them better fathers, and better husbands and professionals, too."[1]

---

[1] Newberger, E., *The Men They Will Become*, Perseus Books.
[2] Gardner, H., New York Review of Books, November 5, 1998.

Healthy Men, Strong Families: Being a Strategic Father Figure

By Howard Hiton

ON A RECENT SATURDAY afternoon, along with a good friend and his two children, I took my two boys for a walk in the forest. It was one of those beautiful late fall days we had this year and the trail was filled with people and dogs. Over and over again, either through direct comment or smiles that said, "Isn't that cute, the daddies are with their kids," the fact that we were men with our children was noted. It struck me that, even today, when it is more common to see fathers with children it is still perceived as a cute anomaly.

The fact is that not only is it endearing to see a dad with his kids, it is essential to the child's development. So much has been made of fathers' absence. What about father presence? It is true that there are many types of families. There are truly absent dads—men that may never step up to their responsibility of fathering. But that is only part of the father picture. There are also stay at home dads, custodial and non-custodial dads, and fathers whose work keeps them from home much of the time. How helpful is it to focus solely on the negativity of father absence? Wouldn't we rather share information that supports increased levels of father involvement? There is a wealth of research that we should be using to educate men about the power of their presence in their children's lives. Here we focus on dads that are in the picture but spend most of their time on the sidelines.

- In one study, preschool age children whose fathers were responsible for 40% or more of the family's child care tasks had higher scores on assessments of cognitive development, had more of a sense of mastery over their environments, and exhibited more empathy than those children whose fathers were less involved.
- Higher levels of father involvement in activities with their children, such as eating meals together, going on outings, and helping with homework are associated with fewer behavior problems, higher levels of sociability, and a high level of school performance among children and adolescents.
- Several studies have documented a positive relationship between the provision of child support and the well being of school age children.

So if father presence holds so much benefit for the child, what holds fathers back? There are many cultural, familial, financial, and personal reasons that fathers may be less involved. Initially we must understand that the importance of father presence is new information. When I have looked for advice from my father, lamenting about the difficulties of parenting young children, he laughs saying that he never really was that involved in day-to-day parenting. For some men this lack of role modeling has led to a lack of confidence in their role as father as well as embarrassment about their difficulty mastering this role. Additionally, women are culturally expected to be enthusiastic about parenting and tend to be more comfortable in the world of relationships. This can lead to a dynamic within families that further pushes mother to the foreground and father to the background. There are also financial issues at play here. Family expectations or workplace cultures may set demands on fathers that limit or even prohibit their involvement with their children. For example fathers may find it impossible to leave work to run their child to the doctor or volunteer at school.

So what can we do?

Informing and motivating fathers is a public health issue. Father involvement has been seen to be particularly important in the first year of life. There are programs in hospital maternity units across the country that works to teach men about the importance of their presence. Early childhood education programs such as Head Start have done a wonderful job of making father involvement a priority. Through staff training, employees are helped to see things from men's perspective to enable them to create an inviting atmosphere for fathers.

Some specific ideas for powerful fathering:

- Act with the knowledge of how important you are in children's lives.
- Make being a father figure your highest priority.
- Tell stories of your childhood.
- Stay connected to your kids even if separated from their mother.
- Model respectful behavior to women. Start with how you treat your kids' mother.
- Tell kids you love them and are proud of them.
- Model good friendships with other men.
- Volunteer in the classroom.
- Work on finding the right balance between being a teacher, mentor and friend.
- Talk to other men about being a father figure.

Reprinted with permission of Howard Hiton, co-author of *BAM! Boys Advocacy and Mentoring* at www.hitonassociates.net and www.BAMgroups.com. Originally in Rational Enquirer of Oregon Teen Pregnancy Prevention Task Force.

Family Rituals: The Ties that Bind

By William J. Doherty, author of *Putting Family First*

IF YOU RECALL YOUR FAVORITE memories of childhood, they are likely to center around family rituals such as bedtime, an annual vacation, or patriotic and religious holidays. Your worst memories might also be connected with these family rituals. Interestingly, many family researchers and family therapists have learned only recently how important family rituals are to the glue that holds families together.

What are family rituals? They are repeated and coordinated activities that have significance for the family. To be a ritual, the activity has to have meaning or significance; otherwise it is a routine, not a ritual. To be a ritual, the activity must be repeated; an occasional, unplanned trip to a cabin would not make for a family ritual, whereas an annual trip that family members look forward to would. Also, a ritual activity must be coordinated; a meal that each person fixes and eats separately would not qualify as a family ritual, whereas one that everyone deliberately eats together would be a family ritual if done regularly and with meaning for the family.

Family rituals give us predictability—the sense of regularity and order that families require, especially those with children. Knowing that a father will talk to his child and read a story every night makes bedtime something to savor.

Family rituals give us connection. The bedtime ritual may be the main one-to-one time between a father and his child. Trips to see grandparents provide the glue in the grandparent-grandchild relationship. A family meal is a place for the telling of family stories.

Family rituals give us identity—a sense of who belongs to the family and what is special about the family. You may know whom your core family members are by who is invited to the Thanksgiving meal. Including non-relatives in core family rituals also makes them "family." Families who do interesting vacations together acquire the self-image of a fun-loving family. They will say, "We are campers" or "We are hikers."

Family rituals give us a way to enact values. They help us demonstrate what we believe and hold dear. Religious rituals are a good example, as is a family's collective volunteering for community work, or expecting the children to join in regular family visits to a grandparent in a nursing home.

Family rituals by definition involve more than one family member. But not all family rituals necessarily involve the whole family. Some rituals involve just two members, say, a married couple's dinner out or a parent reading to a child. Some involve sub-groups, as when my father took my sister and me to Philadelphia Phillies baseball games. Some involve the larger extended family, such as family reunions and holiday rituals. Some involve close family friends, and some involve a larger community like a church/synagogue or a volunteer group.

I like to classify family rituals by the function they play for families, or what needs they serve. Thus, there are rituals for connection or bonding, rituals for showing love to individual family members, and rituals that bind the family to the larger community.

There is no universal yardstick for measuring family rituals for all of our diverse, contemporary families. Remarried families will have different needs than first-married families, as will single-parent families than two parent families. Different ethnic traditions will expect different degrees of flexibility or structure in family rituals. Some families have young children, some have adolescents, and some have no children. Some families are experiencing peaceful periods in their life, and thus feel free to be creative with their rituals, while others are undergoing tremendous stress and need to just hang on to what they have. There is no formula for all this diversity, but at the core of each kind of family are its rituals of connection, love and community.

How can we become more intentional about our family rituals in the face of the time shortage most of us experience? What if you are already an overwhelmed single parent, or a married person who barely has time to talk to your spouse? Will thinking about enhancing your family rituals just make you feel even more guilty than you already are? I offer two general strategies:

1. Make better use of the time you already spend on family activities. You have to feed your children, so start with improving the quality of those feeding rituals. You have to put your kids to bed; work on making it more pleasurable. You probably have birthday parties, holiday celebrations, and countless other family activities. You can work on enhancing their quality while not extending their number or their time burden.

2. Experiment with carving time out of another activity that occupies more than its fair share of your attention. Here is the place for taming

technology. We live in an era of the "Wired American Family." The average American spends over four hours per day watching television, half of our non-sleep, non-work time. Perhaps carve ritual time from there!

Once you capture time for family rituals, how can you put new rituals into place, or turn routines into rituals? Here are some practical ways:

1. Make something happen one time without major comment, and then ask other family members how they liked it and whether they would like to do it again. You might say, "Why don't we try something different this time?" If family members go along with it, they may have a new experience they want to continue. I did this once with my wife and children when I proposed that during the Christmas meal we each express some appreciation to the other family members, as a kind of verbal Christmas gift. I brought it up a few days before Christmas so that everyone could think about what they might want to say. No one objected. During the meal, we had a lovely exchange of appreciations, a real moment of family intimacy. Now it's a Christmas ritual.

2. Elevate a routine into a ritual by giving it meaning. After moving to Minnesota in 1986, my family started going to Davanni's restaurant for pizza with no thought of starting a family ritual. After several months of going every Friday night, we began to realize that we had the makings of a ritual, and decided together to commit to it as a going-out ritual of connection. Even when my kids were in their 20's, they still signaled that they wanted family time by calling home to suggest we do pizza at Davanni's.

3. Negotiate a new ritual or change an existing one. Bring up your idea at a calm moment and without criticism. Just say that you are feeling the need for a change. Say what is missing for you, or what you would add. Make a suggestion to try something different. See if other family members are willing to give this a try for a period of time to see how it works. And do your best to make it special. It may take a while for family members to get used to a new ritual, but give it time. And be willing to make adjustments and compromises that seem to be reasonable and do not defeat the purpose of ritual.

Once you have good family rituals in place, keeping them alive takes work and vigilance. Here is a summary of the major principles I have developed for managing family rituals over time:

- **Adult Agreement:** If you and your spouse or co-parent do not agree on the ritual, it will not work well. Take the time to negotiate the needs, values, and goals of your family rituals with your adult partner.
- **Eventual Buy-In from the Children:** Older children especially may resist changes at first, particularly if the changes diminish their freedom and spontaneity. But a ritual that works well will eventually win the allegiance of the children. If they continue to complain and resist over time, consider overhauling, substituting, or dropping the ritual.
- **Maximum Participation:** The more that family members are involved in planning and carrying out the ritual, the more meaningful it is likely to be.
- **Clear Expectations:** Rituals of all kinds require enough coordination that people know what to do and when to do it.
- **Minimal Conflict:** Although conflict can always pop up in families, the most successful rituals occur without regular tension and conflict.
- **Protection from Erosion:** Entropy threatens all family rituals. Good rituals must be fought for and management means protecting the ritual from the inevitable threats to its consistency and integrity.
- **Openness to Change:** Rituals have their seasons for planting, cultivating, pruning, and harvesting. Intentional families are forever changing while holding on to their important traditions.

Most families have some rituals they enjoy, some they don't enjoy but feel stuck with, and some they could benefit from creating or refurbishing. I encourage you to develop an agenda of current rituals you might want to remodel and new ones you might want to try. The pay-offs for your family can be enormous.

Written for Family Empowerment Network by William J. Doherty, PhD, professor of family social science at the University of Minnesota and a practicing marriage and family therapist. He is author of The Intentional Family: Simple Rituals to Strengthen Family Ties *(1999); and* Take Back Your Kids: Confident Parenting in Turbulent Times *(2000) and co-author with Barbara Carlson of* Putting Family First *(2002). He helped found a grassroots parents' initiative: www.puttingfamilyfirst.org. He is father to a son and a daughter. For reprint requests, contact www.family-empower.com*

At the Heart of Parenting: Eating Together

By Kathy Keller Jones, MA

In today's busy world, what was once considered an inevitable part of family life—eating together—is becoming an "endangered species." In the busyness of our modern consumer-driven world, we either defend our family time or we lose it. When we eat together regularly, as in all family rituals, the family's culture is created and maintained, and family life is enhanced by the sense of order, the emotional bonding, the sense of being part of a larger whole, and the modeling of family values and communication. When we spend time together, the family provides a critical counterpoint to the negative aspects of the consumer culture which teaches a maladaptive attitude of personal entitlement: "I will fuss as much as necessary to have my own way and have it now." Contrast this with the sense of teamwork and belonging that can come when family members work together to plan, prepare and enjoy good food. Eating together is one of the critical ways we can support our children of all ages as they grow and find their way in the world.

Becoming organized enough to share regular meals can be a challenge, but it is also a step which can help us become more proactive in many areas of our lives. As our ability to plan ahead and organize the week improves, the entire family benefits since their needs for order and security are met. As our children enter elementary school, they too need to learn to look ahead and plan the week, and family meetings can become a vehicle for this, as long as they are kept short and end with fun. I was inspired by one large blended family who organized eating together in the following way: the father cooked breakfast every morning and oversaw the bagged lunch preparation. Each week an older and younger team (parent and child or older child and younger child) signed up to be in charge of each dinner, which included planning the menu, listing and shopping for the items needed, cooking and cleaning up. Most families have

fewer family members than my friends had, but it is a reminder that meals provide wonderful opportunities for learning about teamwork. Meals are family affairs and even the youngest children can help out in some way. Some families, for example, call the kids 10 minutes

before the meal is ready and have the kids prepare the table. Others ask everyone to stay in the kitchen until cleanup is 100% done and then they all sit down and do quiet work/homework together. Dinner and work time are times when TV screens and phones are off. (For adolescents, the computer can be at hand, and in sight, for writing and research.)

Why is eating together so important? Family dinners are incredibly powerful protective factors for our children and adolescents. Research by the National Center on Addiction and Substance Abuse (CASA) at Columbia University (2007)[1] has clearly shown that children who eat 5 or more weekly dinners with their family are significantly more successful than kids who eat 1 or 2 meals weekly:

- They are less likely to smoke, drink or use illegal drugs. The fewer family dinners a teen has in a typical week the more likely they are to use.

- They have higher grades.
- They are at lower risk for depression and thoughts of suicide.
- They are more emotionally content and have fewer behavior problems.
- They have healthier eating habits and fewer eating disorders
- They are less likely to have sex at younger ages.

These findings held regardless of gender, socio-economic status, and whether there were one or two parents in the household[3]. A University of Michigan longitudinal study of how children use their time (1999) [2], found that mealtime at home was the strongest predictor of achievement and behavior. Mealtime was more powerful than time in school, studying, church activities, playing sports or art activities! Family meals directly compete with the problematic tendency for teens to bond exclusively with peers and leave adults out, thus putting themselves at risk.

The key ingredients of family meals involve gathering together without distractions and having face-to-face interactions. Of course, families with very young children may only be approximating this ideal while they teach the basic skills of sitting and staying at the table for 15 to 20 minutes. Over time, however, family meals are an opportunity to share the "best and worst" thing that happened that day and to learn to listen to others. Some families have the delightful habit of sharing one thing about the day for which they are grateful. Telling and creating family stories can take place during meals and greatly enrich our children's language and concept development while creating community. Without saying a word, parents are modeling a healthy relationship to food. As a counselor, I have found that children are less likely to exhibit behaviors related to food disorders when they eat daily family meals. Although the companionship at family dinners is more important then the quality of the food, families with frequent meals together expose children to more natural and homemade foods and therefore the entire family is less likely to become overweight. When we snack or eat meals individually, we are more likely to eat lower quality, more highly processed and thus less nutritious foods[4]. In the CASA, study[1] 84% of teens surveyed said they would rather eat dinner with their family. Let's make eating together a top priority; it is at the heart of good parenting!

1 CASA., *"The Importance of Family Dinners IV,"* 2007. www.casacolumbia.org.

2 Sandra L. Hofferth, *"Changes in American Children's Time, 1981–1997,"* U. of Michigan's Institute for Social Research, Center Survey, January, 1999.

3 Council of Economic Advisors to the President. *"Teens and Their Parents in the 21st Century: An Examination of Trends in Teen Behavior and the Role of Parental Involvement."* May, 2000.

4 Make Healthy Eating Fun for Kids. www.nationalfamilymonth.net/JoinTheFight/MakeHealthyEatingFun.pdf

Tips on Running a Successful Family Meeting

By JoAnne Nordling, MS, MEd

THE PURPOSE OF THIS article is to give you some basic guidelines on how to run successful family meetings, meetings that will give you and your children the opportunity to 1) Learn the art of problem solving, negotiation and compromise, 2) Share responsibility for family operating rules, and 3) Strengthen emotional bonds among members of the family.

Schedule a regular meeting time, rather than holding family meetings only when a crisis arises.

Weekly meetings held on a regular basis help ensure a calm and supportive atmosphere. Before holding your very first family meeting, ask each member of the family when would be the best time to meet. There-after, before the closing of each meeting, ask the family, "Shall we meet at the same time next week?" Give everyone a chance to check their schedules. Then write the date on a calendar, which you display in a prominent place, such as the refrigerator door.

No voting is allowed at family meetings.

While voting is a great system for a nation, voting in the intimate family setting can tear the group apart. Whenever there is a vote, someone wins and someone loses. People who lose are likely to feel misunderstood and put down. The losing minority will also often resist the will of the majority, and sabotage in subtle and not so subtle ways.

The process of searching for a solution is more important than actually finding a solution. Not voting means that the meeting might end with everyone still not agreed on a solution. Believe it or not, this is perfectly okay. The most important outcome of the meeting is that every individual in the family has had a chance to speak and to be heard. People of all ages who have their needs met for being treated as competent and respected human beings are much more likely, in the long run, to be cooperative and trusting members of the group.

Do not let yourself be baited into a power struggle by getting involved in an argument with any other member of the family. This is probably the hardest idea to put into practice, but is a rock-bottom necessity for conducting a successful family meeting. Remember that when children are nervous about being blamed for the problem, it is common for them at first to attempt to sabotage the process. And when a child makes some apparently outrageous and self-indulgent remark in an attempt to deflect blame, the indignant adult can hardly resist trying to "talk some sense" and saying "listen to reason."

Here's an example of how two parents sabotaged their first attempt at a family meeting. Every night when the mother, Naomi, got home from work, she walked into a messy house where her four children had left behind a trail of books, clothes, and half-eaten food. At the family meeting, she presented the problem to her kids, being careful not to place blame, and used good describing language to state the problem, "When I come home from work, I see coats and books and food in the living room and dining room. I get so tired when I come home to a messy house. I need some help in figuring out a plan for keeping things picked up." Her thirteen-year-old daughter said, "Why can't the baby sitter pick things up?" The ten-year-old son added, "Why should I have to work on this? I never leave my stuff around."

Imagine Naomi's feelings. She immediately launched into a lecture to her daughter on the need for everyone to be responsible for his or her own things. Next, her husband told their son (in a sarcastic tone of voice) that even if the son was Mr. Perfect, which he clearly was not, he had an obligation to participate in the meeting to help his mother find a solution. All doors to communication promptly slammed shut. Here's how the parents might have sidestepped their children's attempt to sabotage the meeting:

Daughter's attempt to sabotage:

1. Describe what your daughter just said by repeating her exact words: "You think the baby-sitter should pick things up." Try to look thoughtful and keep calm. Turn to the rest of the group and ask, "Anybody else have any ideas?" Or,

2. Use an inner-reality listening response. If you can't think of anything to say, just say, "Hmm…" Then turn to the group and ask, "Anybody else have any ideas?" Try to keep your tone of voice accepting and unemotional.

Son's attempt to sabotage:

1. Describe what he just said, "You never leave your stuff around so you don't think you should have to work on the problem." Keep your voice even and calm (no sarcastic overtones please!). Turn to the rest of the group and ask, "Anyone have any ideas?" Or,

2. Use an inner-reality listening response: "Hmm…" If you think of it, you can add, "You don't think it's fair." Then ask, "Anybody else have any ideas?" Your new response to these kinds of self-indulgent statements opens up lines of communication and reduces power struggles.

Establish a relaxed and upbeat atmosphere for the meeting. It's okay to sprawl on the floor.

Use an opening ritual. Rituals should be done on a regular basis so they help set the mood for the meeting to follow. Rituals can be as simple as tinkling a bell, turning off the fluorescent lights, passing out the popcorn, lighting a candle, or building a fire in the fireplace.

Ruth, who grew up in a Jewish family, looked forward to the meetings her parents held when she was a child. These meetings always opened with a short reading. Then each person was asked to tell something interesting that had happened to them during the week. Ruth remembers how important she felt when her opinion was asked for and listened to.

Involve everyone in setting the agenda. Use a blank sheet of paper and fasten it to the refrigerator door. Tell everybody this is the place to write down items anyone, whether parent or child, wants to discuss at the next family meeting (or use a shoebox with a slot on top.) If children are only writing down problem topics, be sure to add at least one fun topic like, "Should we do something fun together as a family next week?" or "Something that happened recently that made you feel happy or proud."

Keep focused on the general problem. Emphasizing specific names makes it easy to turn the meeting into a blaming session, where the "good guys" blame the "bad guys" and the "bad guys" blame everybody else. Try to keep the group focused on the general problem of teasing, for example, instead of on the specific complaints.

Watch out for hidden agendas. If mother comes to the meeting convinced she has already found the correct solution for convincing her children to pick up their clutter, it will be almost impossible for her to listen to their ideas. Since children are smart, they will soon realize mother is not able to listen to their ideas.

Use brainstorming to think about possible solutions. Even though it is okay if a solution is not found, it is important to sincerely explore all possibilities for a solution. Have the recorder for the week write down all ideas so they can be referred to throughout the process. 1) Clarify the problem so that everyone agrees as to the exact nature of the problem. 2) Brainstorm possible solutions; accept and write down even the zany ones. 3) Attempt to choose a solution from your list. Remember, every single person in the family must agree on any proposed solution. If no unanimous solution is found, just say, "Well, at least we tried and we did a lot of good thinking about it. Maybe someone will come up with a good idea this coming week. In the meantime, we'll just have to keep on doing it the way we always have."

Rotate leadership of the group when you think your children are ready. Adults have to continue to exercise informal leadership in all areas that are beyond the capabilities of a child, but you will be amazed at the extent to which your children will learn effective leadership and human relationship skills by observing your behavior as you participate in the family meeting.

For more information on how to conduct family meetings and brainstorming sessions, read the entire chapter on family meetings in Taking Charge: Caring Discipline That Works, at Home and at School, *4th ed. by JoAnne Nordling. A videotape featuring the author and two examples of family meetings is also available from Parent Support Center (503) 796-9665. CDs and audiotapes are available from North American Parenting Institute at (616) 738-0848 or www.parenting-institute.com.*

Reprinted with permission from JoAnne Nordling, the author of *Taking Charge: Caring Discipline That Works, at Home and at School* and director of Parent Support Center at www.parentsupport.org.

THERE ARE MANY THINGS you can do and say to teach your

9 Steps to Raising Money-Smart Kids
By MFS Heritage Planning

THERE ARE MANY things you can do and say to teach your children good money sense. Having once been a child yourself, you can always fall back on stories of how you used to earn, save, and spend money all those years ago. You can fill their heads with lessons on how important it is to be careful and wise with their money. However, the bottom line is that there's no better teacher than experience. The key to teaching your children one of the most important lessons of their lives is to have them learn by doing.

Following are a handful of ways you can encourage your children to save and manage money. In addition to the short-term benefit—namely, having children who realize that money doesn't grow on trees—you'll be instilling in them a healthy dose of financial responsibility that they can carry with them through adulthood.

1. Get children interested in money early
When your children are very young (perhaps at age three or four), show them how to tell different coins apart. Then give them a piggy bank they can use to store up their change. A piggy bank (or even a wallet or a purse) is a tangible place to keep their money safe.

Using a clear bank is probably best, as this will allow your child to hear, feel, and see the money accumulating. This visual experience is the child's equivalent of an adult reading the daily mutual fund prices in the newspaper or examining a quarterly retirement plan statement.

Once the saving has begun, let children spend money on treats, buying things both when there are just a few coins in the bank and when it's completely filled. This way, they will come to realize that a little bit in the bank buys a small treat, but a full bank enables them to purchase something special.

When your children are a little older, try playing games to help them understand the difference between "needs" and "wants." When riding past billboards or watching television, for example, ask them to identify whether each product advertised is a "need" or a "want." Tally their score, and when they've accumulated enough points by guessing 10 or more correct answers, treat them to a "want."

> ### Key Points
> **Children learn by doing. Give them as many opportunities as possible to**
> - **save money**
> - **spend money**
> - **earn money**
>
> **Guiding them through real-life transactions is the best way for them to gain an understanding of the value of money and the importance of managing money**

2. Make saving a habit
To get children off on the right foot, make a house rule of saving 10% or more of their income, whether the source of that income is earnings from a neighborhood lemonade stand, their weekly allowance, or a part-time job.

If started early enough in the child's awareness of money, your plan shouldn't run into much resistance. However, if you don't set some sort of guidelines, chances are pretty slim that a child will take the initiative and save on his or her own.

For proof, all you have to do is think back to when you were a child. Can you honestly say you would have saved the money you received from a relative on your eighth birthday without a parental directive to do so?

Chances are, you would have spent that money at the first candy shop you walked by. Like any positive behavior you try to instill in your child, saving money is a learned skill.

3. Open a savings account in a child's name
Like a piggy bank, a bank savings account can show kids how their money can accumulate. It can also introduce

them to the concept of how money can make money on its own through compound interest. Start by giving your child a compound interest table (available for the asking at most banks) to let them anticipate how their money may grow.

Be sure to plan regular visits to the bank. Although these days many people find it easier to save via direct deposit, having your young child see you make regular, faithful trips to the bank can shape his or her own saving behavior.

Being able to participate in something a grownup does will make any youngster feel mature and responsible. In case you haven't noticed, children who accompany their parents to the bank invariably want to "fill out" their own deposit slips. Why not do it for real?

4. Encourage goal setting

Have your kids write down their "want" list, along with a deadline for obtaining the items on the list. For example, your child may want inline skates by the end of the summer or a mountain bike by next year. Visualizing may give kids the added motivation they need to save.

You might also contribute a matching amount every time they reach a certain dollar amount in savings by themselves. Such a proposition sounds just as appealing to a child as it would to you if your boss told you the company would kick in a dollar for every dollar you saved over $10,000.

Not only will such an arrangement make them work harder to reach their goals, it might also prevent them from thinking they'll be old and gray before they save enough for an item on that wish list. After all, a year is an eternity to a young child.

5. Give regular allowances

Allowances give kids experience with real-life money matters, letting them practice how to save regularly, plan their spending, and be self-reliant. Of course, you should determine the amount of allowance you think fits their age and the scope of their responsibilities.

Some parents feel they don't have to pay allowances because they generously hand out money when their kids need it. But surveys have shown that kids who got money from their parents as needed saved less and were broke more often than children who earned allowances, even when the total amounts children in each group received were the same.

While you'll naturally decide for yourself when to start allowances and how much to offer your children, consider the following guidelines:

- **Don't grant too much independence by telling them they can spend their allowances on whatever they wish.** Make them save at least some of their allowance, and then advise them to spend the rest wisely.
- **Don't take away allowances as punishment.** Allowances are an educational tool, not a disciplinary one.
- **Carefully consider raise requests.** Discuss with a child why he or she is making such a request. Spare yourself weekly petitions for raises by telling your children they can only ask for raises twice a year, and then stick to your rule.
- **Don't reveal too much about your own finances when justifying reasons not to grant a raise in allowance.** Simply explain that your own budget is limited and that there is no extra money for a higher allowance.
- **Don't be too generous.** Too much money in a child's hands can breed careless spending habits.

6. Help plan a budget

Have your children write down what they'll buy during the week and how much each item costs. Then write down their weekly incomes. If they don't match up, they'll have to prioritize their "needs" and their "wants."

To give younger children practice making tough decisions, allow them just one special treat—which they pick out themselves—at the grocery store. Having to face 10 or more aisles knowing they can choose something from only one helps children understand that spending means making choices.

Just as you know fixing a leaky roof might mean postponing your Caribbean vacation, your children will realize that opting for an action figure during a store visit means they won't be able to enjoy a candy bar on the way home.

7. Encourage money-earning ventures
To help your children earn money beyond their weekly allowances, suggest to them that they find creative ways to make money. Encourage them to do special household chores or to seek jobs in the neighborhood such as raking, mowing, pet sitting, or shoveling snow.

Many people in your neighborhood—particularly elderly residents—would love to have a "regular" person doing things for them they can no longer do. This is a perfect opportunity for your child to earn some money and to do something for someone in need.

Even though by the teen years many children begin earning money on their own by working part-time jobs, continue to encourage that entrepreneurial spirit. To supplement his or her income and help pay car insurance, for example, a teen might consider starting a car pool to and from school and charging passengers a nominal fee each week.

8. Show them the effects of inflation
To show your children how prices have risen over the years, take them to the library to look up ads—for movie tickets, bikes, sneakers—in the newspaper archives (try finding the year they were born). In addition to being a trip down "memory lane" for you, it can serve as both a financial awakening and a history lesson for your children.

Once armed with the knowledge that things will almost certainly rise in cost, your children can use their math skills to see how much items they're saving for will cost in the future. For example, a bike that costs $150 today might cost $180 in five years, with 4% inflation.

If they're old enough, let them know there are ways to keep ahead of rising prices, such as investing in mutual funds, which historically have grown faster than inflation over time (although past performance is no guarantee of future results).

Of course, you should also tell them of the risks involved in investing. Let them know that the value of mutual funds fluctuates over time and that they have just as good a chance of losing money as they do of earning money. This will discourage them from thinking that investing is a sure thing, and encourage wise spending.

While investing may not hold any interest for them at this point in their lives, it's important that they know such financial opportunities exist.

9. Most importantly, give them a head start
The money habits your children learn—and witness from mom and dad—will certainly carry over into adulthood. While you may be proud of the 12-year-old who saves enough to buy a $400 bike, you might be even prouder of the 22-year-old who can move into her first apartment without having to ask mom and dad for a loan, or the 32-year-old who can draw on his savings and investments to put a 30% down payment on his first home. When those financial successes come, your son or daughter might even turn to you and say, "Thanks, I owe it all to you."

Resources
- **The National Association of Investors Corporation (NAIC)** find out how your child can join or start an investment club www.better-investing.org

- Karlitz, Gail; Honig, Debbie; and Lewis, Stephen, *Growing Money: A Complete Investing Guide for Kids*. (Price Stern Sloan Publishing, 1999)

- Godfrey, Neale S., *Neale S. Godfrey's Ultimate Kids' Money Book*. (Simon & Schuster, 1998)

- Otfinoski, Steven, *The Kid's Guide to Money: Earning It, Saving It, Spending It, Growing It, Sharing It*. (Scholastic Trade, 1996)

By the numbers
- **One-to-one.** Matching a child's savings dollar for dollar when they save for a big ticket item like a bike or a new computer game can be a great motivator.
- **Two times a year.** Let your children ask for a raise to their allowance only twice a year. They'll learn that money is a serious topic of conversation.
- **Six is a good age** to start paying an allowance. By first grade most children can appreciate that money can buy things—it's a valuable lesson to learn early on.
- **Ten percent of the money your child receives**—as a gift, allowance, etc.—should be earmarked for savings.

Nourishing Healthy Masculinity

Nourishing Healthy Masculinity

"For most men, masculinity is all about displaying competence and fearlessness. But this is a difficult posture to maintain. Men not only fear, they are scared that others may discover their fears. Thus men learn to hide behind a precarious posture, an air of cool confidence, a stance of toughness and self-reliance."
—From *The Contemporary Crisis of Masculinity*

"Sometimes just because you're a guy, people treat you like you're a little hoodlum. I think if they opened up their eyes, they'd see that most of us are actually pretty good people."—Boy quoted in *Real Boys* by William Pollack

"The making of friends, who are real friends, is the best token we have of a person's success in life."
—Edward Everett Hale

GOALS

- To discuss our standard cultural view of masculinity and the impact on individuals who do and do not conform to this exisiting standard
- To help your son to be himself and to resist gender stereotypes
- To present information on how testosterone affects males
- To understand boy's sexual developmental stages
- To explore homosexuality and other alternative sexual orientations, and the struggles in dealing with these issues
- To explore boys' friendship styles and ways to promote healthy relationships

3

OVERVIEW

Watching our sons awaken into young men can be both wonderful and terrifying for parents. On the one hand, it is exciting to share with our sons their sense of empowerment as they experience their emerging manhood. On the other hand, it can scare the daylights out of parents to watch their son become a sexual being, do daring activities, or lose his temper in a physical way. We worry about whether our teenage boys will be able to channel their aggression and risk-taking positively or whether it will get them into trouble. It pays for parents to think about how they are teaching their boys to grow into men, especially if they want to ensure that their sons are receiving the lessons parents most want to be imparting. For this reason we are focusing an entire chapter on nurturing healthy masculinity.

Whereas girls have problems feeling valued and empowered in our culture, boys have different kinds of problems. They tend to face cultural "masculinity barriers" at a young age when they try to fit themselves into the strict male image of stoicism and aggression that our culture imposes upon them (see "Boy in the Box", Chapter 1). This so-called "gender straightjacket" results in boys having great (hidden) insecurities about their masculinity, while paradoxically, they feel empowered and secure about taking on the preferred, male role in our culture. Helping boys to be who they can and want to be requires looking carefully at how we train them to become men. Families who want their boys to be able to express themselves fully and deeply will need to offer their boys a new model of masculinity that encourages connection and sensitivity, as well as confidence, independence and strength.

Here are a few reasons why it is important to challenge our culture's concept of masculinity and address what kind of positive impact parents can have in the process of making a boy into a man:

- **Violence, for the most part, is perpetrated by men; 90% of the aggressors and 75% of the victims are males.** There is something about being male that is strongly linked to aggression. To what extent is this true because of the way we socialize males or because of inborn tendencies?

- **Boys get mixed messages about how they "should" act.** There is pressure on the one hand to be cool, confident and strong (to stay in the "boy box") and on the other to be egalitarian, sensitive and open with feelings (to be out of the "boy box"). How can boys resolve these two opposite expectations?

- **Unrecognized depression in men.** Men aren't allowed to show weakness or vulnerability, so they suffer in silence and don't get the help they need or deserve.

- **Our culture resists men doing anything "female."** Men are ridiculed for sharing feelings, being sensitive, showing any feminine traits or doing "female" jobs. Men struggle when they become stay-at-home dads or enter traditional female careers, like nursing or elementary education.

Masculinity is thought by many researchers to be largely learned through cultural practices. Boys are taught from an early age how to act in ways that are considered masculine. Masculinity does differ with each culture. The problem with masculinity in our culture is that it can become a "gender straitjacket," where men are ridiculed for expressing any feelings, behaviors, or actions that are considered feminine. The article, **"Masculinity"** (p. 4:11), helps explain how this masculine code is transmitted and how parents can create a more holistic experience of masculinity for their sons. It also reminds us of the many masculine traits which are positive additions to all of our lives, such as fairness, leadership, ego strength, separating disagreements from friendship, releasing anger, self-sufficiency, sense of humor, resourcefulness, risking for the sake of one's beliefs, and many more. **"Men, Masculinity, and Media: Some Introductory Notes"** (p. 4:16) elaborates on the enormous impact of the media on the current masculine code of behavior. Our boys suffer greatly from masculine training that teaches them to bottle up feelings, disconnect from their fears, and avoid close and nurturing relationships. It is helpful for parents to understand how this training increases their boys' chances of violence, depression, suicide, sexual promiscuity and other risky behaviors, so that they can counter it effectively from a young age.

The question of how much of a boy's behavior is influenced by nurture and how much by nature is one that is not easily answered.

> A famous psychology professor told a reporter that he had studied the Nature versus Nurture question with great care, reading all the literature, and had come to the conclusion nature wins—by a score of 53% to 47% ... Clearly everything we do is influenced heavily by both. When asked why it is that there is such an exclusive determined hunt for a biological culprit, he said, 'Well, people are looking for simple answers.'
>
> —Michael Thompson, author of *Raising Cain*

Why is it Important to Know about Brains?

Marvelous new brain imaging studies are giving us more and more information about the differences between male and female brains. Our sons' and daughters' brains have different strengths and capabilities due in part to the pre- and post-natal influence of testosterone and other hormones. Studies of boys and girls exposed to testosterone in utero add additional information. These studies found that developing brains of either sex exposed to testosterone tended to result in children who are more active and better at spatial orientation. Brain scans show differences in the corpus callosum of males and females, the structure that connects the two sides of the brain. It is much larger in females than males—allowing for more connections to be going back and forth at the same time. Men, as a population, have more difficulty multi-tasking than women and less natural ability with complex social and emotional communication, and this decreased connection between the two sides of the brain may explain it. Brain scans also show that when men are asked a question, say a math problem, only one side of his brain is typically activated in answering, whereas in a woman both sides tend to be involved. There is some evidence that prenatal testosterone also compacts parts of the male brain connected to communication and understanding emotions[1], while enlarging the spatial, action and sexual areas of the brain. Many researchers feel that this is the reason that boys tend to excel at spatial skills, but may need extra coaching when it comes to social skills and

feelings. Finally boys' brains tend to mature more slowly than girls'[1]. Michael Gurien describes the implications of the boy-girl brain differences in the following way:

> The boy's brain tries to recreate itself in the outside world by creating and playing games – like basketball and football, etc.—that fill large spaces and challenge the male brain to hone its skills at moving objects through space. The girl's brain tries to recreate itself in the outside world by creating situations and playing games—like house, doll life, imagined community life—that use lots of verbal skills, require lots of one-on-one communication between actors and involve overtly complex emotional behavior...[2]

In spite of real brain differences between the sexes, these are only tendencies, and brains are flexible devices that are affected by everyday experiences. Being aware of brain characteristics in our sons can help us to capitalize on their strengths and teach in the areas of relative weakness.

Boys' higher level of testosterone affects their brains and their behavior—action takes precedence over talking. What does the research show about the effects of testosterone on aggressive behavior? Harvey Klivett, MD, a pediatric endocrinologist, did a literature search on the proven effects of testosterone and summarized these results in **"Masculinity and the Role of Sex Hormones"** (p. 4:18). He found that although boys are attracted to more aggressive and physical play, there is no clear evidence that testosterone is linked to violence.

What we do know about testosterone is that it is a sex hormone present in larger doses in males than females. These research-proven effects include:
- Deepens voice at puberty,
- Triggers normal development of male sex organs,
- Stimulates growth of hair on the face, chest, genital area and underarms,
- Increases lean body mass and cuts down on body fat,
- Increases sex drive,
- Increases bone density and growth,
- Increases energy and vitality.

The jury is still out on how much of our behavior is determined biologically versus culturally. A child's development—how he turns out—depends on many factors. The characteristics and temperament a boy is born with and the responses he gets from those around him shape him into who he will become. What we do know in this debate is that we adults have the power to create a healthier masculine image for our boys, one where a balance of masculine and feminine traits are celebrated and accepted without shame. Parents can encourage their sons to express a full range of emotions, refrain from shaming sons for expressing vulnerability, and find an alternative, healthier expression of masculinity to share with their boys. They can also create home environments that are accepting and that model respectful relationships between men and women.

Does a boy need a man to teach him how to grow up?

Many of us have heard that it is important to have a man in your son's life. We know, however, that a boy will become a man even if he is surrounded by 500 women and no men. What kind of man he becomes is influenced by all the people—children, men, and women in his life. If we want to teach him to be a strong, respectful, honest, forthright, caring man, we expose him to people who have these qualities. (See "The Myth of the Male Role Model" in Chapter 3.) Your son will thrive if he has one loving parent who really understands him. (If he has more than one, that is a bonus.) "**'Listening' to Your Child's Behavior**" (p. 4:20) will remind you how to bring your son's unspoken beliefs, needs and feelings to light so he will feel loved and heard.

Puberty

As parents it is important for us to know about the progress of sexual development in our budding young sons. "**Pubertal Development in Boys**" (p. 4:21) describes the sequence of events in boys' puberty and the range of age at which these occur. The article also outlines the emotional changes your son may experience during puberty and how you may adjust your parenting. The handout "**Surviving Puberty: A Handout for your Son**" (p. 4:23) is included as a way to share this important information with your sons. For

additional information, please see our list of further reading resources. Finally, the article "**How I Dealt With My Teenager's Sexuality**" (p. 4:24) outlines a practical approach to talking to your teen about your values and expectations around sexual behavior. Responsibility, respect, and safety in sexual behavior must be taught like any other skill, even if in the final analysis it is your teen's personal decision.

Boys and Alternative Sexual Orientations

Teenage boys are grappling and experimenting with their sexual identity. Although most are heterosexual, up to 10% of our sons will be gay, transsexual, transgendered or bisexual. (The currently politically correct term to use when referring to non-heterosexuals is GLBT: gay, lesbian, bisexual, transsexual, transgendered.) This means that one out of every four families will have an immediate family member with an alternative sexual orientation. Research supports that the origins of alternative sexual orientations are inborn, not created. There has never been proof that growing up in an all-female household, having exposure to homosexual men or even being the victim of pedophilia (most pedophiles are heterosexual) has ever turned someone from heterosexual to homosexual.

What is tragic is what happens to a son when his family cannot accept that he is gay. Gay youth have a much harder time during adolescence on many fronts, not the least of which is the alienation from their families and loved ones that many endure when they "come out." Overall, a youth with alternative sexual orientation is at higher risk than most youth for a host of serious problems:
- 69% suffer from anti-gay abuse;
- 40% suffer from physical violence due to their sexual orientation;
- 48% run away or are thrown out of the home;
- 20% are physically assaulted by family members because of their sexual orientation;
- 42% attempt suicide;
- 33% of all completed suicides are youth with alternative sexual orientations.

Keep in mind:
- Many parents may suspect their son is gay and

look for signs to prove it. However, there are many heterosexual men and boys with effeminate qualities. There are many boys who engage in homosexual experimentation who ultimately end up being heterosexual. You may be making more out of these signs and normal adolescent exploration than is warranted.

- GLBT youth often take years (often until their mid-20s) to fully understand their sexuality.
- GLBT youth themselves recommend that parents wait until their child is ready to tell them about their alternative sexual orientation. You can foster this by letting him know that you would love him regardless of his sexual orientation. One might say, "If I had a kid that was gay, I would be OK with that." The advantage to establishing this level of comfort is that your son might tell you earlier and you can help protect him.
- When a boy first recognizes that he is GLBT, his first step will be to work through his own deep-seated homophobia. This can be very painful.

A significant problem for our GLBT youth is that they don't have very many role models proving that they can have both an alternative sexual orientation and a productive, happy life. We know from those willing to take the risk of revealing their sexual orientation that GLBT individuals are found in every kind of profession, from elected officials to football players. As parents, what we want for our children is that they be happily adjusted and productive citizens. It is important that this be conveyed to both our straight and our GLBT youth, and that all young people understand that being gay and happy are not mutually exclusive conditions. Furthermore we need to convey to our children that using the word "gay" or "fag" as a putdown or a casual remark may contribute to homophobia and be potentially hurtful to GLBT youth who hear them. The article **"What If My Son Is Gay (GLBT)?"** (p. 4:25) goes into greater depth about sexual identity development and the special needs of adolescents with alternative sexual orientations.

Boys' Friendships

Boys' friendships are a very important part of their development and well-being. **"The Nature of Boys'** **Friendships"** (p. 4:30) contrasts boys' and girls' friendships. Boys socialize in action-oriented groups. Boys enjoy the order of competitive games with set rules and procedures. In fact, in life in general, boys enjoy order and feel insecure or act wild when not enough structure is provided. They want to know what the rules are and who is in charge, which leads to a pecking order among boys. (Similarly, when it comes to parenting, boys want to know what the rules are, what the consequences are, and whether you are going to enforce them. Structure helps boys relax and feel safe.) Boys' popularity is based on sports, stature, and a sense of humor or quick tongue. It is important for parents to know that rough-housing, "teasing," and "razing" are an important part of the fabric of male friendships. William Pollack emphasizes the importance of close friendships to our older boys as described in **"Boys and Their Friendships"** (p. 4:31):

So it seems that boys may follow their own formula for friendship: start with action and energy, throw in loyalty, laughter and 'doing together.' Add covert verbal expressions of caring, earnestness, and hidden physical touching—and you get a good friend.[3]

One of our challenging times as a parent is those inevitable times when our child is not getting along with his peers, doesn't have a friend, or selects a friend we don't like or trust. It is easy for "mother/father bear" to jump in to protect and rescue, when what our kids need most is guidance. As parents, we need to acknowledge that our kids have the prerogative to choose their friends. Then we can focus our efforts on healthy friendship skills. Here are a few tips from the **"Supporting Healthy Friendships"** (p. 4:32) article:

1. Get to know your child's friends, especially those you are unsure about.
2. Make it comfortable for kids to be at your home.
3. There is not a "right" number of friends. One or two friends can be enough.
4. Encourage kids to be friendly and fair to everyone. As your children get older, help them distinguish under what circumstances they can trust each of their friends and develop the ability to set appropriate limits with friends.
5. When your boy fights with a friend, listen carefully

and empower him to solve his own problems. Focus on support rather than rescue. **"The Peer Problem and Social Pressure"** (p. 4:33) discusses both the positive and negative effects of peer pressure on our sons.

Boys particularly benefit from coaching around interpersonal skills and conflict management, as was mentioned earlier in this chapter. In the 40 Developmental Assets in Chapter 1, boys show a huge gender gap from girls on several assets which are critical to friendship: interpersonal competence, peaceful conflict resolution, and caring. Sixty percent of girls reported that they had empathy, sensitivity and friendship skills while only 26% of boys reported having those skills; a gender gap of 34%! Twenty-five percent fewer boys (31% total) felt that they had skills for peaceful problem solving and only 32% of teenage boys felt they were caring people compared to 54% of girls. **"Relationships with Family, Friends,**

Self, and Others" (p. 4:34) describes specific, practical relationship skills that you can model and teach to your sons. Positive discipline coach Glenda Montgomery's article **"When Our Kids Fight with Friends"** (p. 4:37) can help us to strengthen our children's social skills in times of conflict, through listening, coaching and encouraging.

Our boys also benefit from "home alone" time to regroup, process, and get grounded and **"Fun Things To Do When You Are Alone"** (p. 4:38) lists several ways to strengthen one's relationship with one's self. Understanding our boys and their physical and psychological development puts us in the best possible position to teach them to express themselves fully in a model of masculinity that embraces connection and caring as well as strength and independence.

---

[1] Brizendine, L., *The Female Brain*, pp. 14, 24.
[2] Gurion, M., *The Wonder of Boys*, p.16.
[3] Pollack, W., *Real Boys*, p. 195.

THE 40 DEVELOPMENTAL ASSETS Essential to Every Young Person's Success

A healthy attitude about self—based on who you are rather than who you think you should be—would be fostered by the following assets, which promote social competencies and positive identity. With these assets present, perhaps we would see less homophobia, violence, and other stereotypical masculine behavior.

- **Asset #1   Family Support:** Family life provides high level of love and support.
- **Asset #14   Adult Role Models:** Parent(s) and other adults model positive, responsible behavior.
- **Asset #26   Caring:** Young person places a high value on helping other people.
- **Asset #28   Integrity:** Young person acts on convictions and stands up for his beliefs.
- **Asset #33   Interpersonal Competence:** Young person has empathy, sensitivity, and friendship skills.
- **Asset #34   Cultural Competence:** Young people know and respect people of different racial and cultural backgrounds.
- **Asset #35   Resistance Skills:** Young person can resist negative peer pressure and dangerous situations.
- **Asset #36   Peaceful Conflict Resolution:** Young person seeks to resolve conflict nonviolently.
- **Asset #37   Personal Power:** Young people believe that they have control over things that happen to them.
- **Asset #38   Self-esteem:** Young people feel good about themselves.

CIRCLE QUESTION

What messages is your son receiving about masculinity?
What do you see in your boy's life that keeps him in the "boy box"?

POSSIBLE DISCUSSION QUESTIONS

1. Whether "boys will be boys" is cultural or biological in origin, what can we do to promote a healthy view of masculinity in our culture?
2. What can parents do to encourage their son to be who he wants to be even if it means stepping out of the "boy box"?
3. What are your perception of the effects of testosterone on boys and men?
4. How comfortable do you feel with your son's sexual development? How has (or will) his physical maturity change your attitude toward him or cause you to treat him differently?
5. Where do you notice homophobia in the boys around you? What makes it hard to challenge homophobia when you see it?
6. When boys say, "That is so gay." (meaning "lame") how can we convey to them that it can contribute to homophobia and be potentially hurtful to GLBT youth who hear them?
7. How can we help prevent homosexual youths from being harassed at school? In the community?
8. Discuss some of the differences you see between male and female friendship? As a mom, do you sometimes feel uncomfortable observing your son's friendships?
9. Does your son have friends of different ages? If not, how could you foster this?
10. Describe a conflict with a friend that you have helped your son through. What seems to work and not work?

PUTTING IT INTO PRACTICE

- Be aware that your son may feel pressure to be cool, confident and strong and, at the same time, egalitarian, sensitive and open with his feelings.
- Encourage and support your son to be who he is—even if it is outside the box.
- Be aware of the signs of depression in male youth.
- Create a safe place for boys to be themselves in a group (a club or support group).
- Break down barriers wherever you can—catch yourself when you perpetuate the masculine stereotype.
- Be supportive of gay youth in your school and community.
- Teach your son to respect all people regardless of sexual orientation.
- Model the behaviors you would like to see in your son—respect, acceptance of diversity.
- Make your home friendly and welcoming for your kid's friends.
- Ask your son what qualities he looks for in his friends and which friends have them.
- If you are concerned about his relationships with his friends, try to put yourself in situations where you can be with them—car pools, camping trips, etc.
- Have a multi-family gathering inviting the families of your son's friends—play games together, eat together etc., where adults are mixed up with the kids.

PUTTING IT TOGETHER—YOUR VERSION

Write down three or four ideas you have been inspired to implement in your own life after reading and discussing this chapter.

1. _____

2. _____

3. _____

4. _____

FURTHER READING

What's Happening to My Body? Book for Boys by Lynda Madaras

I Don't Want to Talk About It: Overcoming the Secret Legacy of Male Depression by Terrance Real, PhD

Why Men Are the Way They Are by Warren Farrell, PhD

Raising Boys: Why Boys are Different and How to Help Them Become Happy and Well-balanced Men by Steve Biddolph

Real Boys: Rescuing our Sons from the Myths of Boyhood by William Pollack (see Chapter 8, "The World of Boys and Their Friendships")

Best Friends, Worst Enemies: Understanding the Social Lives of Children by Michael Thompson

The Friendship Factor by Kenneth H. Rubin

Teaching your Child the Language of Social Success by Stephen Nowiki Jr., Marshall Duke, and Elisabeth Martin

The Unwritten Rules of Friendship: Simple Strategies to Help Your Child Make Friends by Natalie Elman and Eileen Kennedy-Moore

VIDEOS

Tough Guise: Violence, Media and the Crisis of Masculinity by Jackson Katz Media Education Foundation at www.mediaef.org

Masculinity

By Jody Bellant Scheer, MD

MASCULINITY IS DEFINED differently by different cultures, and is culturally, not biologically, prescribed. This means that boys are taught from an early age how to act in ways that are considered "masculine" in their own society. Our culture's current codes of masculinity and femininity originated in the Victorian era and have exerted influence over male and female behavior, albeit with some changes, since the 19th century.[1] Dr. Pollack, a psychologist who wrote *Real Boys,* calls the outdated, constricting assumptions, rules and models about boy behavior "The Boy Code."[1] This code becomes a "gender straightjacket," a strict ordering of feelings, behaviors and actions that are acceptable among males. Feelings, behaviors and actions that fall outside the "boy code" are deemed feminine and therefore unmanly. In short, the Boy Code consists of four main injunctions:

"The Sturdy Oak" men should be stoic, stable, independent. A man never admits weakness, shows pain, or grieves openly.[1]

"Give 'em Hell": This is a stance based on a false self, one of extreme daring, bravado and attraction to violence, which encourages risk-taking behaviors.[1] This injunction stems largely from the myth that boys are biologically wired to act like "macho, high-energy, even violent supermen."[1]

"The Big Wheel": "This is the imperative men and boys feel to achieve status, dominance and power. Or understood another way, the 'big wheel' refers to the way in which boys and men are taught to avoid shame at all costs, to wear the mask of coolness, to act [at all] times as though everything is all right."[1]

"No Sissy Stuff": "Perhaps the most traumatizing and dangerous injunction thrust on boys and men is the literal gender straitjacket that prohibits boys from express-ing feelings or urges seen (mistakenly) as feminine—dependence, warmth, empathy."[1] Such feelings are taboo, and when boys break under the strain and display them, they are met with shame and ridicule instead of empathy. They are often taunted and threatened for failing to act

and feel stereotypically masculine.[1] So, boys become determined never to act or feel outside of their gender straitjacket, and they bury their "feminine" feelings.[1]

Because the "boy code" is so subtly a part of the fabric of our society and is passed on unwittingly by families of all types, even in progressive communities, most boys don't know they are living by this code.[1] However, when they act outside of the code, they are quickly reminded of their transgression, and may even suffer ostracism from those who love them the most: their parents.[1] As boys learn to mask their deepest feelings and thoughts, their insecurities and fears, and their real selves in order to abide by the "boy code," they make a bold and inaccurate statement to the world that everything's fine, even when it isn't.[1] This process of masking teaches boys to disconnect from their vulnerable feelings and fears, as well as from close and nurturing relationships. The result can be that boys' bottled up or hidden vulnerabilities can explode into violence, behavior disorders and/or covert depression, all of which are far more prevalent in boys than girls.[1,2] This demonstrates how poorly some boys fit within their gender straitjacket.

Additionally, boys pay a high price for our society's practices that reinforce a boy's grandiosity, his male privilege, his "better than" position.[2] Boys, suffering from a kind of relational impoverishment due to their masculine training of disconnection, often mask their insecurities with bravado or addictions in order to provide the illusion of connection or dominance.[2] Dr. Real, a psychologist and author of *I Don't Want to Talk About It,* summarizes: "The paradox for many boys and men lies in that one must dominate in order to belong. We have grown accustomed to think all this [male] jockeying is principally about power. But I believe that underneath, it is really an attempt at connection. In the hierarchical world of boys and men, some degree of power is a necessary security; it insures against the dread of either subordination or abandonment. Being one up means that you won't wind up picked upon. But power is not the driving force here, belonging is. The greatest cost of the less than/better than dynamic of traditional masculinity lies in its deprivation of the experience of communion."[2] This dynamic is most evident in domestic abuse, where a man's sense of entitlement and power spills over into family life, and he finds that his desire to control his wife and children prevails over his need to create intimate connections with them.

The relationship between masculinity, violence and male depression will be discussed in greater depth in Chapter 7, "Keeping Him Safe." Here we'll discuss how our culture's code of masculinity relates to boys' gender identity, psychology, sexuality and self-esteem.

Gender Identity

Our society's outdated social codes tend to strictly define emotions, behaviors and characteristics as either masculine or feminine. The truth is, though, that boys and girls are born with an equal capacity to feel a whole range of emotions and to act in a whole range of ways that can be classified as both masculine and feminine. The term "gender identity" refers to an individual's broad sense of his or her own combination of masculinity or femininity.[3]

Gender identity has three main components: core gender identity, sex role identity and sexual partner orientation.[3] Although the majority of our children will be heterosexual individuals, at least 10-12% of our children, as well as all people in all cultures, will be homosexual, bisexual, transgendered or transsexual.[1,4] Parents need to remember that all children are valuable human beings regardless of their gender identity, and deserve the same kind of love, nurturing and support as heterosexual children, even though you may be fearful or disappointed in having discovered this. It is also important to understand that your son may have many effeminate qualities, and also be a perfectly ordinary, heterosexual man, who also needs your love, respect and support. Our culture lays a terrible burden on men around masculinity, expecting them to be strong, tough, stoic and brash. These qualities certainly have their advantages at times, but a good father,

friend, or lover also needs to be nurturing, empathic and connected. Again, by remembering that all people have a balance of masculine and feminine within them, it will be easier to help our boys (and girls) weather the difficulties of growing up. We can also encourage our boys to experience a whole range of emotions and behaviors that the "boy code" would forbid, and in doing so, offer a new definition of masculinity that is healthier, happier and more balanced.

Psychological Development of Masculinity

Men in our culture are often fearful about not being masculine enough, in fact, men seem vulnerable to a kind of "femininity phobia," in part due to the shaming, ostracism and teasing they receive when they act outside of the "boy code."[1,3] The reality is, however, that men do have desires to experience those aspects of themselves (such as the desire to be passive and to be taken care of, for example) that our culture conventionally associates with femininity.[3] Likewise, women want to experience parts of themselves (such as power, assertiveness, etc.) that our society labels as masculine.[3] These desires can be called cross-gender impulses, and are universal.[3] It is a reality that men and women are not just masculine or feminine, but in some sense both.[3] This can be more easily understood if you look at the psychological development of young children. 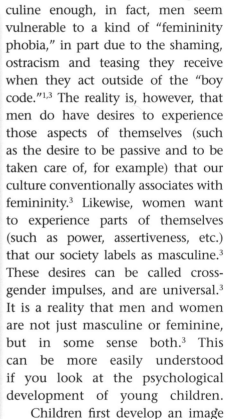 Children first develop an image of themselves as they identify with loved ones.[3] Babies' first love object is usually mother: they identify with and want to be just like her. It is easy to see how this process will differ a bit for baby girls and boys, as girls will grow up to be women and can more easily mirror themselves in their mothers' image. To secure a sense of masculinity, however, a boy must disidentify with his mother at some point, and identify with his father (or another important male in his life).[3] The young boy's developing sense of masculinity finds its first model in his beloved father, in whom he sees a mirror of himself.

However, boys also develop a healthy sense of who they are from mirroring certain aspects of their relationship with their mother. Being taken care of passively without having to DO anything is a big part of any baby's healthy experience. The problem for boys in our culture, with its strict divisions of sex role identity, is that this very desirable experience promotes identification with the feminine. "So, to feel masculine, the little boy has to put behind him his first intimate experiences with his mother and all the feelings and wishes that were part of it. In light of this early development, masculinity is like a house built on a hidden foundation ... for the foundation of the house is feminine."[3] This helps explain why men can be so worried about their "feminine" impulses, as these threaten their feelings of masculinity.[3] Also, this helps explain why so many men (as well as psychologists) have worried that a boy's attachment to his mother will derail his masculinity (a concept that is completely without scientific backing).[1] Dr. Pollack, in *Real Boys,* points out that our culture's rules of masculinity encourage the premature separation of boys from their mothers' love, nurturance and support.[1] Contrary to creating more masculine men, this practice produces boys who give up their attributes of "dependency, expressiveness and affiliation—all the self concepts and skills that belong to the relational, emotive world."[2]

As a consequence, our boys and men grow up with and suffer from a sort of relational impoverishment due to this disconnection from the feminine qualities of emotional expression and interpersonal connection.[2] A healthier masculine image for our modern culture would be one where a balance of masculine and feminine traits were encouraged and celebrated in our boys and men. Dr. Real, author of *I Don't Want to Talk About It,* and a psychotherapist specializing in men's depression, sums it up as follows: "My work with depressed men has led me to turn the conventional thinking about sons and their fathers on its head. If we give credence to the research detailing the centrality of affection in father-son relations, and the relative irrelevance of the father's 'masculinity,' it becomes clear that boys don't hunger for fathers who will model traditional mores of masculinity. They hunger for fathers who will rescue them from it. They need fathers who have themselves emerged from the gauntlet of their own socialization with some degree of emotional intactness. Sons don't want their fathers' 'balls,' they want their hearts."[2] Contrary to the "boy code," research has shown that what our boys need most during their developing years is a constant source of love, nurturing and connection from both their fathers and mothers.

Masculinity and Adolescent Sexuality

The conventional view of society is that a boy must separate from his family and learn to stand on his own to become a man.[1] This view is especially harmful to our adolescent sons, who are entering the most confusing and perilous time of their lives in the midst of hormonal and emotional turmoil, and often without the love, connection and support of their families, friends and communities.[1] Boys reach adolescence faced with a confusing, double standard of masculinity: they are encouraged to become both the strong, stoic, and tough traditional male, as well as the empathic, sensitive and egalitarian "new age" man.[1] The problem is, boys never know which role to enact, as they face rejection and ridicule no matter which role they play. The emergence of sexuality adds a new layer of confusion to the adolescent boy's conundrum. He feels pressure from society, his peers and from the media to perform as a man (to have sex), yet he is also urged to respect girls' emotional and sexual needs over his own.[1] Adding to the confusion is the fact that boys really don't know if they are capable of sex until they have it, and the fear of impotence, the ultimate masculine humiliation, is never far away in every boy's mind.[1] As a result, boys look at their first sex act very differently than girls. "Boys tend to see it as a confirmation of their masculinity, and only become relaxed and emotionally vulnerable after they feel secure about their physical ability to have intercourse, and feel that the act of sex won't shame them in any way. Boys open up after sex (often long after), just the opposite of girls."[1]

Because of these factors, boys can be easily labeled as sexual predators or sexually toxic.[1] However, it is important to remember that boys' behavior "is a compromise between a desire for connection and the fears of rejection and shame around being abandoned, when the ultimate humiliation as a man is possible and the least amount of honesty is allowed."[1] It is also important to recognize that boys "have their own very real confusions about sexuality and the male double standard that both pushes boys to prove themselves and then castigates them when they do,"[1] all during a time of life when they are encouraged to face their problems all on their own, without adult advice or support.

By puberty, the fact is that most boys feel they have been taught little or nothing about dating, sex and sexuality, that they don't have the relationship that they would like with their parents, and that there is no one to talk to about their feelings and sexual development.[1,2] Many boys, faced with so many confusing issues to deal with on their own, will turn to sex, drugs or alcohol to cope. These behaviors can be used as a desperate attempt to connect with others, as well as a way to numb the pain of their confusing emotions.[1] Without solving any of the root problems causing their distress, these boys now have a whole new array of difficulties and risks associated with addictive behaviors. Their negative behaviors often further alienate them from their most logical source of support: their parents.

How can parents help their sons navigate this treacherous journey of masculine sexual maturity? First of all, it is critical to maintain connection with our sons, letting them know that we will love and respect them as they individuate, even if they choose differently than we would like. Because boys often retreat behind of a mask of hostility or dispassion, this will mean that parents will need to keep trying in many different ways to continually connect with their sons. Make regular dates with your son, as boys often find it easier to open up to you if you are doing something together.[1] Find lots of opportunities to tell your son you love him and be careful to create a home environment that is a safe haven from ridicule and shame.[1] It is important to discuss the complexities of adolescence honestly with your son, and to admit to your own confusion.[1] Share your own stories, so he can understand that you, too, are a fellow survivor of adolescence.[1] Listen empathically, and be patient, nonjudgmental and attentive. Encourage your son to express a full range of emotions and vulnerable feelings by modeling these behaviors yourself. Lastly, don't put off talking to him about sex, drugs or other tricky topics, as the payoff may be saving your son's life and good health. Be honest about your own embarrassment with such subjects, and stay factual and matter-of-fact. Remember that a parent is most effective when supporting and guiding a son in making his own decisions. We can listen, guide, set clear limits on what WE will do, and respect that our teens may act differently than we would. It is a great act of unconditional love to support a son while he makes a choice we are at odds with. A long-term outcome of intimacy and mutual respect, however, is the reward.

The Best of "Masculinity"

Dr. Warren Farrell is a psychologist who has studied masculine and feminine roles within our society since the mid-1960's. He states, in his book *Why Men Are the Way They Are,* that he has critiqued traditional masculinity for years because it has been taken to the extreme. "And, taken to the extreme, it creates anxiety, homicide, rape, war and suicide: not taken to the extreme, it has many virtues not to be tossed out with the bathwater."[5] To present a balanced view of masculinity, I thought it would be only fair to end this discussion with some of the advantages of male socialization, of which there are plenty. These benefits can boost a boy's self-esteem and feelings of competency. Below is a list paraphrased from Dr. Farrell's own observations.[5]

Giving/Generosity: Men are socialized to give of money and effort to support their families and community. They pick up tabs, work (often in dangerous, dirty or unfulfilling jobs) to pay for homes and family, mentor children and coworkers, and provide countless other acts of service to their loved ones.[5]

Fairness: Male socialization teaches the value of a care-ful system of rules in which anyone can work to gain advantage.[5]

Nurturing: Males nurture by finding solutions to problems and supporting wives while they bear and raise children, and/or work full or part-time.[5]

Modeling Vulnerability through Coaching: Children feel nurtured by the fact that Dad cares enough to be "the coach." Coaching demands vulnerability— as a dad may be teased, mocked, and/or judged in front of his kids.[5]

Leadership: Male socialization has trained millions of leaders to lead thousands of businesses that now provide millions of women (and men) with opportunities for leadership that might not have existed if not for male leadership.[5]

Outrageousness: Men are socialized to get female attention by standing out. One can stand out by being outrageous, and being outrageous helps to break barriers that allow everyone more opportunity to experiment with discovering themselves.[5]

Ego Strength: Male socialization teaches men to quickly recover from bad experiences. In order to succeed, the pressure on men is to learn to reflexively self-correct after a loss, creating ego strength.[5]

Keeps His Emotions Under Control: This male trait comes in very handy under crisis situations.[5]

Separating the Issue from the Friendship: The best part of male competition is insight into the game of life —a philosophical distance allowing men to separate the roles they play (lawyer, teammate, husband, opponent) from their friendships. They are able to oppose each other, not take it personally, and then go to the ball game afterwards.[5]

Expression of Anger: Men's tendency is to release anger in intense, quick shows of emotion, then after a subsequent calm that follows the storm, grudges are often not held. This intensity, like all powerful energy, can be harnessed into powerful lovemaking.[5]

Keeps His Complaints about His Relationship within the Relationship: Men are socialized not to talk about their relationships with other men, which means that a man tends not to break a woman's confidences, and he tends to confront her on issues instead of talking about them with others.[5]

Risks His Own Life for the Sake of His Beliefs, His Wife, His Kids, His Country: Men are socialized to risk their own lives for the women they love, for their country during times of war, for loved ones in the line of danger, for their own desires to be strong heroes, for money and as a way to make a living. Male superheroes embody this (i.e,. Superman, Batman).[5]

Self-Sufficiency: Men are expected not only to be self-sufficient (no such thing as a "career man"—this is taken for granted), but to take care of wife and family as well. Because of a man's training to take care of himself and others, millions of women have been freer to look at their own values (and to criticize men) than they would be if they had to support him.[5]

Self-Starting: Men are socialized to take the initiative. This is a positive trait, as it helps men to create change for themselves, to compete for better jobs, to be active in the pursuit of their desires.[5]

Risk-Taking: Male socialization teaches men to risk and be willing to fail a lot, all for the hope of success. [5]

Challenges Authority: Males are socialized to challenge authority, and risk rejection by challenging it. This builds strong ego strength.[5]

Sense of Humor: One of the best things that emerges from men's training is to see life as a game and be able to laugh at the game as well as themselves.[5]

Resourcefulness: While males' tendencies to turn "no" into "maybe" and "maybe" into "yes" has a negative side in the sexual arena (often called rape training), but in the business arena, this trait can be very successful.[5]

Enjoys the Woman, Not the Potential: Men, due to their diminished focus on commitment, are more willing and able to enjoy fully the "here and now" in relationships, instead of postponing a full emotional and sexual letting go until he is persuaded that she is Ms. Right. Men are socialized to enjoy women, as such, they put less pressure on women to "perform" and/or "commit."[5]

Plays with Kids on Kids' Terms: Dads tend to combine physical risk with physical protection in their rough and tumble play, encouraging their kids to test their physical boundaries without risking their lives. This may push play to the point that mothers are uncomfortable, but this kind of play is an important part of kids' development.[5]

Changes without Blame: Men have been socialized to make many changes in behavior over the past 40 years, and while they may not have made as many changes as women, most of them have accomplished these changes without blaming or maligning women.[5]

References:
[1] *Real Boys: Rescuing our Sons from the Myths of Boyhood* by William Pollack, PhD
[2] *I Don't Want to Talk About It: Overcoming the Secret Legacy of Male Depression* by Terrence Real, PhD
[3] *Mapping the Terrain of the Heart* by Stephen Goldbart, PhD, and David Wallin, PhD
[4] *"Just the Facts About Sexual Orientation & Youth: A Primer for Principals, Educators and School Personnel,"* www.apa.org/pi/lgbcpublications/justthefacts.html
[5] *Why Men Are the Way They Are* by Warren Farrell, PhD

Men, Masculinities and Media: Some Introductory Notes
By Jackson Katz

THE CLIMATIC SCENE in the Wizard of Oz where Toto pulls back the curtain to reveal a nervous, tragic man pretending to be the Great and Powerful Oz represents more than just a classic moment in American cinematic history. It is also a powerful metaphor for looking at masculinity in a new way not as a fixed, inevitable, natural state of being, but rather as a projection, a performance, a mask that men often wear to shield our vulnerability and hide our humanity.

In fact, the poses we strike and the images we create can tell us a great deal about what's going on in individual men's lives and about our culture as a whole. That's why it is important for us to pull back the curtain and take a sober look—both at the images themselves and what's behind them.

These images tell a story—actually part of a story—about what's been happening with American men over the past generation. The last quarter of the 20th century has been marked by rapid and seismic changes in gender and sexual relations. In the brave new world in which we live, at the dawn of the 21st century, these changes have created new life experiences and identities for whole generations of women and men. It has been well documented that the enormous baby boom generation catalyzed the modern multicultural women's movement, which is one of the key transformative social movements in human species history.

Young people in the US who came of age in the 1970's, 80's and 90's, including the younger boomers, Generation X, and the so-called millennium generation, are the first generations to have grown up with this movement, not simply to have reacted to it, but literally to have grown up with it. Consequently, many young men of all races and ethnicities have embraced new notions of sexual equality, and are pioneering new ways of being in egalitarian relationships with women, as friends, lovers and husbands, classmates, colleagues and fellow workers.

Not surprisingly, however, some men have reacted very poorly to these changes. It's not just an extreme movement in foreign cultures—like the Taliban in Afghanistan—where we can see male backlash played out.

> Bottom line, if you want to understand what is going on with masculinity in contemporary America, you have to look at what's going on in the media.

Many US men of varying class and racial backgrounds, have been decentered and threatened by women's increased assertions of strength, integrity and social and economic power. One manifestation of the backlash is the pandemic rates of violence perpetrated by men and boys against women and girls, rates that have persisted despite decades of feminist antiviolence activism.

Through a gradual social change, a proliferation of mass media images has helped structure the way we think and react to the shifting gender terrain. The post-sixties generations are immersed in a world of media imagery whose scope and variety is, to say the least, historically unprecedented. The bottom line, if you want to understand what's going on in contemporary American masculinities, you have to look at what's going on in the media.

Over the past couple of decades, cultural theorists such as Raymond Williams have argued that while it's people who produce the images that bombard us daily on TV, on billboards, in video games and in film, it is equally true to say that this virtual landscape of images, in some sense, produces us. This means that we're not just consumers of these images; we don't simply make our way through the thousands of images we see daily and pick and choose what we like and don't like. These images have a profound impact on who we are and on our tastes, attitudes and the kinds of choices we make.

Feminists who have analyzed media content to date have primarily focused on images of women, and what we can learn from them about women's lives. This is crucial and important work. But until recently there has been relatively little attention paid to images of men. Consider the pioneering feminist media literacy work of Jean Kilbourne or the work of Naomi Wolf on western constructions of female beauty. As these and other feminist theorists and activists have long maintained, images of women's bodies as represented in the mainstream media are thinner, more waifish, and younger than women's bodies in the real world. Showing women this way is a means of symbolically taking power away from them, because thin, waifish women literally take up less space in the world, and hence are less threatening. These images, feminists remind us, are flooding the visual landscape at a time when women are challenging traditional male power on many different fronts.

Only in the past decade, as queer theorists and pro-feminist men's studies scholars have taken up the subject, has there been any significant attention paid to how men's bodies are represented and what that suggests about recent developments in men's lives. It is axiomatic that for every story about women's lives, there is a corresponding story about men's. For example, while images of women have been thinner and more waifish, images of men have gotten bigger, stronger, more muscular and more violent. What accounts for this?

Young men for the past several decades have been challenged by women in areas that our fathers and grandfathers never were—in education, the workplace, business, and the professions. But one area where men as a group continue to assume they have a significant advantage over women as a group is in the area of physical size and strength. As a result, physical size and strength for many men have become increasingly important to proving manhood. This is borne out by a review of changes over the past generation in the body morphology of male action film stars, the musculature of the dolls that young boys play with, as well as the exaggerated strutting and posing of many rock and rap performers.

Tough guy posing, even though it's often just an act, also has the effect of keeping men in line. Fed by a constant stream of images formed by the Marlboro Man ethos of the "real man" as a stoic, rugged individualist, millions of boys and men learn early on that acting like a man means you don't complain, you don't admit weakness, you don't ever let others see the anxious man behind the curtain. This sort of conditioning starts very young, as does the pressure on boys and young men to compete—in school, in sports, in their social milieu—to live up to their fathers' visions of them as manly men.

But the pretense of omnipotence and invulnerability that is implied by ubiquitous images of physically powerful males is not just emotionally stultifying. It also gets a lot of men—and boys—killed. Richard Majors and Janet Billson have examined one angle of this phenomenon with their concept of "cool pose." The cool pose is a style affected by poor urban black males who have few resources (middle-class income or the expectation of one, education, workplace authority,

social status) to earn respect as men beyond their bodies and their ability to strike a pose of "cool," "badness" or violence.

But it's not just poor black males and other men of color who fall into a hyper-masculine posture to compensate for their disadvantages in other areas of life. Poor and working-class white men are also denied opportunities available to more privileged middle-class males. White suburban, middle-class males are the leading purchasers of rap music, including misogynous "gangsta" rap; these young men take poses that grow out of mean city street culture and adopt them to their lives in relatively (at least superficially) nonviolent suburban communities.

Over the past 10 to 15 years, there has been an outpouring of scholarship, books, articles and discussion about masculinities, the gendered nature of men's lives, and how men have and have not adjusted to the changes catalyzed by feminism. This work has accelerated the long-term feminist project of shining the spotlight on the intimate workings of the dominant group, men. The purpose is not to push women aside and put men back on center stage, but to understand the ways that male dominance functions, in the hope that this understanding can hasten the process of breaking down sexual inequality and improving the lives of women and men.

Furthering our understanding of the ways that media imagery helps shape the construction of masculinities is a critical part of this effort. The more we can, like Toto, deflate the power of the unrealistic images that dominate our visual landscapes, the better we'll be able to face honestly the ongoing challenges of our time.

References:
- Connel, R.W. (1987) *Gender and Power*. Stanford, CA: Stanford University Press.
- Kilbourne, J. (1979) *Killing Us Softly: Advertising's Image of Women*. Cambridge, MA: Cambridge Documentary Film.
- Majors, R. and Billson, J. (1992) *Cool Pose: the Dilemmas of Black Manhood in America*. New York: Lexington Books.
- Williams, R. (1981) *The Sociology of Culture*. Chicago: University of Chicago Press.
- Wolf, N. (1991) *The Beauty Myth: How Images of Beauty Are Used Against Women*. New York: William and Morrow.

Reprinted with permission by Jackson Katz. Jackson Katz, lecturer, anti-violence educator, anti-sexism, narrator of *Tough Guise* video from National Media Education. Check out www. jacksonkatz.com.

Masculinity and the Role of Sex Hormones
By Harvey Klevit, MD

Masculinity is one of those things you know when you see it, encounter it or even smell it, but is difficult to define. For purposes of this chapter we define masculinity as all of those features attributed to the male sex and gender. Sex is related to physical characteristics determined by anatomic and hormonal factors. It includes anatomy, physiology, reproductive function and genetic factors. Gender, on the other hand, is regarded as behavioral expressions of an internal psychological conviction that one is either male or female. Noted psychologist John Money defines gender role as "everything that a person says and does to indicate to others … the degree that one is either male or female…."

Role of Testosterone in Human Sexual Development and Differentiation

Boys are made of "snips and snails and puppy dog tails" and have Y chromosomes contributed by their fathers in each and every cell of their bodies. Girls are "sugar and spice and everything nice," but lack a Y chromosome in any of their cells. This is the basic genetic difference of the sexes. Vive là difference! Thus every "normal" male has 46 chromosomes (autosomes) plus two sex chromosomes, an X and a Y, in the nucleus of each cell. Girls likewise have 46 autosomes but have 2 X-chromosomes. The Y chromosome contains genes that direct the undifferentiated gonad in all individuals to become a fetal testis at about the 4th to 6th week of pregnancy. In the absence of a Y chromosome as in normal XX females or in abnormal conditions where there is only one X chromosome, the fetal gonad will not become a testis. It either becomes an ovary when there are 2 X-chromosomes or does not develop at all. So, no Y, no testis.

What's so important about having a fetal testis? The fetal testis has a certain type of cell, which under proper conditions will produce large quantities of male sex hormones, the most important of which is the steroid testosterone. It is interesting that the mother's placenta produces another hormone, chorionic gonadotrophin, which whips the fetal testis into action.

Male and female fetuses are virtually identical anatomically until the end of the first trimester of pregnancy when the male's supply of testosterone stimulates the primitive phallus to enlarge and differentiate into a penis. The latter can be detected by ultrasound visualization and can be used to determine the sex of the fetus. Only a small remnant remains in the Y-less female, which will become her clitoris. The external genital structures are further developed as a result of testosterone's effect on the primitive "labial folds." A male gets a scrotum and in the female the labial folds persist as the labia majora. If, for a variety of reasons, a female fetus has excessive amounts of testosterone or other male hormones in her system, she too will undergo labioscrotal fusion and clitoral enlargement and might be mistakenly assigned a male sex at birth in spite of her feminine internal anatomy.

But that's not the whole story of the role of the fetal testis, that thing created by genes on the Y chromosome. The internal genital structures in males and females differ greatly. Normal females possess a uterus, Fallopian tubes, and a vagina. If an animal's gonads (ovaries or testes) are removed surgically early in pregnancy, it will be born with female internal structures regardless of gender or chromosomal sex. A substance in the fetal testis called "Mullerian inhibiting hormone" prevents males from having female internal structures and allows their testosterone to go to participate in the production of male structures such as the sperm-carrying vas deferens and semen-storing seminal vesicles. All others, normal females or anyone lacking a fetal testis, will be allowed to have a uterus, fallopian tubes and a vagina. It has been said that the female is the "default sex."

Androgenic Properties of Testosterone

Testosterone has the well-known properties of making men big, swarthy, muscular, "horny" and, at times, downright disgusting. It is the stuff of adolescent boys, weight lifters, sumo wrestlers and Shaq. It has been known for many years that testosterone and other "anabolic steroids" are responsible for the development of secondary sex characteristics at puberty. These include deepening of the voice, penile enlargement, acne, body odor, and increased growth velocity and musculature and pubic/axillary hair in both sexes. There are marked variations in the timing of pubertal development and both precocious as well as delayed onset are causes of great concern among families. It is socially devastating for a boy with delayed onset of puberty to share a gym class shower with a fully developed pimple faced "bull." In most cases the immature boy is perfectly normal and when his testosterone is turned on, he may end up bigger and tougher than his shower mate.

Behavioral Properties of Testosterone

It does not require a behavioral specialist to observe that males beyond infancy well into adolescence and adulthood play a more dominant role in society. They tend to be more aggressive, engage in more physical play and to sum it up, are macho. It has long been recognized that males are more interested in and perform better at mathematical and problem-solving skills, while females tend to be superior at reading, writing and other verbal skills. Why did boys of past generations prefer "cops and robbers" to hopscotch or jumping rope (which certainly requires some athletic ability)? It remains unclear to what extent these attributes are related to hormones of any kind. Perhaps boys are better at figuring out how to build model airplanes or make a kite fly because of parental expectations or peer conformity, not because they are inherently better at it.

Some prominent neuroscientists assert that gender differences in math aptitude or spatial relations are related to anatomic differences in brain structure, which in turn may be related to hormonal influences. The corpus callosum is a structure in the brain separating the right and left cerebral hemispheres and carrying millions of nerve fiber connections between the two sides. The female corpus callosum is significantly larger and may play a role in gender-related academic propensities.

As far as aggressive behavior is concerned, that too may be a learned attribute. Recent studies where adult males were given very large quantities of testosterone for weeks failed to show measurable degrees of increased aggressive behavior. In animals, exposure of the female fetal brain to testosterone produces male-type sexual and mounting behavior in spite of female anatomy.

It is impossible to predict behavioral characteristics in individuals by simply measuring testosterone levels, although a number of circumstances appear to be associated with increased hormone levels. Testosterone in the blood of athletes and even chess players appears to increase prior to a competition and remain elevated in winners, but diminish in losers. Testosterone in recently divorced men increases to a higher level than when they were happily married; could this be an evolutionary phenomenon to adjust fecundity?

Testosterone causes masculine secondary sexual characteristics, increased sexual drive, more active, rowdy physical play and influences the brain to enhance spatial skills. It does not produce antisocial aggression and violence. Nevertheless our parenting and nurturing of our sons is important to foster peaceful problem solving, interpersonal skills and empathy for others.

Harvey Klevit, MD is an endocrinologist who investigated the research-proven effects of testosterone for Full Esteem Ahead.

Written for Family Empowerment Network by Harvey Klevit, MD. For reprint requests, contact www.family-empower.com.

"Listening" To Your Child's Behavior

By Jody Bellant Scheer, MD

Parenting is a bit like veterinary medicine: children often do not tell us directly what they are thinking, feeling or needing and it is up to parents to figure it out for themselves by "listening" to their kids' behaviors. While we may perfect this kind of "listening" with our preverbal toddlers, it is also a useful tool for understanding older children, especially our sometimes gnarly, nonverbal teenagers. Becoming good observers of our children's actions and misbehaviors can provide us with valuable insights into our children's hidden beliefs, feelings and needs, making it easier for us to support and encourage them.

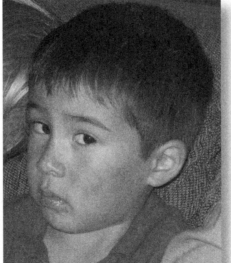

It is important to realize that at the core of ANY behavior is a positive intention, which is to find love, respect and a sense of belonging. Behaviors are the result of a person's unique belief system that is created to meet these universal human needs. Children (like adults) are prone to developing mistaken beliefs about how to earn love and respect. Acting on these mistaken beliefs can be self-defeating. This is because humans tend to be good perceivers but poor interpreters. A child, for example, may perceive that Mom is gone a lot at work, and interpret that the only way to get love is through misbehavior. Though based in a need for love and significance, misbehaviors don't ordinarily create the desired loving response from parents. Likewise, teenagers may perceive their parents' fear, lectures and restrictions in response to their desire for increased autonomy, and interpret this to mean that they are disliked and disrespected at home. They then look to their peers for love and respect, and act with retaliation, withdrawal, or by acting out towards their parents. These behaviors do nothing to build the trust and acceptance that a teen really wants with his parents.

"Listening" to a child's behaviors can help parents play a vital role in helping children to challenge their mistaken beliefs, to recognize their feelings and needs, and to develop positive behaviors that will get them what they really want. This can be accomplished by making a guess about what mistaken belief, unspoken need or feeling is underlying a child's behavior, and talking about these hunches with our children. Making an empathic connection in this way often results in our kids opening their hearts and minds to us.

A helpful way to do this is by asking questions in the following format: Are you feeling (x) because you would like (y)? This technique works only if you avoid blaming yourself for your child's behavior, refuse to take her behavior personally, and avoid shaming the child by using negative judgmental words. Examples of this technique might be, in the case of a child who just hit her sister: Are you feeling angry because you would like to play alone? Are you feeling sad because your friends left without you? Are you feeling frustrated because you would like to play with me instead of your sister? Each of these responses could be true for the child: the clues must come from observing the child's behaviors, social interactions and nonverbal behavior. The difference between this kind of approach and one that uses punishment is that the child will be encouraged to explore her own (often unconscious) feelings, needs and beliefs, such that the next time she is tempted to swat her sister, she will be more able to make a positive behavioral choice instead. Punishment may stop a misbehavior in the moment, because the child is caught up in crying, plotting revenge or wallowing in self-pity, but it does little to inspire thoughtful reflection upon the reasons for and consequences of misbehavior.

By "listening" to our children's behaviors and bringing to light our children's unspoken beliefs, feelings and needs, our children will feel our compassion and empathy, will feel loved and heard, and will be more willing to cooperate with us to create positive personal choices. Children also receive a clear message that they are significant, special and worth our time.

Jody Bellant Scheer is a mother to 3 young adults and a pediatrician in a Neonatal ICU.

Pubertal Development in Boys

By Kathy Masarie, MD

THERE ARE FOUR main events that occur during puberty:
- Sexual organs mature and additional sexual characteristics develop.
- A wide range of emotional changes take place.
- A significant growth spurt and weight gain occur.
- Reproduction becomes possible.

In boys there is no single dramatic event that makes it clear that puberty has started. There is a typical sequence, however. The average age of the onset of puberty is eleven or twelve, but the range is from nine to sixteen. One twelve-year-old boy may be very tall, muscular and have a lot of pubic hair. Another may have just barely started. It seems that a big influence on when a boy starts is related to his family, when his mother and father started puberty. No matter when a boy starts puberty, he may develop rather quickly in a couple of years, or he may develop slowly over five or even more years.

Boys can go through the changes in different order. For most boys the first change to take place is enlargement of the testicles, which starts at age 11 and continues until about age 18. Penis enlargement usually begins about a year later and continues until about age 16. Pubic hair usually does not begin to appear until age 13½, although some 11-year-old boys show signs of early pubic hair. If there are signs of pubic hair development before age 10, a call to the physician is in order. Testosterone, which is responsible for the enlargement of the penis, testicles and growth of pubic hair, is also responsible for the development of axillary and facial hair, voice change, adult body odor, acne and increasing muscle mass at about age 15.

Half of all boys will experience some enlargement of one or both breasts. Commonly there may be a lump and/or even tenderness under one or both nipples. While this can easily be explained on the basis of hormonal changes, it is often very embarrassing. Your son will need your help and support without having undue attention drawn to their condition. For some boys, tender and large breasts inhibit him from doing sports. Obesity may exaggerate the problem to the point some boys have considered cosmetic surgery. Usually the condition resolves itself within a year, but many last two years and even into adulthood.

Soft adult penises are usually between 3¼ and 4¼ inches long. When they are hard, most adult penises vary from four to eight inches long. Some may be shorter or longer. Six inches is the average length of a hard penis. With the onset of puberty, a boy may begin to have erections frequently. This may happen when he is sexually excited or for no reason at all (called a spontaneous erection). These "spontaneous erections" can be particularly embarrassing, but usually go away after a few minutes on their own. Once a boy has his first ejaculation, he is fertile and physically able to father

Sequence of events at puberty	Average Age	Range
Growth of testis	11.5	9.5-13.5
Pubic hair	12.3	9.5-15
Growth of penis	12.5	11.5-14.5
Height spurt	12.5	10.5-16
Auxiliary, facial hair, subareolar breast tissue	14	12-17
Full growth of penis and voice change	15	13.5-16.5
Full growth of testis	16	14.5-18

children. This often occurs for the first time during sleep, which is called a nocturnal emission or "wet dream." (The boy may wake up to this sticky fluid and worry that he has wet the bed.)

Summary of Physical Changes:
- Experience growth spurt between 13 and 14 years old (on average),
- Grow larger ears, hands and feet,
- Grow larger penis and scrotum around 12 years old,
- Develop very sensitive testicles (balls),
- Develop (temporarily) larger and more sensitive breasts (yes, breasts),
- Experience more frequent erections,
- Experience ejaculations and "wet dreams,"
- Develop larger muscles and broader shoulders.

Masturbation

Girls and boys touch their sex organs for pleasure from the time they are babies. The clitoris is designed to give women and girls great pleasure when touched. The penis, especially the tip of the penis, gives men and boys great pleasure when touched. Masturbation, touching our sex organs for pleasure, is a normal, healthy part of life. However, some people choose not to masturbate. And some people are ashamed to admit that they do. Masturbation is not harmful, in any way. It is a healthier outlet for sexual arousal than having sexual intercourse or oral sex before a girl or boy is ready. Many boys masturbate one or two times a day.

Sexual exploration at this time may include mutual masturbation and other homosexual encounters. This shouldn't be construed as correlating with homosexuality. These homosexual encounters most often merely reflect a time of experimentation with new feelings and a new drive.

Relationships

The emotional changes of puberty appear to parallel physical changes. In their early teen years, boys compare their secondary sexual changes, like penis growth and pubic hair with those of other boys. These body changes become a major preoccupation.

Attaining independence from parents is a necessary and central task of adolescence. As boys decrease their dependence on their parents, they increase their dependence on others. For some, these "others" are exclusively their peers. What is best is if they have other adults to turn to for this new support they need: youth

leaders, teachers, counselors, neighbors, etc. Initially the peers boys hang out with are other boys. Eventually they start dealing with the struggle of dealing with girls. Dealing with feelings of sexual drive, attaining some social sophistication and relating to members of one's own peer group about sexual matters all become areas of concern for the teenager. Those emotionally immature boys and girls enter intense relationships to feel good and appear mature. There is little concern about the feeling of the partner and such relationships are often intense and short-lived. The onset of a mature heterosexual relationship does not come about until the end of adolescence or even later. For this to happen, a boy needs to realize a degree of autonomy and develop caring feelings for another.

The parents must support the move toward independence. On the other hand, if a child feels he is being pushed too fast by what he sees in the media and what his peers say they are doing, he might feel anxiety, loneliness and abandonment. A boy may guard himself against these feelings by not truly achieving the necessary independence. If he acts impulsively and pushes boundaries too far, it forces intensive parent involvement with a crack down on rules to reel him back in. Another way a boy might manifest problems with separation is in the way he handles going off to college or breaking up with a girlfriend. He might panic or get depressed. Feelings of abandonment are acute and are often dealt with in a self-destructive fashion.

Summary of Emotional Changes
- Experience moodiness:
  - o For females, changes in their estrogen levels can cause mood swings,
  - o For males, changes in their testosterone levels can cause mood swings.
- Are concerned about how their bodies look, how other people look and how they compare to self, and what other people think in general
- Feel awkward or embarrassed, especially in times of change
- Feel sexual attraction and arousal very easily
- Experience sexual curiosity and attraction in other people (like crushes!)
- Usually become more emotional and react to situations more intensely than before
- Typically try to gain more independence from parents.

Surviving Puberty: A Handout for Your Son
by Kathy Masarie, MD

Puberty can be challenging if you are not prepared for what is happening to your body and either don't have someone you can reliably turn to for advice or are uncomfortable talking about it. Here are some guidelines to help:

1. Look for information you need to understand what is happening to your body.
   * Ask questions of people you trust.
   * Check out the web:
     www.teenwire.org; www.iwannaknow.org/puberty/boys.html; www.frombirthtopuberty.com
   * Look up information in books such as *The "What's Happening to My Body?" Book for Boys: A Growing-Up Guide for Parents & Sons* by Area Madaras and Lynda Madaras.
   * Call your local Planned Parenthood health center at 1-800-230-PLAN.

2. Respect your body. What are you going to do about alcohol, drugs, cigarettes, and other addictive stuff?
   * Smoking, using drugs and drinking alcohol harm your body and can lead to illness and early death.
   * If you love junk food, eat it infrequently and in moderation. Two slices of pizza with a side salad is healthier than four pieces of pizza.
   * If you must lose weight, do it sensibly. Eat several reasonably sized meals a day. Studies show that people who skip breakfast end up eating more overall than those who don't.
   * Exercise 3-4 times a week. Walking is great and easy.

3. Accept the changes you see in your body. Try not to compare yourself with others. Know that everyone goes through puberty at his or her own rate.

4. If you are feeling down or confused about something, talk to somebody. Don't suffer in silence.

5. Your parents can give you a lot of support and information if you give them a chance. They are more interested in your well-being than anyone.

6. **Wait to have sex until you are ready. Don't be pushed into it.**
   * Sometimes, it seems that having sexual intercourse is more important than anything else. It isn't.
   * Sometimes, it seems that having sexual intercourse will solve all our problems. It won't.
   * Sometimes, people have sexual intercourse before they're ready and when they don't really want to. It's not worth it.
   * We have to remember the risks of sex, and especially unsafe sexual behaviors, no matter what people say, no matter how "turned on" we are. An accidental pregnancy can change everything. Getting a serious sexually transmitted disease can damage your health for the rest of your life.
   * Before things get really sexy, or you feel pressured, take time to think about your dreams and plans for the future. Think about what they mean to you. Then ask yourself and your partner if you are ready. If not, then cool down.
   * Sex can be exciting, satisfying, caring and rewarding—especially when you plan ahead and wait until you're ready for it. If you know what you're doing, and if you stay in charge, you can feel empowered.

How I Dealt with My Teenager's Sexuality

By Jody Bellant Scheer, MD

PARENTING IS FULL OF surprises and awakenings. Just as kids grow and change, parents must grow and change to keep up. Providing our kids with the experiences and knowledge they need to succeed in contemporary culture is a challenge parents must constantly face. Teenage sexuality is probably one of the most emotional challenges a parent will face in trying to balance one's own values, wishes and desires with those of our kids and with the realities of the world. Our kids live in a sexualized culture, unprecedented in any previous era. The media and teenage peer culture encourage ever-younger kids to experiment with sexual intercourse without stable relationships, marriage, contraception, safe sex or even emotional attachments. Rates of pregnancy and sexually transmitted diseases, including AIDS, occur in our culture's teenagers at rates far above those of any other developed country in the world. Faced with my own three teenagers' developing sexuality, I turned to my medical training background and experience with positive parenting. Now that they are young adults, they admit they're thankful for how I approached this subject, even though it did make them uncomfortable many times.

My approach to sexuality differed little from any other aspect of my parenting, other than it made me a lot more uncomfortable! However, I was committed to talking about sexuality and all of its ramifications, so I made it a priority to start talking about sex with my kids from the time they were little. As they approached puberty, I often brought up such discussions as we watched movies or TV shows together, where sexual behaviors were shown or hinted at. I made sure to provide my kids with accurate information about their bodies, puberty and sexual function, and I shared my values and opinions with them. Since I deal with the ramifications of unprotected and unsafe sex daily in my job, I shared stories from my work as well.

Finally, though, each of my kids started a dating life and each one of them, at some point in high school, developed a steady relationship. How different it was for me when it came time to deal with a potential sexual relationship, rather than a hypothetical one, and I needed all the positive parenting skills I could muster. Though this approach was diametrically opposed to the way I was raised, I was convinced that making my children's sexuality their own business AND responsibility was the best way to ensure that they would make sensible and healthy decisions.

My strategy was simple. First, I shared my own values, which included the opinion that intercourse is an adult behavior that carries with it a host of benefits, risks and responsibilities. I acknowledged the pleasures of sexual relationships. I also outlined what I considered the minimum of sexual responsbility: some sort of committed relationship, sharing of important sexual history (such as sexually transmitted diseases), testing for HIV, use of contraceptives, making plans in the event of an unplanned pregnancy, and being responsible about getting and paying for adequate medical and reproductive healthcare. People who were not responsible, or who couldn't talk with their partners about these details, were not ready for sex.

Secondly, I reiterated that I respected that my kids would and could make their own decisions about sex. I conceded that, although I didn't think they were ready at the time, they might feel otherwise. I noted that while I respected their ability to choose to become sexually active, I did not exempt them from being responsible about their sexuality. I talked about the many ways to be sexual without incurring the risks of intercourse. I also reminded my kids that the results of their sexual activities affected their lives way more than mine. I asked them to think wisely before acting.

Lastly, I explained that while adults can make independent decisions, and their sexual activity was none of my business, it really was my business to know about any sexually active kids who lived under my roof and who depended on me for their economic, emotional and bodily welfare. Part of becoming an adult is being accountable for one's actions. I did ask my kids to confide in me if they were thinking a relationship might be turning sexual. (Contrary to our society's puritanical myths, I believe that most couples KNOW when they are in a relationship on the verge of sexual intercourse.) I wanted to know that they had carefully considered this step and had been responsible in planning for it.

This approach has worked very well. It even scared off a suitor or two, when I included them in our "family discussions." Responsibility and respect around sexual behaviors must be taught, and the lessons are best learned at home in communication with parents. The payoff of this approach for me is my three healthy young adult children, who, to the best of my knowledge, have been responsible, safe and respectful in their significant relationships.

What If My Son Is Gay, Bisexual, Transgendered or Transsexual?

By Jody Bellant Scheer, MD

WHAT DOES A PARENT do if they know or suspect their son is gay, bisexual, transsexual or transgendered? How does a parent move beyond their own shock, disbelief, sorrow, fear or anger when their son questions his sexuality? These are questions that haunt many parents, because in every culture, between 10-12% of all people do find themselves to be lesbian, gay, bisexual, transsexual or transgendered (also known as GLBT).[1,2,3] In reality, this means that one out of every four families will have an immediate family member who has an alternative sexual orientation.[3] Commonly, after a GLBT child discloses his/her sexual orientation or confusion, parents find themselves suffering from guilt, depression and disappointment, and may be unwilling to accept the reality of their children's sexuality. This process is akin to grieving, during which one must shift an expected and accepted view of your child to a new one that is more honest, but which is tainted with fears, stigma and prejudice. It is helpful to step back a bit during this process and ask yourself what is more important to you: loving and accepting your gay, bisexual, transsexual or transgendered (GBT) son as he is, or loving and accepting only your idealized image of your son. This sets the stage for allowing yourself to give your son what he really needs and wants as he navigates the challenges of adolescence: your love and support.

GLBT adolescents have an especially hard time navigating the teen years safely. They must explore and establish their core identities in a hostile environment, where the stigma of alternative sexual orientation deprives them of healthy role models, and where rejection, violence and harassment (verbal, sexual and physical) are commonplace. GLBT youngsters find themselves very lonely and isolated, and often think that there is no one who understands them or who can help them sort through their sexual feelings. GLBT youth are at higher risk than other youth for suicide, sexual abuse, teen pregnancies, substance abuse, depression, anxiety, homelessness, violence, promiscuity and prostitution. These stressors only add to the already high distress typically created as kids this age experiment, explore, take risks, seek peer approval and individuate.

It is a great act of unconditional love to work with your son to explore and understand his sexual identity, and it may save his life to do so. Dr. Pollack, in his book *Real Boys* states, "If we want to help boys when they are uncertain of their sexuality, if we want to show them that we love them no matter what they discover about themselves, if we want them to feel positive about who they are as young people and as adults, I believe that the most helpful thing we can do is teach all of our boys, gay or not gay, that homosexuality is nothing to fear and nothing to hate. We need to help our sons, in particular, to puncture old myths about homosexuality and teach them that no matter what their sexual orientation may be, they can be successful, strong, happy, 'real' men."[1]

With this in mind, I would like to discuss alternative orientations as variations of normal sexual development and how proposed treatments to 'cure' homosexuality can cause more harm than good. I will discuss the process of normal adolescent sexual identity development for GBT boys and how a boy's disclosure of his alternate orientation can affect family dynamics. Finally, I will discuss the special challenges and difficulties experienced by GBT adolescents and how parents can help themselves and their sons to learn effective coping skills.

Alternative Gender Identities Are Variations of Normal Sexuality

Gender identity, already discussed in detail in my previous article on masculinity, consists of core gender identity, sex role identity and sexual partner orientation. About 10-12 % of all people in all cultures will have GLBT gender identities, so it is easy to conclude that these are simply variations of normal sexual development amongst human beings.[1,4] This concept is supported by a growing body of scientific literature that suggests that GLBT gender identities are inborn or set in place very early in development.[1,4,5] There is no evidence that gender identity is created by parental inadequacies, sexual abuse, coercion, or personal choice.[1,4,5,6] Most heterosexuals testify that their gender identity tends to form with very little conscious thought, and certainly not by choice. GLBT individuals tell us much the same. However, developing a healthy and viable alternative sexual identity does tend to be a draining, secretive and lonely process for GLBT young people, due to the cultural stigmatization involved.[1,2,6]

Reparative Therapy and Transformational Ministry Can Be Harmful

Reparative (or conversion) therapy is a form of psycho-therapy aimed at eliminating homosexual desires and is used by people who think homosexuality is a mental disorder, and as such, think that it can be "cured."[2,3] This is currently a position that is actively opposed by the official American Associations of Medicine, Pediatrics, Psychiatry, Psychology, Social Work, and Counseling for a variety of reasons.[4] Sexual conversion therapy has not proven to be successful and is associated with numerous long-term harmful effects.[4,5] Reparative therapy can create even more confusion and anxiety for GLBT individuals by reinforcing the negative thoughts and emotions with which they are already struggling.[5] Reparative therapy does not help patients to see that a happy, fulfilling life can be achieved with an alternative sexual orientation, and it does not help a person develop appropriate coping strategies.[4,5]

Likewise, Transformational Ministry is the use of religion to eliminate homosexual desires.[4] This movement began in the 1970's in conservative Christian denominations who felt that religious faith and GLBT sexuality were incompatible.[4] This movement is not broadly accepted in religious institutions, many of whom openly accept gay parishioners with messages of love and acceptance.[4] As well, many GLBT people maintain an active and deep religious faith, and find comfort in their spiritual beliefs. Transformational ministry may help some people repress their sexual orientation, but it is no more successful at "curing" homosexual desires than reparative therapy.[4] However, it can be even more damaging to an individual's self-esteem if they truly come to believe that their God would somehow have made them in a way that is undeniably despicable. This only adds to the isolation, despair and stigmatization of GLBT persons attempting to achieve a healthy sexual identity.

Sexual Identity Development in GLBT Adolescents

Researchers, Caitlin Ryan and Donna Futterman, explain that "Adolescence is a time of exploration and experi-mentation; as such, sexual activity does not necessarily reflect either present or future sexual orientation."[7] Confusion about sexual identity or orientation is common among teenagers, and this often manifests in a variety of exploratory sexual activities during this time.[7] "Many youth engage in same-sex behavior: attractions or behaviors do not mean that an adolescent is lesbian or gay. Moreover, sexual activity is a behavior, whereas sexual orientation is a component of identity. Many teens experience a broad range of sexual behaviors that are incorporated into an evolving sexual identity, consolidated over a period of time."[7]

The process by which most adolescents come to develop a GLBT identity is usually painful and anxiety producing.[2] Moreover, claiming a GLBT identity may take many years beyond adolescence for many people.[2] The average age of self-identification as GLBT appears to be dropping in recent years, from an average of 19-23 years some years ago to approximately 16 years of age currently.[7] The age of first awareness of homosexual attraction is also dropping, from 13-16 years of age previously to 9-10 years currently.[6] Studies also show that between 1 and 6% of 7th- to-12th-graders describe themselves as GLBT, with the numbers increasing as students get older.[6] Uncertainty about sexual orientation is also common and declines with age (26% of 12-year-olds and 5% of 17-year-olds, respectively).[6] Developing a sexual self-concept is a key task of adolescence[6] and the process of establishing a sexual identity for most GLBT adolescents is characterized by extreme emotional turmoil—due to the guilt, uncertainty and isolation that most of these children feel.[7] Parents can better understand their GBT sons if they familiarize themselves with the following six stages of sexual self identification that all children go through:

Stage 1: Identity Confusion: during this phase, there is a lot of confusion, questioning and search for information. School librarians note that books on alternative sexual orientation tend to disappear all the time without being checked out.[2]

Stage 2: Identity Comparison: at this stage, individuals accept that there is a possibility that their homosexual/alternative feelings might be a part of themselves. There is still a lot of questioning, denial and rationalizing. The task here is to deal with the alienation that occurs when a teen becomes aware of his/her difference from others, senses his/her not belonging to the greater peer group, and feels isolated and alone.[2] Middle school students in this stage are especially vulnerable due to their overwhelming need to belong.

Stage 3: Identity Tolerance: the child moves toward his first statements of "I am GLBT." This movement towards GLBT identity resolves some of the turmoil of earlier stages, but creates a greater comparison between self and others. This usually occurs when adolescents are at an age where they need lots of peer support and approval, so this can be very trying. GLBT teens at this stage often scrutinize their every move in order to guard their secret. They may become asexual, try to change themselves by having sex with the opposite sex, have covert relationships, or give way to impulsive, unsafe acts such as unprotected sex. Positive gay experiences are crucial at this stage to the development of some degree of self-acceptance instead of self-hatred.[2]

Stage 4: Identity Acceptance: the adolescent accepts that he/she is GLBT and looks for increased contact with other GLBT people. This can be a difficult task for some teens, especially in small towns. Social isolation can be nearly unbearable in this stage. Many teens will leave home, run away, move to urban settings, and drop out of school at this phase. Support groups and counseling can be of great help in this stage.[2]

Stage 5: Identity Pride: adolescents develop a strong identification with gay sub-culture and may devalue heterosexuality. This stage is very difficult for school age adolescents, due to their dependency and the reality of their circumstances.[2]

Stage 6: Identity Synthesis: one moves from an "us and them" mentality to a less rigid, less polarized view of the world. Similarities of homosexuality and heterosexuality are accepted, and behaviors are more inclusive and cooperative. A healthy, hopeful view of life as a GLBT adult develops. Again, this is a difficult stage to accomplish for school-aged adolescents.[2]

Coming Out (A Boy's Disclosure of his Alternative Sexual Identity)

A boy will choose to tell you about his feelings of being GBT when he feels ready to be honest with you and when he has the courage to withstand what will almost always turn into some kind of family crisis.[2,4,5,8] What he fears most is rejection, disappointment, stigmatization or violence from the people he loves the most: his parents and family. That is why, most commonly, GBT adolescents will disclose their sexual identity first to other GBT peers, then to close heterosexual friends, other close family members and lastly to siblings and parents.[4] Fears of rejection and violence are well-founded: 46% of GLBT youth in one study were rejected by heterosexual peers after coming out,[6] and 20% of GLBT youth in another

study reported physical violence at the hands of family after disclosing of their sexual orientation.[9] For these reasons, it is imperative that adolescents be thoughtful regarding the costs and consequences of disclosing sexual orientation to others.[2] Likewise, parents will need to allow their GBT son full control over deciding when and to whom to come out. If you suspect that your son is GBT, it is also best to wait for your child to bring the issue up with you.[3] This might be facilitated by taking the time to educate yourself on GLBT issues, and by initiating thoughtful general discussions that affirm your support for all young people, regardless of sexual orientation. Counseling may be especially helpful for adolescents (and families) during this period of time.

It is important for parents to realize that your GBT son is the same person he always was, and your new understanding of him won't change that.[8] If you are a loving and caring parent, your understanding of your child's sexual orientation should improve your relationship with him.[8] Whether that happens or not depends on you. "This new revelation can be a starting point for a whole new level of parent-child interaction and closeness, or it can be a point of contention and argument. It all depends on how accepting you choose to be."[8]

A child's coming out does impose a whole new array of feelings, emotions, fears and stigmas on families. Parents often have difficulty accepting their teen's homosexuality for some of the same reasons that the adolescent wants to keep it secret.[5] Parents may be unprepared for long periods of uncertainty and exploration by adolescents who are unclear about their sexual orientation (i.e., sons who are in stages 1 or 2 of sexual identity formation).[2] Families may be newly faced with a confusing array of questions about setting appropriate limits on behaviors of their GBT adolescents (such questions arise as, are sleepovers OK? Or, are younger children safe with my son? etc.[2] One of the best places to find support for yourself is from other parents who have lived through what you are going through. PFLAG (Parents, Families and Friends of Lesbians and Gays, Inc.) is a non-profit organization with a website (www.pflag.org) and local chapters in most states. Their mission is to educate and support families and GLBT individuals, as well as to create a society where diversity is celebrated and where everyone is embraced.[3]

Special Risks of Having an Alternative Sexual Orientation

One of the wonderful benefits of knowing about your son's alternative sexual orientation is that you can be an advocate for him while he manages a stigmatized identity within his community. GLBT adolescents face higher risks than do their heterosexual peers of psychological disturbances, self-destructive behaviors and victimization with violence.[6] They live in a largely homophobic world: 69% of GLBT youth experience anti-gay abuse, 40% suffer from physical violence due to their sexual orientation, and they are five times as likely as heterosexual youth not to attend school due to fear.[7] Gay slander is used commonly in our society against anything disliked or undesirable, highlighting the devaluing of anything associated with being gay.[6] On average, a GLBT student will hear 25 anti-gay slurs per day.[6,7] It is no wonder that so many GLBT youth drop out of school or do poorly academically.

Health risks are also elevated. The suicide risk for GLBT youth is high: 30% of completed youth suicides in America are among GLBT youngsters, 42% of all GLBT adolescents have attempted suicide, and GLBT youth attempt suicide four times as often as their heterosexual peers.[7] In addition, GLBT youth are at higher risk than heterosexual youth for sexual abuse, having intercourse before age 14, having frequent sex with members of both sexes, being both pregnant and having multiple pregnancies (girls), using no contraceptives or condoms, and being involved in prostitution.[6,10] HIV infection and AIDS are definite risk factors for GLBT youth having unprotected sex. Currently, 20% of all AIDS cases are occurring in young people who acquired their infections as teens.[1] Substance abuse occurs in GLBT youth at rates 35% higher than in their peers.[7] Perhaps most sadly, GLBT youth commonly face hostility and harm in their own homes: 48% of GLBT youth run away from home or are thrown out, 40% of all homeless youth are GLBT, and 20% of GLBT youth have been physically assaulted in the home.[9,11]

The extra risks suffered by GLBT youth cannot be attributed to homosexuality itself, but rather to society's misunderstandings of homosexuality.[1] Dr. Pollack, author of *Real Boys* summarizes: "The stereotypes and stigmas that burden gay people ... lead many adults to develop irrational fears about gay people and even to hate them for no rational reason. I have found that this homophobia—not homosexuality itself—is what makes the lives of gay people so difficult."[1] Facing the humiliation of society's homophobia with the help and support of a family standing behind and beside him can provide a GBT adolescent with an important framework upon which to build self-esteem, and healthy behaviors.[7] What better reward could there be for a parent who,

having worked hard to rise above their own issues of homophobia, than becoming a cherished lifelong source of unconditional support for their son?

What Parents Can Do To Help Their GBT Sons

As William Pollack emphasizes the most important thing that parents can do for a GBT son is to remind him of their love for him. "Acceptance is critical to not losing your gay son ... either emotionally or physically."[1] "If a boy is given the love and support he so desperately needs at this crucial time, if he is assured that his sexual orientation will never change the way he is thought of or how much he is cared about, [parents will be] doing the best thing they can to restore his sense of self worth, to preserve his faith that you can be trusted even with his most challenging feelings and struggles, and ensure that his adult romantic relationships, whether gay or straight, will be as happy, healthy and fulfilling as possible."[1]

However, this is easier said than done for many parents. What if you, as a parent, have already reacted with words of shame, pain, or anger? What if you feel you could have done a better job of supporting your son in his disclosure to you? How can you support your son if you are in an overwhelming stage of grief yourself? In all these cases, it is very helpful to first educate yourself as best you can about gender issues and alternative sexual orientations.[1] Read books, do research on the Internet and talk with other parents or a family counselor. Being able to recognize your own feelings and issues around the subject of homosexuality and gender identity is an important first step to learning how these emotions are affecting the way you are treating your son.[1]

Steven Covey, in his book *The Seven Habits of Highly Effective People*, states, "Begin with the end in mind."[12] Consider what kinds of messages you want your son to gain from your conversations and make sure that your message of love and concern comes first. Don't be afraid to apologize for your own behaviors or comments. It is always all right to be honest about your own emotions and thoughts, even if they are negative, if you also identify what it is that you want for your son, and what you will do to achieve that. For example, you can identify your own disappointment and fear over the news of his homosexuality, as long as you also share with your son that the reason you are afraid is that you worry he won't have a safe and happy life, and that you commit to working with him to find ways to achieve happiness. Your fears will undoubtedly be very similar to the ones that your son shares, and to know he has an ally in facing them will be a godsend. This formula will

likely not work if your wants and actions are judgmental or self-centered (for example: you are worried what the neighbors, the boss, or your friends will think, so you will demand that this secret stays within the family!). Again, it is very helpful to spend some time understanding your own thoughts, feelings, and motivations before setting a course of action. This is an excellent way to line up your values with your actions, and to work on continuing an honest and loving relationship with your son.

Finally, be sure to protect your son. Make sure that he is safe in his current school; if not, help him to find an alternative education. Support school-based interventions such as diversity training and peer support groups. Get to know the GLBT resources in your own community, and refer your son to these. Address safe sex with your son: you may strongly emphasize abstinence, but your son's life and health depend on having access to accurate and responsible sexual information.[12] Listen to your son compassionately and regularly. Listen to your own words, and refrain from gay-bashing statements or remarks. Recognize that you are responsible for your own negative feelings, and seek professional help for yourself or anyone in your family who needs help diffusing them.[3] Develop trust and openness with your son by allowing him to discover and choose his own lifestyle and sexual identity.[3] Support loving relationships within your own family and for your son.[3] Defend him from anti-gay discrimination and don't forget to say "I love you" often.[3] The goal of unconditional positive regard for all human beings is a noble one for mankind, but it is an especially challenging and rewarding one for parents to practice with their sons who are gay, bisexual, transsexual or transgendered.

Resources:
[1] *Real Boys: Rescuing our Sons from the Myths of Boyhood*, by William Pollack, PhD, 1998, Henry Holt and Co., New York, NY.
[2] "Counseling Issues with Gay and Lesbian Adolescents," by Janet Fontaine and Nancy Hammond, *Adolescence*, Vol. 31, 12/02/96. Reprinted on the website of youth.org, a site run by volunteers and created to help self-identifying gay, lesbian, bisexual and questioning youth. See www.youthorg/loco/PERSONProject/Resources/OrganizingResourcescounseling.html
[3] From the website of PFLAG, Inc., the national organization of Parents, Families and Friends of Lesbians and Gays, 1726 M. Street, NW Suite 400, Washington, DC 20036, www.pflag.org
[4] "*Just the Facts about Sexual Orientation and Youth: A Primer for Principals, Educators and School Personnel.*" Reprinted by the American Psychological Association at its website: www.apa.org/pi/lgbc/publicationsjustthefacts.html.
[5] "Gay and Lesbian Adolescents," January 2002, American Academy of Child and Adolescent Psychiatry Facts for Families, #63, www.aacap.org/publications/factsfam/63.html
[6] "Lesbian, Gay, Bisexual and Transgender Youth Issues," from SIECUS Report, Vol. 29, No. 4, April/May 2001. Reprinted by the Sexuality Information and Education Council, at its website: www.siecus,org/pubs/factfact0013.html
[7] "Lesbian and Gay Adolescents: Identity Development," by Caitline Ryan, MSW and Donna Futterman, MD, 1998. Reprinted on the website of The Prevention Researcher, where in depth research is presented on at risk youth, at www.tpronline.org
[8] "My Child is GAY! Now What Do I Do?" by Scott Bidstrup at www.bidstrup.com/pardata.htm
[9] "Issues for Gay and Lesbian Adolescents," by Richard Niolan, PhD at www.psychpage.com
[10] "Gay, Lesbian, Bisexual, Transgender Youth Suicide," by Laurie Lindop, reprinted at www.healthyplace.com
[11] "Working with Gay, Lesbian and Bisexual Youth," reprinted on the website of the Long Island Crisis Center, at www.licrisiscenter.org/comm.htm
[12] "Sexuality and Adolescents: A Handout for Parents" by Richard Staples, CAGS, reprinted at the website of the National Mental Health and Educational Center, at www.naspcenter.org

The Nature of Boys' Friendships

"Start with action and energy, throw in loyalty, laughter, and 'doing together.' Add covert verbal expressions of caring, earnestness and hidden physical touching—and you get a good friend."

— Author William Pollack, PhD, *Real Boys*

- Boys play and socialize in packs or tribes.
- Boys typically have "side-by-side" relationships, using action-oriented behavior to express their connection to other boys.
- Boys engage in active competitive games, with set rules and procedures to enhance camaraderie.
- Boys use nonverbal bonding and affectionate insults.
- Pecking order is important to boys.
- Humor is used to gain popularity.
- The top three popularity traits[2] in boys are: 1) sports; 2) stature; and 3) humor.

The Nature of Girls' Friendships

"Female friendship is most of all about sharing who we are....
It doesn't matter to me what I do with my friend, as long as I am with her."

—Janet F. Quinn, Nurse, Professor, Researcher.

- Girls are relationship-oriented, concerned more than boys with their standing among friends.
- Girls tend to socialize in pairs which exist within larger cliques.
- Girls have "face-to-face" relationships, where they center their play around talking and socializing within a small circle of friends.
- Friendships solidify via shared confidences and feelings.
- Girls need constant reassurance from one another that they look good and fit in.
- Girls are swayed by their friends more easily than boys are[1].
- The top three popularity traits[2] in girls are: 1) looks; 2) clothes; and 3) charisma.

[1] Interview with Dianne Hales on peer pressure, *Daughters*, Vol. 6, No. 5, July 2001.
[2] Michael Thompson found one study that showed the top three traits of popular 4th grade boys and girls. Those traits are listed in the nature of boys' and girls' friendships above.

Boys and Their Friendships

By Kathy Masarie, MD

CLOSE FRIENDSHIPS ARE extremely important for boys. This may seem contrary to gender stereotypical ideas of what male friendships may look like, but William Pollack, author of *Real Boys, Rescuing our Sons from the Myths of Boyhood*, finds that boys yearn for friendships with other boys. These friendships operate under different parameters and are demonstrated differently than girls' friendships. He suggests that we analyze boy's friendships differently than those of girls, as the standards for intimacy and attachment are quite different.

It is common knowledge that boys have public, action-oriented relationships with one another. Boy friendships tend to thrive in active, competitive play with clearly established rules. Teasing and arguing are part of the play but do not hold the same meaning as these actions would in girl friendships. A well-developed sense of fairness governs the play. Through competitive, rowdy play, boys become intimate with one another as well as develop a stronger sense of self.

Pollack asserts that boys also have intimate, private relationships with other boys. Boys express their natural empathy in different ways than girls do. This may involve a male friend cheering them up or even teasing them for feeling down. Direct expressions of sympathy are avoided in order not to appear condescending. Privacy is key to these relationships in order for boys to avoid the possibility of shame and embarrassment.

Pollack refers to the "unwritten rules of masculinity" that guide boys' development. Boys live in fear of being perceived as feminine, weak, dependent, sad or homosexual. Consequently, boys must be very careful how they express emotions with one another, how they express physical affection and/or say caring words to each other.

Pollack also discusses his findings that young pre- and adolescent boys are capable of forming important platonic friendships with girls. These relationships are crucial for boys' emotional support and good for their self-esteem. With girls, a boy can experience a "safe space" to break the boy code of toughness, express himself openly and just be who he is. These platonic relationships help boys learn to be "bilingual in gender, able to hear and speak the feminine with the same empathy and comfort as they speak and hear the masculine."

Parents who openly share their stories of friendships with boys when they were young, can help encourage their son to seek similar healthy relationships in his own life.

It is worth reading the entire chapter of "The World of Boys and Their Friendships" in William Pollack's book *Real Boys* for an insightful look at critical ingredients of boys' friendships and to gain understanding from a boy's point of view. *Stand By Me* is a great movie for you and your son to see.

To Summarize with Two Quotes from *Real Boys:*

"So it seems that boys may follow their own formula for friendship: start with action and energy, throw in loyalty, laughter and 'doing together.' Add covert verbal expressions of caring, earnestness, and hidden physical touching—and you get a good friend." (p.195)

"Boys and men have had to learn to walk a fine line: to have intimacy without sentimentality, closeness without long conversations, empathy without words. Once we can read this code of boys' friendships, we can see that boys on a soccer field are engaged in sociable activity, building friendships that matter." (p. 198)

Supporting Healthy Friendships

By Kathy Keller Jones, MA

As PARENTS, IT IS normal to be invested in our children's friendships. We all want our kids to be well-liked. Some of us even venture into wanting our kids to be popular. One thing that is very true for our children is that every one of them is unique. What attracts them to one kid and not another is sometimes a mystery.

Suggestions:
- **Your kids will choose their own friends.**
- **If you don't like a friend or friends they choose, find ways to spend time with those kid(s).** You may start to see what your child sees and actually like them. You may have a good influence on them and be a person they turn to. You can encourage them to play at your house.
- **If you are worried about the negative influence of a friend, do the same as above and really strive to keep communication open with your child.** Under some circumtances with younger children, you may restrict play to your house and school.
- **When your child has a fight with a friend, listen attentively and with caring and empower your child to solve his/her problem.** Focus on support rather than rescue. You are your child's consultant and they need to feel free to come to you when they are feeling overwhelmed by any size problem.
- **If your child and a friend get in trouble, make sure you are calm and have remembered that mistakes are great learning opportunities before you help with processing the situation.** Be empathetic about the fact that they have a problem and support them in making amends and experiencing logical consequences.
- **There is no right number of friends. Some kids will have one or two and others will have more than they can handle.**
- **When your child says, "no one will play with me," listen very carefully and allow space for the story to unravel. Often kids exaggerate from one kid who wouldn't play with them that one day to "I don't have any friends." Remind them that every day is a new day.**

Prevention Strategies
- Teach your child to be friendly and fair to everyone and to use the Golden Rule.
- If your child has trouble making friends, expose them to new and different environments. You may find a child who doesn't do well in a crowded school does extremely well in scouts or a youth group.
- Don't force your child to play with your friend's children. It helps if your families spend time together when your children are young so they grow up like cousins, or if you allow the children to bring along other friends who are inclusive.
- Clothing styles are very important to help a child feel comfortable and "fit in." Let them choose the style.
- Stock your place with good food and provide space and acceptance so your kid will hang out with his friends at your house. This is a great investment of energy in the long run.
- Watch your baggage. You may hang onto friends forever, but your child may move on to new ones frequently. Accept his/her style.
- If a parent has a chemical dependency problem, it can make it very difficult for your child to have friends over. The environment can be embarrassing and unpredictable. Get help.
- As they get older, kids need to learn how to be friendly with a peer who tends to get them in trouble. They need to know under what circumstances they can trust that friend and have a good, safe time.
- Clear behavioral expectations are important for all of our children, but especially our sons. Communicate how you expect them to behave at home and wherever they go.
- When your child needs help with social skills, role-playing, rehearsing and direct teaching can be very important, especially in today's times when they are exposed to so much negative modeling.

For more information see the texts listed below.

Resources:
The Friendship Factor by Kenneth Rubin
Best Friends, Worst Enemies by M. Thompson, et. al.
Positive Discipline from A to Z by Jane Nelsen

Peer Pressure

By Kathy Masarie, MD

PEER PRESSURE HAS the potential to be positive or negative. Although we often think of peer pressure in terms of alcohol and drugs during the teen years, peer pressure starts much earlier. When working with students, we often try to get them to use peer pressure to stop such negative behavior as bullying. We also try to get the bystanders to join together and not do what they view everyone else to be doing. However, all children have a need to belong and for some, this need can overpower everything they have been taught about right and wrong.

The best thing a parent can do is to strengthen a child's sense of self and give them the skills to maneuver these tricky situations.

1. Teach decision-making and give them some power. Let them practice making decisions on things that may be important to them, but not you, such as what day to clean their room, what sport to play, and their homework schedule.

2. Help choose their peers! Help them to get involved in groups or clubs with children who have similar interests and involved parents. In each group, there are positive role models.

3. Teach him the social skills to stand up to his friends. Most likely, the first person who tries to get him to break the rules, skip school, or use alcohol is not going to be some stranger down the street or casual acquaintance. It will be a good friend. Teach him how to safely get out of an unsafe situation and still keep a friend. When friends are hinting around about doing something, teach them to ask direct questions and label the behavior: "That's stealing," or "That's against my family rules." Have them feel free to use you as an excuse to exit the situation or suggest something else fun to do.

4. Don't be too critical of his friends. Get to know them first. Remember: the more you criticize, the more interesting the friend becomes.

5. On the other hand, support the friendships you like. Encourage your child to spend more time with children whose families seem to have the same values. And make sure that your children know what you believe in—lead by example, not words. Be clear about what you feel is right and wrong and don't leave anything out.

6. Get to know other parents. The better you know them, the more comfortable you will feel about having your child spend time with them. You will also feel more comfortable calling them with a problem or question.

7. Use natural and logical consequences. It is so much easier than trying to devise a punishment for misbehavior.

8. Be on the job! Always know where your child is and whom they are with. Although this is a given when they are quite young, it is even more important in middle and high school. Children who are supervised and know their parents are interested are better equipped to say "No."

Resources:
"The Peer Problem and Social Pressure," Family Life (10/99) by Steve Biddolph
Best Friends, Worst Enemies: Understanding the Social Lives of Children by Michael Thompson

Relationships with Family, Friends, Self, and Others

By Barbara A. Lewis, author of *What Do You Stand For? A Kid's Guide to Building Character*

"Personal relations are the most important thing forever and ever." —E. M. Forster

YOU MAY HAVE heard or read about the three-year-old boy who fell into a gorilla exhibit at the Brookfield Zoo in Illinois in 1996. Binti Jua, an eight-year-old female gorilla who was carrying her own baby, Koola, on her back, hurried over to the unconscious boy, who had climbed a railing and fallen 18 feet. Binti gently picked him up, cradled him in her arms, and held him. Then she carried him over to the door where the zookeepers could reach him, and carefully placed him on the floor. She continued to protect him from the advances of the other gorillas until help came.

Onlookers were astounded at the seemingly understanding and sensitive behavior of the mother gorilla toward the human boy. Some animal behavior specialists think that Binti might have acted differently if the boy had been running around in a threatening way, because gorillas, while not normally aggressive, will act to defend their territory and their babies. Nevertheless, Binti's behavior sparked a lot of discussion across the country.

It's difficult to know why Binti behaved the way she did, because she can't tell anyone how she felt at the time. Is it possible that Binti protected the boy because she had her own baby and had experienced the mothering instinct? What do you think?

You first learned about loving and caring in your relationship with your parents and family. When you are loved and nurtured, you can love and nurture in return. Babies who aren't loved and nurtured don't grow as well, and sometimes they die. If they live to be adults, they often have a difficult time developing relationships with other people.

You probably received tender loving care from your parents, and you're all set. But what if you didn't? What if your relationships with family members weren't as nurturing as you might have hoped or wanted them to be? Here's good news: You can *learn* to develop good relationships with your family, friends, yourself, and

other. Following are some tips and suggestions you can try:

12 Ways to Start and Strengthen Relationships[1]

1. **Be a person of good character.** When you're positive, honest, loyal, and respectful, other people are naturally drawn to you. They recognize you as someone worth getting to know.

2. **Be kind and caring.** Notice and reach out to other people, especially when they're hurting. *Example:* Your friend is caught cheating on a test and he's embarrassed and ashamed. You might write a note telling him something you admire about him. By doing this, you're not condoning the cheating. Instead, you're letting him know that you still see his good qualities.

"The greatest healing therapy is friendship and love." —Hubert Humphrey

[1] Sometimes people who haven't been loved and cared for need professional help learning how to love and care for others. If you think you might need professional help, talk to an adult you trust—a teacher, school counselor, religious leader, family member, or a friend.

3. **True love is unconditional.** You love your friend even when she makes poor choices. You love your little brother in spite of the fact that he constantly raids your hidden cache of candy. IMPORTANT: Unconditional love doesn't mean that you sacrifice your beliefs or values for another person. You can stay true to yourself and be a true friend.

"If we would build on a sure foundation in friendship, we must love our friends for their sake rather than for our own." —Charlotte Brontë

4. **Be a good listener.** Show that you're interested in other people and their lives. Ask questions about their talents, passions, plans, goals, hopes, dreams, fears, and anxieties; find out what makes them happy or sad. Example: If your sister suddenly starts spending a lot of time alone in her room, try to find out why. She might not be willing to tell you when you first approach her. But if you're patient, persistent, and kind, you'll eventually gain her confidence and she may tell you what's bothering her.

"You can make more friends in two months by becoming interested in other people than you can in two years by trying to get other people interested in you." —Dale Carnegie

5. **Spend time together and share experiences.** As much as you might like and appreciate another person—a parent, sibling, close friend, or acquaintance—your relationship won't grow if you don't do things together and connect in other ways. You might plan special adventures to share—or you might spend quiet time together reading, doing homework, studying, or watching the clouds go by.

6. **Recognize when you have problems with others.** The first step in healing a wound is acknowledging that one exists. But don't just scratch it or put a band-aid on it and hope it will go away. Try to find the cause of the wound. Was it something you said or did? How can you make up for it? Was it something another person said or did? How can you find out what's bothering him or her, and what, if anything, can you do to make things better? What might you do to improve the relationship?

7. **Be willing to compromise.** When you compromise with another person, you *both* get something you want. You might not get *everything* you want, but you reach an agreement that seems fair to everyone involved. *Example:* You're 15, and your dad still wants you to be home each night by 8:30 p.m. You'd like to be able to stay out later. You and your dad sit down together to talk about your curfew. You each express your point of view, and you listen carefully to each other. You agree to a compromise: 8:30 p.m. on school nights (unless there's a school activity), later on Fridays and Saturdays. Neither you nor your dad gets *everything* you want, but you both get *something* you want.

8. **Talk about your feelings**, especially when problems arise. Be assertive. Address the problem without blaming the person. *Example:* A friend borrows $10 from you and doesn't pay it back. You might say "I'm wondering how soon you'll be able to pay back the $10 I loaned to you. I have to buy some books tomorrow and I really need the cash. Could you have the money for me by tomorrow morning?" Or you might say "You're such a loser! You never pay me what you owe me. Don't ever ask me for a loan again!" Which approach is most likely to get your $10 back?

9. **Don't play the blame game.** If you think your parents, siblings, friends, and others have wronged you in any way, try to forgive them. Let it go.

There's a story about an old man who gathered kindling for a living and sold it to others. He was an angry guy who held many grudges. Whenever someone did something mean to him, he wrote the person's name on a stick and put the stick in a sack on his back so he could eventually get even. At night, he'd pull out all the sticks and plan strategies for revenge. Often just thinking about what he might do to get back at someone made him feel better. One day, as he was climbing a hill to collect dead branches from a tree, he lost his balance from the burden of sticks on his back and fell backwards to the bottom of the hill.

Holding grudges can weigh you down. When you let things go, you're free to move on and improve your relationships.

10. **Try not to judge others**, not even when you're absolutely, positively sure that you're right and they're wrong. Nobody's perfect all of the time—not even you. It's your job to improve *yourself*, not everyone else you know.

"Every man should have a fair-sized cemetery in which to bury the faults of his friends."
—Henry Brooks Adams

11. **Expand your circle of friends** to include people who are different from you. Sometimes these friendships can bring the most rewards. You'll learn to see things from a new perspective. You'll become more tolerant and accepting. Your world will grow in many positive ways.

12. **Be friendly.** You might say "But I'm too shy!" Or "Being friendly is too risky. I don't want to get hurt." Many people are shy or go through periods in their lives when they're shy. Being shy is okay. And most people are afraid of getting hurt—so you're not alone. But if you want to be friendlier, here are some tips you can try:

Friendliness starts with a simple "Hello." Say "Hello" (or "Hi" or "How's it going?" or whatever feels comfortable to you) to people you see often, even if you don't know them well. Practice by standing in front of the mirror and watching yourself. Practice on your family. Tell your mom or brother that this is your goal. Try doing it

once a day, then three times, and so on. The more you do it, the easier it gets, like learning to ride a bike.

Reach out to others. Join groups, organizations, and clubs. Sit with someone you usually don't sit with at lunch. Get a pen pal. Call someone on the phone.

Include others. Look for people who are left out of activities and groups and invite them to join you. The more people you're nice to, the more friends you'll have. I know a young man who once ran for president of his high school. He didn't hang out with the popular group, but he always talked to everyone and looked for people who were alone so he could include them. Some students laughed when he ran for school president, but they didn't laugh when he won.

Eye contact. If you look at people when you say "Hi" or talk with them, they'll pay more attention to you. Practice on your family. Practice in the mirror. Try making eye contact with teachers, then with friends, and so on.

Names. Learn and remember them. To most people, the most beautiful sound in the world is the sound of their own name. When you first meet someone new, repeat his or her name. To help you remember it in the future, make up a mnemonic or "hook." *Example:* You're just met someone named Justin Harmon. You might think "*Justin* is *just* and he *harmonizes* well." It's corny, but it works.

Don't focus only on yourself. Think of the person you're with. If you hang a picture of yourself in your window, you can't see through it to the world (and the people) on the other side. Ask questions and listen to the answers.

Smile. Your smile might warm up a person who doesn't know you exist. If you combine your smile with eye contact, you might start a fire of friendship. If you're not used to smiling very much, you may need practice.

Excerpted from *What Do You Stand For? A Kid's Guide to Building Character* by Barbara A. Lewis, copyright © 2005. Used with permission from Free Spirit Publishing Inc., Minneapolis, MN; 1-800-735-7323; www.freespirit.com. All rights reserved.

When Our Kids Fight with Friends
based on the approach of the *Positive Discipline* books by Jane Nelsen
By Glenda Montgomery

ONE OF THE MOST difficult times to be a parent is when we witness our child experiencing the intense emotional pain which is inherent, at times, in human relationships. We all remember that gut-wrenching feeling that accompanies the trauma of fighting with or being rejected by our friends. So, as concerned parents, we will often leap into what I call my "mother bear" mode: bristling, ready to pounce, eager to protect and to rescue. However, as difficult as it is for us, what is most helpful for our children in these times is to allow them to experience the trials, tribulations and challenges that come along with the joys of friendships. Rather than being a rescuing mother bear, we are more helpful and productive long term if we choose the roles of listening heart, coach and cheerleader.

As a listening heart, we listen with empathy, identifying with our child's emotions. We refrain from judging the behavior of our own child or of the other child involved. We refrain from treating our children like victims or they will begin to see themselves as victims. We don't explain other points of view at this point, we just LISTEN. This is extremely hard to do but unless we listen in this respectful way, we will risk losing our child's confidence.

As a coach, we can be available to encourage our children. We can help them to brainstorm some potential solutions or action plans. We can describe some ways we might have approached a similar problem when we were little. We can stimulate creative thought and ways of looking at other points of view. But we cannot force our child to take our advice. We are *available as needed,* but the creation of plans or any action must come from our child, not from us.

As a cheerleader, we can let our children know that we have faith in their ability to confront difficult situations, deal with pain, and be strong enough to withstand rejection. We can celebrate with them when they have successes, and let them know that no matter what, we love them completely.

When we listen, encourage and offer faith in our children's abilities, rather than jumping in and making the problem go away, our children learn that:

- They can handle emotional pain and that it eventually does lessen and go away,
- They can deal with rejection and the whole world does not fall apart,
- They are capable human beings, able to solve friendship problems,
- They can fight with friends AND make up with friends,
- They can stand up for themselves.

This is the time for our children to learn about themselves and the world of human relationships. They need practice and support. Should your child be the victim of bullying, abuse, sexual abuse or racism, you **would** need to step in and take an active role in getting help, as this trouble is beyond a child's ability to manage. However, in cases of normal relationship turmoil, do choose to be a listening heart, a coach and a cheerleader. Keep that "mother bear" at bay and then stand back, allowing your children to build their friendship skills, their problem-solving skills and their faith in themselves.

Reprinted with permission of Glenda Montgomery, parent coach and Certified Positive Discipline Instructor in Portland, OR and mother of a teenage boy and girl. All rights reserved. www.positiveparenting.pdx

Fun Things To Do When You're Alone

By Barbara A. Lewis

"Friendship with oneself is all-important, because without it one cannot be friends with anyone else in the world."
—Eleanor Roosevelt

To *have* a good friend, you must *be* a good friend. And that means with yourself as well as others. Here are some ways to strengthen your relationship with Y-O-U:

- Find a quiet, private place where you can hang out with yourself and just think—an attic, basement, tree, under the porch, under your bed, or in your closet.

- Write in your journal about how you feel about things that happen to you each day or each week. Or write poems, stories, or letters to yourself.

- Dress up in a friend's or parent's clothes, or go to a department store or sports shop and try on clothes you don't normally wear.

- Do something physical. Jog, practice throwing, shoot baskets, kick balls, skate, walk, lift weights, swim, dance, or whatever gets your heart beating and your blood circulating.

- Draw or paint. Copy characters from comic books or the comics section in your local newspaper. Check out books on drawing from your library and practice. Instead of *writing* in your journal, try *drawing* in your journal.

- Surprise your parents and wash the dishes, clean out a closet, or bake a treat.

- Practice a skill you'd like to learn, such as singing, dancing, playing a musical instrument, doing card tricks, or blowing bubbles.

- Make something, such as jewelry, wood carvings, model cars or airplanes, or clothes.

- Read something. Read anything that interests you — books, comic books, encyclopedias, cookbooks, newspapers, magazines,

- Make a time capsule. Bury it in your backyard or hide it on a closet shelf. Plan to dig it up or take it out in five or ten years.

- Lie in your bed, under the clouds, or somewhere you're comfortable and just dream. Listen to soft, soothing music and let your mind wander.

Excerpted from *What Do You Stand For? A Kid's Guide to Building Character* by Barbara A. Lewis, copyright © 2005. Used with permission from Free Spirit Publishing Inc., Minneapolis, MN; 1-800-735-7323; www.freespirit.com. All rights reserved.

Nurturing Emotions and Compassion

1

2

3

4

5

6

7

8

9

10

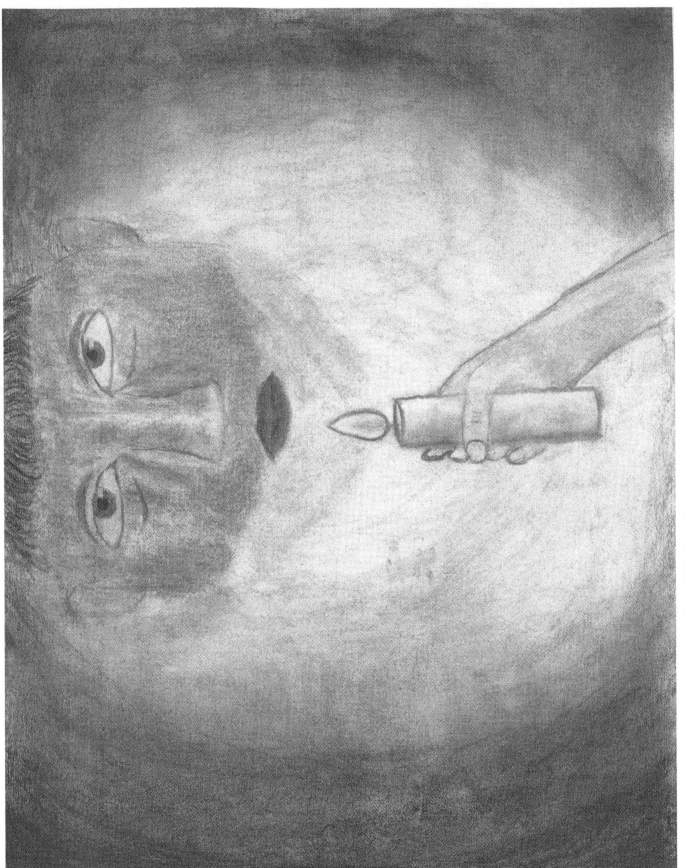

Danny Walinsky, 7th Grader, Rosemont Ridge Middle School

Nurturing Emotions and Compassion

"It is said that, at thirteen, girls lose their voices, but at five, boys lose their hearts."
—Terrance Real, *I Just Don't Want to Talk About It*

"What 'real' boys actually need from infancy forward is complete and unconditional empathy and understanding for a full range of feelings. Love is the core of each and every boy." —William Pollack, *Real Boys*

"Empowered mothers are a key to resolving society's confusion about masculinity and emotion, and creating a new real-boy code. By empowering the mothers, you empower the sons. Mothers help make boys into men."
—William Pollack, *Real Boys*

"To be nobody but yourself—in a world which is doing its best, night and day, to make you everybody else— means to fight the hardest battle which any human being can fight, and never stop fighting." —EE Cummings

"Positive self-esteem operates as, in effect, the immune system of spirit, providing resistance, strength, and a capacity for regeneration." —Nathaniel Brandon

GOALS

- To give parents insight into the unique ways that boys communicate and to offer tools to help them share their feelings

- To recognize the important role of parents in helping their sons express feelings, control their anger, resist impulses, and make friends

- To realize the value of empathy, personal character, friendship, and a place to "be yourself" in developing emotionally secure and productive boys

- To empower our boys with resiliency and healthy self-esteem

OVERVIEW

"Love is the core of each and every boy." Is this really the way most people in our culture view young boys and men? Do our personal experiences and/or the thousands of media images that we are bombarded with each day suggest that the core of masculinity is love? Hardly! However, those of us with sons luckily know that our boys do have a "loving core," although we may tend to see it less and less often as they grow into men. In fact, our culture's masculine training teaches our sons to be distant, stoic, unfeeling, aggressive, even violent, effectively undermining our boys' relational lives.

Cultural Conditioning

Boys are actually very emotional beings. Dr. William Pollack goes into great detail in his book, *Real Boys*, about how this emotional freedom drastically changes or disappears as boys grow up in a culture that encourages male aggression and stoicism. Pollack calls this masculine training the "boy code," where it is culturally taboo for boys to be overtly emotional (unless that emotion is anger or aggression, of course) and where boys are taught to buck up and repress feelings for fear of being ridiculed. This fear guides outward behavior. Boys who are caught up in the "code" or "boy box" are encouraged to be tough, dominant and strong. Boys who do not follow the code are called "sissies" or worse. This fear of shame causes boys to repress emotions and steers young men to silence, solitude and distrust. This results in a society of men who are preconditioned to struggle with their feelings and how to appropriately express them.

Here is a story from Terrance Real's book, *I Don't Want to Talk About It, Overcoming the Secret Legacy of Male Depression* (pages 133-4). It is a chilling story of what goes on in our lives every day and how insidious the lessons are that we inadvertently teach our sons about how to suppress their emotions.

Janie and her sons sit at the dining room table. Janie's husband, Robert, who is fatigued and somewhat depressed, joins them after a long day at the office followed by a hectic commute home. Janie wants to talk to Robert and the boys about their days and hers. Robert wants to "relax," that is, to be left alone. After a few abortive efforts, Janie gives up and, rather than confront Robert, compensates for his lack of interest with redoubled efforts toward the kids. The boys, particularly the oldest, pick up Dad's cue and freeze out their mother with monosyllabic responses. Janie, reluctant to "smother," willing to give her men "their space," eventually amiably withdraws. She putters about the kitchen and cleans up while Robert listens to the news and the boys go off to sports or video games or homework. This transaction is seamless. There occurs, in this family, hardly a ripple of overt discontent. And yet, as Janie and I work together to deconstruct this simple, everyday scene, it begins to seem nothing short of chilling. What have Janie's sons learned about what it means to be a man?

They have learned not to expect their father to attend to them or to be expressive about much of anything. They have come to expect him to be psychologically unavailable. They have also learned that he is not accountable in his emotional absence, that Mother does not have the power either to engage him or to confront him. In other words, Father's neglect and Mother's ineffectiveness at countering it teach the boys that, in this family at least, men's participation is not a responsibility but rather a voluntary and discretionary act. Third, they learn that Mother, and perhaps women in general, need not be taken too seriously. Finally, they learn that not just Mother but the values she manifests in the family—connection, expressivity—are to be devalued and ignored. The subtext message is, "engage in 'feminine' values and activities and risk a similar devaluation yourself." The paradox for the boys is that the only way to connect with their father is to echo his disconnection. Conversely, being too much like Mother threatens further disengagement or perhaps, even active reprisal. In this moment, and thousands of other ordinary moments, these boys are learning to accept psychological neglect, to discount nurture, and to turn the vice of such abandonment into a manly virtue.

The Search Institute has documented this emotional trend in boys in their Developmental Assets research. Boys lag significantly behind girls in more than half of the assets that measure interpersonal skills and social competencies, and do more poorly as they grow older.

Modeling Compassion

Boys who do score high on caring and friendship skills have one commonality: how they were raised. They have learned, usually from their parents and families, to be able to put themselves in other people's shoes. The skills of empathy and compassion are learned through a process of parental modeling and encouragement. Parents who make it a personal priority to help their sons learn interpersonal skills can be enormously effective in helping their boys to be aware of and to connect with their loving core.

Given that Family Empowerment Network is about prevention, how can the seeds of compassion and intimacy be rekindled and encouraged in our own sons? Any parent who wants to raise a compassionate son must first make the commitment and then find ways in their daily life to do so. **"Passionate Parenting...Discovering Your Exceptional Selves"** (p. 5:13), written by a personal development specialist, encourages all parents to focus on and celebrate the exceptional qualities within themselves and their children as a way to enrich their family relationships.

How we parent is one of the important ways that we model respect for feelings and needs. As our children become teens, we can model respect by shifting our parenting style into a "parent coach" style. Diana Sterling's article on her book **"Parent as Coach Approach"** (p. 5:15) introduces us to a model which encourages parents to focus on respecting, listening, understanding, appreciating, and supporting their budding teenager. This will then provide your son with a solid base from which he can know himself, and become increasingly responsible and independent.

Understanding Anger

We know that boys experience a full range of feelings, yet when they are asked to make a list of feelings, boys can often name only three or four rather than the dozens that many of us experience. One phenomenon commonly seen in our nation's boys and men is that of "funneling." Since anger is the one feeling that boys are allowed to express openly, it often becomes the funnel for all the other feelings that boys don't think they can safely express without shame or ridicule. Funneling starts at a very young age. This dynamic gives their anger tremendous power and makes it both frightening because it can lead to violence, and a relief because at least he is expressing something. This coping mechanism continues into adolescence and adulthood, where many men find it difficult to express a full range of emotions other than anger in intense emotional situations.

The article, **"Coping with Anger and Impulsivity"** (p. 5:16) discusses the difficult task of teaching boys to manage these powerful emotions in socially acceptable and healthy ways. Parents can help their sons to do so by helping them to first recognize and name all their feelings. When they do feel anger or impulsiveness, it is important to learn to pause for thinking before lashing out ("Cool Down" and "Think First"). This pause is an essential element in being able to consider the impact one's behavior has on others, and to be accountable in how you choose to direct your response. Boys who are held accountable by their parents for their angry behaviors are more likely to develop socially acceptable forms of emotional release. At times you may feel overwhelmed by the power of your teenage son's anger, coupled with his new size and strength. Remember to avoid either totally backing down and giving in, or getting in numerous angry arguments. Instead, work on shifting the energy back into a respectful place by staying present

Feelings Funnel

from *Boys Will Be Men* by Paul Kivel

but not getting drawn in. When necessary, reschedule the discussion for a time in the immediate future (like after dinner) when you are both calm.

Connecting with Boys

It is important to remember that boys want to be emotional. They want to have close relationships that are both safe and open. They want close relationships with family members and friends of both genders. They long to talk in safe environments that are free from the fear of shame. Boys benefit from being taught how to open up and release the tension that builds up from unspoken emotional repression. They benefit from being "allowed"' to learn how to express themselves, and to do so at their own pace. This is particularly true of boys who have had little success in forging positive solid relationships. Dr. Pollack introduces three communication concepts that we believe can really help parents to connect emotionally with their boys:

1. Action Talk

Boys open up and develop closeness and friendship through action. Pollack suggests that casual interaction with boys in activities leads to a natural development towards a close relationship in which the boy feels safe. Through this security of action, without confrontation, boys are able to open up and a bond develops. Therefore, activities and common interests can be used as a springboard towards healthy emotional bonds.

2. Shame-free Zones

Our boys need places where they can be themselves, and say what they feel without being made fun of by their peers. The obvious first step is to be careful about how we communicate with our sons, especially in front of an audience. For example, avoid confronting them about a "misdeed" in front of anyone, even their siblings, if possible. Another step is to help find groups where they feel comfortable:

- a youth group in your religious organization,
- sports where the coaching is healthy,
- after-school classes in drama, art, pottery (mud club), reading, or chess,
- non-competitive exercise clubs such as weight lifting, running for fun, ultimate Frisbee,
- boys' support group.

If you can't find a place for your son, create one. Running an after-school club can be a blast and a great way to learn about your son's culture. This will be covered in more depth in the last two sessions of the parenting guide.

3. Timed Silence

When something embarrassing or emotionally intense happens to a boy or a man, they often need time to process it silently and alone before they are ready to talk. This is called "timed silence." This is probably one of the most useful techniques for mothers to understand. Mothers have a natural tendency to "pursue" or go after an explanation with vigor when they are worried about their sons. This can have the exact opposite effect of shutting him down. When our sons come home on the verge of tears or upset, we want to know immediately "What's wrong?" It may be best to wait for awhile.

Emotional Intelligence

As Dr. Pollack suggests, part of supporting healthy emotional skills is to help our boys to understand all their feelings and to learn emotional self-control. Boys are born with the capacity for a full range of feelings, yet as they grow older the dictates of masculine training encourage them to express few of them and condones the expression of only one: anger.

The article **"Emotional Intelligence: Helping Children to Work with Feelings Not Against Them"** (p. 5:20) discusses how parents can work with their sons to recognize their feelings and cultivate their "emotional intelligence." Emotional intelligence is the ability to sense someone's emotions and to respond accordingly. It is critical for success and happiness in life. Daniel Goleman, author of *Emotional Intelligence*, provides a synthesis of brain and behavioral research and concludes that our emotional intelligence or "EQ" may be *more important* than our IQ. Our brains develop emotional abilities long before cognitive abilities. As a result, our emotions often take a leading role (without much thought) in our behaviors. Three factors make up a person's EQ and are consistent with much of the research about the characteristics of healthy self-esteem:

- self-awareness (an ability to step back from emotions and experiences and analyze them),

- self-discipline (an ability to withstand emotional storms and to think before acting),
- empathy (an ability to understand how another person feels).

The ability to delay gratification is a critical part of emotional intelligence and a life skill which can be difficult to learn in today's consumer culture. We can help our children practice this skill by having realistic expectations and challenging children to wait for small delays (e.g. waiting for muffins to cool) and building up their ability (e.g. saving for several months for something important). We can talk about the importance of patience to people of all ages.

Here are some suggestions for ways that parents can help their sons develop emotionally:

- Share thoughts and feelings about books, TV shows, movies, the news, family life, etc.
- Discuss the emotions involved in stories and the feelings they create. Ask "How do you think (x) felt when (y) happened?".
- Create a feeling word list to widen the range of a boy's vocabulary and awareness of his feelings.
- Look at different facial expressions on people in pictures or on TV without the sound and talk about the emotions you think that person is feeling and why.
- If you can stay neutral with no blaming, discuss emotional outbursts after the storm has settled. Watch out for women's tendency to pursue (talk too much) about emotional topics and men's tendency to withdraw.
- Keep dialogues open-ended, which allows boys to express otherwise repressed emotions.
- Start general conversations with simple questions like "Have you ever felt …" or share your experiences "I felt …."
- Have these discussions while doing something active, rather than as a confrontation.
- Model and articulate healthy responses to emotions like anger and disappointment, as well as empathy, caring and giving, so our boys can see how others express emotions in their lives.

Again, it is important to set up your home as a "shame-free zone," where your son feels free to express a wide range of emotions without the fear of shame or ridicule. If he feels supported in being a fully emotional human being at home, it will be much easier for him to function out in the world with these same skills. Howard Hiton, co-author of *BAM! Boys Advocacy and Mentoring: Helping Boys Connect Through Physical Challenge and Strategic Storytelling,* wrote **"Staying Connected to Boys"** (p. 5:21) to give parents practical tips on staying connected to our sons as they struggle with their masculine identity. We need to watch for subtle openings and it helps to talk "shoulder to shoulder" with them. For example, driving in the car can be an ideal setting for conversation.

Cultivating Compassion

There are many ways in which we can develop our boys' abilities to be compassionate and empathetic. **"Cultivating Compassion in Boys"** (p. 5:22) reminds us that boys are kind and have big hearts, that they want our undivided attention and help understanding their feelings, when they are ready to talk. We can also create family expectations that encourage family caring (appreciations, no puts downs) and rules about how to deal with conflict in a caring and respectful way. **"Compassionate Connection"** (p. 5;24) by Inbal Kashtan, author of *Parenting from Your Heart: Sharing the Gifts of Compassion, Connection and Choice,* is one of the most powerful approaches for understanding temper tantrums, silent treatment and other "behaviors that are less than wonderful." Compassionate communication (Nonviolent Communication) takes feelings as a signal that an underlying need or value is not being met. Exploring these unmet needs is an amazing way to empower yourself and your child with self-awareness and self-empathy, as well as empathy and connection for others. By getting connected to the values and needs that are behind our reactions, we can then look at what is going on beneath the "behavior storm" or "brick wall" in the other person. When we operate from a place that everyone's needs matter equally, we also model "power with" vs. "power over," and a deep respect for our sons. Empathy cannot be taught, unless it is experienced, received and felt first-hand. When our sons see that we can "step into their shoes," they become empowered with skills to give empathy. We feel that compassionate communication is a powerful approach for this.

Developing interpersonal skills and social competencies in our sons is a process that requires that parents take an active role in teaching the skills of self-awareness, self-discipline, and empathy, as well as sharpening our sons' facility with a wide range of emotional experiences. For parents this is a long-term project, the outcome of which can be a son who is compassionate and kind as well as resilient, capable and morally strong.

Resiliency and Healthy Self-Esteem

Self-esteem is a term that has been used to describe many aspects of a person's self-concept and their positive or negative adjustments to their world. As a rule, boys struggle less with this than girls. The Search Institute survey of over 1.5 million youth tell us that self-esteem is one of only three assets (out of 40) that is more likely to be found in boys than girls. Also, Mary Pipher, author of *Reviving Ophelia*, shares that although boys and girls may both struggle with low self-esteem, a boy will still act; for example, he will still go out for basketball and still ask a girl for a date.

Self-esteem can be seen as a measure of how much a person really believes that they are whole, lovable, capable and magnificent at their core, in spite of what they do, or how they look. Boys with healthy self-esteem tend to handle conflicts and resist negative pressures better, enjoy life more, and are generally optimistic and realistic. Parents can help their sons develop a positive sense of self by supporting them to learn from their own experiences, by encouraging them to keep trying and working towards success, and by loving them unconditionally.

Parents create the background against which children initially explore their self-worth and capabilities. The messages that we send them verbally, physically and emotionally can take a great toll on their self-esteem if we are overly critical. Researchers have studied the messages that 2-year-olds receive throughout the day by placing recording devices on them that monitored all their verbal interactions. Eighty percent of the average daily verbal interactions with these toddlers consisted of negative and/or punitive messages! An interesting experiment for parents wanting to become aware of the flavor of their interactions with their kids is to carry around two punch counters, one in each of two pockets. On one counter,

keep track of positive messages and interactions with your child. On the other counter, track your negative messages, interactions, judgments, and demands. Analyzing a few days of data will give you a good way to assess your own parenting style, and to really look at how you might better create a positive, caring, and unconditionally loving climate for your child to grow up in. Remember from Chapter 3 that we all need at least four positive attentions for every negative one to feel and act well, and that paying attention to another's neutral (rather than positive or negative) behavior most clearly gives the message that they are loved just because they exist.

Do we support the inherent goodness of our children, or do we berate them with our words and actions? Do we allow them to experience the consequences of their own actions and to learn from them, or do we try to control them with our own well-intentioned ideas of how to behave? It is easy to imagine why it is so hard for the average person to believe he is whole and worthy just how he is when his environment is constantly telling him otherwise. One wonders how children might grow up differently if they were instead surrounded by encouraging and accepting words and messages. Supporting your son's developing self-esteem can mean simply choosing your messages carefully when you speak with him. His self-esteem will also be enhanced when you show him that he has worth in spite of his behaviors, encouraging him to believe in himself, raise him to be capable and accountable for his own life choices, and model healthy self-esteem yourself. Self-esteem is not something that you can buy and not something that you can GIVE to your children. It is derived from a child's own exploration of self within his own world, and the degree to which he believes in his capacity to learn, grow and thrive in spite of adversity. It is important to recognize that if you as the parent have low self-esteem, it is often passed on to your child by your self-deprecating comments and actions. Therefore, another way to build self-esteem in your child is to start with yourself. *Breaking the Chain of Low Self-Esteem* by Marilyn Sorenson is a helpful resource.

Supporting our son to develop resiliency is another way to empower him with skills to handle challenges. **"Developing Capable People Guidelines"** (p. 5:30) based on the work of Jane Nelsen, author of *Positive*

Discipline, and Stephen Glenn, author of *Raising Self-Reliant Children in a Self-Indulgent World,* lists seven characteristics of resilient people and some of the parenting skills that help develop these skills:

1. Strong perceptions of personal capabilities,
2. Strong perceptions of significance,
3. Strong perceptions of personal influence over life,
4. Strong intrapersonal skills (e.g. self-control),
5. Strong interpersonal skills,
6. Strong systemic skills,
7. Strong judgmental skills.

Resilient behaviors develop slowly over time, so as parents, we have to be patient and steady about communicating what we believe. We also need to be aware that mistakes and hardships handled wisely actually strengthen our children. **"10 Tips for Building Resilience in Children and Teens"** (p. 5:31) reviews practical ideas on setting up an environment in which your child can learn these skills.

In supporting your child's developing self-esteem and resiliency, it is important to understand development, including the evolution of their "moral intelligence".

"Why Kids Do What They Do: How Parents Can Use This Knowledge to Strengthen Their Child's Self-Esteem" (p. 5:33) explains the basic stages of moral development written about by Laurence Kohlberg, a developmental psychologist. Our younger children are in self-centered stages and gradually grow into a more rule-oriented morality. Some adults stay stuck in rule-oriented morality at levels 3 and 4. Other people attain the most advanced stages based on universal principles and personal integrity at levels 5 and 6. It's exciting when we see teens and young adults moving into those levels. Michele Borba is an expert on building moral intelligence. Her article gives practical ideas on how to build our children's moral IQ: **"Building Moral Intelligence: 10 Tips for Raising Moral Kids"** (p. 5:35).

Many boys in our culture struggle hard to hold onto their true compassionate selves as they grow into men. The reward for parents who help their sons with the difficult challenges of growing into whole, emotionally capable men will be the many years of dynamic, empathic and respectful connections they will enjoy with their sons in all the years to come.

THE 40 DEVELOPMENTAL ASSETS Essential to Every Young Person's Success

There are at least nine assets that will help provide our sons with the external support and internal strength they need to thrive emotionally. Some assets may be more powerful than others and one thing is clear … connection counts. Having a relationship with your child that allows communication to flow freely (Asset #2) is one of the most powerful ways to protect your child from harm. Relationships and connections with other adults and peers (Assets #3, 15, 33 & 35) are a vital part of any child's well-being. It is important to have friends of all ages too. Character building and social competency (Assets # 26, 27, 33-36) help to develop and retain our son's empathy, compassion, and caring through the years when our sons usually exhibit a decrease in these traits.

- **Asset # 2 Positive Family Communication:** Young person and his/her parent(s) communicate positively, and young person is willing to seek advice and counsel from parent(s).
- **Asset # 3 Other Adult Relationships:** Young people have at least three other adults in their lives giving them support in addition to parents.
- **Asset # 15 Positive Peer Pressure:** Young person's best friends model responsible behavior.
- **Asset # 26 Caring:** Young person feels that it is important to help others and make the world a better place.
- **Asset # 27 Equality and Social Justice:** Young people believe in fairness and equality and are committed to social justice.
- **Asset # 33 Interpersonal Competence:** Young person has empathy, sensitivity, and friendship skills.
- **Asset # 34 Cultural Competence:** Young people know and respect people of different racial and cultural backgrounds.
- **Asset # 35 Resistance Skills:** Young person can resist negative peer pressure and dangerous situations.
- **Asset # 36 Peaceful Conflict Resolution:** Young person seeks to resolve conflict nonviolently.

CIRCLE QUESTION

In what situations do you and your son connect well? Do you feel included in the important things going on in his life? If not, what can you do to foster increased "action talk" situations and connection time?

POSSIBLE DISCUSSION QUESTIONS

Emotional Empowerment

1. Describe times when you feel connected even when few words are spoken.
2. What will you do to cultivate emotional awareness and empathy with the boys in your life?
3. Describe "action talk," "shame-free zones," and "timed silence." Have you had success using these approaches?
4. In what types of situations do you find yourself and/or your son getting emotionally out of control? Do you share your feelings with your son? Do you share a broad range of feelings (especially Dads)?
5. Using Compassionate Communication, pick a particularly volatile situation, especially one with strong anger. What were your son's feelings behind the anger and the underlying unmet needs (from the list in Chapter Three)? What were your feelings and needs in that situation?
6. Do you allow your son to respectfully disagree with you? How do you handle conflict?
7. Moms—do you find yourself pursuing your son in an emotionally tense situation? Dads—do you find yourself withdrawing from emotionally tense situations?
8. Describe the compassion you see in your son. What ways can you foster that?
9. Parent often find that boys open up and share more about their lives when they are driving together. What are the factors in this situation that make it easier for boys and men to communicate?
10. Where does your son have a safe haven or "shame-free zone" for expressing himself such as accepting friends, youth group, Scouts, after-school clubs …?

Modeling

11. How do you express "passionate parenting," described in the first article, outside of participating in this discussion group? How are you doing at modeling "what you want to see" in your son, especially compassion?
12. Talk about situations where "coaching your kid" may be the best approach.
13. Do you openly share your feelings, vulnerabilities and stories about how you struggled as a child?
14. Who are the positive and negative male and female role models in your son's life? How have they influenced your son's character development? Have you discussed these people with your son?
15. What has your son taught you? How have you grown as a result of parenting?
16. What are your celebrations and your regrets in your relationship with your son?

Values and Empowerment

17. Do you have concerns about your child's self-esteem? About yours?
18. How can you help your son to develop and trust his inner voice, intuition and feelings?
19. How do you bring your values into everyday life and language? What tools, approaches do you use to promote them?
20. At what stage of "moral development" is your son and the other members of your family? How does this awareness help your parenting?

PUTTING IT INTO PRACTICE

- Model effective listening and communication skills. Share stories, feelings and underlying needs.
- Wait until you cool off if you are angry with your son. Talk to your son using non-intimidating language.
- Realize that boys take time to share their feelings and open up. Don't rush their response. Allow silence!
- If your son finds it tough to talk, use "action talk"—go for a walk, do an activity that allows the boy to relax, connect and open up. Boys open up, share and show their love through action and doing.
- Talk about your own experiences so that he can see that you, too, have gone through tough times and can relate to any troubles that he might be experiencing.
- Listen to your boys. They are eager to be heard.
- Model emotional literacy and emotional intelligence.
- Show respect and give them your time. At least once a day, give your boy focused attention.
- Use positive physical affection. Hug your boy, even after he becomes a teenager.
- Allow your boy his emotions. If you negate, shame or tease him in regard to his feelings, he may bury his emotions further. If he is sad, acknowledge the feeling. Show empathy and understanding. Let him feel safe so that he can be vulnerable and honest without fear or shame.
- Use an emotional vocabulary. Share impressions of stories, TV and movies.
- Think carefully about the messages you give your son about his worth, his abilities and his capacity to succeed. Create a positive and nurturing environment for him to learn, make mistakes and grow up in.
- Provide a wide range of positive male and female role models so your boy sees that there is no single way to be a man or a woman. Most of the problem-solving skills he will acquire will be from examples.
- Connect your son with adult mentors.
- Support your son to explore his interests and to find his passion.
- Live your own life with passion and according to your values, so you will be a good role model for your son, no matter how you balance your home, work and social life.
- Fathers: participate in traditional female activities…cooking, grocery shopping, cleaning. Mothers: participate in traditionally male activities…mow the lawn, fix the bike, play catch, coach.
- Have a multi-family gathering inviting the families of your son's friends—play games together, eat together, where adults are mixed up with the kids.
- Work with your son on a fundraising project and encourage volunteering to foster compassion.
- Take Your Child to Work on the fourth Thursday of April each year (or take someone else's child).

PUTTING IT TOGETHER—YOUR VERSION

Write down three or four ideas you have been inspired to implement in your own life after reading and discussing this chapter.

1. _____

2. _____

3. _____

4. _____

FURTHER READING

Emotional Empowerment

Raising Cain: Protecting the Emotional Life of Boys by Dan Kindlon, PhD and Michael Thompson, PhD

Speaking of Boys by Michael Thompson, PhD

Raising Boys: Why Boys are Different and How to Help Them Become Happy and Well-balanced Men by Steve Biddolph

A Fine Young Man: What Parents, Mentors and Education Can Do to Shape Adolescent Boys into Exceptional Men by Michael Gurian

I Don't Want to Talk About It, Overcoming the Secret Legacy of Male Depression by Terrance Real

Challenges: A Young Man's Journal for Self-Awareness and Personal Planning by Bingham, Edmondson, and Stryker

BAM! Boys, Advocacy and Mentoring by Howard Hiton, Peter Mortola and Stephen Grant

Emotional Literacy by Daniel Goleman

Nonviolent Communication, the Language of Love by Marshall Rosenberg

Parenting from Your Heart: Sharing the Gifts of Compassion, Connection and Choice by Inbal Kashtan

Self-Esteem and Resiliency

The 6 Most Important Decisions You'll Ever Make by Sean Covey

Self-Esteem, a Family Affair by Jean Illsley Clarke

The Handbook for Building Healthy Self Esteem in Children and *Breaking the Chain of Low Self-Esteem* by Marilyn Sorensen

Stick Up For Yourself! Every Kid's Guide to Personal Power and Positive Self Esteem by Gershen Kaufman and Lev Raphael

Building Moral Intelligence: A Parent's Guide to Teaching the 7 Essential Virtues by Michele Borda at www.moralintelligence.org

What Do You Stand For? A Kid's Guide to Building Character by Barbara A. Lewis

Passionate Parenting ... Discovering Your Exceptional Selves

By Kris King

"DISCOVERING THE *ways in which you are exceptional, the particular path you are meant to follow, is your business on this earth..."* said Bernie Siegel, MD, a pioneer in supporting cancer patients to change their perception of themselves from being victims of cancer and disease, to being exceptional and courageous patients. I agree with Dr. Siegel. I believe it is our task to accept and explore our own unique talents and gifts... to live our lives becoming more truly our best selves each day *now*...not waiting for a catastrophe to wake us up.

And yet so much of what happens in our lives has nothing to do with these discoveries of your exceptional nature. Much of what we are taught in life is devoted to directing, restraining, and containing ourselves to fit into a certain pattern that is called "culturally acceptable." Am I saying that learning to follow the rules isn't important? No...I think some rules are vitally important to our health, welfare and to our community.

What I am saying is that through our ac-culturation and learning process sometimes the uniqueness, the spunk, the creativity and the dignity of the individual are sacrificed. The intention is good, to create structure, predictability and safety. The results are not always so good...individuals who feel controlled and dependent upon authority figures, bored, and fearful of being judged and not belonging.

I believe we must live and behave in such a way that our children (our own and those we have a responsibility to) learn to appreciate their own magnificence and learn to take action for themselves that **repeatedly reaffirms their accountability, magnificence, and capabilities.** That sounds like a tall order when faced with an irate toddler or teenager! And how do we do this, if we have not learned how to do this for ourselves?

To become an exceptional parent...or to assist others in becoming exceptional people, we must decide that

discovering our own uniqueness is valuable, possible, and worthy of our time and energy... because it will take time and energy! From there on, it is a matter of learning ways that work and using them everyday with ourselves and in our interactions with everyone, especially our children!

The ways that work are simple things, simple actions that show how much you care and what you stand for. Simple things like:

- **taking ownership of your own behavior**, rather than blaming others,
- **receptive listening, rather than judging and rebuttal,**
- **telling the whole truth,** instead of editing or lying,
- **respecting,** rather than disregarding,
- **loving uncondi-tionally,**rather than expecting,
- **creating clear agree-ments and keeping them,** rather than forgetting,
- **encouraging,** rather than controlling,
- **celebrating,** rather than criticizing.

Simple to understand, perhaps not so simple to apply, especially in those moments when you feel the most challenged. However, isn't it amazing we want our kids to practice self-control, when we ourselves cannot? Imagine in those moments of feeling most challenged that you stop, breathe, and take ownership of your own behavior. For example,

"I just noticed that I am speaking loudly and using critical language as I am talking to you. I apologize. I think it is something I do with you when things don't go the way I want them to. I think I am afraid of conflict and don't know how to handle it very well. I feel sad and concerned that I do this with you. What I want is to understand you and for you to understand me. I want to really hear what you are saying. I want to make clear agreements with you

that we both keep to build trust between us. How do you feel about what I just said?" And then, really listening.

This may sound like a mouthful to you and I want you to know with practice you will transform not only the way you communicate, but the level of trust, clarity, love and cooperation between you and your child.

"Those who preserve their integrity remain unshaken by the storms of daily life. They do not stir like leaves on a tree or follow the herd where it runs. In their minds remains the ideal attitude and conduct of living. This is not something given to them by others. It is in their roots . . . it is a strength that exists deep within them."
—Unknown Native American

Why wait to be sick or to have a life-changing event come along before you accept and appreciate that you and your daughter are truly exceptional people? Use the actions listed above with yourself and your child for a few days, or a lifetime, and you will be amazed at what you will discover about yourself and your daughter!

With love and gratitude,
Kris King

Note:

The communication technique being demonstrated in the example above can be summarized in the following way:
- Observing what I am doing right now.
- What do I think this is about?
- How am I feeling right now?
- What is it that I really want for myself and for my child?
- Checking for understanding, making sure that my child understood what I said.
- Listening carefully for her feelings and needs.

This technique is powerful because it allows a person to slow down, to carefully attend to everyone's feelings and needs, and to establish empathy with the other person. This sets the stage for successfully resolving conflicts, being accountable for your own behavior, and creating more trust and connection in your relationships.

Kris King is owner of Wings Seminars/Innovative Learning Group, a Personal Development Center headquartered in Eugene, OR that offers experiential seminars in personal development and communication skills. Kris works with individuals, organizations and business communities in the areas of transformational education, leadership development, teen leadership training, professional and personal coaching, and spiritual renewal. Innovative Learning Group's mission is to inspire and support positive change, creating an abundant, loving and respectful world community. More information can be found at www.wings-seminars.com.

Written for Family Empowerment Network by Kris King, owner of Wings Seminars/Innovative Learning Group. Wings is a Personal Development Center that offers experimental seminars in personal development and communication skills. Please contact Kris King at www.wings-seminars for reprint permission.

Parent as Coach Approach

By Diana Sterling, author of *Parent as Coach*

DO YOU WANT your children to be authentic, to find their passions and manifest their dreams? Imagine your children knowing that what they experience is a result of a choice they have made. How can we teach our kids to be strong, resilient, self-aware and take responsibility for their own lives? How can we support our children to think through their decisions, to practice their "choice muscle?"

Most of us learn by trying out different ways and discovering for ourselves what is the best fit for us. As parents, the idea of allowing our kids to "figure it out" can be scary, especially for those of us "helicopter parents" who tend to hover and rescue. As your child's abstract brain develops, their need to become independent beings. Parents find their old parenting style is not working. An approach that can be quite effective is to become a "parent coach." A good resource to support you on this is my book, *Parent as Coach: Seven Ways to Coach your Teen in the Game of Life*. It is based on the poem below, written by teens who shared what they learned from the coaching they received from Diana.

The Parent as Coach® coaching philosophy is based on the belief that we first need to understand what human beings are in order to teach and coach them. This includes often misunderstood teens! From this place of understanding, we learn to offer support, ideas, new perspectives, plans for moving forward, and a host of tools and formats to help people create fulfilling and meaningful lives. Above all, we offer love and compassion

> **Young people require adults who can help them to find their own way**

to all we serve and come in contact with.

Instead of teaching how to manage and control teens, our model helps us as adults appreciate the unique perspective of teens and young adults and to express respect, understanding, and support for who they are right now. This produces uncommon effects of the young person actually feeling respected and heard, which in turn allows an accelerated path for the young person to grow, learn, and produce positive choices and outcomes.

The Parent as Coach® Approach does not dictate how to grow up; instead, the parent learns how to guide young people to their own positive decisions, solutions, inherent gifts, and the path to a meaningful and purposeful life.

What our young people need is adults who can help them find their own way.

- Teens do not want or need adults who tell them, exactly how, what, and where to do this and that.
- Teens who feel heard and respected can more readily access their own sense of self and create lives of joy and meaning.
- When teens feel understood they work harder, display more interest and curiosity, and are far more compassionate and easy to get along with.
- When teens feel that they are seen as responsible, they become more responsible.
- When teens feel appreciated, they are more willing to feel and show gratitude.
- When adults open the lines of communication through the Parent as Coach® role, the result can be harmonious and loving relationships that both parents and teens treasure.

As parents it is our responsibility to help our young people to build the confidence to handle the ups and downs of life, the courage to take on new adventures, and the capacity to develop compassion for all living beings. Join the **Parent as COACH®** movement! For more information: www.parentascoach.com

---

A Message to Parents
If you Respect me,
I will hear you.
If you Listen to me,
I will feel understood.
If you Understand me,
I will feel appreciated.
If you Appreciate me,
I will know your support.
If you Support me as I try new things,
I will become responsible.
When I am Responsible,
I will grow to be independent.
In my Independence,
I will respect you and love you all of my life.
Thank you, Your Teenager
From Parent as Coach

Reprinted with permission from Diana Sterling, CEO of New Generations and author of Parent as Coach: Seven Ways to Coach Your Teen in the Game of Life. Visit www.parentascoach.com for more information.

Coping with Anger and Impulsivity

By Kathy Masarie, MD

Anger: a feeling of great annoyance or antagonism as the result of some real or supposed grievance; rage; wrath
—The Collins English Dictionary, 2000

"The world we presently live in has chosen to ignore the message that patience is a virtue. We want things instantly, and if we don't get our own way, we have a tendency to flare up with anger. All too often that anger results in our own personal destruction and humiliation or the destruction of others."
—John Crudele & Dr. Richard Erickson

Aggression: 1) violent action that is hostile and usually unprovoked, 2) deliberately unfriendly behavior, 3) act of initiating hostilities, 4) disposition to behave aggressively, 5) feeling of hostility that arouses thoughts of attack
—WordNet Dictionary

"ANGER IS A NORMAL and natural emotion that arises from our interpretation of the 'fight or flight' arousal we all experience at times," according to Michael Obsatz, author of *Raising Nonviolent Children in a Violent World*. "It is a warning signal that lets you know when something is going on around you that needs your attention." We feel angry when our boundaries are being violated or we feel some injustice. Violent individuals do not know how to vent their anger appropriately. They often interpret events in a negative or blaming way and become cynical and hostile. Their stress builds to a boiling point and a violent explosion occurs.

It is common to worry about anger in perpetrators of violence or aggression. But this emotion is also operating within the psyche of the victim. Anger may be even more pronounced in victims because they are the ones who have the least control, and anger commonly occurs when someone feels powerless in a situation. According to Jane Nelsen in *Positive Discipline Solutions From A to Z*, "When children are bossed or controlled and have no choices, they will probably feel angry." In a similar way, victims of aggression will also likely feel anger.

When this occurs, a child victim may turn this anger outward by acting aggressively toward others. Or the child may turn the anger inward, which can lead to depression, anxiety, eating disorders, social withdrawal or suicide. In a 2001 study reported in *Adolescence* magazine, results indicated that adolescents who internalized their anger were more likely to be depressed and to experience feelings of hopelessness. In addition, teens who internalized their anger made more serious suicide attempts than did those who externalized their anger. Teens who externalized anger, however, were shown to have a higher-than-average addiction to alcohol and drugs.

Does this mean it's better for your child to externalize his anger and act aggressively in order to avoid the serious implications of internalizing that anger? Obviously not, but what are the other choices? Here are some suggestions for helping your son identify and deal with normal angry feelings and for learning some safe, non-violent responses to these passionate emotions and sometimes aggressive behaviors.

Model coolness

- Parents, your kids are watching! How do you act when you are in a crisis, after a hard day with your patience sagging, or when you think no one is watching?
- Do you follow the same rules you set for your

kids? Do you talk only when calm and treat your son with respect and dignity, even when he is misbehaving?

- Have you made a strong commitment to teaching self-control and healthy anger management by example? When angry yourself, do you treat your spouse and loved ones in a way you'd like your son to treat you?

Acknowledge anger

- Let your son know that anger is a normal and important feeling and that its purpose is to act as a signal that his needs are not being met.
- Encourage your child to express his anger in words. Those who can't, may need to draw it.
- Show him that you really have listened by repeating what he has said and expressing some understanding of his feelings.
- Discuss the reason for being angry. Help him to see that it's a normal reaction to having our boundaries, our needs or our sense of justice violated.

Watch for the warning signs

- Try to relieve stress before it becomes an angry outburst by recognizing your own early signs of distress that usually precede loss of control. That way you can do something to calm yourself down instead of blowing up.
- Become aware of the physiological signs of stress: flushed cheeks, rapid breathing, dry mouth, etc.
- Become aware of the physical signs of stress: clenched fists, loud voices, hunched shoulders, aggressive stance, etc.

Encourage healthy outlets

- Let him cool off. Encourage "time-outs" as a way to regain self-control, not to punish or humiliate.
- Teach the use of self-talk, such as "I can calm down," "Slow down," "Keep control," "Be cool," "Be calm."
- Teach relaxation techniques, such as taking deep, slow breaths, contracting and relaxing muscles (such as the fists), or visualizing a calming experience or place.

- Exercise! Physical activity helps expend energy, as anger and aggression create lots of energy. Have kids beat pillows or a punching bag, let them scream out their frustration in a designated place, etc. Taking an active "time-out" (such as running around the perimeter of the house, for example) helps dissipate anger along with the desire to seek immediate retaliation.

Look for those things that tend to trigger anger

- Desensitize yourself to these triggers by convincing yourself that you won't be bothered by it. Choose not to become enraged.
- With children, it is very important to help them identify and validate their emotions as they are feeling them. If we can point out—you feel sad, you feel disappointed, etc., we help our sons to identify all their emotions including anger. And, by recognizing anger, boys are more able to make conscious choices about how to respond to their anger, rather than just internalizing it or blowing up.

Long-term solutions to anger management

- Focus on finding creative solutions to deal with anger.
- Distract him by involving him in something that requires attention and energy.
- Share a lesson about how you managed your anger in a similar situation.
- Suggest he write a poem, story, letter or draw a picture that describes the anger. Consider tearing up the paper afterwards as a symbolic way to "throw your anger away."
- Establish a house rule to "Talk only when calm,"

or remind your children that your house is a "No-hit, no-hurt home." While exact words might later be forgotten, yelling, hitting and out-of-control behaviors rarely are.

Teach and Practice the 1+3+10 Rule:

- This is one of the most effective formulas for self-control in both kids and adults, according to Dr. Michele Borba, author of *No More Misbehavin' - 38 Difficult Behaviors and How to Stop Them.*
- Here's how it works: As soon as you feel you're losing control (when you feel your stress warning signs), do 3 things:
  1) Tell yourself inside your head to "Be Calm".
  2) Take three deep, slow breaths from your tummy (getting oxygen to the brain helps to calm you down).
  3) Count slowly to ten inside your head.
- Putting this together makes 1+3+10: an easy way to stop the tide from anger to outburst.

Work through the following questions/ideas together with your son to help him learn to vent his anger nonviolently

- What makes you really mad?
- When was the last time you were really mad? How did you handle it?
- Brainstorm 5 nonviolent ways of venting anger.
- What are some of the benefits of anger? How can anger teach you some things about yourself?
- List 5 ways of venting anger that are hurtful and destructive to yourself or others.
- Role-play a situation that might make your child angry—such as a friend being unfair in a game—and brainstorm some new ideas on handling the situation.
- Help him practice calming himself down and figuring out nonviolent ways to vent his feelings.

It is important that your child understand that angry and aggressive feelings are normal, and that there are healthy ways to display and manage these feelings. By learning self-control, your son will feel more confident about responding to anger in an appropriate manner that lets him remain in control of himself, while retaining a sense of personal power and dignity.

Impulsivity

Dr. Michael Obsatz, who wrote *Raising Nonviolent Children in a Violent World,* believes that many children do not learn to control impulsive behaviors. They watch adults who act impulsively while driving, watching a sports game or shopping—to name a few. They watch movies and TV programs which not only show impulsive and selfish behavior, but show people being rewarded for these behaviors. "When we act impulsively, we act without thinking. We don't consider our options, the consequences of our behavior or how we affect others." While "impulsive behaviors can be positive, loving and life-affirming, they can also be self-destructive and hurtful to others. We may move quickly into anger or quickly follow through on a thoughtless act without thinking about the harm it may cause another."

Impulse control requires a certain level of experience and maturity. A child needs to be able to consider the outcome of his behavior, as impulse control means not always getting your own way, and it requires finding safe, nonviolent alternatives for the expression of disappointment, frustration or rage. Children need support, guidance, and tools to learn how to stop, take a time-out and think before they act.

So, how can parents teach their children to control their impulses? Dr. Obsatz recommends the following:

- Parents can discuss with children "both positive and negative impulsive behaviors—such as driving without considering other drivers, fighting back when you feel wronged, buying on impulse and sending flowers to a friend." What makes some of these behaviors okay and others unacceptable? What are some other, more acceptable ways, to express our feelings at these times?

- Role-play with children about how to stop themselves when they are acting impulsively. Practice deep breathing or time-outs.
- After a cooling-off period, they can use reason to consider other ways to handle a situation or communicate their feelings without hurting someone either physically or emotionally.
- Most importantly, adults must model the behavior they desire to see in their child. They must show children that they can control their own impulses. They may need to tell their child when they've done it —"See, I just stopped myself from shouting at that bad driver," then tell him why they believe it was a wise decision and how glad they are that they took a time out before reacting.

Controlling anger and impulses are key skills that parents can teach and encourage in their sons. While many in our culture never become competent in these pro-social skills, those kids and adults who do will experience unequaled success, connection and happiness in their lives. Imagine how much your own close relationships would be enriched if your family practiced consistently safe, respectful and conscious conflict resolution. The benefits of such personal accountability around anger and impulse control can be summed up in the following quote:

> *"Real Freedom is the ability to pause between stimulus and response, and in that pause, to choose."*
> —Rollo May, author of *Love and Will*

To teach your son to be accountable for his reactions to anger and impulses, and you will empower him to have deep and meaningful friendships and an actualized, authentic life.

Resources:
- *Adolescence,* 2001 Spring; 36 (141): pages 163-70.
- *Building Moral Intelligence: The Seven Essential Virtues that Teach Kids to Do the Right Thing,* by Michele Borba, Eddy. (Jossey Bass, 2001)
- *Cliques: Eight Steps to Help Your Child Survive the Social Jungle,* by Charlene C. Giannetti and Margaret Sagarese (Broadway, 2001)
- *Journal of Psychosomatic Research,* 2000 Oct; 49(4): pages 247-53.
- *Positive Discipline Solutions A to Z,* by Jane Nelsen, Ed.D, (Prima Lifestyles, 1999)
- *No More Misbehavin' - 38 Difficult Behaviors and How to Stop Them,* by Michele Borba, Ed.D. (Jossey Bass, 2003)
- *Raising Nonviolent Children in a Violent World,* by Michael Obsatz, PhD (Augsburg Fortress Publishers, 1998)

Emotional Intelligence: Helping Children Work with Feelings Not Against Them

By Gretchen Randolph

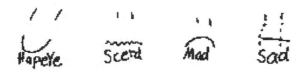

DANIEL GOLEMAN'S book *Emotional Intelligence, Why It Can Matter More Than IQ* was on the NY Times and international bestseller list for months. Its relevance was made more obvious by the dramatic upsurge in the violent acts of school shootings , mostly done by boys (and men).

Most of us are more familiar with the concept that Intelligence Quotient (IQ) measures one's intellectual potential. Goleman's book was the first easily understood explanation of brain research showing the profound influence feelings have on thinking. He coined the term "emotional hijacking" to describe how emotions can respond faster than thinking and take over control. Goleman believes all parents and children need to understand emotions and how to counteract these sometimes destructive forces.

While IQ is predominately genetically determined, one's EQ (Emotional Quotient) is largely formed by developmental experiences. Recent physical findings show that at birth a massive portion of the brain circuitry is awaiting definition. This remarkable plasticity is like a computer's hard drive that requires programming to make it work. Different software makes the computer behave in vastly different ways. For parents and children this is an absolutely vital message. How parents relate to their children can establish permanent neurological patterns in their child's brain that influence their emotional responses. If your children understand how to work with their feelings, they will have greater opportunities to excel in life. Regardless of your children's ages, everyone in the family will benefit from learning more about feelings, and purposefully dealing with them in relationships.

Keep the following in mind as you add to your emotional skills.

- Feelings are a natural part of us. We can't stop them, but we can process them to enliven our lives.
- People are different. Feelings contain information about ourselves and can help teach us who we are.
- Feelings constantly change—influenced by other aspects of ourselves such as our experiences, our bodies, and self image.

- Sharing feelings can create a closer bond between parent and child.
- In short, feelings are a process. They draw on internal experiences that with practice, each of us can know more fully.
- To understand and work with our feelings let's think of them in three phases.

Feeling ➡ Thinking ➡ Action

- **Feeling** - First, cultivate the ability to stand back and observe one's feelings. If a situation is bothering your child, help him to identify and recognize his feelings.
- **Thinking** - Next, encourage him to pull back, give himself time to think about what he is feeling and to understand what the feeling is telling him about himself. This is a complex step and children often need help with developing purposeful habits of thinking about their feelings. There are varied styles for this. Some options are to talk with others, draw pictures, make up songs, exercise, write in a diary or take a time out, away from distractions.
- **Action** - Last, consider what action to take (if appropriate). Together these three steps can decrease emotional intensity, foster a self-observing attitude, and draw forth the information the feelings give us. Feelings can then empower a child toward constructive action.

Emotional intelligence skills enable children to work **with** their feelings not against them. While this appears simple, we are complex beings and these concepts are not easy to implement or communicate. These are challenging times to raise children, and we have many concerns about our youth. In spite of the utterly depressing daily news as a psychotherapist and parent, I have never been so optimistic about a book and its impact on cultural awareness. Daniel Goleman has begun a revolution, bringing the power of emotions to our attention. Now we have direction and tools for building Emotional Intelligence.

Gretchen Randolph, PhD, N.P., works with all ages in psychotherapy and preventative counseling. She lectures on Emotional Intelligence, has two children's books, and a video "How to Work with Feelings."

Reprinted with permission from Full Esteem Ahead, *Wings*, Fall 1998

Staying Connected to Boys
By Howard Hiton

- Watch for subtle openings to more emotional content.

- Use self-disclosure (sharing stories and experiences about yourself) and non-threatening topics to establish trust.

- Be patient.

- Stay centered.

- Boys do not identify and express feelings as quickly as girls. They might not be clear right away as to what they feel. Allow boys time to finish a situation then talk about it afterward.

- Learn about youth culture and, in particular, young men's culture. Read, ask questions, and listen.

- Women, watch your tendency to pursue. Allow your boy space.

- Men, watch your tendency to get disconnected. Get involved and stay involved in your boys' daily lives.

- Honor a boy's need for silence.

- Timing is everything. Ask, step away, and give them time to come to you. Allow boys to walk away then return.

- Allow boys to express with movement and activity. Talk "shoulder to shoulder" with them.

- Boys are shame phobic. Find places to talk that are "shame free."
- Allow boys to talk about feelings indirectly. Use metaphor, stories, and share your personal examples when relevant.

- REALLY LISTEN!

Cultivating Compassion in Boys

By Judy Brodkey

I love to visit David, my four-year-old nephew who lives in California. Toward the end of one visit, I was sitting on the floor when I felt something soft tickling my nose. David was walking around me, draping his blanket over me as he went. "What are you doing?" asked his perplexed mom. David replied, "I'm casting a magic spell so when Judy goes back to Portland she can feel my hugs and kisses anytime and she'll feel better."

Boys are compassionate. Boys are kind. Boys are caring. Boys have big hearts. As boys grow older, it often looks otherwise to the casual observer. Many boys appear angry, withdrawn, mean, non-caring, distant, or unkind.

The Search Institute (www. search-institute.org) has identified 40 Developmental Assets, building blocks that young people need in order to grow up healthy, caring and successful: external assets including such things as family support, adult role models, and creative activities and internal assets including integrity, honesty and a sense of caring. The Search Institute found the percentage of boys with the "caring" asset drops significantly between elementary school and high school, with only 25% of 12th grade boys still having the "caring" asset.

What happens to transform a boy with a compassionate, gentle soul into a teenager who appears uncaring? Boys get hurt in a multitude of ways. They may be left alone, isolated, teased, humiliated, criticized, shamed, judged harshly for their exuberance, taunted, bullied, hit, sexually abused and much more. Many get targeted for showing feelings and learn to act tough. They receive countless messages about what it means to be male, and many of those messages are lies. Many boys have the added burden of racism and class issues bearing down on them. Boys work very hard to hold onto their true, compassionate, and kind natures in the face of these and other obstacles. As caring adults, we can do a lot to cultivate the seeds of compassion that are inherent. Above all, we need to treat boys with respect, kindness and compassion.

Listen to boys. My nephew David loves to talk to any adult who will listen. Boys naturally want to connect with others and share their ideas and feelings. David has a lot to say, but sometimes adults don't listen very well. Listening well means not criticizing, interrupting, or rushing to share our own thoughts. It means reflecting the feelings he sometimes half expresses. When we really listen, David knows someone cares, and that he is important and not alone.

Sam, an eleven-year-old, attended a two-week overnight camp last summer. Early in the session, his parents heard that Sam wasn't happy and wanted to come home. They wrestled with what to do. After a mid-session visit to the camp and after listening to their son for a long time, they decided the camp wasn't a good place for Sam. He came home with them, had a great rest of the summer, and learned his parents would truly listen and respect his thinking and feelings.

Help boys show and understand their feelings. As a culture, we often deny that boys have certain emotions. If they show sadness or fear, or even if they show too much exuberance, we sometimes become uncomfortable and try to get them to stop. "Big boys don't cry" is a message most boys have heard. Each time we minimize, ignore, or criticize a boy for showing feelings, that boy becomes a little more cut off from himself. That, in turn, will eventually make it more difficult for a boy to have compassion for himself and others. Listen to a boy when he makes any attempt to share his feelings, don't abandon him, and help him talk through those feelings.

It's helpful when adults—men in particular—model a range of emotions. When men show sadness, fear, joy or other feelings, boys learn their own feelings are normal and not shameful, and they learn to accept those feelings in others.

Find ways to stay physically close and affectionate with boys. Boys want and need hugs, affection and other physical closeness. Some adults, especially women, become uneasy in the presence of energetic, physical boys. We may need to push past our fears to learn new ways of being physically close. We can learn to play wrestle, shoot hoops, and have pillow fights. There are many ways to play hard, stay connected, and have fun with boys.

Remember that boys are good and magnificent human beings. Celebrate boys! When your son prances around the house with a make-believe sword, remember his goodness and what a wonder he is. His play is normal and not an indication he's going to become a rapist or murderer. Look for ways to let boys know how much you like them and that you believe in them. Encourage their passions and appreciate their strengths.

Help boys learn to pay attention to their bodies. Boys feel physical pain when injured, but our culture teaches them to ignore their bodies. Help boys learn to pay attention to their bodies when they are sick or injured. Messages such as "You're not really hurt," "It doesn't hurt that bad" or "Only girls cry when they are hurt" distract a boy from what is happening and cut him off from his own intelligence. Not only are these messages harmful to a boy's own well-being, but these messages make it easier for a boy, in turn, to ignore or disrespect what's happening to other people and their bodies.

Eliminate anti-male comments from your vocabulary. This includes such comments such as "You know how boys are," "They just think with their penises," "Boys can't be trusted" and "Men are jerks." When boys are given messages that maleness is "bad," it makes it harder for them to know and act on their own goodness.

Never shame or humiliate a boy. Last summer, a ten-year-old boy riding in a bicycle race rounded a corner too fast and fell down hard on concrete. I saw he was conscious but very shook up. Although nothing appeared broken, he was bruised and bleeding in several places. I stayed close and listened to him while he cried softly. Several adults soon came over. They told the boy to stop crying, paid little attention to his injuries and discounted his pain. One woman who knew the boy asked him repeatedly whether he wanted to continue the race. Three times, he answered, "No." Finally she shamed him with the taunt, "Your sister would never be a sissy and give up like this." The adults thrust the bike into the boy's hands and he had no choice but to keep riding. That day, one boy got a big lesson in lack of compassion.

Involve boys in community service. Enlist boys' help in projects that involve being kind to others. They can take a meal to a sick neighbor, help plant a community garden, or donate old toys to a shelter. *Hands On Portland* (503-234-3581) is a great community resource that offers family-friendly volunteer opportunities.

Help boys learn problem-solving skills. Find teachable moments to help boys think through and solve problems non-violently. Some organizations offer programs that teach kids mediation and other problem-solving skills. These skills help boys learn "emotional literacy" that will prepare them for situations that call for compassion and clear thinking.

Minimize boys' exposure to television and other media that present meanness and violence as normal or humorous. If your son watches these shows at all, watch with him and then engage him in conversation about the difference between fantasy and reality, and the implications of meanness and violence. Contact the Northwest Media Literacy Center (503-452-7333) for more information.

Be an advocate for boys. Work with schools, coaches, community centers, and others to ensure that boys are treated with kindness and compassion.

My nephew David's spell continues to work magic. I can feel his hugs and kisses anytime I want. Even more importantly, his magic spell is a constant reminder of his goodness and the importance of cultivating compassion over the coming years as he faces new challenges that every boy inevitably encounters. Nothing could be more important in his life—or mine.

Judy Brodkey is a life coach who does program coordination, facilitation, and teaching/training in addition to coaching. She can be reached at 503-234-1012 or J246brodkey@aol.com.

Reprinted with permission from Full Esteem Ahead, *Wings*, Winter, 2003.

Compassionate Connection

By Inbal Kashtan, author of *Parenting from Your Heart: Sharing the Gifts of Compassion, Connection, and Choice*

Attachment Parenting and Nonviolent Communication

How do we deal with a two-year-old when he grabs every toy his friend plays with? What do we say to a four year old who screams in rage when her baby brother cries? How do we talk with a ten-year-old about the chores he has left undone, again? What strategies will keep our teenager open with us—and safe?

NONVIOLENT COMMUNICATION (NVC), sometimes referred to as Compassionate Communication, offers a powerful approach for extending the values of attachment parenting beyond infancy. A process for connecting deeply with ourselves and others, and for creating social change, NVC has been used worldwide in intimate family settings as well as in organizations, schools, prisons, and war-torn countries.

NVC shares two key premises with attachment parenting: human actions are motivated by attempts to meet needs, and trusting relationships are built through attentiveness to those needs. Both premises contrast with prevailing child rearing practices and with the assumptions about human beings that underlie these practices. Instead of focusing on authority and discipline, attachment parenting and NVC provide theoretical and practical grounds for nurturing compassionate, powerful, and creative children who will have resources to contribute to a peaceful society.

Human Needs and Human Actions

Unlike conventional views of babies as manipulative and in danger of being spoiled, attachment parenting suggests that our babies' cries are always attempts to get their needs met. NVC, too, shifts attention away from judgments about our own and others' actions (as manipulative, wrong, bad, inappropriate—or even good), focusing instead on our own and others' feelings and needs. (See end of the article, "The Steps of NVC.") Consider the following common situation:

A child, Anna, leaves her clothes and toys strewn about the house. Dad may reprimand, remind, offer

incentives, or punish. These tactics may or may not lead to the immediate outcome he intends. They will, however, likely result in unwanted long-term outcomes, such as hindering Anna's intrinsic desire to keep her home orderly and impairing the sense of connection and trust in the family.

Anna's mom may choose to say nothing out of confusion about what might work. Not getting her needs met, and lacking trust that her needs even matter to Anna, Mom might feel resentful and frustrated. The relationship is again impaired, and Anna loses the opportunity to practice finding solutions that will work for everybody—a powerful skill she needs in order to live in harmony with others.

NVC offers parents two key options that foster connection: empathy for others' feelings and needs and expression of one's own. In this situation, Dad can guess—and thus connect with—Anna's deeper feelings and needs. He can ask, "Are you excited because you want to play?" Or, "Are you annoyed because you want to choose what to do with your space?" Often, simply shifting to an empathic guess of the child's feelings and needs eases the parent's reaction. Dad no longer sees Anna as an obstacle to getting his needs met; rather, he is ready to connect with this other human being. For Anna, having the experience of being understood may nurture her willingness to listen to Dad's feelings and needs and to contribute to their fulfillment.

Mom may choose to express her own emotions. She may start with an observation: "I see clothes, books, markers, and toys on the living room floor." The observation, instead of an interpretation or judgment ("the house is a mess"), can make a tremendous difference in Anna's readiness to hear Mom's perspective. Then, when Mom follows with her feelings and needs instead of going immediately to a solution, she humanizes herself to Anna: "I feel frustrated because I enjoy order in the house." Mom clearly expresses that her feelings are caused *by her own unmet needs, not by Anna's actions, thereby taking full responsibility for her feelings and for meeting her needs. She continues with a doable request: "Would you be willing to pick up your things and put them in their places?" Or if she wants to explore the broader pattern: "Would you be willing to talk with me about how we can meet your needs for play and choice and my need for order?"*

Even if Anna were not willing to talk at that moment, her parents could continue to use empathy and expression until mutually satisfying strategies were found—in that moment or over time. In fact, one of the most profoundly connecting moments in relationships can occur when one person says "No" and the other empathizes with what that person is implicitly saying "Yes" to: "When you say you don't want to talk about this, is it because you want more confidence that I care about your needs?"

Every interaction we have with our children contains messages about who they are, who we are, and what life is like. The parent who takes a toy away from a toddler who just took it from another child while saying "No grabbing," teaches her child that grabbing is okay—for those with more power. Instead, in both words and actions, a parent could convey three key things: I want to understand the needs that led to your actions, I want to express to you the feelings and needs that led to mine, and I want to find strategies that will meet both of our needs.

By hearing the feelings and needs beneath our children's words and behaviors, we offer them precious gifts. We help them understand, express, and find ways to meet their needs; we model for them the capacity to empathize with others; we give them a vision of a world where everyone's needs matter; and we help them see that many of the desires that human beings cling to—having the room clean, right now!, watching television, making money—are really strategies for meeting deeper needs.

Allowing ourselves to be affected by our children's feelings and needs, we offer ourselves the blessing of finding strategies to meet our needs that are not at a cost to our children. Conversely, by sharing our inner world of feelings and needs with our children, we give them opportunities all too rare in our society: to know their parents well, to discover the effects of their actions without being blamed for them, and to experience the power of contributing to meeting others' needs.

Power With versus Power Over

When we want our children to do something they don't want to do, it is almost impossible to resist the temptation to use the enormous physical and emotional power we have over them. Yet attempting to coerce a child to do something she doesn't want to do neither works effectively in the short term nor supports our long-term needs. (The only exception comes when there is threat to health or safety, in which case NVC suggests that we use non-punitive, protective force.)

Marshall Rosenberg, founder and education director of the Center for Nonviolent Communication, asks parents two questions to point out the severe limitations of using power-over tactics such as reward and punishment: "What do you want the child to do?" and "What do you want the child's reasons to be for doing so?" Do we really want our child to do something out of fear? Guilt? Shame? Obligation? Desire for reward? Most of us have experienced the deadening effect—and the ensuing anger and resentment—of doing things out of these motivations. Human beings do not respond with joy to force or demands. It follows that if people get their needs met at a cost to others, there is an attendant cost to themselves. Our needs are met most fully and consistently when we find strategies that also meet others' needs.

While helping us meet our needs without coercion, NVC also helps us resist giving in to our children's every wish by teaching us to express our feelings, needs, and requests clearly, and to expect our needs to be considered. When we consistently express our commitment to attending to everyone's needs—not just theirs, not just our own—we model a way of life to our children and create power with them: the power of choosing to contribute to making life more wonderful for everyone.

Neither coercive nor permissive, NVC focuses on human needs and helps us realize that we, our children, and all human beings share these needs. I draw profound hope from the knowledge that by living this way, I can foster harmony in my family—and contribute to peace in our troubled world.

Copyright © Inbal Kashtan. Excerpted from her book, *Parenting from Your Heart* and also published in *Mothering*, Jan/Feb 2002.

Parenting for Peace

When my son was four years old he asked me to read a book about castles that he had picked up at the library. He picked the book because he loves the Eyewitness series and was methodically going through as many of those books as we could find, irrespective of their subject matter. I didn't like this one. It depicted not only castles but also knights, armor and weapons of all kinds used in battles in centuries past.

I am not ready for weapons. One of the things I enjoy about my son not going to preschool and not watching TV is that his exposure to violence has been extremely limited. He has never said the word "gun" or played pretend violent games—yet. He doesn't know about war and people purposely hurting one another—yet. But here was the castle book, and he wanted to read it.

I am not trying to shield my son from the reality of violence and suffering in the world—but I am in a (privileged) position to choose, often, how and when these realities enter our lives. I read him some of the book, with numerous editorials. But when he asked to read the book again a few days later, I found myself saying that I feel a lot of sadness about people being violent with one another because I believe human beings can find peaceful ways to solve their conflicts.

Questions, of course, ensued. In response to one of my son's questions, I shared with him that my sadness was related not only to the past, when there were knights and castles, but to the present as well: people in the area where I grew up, Israelis and Palestinians, are also fighting. "Why are they fighting?" my son asked. "Because they both want the same piece of land and they haven't figured out how to talk about it," I replied. "I'll teach them!" he volunteered. "What will you teach them?" I asked. "I'll teach them that they can each have some of the land, they can share," he replied easily. "The only problem," he continued, "is that I don't know how to find them."

I felt a mixture of joy and grief at his words. How wondrous to hear from my son—and from so many children—a desire to contribute to the world and a trust in the possibility of solving conflicts peacefully. Yet how apt his words were—"I don't know where to find them." How do we find the hearts of "enemies" so we can reach them with a message of peace? How do we find our own hearts and open them to those whose actions we object to profoundly?

This search for our own and others' hearts is at the core of my hope for peace and has been the greatest influence on my parenting, including the decision to practice attachment parenting when my son was a baby. It has also led me to teach a process called Nonviolent Communication (developed by Dr. Marshall Rosenberg and taught around the world). I lead workshops for parents, couples, teachers, social change activists, and others who want to connect more deeply with themselves and with others and who want to contribute more effectively to mutual understanding, safety and peace in families, schools, organizations, and in the wider world.

My experience convinces me that what happens in our families both mirrors and contributes to what happens in our societies. Just as "enemies" fail to see each other's humanity, so we, too, at times fail to relate with others, even loved ones, with compassion. Probably the primary challenge most parents tell me about is, though they yearn for peace and harmony in their families, they find themselves getting angry with their children more often and more quickly than they would like. Because the problem-solving model we follow so often relies on threat of consequences or promise of reward, it's almost guaranteed that anger will crop up regularly. For what children learn from this model is not cooperation, harmony and mutual respect; it's more often the hard lesson of domination: whoever has more power gets to have his or her way, and that those who have less power can only submit or rebel. And so we continue the cycle of domination that is leading human beings close to self-destruction.

What alternative do we have? As parents, we have a remarkable opportunity to empower our children with life skills for connecting with others, resolving conflicts, and contributing to peace. Key to learning these skills is our concept of what human beings are like. Nonviolent Communication teaches that all human beings have the same deep needs, and that people can connect with one another when they understand and empathize with each other's needs. Our conflicts arise not because we have different needs but because we have different strategies for how to meet our needs. It is on the strategy level that we argue, fight, or go to war, especially when we deem someone else's strategy a block to our own ability to meet our needs. Yet Nonviolent Communication suggests that behind every strategy, however ineffective, tragic, violent or abhorrent to us, is an attempt to meet a need. This notion turns on its head the dichotomy of "good guys" and "bad guys" and focuses our attention on the human being behind every action. When we understand the needs that motivate our own and others' behavior, we have no enemies. With our tremendous resources and creativity, we can and—I hope—we will find new strategies for meeting all our needs.

We can teach our children about making peace by understanding, reflecting, and nurturing their ability to meet their needs while we also understand, express and attend to our own. One of the needs human beings have is for autonomy, for the ability to make decisions about things that affect us. This leads us on a path of self-interest and a search for confidence and power. Yet if we nurture this need in our children to the exclusion of others, it can be difficult for us to get our own needs met. Thankfully, our need for autonomy is balanced by another shared human need, for contribution to others. This need leads us on a path of consideration, care and generosity to others. NVC enables us to look at both needs (and many others) and find a way to balance them with each other so that we recognize our need to give, to consider others and contribute to them, as an autonomous choice. When giving is done freely, out of mutual care and respect, it does not conflict with autonomy and choice, but rather complements them.

From this perspective, parents may find that we don't need punishments or rewards in parenting our children—we can instead invite our children to contribute to meeting our needs just as we invite ourselves to contribute to meeting theirs: with joy and willingness instead of guilt, shame, fear of punishment or desire for reward. This is not permissive parenting—it is parenting deeply committed to meeting the needs of both parents and children through a focus on connection and mutual respect.

Transforming parenting is hugely challenging in the context of the daily, overwhelming reality of parenting. Yet this transformation enables a profound depth of connection and trust among family members. Perhaps more poignantly for me, choosing to parent this way gives me hope for peace for our world—perhaps for our children's generation, perhaps for future generations, when human beings have learned to speak the language of compassion. As the world enters our home and my son's exposure to life's realities grows, I hope he will sustain these lessons and carry them into his own life. I hope he will know that the path to peace is most effectively followed not by rewarding the "good" guys and punishing the "bad" ones, but by striving to find strategies that will meet people's needs—not just our own, but everyone's. I hope he will have the confidence and trust in his own peaceful resources and in human beings' capacity for peace. I hope he remembers that we can find other people's hearts by seeing their humanity.

Copyright © Inbal Kashtan. Excerpted from her book, *Parenting from Your Heart* and also published in *Paths of Learning* (Spring 2003).

Transforming Children's Anger

NVC invites us to explore a different paradigm when we face challenges with and between our children: connection and compassion for all, of mutual care and the possibility of contributing to everyone's needs. Perhaps most importantly for our troubled times, this paradigm supports children with models and skills for making peace in our world.

How does this paradigm shift work in real-life families who practice NVC? Here is a story from one mother of three boys, who participated in BayNVC's family camp in 2004:

My 13 year-old son, David, was really angry one day and about to hurt one of his twin younger brothers as they sat near each other on the couch. So, I did what I now do whenever physical violence is about to happen between them and got in the middle of the two. David was breathing heavily and had his fists clenched as he sat in a chair next to me. His brother was on the other side of me on the couch. I went with habit and started to tell David about anger management and how he needed to go for a walk or go to his room until he cooled off. He continued to breathe heavily and clench his fists.

Then his brother said something like, "David did you just want to be included?" I realized then that what David needed was empathy and started guessing, too. My first guess simply echoed what his brother already guessed: "Are you needing to be included?" I saw David's fist relax just slightly. I guessed again: "Are you needing to feel that you belong?" His fist relaxed even more and his breathing began to slow down some. Then I guessed that his need for belonging had been unmet for a really long time with his twin brothers.

David's fist relaxed more along with his body. Then I guessed that maybe if his need for belonging were met, his need for love would be met, and tears began to roll down his cheeks.

I will be forever grateful for the tools of NVC for allowing me to get to this place of awareness and healing with my son.

I celebrate this mother's honesty about her struggle to remember to turn to connection. Like most of us, she has habits that point in another direction. Yet she is willing to be awakened by her son's initiative and remembers to return to the focus on the heart. This reinforces my trust in the possibility of transformation for all of us. We can always be reminded and can always choose to return to connection. I also celebrate this mother's modeling for her sons. It's her dedication to trying, again and again, to focus on holding everyone's needs with compassion and care that made it possible for her son to do the same when she could not.

The Steps of NVC

Expressing Ourselves:
NVC includes stating our observations, feelings, needs, and requests.

Step 1—Observations: Descriptions of what is seen or heard without added interpretations. For example, instead of "She's having a temper tantrum," say "She is lying on the floor crying and kicking."

Step 2—Feelings: Our emotions rather than our story or thoughts about what others are doing. For example, instead of "I feel like you're irresponsible," which includes an interpretation of another's behavior, say "I feel worried." See **Feelings Inventory** (p. 3:30).

Step 3—Needs: Feelings are caused by needs, which are universal and ongoing and not dependent on the actions of particular individuals. State your need rather than the other person's actions as the cause; for example, "I feel annoyed because I need support" rather than "I feel annoyed because you didn't do the dishes." See **Needs Inventory** (p. 3:30).

Step 4—Requests: Doable, immediate, and stated in positive action language (what you want instead of what you don't want); for example, "Would you be willing to come back tonight at the time we've agreed?" rather than "Would you make sure not to be late again?" By definition, when we make requests we are open to hearing a "No," taking it as an opportunity for further dialogue.

Example of NVC Statement:
Original statement: "You're irresponsible! You made me so worried when you didn't get home on time! If you come home late again, you'll be grounded."

NVC statement: "When you came home at midnight after agreeing to come home at 10 p.m., I felt so worried because I need peace of mind about your safety. Would you be willing to spend time right now coming up with a plan that will give you the autonomy you want and also help me feel more peaceful?"

Empathizing with Others:
In NVC, we empathize with others by guessing their feelings and needs: "Are you feeling ____ because you need ____?" Instead of trying to "get it right," we aim to understand. In the example above, the teen's response may be, "No!" The parent can then switch from expression to listening with empathy: "Are you feeling annoyed because you need your ability to choose how to spend your time to be trusted?" From here, the dialogue can continue with empathy and expression until both people's needs for connection and understanding are met.

© by Inbal Kashtan.

Inbal Kashtan, co-founder of BayNVC and the NVC Leadership Program, focuses on training for trainers and occasionally also workshops and retreats for parents, couples, and the general public. She is the founder of the Center for Nonviolent Communication's Peaceful Families, Peaceful World project, and the author of Parenting from Your Heart: Sharing the Gifts of Compassion, Connection, and Choice, *a booklet about parenting with NVC. She also has a CD,* Connected Parenting: Nonviolent Communication in a Family Life. *Both are available at www.baynvc.org. For more information about Nonviolent Communication see www.cnvc.org. For more information about Inbal's work, see www.baynvc.org.*

DEVELOPING CAPABLE PEOPLE
Guidelines
from the book *Raising Self-Reliant Children in a Self-Indulgent World*
by H. Stephen Glenn and Jane Nelsen

Seven Strategies for Developing Capable People

1 *Recognize* that the rate and intensity with which knowledge, technology, and lifestyle are changing have created conditions in which resiliency and personal resources are critical to effective living and learning.

2 *Encourage* the development of seven resources of highly resilient and capable people:
   a. *Strong perceptions of personal capabilities.* "I am capable of facing problems and challenges and gaining strength and wisdom through experience."
   b. *Strong perceptions of significance.* "My life has meaning and purpose, and I contribute in unique and meaningful ways."
   c. *Strong perceptions of personal influence over life.* "I can influence what I do in life and am accountable for my actions and choices."
   d. *Strong intrapersonal skills.* The ability to manage personal emotions through self-assessment, self-control, and self-discipline.
   e. *Strong interpersonal skills.* The ability to communicate, cooperate, negotiate, share, empathize, listen, and work effectively with people.
   f. *Strong systemic skills.* The ability to respond to the limits and consequences of everyday life with responsibility, adaptability, flexibility, and integrity.
   g. *Strong judgmental skills.* The ability to make decisions based on moral and ethical principles, wisdom, and understanding.

3 *Provide* opportunities in homes and classrooms for children to develop the significant seven. Strategies such as family/class meetings, mentoring, and firmness with dignity and respect can provide opportunities for children to develop all of these resources.

4 *Create and use* rituals, traditions, and service projects as opportunities for growth and empowerment for children.

5 *Increase the use* of dialogue (a meaningful exchange of ideas and perceptions) as the essential process for encouraging closeness, trust, and learning: "What are your thoughts about that?" *Avoid* "Did you? Can you? Will you? Won't you? Is everything okay?" etc. Instead *use* "What? How? When? In what way ___?" etc.

6 *Build closeness* and trust, and convey respect by avoiding the *Five Barriers* and using the *Five Builders* instead:

Barrier #1: *Assuming:* Acting on limiting assumptions about what a person can or can't do, say, think, etc. "I didn't tell you because you always get upset." "You always think ___." "You're too young to try that!" etc.

Builder #1: *Checking:* Giving people a clean slate: "How do you want to deal with this?" "What are your thoughts about _____?" "What will you need to have ready for _____?" etc.

Barrier #2: *Rescuing/Explaining:* Problem solving for a person: "_____ is what is happening." "_____ is why it is happening." "_____is how to deal with it." "Do it this way." etc.

Builder #2: *Exploring:* Problem solving with a person by letting them try something and then asking: "What did you experience in that situation?" "Why is that significant?" "How might you apply what you have learned in the future?" etc.

Barrier #3: *Directing:* Telling people what to do: "Pick up your shoes." "Put that away." "Don't forget your lunch." "Be sure and _____." etc.

Builder #3: *Inviting:* Asking for participation/assistance: "I would appreciate any help you could give me in straightening up the room." "How do you plan to _____?" "What will you need to do in order to _____?" etc.

Barrier #4: *Expecting: (too much too soon)* Using potential as a standard and discounting people for not being there already: "I was expecting this room to be spotless." "You should know that already." "I appreciate ____ but you forgot ____." etc.

Builder #4: *Celebrating:* Focusing on effort progress and/or what was gained by trying: "I appreciate the effort you have made to clean up this room." "What did you learn from trying to do that?" "What progress do you see yourself making?" etc.

Barrier #5: *Adultism:* Using stereotypes when dealing with people: "Teenagers are like that." "You know better than that! Surely you realize!" "You are too young to appreciate that." "Grow-up!" "Why are you so childish." etc.

Builder #5: *Respect:* Allowing for people's uniqueness and individuality: "What is your perception of _____?" or "Let me check out what you think." "How do you see this issue?" etc.

7 *Improve* your relationships 100% by avoiding the *Five Barriers.* Where can you get that kind of return for doing less? Replace the Barriers with *Builders* and double the positive impact of your contributions!

Reprinted with permission of Stephen Glenn and Jane Nelsen, EdD, MFT, authors of *Raising Self-Reliant Children in a Self-Indulgent World* at www.empoweringpeople.com. For information on lectures or seminars, contact jane@positivedisipline.com.

10 Tips for Building Resilience in Children and Teens

By American Psychological Association

WE ALL CAN DEVELOP resilience, and we can help our children develop it as well. It involves behaviors, thoughts and actions that can be learned over time.

Following are tips to building resilience.

1. Make connections

Teach your child how to make friends, including the skill of empathy, or feeling another's pain. Encourage your child to be a friend in order to get friends. Build a strong family network to support your child through his or her inevitable disappointments and hurts. At school, watch to make sure that one child is not being isolated. Connecting with people provides social support and strengthens resilience. Some find comfort in connecting with a higher power, whether through organized religion or privately and you may wish to introduce your child to your own traditions of worship.

2. Help your child by having him or her help others

Children who may feel helpless can be empowered by helping others. Engage your child in age-appropriate volunteer work, or ask for assistance yourself with some task that he or she can master. At school, brainstorm with children about ways they can help others.

3. Maintain a daily routine

Sticking to a routine can be comforting to children, especially younger children who crave structure in their lives. Encourage your child to develop his or her own routines.

4. Take a break

While it is important to stick to routines, endlessly worrying can be counter-productive. Teach your child how to focus on something besides what's worrying him. Be aware of what your child is exposed to that can be troubling, whether it be news, the Internet, or overheard conversations, and make sure your child takes a break from those things if they trouble her. Although schools are being held accountable for performance on standardized tests, build in unstructured time during the school day to allow children to be creative.

5. Teach your child self-care

Make yourself a good example, and teach your child the importance of making time to eat properly, exercise and rest. Make sure your child has time to have fun, and make sure that your child hasn't scheduled every moment of his or her life with no "down time" to relax. Caring for oneself and even having fun will help your child stay balanced and better deal with stressful times.

6. Move toward your goals

Teach your child to set reasonable goals and then to move toward them one step at a time. Moving toward that goal —even if it's a tiny step —and receiving praise for doing so will focus your child on what he or she has accomplished rather than on what hasn't been accomplished, and can help build the resilience to move forward in the face of challenges. At school, break down large assignments into small, achievable goals for younger children, and for older children, acknowledge accomplishments on the way to larger goals.

7. Nurture a positive self-view

Help your child remember ways that he or she has successfully handled hardships in the past and then help him understand that these past challenges help him build the strength to handle future challenges. Help your child learn to trust himself to solve problems and make appropriate decisions. Teach your child to see the humor in life, and the ability to laugh at one's self. At school, help children see how their individual accomplishments contribute to the wellbeing of the class as a whole.

8. Keep things in perspective and maintain a hopeful outlook

Even when your child is facing very painful events, help him look at the situation in a broader context and keep a long-term perspective. Although your child may be too young to consider a long-term look on his own, help him or her see that there is a future beyond the current situation and that the future can be good. An optimistic and positive outlook enables your child to see the good things in life and keep going even in the hardest times. In school, use history to show that life moves on after bad events.

9. Look for opportunities for self-discovery

Tough times are often the times when children learn the most about themselves. Help your child take a look at how whatever he is facing can teach him "what he is made of." At school, consider leading discussions of what each student has learned after facing down a tough situation.

10. Accept that change is part of living

Change often can be scary for children and teens. Help your child see that change is part of life and new goals can replace goals that have become unattainable. In school, point out how students have changed as they moved up in grade levels and discuss how that change has had an impact on the students.

Reprinted with permission from the American Psychological Association. Documents from apahelpcenter.org may be reprinted in their entirety with credit given to the American Psychological Association.
www.apahelpcenter.org/featuredtopics/feature.php?id=39&ch=2

Why Kids Do What They Do:
How Parents Can Use This Knowledge to Strengthen Their Child's Self-Esteem
By Jody Bellant Scheer, MD

ALL BEHAVIOR HAS, at its core, a positive intention: that of getting a person's needs met. Behaviors, therefore, can be seen simply as the strategies a person chooses for meeting their needs. When babies are born, they have no capacity for words, but they are actually very good communicators, which is a very good thing because they are completely dependent upon others to get their needs met. Imagine our reaction if we went to pick up a squalling baby in the middle of the night, and she stopped just long enough to bellow, "Where's my milk?? I'm hungry, you lazy bum!!" This baby would be embarking upon a suicidal form of behavior, as very few of use would be willing to answer to this request 8 to 12 times per day! But babies actually have very good strategies for getting their needs met and for invoking feelings of love and concern in their caregivers, which is why they so successfully survive!

Somewhere along the way to toddlerhood, children start to get "socialized" and develop language skills. They continue to be motivated to get their needs met, and they develop strategies to do so which are much more complex than a baby's crying, smiling and cooing. Often, children learn strategies that are not likely to get them what they want, and that may even elicit anger, irritation, or other negative emotions in their caregivers. If children develop too many of these unsuccessful strategies, they begin to have troubles getting their needs met. The result is that they feel badly about themselves, and they start to perceive that they are somehow not worthy or able to get what they need in life. They may act out, withdraw or give up under these circumstances, and develop what many people describe as problems with their self-esteem. Parents who can help their children to identify what their needs are, who can redirect their children's inaccurate beliefs about themselves to more self-serving ones and who can encourage their youngsters to find successful strategies to meet their needs, can be of tremendous help in building

their children's self-esteem and positive adjustment to their world.

A famous psychologist, Lawrence Kohlberg, developed a theory of moral development, which attempts to explain why people do what they do. This theory helps to explain what kinds of strategies people choose in order to get their needs met. There are six stages of moral development: these stages are experienced in ascending order throughout life, although no more than 25% of adults tend to make it to the highest two levels. Understanding this model can help parents to understand both the positive intention AND the motivating force behind their child's behavior.

For example, most young children operate at levels one and two, which are the "reward-punishment" and "reward-reciprocity" stages. Kids at these stages do what they do to avoid the pain of separation or disconnection, to seek rewards, or to exchange benefits. Behavior is controlled by authority figures external to themselves (parents, school teachers, bosses, etc.). Starting in middle school, kids move into the "good boy/bad boy" stage, where control of behavior is still external, but the drive for behavior is to gain approval of significant others. One can see the increasing importance of peers as motivators for behavior at this stage. Stage 4, the "law and order stage," is driven by a desire to belong to a larger group or society, and to avoid censure and guilt. Behaviors are motivated by wanting to conform to rules, laws, customs, social values, and/or religious tenets. Control of behavior still resides in authority figures external to the self. This stage often first appears in young adults, the majority of whom will remain at this level of moral development throughout life.

The final two stages depend on self-discipline. Control of behavior is internal, within the self. Behaviors are chosen due to their positive effects on humanity (stage 5) or due to their consistency with universal values and principles (stage 6). Social unity and personal integrity are the driving forces behind behaviors for people operating within these two stages. Generally, only a few adults are able to operate from these levels and, in fact, only a few visionaries are capable of consistently acting from level 6.

Understanding this guide to moral development can help parents to understand the positive intentions behind their child's behaviors. A child in stage 2, when faced with the opportunity to sacrifice his own hard work and efforts to help others, may not perceive this as meeting his own needs. He may need a more concrete or immediate reward to motivate him towards good works. Likewise, it is easier to have compassion for a child when he acts outside of his parents' moral code and acts instead in accordance with his peers, if you also understand that he is well entrenched in stage 3 of moral development. Again, all behavior has a positive intention: which is to meet one's basic human needs. The choices of strategies to meet these needs, however, will depend on many factors: the person's age, experience, family, culture, and stage of moral development. While strategies may have

positive or negative outcomes, the ability to separate the need (with its positive intention) from the strategy will help adults to parent in a nurturing way, building their child's self-awareness and self-esteem.

How can this knowledge be used to support your child's self-awareness and self-esteem? First of all, parents can better understand their kids' irrational beliefs about themselves and about how to get their needs met, especially when they are misbehaving. If we assume that ALL misbehavior is really a tragic attempt to meet an unmet need, it is easier to interact with a child and his behaviors in a more positive, non-punitive and supportive manner. By helping the child to look for his unmet need while acknowledging his right to have his needs met, a parent can help a child to look for alternative behavioral strategies that would be more likely to get him what he wants. This helps the child to know himself, to be self-aware, and to get his needs met without feeling badly about himself. Ultimately, this is the basis for developing healthy self-esteem.

A Simplified Version of Kohlberg's Stages of Moral Development: Why Do We Do What We Do?

Stage:	Categories:	Control:	Behavior	Drive (Need):	Common Name of Stage:
6	⇑	Internal	Consistent with my chosen highest universal principles and values	Personal Integrity; Guided only by your own conscience	"Universal Principles Stage"
5	Principled Reasoning	Internal	Has a positive effect on humanity. Based in fairness, justice & truth	Social Unity; Faith in individual rights and democratically decided laws	"Social Contract Stage"
4	⇑	Peers (External)	Conforms to laws, customs, social values, authorities, religious beliefs	Belonging; Avoidance of censure and guilt	"Law and Order Stage"
3	Rule-Oriented	External authorities	Seeks approval of significant others, peers	Approval	"Good Girl/Bad Girl, Good Boy/Bad Boy Stage"
2	⇑	External authorities	Seeks rewards (my actions are OK as long as I get what I want + I don't get caught)	Reward or reciprocity (I'll scratch your back if you'll scratch mine)	"Reward-Reciprocity Stage"
1	Self-Centered	External authorities	Seeks to stop the pain of separation/disconnection	Avoid the pain of separation or disconnection.	"Reward-Punishment Stage"

Building Moral Intelligence: 10 Tips for Raising Moral Kids

By Michele Borba, author of *Building Moral Intelligence: The Seven Essential Virtues that Teach Kids to Do the Right Thing*

1. Commit to Raising a Moral Child

How important is it for you to raise a moral child? It's a crucial question to ask, because research finds that parents who feel strongly about their kids turning out morally usually succeed because they committed themselves to that effort. If you really want to raise a moral child, then make a personal commitment to raise one.

2. Be a Strong Moral Example

Parents are their children's first and most powerful moral teachers, so make sure the moral behaviors your kids are picking up from you are ones that you want them to copy. Try to make your life a living example of good moral behavior for your child to see. Each day ask yourself: "If my child had only my behavior to watch, what example would he catch?" The answer is often quite telling.

3. Know Your Beliefs & Share Them

Before you can raise a moral child, you must be clear about what you believe in. Take time to think through your values, then share them regularly with your child, explaining why you feel the way you do. After all, your child will be hearing endless messages that counter your beliefs, so it's essential the she hears about your moral standards. TV shows, movies, newspapers, and literature are filled with moral issues, so use them as opportunities to discuss your beliefs with your child.

4. Use Teachable Moments

The best teaching moments aren't ones that are planned—they happen unexpectedly. Look for moral issues to talk about as they come up. Take advantage of those moments because they help your child develop solid moral beliefs that will help guide his behavior the rest of his life.

5. Use Discipline as a Moral Lesson

Effective discipline ensures that the child not only recognizes why her behavior was wrong but also knows what to do to make it right next time. Using the right kind of questions helps kids expand their ability to take another person's perspective and understand the consequences of their behavior. So help your child reflect: "Was that the right thing to do? What should I do next time?" That way your child learns from his mistakes and grows morally. Remember your ultimate goal is to wean your child from your guidance so he acts right on his own.

6. Expect Moral Behavior

Studies are very clear: kids who act morally have parents who expect them to do so. It sets a standard for your child's conduct and also lets her know in no uncertain terms what you value. Post your moral standards at home, then consistently reinforce them until your child internalizes them so they become his rules, too.

7. Reflect on the Behaviors' Effects

Researchers tell us one of the best moral-building practices is to point out the impact of the child's behavior on the other person. Doing so enhances a child's moral growth: ("See, you made her cry") and highlights the victim's feeling ("Now he feels bad"). The trick is to help the child really imagine what it would be like to be in the victim's place so she will be more sensitive to how her behavior impacts others.

8. Reinforce Moral Behaviors

One of the simplest ways to help kids learn new behaviors is to reinforce them as they happen. So purposely catch your child acting morally and acknowledge her good behavior by describing what she did right and why you appreciate it.

9. Prioritize Morals Daily

Kids don't learn how to be moral from reading about it in textbooks but from doing good deeds. Encourage your child to lend a hand to make a difference in his world, and always help him recognize the positive effect the gesture had on the recipient. The real goal is for kids to become less and less dependent on adult guidance by incorporating moral principles into their daily lives and making them their own.

10. Incorporate the Golden Rule

Teach your child the Golden Rule that has guided many civilizations for centuries, "Treat others as you want to be treated." Remind him to ask himself before acting, "Would I want someone to treat me like that?" It helps him think about his behavior and its consequences on others. Make the Golden Rule become your family's over-arching moral principal.

Dr. Michele Borba is an educational consultant and author who has conducted parent and teacher seminars to over a half million participants. Her latest book is Building Moral Intelligence: The Seven Essential Virtues that Teach Kids to Do the Right Thing *(Jossey Bass Publishers). Information on her publications and seminars can be accessed through her Web site, www.moralintelligence.com.*

Teaching Him 6

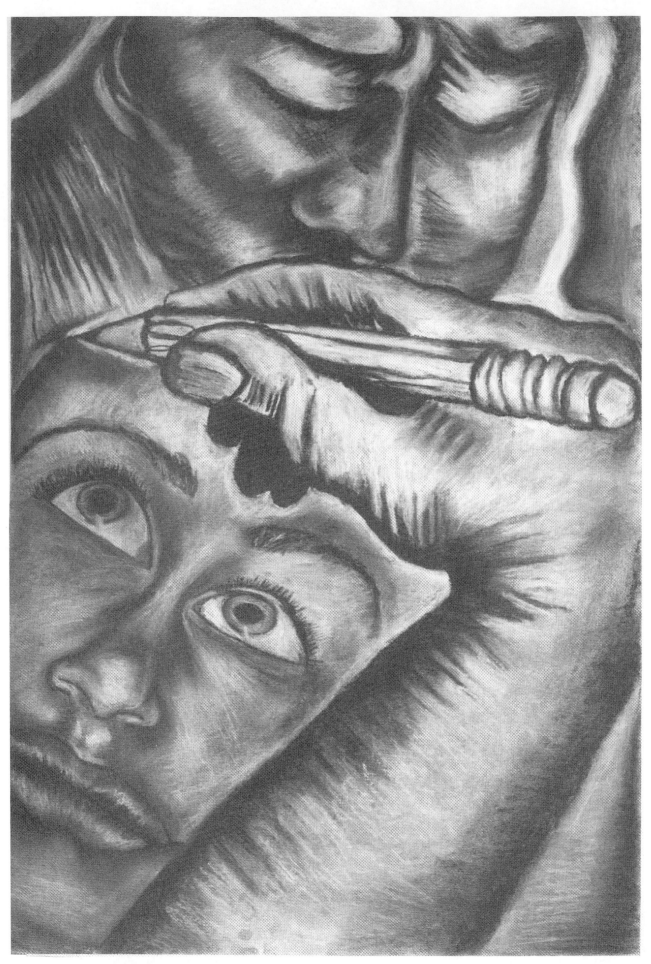

Sally Nelson, Class Instructor & Children's Art Institue Teacher

Teaching Him

> "People don't care how much you know—until they know how much you care." —John C. Maxwell
>
> "The secret of education is respecting the pupil." —Ralph Waldo Emerson
>
> "Overwhelmingly, recent research indicates that girls not only out-perform boys academically but also feel far more confident and capable. Indeed the boys in my study reported, over and over again, how it was not 'cool' to be too smart in class, for it could lead to being labeled a nerd, dork, wimp or fag."
> —William Pollack, *Real Boys*
>
> "I'm not a bully. I was only teasing." —Suellan Freid, *Bullies and Victims*
>
> "I get a little down but I'm good at hiding it. It's like I wear a mask. Even when kids call me names or taunt me, I never show them how much it crushes me inside. I keep it all in."
> —Adam's confession from *Real Boys* by William Pollack

GOALS

- To discuss ways to positively impact your son's learning

- To raise the awareness of parents and teachers about the unique ways in which boys learn and behave so that more nurturing home and school climates can be created for boys

- To recognize the destructive power of verbal, physical and relational aggression and to learn about ways to reduce this problem

- To recognize the value of the partnership between families and schools in preparing children for the future

OVERVIEW

Going off to school marks an important milestone in the life of a child. A child moves from the nurturing environment of hearth and home into the larger society of his culture when he starts school. At school, he encounters a diversity of values and experiences that help him to expand his world, and learn about what his culture expects from its young people. Ideally, our educational system works in partnership with parents to support the intellectual, social, psychological and emotional development of our nation's children. Feeling connected to school is the second largest major factor, after family closeness, that protects boys from emotional distress, drug abuse and violence (1997 national longitudinal study "Protecting Adolescents from Harm"). Parents who think of school as a collaborator in preparing their children for the future can reinforce their son's learning and school activities. Parents are in the best position to monitor the psychological and social well-being of their children, and to assist the school or intervene if these needs are not being met. Parents who take an active role in their children's schools can ensure that the educational environment is accepting, caring and supportive, and one that encourages all students to succeed.

Developmental Asset-Building in Schools

Developmental Asset-building within a school is one manner in which communities can maximize success for all their students by encouraging respectful relationships, creating caring environments, and building successful programs and practices. In fact, 5 of the 40 Developmental Assets relate directly to commitment to learning. They are:

- Achievement Motivation—Young people try to do their best in school.
- School Engagement—Young people are enthusiastic about learning and come to school prepared.
- Homework—Young people in middle and high school spend at least one hour per day completing homework.
- Bonding to School—Young people care about their school.
- Reading for Pleasure—Young people enjoy reading on their own for at least 3 hours per week.

Young people who have these assets will be more successful in school and less likely to engage in risky behaviors. Asset building in schools is a great way for school staff, parents and communities to encourage success for all children.

Within a school community, respectful, high-quality relationships are more strongly correlated with student academic success than are the presence of high-powered programs. The article **"Great Places to Learn: How Asset-Building Schools Help Students Succeed"** (p. 6:14) reminds us that children who feel valued and cared about, who have numerous positive role models, and who feel connected to their school are more able to learn and excel. Teachers and parents are both in excellent positions to help build assets within their kids' schools. **"Asset Building Ideas for Teachers"** (p. 6:16) offers several suggestions to implement in the classroom. **"Every Student a Star"** (p. 6:18) outlines how staff in a Texas middle school of 900 kids reached out to "leave no child behind." The principal first put every child's name on a bulletin board and then asked each teacher to place stickers by the names of the 10 kids they felt closest to. What they discovered was that the students who were the most outgoing received the bulk of the stars. More than half of the kids, including those who needed attention the most, received none. The teachers then divided up the kids with no stars and brainstormed about ways they could establish some sort of meaningful connection with them.

Parents are just as capable of creating assets within their kids' schools. Asset building at a school benefits your own child as well as others; it helps create a community where all children feel cared for no matter what their home environments are like. School volunteers often become important mentors for high-risk children whose success depends on finding positive role models outside of their home environments. Parents do not need to have oodles of time or money to become meaningfully involved in their kids' education. Working parents, who face an additional challenge staying connected to their child's school, may be able to broker paid time off in order to volunteer in a classroom.

They can also be involved in nighttime or weekend activities.

There are as many ways to be involved in schools as there are parents, and taking the initiative to find some small way to contribute to your son's school will greatly benefit both your child and your community. Here are some asset-building ideas that can be organized by parents working with school staff:

• Greet kids as they arrive at school.
• Arrange a school-wide spaghetti dinner to welcome incoming 6th-grade students and their parents.
• Coordinate a community service day with speakers and parent-led volunteer opportunities.
• Attend open houses and join parent organizations.
• Incorporate Art Literacy—a parent-run art history program.
• Create appreciations for teachers.
• Tutor and mentor students.
• Organize evening school-wide festivals or dances.
• Help in classroom.
• Teach/facilitate an after-school or lunch recess class/club.
• Organize the school's recycling program.
• Start parent-led, grade-level monthly discussion of timely topics.

Small actions can create a huge ripple effect in your community and can increase the number of assets for your child and his school. The power of parents to improve their children's education is really quite unlimited. "**At Home in Our Schools**" (p. 6:19) is an article that outlines a novel way of creating a sense of community within our schools. A sense of fun and shared community is enhanced by implementing educational activities where the goal is to have everyone participate, where students work collaboratively with families and other students, and where everyone wins and nobody loses. Included in this article are examples of family-focused activities that parents anywhere can initiate in their schools.

Ten months of the year our neighborhood schools are teeming with activity between the hours of 8 and 3, but think of the potential schools have for community-building when class is not in session. Your school can become a community resource where the doors are "always open" to meet the needs of local children, families, and community members. In some regions of our country, school communities have collaborated with cities and counties to create Community Schools, where schools are used when they are traditionally closed. Community Schools can offer school year and summertime activities, homework and reading clubs, tutoring, mentoring, family fun nights, health fairs, and educational activities for the community. Community Schools increase academic success, encourage family involvement, support families, involve community resources and local businesses in schools, and foster local collaboration to benefit schools and optimize their use as a public resource. In some counties, high schools are the sites of health clinics which offer free health and mental health services for local teens.

The way schools are structured can make a big difference in how readily children (or parents) can bond to school. Recall that "Bonding to School" is an asset and protective factor for teens. Community-building becomes increasingly difficult as schools increase in size. Small schools may not be the most financially viable model, but they do create the critical sense of being known and valued. "**Thinking Small in a Big School**" (p. 6:21) describes a federally-funded initiative to create smaller communities and better bonding within large high schools. A national trend to keep middle school children in their elementary schools, thereby returning to the older K–8 model, echoes the importance of keeping students bonded to school and school values (kindness, respect, hard work, connection to adults) as they move into adolescence. "**TRIBES: A New Way of Learning and Being Together**" and "**Fostering Cooperation and Compassion in the Classroom**" (pp. 6:22-6:23) are included to offer a look at educational models designed to create schools that are safe, respectful containers in which children can learn. As schools decrease competition, increase collaboration and improve relationships, students learn skills that will help them succeed in all aspects of their lives. To be bonded to school, our children need to feel that they can be themselves at school and that people care about them.

Recent education trends, fueled by an emphasis on test performance, often ignore developmentally appropriate practices and push formal academics for younger and younger children while withholding the arts and recesses. This is counterproductive for our sons and daughters. Education is not about force-feeding information to our children, but is about involving the whole person in the process of learning. Children (and adults) need breaks and physical activity to feel content and mentally alert and to retain new information. Furthermore, we need to acknowledge the importance of kinesthetic learning which only occurs when children move their bodies. Playgrounds at recess offer rich opportunities for this learning. As parents we have an important role: to be aware of educational trends that are counter-productive and to advocate for healthy, effective practices that educate the whole child. The importance of arts education for our children is poignantly expressed in the article **"The Power of Arts Education"** (p. 6:24).

"The Turning Point: Boys' Night Out" (p. 6:25) describes a very successful program for 6th-grade boys entering middle school where they spend an overnight together at their school. Dads, older teens, volunteers and the boys themselves offer a flurry of activities that helps bond the kids together and set a positive tone for the rest of their middle school years. Many good memories are created for the boys, teens and dads alike. Again, parental advocacy for such programs is instrumental in creating similar opportunities for the children at your kids' schools.

Another way to increase our children's bonding to school and community is to offer them "place-based education" (see *Place-Based Education: Connecting Classrooms & Communities* by David Sobel). In place-based education, students learn **in** the community: for example, through researching its history, researching and reconstructing a local watershed, or improving habitat for wildlife in an empty lot or at the edges of the schoolyard. Students become actively involved in their community and become resources to the community. David Sobel describes place-based education in this way:

> *Place-based education is the process of using the local community and environment as a starting point*

to teach concepts in language arts, mathematics, social studies, science, and other subjects across the curriculum. Emphasizing hands-on, real-world learning experiences, this approach to education increases academic achievement, helps students develop stronger ties to the community, enhances students' appreciation for the natural world, and creates a heightened commitment to serving as active, contributing citizens.

Getting our children involved with their world rather than simply observing it is more likely to honor the multiple types of intelligence our children possess.

Character Education and School Success

Parent-school partnership is also critical in helping children develop positive character traits. The six pillars of character education (www.charactercounts.com) provide us with a shared vocabulary for teaching ethics: trustworthiness, respect, responsibility, fairness, caring and citizenship. Parents of all religious backgrounds agree with these core values. **"Character Counts! From the Inside Out"** (p. 6:26) describes how a character education program was designed at an elementary school with the intent of encouraging ethical behavior and reducing discipline referrals. Can you imagine what kind of impact a similar program could make in the caring environment of your own child's school?

Schools that emphasize Service Learning as part of their curriculum help develop the character of their students while creating a bond between the school and the community. School service learning can happen at many levels:
- Within school service: recycling, school buddies, gardening, teacher assistance,
- Whole class projects: sandwiches for the homeless, pulling ivy at the park,
- Family service projects: organize recycling, build bird feeders, family garden,
- Community projects organized by students,
- Volunteering at a local agency (see Ch. 10).

Service learning connects students to their community in ways which allow them to see themselves as people who are making a positive difference. These experiences empower and encourage them to develop the skills and motivation to become responsible citizens.

Character education could also be helpful in curbing the widespread practice of cheating, an ethical problem that many schools have had to approach as a singular issue, as noted in **"Cheating in High School is Widespread, High-Tech and Contagious"** (p. 6:27). Many adolescents struggle with impulsive behaviors such as lying, fibbing and cheating, and unfortunately these are facilitated by modern technology such as cell phone texting, Internet access and instant messaging. As parents, however, our role is to stay true to basic values through modeling and using calm respectful communication and consequences when needed.

Helping your child learn how to learn and study effectively is an important parenting role. You are your son's consultant, providing the structure he needs to be successful in school. Some of our sons are "self starters" and need very little supervision with homework at any age. However, most children benefit from family routines for planning the week (at a family meeting) and weeknight family quiet times when all distractions (except music) are turned off and everyone is doing homework, reading or writing. Don't be surprised if at some point you have to track your son more carefully, communicate with teachers, and insist that 100% of homework is completed before fun begins. When your son has been absent for a period of time or gets behind, he will also need your support in designing a plan to catch up. **"Helping Our Children Learn Study Skills"** and **"Time Management from a Different Point of View"** (pp. 6:28-6:30) offer some good tips for helping children succeed at school.

While it is important for our children to do reasonably well at school, sometimes parents get too focused on grades and lose track of the bigger picture. Being bonded to school and home is actually more important than getting A's, because the bonding is the protective factor that helps keep your teen making safe and reasonable choices during adolescence. This means that if homework completion starts to become a power struggle with your teen, you may need to shift to more of a coaching strategy, which minimizes nagging and recognizes that

homework is a contract between your teen and his or her teacher, and involves natural consequences. Teens generally need more support and less pressure from us in navigating the complexity of this developmental period. If school is not going well for them, sometimes it is because they are not getting their needs met in that school; they may need a smaller magnet school or our older teens may be ready to move out of high school and get their credits from your local community college.

Parents are also wise to supervise the number of hours their sons work in the community as they reach the teen years. A part-time job can be a source of great growth and pride for a boy, as long as the number of hours worked during the school year remains at less than 15 hours per week. Working enables teens to learn lifelong work and money management skills and gives them a role in the community as well as exposure to future career possibilities. You can check out your state's rules about teenage workers at www.familyeducation.com. However, working too many hours (more than 20) during the school year is associated with lower grades and sleep deprivation and interferes with extracurricular activities and social relationships. Contemporary research shows a direct link between the number of hours worked and the likelihood of dropping out of high school *(Student Workers in High School and Beyond* by Stephen Lamb, et. al.). Parents are an essential resource in helping their sons maintain a healthy balance between their studies and work. Our sons also need help in learning to handle stress and to "de-stress" in healthy ways. Our teens are often happy when they are busy with school and many activities, but at times they can feel overwhelmed by their lives. Teach and model living a balanced life.

Boy-Friendly Education

An area of concern to parents of boys is the falling academic achievement that boys have been exhibiting worldwide over the past 30 years. For the past three decades, educators and social scientists have focused on improving the academic performance of girls, while failing to notice that our schools are not adequately serving the needs of our boys. Boys may dominate as the top academic all-stars in science and math, but there are actually more than twice as many boys as girls who are in the lowest rungs of academic achievement. Boys now rank 1 to 2 years behind girls in reading and writing skills, they drop out of school 4 times more often than girls, and are held back a grade 50% more often than girls. In addition, boys are much more likely than girls to be labeled as learning disabled, emotionally disordered or behaviorally at risk in our schools. For example, two-thirds of all children currently requiring special education are boys, almost three quarters of all school suspensions are meted out to boys, and serious emotional disorders are up to 10 times more likely to be diagnosed in boys. Why are boys having so many problems with modern schooling? Is it due to characteristics of male biology, or more likely, are current educational expectations and cultural practices a poor fit for our boys?

There are a host of possible explanations for the problems that boys have in schools based on biologic tendencies and cultural practices. It is clear from recent research that boys' brains are different from girls and, as a result, they may mature at a slower rate and have different aptitudes for learning. Boys tend to require more physical activity than girls, making it difficult for them to sit still for long periods in the classroom. Boys also tend to encode emotional information in the brain in ways that make it harder for them to manage impulsive behaviors, which can be disruptive to classroom activities. These tendencies may be related to boys' increased referrals for problem behaviors and hyperactivity within schools. Boys also tend to learn better with active, hands-on activities, and have more difficulties hearing and processing verbal instruction than girls. As a result, boys adapt more poorly than girls to traditional, didactic teaching methods that emphasize passive learning and lectures. To make matters even more difficult, boys' masculine training to be strong, independent and tough tends to disconnect them from making the close connections that are helpful for keeping them invested in school. Furthermore, traditional schools tend to reinforce behaviors such as obedience, conformity and passive learning, which are behaviors generally associated with a stereotypical female role. This puts boys in conflict with their gender role, which can then lead to low achievement and poor self-esteem. Noisy, disorderly environments are also known to be an academic risk factor for boys since boys generally like order and clear expectations. All these factors can add up incrementally to undermine the overall academic success of our boys in our contemporary schools.

Schools and parents can do a lot to ameliorate the problems that boys face in academics by immersing boys in the joys of reading and writing and creating boy-friendly classrooms. The article "Our Sons are Faring Poorly in School: What Can We Do About It?" (p. 6:31) addresses how to do this at length. Solutions include providing curricula, textbooks and reading materials that are interesting to boys, emphasizing hands-on learning opportunities, encouraging classroom discussions and debate, ensuring that physical activity is built into learning activities, and encouraging male bonding in the classroom by providing positive male role models and mentors, as well as experimenting with all-male classrooms in some circumstances. Schools also need to create safe emotional environments for boys by encouraging/allowing them to express their fears and vulnerabilities without fear of shame or ridicule so that their relational skills can be enhanced. Dr. Howard Hiton has researched the problem of boys' underachievement at length and suggests several key strategies. These are reviewed in his "Summary of Strategies to Help Boys Learn" (p. 6:39). His suggestions include increasing boys' connection to school, improving boys' academic performance by tailoring literacy instruction to boys' needs and interests, addressing boys' behavior by directly teaching social and impulse control skills, and providing boys with more positive male role models (see *Building on Strengths* at www.hitonassociates.net). Boys' writing (and drawing) often contains more violent images than that of their female peers, and as parents and teachers we need to be careful not to shut down boys' creative process by overreacting. (For more information on teaching literacy to boys, see "Further Reading" at the end of the overview.) Dr. Hiton emphasizes the essential role of male teachers and mentors in the lives and academic success of our boys. Parents are an invaluable resource for making sure that their own local teachers, administrators, schools and community understand the plight of boys in school. By entering into a partnership with their schools, parents can ensure that their sons receive an appropriate and equitable education by encouraging more boy-friendly practices and curricula.

Relational Aggression in Schools

Learning environments need not only to be openly supportive of boys; they need to ensure safety from harm, harassment and ridicule. Twenty percent of kids sit in class every day in fear of being bullied (Garity, *Bully Proofing Your School*, Intervention in School and Clinic, 32 (4), pp. 235-243, 1997). No one can learn in the face of fear and intimidation; however, physical, verbal, non-verbal and relational bullying occur at alarming rates amongst our youth. The fear of bullying causes many children to miss school in America each day. While most schools do a good job of disallowing physical bullying, other forms of bullying are rampant and can be just as traumatic for children. Verbal bullying includes name-calling, teasing, insults, putdowns, and making threats. Non-verbal bullying carries similar messages but does so with gestures or dirty looks instead of words. Relational bullying uses gossip, cliques, rumors or other group activities to ostracize, make fun of, humiliate or harass anyone deemed "different" or "not belonging." Relational aggression is unique in that it is used as much in close relationships as it is against one's enemies. Often, the price of belonging to a clique is the requirement to commit relational aggression against others both inside and outside the group. What can parents do about the problems of bullying within their own children's lives and schools?

The first step is to learn about bullying and then raise awareness of this problem in others. To help you with this, we have summarized the key concepts about peer aggression and its solution in the article **"The Problem with Peer Aggression in our Schools Today"** (p. 6:41). There are skills individual parents, teachers, counselors and administrators can learn to help intervene effectively when a bullying incident occurs.

Anti-bullying programs can operate with great success, and parents can be instrumental in insisting that they exist. However, the most effective approach to the problem of aggression is to raise the social norm of the school to higher standards for how people treat each other. The only way this can happen is for the entire school community, from the school board to the youth themselves, to implement sustainable interventions and programs to reduce aggression. Many schools with such programs have reduced bullying and relational aggression tremendously and have successfully created a culture of caring within their school community. Our children must be taught the power of bystanders to avoid allying themselves with bullying, and, on the contrary, to speak up for kindness. This takes courage, confidence, empathy, ingenuity, and communication skills—qualities that will benefit our children throughout their entire lives.

The journey through school is an important rite of passage for your child. However, the quality of a child's education tends to correlate strongly with the quality of parent involvement in their school community. Parents who partner with schools to improve education truly create benefits for all the children and families within their community. It is the sincere hope of Family Empowerment Network that parents will be inspired to find many small or large ways to get involved in their children's schools. This *Raising Our Sons* discussion group is a perfect place to start networking together and brainstorming ways for each participant to get involved in improving the lives and education of the children in your own school. Research has proven the benefits: your son's life and academic success will be greatly enhanced by your efforts to stay involved.

THE 40 DEVELOPMENTAL ASSETS Essential to Every Young Person's Success

The 40 Developmental Assets are research-proven building blocks that support the healthy development of our youth and help them to grow up to be caring and responsible. The following assets relate directly to a child's academic success and experiences at school:

- Asset #5 **Caring School Environment:** School provides a caring, encouraging environment.
- Asset #6 **Parent Involvement in Schooling:** Parent(s) are actively involved in helping young person succeed in school.
- Asset #9 **Service to Others:** Young person serves in the community, one hour or more per week.
- Asset #10 **Safety:** Young person feels safe at home, school, and in the neighborhood.
- Asset #12 **School Boundaries:** School provides clear rules and consequences.
- Asset #21 **Achievement Motivation:** Young person is motivated to do well in school.
- Asset #22 **School Engagement:** Young person is actively engaged in learning.
- Asset #23 **Homework:** Young person spends at least one hour on homework each school day.
- Asset #24 **Bonding to School:** Young person cares about his school.

CIRCLE QUESTION

Share one positive experience your son has had in school,
where he has really blossomed and grown.

POSSIBLE DISCUSSION QUESTIONS

1. How do perceive your school is doing with educating your child and with partnering with parents?
2. How is your child's school doing with building Development Assets? How can you get involved to increase assets at your child's school?
3. In what ways does your child's school show they care about their students? Does your child and do you perceive it as a nurturing, caring place?
4. What kinds of community-building activities occur at the school? What would you like to see?
5. What are some specific steps parents can make to enhance communication between home and school?
6. What strategies have helped your child with study skills, time management, and balance of activities?
7. Is character education being taught in the school? How effective is it? How can you help?
8. In what ways can overt and subtle expectations imposed by parents and teachers limit the growth and development of boys (and girls)? Did this happen to you growing up?
9. How does your school manage equity issues in education?
10. What are the key differences between bullying and a conflict? Why is it sometimes hard to tell? How would your parenting be influenced by knowing whether it's bullying or a conflict? Share examples.
11. How much peer aggression goes on at your child's school? What is your school doing to address this problem? Discuss the power of empathy and of addressing the "school climate" for systemic change.
12. How can you empower your child to help reduce peer aggression as a bystander? As an aggressor? As a target? What can you do to help reduce peer aggression at your child's school?

PUTTING IT INTO PRACTICE

- Have your child name people at school who show they care about students. Write a personal note of thanks and appreciation to everyone your child names.
- Help your child explore all the options for education available to him at his school or elsewhere if his current school is not serving his needs. He may not be aware of interesting opportunities.
- Nurture a sense of school ownership in students; include them in decision-making.
- Volunteer in your child's school: classroom, library, office or on PTA activities.
  If you work full-time, consider taking a half-day off to go on a field trip or offer to help from home occasionally.
- Engage your child in conversations about what she is learning in school.
- Make learning a family affair. Share each other's hobbies and interests.
- Attend all of your child's parent-teacher conferences, open houses, and community nights.
- Help your child explore all the options for education available to him at his school or elsewhere if his current school is not serving his needs. He may not be aware of interesting opportunities.
- Encourage your place of business to give employees time off to volunteer in a school.

- Plan extracurricular activities that bring students, teachers, administrators and staff together for fun and fellowship (e.g., a Bike Safety Fair, Ice Cream Social).
- Encourage your son to gain skills outside of the "stereotypical male role."
- Discuss with your child the peer aggression he sees in his school and empower him with information on how to make a positive impact.
- Talk with your son about the differences between groups of friends and cliques that emphasize sameness, exclusion and meanness. How can you tell when your group starts becoming a clique?
- Recognize the difference between friendship and popularity and that friendship is more important.
- Monitor yourself and your family and friends very closely to just notice target, bully and bystander behavior.
- Take a step at being the "gossip-stopper."
- Discuss the difficulty of keeping story-sharing, teasing or razzing and exclusion in the "healthy" realm to avoid hurting others inadvertently (both with adults and children).
- Share stories about how you struggled, learned and/or succeeded in supporting a target? A bully? A bystander? What worked best?
- Discuss situations where you (or your child) as bystanders wish you would have stepped up and helped a targeted person.
- Be a good listener and empathize with your child's social pain, but keep it in perspective.
- Try not to worry too much!

PUTTING IT TOGETHER—YOUR VERSION

Write down three or four ideas you have been inspired to implement in your own life after reading and discussing this chapter.

1. _____

2. _____

3. _____

4. _____

FURTHER READING

General Education

Challenge Newsletter: Dept of Educ. publication to Creating Safe and Drug Free Schools at www.thechallenge.org

ERIC: Education Resource Information Center at www.eric.ed.gov/

PTA: Parent Teacher Resources at www.pta.org/parent_resources.html

Search Institute: Building Assets in Schools at www.search-institute.org/education

Essential Assets for You at www.essentialassetsforyou.com/education.htm

Great Places to Learn: How Asset-Building Schools Help Students Succeed by Search Institute

You Have to Live It! video by Search Institute, identifies three themes for asset building in schools

Teaching with the Brain in Mind by Eric Jensen

Seven Kinds of Smart: Identifying and Developing Your Multiple Intelligences by Thomas Armstrong

Raising Lifelong Learners: A Parents Guide by Lucy Calkins and Lyle Bellino.

The Essential Difference: The Truth About Male & Female Brains by Simon Baron-Coven

Place-Based Education: Connecting Classrooms & Communities by David Sobel

What Do We Say? What Do We Do? Vital Solutions for Children's Educational Success by Dorothy Rich, EdD

At Home In our Schools: A Guide to School-Wide Activities that Build Community, ideas from the Child Development Project by Alfie Kohn at the Developmental Studies Center

Ways We Want Our Class to Be: Class Meetings that Build Commitment to Kindness and Learning by Developmental Studies Center

Among Friends: Classrooms Where Caring and Learning Prevails by John Dalton and Marilyn Watson

Your Hyperactive Child: A Parent's Guide to Coping with Attention Deficit Disorder by Barbara Ingersoll, PhD

Overcoming Underachieving: A Simple Plan to Boost Your Kids' Grades and End the Homework Hassles by Ruth Peters, PhD

The Pressured Child: Helping Your Child Find Success in School and Life by Michael Thompson, PhD and T. Barker

Is Your Teen Ready for a Job? and *The Five Worst Jobs for Teens* at www.familyeducation.com

Literacy

Misreading Masculinity: Boys, Literacy and Popular Culture by Thomas Newkirk

Boy Writers: Reclaiming Their Voices by Ralph Fletcher

Imagination and Literacy, A Teacher's Search for the Heart of Learning by Karen Gallas

Reading, Writing and Gender: Instructional Strategies and Classroom Activities that Work for Girls and Boys by Gail Goldberg and Barbara Roswell

Character Education and School Success

What Do You Stand For? A Kid's Guide to Building Character by Barbara Lewis

Character Counts by Josephson Institute Center for Youth Ethics at www.charactercounts.org

Gender-Focused Education

Masculinity Goes to School by Gilbert and Gilbert

Boy Smarts: Mentoring Boys for Success at School by Barry MacDonald

Building on Strengths: Helping Boys Succeed in Portland Public Schools by Howard Hiton. Free copy at www.hitonassociates.net/publications/publications.php

Addressing Relational and Verbal Aggression

Schools Where Everyone Belongs by Stan Davis, one of the best, positive resources for primary and middle schools

Cliques: 8 steps to Help Your Child Survive the Social Jungle by Charlene Giannetti and Margaret Sagarese

Bully, Bullied and Bystander: From Preschool to High School—How Parents and Teachers Can Break the Cycle of Violence by Barbara Colorosa

Nobody Left to Hate: Teaching Compassion after Columbine by Elliot Aronson

Best Friends, Worst Enemies: Understanding the Social Lives of Children by Michael Thompson

Mom, They're Teasing Me: Helping Your Child Solve Social Problems by Michael Thompson

The Bully-Free Classroom by Allan L. Beane

Books for Children and Teens

How To Do Homework without Throwing Up by Trevor Romain

Get Off My Brain: A Survival Guide for Lazy Students by Randall McCutchen

The Teenage Liberation Handbook: How to Quit School and Get a Real Life and Education by Grace Llewellyn

Keeping Ahead in School: A Student's Book about Learning Abilities and Learning Disorders by Mel Levine, MD

Great Places to Learn
How Asset-Building Schools Help Students Succeed
by Neal Starkman, PhD, Peter C. Scales, PhD, and Clay Roberts, MS

School must be more than just a place to learn—even a great place to learn. It should be a place to belong.
—Sara Pierce, Senior, Overland HS, Aurora, Colorado

HOW CAN A SCHOOL build Developmental Assets? The obvious thought might be for the school to concentrate on the five Commitment-to-Learning assets that are part of Search Institute's 40-asset model. Those five assets describe students who care about their school, are actively engaged in learning, are motivated to do well, hunker down over homework each school night, and read for their own enjoyment.

Yet research suggests that practically all the assets play some role in helping to create and sustain a climate for improved student learning. Although schools can't directly affect all 40 assets, they can have a direct impact on more than half, including the assets that research indicates are very important in promoting academic success (see chart).

A look at the key assets related to academic success reveals that most involve *relationships* more than they do *programs*. They are about how students are treated as individuals, how much they feel valued and cared about, the kinds of positive role models they have, and how connected they feel to their school. Researchers have repeatedly found that schooling is as much social—how students relate to each other and to the adults around them—as it is intellectual.

Yet most students do not experience most of these key assets. In fact, only 7 of the 22 Developmental Assets that schools can directly influence are experienced by half or more of students. For example, only a minority of students surveyed report experiencing school as a caring place, where students genuinely care about each other, and where students get care and encouragement from their teachers.

How can schools go about changing this? *Great Places to Learn: How Asset-Building Schools Help Students Succeed* identifies three strategic areas for action and offers stories from the field. Read on for a sample.

Forming Relationships

No matter who you are, you can potentially form a respectful, asset-building relationship with a young person. In fact, young people can form such relationships

Assets at Work at School

Assets Schools Can Most Directly Affect	Percentage of Youth Who Report Experiencing Asset*
School Engagement	64%
Achievement Motivation	63%
Positive Peer Influence	60%
Youth Programs	59%
Safety	55%
Bonding to School	51%
Service to Others	**50%**
School Boundaries	46%
Homework	45%
Peaceful Conflict Resolution	44%
Interpersonal Competence	**43%**
Other Adult Relationships	**41%**
High Expectations	41%
Resistance skills	37%
Parent Involvement in Schooling	29%
Planning and Decision Making	29%
Adult Role Models	27%
Caring School Climate	25%
Youth as Resources	25%
Reading for Pleasure	24%
Community Values Youth	**20%**
Creative Activities	19%

*Assets in boldface are those that research suggests are most important to academic success. *Sample of 99,462 6th- to 12th-grade youth surveyed in the 1996-1997 school year. Figures from Peter L. Benson, Peter C. Scales, Nancy Leffert, and Eugene C. Roehlkepartain. 1999. A Fragile Foundation: The State of*

that benefit both themselves and others. Consider, for example, the case of the boy who became a mentor.

Hilde Newman, a social worker at Dry Creek Elementary School in Englewood, Colo., tells the story of a boy (we'll call him Max) who had a number of emotional, learning, and motor problems. He was becoming increasingly difficult to teach—or even have in a classroom. But something happened; somebody looked for and found the positive in Max. One of the teachers told Newman that Max did great in her room.

Asked what was different about the situation there, the teacher revealed that the other students in the room were younger than Max, and he seemed to really enjoy working with them and being a leader.

So Max was given the responsibility of teaching several kindergarten students, and he became a mentor. The improvement in Max was dramatic. He began to walk taller, to show more tolerance for behaving in class, and to concentrate on his own work. "He loves helping out," says Newman, smiling. "He told me, 'I've got it worked out. I've got a plan for the kids.'" He was being treated as a resource, not as a problem, and as a result he more than fulfilled people's expectations and blossomed.

Creating an Environment

Lots of little changes are what add up to an asset-rich environment in which students experience comfort and warmth alongside challenges and boundaries. At New Richmond High School in rural New Richmond, *Wise,* an asset-building approach, has brought about wide-ranging innovations, from including students on the hiring committee for new faculty to adding comments about student strengths on each report card.

And for each new student who enrolls, New Richmond extends a warm welcome, sending out a letter of introduction to staff that might go something like this:

Hello! Let me introduce "Marcia," a new student at New Richmond High School. Marcia likes to read and write and indicates that some of her greatest assets include Planning and Decision-Making, Interpersonal Competence, and Cultural Competence.

Sometimes peaceful Conflict Resolution is a challenge for Marcia. When she experiences a conflict with staff, it's helpful for both the staff person and her if another person is there to help work through the conflict. Marcia is also working to improve her assets in the category of Support.

Using Programs and Practices

Asset-building is not itself a program or a practice; it's a philosophy that informs and shapes how we "do" school and a framework that helps schools organize their efforts on many fronts. But many programs and practices can contribute significantly to making a school a great place to learn. Some of these include service learning, peer mentoring and counseling, and youth leadership activities.

Consider Mitchell Elementary School in Denver, Colo., which has created a number of entrepreneurial programs that give learning a real-world flavor. Students

can see the concrete results of their hard work while at the same time building such assets as responsibility, planning and decision-making, and sense of purpose.

The budding young businesspeople run the Mitchell Mart, where they sell flowers and vegetables they've grown in their own garden behind the school; the school store, in which they sell school supplies to other students; and a vinyl-letter business called SPELL, for Students Producing Educational Letters in Learning. Mitchell Elementary School entrepreneurs can also be spotted pulling a red wagon through the school halls. They're headed to make deliveries for the teacher-supplies warehouse, as well as toward a brighter, asset-rich future.

School Resources

Great Places to Learn: How Asset-Building Schools Help Students Succeed, #722, 216 pages, $29.95.
"You Have to Live It." Building Developmental Assets in School Communities, #723, 27 minutes, VHS, $24.95.
Call Search Institute at 877-240-7251 to order.

Reprinted with permission from Neal Starkman, PhD, Peter C. Scales, PhD, and Clay Roberts, MS, "Great Places to Learn," *Assets: The Magazine of Ideas for Healthy Communities and Healthy Youth.* Copyright ©Autumn 1999 Search Institute®, Minneapolis, MN; www.search-insitute.org. All rights reserved.

Every Student a Star
School Staff Reach Out to the Forgotten Half
By Search Institute, from *Assets* Magazine

ALL KIDS ARE OUR KIDS—AREN'T THEY? Recently, Principal Randy Adair at Benold Middle School in Georgetown, Tex., decided to see to what degree the school was truly embracing that philosophy. He began by posting the names of all 900 Benold Students on the walls of the school cafeteria during a staff planning meeting.

"I said that we were going to do an exercise to let the staff know that all really does mean all," says Adair, referring to that title of the book by Search Institute President, Peter Benson. "I gave each teacher ten stickers and asked them to put a star next to the students that they had the closest relationship to."

After completing the task, the teachers and principal stood back and surveyed the cafeteria walls. What they discovered was that a quarter of the students had more than one star next to their names, but more than half didn't have any stars at all! "My immediate reaction was sadness," says sixth-grade language arts teacher Mindy Ellerbee. "We found that the more outgoing students had all of the stickers, and a number of those students who really needed our attention didn't have any."

The staff then brainstormed about those students who didn't have a connection to a staff member, identifying small ways to reach out without necessarily drawing attention to what they were doing. "A lot of these kids don't want a mentor and are suspicious of adults based on their own past relationships," says Adair. He acknowledges it can be a challenge to build bridges to such youth, especially those in high-risk situations who find learning and bonding to the school community difficult.

"I asked the teachers to put a star next to the names of the kids that they would start a relationship with in some way," says Adair. "To start, it could be as simple as saying 'Hi!' to that young person in the hall." Adair calls this strategy "the silent mentor concept."

Ellerbee is taking small steps to connect with her silent mentee, who struggles with low self-esteem. "My goal is not to be any different in his eyes but to raise my awareness of his needs," she says.

Adair says these new relationships will not only improve student self-esteem but will also allow them to excel academically. Ellerbee agrees. "I've found that by talking more about the Assets and raising the level of respect, student put more effort into their work than ever before," she says. "I believe it's because they get the sense that teachers care. The improved performance of Ellerbee's new star in her classroom is proof positive for her.

Asset-Building Ideas for Teachers

By Search Institute, from *Pass It On! Ready-to-Use Handouts for Asset Builders*

TO TEACH IS TO TOUCH a life forever. Teachers have the potential to be powerful asset builders. In addition to the Commitment-to-Learning assets (21-25), five other assets (3: Other Adult Relationships; 5: Caring School Climate; 8: Youth as Resources; 12: School Boundaries; and 14: Adult Role Models) focus on the important role of a teacher. Below are some suggestions for what teachers can do to build assets. These suggestions are intended to give you some ideas for how to get started. They may need to be modified or adapted depending on the grade you teach; whether you are a classroom teacher, specialist, or resource teacher; and the nature of your school environment.

Asset Building in General

- Post the list of assets in your classroom.
- Devote a bulletin board in your classroom to asset-building messages.
- If your community has an asset-building initiative, get involved.
- Train all volunteers and support staff you work with to the asset framework.
- Plan asset-building learning activities as part of the curriculum (for example, service learning projects, social skills training, or setting aside time to read for pleasure).
- Put an asset-building message on your computer screen saver. One school used the slogan, "Wrap Your Arms around Cherry Creek Kids . . . Build Assets!"

Support

- Greet students by name when you see them.
- Send a letter to parents about the idea of asset building, and then use assets as springboards for discussions in conferences with parents and students.
- Meet with other teachers and brainstorm ways to help students succeed. A school in Wisconsin set up DATES (Developing Assets to Encourage Success) meetings that are designed to help students who are struggling academically.
- Encourage access to at least one caring adult for each student in the building. Homerooms can facilitate this.
- Provide asset-building resources for parents.

Empowerment

- Teach students about the 40 Assets and help them set goals for assets they want to develop (two resources for this are *Me@My Best* and *Take It to the Next Level,* published by Search Institute).
- Provide opportunities for service learning. Help students plan and make decisions about providing service to others.
- Empower students by encouraging them to tell their stories through written and visual autobiographies.

Boundaries and Expectations

- Work with students to set school boundaries or rules. Post a written set of the rules in conspicuous places: hallways, classrooms, the lunchroom, the gymnasium, and other common areas. Create copies of the rules and have an agreement form for students and parents to sign, indicating their willingness to stay within the boundaries.

- Set high and clear expectations for student behavior and learning outcomes.

Constructive Use of Time

- Create visual symbols of assets. For example, cooperative murals can show the importance of working together to strengthen the community. Art students can create self-portraits that reflect their assets.
- Thank other teachers, staff, and students when you catch them building assets.
- Demonstrate sensitivity with respect to student involvement in extracurricular activities. Some teachers make it a practice to always allow at least two nights for students to complete assignments.
- Read biographies or view videos or films about musicians and other artists. Discuss the assets students see in these people's lives.
- Discuss current music, movies, or arts and entertainment and the messages they send. Do they build assets or not?

Commitment to Learning

- Discuss the assets of characters in stories, history lessons, and current events. For example, when studying Romeo and Juliet, talk about how asset deficits can lead to tragedies. Change the tale by building assets for the two main characters.
- Use assets as the focus for assignments.
- Choose a quote of the day with an asset focus and ask students to talk about it.
- Introduce students to web sites that have asset-building themes.
- Read biographies of people who have realized their dreams. Talk about the assets that helped those people succeed.

Positive Values

- Ask students to gather information about their heroes—famous or not. Then have small-group or class discussions about what values these heroes seem to have and how those values guide who they are and what they do.

- As a class, create a list of shared values. See the Positive-Values assets (26-31) as a place to start. Talk about what it takes to uphold these values. Set boundaries and expectations based on these values.

Social Competencies

- Provide a process in the classroom for mutual goal setting and evaluation. Such a process empowers students and actively engages their learning.
- Encourage planning through the use of student agendas and calendars.
- Use resources in your community to help teach Cultural Competence (asset 34). Consider having students organize a diversity-awareness week, a cultural fair, or some other way of learning about each other's backgrounds and cultures.
- Don't let students get away with bullying or fighting. Talk to them about how to solve conflicts peacefully.

Positive Identity

- Use "strength interviews" with students to help them identify their assets and their sources of support.
- Attend concerts, programs, and activities your students are involved in.
- Congratulate successes with a written note, a call home, or verbal praise.
- Create life-planning portfolios that follow a student from the end of one school year to the beginning of the next school year and include goals, dreams, and hopes. They can be an important tool for the student—and for teachers—to keep track of accomplishments and challenges.

The Developmental Assets are positive factors within young people, families, communities, schools, and other settings that research has found to be important in promoting the healthy development of young people.

Reprinted with permission from *Pass It On! Ready- to-Use Handouts for Asset Builders* [#28]. Copyright @1999, 2006 Search Institute®, Minneapolis, MN; www.search-institute.org. All rights reserved.

At Home in Our Schools
A guide to school-wide activities that build community
Ideas for Parents, Teachers, and Administrators from the Child Development Project
at the Developmental Studies Center

Creating a Sense of Community

While many of the community-building ideas presented here will be familiar, what may be new is the emphasis on the relationships that form and foster a sense of community—relationships that include everyone, avoid competition, and respect differences but lessen hierarchical divisions between older and younger students, staff members and students, and teachers and parents. As you read the pages that follow, think about your goals for community building and about the school-wide activities your school already sponsors.

Then think about ways in which small shifts in focus may better align these activities with your goals.

Consider the following example of how these essential ingredients might be realized in an actual activity, such as your school's annual science fair. How can the "traditional" science fair—in which children compete to create the "best" project in the hope of winning an award—be given a CDP "twist" to create an environment where everyone is included, everyone works cooperatively, and everyone wins?

Traditional vs. Noncompetitive	
"Traditional" Science Fair	**Noncompetitive Science Fair**
• Individual students create science projects that are displayed in a central area, such as a gym or a library. Students and families view the projects. Prizes are awarded to "outstanding" projects.	• Science experiments and activities are set up around the school in different classrooms. Students and families visit the classrooms and try out the activities. Students and families become more comfortable in school and experience a collaborative learning atmosphere—everyone is a learner.
• Competitive • Goal is to win • Students work individually	• Collaborative • Goal is to participate • Students work with families and other students
• Parents observe • Teachers judge • Some people win, some people lose • Excludes students and families unwilling to compete	• Parents participate • Teachers participate • Everyone wins, no one loses • Includes everyone

Family Projects Fair

A Family Projects Fair begins with families deciding on a cooperative project to do at home—for example, they might document a project that they work on together, such as planting a garden; create a project such as a science experiment or model; or make a display about a family interest, such as baseball or rock collecting. The emphasis should be on the process of working together as a family, rather than on the resulting "product." Families then show their projects at school for the Family Project Fair, during which they can both explain their work to other families in the school community and learn from the other families' projects.

Family Math Night

Family Math is a widely used parent involvement program developed by EQUALS at the Lawrence Hall of Science of the University of California at Berkeley. Together, parents and children attend a series of hands-on workshops where they use math manipulatives such as blocks, pennies, and other easy-to-find objects to understand more about numbers and space and to develop strategies for solving mathematics problems.

Working for a Cause

Each school picks a "helping opportunity that interests its students and staff—such as collecting supplies for disaster victims, raising money for a cause, or working together on a community service project such as a toy drive or walk-a-thon. Students apply their considerable energy and ingenuity to a cause that lets them reach out and contribute to the wider community.

Family Read-Aloud

Family Read-Aloud brings students, families, teachers, and school staff members together in a comfortable environment to enjoy reading. This event helps unite the entire school community around the importance of reading without setting up a competition among students and classes.

Family Science Night

Family Science Night is a high-involvement "messing around" time for children and their parents. Together, families make their way from classroom to classroom exploring a variety of hands-on science activities that students have created in class during the weeks leading up to the event.

These are summary excerpts describing some community-building ideas. Full details on ways of implementing these projects can be found in the book, *At Home in Our Schools: A Guide to School-Wide Activities That Build Community* by Alfie Kohn.

Reprinted with permission from Developmental Studies Center, 2000 Embarcadero, #305; Oakland, CA 94606, 1-800-666-7270, www.dvstu.org. Copyright 1994. All rights reserved.

Thinking Small in a Big School

By Linda West

TRAGIC INCIDENCES OF violence on school campuses prompted Congress to fund the development of small, safe and successful learning environments within large high schools. Three-fourths of high schools have over 1,000 students and half have over 1,500. Researchers and educators believe that large, impersonal schools may lead to increased apathy, isolation and alienation.

The Smaller Learning Communities Initiative is a $45 million federal grant program to develop smaller learning communities so that all students receive more personalized attention in order to make a successful transition to college, careers and productive citizenship. US Dept. of Education research supports that smaller learning environments result in increased student achievement, attendance and connectedness, and a decrease in disciplinary actions, drug and alcohol use.

Across the country, schools are examining ways of reorganizing their use of time, space and student/staff relationships to create safer and more effective learning environments. Southridge High School (SHS) near Portland, Oregon, is one such high school. SHS was designed to house its 1,800 students in 4 smaller, more personalized learning communities of 450 students each. In its second year of the Smaller Learning Communities grant, SHS is seeing the results: student achievement, test scores and academic rigor have increased, absentee and dropout rates have decreased. Says principal, Sarah Boly, "It's about re-inventing the 'American High School.' Smaller learning communities have the greatest potential for personalizing learning and are very supportive of humane treatment of kids. To create a small school, you have to create a democratic school."

So what are the key elements of the SHS initiative? Increase personalization of education and relationships with adults by:

- The neighborhood structure that includes a core group of teachers, parent volunteers, and an advisor, counselor and administrator who provide the student's base for four years.
- More in-depth teacher contact by having 5 classes a day for 70 minutes. (Many schools have 6-8 periods with educators facing upwards of 170 students daily!) Teachers and students alike get to know each other better. In the 9th/10th grade, Language Arts and Social Studies are teamed: teachers have the same students in both classes.

> "To create a small school, you have to create a democratic school."

- Assignment of an advisor with whom each student meets 2 to 3 times each week for 4 years to obtain academic support, conduct career and college planning and address important school climate issues. Each advisor has 25 students of all grade levels and a Link Crew Leader, who is a senior trained to serve as a big brother/sister to freshmen.
- Offering of Career Academies: Students focus their studies in one of 6 Career Academies ranging from Science and Technology to Arts and Communication. Students work closely with their Academy Advisor to pursue an individualized course of study that includes a senior project and field experience.
- Completion of a Service Learning requirement: In order to graduate, every student completes at least 60 hours of community service that is tied to their course work, thus making their schooling more authentic and relevant.
- Offering a variety of courses and programs: Based on a trimester schedule, students graduate with 30 credits, as opposed to the standard 24. Students are encouraged to explore their interests, pursue their dreams and prepare for college and career. A strong International Baccalaureate program allows students to earn a full IB diploma or follow their passion in a particular subject area. The Learning Center offers 9th and 10th grade students a daily study period with a peer tutor, resulting in both academic and social success. Students sit in small table groups, not individual desks, emphasizing discussion and interaction, not isolation. Teachers team and make inter-disciplinary connections.
- Valuing student voices: As members of staff committees, students raise questions, address key issues and make proposals on issues ranging from advisory topics to discipline policies.

At SHS, the Small School grant has enabled staff to look at other model programs and collaboratively examine their own teaching. The SHS staff are committed to small school reform that has proven so effective in their work with students.

Linda West is a high school teacher in Beaverton, Oregon.

Reprinted with permission from Full Esteem Ahead, *Wings*, Winter 2002.

TRIBES: A New Way of Learning and Being Together

By Nancy Huppertz

A CLASSROOM IS A microcosm of a community. The members are together on a regular basis, in the same place, and must function together to attain group and individual goals. At the elementary level, the group is usually intact for 5 to 6 hours each day. At the secondary level, groups are together for only 50 or 90 minutes, but they are together every day and, to be most successful, must function harmoniously.

Teachers are trained well in their content areas. They know what to teach and most have acquired skills in how to get the information across to students. What most teachers lack is the skill to turn a room full of individuals into a group that functions well for all its members. What happens in the classroom each day is an important part of a student's educational experience not only cognitively, in terms of the content taught, but emotionally and socially, how it feels to be in the classroom, how s/he is treated by the teacher and other students and whether s/he feels an integral part of what is going on.

TRIBES is a national program that trains teachers how to build community in the classroom. The goal is to make all students feel welcome and viable, to feel as though they are regarded and treated in a positive manner by the teacher and other students, and to have the knowledge, skills and resilience to be successful in a rapidly changing world.

TRIBES is not a curriculum, but a process that uses three phases and a set of community agreements to transform a room full of isolates into a group.

TRIBES begins with INCLUSION. Teachers learn how to take the time to build caring and support within the group by allowing students to get to know each other. A skilled TRIBES teacher knows how to encourage students to participate in inclusive activities without feeling that they have to reveal personal information if they do not wish. Barriers between diverse students begin to crumble as they begin to know and enjoy their similarities and respect their differences.

The next phase of TRIBES is INFLUENCE. Teachers give students a sense of value and offer meaningful participation by modeling and teaching communication skills, some as basic as taking turns speaking, rotating responsibilities in small groups, asking questions, listening, disagreeing without rancor, and problem-solving. TRIBES teachers know not to assume that the students already have these skills. Many adults do not.

Finally, TRIBES recognizes the importance of APPRECIATION. Time is taken to express thanks to other members of the group for working together and students are taught to value the contributions and celebrate the achievements of others.

The community agreements taught early on in TRIBES classrooms include: attentive listening, appreciation, no put-downs, mutual respect, and the right to pass.

Judi Mackey, a middle school principal in the state of Washington, sponsored a TRIBES training for her entire staff. The staff was so enthusiastic about the concepts and process that they began using them in staff meetings as well as in their classrooms. A year later, Principal Mackey reported a decline in absenteeism among students and staff and a reversal in attitudes of substitutes previously reluctant to come to her school—all attributed by Mackey to the implementation of TRIBES.

Schools throughout the US and Canada are using TRIBES to create safe and non-violent schools, engage students in the prevention and management of conflict, make cooperative learning work well, teach students collaborative social skills and provide inclusion and respect for multicultural populations. TRIBES was developed and written by Jeanne Gibbs.

Parents who would like to see a TRIBES training occur in their child's school may contact CenterSource Systems at 1-800-810-1701 to get the name of a TRIBES trainer in their area. The trainer can provide complete information about TRIBES to the principal and may be willing to do a brief overview of TRIBES for a parent group or faculty meeting. Check out the web site at www.tribes.com.

Nancy Huppertz is a gender equity specialist who runs Apogee Training and Consulting, consulting firm specialists in gender equity issues for organizations and schools throughout the United States.

Reprinted with permission of Full Esteem Ahead, *Wings*, Winter, 2002.

Fostering Cooperation and Compassion in the Classroom

By Kathy Keller Jones, MA

IN MANY HIGH SCHOOLS and middle schools around the country, the academic environment encourages students to compete against each other for grades and teacher attention. Students have 6-8 classes like this a day and the competition in the classroom exacerbates competition outside the classroom. Everything becomes a competition: the car you drive, the clothes you wear, the sports you play. This highly competitive atmosphere creates a situation of winners, losers, and those in the middle. The winners and those in the middle will distance themselves from the losers, often teasing and taunting then. We've seen these situations escalate in cases like Columbine and Springfield.

Many schools have tried to counteract the effect of too much competition. In fact, in elementary and preschools, children are encouraged to share, treat others with respect and cooperate, even nurturing students with outdoor classes. All children are included, even those with learning disabilities or physical handicaps. Unfortunately, teaching inclusion and using cooperative learning techniques become less common as children grow older. It is hard to find a high school that has successfully dealt with the negative impact of competition.

The "jigsaw classroom" is a cooperative learning structure and has been used successfully for over 30 years. It was developed by Elliot Aronson, author of *Nobody Left to Hate: Teaching Compassion after Columbine*. The jigsaw classroom is designed to reduce competition and increase cooperation among students. It is successful, because unlike other cooperative learning environments, it requires everyone's cooperation to produce the final product. For example, if in the name of cooperation, we simply put a group of students together to work on a project, the one or two most motivated students will do most of the work and they will resent that they have had to carry the load. The less able and less motivated students will do less, learn less, and end up feeling inadequate. While it seems like this model should have created cooperation, it didn't.

The jigsaw classroom works like this: the class is divided into small groups of 5-6 students. Each group is assigned the task to learn, for example, about World War II. Each member of the group is assigned a different area to become an expert in. For example, one student researches Hitler's rise to power, another is assigned to learn about concentration camps, the others research Britain's role, the Soviet Union's role, Japan's role and the atomic bomb. Each student goes off to research their given area. Then a student researching the atomic bomb may work with students who are also assigned to learn about the atomic bomb but are from different groups. This helps ensure that information is complete and accurate. After all the students have researched their individual areas, the groups reconvene to share their information. Even the students who didn't do their research well, but went to the group meeting on their subject, will have valuable information to share. Each group member has to listen intently to the person reporting or they will not be able to learn the information they may need for the test that follows.

There are many benefits to this style of learning. The jigsaw classroom (www.jigsaw.org) is an efficient way to learn material, but more importantly, it gives every student an important role and requires that everyone listen attentively. Only teamwork can achieve the desired outcomes, and individual and group goals become intertwined. Each student ends up collaborating successfully with a variety of classmates, some of whom s/he might not normally interact with. Ideally a sense of belonging will be created within the classroom. In the same way that competition in the classroom exacerbates competition outside the classroom, cooperation, empathy, and compassion in the classroom will lead to cooperation, empathy, and compassion outside the classroom. Our children of all ages need to be taught in ways and about topics that foster the development of compassion, respect, and cooperation.

Resources:
   Check out www.jigsaw.org.
   Nobody Left to Hate by Elliot Aronson

The Power of Arts Education: Everything I Need to Know I Learned from My Dance (Art) Teacher

By Georgia Harker

TRYING TO "REACH" our teens, we often listen to their words but miss their meaning. Just like the rest of us, our children communicate in many ways. Encouraging and supporting our adolescents' continuing involvement with the arts is one way to "hear" what they are trying to say and teach life skills.

Linda Smith, my dance teacher, taught me that my dancing is a unique, personal, and important form of expression, but that the underlying experiences are universal. I learned to:

- Not automatically accept my first solution to any problem.
- Keep building my skills to perform my best work.
- Use eye contact.
- Present my work and myself confidently.

Through the arts we learn many things. As a parent and an artist, I'm continually reminded of the power and importance of the arts and arts education in our children's lives. When there are opportunities for self-expression, risk-taking, problem solving, and imagination in a supportive environment, good things happen.

Jan von Bergen, a teacher at the Arts and Communication High School in Beaverton, Oregon, has taught art for 22 years. She believes very passionately that "one of the worst things you could do to teenagers is to take away their expressive outlets. They are vital. It would be like cutting their heads off!" She thinks art education encourages students to dig within, to push themselves, and to improve at something. She believes this is great for building self-esteem.

How does Jan encourage healthy self-esteem in her students? "My approach is always, 'tell me about that,' not, 'what is that?' In spite of teenagers' apparent bravado, they are really very sensitive. You can inadvertently put the kibosh on something that would have been great, by seeming to criticize it. What matters most is not what I see in their work, but what they are trying to create."

Art, music, and theater classes can be havens for students who don't shine in the prescribed ways most schools emphasize. I still harbor a crush on a tall, charming guy I knew in high school. While barely passing most of his other classes, he produced amazing and ambitious creations in Mr. Morrison's art class. Howard Gardner, Harvard education specialist and author, might say my friend displayed "high degrees of visual/spatial and kinesthetic intelligence." Gardner's research into the brain and learning styles led him to identify seven different forms of intelligence, and to call for radical changes in how we teach and raise kids.

In his book, *The Unschooled Mind*, Gardner says that different people learn, think, and respond to the same stimulus differently. We want to acknowledge that and help children build on their strengths. For teens who are more spatially, musically, or kinesthetically oriented, involvement in the arts may be the vital link with school and learning. "To the extent that students feel good about themselves, feel productive, have an opportunity to be critical and creative in the arts," he says, "these can have positive spin-offs in the class and in school."

Anna Montgomery is a family friend whose self-confidence was clearly bolstered by her decision to attend a small, arts-oriented high school. She thought she would feel lost, or be labeled "weird" at a large school, where she finds most of the energy and attention go into fashion and sports. She likes being in a place where self-expression is valued and expected.

Jan von Bergen has great advice for parents: "Allow for different approaches! As much as possible in school and in life, present the important concepts and goals you'd like them to achieve. Then let them decide how to get there. Allow for growth. Help them to take chances, and to stretch out of their comfort zone. Otherwise, they'll never reach new levels of understanding and achievement."

Georgia Harker is a designer and writer who works with her husband Chris, for Cayuse, their software company. She has a daughter and a son.

Reprinted with permission from Full Esteem Ahead, *Wings*, Winter 1999.

The Turning Point: Boys' Night Out

By Kathleen Janicki and Janet Cathcart

WHAT HAPPENS WHEN you stay up late with 60 sixth-grade boys: tons of fun, exemplary behavior, making new friends, seeing old ones and building healthy relationships. That's what students experienced at the 2nd Annual *Turning Point* at Athey Creek Middle School in West Linn, Oregon. It was a tremendous success for students and parents alike. The *Turning Point* is a sixth-grade sleep over and part of the school's character development program. There is one night for all of the sixth-grade girls and another for all of the sixth-grade boys. The two events were organized by Athey Creek's Parent Teacher Student Association. This idea stemmed from the *Girls Night Out* curriculum produced by Cindy Eaton, a teacher who has developed a program to help spread the word on this wonderful idea. Athey Creek successfully adapted it to include boys last year.

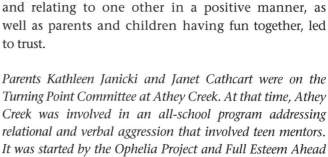

Turning Point was designed for students to get to know one another in a friendly and safe environment. Teen mentors from the local high school headed up small groups. Each group was designed to include students who did not know each other well. They started things off with creative activities designed to help them learn about each other and to break down barriers that traditionally support "cliques."

The Boy's *Turning Point* drew 60 sixth-grade boys as well as 20 dads (who managed to survive on a few hours of sleep). It is hard to know who had more fun, the kids or the dads! Teen boys mentored small groups of the sixth-graders. Nick Jones, a former NBA player, inspired the boys with his candid dialog. The evening flew by in a flurry of activities from hip-hop dance lessons to midnight basketball to juggling lessons, relay races, foosball, movies and, of course, LOTS of eating. Having so many dads involved was the key to making

this evening such a success. Although tired the next morning, the boys left with smiles and enthusiastically urged the school to hold the event again next year.

In order to pull off this kind of successful experience for students, many parents must be involved. The Athey Creek planning committee for the boys' and girls' overnights was comprised of three coordinators, a teen who took charge of getting teen mentors from the local high school, fourteen moms and five dads. The parents who went without sleep at the two events were very grateful for the fresh batch of parents who came the next morning to serve breakfast and help clean up. Community neighbors and businesses also played a role, generously donating from their hearts—food, supplies and financial support.

Most impressive were the students themselves, who responded beyond expectations, participating with enthusiasm, and reminding all of the parents why we volunteer. They demonstrated that the goal of the evening, learning about and relating to one other in a positive manner, as well as parents and children having fun together, led to trust.

Parents Kathleen Janicki and Janet Cathcart were on the Turning Point Committee at Athey Creek. At that time, Athey Creek was involved in an all-school program addressing relational and verbal aggression that involved teen mentors. It was started by the Ophelia Project and Full Esteem Ahead at an in-service given in August 2000. Boys' and Girls' Night Out are a fabulous way to break down cliques and teasing.

Reprinted with permission from Full Esteem Ahead, *Wings,* Winter 2002.

Character Counts! From the Inside Out

By Liz Swinea, School Principal

"NOT ONE MORE THING! Our plate is full and overflowing!" teachers are saying. They are bombarded with information, technological advances, and more and more pressure for accountability for student achievement. How can they possibly be expected to teach one more thing? And of all things, why character education? I believe we can't afford to not teach character education, purposefully, systematically, and pervasively. With violence, substance abuse, and delinquency on the rise, there is a sense of urgency to reduce the risk factors that contribute to these problems, while promoting protective processes as preventive measures. Character development—a firm understanding of and commitment to core ethical values is one such protective measure. It is essential to inform and to energize conscientious, proactive decision-making.

The staff of Lincoln Elementary School identified character education as a means through which we would raise achievement and decrease disciplinary referrals. We specifically chose *Character Counts!*, a nationally recognized, community-based program directed toward developing character in children. Founded by Michael Josephson, the *Character Counts! Coalition* is a project of the Josephson Institute of Ethics. It identifies Six Pillars that "clearly define us at our best"—trustworthiness, respect, responsibility, fairness, caring, and citizenship.

To initiate our Character Counts! program, we compared it to the Wizard of Oz, since we felt that the story line and characters were familiar to most kids. In our version, Dorothy is looking for someplace special, where character counts. The Scarecrow, Tin Man, and Lion represent the thinking, compassion, and courage it takes to be a person of character. They follow the yellow brick road through the Pillars of Character, only to discover that it's up to them to make their school, families, and community a place where character counts. The script was the brainchild of teachers, Cindy Robnett and Kathleen Augsburger.

Each month we study a Pillar of Character, integrating it throughout the curriculum, from reading to math to P.E. Everywhere on campus, kids are "caught" being persons of character and are awarded a coupon, which goes into a weekly lottery for prizes. Daily announcements include brief comments about what character looks like and sounds like—at school, at home, and downtown. We've created a "citizenship" grade on the report card. To earn an A, students must not only follow the rules, they must also provide two hours of community service. We celebrate quarterly success, and students who earn A's three of the four quarters are inducted into the Kids' Character Counts! Club.

Parent involvement is an integral part of our program. Through newsletters from school, and a page in our local newspaper, we keep parents and the community informed of the monthly pillar. We identify vocabulary, and the do's and don'ts specific to the current pillar. This year we'll sponsor several parent seminars to encourage support and to invite input on improving the program.

We've encouraged community involvement by posting kid-made posters in our stores, and requesting patrons to ask our kids about the Pillar of the Month. Kids' Club members march in our community's annual parade in June. As we emphasize community service, we're supporting the community's swimming pool enhancement campaign, setting a goal of $2000 in our own "Pennies for the Pool" project.

The responsibility to teach our youngsters about character rests with all of us—parents, schools, and community members. Yes, it does take a village to raise a child. Thank goodness, we're in it together—for kids' sake!

Elizabeth Swinea ran this program as principal of Lincoln Elementary in Coquille, Oregon. The Character Counts! website is www.charactercounts.org.

Reprinted with permission of Full Esteem Ahead, *Wings*, Winter 1999.

Cheating in High School is Widespread, High-Tech and Contagious

By Kathy Masarie, MD

HIGH SCHOOL STUDENTS today find themselves in a competitive environment where grades and test scores determine their eligibility for graduation, upscale scholarships, university admissions and favored academic status. Faced with family and academic pressures to succeed, many students are cheating as a convenient and efficient way to get ahead.

Cheating has become much easier for students now that they have access to computers and the Internet. Numerous websites offer tips on how to cheat and others sell downloadable term papers for $10-$15 apiece. The Internet acts as a multi-billion page encyclopedia, offering endless cut and paste opportunities for students who plagiarize to enhance their own writing.

Classroom cheating has also hit the high-tech age. Students can use small fonts to create crib sheets on business or note cards, which they then use to cheat on tests. Palm pilots can be used to "beam" answers to each other, and calculators can be programmed with algebraic formulas that are supposed to be memorized.

"Students are getting a bottom-line mentality that grades matter, not learning," states Elizabeth Kiss, director of the Kenan Institute for Ethics at Duke University. She notes that cheating starts at ages 11-13, when schools begin to place more emphasis on grades.

Michael Josephson, founder of Josephson Ethics Institute notes that kids do not grow out of cheating. "In fact," he says, "they grow into it. Cheaters are more likely to lie on resumes, expense reports and insurance claims."

The problem of cheating has always been around, but it is getting more common and more acceptable in recent years. A 2002 study by the Josephson Ethics Institute found that 74% of 12,000 high school students nationwide had cheated on a test in the previous year. This represented a 21% increase over a decade before. As well, 38% of the students admitted to stealing from a store within the past 12 months, and over 80% admitted to lying to parents and teachers. Of these students, 43% of them agreed with the statement that "a person has to lie or cheat sometimes in order to succeed." This is a substantial increase from just two years previous, and indicates a growing cynicism amongst our young people.

Josephson notes, *"The evidence is that a willingness to cheat has become the norm and that parents, teachers, coaches and even religious educators have not been able to stem the tide. The scary thing is that so many kids are entering the workforce to become corporate executives, politicians, airplane mechanics and nuclear inspectors with the dispositions and skills of cheaters and thieves."*

A similar 2001 study by Donald McCabe of the Rutgers University Management Education Center found that 75% of 4,500 high school students had engaged in serious cheating, up from 50% in 1993 and 25% in 1963. This study also found that more than half of the students had plagiarized work they found on the Internet, and a similar number did not see anything wrong with cheating. When students were asked why they cheat, most cited academic pressures and the poor examples set by the adult world. McCabe notes, "I think kids today are looking to adults and society for a moral compass, and when they see the behavior occurring there, they don't understand why they should be held to a higher standard."

What can parents and teachers do about this phenomenon of cheating? First of all, it is important to make your values of trust and integrity clear to your students. Children not only need to hear that cheating in any form is a serious offense; they need to watch adults be good role models in their own lives. Kids notice when adults act in untrustworthy or dishonest ways, and frequently copy what they have learned. Honesty, trust and integrity are best taught by example.

Websites, such as www.nocheating.org, offer tips, advice, and free pamphlets to help adults teach values that counteract cheating. Teachers can also educate kids about plagiarism and utilize a number of website services that check term papers with search engines to identify plagiarism. Parents and teachers can help by emphasizing learning over class standing and grades. This may mean taking an active role in redirecting your own academic emphasis and goals for your child, as well as influencing that of your child's teachers and the local school system. Helping your child to get organized is a big help for kids who cheat due to time crunches and/or overextended schedules. This could mean helping your child to schedule time on the calendar to work on bigger projects, limiting extracurricular activities, or brainstorming with your child about ideas and research.

Most of all, it is important for parents to resist the urge to do homework for their child. One study of middle schoolers found that 33% turned in work done by their parents. This sets a terrible example, as it involves kids in cheating with the sanction of their parents and robs them of an opportunity to learn for themselves.

Josephson summarizes: *"The biggest single factor in escalating academic dishonesty is the failure of parents and teachers to diligently teach, enforce, advocate and model personal integrity. It's the adults, not the kids, who have the greatest responsibility to create an ethical culture that nurtures the virtues of honor, honesty and fairness."*

Helping Our Children Learn Study Skills

By Susan Wellman, founder of *The Ophelia Project*

My child wants me to be with her when she studies. I need that time to get things done around the house. How important is it that I study with her?

My son is totally disorganized when he studies. I tell him to clean off his desk; he tells me he likes to work that way. I don't know what to do about it.

Studying each night in our home has become a war zone. Our kids want us to help them, but when we do they just get mad at us. I also have to hassle them to get off the phone or away from the TV. They argue that they study better in front of the TV. It's making me crazy and I'm about to give up entirely. What do you recommend?

DO THESE SOUND like they could have come from your home? You're not alone. All parents struggle with the homework issue. Here are some tips to help parents create a good study environment at home:

1. Choose a good study site where the whole family can be together rather than having children working alone in their rooms.
2. Create a "distraction-free" zone during study times. Turn off the phone so you don't even hear it ring. If your child needs background noise to study, turn the radio on low volume.
3. Make this a time when everyone in the family is studying or reading. Reading together as a family is one of the best ways to encourage the activity.
4. Create an aura in your home where learning is "what we do in our family," just like "we use napkins instead of our sleeves" or "we listen when someone has a concern."
5. Make "learning" not "homework" the task.
6. Correct homework only if your child asks for help and if this is a peaceful activity between you and your child. Reassure your child that the goal is NOT to get everything right. It is to learn the material, eventually, not necessarily all at once.
7. When your child is "stuck" (angry, frustrated, self-deprecating, bored), try these tips:
   - Show a genuine interest in what your child is learning.
   - Ask your child questions that he/she CAN answer—be the learner and allow your child to be the teacher. If you are both clueless about an assignment, suggest questions the child can

ask the teacher the next day and be eager to hear the answers when your child returns.
   - When you or your child can't do something, use that moment to role model effective problem-solving skills—ask questions, seek answers, practice and acknowledge that the learning process involves stretching and not always being able to do something right away. If your child can always do the work, he/she is not being challenged.
   - If you see a problem, speak directly with the teacher rather than venting your concerns to your child.
   - Keep the dialogue with the teacher open until you both feel the child is "on the right track." Email works well for many teachers.
8. At dinnertime, make it a ritual for everyone in the family to share one thing new they learned today and one thing they don't understand yet.
9. Create family mantras about school, studying and learning.
   - We are learners and readers.
   - School is an opportunity to learn.
   - Learning is a life-long adventure and it is fun!
   - It's perfectly OK to make mistakes or not learn something right away.
   - Each time you will do a little better.
   - It's not your grades that count.
10. Create a reward at the end of study sessions (not video games), such as:
   - A half-hour family TV program that you all watch together,
   - A bowl of popcorn, dessert or piece of fruit,
   - Play a game or do a hobby,
   - Read to your child from a great book,
   - A phone call to a friend.

Susan Wellman, founder of The Ophelia Project, *has brought relational and verbal aggression prevention into schools all over the country. Previous to this, she taught study skills, then high school and college English. She lives in Erie, PA, is mother to a son and daughter, and has five grandchildren.*

Reprinted with permission of Full Esteem Ahead, *Wings*, Winter 2002.

Time Management from a Different Point of View

By Marydee Sklar, Organizing Coach, Teacher and Tutor

BELIEVE IT OR NOT, you can teach your child time management skills. The trick is to use strategies that match your child's thinking. If you're a parent who is always on time and always plans ahead, your approach using lists and priorities won't work with a child who floats through time. Lecturing them just goes in one ear and out the other. If you're a parent who struggles with being on time and meeting deadlines and you have a child who is also challenged by time issues, there's hope! This article gives you family-tested ideas to help you teach your child the critical life skill of time management.

I've found it useful to divide learners into two groups, based upon behavioral characteristics. By looking at behavior, I have clues about how the learner's brain works. I label these two types of learners as auditory thinkers and visual thinkers.

In my role as a learning coach, I specialize in visual thinkers. This is the group of learners who typically have the most challenges connected to time. Auditory thinkers, on the other hand, seem to have internal clocks and can more easily manage themselves using traditional homework strategies.

If your child exhibits most of the behaviors listed in the box, you can describe your child as a visual thinker. It is critical for visual learners to be taught about time management using methods that match their visual brain. I know this because I am a visual thinker and have visual thinking children. The ideas I use as a learning coach came from problem solving within our family. The list of tools

and ideas below are effective because they keep time in the sight and mind of the visual thinker. I recommend the book, *Mapping Inner Space: Learning and Teaching Visual Mapping (Zephyr Press, 2001)*, by Nancy Margulies for more ideas about visual learning and teaching.

Time Tools and Tips:

- "Face clocks" and wristwatches: Have one in every room, even in the shower! They show how much time remains to finish a task. They help the visual thinker see ahead so they can be on time.

- Beeping digital timers: The continual beeping breaks into the visual thinker's world and brings them back into the present. It works as a reminder to change activities. Visual thinkers have no clue about how long a task really takes, so timing a homework assignment is a good exercise for a child. They'll find that if they stay focused and try to "beat the timer" they'll have time left over for fun!

- Use an assignment book that shows the whole month at one glance. Record assignments on the date they are due. This helps them to look ahead and not forget assignments. Dates for extra-curricular activities, parties and family events should also be written on the calendar.

- Use "to do" lists that are divided into 30-minute increments of time. Block out the time that is taken by activities like sports, dinner and chores. The empty

TRAITS OF A VISUAL THINKER:
- Big picture, creative thinking—not sequential linear thinking
- Spoken and written language lacks continuity of thought
- Usually late; NOW is important
- Last minute or late projects, produces lower quality work
- Trouble planning ahead; lots of procrastination
- Distractible
- Lists and prioritizing don't help scheduling
- Argues with, or ignores verbal reminders to work

TRAITS OF AN AUDITORY THINKER:
- Sequential details
- Organized "linear" language
- Usually on time or early
- Completes projects on time; has time for quality work
- Stays on task
- Works well with lists and reminders

space is where they have time for homework. Once the work is done, the leftover spaces are for fun!

- Plan ahead by planning backwards using the monthly assignment calendar. For bigger assignments and projects, use Post-it-Notes to represent each step.

On each individual task note, write the estimated time required to complete each part of the project from its beginning, through revisions, to the end. Begin by placing the "Done!" note on the calendar space two days before the actual due date. These two days are a cushion for unexpected complications like the printer dying. Then, put all of the remaining Post it-Notes on the calendar by working backward to the beginning task. Your child will have to decide where there is time to work on each piece. After this exercise, your child can concretely see the time needed to complete the project. They know when they have to begin and how they must fit it in with the rest of their life.

Developing good time management skills is a process that has to be learned and practiced in steps, especially for a visual thinker. A child, who can use time well, will feel less stress and be more successful reaching their goals. Be patient with yourself and your child as you teach and model time management skills. Time spent developing these skills is time well spent.

Marydee Sklar is a state-licensed teacher and reading specialist. She coaches individual children and adults who need help with learning, writing and time management. She conducts workshops and gives presentations for groups. You may reach her at marydee.sklar@comcast.net.

Resources

Beat Procrastination and Make the Grade by Linda Sapadin
The Procrastinating Child: A Handbook for Adults to Help Children Stop Putting Things Off by Rita Emmett
Perfectionism: What Is Bad about Being so Good by Free Spirit Press
Taming the Tiger (of Stress) by Free Spirit Press

Reprinted with permission of Full Esteem Ahead *Wings*, Winter 2002.

Our Sons Are Faring Poorly in School: What Can We Do About It?

By Jody Bellant Scheer, MD

Current Underachievement in School by Boys is a Contemporary Global Trend

It is a commonly held belief that boys and men benefit from power relationships in modern society that give them disproportionate advantages over girls and women in every arena. Currently, this view cannot be substantiated in at least one important area: that of males within our educational system, from elementary school through college. For at least the past decade, in fact, girls have outperformed boys in most measures of academic achievement.[1] In addition, girls drop out of high school at lower rates, participate more often in academic extracurricular activities, attend college more often, and now earn the majority of scholarships and college degrees.[1] Girls may have encountered educational difficulties in previous decades, but it now appears that they have caught up and a new educational "gender gap" has emerged: that of boys who are falling to the bottom of the heap in great numbers and failing in school.[2] This is not just a problem in the United States, it is part of a global trend of male academic underachievement that can be seen in most other developed countries as well, including Western Europe, Australia, New Zealand and Japan.[3]

Understanding this academic underachievement of boys is a great and complex challenge for educators, legislators and parents alike who would like their sons, as well as their daughters, to have successful educational experiences. To better understand this phenomenon, it is helpful to first look at how boys are actually doing academically. Then, reviewing recent advances in brain research can show us how boys and girls have structural and neurological differences that affect learning. Equally helpful is to look at how cultural constraints on behavior and gender-based concepts of masculinity can deeply affect academic success for boys. Often dismissed in research on academic resiliency and school success are the effects of family structure and social, racial and ethnic factors. Lastly, it is important to look at schools and educational settings where boys (and girls) are already doing well, so that we can know what to advocate for in our own schools to help our sons become successful students. In this era of "leave no child behind," it is especially important for parents, educators and schools to be knowledgeable about the special characteristics and educational needs of our boys, so academic changes can be implemented in our communities that will positively impact the academic futures of our sons.

The Current State of Affairs: Just How Far Are Boys Falling Behind in Academics?

Boys as a group have been losing ground academically for years, and although there is a preponderance of male all-stars in the top 10% of math and science performers, the same is not true for reading and writing. Overall, there are also twice as many boys as girls who fall into the lowest rungs of academic achievement.[2] Since at least 1992, boys have posted lower overall grades and class marks than girls, and do significantly less well in assessments of reading and writing skills.[1] The typical boy is, in fact, one-and-a-half years behind the typical girl in reading and writing.[4] Boys still maintain a narrow advantage on standardized testing in math and science, but girls now take more higher-level math and science courses than boys.[1] Finally, boys are doing more poorly in school than girls across all socioeconomic levels, though the differences are smaller in more affluent groups.[5]

There are other indicators that boys are not doing well in school. First of all, "the over-representation of males in special education classes and in virtually every other category of emotional, behavioral or neurological impairment is undisputed" amongst educators and researchers.[1] Two-thirds of all children requiring special education are boys,[2,3,6] boys receive 71% of all school suspensions,[6] and boys are up to 50% more likely to be held back a grade than girls.[6] Boys are up to ten times more likely than girls to be diagnosed with a serious emotional disorder, especially attention deficit hyperactivity syndrome, and have 2 to 3 times the incidence of communication disorders, such as stuttering or dyslexia.[4,6] Boys are twice as likely to be labeled as learning disabled, are three times as likely to be the victim of violent crime, and are 4 times as likely to commit suicide.[6] Boys are 3 times as likely to be autistic, and are more commonly schizophrenic, delinquent, and perpetrators of criminal acts or homicide.[4] Additionally, boys are less commonly involved than girls in student government, honor societies, school newspapers, leadership roles, and extracurricular academic clubs and activities.[1] The only activity where boys are involved in greater numbers than girls is sports.[1] Not surprisingly, a 1998 study by the Horatio Algiers Association found that only 37% of highly successful students were male, and that males made up an overwhelmingly large majority (70%) of disillusioned students.[4]

Dr. William Pollack, a professor of psychology and author of the book, *Real Boys*, has researched the dilemma of boys' academic underachievement at length, and notes that "behind all these statistics lies an irrefutable yet under discussed reality: boys have a significant problem with their self-esteem as students."[2] This problem tends to worsen over time, such that "adolescent boys suffer from a crisis in self-esteem that seriously threatens their capacity to learn, achieve, and feel successful."[2] Feeling disempowered, males tend to graduate less often from high school, and the number of males going on to college has been dropping dramatically over the past 20 years. Women now outnumber men at all levels in postgraduate education: only 44% of college students are male, and men earn only 45% of all bachelors and master's degrees.[1] For African-American young men, this problem is even more pronounced: they earn only one third as many postgraduate degrees as do African-American women.[1]

One question comes to mind in light of this cascade of statistics. How could the educational crisis amongst our sons have gone so unnoticed over the past few years? Why do so few parents or educators even know of this problem?

There are several possible explanations. The disadvantage of girls in classroom environments has been a hot topic for the past three decades. One inadvertent assumption made by many who have championed the efforts that have helped girls to make substantial academic gains in recent years, is that if girls are doing poorly in school, boys must be doing great.[5] This simply isn't true. By pitting the interests of boys and girls against each other, many have failed to see that many of the conditions that caused girls to fail in the classroom are the same ones that are detrimental to boys.[7] Other people fail to be concerned about the problems boys are having in school because they rationalize that the gender differences that favor girls in school are more than offset by labor forces favoring boys in the workplace.[5] This

is an insensitive rationale that ignores the plummeting self-esteem and success of half of our nation's students. Our sons and daughters equally deserve to have their academic needs understood and attended to. Still others have ignored the academic underachievement of boys as part of a cultural, fixed notion that "boys will be boys."[8] Poor achievement, delayed maturity, aggression and disruptive behavior are accepted by some as inevitable for males, thereby removing any responsibility to help remedy these problems.[8] Again, there is little evidence to support this notion, which is overtly sexist. Lastly, many schools, teachers and parents are simply unaware of the academic problems boys are having, and don't understand that the learning styles and educational needs of boys differ from those of girls.[2] After spending 30 years implementing successful interventions to improve the academic performance of our daughters, it is high time to address our nation's contemporary crisis in the education of our sons. Our sons deserve no less than an excellent academic education that empowers all of them to succeed.

Boys' Brains Are Different: How Does This Impact Learning?

Recent research has discovered differences in the brains of males and females, as well as gender differences in the way information is processed. For example, the corpus callosum, a bundle of nerves that connects the two sides of the brain is up to one-fifth larger in females.[9] As well, the cerebral cortex, responsible for higher level thinking, is larger on the left in males and on the right in females.[9] This may well account for the way women can more easily accomplish multiple tasks at one time than men, as well as have an easier time verbalizing emotions and feelings. It may also explain why math and science skills come easier to males, with more left brain connections, and why English and art skills are more easily acquired by females, who have larger right brains.

Brain maturation occurs at different rates between the sexes, and in most aspects of developmental chronology from infancy to young adulthood, girls' brains mature earlier than boys.[9] As a result, girls tend to acquire complex verbal skills as much as a year before most boys.[9] Testing has also shown that a resting female brain is as active as an activated male brain, which gives girls yet another learning advantage.[10] While female brains excel at memory and sensory intake, boys do better at spatial tasks and abstract reasoning.[10] As well, boy's brains secrete more serotonin, a brain chemical that makes them more fidgety than girls.[9] Boys tend to be poor auditory learners, having problems hearing and processing verbal instructions from very early on, and are better kinesthetic learners, while the opposite tends to be true for girls.[2,5] As a result, at entrance to kindergarten, girls are more able to stay on task, better able to pay attention and are more eager to learn,[3] while boys tend to be more physically active and need to have hands-on opportunities to manipulate objects in space in order to learn.[10] Throughout their education, boys are more prone to behavior problems when required to sit for long periods of time or when they are forced to learn via verbal, didactic methods of teaching that do not encourage active participation, discussion or debate.[2,10] Hence, this explains the large numbers of boys with behavior and conduct disorders and who are referred to special education.

New technologies in brain scanning have also allowed us to understand differences in the way males and females process emotional information. Using brain scans, emotional information in females has been shown to move quickly from the limbic (emotive) center up into the cerebral cortex (the thinking center), where it is likely to be noticed, verbalized and processed.[9] This may explain why girls have a much higher tendency to talk about their problems and ask for help when they are feeling depressed or upset, and thus are more likely than boys to get help for their problems.[9] Boys tend to send emotional information from the limbic center directly down to the brain stem, where the response to distress is more likely to be either physical aggression (fight) or withdrawal (flight).[9] Hence, it is easier to understand why boys have a harder time managing their impulsive behaviors, why they often respond to personal distress or conflicts with physical aggression, and why they often show their affection through action, such as by bumping into others.[2,9] These male behaviors can all be disruptive within a classroom setting, and tend to get boys into trouble at much higher rates than girls in school.

Such insights into brain and developmental differences can help us to understand why boys might be having problems with academic success. Because traditional teaching methods in schools generally require quiet, focused learning activities, boys have a tendency to lose interest, get fidgety and get into trouble.[2] Because girls brains and fine motor skills are more mature at entry into school, language and reading instruction are easier for girls to assimilate.[3] Boys learn early that reading

and writing are for girls, even though both of these disciplines are essential for becoming successful lifelong learners.[2] By the third grade, when boys might otherwise be starting to catch up developmentally with girls, boys' academic self-esteem has already been dealt a big blow.[2] Add to this the fact that when schools and educators do not modify teaching techniques to engage boys and meet their special needs, many of boys' natural tendencies to be physically active, impulsive and unfocused will be disruptive to the classroom. Teachers, unwittingly, may label these boys as "bad," or as academic failures.[2] Dr. Pollack, author of *Real Boys* states, "What I find tragic is that by failing to understand and appreciate each boy's characteristic learning style in an empathic way, we make it hard for him to feel confident about himself and flourish as a student. Moreover, when he subsequently withdraws from classroom activities or begins to rebel or act out, we often deal him a second blow by interpreting his natural response as the sign of a learning disability or so-called hyperactivity, when in reality it's shame, boredom, or restlessness."[2] Understanding the differences between male and female brains and development can be of immense help to parents and educators who wish to craft teaching techniques that are more "boy-friendly" and which will engage the brains and intellect of all our children.

Boys' Training to "Become a Man" Is Difficult: How Does This Affect Learning?

Boys and girls are socialized in very different ways, such that by the time they get into school, they are two very different entities on the whole.[11] The acculturation process of imparting the "rules of manhood" to our boys involves a process of hardening, or of toughening boys up, whereby males are encouraged to appear strong, tough, invulnerable, and confident, even when they aren't.[2] Strict rules of masculine behavior, restricting the expression of emotion and vulnerability, are enforced unwittingly by parents, teachers and children alike through a system of shame and ridicule.[6] For this reason, the acquisition of masculinity is much like putting on a gender straightjacket, which limits a boy's full human experience as he learns to deny and reject any qualities in himself that might be construed as feminine.[2]

What happens in this process of "becoming a man" is that boys lose many of the connections that are so necessary to keeping them invested in school and safe from harm. This is evident in the research of Dr. Judy Chu at NYU. At age 4½ , she found that boys were more able to have close relationships and to talk about those relationships than later in life.[3] In her study, Dr. Chu found that boys' social skills deteriorated as they grew older, when they began to show more and more "pretense" and engaged in "machoistic" fantasies while covering up their emotions and vulnerabilities.[3] Couple this with the fact that when boys misbehave, the tendency is to punish rather than to look behind the misconduct to find out what boys' genuine emotional needs are.[2] Dr. Pollack, author of *Real Boys*, concludes that the myth of boys' "toxicity" is still entrenched in many school systems, teachers and administrators.[2] Hostility towards boys and their often disruptive behaviors can lead to a disconnect between boys and their teachers and schools.[2] This sets them up for academic failure, as well as high-risk behaviors. In a 1997 national, longitudinal study, "Protecting Adolescents from Harm," perceived school connectedness was the largest major factor (after family closeness) that protected boys from emotional distress, drug abuse and violence. [2]

The fact is, however, that many boys become disconnected from their teachers and from their schools as a result of their gender-based difficulties in adapting to traditional education.[2] "Traditional school reinforces obedience, conformity and passive learning that favors the behavior of girls who conform to the traditional female stereotype. For many boys, this creates conflict between their gender role and their role as a student, which can lead to dissatisfaction, low achievement and poor self-esteem."[12] Furthermore, "a lot of the way boys communicate is through action, and a lot of the way schools try to structure teaching is through talk. Sometimes, you get a disconnect as a result."[11] In learning environments biased against their strengths, boys may get turned off or become frustrated, attempting to get their needs met via negative attention-getting behaviors.[3,6] "This completes the cycle of failure, as boys are now labeled as troublemakers or hyperactive."[6] Dr. Pollack concludes "when boys feel in conflict with their schools and don't do well, it deeply affects their self-esteem as learners."[2]

Another way that gender politics affect boys' learning is through the common misconception that boys are somehow flawed. When boys don't perform well within our traditional educational environments, our tendency has historically been to label them as somehow defective (i.e. learning disabled, special needs, hyperactive, etc.), instead of questioning our teaching methods for flaws.[2] Boys' academic underachievement

has then been shrugged off without much alarm with the excuse that "boys will be boys."[8] This pivots on a fixed notion of masculinity that involves aggression, fighting, delayed maturity and poor achievement as inevitable consequences of being male.[8] This is an example of the "deficit model of masculinity," where boys are considered to be lacking in proper qualities that can be addressed only by changing them so that they are more like girls.[5] This reflects a futile, outdated and biased way of thinking that limits the success of our boys in education through a cycle of blame and denial. A better option might be to look at how our schools could work to expand our current concepts of gender roles such that both boys as well as girls could attain higher levels of academic performance.

For example, boys readily respond to societal expectations that math and science are "boy" subjects, and English and art are "girl" subjects.[7] This lessens boys' resolve to succeed in reading and writing, where boys' achievement lags far behind girls'.[2] It is also a common masculine trait, especially in middle school and beyond, to be reluctant to excel in any subject at school other than sports, for which boys can ensure peer approval.[12] In these ways, a boy's masculine training can be very limiting. Likewise, due to cultural conditioning and gender expectations, schools often ignore the social and emotional needs of boys.[2,13] Boys' masculine training makes it harder for them to recognize and verbalize such needs, and they tend to hide their depression, anxiety and fears, as well as bottle up their emotions.[13] All too often, these emotions then erupt as anger, violence, aggression, delinquency or high-risk behaviors, for which boys get punished or referred to special education.[13] Our schools could take a proactive approach to these problems by teaching boys better communication, relationship and dispute resolution skills, and by discussing with them the ways in which gender roles have historically restricted behavior and created harm in our lives. Creating more flexible gender roles and broadening expectations for both genders within our school systems would help our boys and girls feel more confident as men and women and as lifelong learners.[7] "If we want to have happy, caring, loving and empathic boys, we have to start by being empathic to boys and what their needs are, rather than seeing them as deficient and not fitting into our models."[11] Dr. William Farrell, a psychologist and expert on the men's movement reiterates, "Our genetic future is dependent on encouraging men to become nurturer-connectors. This will evolve not from men and women blaming each other, but from both sexes making a transition from following rigid roles to negotiating trade-offs in a multi-option world. For the past three decades, we've introduced our daughters to a multi-option world; now it's time to introduce our sons." [13]

Family Structure and Social Factors: How Do These Affect Learning?

Modern strategies to improve children's educational performance have often relied on standardized testing as a tool of measuring success. Unfortunately, such testing can fail to take into account the numerous confounding factors that affect each child's academic success and make it all too easy to blame or shame schools and teachers as the root cause of boys' academic failure.[8] The reality is that each boy's educational success is a factor of many overlapping and complex social, economic, political and academic influences that shape his life. It is simply unfair to blame teachers unilaterally for the poor performance of a child who lives in an impoverished neighborhood, goes to a poorly funded public school, is chronically undernourished, speaks English as a second language, and lives in a state of constant family and neighborhood disruption and fear. Improving the academic performance of all our children will require the full support of parents, educators and community alike, and may require the restructuring of various economic, social and political circumstances that may be limiting our nation's children from living up to their full potentials.[8]

The following social and family factors have been shown in research to correlate negatively with academic success in boys: changes in family structure, living in a single-parent home, being of lower socioeconomic status, and family instability.[5] Absent fathers, a national epidemic given the preponderance of single parent families led by women, seem to play some role in boys' educational problems as well.[5] Parental characteristics are also important. Studies of boys who are doing well in school have shown that parents who were involved in ongoing learning activities, had high expectations for their sons, and who did not over-pressure their sons had a positive affect on their boys' academic success.[14] These same parents also tended to be involved in supporting their son's literacy through play activities or homework support, and by providing opportunities for the use of personal or public computers for email and Internet use.[14] Racial and ethnic differences can also have a deep impact on academic success, and are

often ignored when researchers analyze the problems of boys' underachievement.[7] What is missing in much of our national research on academic performance is a description of the subgroups of students at highest risk for academic failure, such that specific strategies could be designed to empower these young people for success.[7] By looking into why certain groups of boys are failing, parents and educators could employ positive interventions to reverse negative academic trends.

Lastly, maintaining close parental and emotional ties with our sons is probably one of the most important antidotes to poor academic achievement.[2] Treating our sons with love and empathy, staying involved with our son's schooling, making sure our boys' emotional needs are being fulfilled at home and at school, and making sure that schools don't misjudge our sons should they have difficulties with learning or behavior are potent immunizations against academic failure.[2] Becoming educated on boys' unique educational styles and needs can help parents advocate for boy-friendly practices within their own school districts. This can go a long way towards improving the lives of the many boys in your own neighborhood.

Creating Boy-Friendly Classrooms and Schools: How Is It Done?

Dr. Pollack, author of *Real Boys* and an expert on boy's development, has made a variety of suggestions based on research that would make schools more "boy friendly." First of all, classroom curricula, textbooks and reading material should be developed that are more interesting to a wide array of boys.[2] Hands-on learning and problem-solving techniques work well for young boys, and older boys need a lot of creative and expressive opportunities, such as team projects, computer-based work and class discussions.[2] The slower pace of boys' learning must be respected and built into the structure of classroom dynamics, such that boys do not suffer from poor self-esteem by seeing themselves as "dumber" than girls.[2] Activity needs to be built into learning environments for boys, with increased classroom activity and a minimum of 4 to 5 recesses per day for boys through the fifth grade.[11] Dr. Pollack advocates for the use of single-gender classrooms for boys—especially for those who are slow learners, or who don't do well in traditional classrooms or in academic subjects where boys are traditionally weak.[2] He feels that all-male bonding environments can help boys to feel more connected, less defensive, more comfortable with their rough-and-tumble aggressiveness, and more egalitarian in their attitudes towards gender roles than in coeducational settings.[2] Mentoring programs can be very beneficial for high-risk boys, and having more male teachers in elementary schools and in courses that are often perceived as gender-limited could provide positive role models for our male students.[2] Lastly, Dr. Pollack believes that it is essential to provide safe environments in schools for our sons to be able to express their fears and vulnerabilities without fear of shame and ridicule.[2] Schools should assume that boys' emotional needs are not necessarily being met at home and should provide ways to meet emotional needs within the educational system, especially since modern boys often spend more hours at school and with their teachers than they do at home and with their parents. [2]

A 2000/2001 study in England of school environments where boys were already doing well resulted in a compilation of best practices that seem to encourage the academic success of boys.[14] Among the common features of these successful schools were classrooms where boys had the same teacher for more than one year, literacy teachers who were highly qualified in this area, use of texts which were popular with boys, reading and writing instruction that were closely linked, lesson plans that had clear objectives that were tied into weekly plans, choice of a variety of writing formats when tasks were assigned, and lots of opportunities for class and group discussions.[14] Also, physical activities tended to be built into classroom teaching strategies, teachers shared their own personal reading and writing, and humorous writing and language play (common in boys' writing) were readily accepted.[14] Behavior management similarities included managing behavior by minimizing disruptions and accepting interjections in class sessions and restless behavior as long as boys were on task.[14] This method of looking at learning environments where boys are already doing well offers fertile ground for determining the kinds of teaching strategies that really work for boys.

There are numerous suggestions on how to create classrooms that ideally support boys' needs in Michael Gurian and Patricia Henley's book, *Boys and Girls Learn Differently: A Guide for Teachers and Parents*.[10] This book is the most quoted reference around for its comprehensive review of brain research and for understanding the common and distinct educational needs of each sex.[10] This book's practical suggestions to improve schools for boys include promoting closer bonding, having smaller classes, encouraging more verbalization, isolating boys less, finding ways to get more men involved as role models and mentors in schools, and encouraging peer mentoring.[10] Physical movement helps boys to stimulate their brains, to manage and relieve impulsive behavior, and to engage their whole bodies in emotive processing.[10] Gurian and Henley consider it a profound mistake to cut recess or eliminate physical education for boys.[10] They contest that troublesome boy behaviors can be transformed by simply allowing boys to engage in some type of activity while learning, such as playing nerf ball, handing out pencils, drawing during class discussions, etc.[10] Other suggestions include using multi-generational classes (to normalize boys' scatter of abilities), using teaching teams and teacher-to-teacher support systems, using bonding rituals in the classroom (such as games or songs), listening more to boys, admitting mistakes, giving children choices in decision-making, using integrated studies, and engaging in character education and a judicious mix of same-sex and coeducational classes.[10] Lastly, Gurian and Henley make a big case for adding gender training to the curriculum of schools, so that boys and girls can hear each other speak, start to demystify the opposite sex, and begin to understand how to relax traditional gender stereotypes so to create a safer environment for learning for both sexes on school campuses.[10]

Improving education for boys can also involve talking to boys themselves. Glenn Ryall of Australia surveyed a group of adolescent boys to find out their input on improving education. He found that boys really wanted school curricula to be relevant to their lives after graduation.[15] They also wanted more variety in teaching methods, more class discussions about topics of importance, and more use of audiovisual tools.[15] Boys wanted individual attention from educators, and an overwhelming majority wanted to play a part in deciding classroom and school rules of behavior, which they noted they would be much more likely to follow.[15] Boys felt more secure answering questions if they had time to discuss them with other students first, and enjoyed classroom quizzes (as opposed to tests) and lively debates.[15] Another highlight of Mr. Ryall's research was the importance of breaking down family and gender stereotypes, such that boys could be encouraged to explore a wider choice of subjects in school. Boys were found to be highly influenced in their subject choices by family and peer expectations. [15]

The Australian government has taken a strong stand on the problem of boys' underachievement, where a parliamentary inquiry into the failing academic success of boys led to a report of 24 recommendations issued in June of 2000.[5] These recommendations fell into three major themes, summarized as follows. First, there was a call to rewrite the national gender-equity strategy to a more balanced model that does not seek to achieve gender-equity by changing boys to be more like girls, which is recognized as being a biased and futile approach.[5] Second, boys' lower levels of literacy need to be addressed through teaching strategies that take into account boys' difficulties hearing and processing verbal instruction (an important and unappreciated finding that before this inquiry was not well known in Australia) and through returning to the traditional phonics-based approach to reading instruction.[5] Phonics instruction has been shown to be better suited to children with short attention spans and to be superior in overcoming reading difficulties, especially for boys.[5] Thirdly, the report acknowledged that effective teacher education and training were paramount to delivering good educational outcomes and meeting the needs of both boys and girls.[5] Knowing about the different and special needs of boys is an essential step for educators who can then implement different teaching strategies to engage boys and help them be more successful. The fact that the highest political body in Australia addressed the needs of boys is a hopeful sign that their educational plight will not be forsaken. It may take a similar action in the United States to fully address the future success of our nation's boys.

Single-sex classrooms or schools have been offered up as a solution to many of the problems that boys have in schools. What has become obvious from actual experience is that single-sex education does not in and of itself solve the problems of boys' (or girls') academic underachievement. The success of such schools or classrooms seems more to depend upon having teachers well-versed in gender stereotyping and upon well-designed curricula sensitive to boys' needs. Some educators have championed single-sex classrooms as a way to allow boys to be able to bond more with their teachers and peers, to better develop their communication skills, to be more self-accepting of their slower developmental pace and need for physical activity, to shed gender stereotypes that keep boys' tender and emotional selves hidden, to diminish social distractions and allow for better concentration on academics, to participate in classrooms where machismo is dismissed as buffoonery rather than as heroism or sexual grandstanding in front of girls, and to find a safe haven from the harm of the gender-based use of shame and ridicule.[2,9,16] These benefits have indeed been seen in some single-sex settings.[2,9] However, in other single-sex settings, traditional gender stereotypes have actually been reinforced, with boys tending to be taught in more regimented, traditional, and often militaristic settings, and girls being placed in more nurturing, cooperative and open environments.[16] Also, it has been seen that when separate schools are housed on the same campus, a dichotomous understanding of gender can be created, where girls are seen as "good" and boys as "bad."[16] State and federal laws on gender equity have also been a problem, as these laws are often interpreted to require single-sex schools to have identical curricula, eliminating the flexibility that is essential to create gender-friendly environments.[16] Lastly, some single-sex public institutions are at risk of becoming a new form of tracking or resegregation, especially when designed only for poorly achieving boys.[16] Overall, the academic success of single-sex classrooms and schools appears to be more related to small classes, strong curricula, dedicated teachers and equitable teaching practices, much like coeducational schools. [16]

Indeed, boys and girls may actually have much more in common rather than differences when it comes to improving their academic distress. Dr. Jovanovic, a university professor and gender studies expert, has found that girls tend to benefit from hands-on, active approaches to learning, from cooperative learning techniques, and from performance-based assessments in science and math, subjects where girls have traditionally done less well than boys.[17] It is interesting to note that boys tend to have these exact same educational needs in subjects where they have traditionally done poorly, such as in reading and writing. This fact that there is much commonality amongst the sexes in the mechanisms needed to improve their performance is echoed by educational researchers.

The American Association for University Women has been at the forefront of research on the underachievement of girls. They recently organized a round table discussion in November of 1997, where they invited many of the most prominent educational researchers to address the issue of gender differences in learning.[17] Considerable consensus was achieved at this round table about the structural and organizational features of schools that were beneficial for both genders.[17] Their findings support small school size, a core curriculum approach that emphasizes basic, academic skills for all students, more personal relations among all school members, a school that functions more like a community than a bureaucracy, instruction that is pervasive throughout a school (not isolated to certain teachers' classrooms) that involves students in higher order thinking and encourages and expects students to become actively engaged in their own learning (as opposed to didactic methods of teaching), and a common willingness on the part of teachers to accept personal responsibility for all their students' learning, including a belief that all students are capable of learning what they are taught.[17] These characteristics in a school tended to ensure the academic success of both boys and girls. Again, boys and girls seem to be able to get adequate support for their strengths and weaknesses in schools where their different and individualized learning styles and needs are met.

Summary:

The issue of boys' academic underachievement is extraordinarily complex and multilayered. However, it appears that schools that are flexible in design, are willing to address different gender-based and individual learning styles and tempos within their classrooms, and have teachers who are well-versed in the needs and characteristics of both genders are capable of creating excellent academic outcomes for both boys and girls. Families who support and encourage their boys' education, who love and support their boys unconditionally, and who actively advocate for boy-friendly educational experiences in their sons' schools are equally important to boys' academic success. Again, we are reminded of how it takes a village to raise a child, and a willing and educated community to ensure that all of our children, boys and girls, get a gender-appropriate, successful and excellent education.

References:
1. "Are Boys Falling Behind in Academics? Part I" by Jeanne Bleuer and Garry Walz, 2002 ERIC Digest, www.eric.ed.gov/
2. *Real Boys: Rescuing Our Sons from the Myths of Boyhood* by William Pollack, PhD, Henry Holt and Company, New York, NY, Chapter 10: "Schools, the Blackboard Jumble," pages 230-171
3. "Research: Boys to Men" by Michelle Galley. On the website of Education Week at www.edweek.org/ew
4. "Disadvantaging Boys in Education" by Gregory Flanagan
5. "Getting it Right Some of the Time: An Appraisal of the Report on the Inquiry into the Education of Boys" by Jennifer Buckingham at www.cis.org.au
6. "Rescuing Our Sons from the Myths of Boyhood" an interview with Dr. Pollack on the web at www.canadianparents.com
7. "Educators Urge End to Classroom 'Gender Wars'" by Sarah Stewart Taylor, 4/5/01. Women's E-News website, at www.womensenews.org/article.cfm?aid=502
8. "Boys and Education: Mapping the Issues" by Melissa Spencer
9. "Different Learning Styles of Boys and Girls" by David Wylde 6/20/02
10. *Boys and Girls Learn Differently: A Guide for Teachers and Parents,* a book review by J. Steven Svoboda of this book written by Michael Gurian, Patricia Henley, and Terry Trueman
11. "Schools Don't Accommodate Boys' Learning Styles" by Michelle Galley, an interview with Dr. William Pollack on Educational Week Website at www.edweek.org/ew
12. "The Challenges and Dilemmas Facing Boys in Education Today" by Nigel Lewis and James Edmunds
13. "Our Sons, Our Schools" by Warren Farrell, PhD on the web at www.dadsnow.org/essay/farrell2.htm
14. "Learning From Boys" by Sally Rundell, Literacy Manager, Suffolk Local Education Authority, England
15. "The Education of Boys" by Glenn Ryall. On the web at www.thesource.gov.au/2001_youth_roundtable/educating_outside/reports
16. "California Study: Single Sex Schools No Cure All" by Elizabeth Zwerling, 06/02/01. On Women's E-News website at www.womensenews.org/article.cfm/dyn/aid/571/context/cover/
17. "Understanding Gender Differences That May Occur in Classroom Settings" by Peggy Patten. On the Parent News website, at www.npin.org/pnews/1999/pnew199/inl199a.html

Summary of Strategies to Help Boys Learn

By Howard Hiton, from *Helping Boys Succeed in Portland Public Schools*

Strategy 1: Increasing Boys' Connection to School

- Create safe places for boys to form relationships with others, including boys' discussion groups.
- Improve the communication skills of school staff so they can better work with boys.
- Create boy-centered social events.
- Develop a broad base of boy-friendly, co-curricular activities other than sports.
- Support coaches to make athletics a healthy experience for boys who participate in sports.
- Explore the potential of rites-of-passage activities.

Strategy 2: Improving Boys' Academic Performance

- Incorporate movement into learning activities.
- Emphasize cooperative learning approaches.
- Capitalize on literature that appeals to young men.
- Invite adult men into classes to model that it is acceptable for men to read.
- Consider new ways to evaluate boys' writing that take into account their interests and tastes.

Strategy 3: Addressing Boys' Behavioral Problems

- Make the reduction of teasing and bullying an administrative priority.
- Challenge the peer norm that teasing is acceptable.
- Educate parents to help their sons better deal with teasing and bullying.
- Implement skill-based violence prevention curricula.
- Help all boys improve their social skills.

- Emphasize the development of self-control to help boys curb impulsive behavior.

Strategy 4: Providing Boys with More Positive Adult Male Role Models

- Motivate men to lead the effort to help boys challenge limiting concepts of masculinity.
- Educate families about the critical role that men play in their children's lives.
- Create volunteer opportunities that men find attractive.
- Utilize mentors as role models.
- Educate male teachers about the role they can play in constructing gender identity.

Involving Men

Boys need more positive male role models. Unfortunately, for many boys in many settings, men have been in short supply. In fact, women have historically led the movement to help boys, with little assistance from their male counterparts. In contrast, girls are improving their academic success and expanding their gender roles in large part because of strong woman leaders willing to act as role models and advocates. It will take similar leadership from men to help boys improve their academic success and expand their gender roles toward broader, more inclusive definitions of masculinity.

The challenge is getting men to participate in this effort. Several factors deter men from joining efforts to alter boys' culture. For one, men themselves grew up under the boy code, and many cannot see its harm. Some men even value their experiences within the toughening boy culture, believing that it "helped them become a man." Still others are threatened by the idea of shifting their gender roles. Finally, some men feel that they lack the relationship skills needed to act as a mentor. Men themselves lack models of other men fulfilling these roles.

Another factor contributing to the lack of fathers' involvement in schools is that some men, and particularly men of color, report feeling unwelcome in schools. In discussion groups to prepare this document, diverse representatives from Portland's youth-serving community noted that schools tend to be selective about the type of men they want in the schools. One participant stated, "We say we want men more involved in schools, but what schools are really saying is they want a certain class of men." Society often makes negative assumptions about the man who is available to come to school during school hours, or even about the man who is attracted to serving youth. Yet many youth don't have contact with either a biological or stepfather and are in dire need of father figures.

Just as schools must examine whether their culture is supportive of men volunteering in students' classrooms and activities, men must examine their lives to discover whether they are adequately contributing to their children and their schools. Eli Newberger writes, "The kind of adjustments that need to be made in the lives of boys to nurture them toward good character in their adult life are coherent with—sometimes identical with—the adjustments that will make men more highly aware and nurturing fathers and role models."

Fortunately, a national effort to educate men about their importance in the lives of children, strongly supported by research, is encouraging more men to respond to the call to become active in boys' lives. In community meetings to help plan this report, strong, motivated, and articulate men spoke of their desire to make a difference for today's young men. Men like these do make a difference. Research on fathers is particularly telling. *Child Trends Research Brief* (www.childtrends.org) shares these examples of the critical role that fathers play in their children's lives:

- In one study, preschool children whose fathers provided 40 percent or more of the family's child care had higher scores on assessments of cognitive development, had more sense of mastery over their environments, and exhibited more empathy than those children whose fathers were less involved.

- Higher levels of father involvement in activities with their children, including meals, outings, and helping with homework are associated with fewer behavioral problems, higher levels of sociability, and high levels of school performance among children and adolescents.

- Several studies have documented a positive relationship between fathers providing child support and the well being of school-age children.

In the national public health drive to disseminate this kind of information to fathers, schools are in a central position to help. They can get the word out through newsletters, parenting workshops, and health classes. Schools can access tools like the CD ROM produced by the US Department of Education, entitled *"Father's Involvement in Children's Learning,"* which contains clips of a national conference on fathering, up-to-date research, and innovative strategies to better include fathers in their children's education.

Activities like "Boys' Night Out," and programs like "Real Men Read," described in earlier sections of this report, are excellent ways to get fathers involved in schools. Projects like the "Minority Male Initiative," detailed in the "Keeping Boys Connected" section, can connect young men with adult male role models. Another important resource for boys is the men already working in schools. How can they become more involved in helping boys succeed?

One idea comes from Upstate New York. Sponsored by the Capital Area School Development Association, the "Men Helping Boys" project gathered men from dozens of area schools to reflect on the challenges they faced growing up in order to increase their empathy, the men went on to create programs targeted at helping boys at the schools in which they worked. Results ranged from an effort to promote leadership among middle-school boys, to a program to bring more positive male role models into schools, to a writing program that helps boys reflect on their efforts to become thoughtful, responsible young men. (For more information and reports on specific programs, contact the Capital Area Student Development Association, Husted Hall 211, University at Albany, 135 Western Avenue, Albany, NY 12222.)

Programs to educate male teachers about the limitations of the boy code that often confine boys' culture would fold nicely into teacher education. In an article entitled, "Schooling and the Formation of Male Students' Gender Identities," Robert Smith argues for training male social studies teachers on these issues in order to broaden their understanding of masculinity and model this for their students.

Adult men, who provide models of respectful masculinity, are key to helping boys succeed in schools. It has been said that "Small boys learn to become large men in the presence of large men who care about small boys."

Reprinted with permission of Howard Hiton, author of *BAM! Boys Advocacy and Mentoring* and *Helping Boys Succeed in Portland Public Schools*. See complimentary copy of *Helping Boys Succeed* at www.hitonassociates.net/publications/publications.php. For reprint requests contact www.familyempowermentnetwork.com.

The Problem with Peer Aggression in Our Schools Today

By Kathy Masarie, MD

A deadly combo is a bully who gets what he wants from his target, a bullied child who is afraid to tell, bystanders who either watch, participate in the bullying or look away, and adults who see bullying as teasing, not tormenting, as "boys will be boys," not the predatory aggression that it is . . . . Bullying is not about conflict. It is about contempt for another person. Bullying is a conscious, willful and hostile attempt to harm someone . . . . The cycle of bullying will only be broken when the majority begins to stand up, speak out and step in to stop the cruel acts of the minority.
  —Barbara Coloroso, author of *Bully, Bullies and Bystander*

Once thought to be simply an unpleasant rite of passages, bullying can actually result in long-term social, academic, psychological, and physical consequences.
  The Challenge, Vol. 11 (3)

IN RECENT YEARS, the ways children hurt each other has received national attention. Nearly all of the school shooters were targets of taunting by their peers. An online rejection by a "boyfriend" led a girl to kill herself; the mother, who posed as that "boyfriend" to avenge her own daughter, may go to prison. We wouldn't send our children to schools where there was no policy on physical aggression, yet we routinely send them to schools where verbal and relational aggression is both rampant and unchecked. To 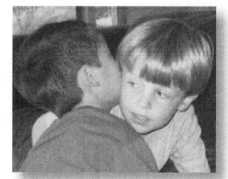 be fair, in former times we didn't have the research to recognize how harmful relational aggression was and we didn't know that verbal taunting could drive someone to extreme acts of violence. Now we do. There is so much we can do, but it takes patience and commitment. And it takes all of us.

While it is easy to dismiss these "stories" as normal rites of passage, research shows that relational aggression is every bit as harmful as physical aggression. Relational aggression is by nature covert, secretive and difficult to detect. Adults struggle to even be able to identify it,

let alone deal with it. Our culture has taken a stand on physical violence in schools and today we rarely see overt fights. However, our children have redirected their aggression to exclusion, gossip, verbal taunting and "sneaky" physical aggression, such as "accidentally" bumping someone.

Forms of Aggression

Aggression takes various forms based on the "weapon" used to hurt another:

- **Physical:** uses physical force such as hitting, tripping, taking a backpack, breaking a pencil.
- **Verbal:** uses words (spoken, written or via email) to tease, taunt, or call names.
- **Relational:** uses the target's social relationships with others to hurt him/her.
  o gossip: spreads rumors about a disliked classmate
  o exclusion: tells others not to play with a certain classmate as a means of retaliation
  o silent treatment: purposefully ignores someone when angry
- **Non-verbal:** uses gestures, dirty looks, eye-rolling, turning one's back to the target

Aggression can also be distinguished as:
- **Direct or overt** (physical and verbal aggression)
- **Indirect or covert** (relational aggression or non-verbal gestures)

There are two additional categories: aggression in self-defense (reactive) versus initiating aggression (proactive). Even the legal system reflects this concern to understand the "motive."

- **Proactive aggressors** are looking for opportunities to bully and to "raise their social status" by putting others down. For example, forming a group to leave someone out.
- **Reactive aggressors** misinterpret ambiguous social settings. For example, when someone in the cafeteria spills a drink on a reactive aggressor, s/he immediately assumes it was done on purpose and acts accordingly by turning around and

punching the child. It can happen when someone has been bullied repetitively and has become suspicious, thinking "everyone" is out to get him/her.

Bully, Bystander, Target

In any aggressive incident, there are three roles: aggressor, target and bystander. The role of the aggressor is obvious: this is the person leading the bullying. The second character is the "target." "Target" implies just that: a person who was chosen, for whatever reason or no reason, to be on the receiving end of the aggression. Using "victim" here implies a helplessness and weakness. Finally, the bystander(s) on the sidelines have three options: join the bullying and encourage the bullying by egging it on, be neutral and observe it from a distance taking no sides, or sympathize with the target. Those that sympathize are often afraid to help because there is a realistic possibility that they will become the next target.

Target Today; Aggressor Tomorrow

It is important to remember that an aggressor today may have been a target yesterday. In today's world, the best defense (to avoid being a target) is a good offense (by becoming a bully). How many kids do both? Research studies show that if you look solely at relational aggression, about 20-30 % of middle and high school students are *both* aggressors and targets. (This is not true for physical bullies, where targets and aggressors usually stay in one role.) So the kid we see being aggressive toward our child today may have been the recipient of our child's aggression for the past month. It is not always easy to figure out where it started and children have more difficulty identifying themselves as aggressors than as targets. One thing that is clear is that "removing the bully" rarely solves anything as there is always another to take his or her place. Nor does "teaching the target to be more assertive" always help since there is always another target to take his/her place.

Peer aggression happens at all ages, including adulthood. How many days do we hear gossip about someone, avoid talking to someone we are angry with, or leave someone out from an activity we are participating in? Or it may go further: we talk about someone disparagingly at the dinner table or tell our kids not to play with that kid who is "from the wrong side of town," which is prejudice and exclusion.

Examples of Aggression

Felicia was bullied continuously from 3rd through 5th grade at a private elementary school and suffered from migraines and stomach aches as a result. Felicia's mother, a single parent, made repeated efforts to get the school to take action. The school's responses: "Felicia is too thin-skinned"... Kids will be kids . . . You're mistaken if you think we can stop this." The bullying continued, with no end in sight. Eventually, Felicia's mother had to place her daughter on "suicide watch" when she threatened to kill herself. Felicia, now 11, no longer attends that school and is on the road to recovery from this long-term abusive situation.

The in-group ruled the social life of a third-grade classroom. Four of the twelve girls decide each day who will be allowed to play with them. The rules change daily, but the best way to get in is to criticize another girl. The girls on the "out" haven't figured out how to create their own friendship groups—they just wait to see if maybe today they'll get lucky and be allowed in.

As a quarterback in football, a seventh-grade boy has friends and social standing. Another boy who covets his position starts spreading rumors, behind his back, that he is gay. Friends start avoiding him. He tells no one, asks no one for help. His grades begin to suffer and he loses focus on the team. The coach replaces him with the aggressor.

When Amanda was in 9th grade, her boyfriend broke up with her. At first she was heartbroken, but when he started dating a classmate she became enraged. She sought revenge by spreading ugly sexual rumors about them, which her fellow students were happy to believe. A few months later, she realized what she had done and apologized to the couple and told her classmates it was all a lie. But it didn't work. The rumors had become "true" to her classmates. She couldn't take it back and she was heartsick. With tears in her eyes, she said she would do anything to help other girls not make the same mistake. She became a teen mentor in her school and helped teach younger students about relational aggression.

At an 8th-grade overnight, a few girls posted some rumors on the Internet about several more "popular" girls who they did not like. On Monday, the aggressors were afraid to go to school. Eventually they admitted their wrong-doing and agreed to meet with the targets to talk. They discussed relational aggression and cyberbullying, and the targets were able to speak clearly about how hurt they were. When it was all over, all the girls felt closer to each other.

The Research on Peer Aggression

Most early studies of bullying were on direct verbal (VA) and physical aggression (PA). Relational aggression (RA) has surfaced since the mid 90's, showing that girls bully as much as boys, it is just that girls use a different, more indirect, form of aggression (RA). What is very interest-ing is that some studies reveal the "underlying beliefs" that allow aggression to continue and become more normal. If you believe something is acceptable, you will continue to do it. Even though kids say relational aggression-exclusion is the most hurtful type of aggression, it is the type most commonly used. Research shows when parents are asked, "Would you rather have your child hit, call names or exclude?" they pick "exclude" even though kids say that hurts the most.

- Boys and girls today view relational aggression as the most acceptable aggression, even in preschool.
- RA is the type of aggression most commonly used at all ages by boys and girls together.
- Kids view relational aggression as the most hurtful type of aggres-sion (physical second, verbal third).
- The research confirms that children who use high levels of relational aggression are more likely to approve of it (compared to children who use low levels of relational aggression). This perpetuates the problem.
- If asked about the best way to retaliate when you were "wronged by someone," all ages and both sexes answered "relational aggression."

Short- and Long-Term Effects of Aggression

The consequences of bullying can be serious. Surprisingly, the outcomes look equally bleak whether you are the target or the aggressor. Research shows that low self-esteem is not always present in aggressors. Those who do have low self-esteem, however, tend to get jealous and frustrated easily, need a lot of attention from other people, need to feel accepted, need to be noticed, and need to gain power and control. Other aggressors may feel very good about themselves and their ability to manipulate others and do not take responsibility for what they have done.

Aggressors who use relational aggression may have a lot of friends, but the quality of friendships is poor. They tend to believe they are "close" to their friends and

don't want to "share" their friends with others. They score high on exclusivity. They are highly jealous and very manipulative, using relational aggression against friends. For example, they may threaten to tell a friend's secrets, a very powerful threat. They will betray a friend if it serves them well. They are low on warmth and caring. These qualities of jealousy and possessiveness extend into romantic relationships of college students. Most of all, they have difficulty recognizing their hurtful behavior. Relational aggression may work very well in the short term but it has serious long-term effects for the aggressor.

Aggressors and targets are <u>both</u> at risk for:
- Depression
- Drug and alcohol abuse and early use
- Eating disorders, poor body image, self-harm
- Violence: 60% of bullies in grade 6-9 had at least one conviction by age 24[1]
- School failure, suspension, dropping out, absenteeism, avoidance, delinquency, disruptive in class
- Peer rejection, loneliness, isolation
- Low attachment to parents and school
- Low self-worth.

Key Ingredients in Bullying
- Imbalance of power
- Repetitiveness
- Intent to harm

In addition to the risk factors listed above, targets suffer other negative effects. Short-term effects include: humiliation, sadness, distressed affect, confusion, anxiousness, psychosomatic symptoms and poor con-centration. The long-term outcomes for targets also include:
- Insecurity about their place in the social hierarchy, which manifests as social avoidance and anxiety
- Lower levels of leadership
- Fear, which may lead to absenteeism, truancy, or dropping out
- Poor self-concept.

Is It Conflict or Is It Bullying?

One of the most frequent questions we hear is how to tell the difference between aggression and conflict. A key feature of aggression/bullying is that there is an imbalance of power between the target and the bully. In bullying, the bully is always trying to have "power over" the target. The power often comes from other children who join in on the bullying. Another feature is intent to harm. The only one who truly knows of equal power, that is conflict, not bullying. Both kids want their way and both kids feel distressed. Conflict resolution skills help with these incidences—hearing each side of the story, helping each to see the other's point of view, brainstorming solutions together. In a conflict, adults may not need to get involved. The intervention in a bully incident is very different: support the target, give clear consequences for the bully, and empower everyone involved with skills to do it differently.

Adults Establish the Social Norms about Bullying

The basic concept of "social norm" is very important because it, more than anything else, is what drives bullying to continue. Social norms are the "expected rules for behavior" and they are driven by beliefs that kids have about the acceptability of a behavior. These beliefs come from the cultural response to behaviors. How would you react to your kid hitting someone versus excluding someone by saying, "You can't come to my birthday party." Even though kids say exclusion is the worst (they would rather be hit or called names), we adults tend to react strongly to hitting but erratically to exclusion. We then have established a "norm" that it is okay to exclude someone. When teachers do not intervene in bully incidents, they create a "social norm" that says it is okay: to bully when you get away with it, put someone down for a laugh, exclude people or spread rumors. Teachers "don't have time to deal with it" but time spent "not dealing with it" is enormous: disciplining bullies, counseling targets, dealing with angry parents—with all of the effort leaving destruction in its wake.

There are social norms within the adult world that perpetuate aggression among adults and between adults and children. Examples include "It's okay to gossip disparagingly about a child who is bullying others and about how 'poorly' that child is being raised by his/her family," and "It's okay to put down a teacher we don't like to our children and other parents."

Intentional versus Accidental Harm

One of the reasons that it is difficult to put a stop to emotional aggression is that it is not black and white. Bullying involves an imbalance of power, but an aggressor may not even realize that he/she is in a one-up position. Because of this, most of us inadvertently

find ourselves a bully, a target and a bystander from time to time.

Here we will explore three areas that we all experience everyday: teasing, gossip and exclusion. On one end of the spectrum, these behaviors are normal, everyday interactions. It is healthy to share stories with each other. It is healthy to tease someone you like. It is healthy to exclude people because there is not room to invite everybody, every time. On the other end of the spectrum is the obvious aggression with "intent to harm," repetition and imbalance of power. Aggressors use the excuse that they didn't mean it to hurt and that they were "just kidding," but the aggressor and the target know the difference. Like any other bullying, the bystanders, target, adults and aggressors themselves need to be involved to stop this kind of aggression. In between these two extremes is the "gray zone" where it is sometimes unclear to the "target" whether the damage was done "on purpose with intent to harm" or done innocently and accidentally. The target feels hurt, but only the aggressor knows their real intent. And if the "accidental aggressor" didn't really mean to do it, s/he may not even know someone was hurt. In this case, the responsibility lies with the "target" to let the person know s/he was hurt. This always works better if the "target" and "accidental aggressor" have a good relationship. Someone who is chronically bullied has an even tougher time deciphering this. After repeated bullying, it is a natural defense mechanism to "be on guard for aggression" and it makes it harder to take things light-heartedly.

Social Types and Friendships

Our children are very different in their friendship needs, partially based on temperament, introvert-extrovert, etc. However, no matter which group a child wants to belong to, there are unwritten rules that the "in-kids" learn in order to fit in. There are five invisible rules or social norms described in *Best Friends Worst Enemies* by Michael Thompson: 1) Be Like Your Peers; 2) You Must Belong to a Group; 3) Be In—Or Be Out; 4) Find a Place in the Social Hierarchy; and 5) You Must Play a Role. He reports on research about the eight essential elements a child receives from his/her relationships with other children. Seven of these can be found in the one-on-one friendships your child finds and establishes: affection, intimacy, a reliable alliance, instrumental aid, nurturance, companionship and an enhancement of self-worth. The eighth element is a "sense of inclusion" comes from belonging to a group. This eighth "essential element" is the one with which parents can directly assist their child. Parents can help find or create groups or "safe spaces" where their child can be accepted for being themselves (e.g., religious youth group, close soccer team, Scout troop or an after-school club). Many of these groups can offer your child a wonderful sense of belonging. Pay attention to the fact that there are other groups, of your child's choosing, that may be detrimental to your child's safety and well-being. Sometimes, members of the group will do daring, foolish or mean things they wouldn't have considered doing as individuals. What is encouraging is that social skills needed to make good friendships and be well-liked can be learned, as you can see in *The Unwritten Rules of Friendship—Simple Strategies to Help Your Child Make Friends* by Natalie Madorsky Elman and Eileen Kennedy-Moore.

Popularity

Popularity—that ever-elusive obsession.... something nearly all kids want but only a small percentage of kids attain. There are two types of popularity: popular-as-dominance ("bad" popular) and popular-as-decency ("good" popular). Good popularity is what we want for our kids—to be liked for who they are as individuals with qualities such as friendliness, ability to share, kindness, assertiveness, and compassion. According to Michael Thompson, parents who focus more on their child's quality of friendships, as opposed to the quantity and their child's popularity status, foster healthy relationships. Why? It

only takes just one good friend to carry you through tough social times. Likeability among one's peers, as opposed to "popularity" with one's peers, is a far more important goal to strive for.

In his book *The Friendship Factor*, author Kenneth Rubin describes popularity as a "reputation bestowed upon an individual by one's social peers." Popular boys are perceived by their peers as those who are the best athletes, wear the coolest clothes, have tough-guy attitudes, have a good sense of humor, and display "advanced" social skills. Popular girls are often described by their peers as attractive, socially competent, fashionable, savvy, financially well off, "sassy," and precocious about boys. The "popularity quest" can wreak havoc on healthy friendships.

Cliques

You can get an idea of the social cliques in your child's school by asking about the school cafeteria, says Margaret Sagarese, co-author of *Cliques, 8 Steps to Help Your Child Survive the Social Jungle*. Most children know who sits where and at which tables they are welcome or not welcome. They could map these out for you, describe the characteristics of each group, and then tell you where they fit in. Asking them, "How does that feel? What group do you want to be in? Why? Which group do you admire most? Which group is mean or a clique?" can give you incredible insight into their lives and help children frame where they fit into the social scene.

Supporting our Children

Some of the most difficult questions we will face as parents are: how to stop your child from bullying other kids, how to protect your child from bullying, and how to empower your bystander to step in and help. The more we explore these roles, the more muddied the waters become. We all play the bystander at one time or another and most people, adults and children alike, have been on the receiving and giving end of hurting others. Every situation that involves potential bullying is unique, which means each situation deserves special consideration.

Support Aggressors: The skills needed to be a bully are the same that are needed to be a leader. When identified, a child who has been bullying can be taught ways to shift his energy into leadership and become an asset to his/her community. Making amends may also be an important

> *"It only takes one friend to buffer the effects of bullying."*
>
> Michael Thompson

part of his or her consequences. You can improve a school by addressing one bully at a time, especially if it is your child, but there is always another to take his/her place. The better goal is to get involved with the PTA and school staff to educate the whole community about bullying and try to establish higher standards of behavior to stop bullying before it starts.

Support Targets: When we ask a group of people why kids get bullied, we get lost in the answers: too fat, too shy, too passive, cries easily, too sensitive, too clueless, too awkward, etc. But we forget the main and really only reason a child is bullied, someone decided to bully them, to solve a problem with aggression rather than non-violently. The focus should be on stopping the bully, not "changing" the target so they won't be picked on anymore. The target should be thanked for reporting the situation. The last thing we want to do is leave targets feeling like it is their fault that they are being bullied.

Support Bystanders: An excellent researcher in the field of bystanders, Wendy Craig, PhD, has shown that bystanders have lots of power when they decide to help. The barriers to helping others in trouble are mostly obvious and the consequences they fear of retaliation by the bully who might then turn on them is very real. Stan Davis wrote a book, *Schools Where Everyone Belongs and Empowering Bystanders in Bullying,* that we recommend you give to your school. He has interviewed hundreds of kids who have been bullied and asked, "What would be the best way somebody watching the bullying could help you?" The overwhelming and surprising answer was "support me afterward." It points to the message Michael Thompson keeps repeating, "It only takes one friend to buffer the effects of bullying."

Teach Empathy: One of the most powerful qualities that will have an impact on decreasing bullying is to foster empathy in our children and in the adults who care about them. Empathy is the "ability to put yourself in another's shoes." Everyone can play a role:
- Adults take the time to intervene when there is an imbalance of power between kids.
- Adults remain neutral and respectful.
- Aggressors learn to get in touch with what they were wanting when they bullied and come up with different strategies.
- Bystanders pay attention to the impact of bullying and intervene (telling the bully to stop, getting

help from an adult and/or comforting the target).
- The target focuses on their underlying needs and receives support to become empowered.

Support School-Wide Interventions
- Educate parents, students, and staff with library books, videos, seminars, monthly newsletter articles, and monthly book clubs.
- Support "safe havens" where kids can be themselves: after-school clubs, lunch clubs, and support groups.
- Create Girls'/Boys' Night Out: 8th graders plan it for incoming 6th graders.
- Host "Mix-It-Up" Day, (www.mixitup.org). Everyone sits in a different place in the cafeteria and engages with people they usually wouldn't talk to.
- Support school staff with supervision in risky areas: playground, hallways, and buses.

Resources:

[1] *Bullying at School: What We Know and What We Can Do* by D. Olweus, 1993, Cambridge, MA: Blackwell
Best Friends, Worst Enemies and *Mom, They're Teasing Me* by Michael Thompson
Cliques: 8 Steps to Help Your Child Survive the Social Jungle by C. Giannetti, et.al.
Schools Where Everyone Belongs by Stan Davis at www.StopBullyingNow.org
The Bully, the Bullied and the Bystander by Barbara Colorossa
Raise Your Child's Social IQ by Cathi Cohen
Teaching Your Child the Language of Social Success by Stephen Nowicki, et.al.
The Friendship Factor by Kenneth Rubin

Making Time for Him

1

2

3

4

5

6

7

8

9

10

Stefani Graap, 8th Grade, Rosemont Ridge Middle School

Making Time for Him

> *"In the end these things matter most: How well did you love? How fully did you live? How deeply did you learn to let go?"* —Jack Kornfield, from *Buddha's Little Instruction Book*
>
> *"You will never find time for anything. If you want time, you must make it."* —Charles Buxton
>
> *"How different our lives are when we really know what is deeply important to us, and, keeping that picture in mind, we manage ourselves each day to be and do what really matters most."*
> —Stephen Covey, author of *Seven Habits of Highly Effective People*
>
> *"If you were starting over today, what would you do differently? Whatever your answer, start doing it now."*
> —Brian Tracy
>
> *"Yet, if we look more closely … you discover that there is only ever this moment. Life is always now. Be still. Look. Listen. Be present."*
> —Eckhart Tolle, author of *The New Earth: Awakening to Your Life's Purpose*

GOALS

- To help you explore your priorities in life, and to make time for these priorities

- To help you become aware of the choices you have regarding busyness, clutter and stress

- To support you to align your actions with your values, so that when you manage your time, you engage in those activities that matter most to you

- To explore your satisfaction with the amount of your life energy devoted to work

OVERVIEW

Families today live in a fast-paced, complex world. It is difficult to find time to spend with kids in a world that encourages both parents to work full time away from home, kids to be in several activities weekly. These same families often lack the support of nearby relatives, adequate daycare options, or a supportive community. Contemporary families are also faced with having to somehow protect their children from the larger culture's values and influences that enter our households through electronic and screen technologies, at the expense of our youth's psyches and innocence. The situation can seem hopeless for many parents, who often feel that if they are asked to do one more thing, they will implode. They may give up, feeling like personal and parental failures, without taking into account that they are simply being battered by societal pressures which are not very family friendly.

There is support out there for such dilemmas. It does require taking the time to figure out what works. Each of us has our own unique issues with time, balance, inner peace and work, and each of us will have unique solutions. The important thing is to pay attention to your intuition, your "inner compass" as a clue to what fits for you and your family. We are constantly changing, as are our sons. Keeping open to new learning and new approaches to what works is helpful.

One answer to family empowerment is to simply take some quiet moments each day to prioritize your time and energy. Focusing your life into what is important and what is not can be liberating and literally life-saving. That is why this parenting guide devotes a whole chapter to "Making Time for Him." To model this concept, we have simplified this chapter. You will note that there are fewer articles to read. Instead, we ask you to take some time to focus on thinking about your own life, looking at how you spend your time, and evaluating what you are getting out of the time you are spending. Do your actions line up with your values? Are you living the life you always dreamed of? Are you able to say "No" to some very good things in life, so that you can say "Yes" to those things that are most important?

The essence of this "time" chapter is illustrated in the following popular story (author unknown, although a version of it is told by Stephen Covey):

A professor stood before his philosophy class and had some items in front of him on a table. When the class began, wordlessly, he picked up a large gallon jar and filled it to the top with fist-sized rocks. He then asked the class, "Is the jar full?" Everyone in the class could see that it was so, and answered, "Yes."

The professor replied, "Really?" He pulled out a bucket of pebbles and poured them into the jar. He shook the jar lightly. The pebbles rolled into all the open spaces between the rocks. Grinning, he then asked the group, "Is the jar full?" By this time, the class was on to him. "Probably not," the students responded. "Good!" he replied. The professor picked up a bucket of sand next and started dumping it into the jar. The sand filled all of the spaces left between the rocks and the pebbles. Once more, he asked the class, "Now, is the jar full?"

"No!" everyone shouted back. Once again, he said, "Good." He then grabbed a pitcher of water and poured in about a quart, until the jar was filled to the brim. Then, he looked at the class and said, "Ladies and gentlemen, the jar is now full. Can anybody tell me the lesson you can learn from this? What is the point of this demonstration?"

One eager beaver raised his hand and said, "The point is, no matter how full your life is, if you try really hard, you can always fit more into your schedule!"

"No," the professor replied, that's not the point. I want you to recognize that this jar represents your life. The big rocks are the important things, those things that, if everything else were lost and only these remained, allowed your life to be full. The pebbles are the smaller things that matter, like your job, your home, your car. The sand and water are everything else…the small stuff. If you put the sand

into the jar first," he continued, "there will be no room for the rocks or pebbles. The same goes for life. If you spend all your time and energy on the small stuff, you will never have room for the things that are most important to you."

"What are the 'big rocks' in your life?" the professor continued. "Pay attention to the things that are critical to your happiness. Play with your children. Take time to get medical checkups. Take your spouse out to dinner. Play another 18. Follow your dreams. Block out time in your schedule for these activities. Amazingly, the other stuff still gets done. Periodically, reflect on how you're doing. Are you putting your big rocks first, or does the small stuff still dominate your life? Set your priorities and when you're planning your month, your week or your day, think back to this story, and take care of your big rocks first."

The first exercise of this chapter, **"Finding Time: An Evaluation of My Values and Activities"** (p. 7:11) relates to this story, and will be used as the basis for your circle question at your next discussion group meeting. How closely do your actions match your priorities in life? Evaluate whether you are getting what you want out of each activity on your list... is each activity worth the amount of time you have invested in it? Are you spending a lot of time doing something that is important but that you are undervaluing? How could your actions and priorities better match up? What kinds of changes could you make to give more time to the activities of greatest value (your big rocks)?

Keep this list of your priorities handy and visible (on the refrigerator, at your desk, etc) and refer to it frequently to help you "choose" the time you want for your son and other loved ones. Becoming a conscious consumer of our culture, as well as a judicious creator of your own life, can cure a lot of contemporary woes: stress, a hectic lifestyle, disorganization, unhappiness, loneliness, and lack of intimacy. By putting your time where it is most important, by keeping your "big rocks in the jar," families can put themselves, their children and their most meaningful activities first in their lives. It may be helpful to do the "Finding Time" exercise on a monthly,

quarterly or annual basis, so that you can track how well you are doing on your quest towards leading a life that you long for, with balance and peace.

People who love what they do enjoy life. Parents who live with passion and intention will inspire their children to do the same. And, kids who are excited about life have within themselves one of the most powerful protections around for avoiding high-risk behaviors. The first two articles in this chapter, **"Modeling a Life Worth Living"** and **"Personal Navigation"** (pp. 7:12-7:14) share ideas about finding passion.

Simplifying your life can often free up time and energy for the "big rocks" that give us the most meaning in life. The article, **"Fifteen Steps to a Simpler Life"** (p. 7:15) is an excellent overview of how to focus on what matters most, how to free ourselves from clutter and how to be more organized. Many of us don't recognize the impact of our "stuff." Not only do we struggle to stay clutter-free, we have to work to afford it, take time to shop for it and have a big enough house to store it, which all takes away energy from our "big rocks."

Today we seem to have too many choices and too little time. Often "time savers" like microwaves, dishwashers, faxes and other electronic devices cause us to pack more into each day. We don't allow them to give us any more leisure time. We tend to pause less and do more. Yet, we do have control over how we use our time. **"Vote with Your Life"** (p. 7:22) talks about how we "vote" every day—with our time, our money and our lives. How do you vote?

Stress is an unavoidable fact of life, and learning to manage stress is a very important life skill for everyone. As parents we need to develop ways of processing some of our stress away from the listening ears of our children. For example, we can process work stress on the way home from work so we can be more present when we are home. Many chores and life obligations can drain us. Housework was a big drain on one Mom. She realized that she was wasting precious mental energy dreading the task. She decided to change her approach. First she evaluated the level of cleanliness that was important to her—clean enough so that she and guests were comfortable. There really wasn't money to hire a cleaning service so she broke down the tasks and the frequency they needed to be done and engaged other family members in the tasks. Her attitude and stress level changed and the house was presentable.

How can we reduce our level of stress and increase our enjoyment? One way is to emphasize connection and relationship. We all get wrapped up in our roles as parents (from homework police to sports fan to chauffeur); we focus on the "doing" and lose track of the importance of "being" together and resetting the rhythm and tone of the family. The pace that matches best with our internal, innate rhythm is the natural speed of children and nature, as Richard Carlson describes in his book, *Slowing Down to the Speed of Life*. Our sons need de-stressing skills just as much as we do, so consider how you can do this together.

- While you are together at dinner, take turns sharing something that troubled you during the day and something that made you happy—share something "good" and something "bad."
- Sharing appreciations is always a good way to shift the focus from our worries to the things in life which are really important.
- When family members are feeling stressed, it pays to get back to basic self-care—exercise, coziness, connection to nature, laughter, restful sleep, good food—a picnic under a beautiful tree, playing catch outside or at a swimming pool, resting together in a hammock, sitting by a fire reading aloud, singing in the car, watching the sun set or the moon rise or the stars come out, going to a beautiful spot and breathing deeply.
- Our children need to know that exercise and deep breathing—even a good walk—helps cleanse the stress chemicals out of our bodies, as do creative activities such as art, music, and writing. Try doing this together.
- We can share skills we have to reduce stress such as getting perspective ("What is the worst that can happen if…?"), prioritizing, mapping tasks out on the calendar, or resetting our inner talk to be more positive.

- If your teen is very driven and rarely misses school, allowing the privilege of a "personal day" now and then can provide time for focusing on calmness, rest and self-care.
- Our sons may enjoy some of the excellent books on stress such as *Fighting Invisible Tigers* by Earl Hipp. *How to Stop Worrying and Start Living* is a very useful book for teens and adults who are inclined toward worry. Sean Covey's book *The 6 Most Important Decisions You'll Ever Make* helps teens thoroughly examine the issues in their lives that are most stressful: academics, friends, parents, dating, addictions and self-worth.

Strangely enough, many of us have fallen into a demanding, stressful, parenting style called "helicoptering" that requires us to protect our kids from all pain, be sure they are always happy and do everything we can to mold them into superstars. This means we must involve our children in countless activities so they can get into the "college of our choice" (eloquently described by Nora Ephron in her book *I Feel Bad About My Neck*). These "helicopter parents" are on call 24/7 and are completely exhausted from their self-generated whirlwind of endless activity. Sadly the outcome is the opposite of what they want; instead the kids resent their parents, lack motivation, and are ill-equipped to problem-solve, make decisions, or become self-reliant. **"How to Ground Your Helicopter Parenting"** (p. 7:23) shares tips on what we can do to reduce this unnecessary pressure in our own life and our kids' lives, and at the same time empower our kids to develop healthy competency and decision-making skills.

A powerful way to reduce stress lies in nature. Time in nature helps us to slow down to a healthy speed of life. In fact, Richard Louv, in his book *Last Child in the Woods— Saving our Children from Nature Deficit Disorder* proposes that contact with nature is an essential part of mental, physical and spiritual health. He says,

> *Unlike television, nature does not steal time; it amplifies it…nature offers healing…inspires creativity…Time in nature is not leisure time, it is*

essential investment in our children's health (and also, by the way, in our own).

Some of our best childhood memories are of time spent in nature. Our children need opportunities to play unsupervised in natural settings and our family deepens from time spent together in nature. Pick a place near where you live and visit it frequently to observe nature. Stay up late and watch the stars. Set up a "nature table" at home with treasures collected outside. Go camping. Sit around a campfire. Visit the beach. Sometimes we forget the importance of unstructured play to both children and adults. "It takes a lot of slow to grow" reminds us that our ingenuity, inventiveness, creativity and imagination flourish in down time. Play is critical to healthy child development and teaches many important relationship and problem-solving skills. Summer is a special opportunity for experiencing life with less stress, for bonding with family and nature, and for developing different sides of ourselves, as described in the article **"Summertime"** (p. 7:24).

Changing your relationship to money and work are examined in the articles **"Your Money or Your Life: Are You Making a Dying or Making a Life?"** and **"Remaking a Living"** (pp. 7:25-7:26) The first explores how work in our society has become so important that we often let our jobs define who we are. Sometimes, by freeing ourselves to think outside the box on the issues of employment, money and security, we can come up with alternatives to doing things the same old way, and create more meaningful life work for ourselves. Family Empowerment Network finds that one of the very best resources for doing this comes from Joe Dominguez and Vicki Robin's book *Your Money or Your Life: Transforming your Relationship with Money and Achieving Financial Independence*. This approach asks readers to contemplate what their life purpose is, and even more importantly, when they intend on enacting it. If not now, then when? Their simple formula shows how ordinary people can simplify their lives, save more money, work less, and increase their happiness and connection with others, while living their dreams. Life is really just a series of choices. By becoming active, conscious participants in these choices, families can jump out of the rat race and into a life of their own choosing.

Many people have found inspiration, peace and purpose in Eckhart Tolle's book, *The New Earth: Awakening to Your Life's Purpose*.

> *Time is seen as an endless succession of moments, some "good," some "bad." Yet, if [you] look more closely, through your own immediate experience, you find there are not many moments at all. You discover that there is only ever this moment. Life is always now... A vital question to ask yourself frequently is: "What is my relationship with the present moment?"*

Our article on **"Mindfulness"** (p. 7:28) elaborates on this concept. By paying attention to what is going on in your and your son's life right now, experiencing it fully and accepting it, one can find a sense of calmness even when there are emotional storms around us. Mindful meditation can happen anywhere and anytime.

Focusing on breathing is a powerful way we can all learn to be present. When our child interrupts us and we react with anger and sharp words, we inadvertently teach our child to do the same. Thich Nhat Hanh, internationally renowned Zen master, peace activist and Nobel Prize nominee suggests we can stop this pattern of "passing negativity down the generations" by saying:

> *Breathing in, I see myself as a five-year-old*
> *Breathing out, I smile with compassion at my child*

He shares this advice with children:

> *Breathing in, I am calm. Breathing out, I smile. Next time you are angry or jealous of your brother or sister, or when you are unhappy with a friend, stop and do this exercise.*

Parents who really want to teach their children how to live fully, how to deal with stress effectively, and how to find balance between family, work, and fun in their lives, must model these behaviors themselves. These parents notice where their time, money, and attention flow, and keep these aligned with their own values.

CIRCLE QUESTION

From the first article of this chapter, **"Finding Time: An Evaluation of My Values and Activities,"** describe how closely your actions and time match your values. Share what "big rocks" you commit to include in your life that are not there now?

POSSIBLE DISCUSSION QUESTIONS

1. Do you think you have enough time to spend with the children in your life? If not, what gets in your way? What are some "small steps" you could take to change this?
2. How do you "vote" with your time, money and life? If you knew you had six months to live, would you live differently? How could you give more time towards putting your "big rocks into the jar of life"?
3. How is your son stressed? What does he typically do to relieve stress? How does his stress affect you?
4. Do you often find yourself asking your child to hurry up? What is his usual response? Is there enough transition time between activities and free time to another allow him to assimilate life lessons and experiences?
5. How are you stressed? What do you typically do to de-stress? How does your stress affect your son and your other family relationships? What are some ways that your family schedule could be less stressful?
6. Do you find yourself drained by "un-dones?" If yes, make a list and focus on doing, deleting, delegating.
7. How can you tell when involved, supportive parenting turns into over-involved, "helicopter" parenting that is actually detrimental to your child?
8. Is healthy eating and exercise a priority in your family? If yes, do you model it by exercising regularly yourself?
9. Do you schedule downtime for yourself? Does your son have downtime?
10. How can we support our son to safeguard his time? Minimal part-time job? Only one sport per season? Cell phone rules? Strive for two nights at home per week? Other suggestions?
11. Would you be willing to take less pay for more time off? If you lost your job tomorrow, how would you feel? Frantic? Relieved? How might you make your work more meaningful?
12. How would you rate your life if your family was happy but your job had lower social prestige? You lived in a smaller house? You drove an old car? You had fewer clothes or gadgets for the house?
13. How might you be able to make your own workplace more family friendly?

PUTTING IT INTO PRACTICE

- Take some time each day to remember your dreams, hopes, wishes and values you had when you started your family. Update your ideas and focus your energy on the most important ones.
- Share your hopes, dreams and ideals with your son, and work on ways to make them happen.
- Place your list of priorities in a visible place and revisit the "Finding Time" activity regularly.
- Have your son and other family members do the "Finding Time" activity, and discuss together how well each of you is doing at matching your values with your time commitments.
- Find others who are on a path of living balanced lives, and ask about their first or subsequent steps.
- Carefully evaluate what you say "yes" to.

- Give yourself permission to do less and find extraneous commitments to jettison.
- Limit your nights away from home.
- Decrease the amount of screen time in your home.
- Practice mindfulness. Learn to enjoy activities in the moment; fully immerse yourself in an activity without watching the time.
- Model the behaviors you want to see in your son.
- Rather than tell your son to hurry up, tell yourself to slow down or start earlier for more transition time.
- Use family meetings to plan downtime fun for everyone.
- Find others in your community interested in the voluntary simplicity movement, and share ideas.
- Read *Your Money or Your Life* or take the Voluntary Simplicity Discussion Course from www.nwei.org.

PUTTING IT TOGETHER—YOUR VERSION

Write down three or four ideas you have been inspired to implement in your own life after reading and discussing this chapter.

1. _____

2. _____

3. _____

4. _____

FURTHER READING

Voluntary Simplicity

The Simple Living Guide: A Sourcebook for Less Stressful, More Joyful Living by Janet Luhrs at www.simpleliving.com

Simplify Your Life: 100 Ways to Slow Down and Enjoy the Things That Really Matter by Elaine St. James

Voluntary Simplicity Discussion Course, Northwest Earth Institute (NWEI) at www.nwei.org, 503-227-2807

Healthy Children, Healthy Planet Discussion Course at www.nwei.org

The Organized Parent: 365 Simple Solutions to Managing Your Home, Your Time, and Your Family's Life by Christina Baglivi Tinglof

Finding Peace Within

The New Earth: Awakening to Your Life's Purpose by Eckhart Tolle

Shelter for the Spirit by Victoria Moran

Inner Simplicity by Elaine St. James

Building Unity by Paul Werder

Slowing Down to the Speed of Life: How to Create a More Peaceful, Simpler Life from the Inside Out by Richard Carlson

Seven Habits of Highly Effective People by Stephen Covey

Addressing Clutter and Stress

Clear Your Clutter with Feng Shui: Free Yourself from Physical, Mental, Emotional, Spiritual Clutter Forever by Karen Kingston

Simplify Your Time: Stop Running and Start Living/ Simplify Your Space: Create Order and Reduce Stress by Marcia Ramsland

Less Stress, More Success: A New Approach to Guiding Your Teen Through College Admissions and Beyond by Ken Ginsburg, MD and Marilee Jones, Dean of Admissions of MIT

Balancing Life and Work

Your Money or Your Life: Transforming Your Relationship with Money and Achieving Financial Independence by Vicki Robin and Joe Dominguez

Getting a Life by Jacqueline Blix and David Heitmiller

The Millionaire Next Door: The Surprising Secrets of America's Wealthy by Thomas Stanley, PhD and William Danko, PhD

Resources for Youth

Fighting Invisible Tigers: A Stress Management Guide For Teens by Earl Hipp

Perfectionism—What's Bad About Being Too Good? by Miriam Adderholdt-Elliott and Jan Goldberg

Create a Personal Stress Management Guide at www.aap.org/stress/teen1-a.cfm

WEBSITES

Northwest Earth Institute at www.nwei.org

Simple Living Newsletter at www.simpleliving.com

Simple Living Network at www.simpleliving.net

The New Roadmap Foundation at www.newroadmap.org (from authors of *Your Money or Your Life*)

Wings Seminars: promote transformational shifts in consciousness at www.wings-seminars.com

Finding Time: An Evaluation of My Values and Activities:

Part 1:

Write here a list of all your daily activities during an average week, along with the approximate times spent on each activity.

When you are done, tally up the time spent on each activity, and divide by 7 to give an estimate of the time spent on each activity daily. List the top ten activities, in order of most time spent on them, in the list at the lower right-hand side of this page.

Part 2:

Write down a list of your top priorities in life:

From your list of priorities, mark the ten most essential ones, and list these in order of importance in the lower left-hand side of this page.

Top Ten Priorities (by importance):

1. _____
2. _____
3. _____
4. _____
5. _____
6. _____
7. _____
8. _____
9. _____
10. _____

Top Ten Activities (by time spent):

1. _____
2. _____
3. _____
4. _____
5. _____
6. _____
7. _____
8. _____
9. _____
10. _____

Modeling a Life Worth Living

By Shann Weston

"FINDING MY PASSION" has never been a one-time event. I used to live and die for horses. Then it was John Lennon. I loved my years of homesteading, raising food and running sled dogs in Alaska. I was an ardent environmentalist. I became an expert on being pregnant and having babies when it was my time. These days, I am passionate about resuming running, writing, and my kids. In coming years I'll expect new passions. Recently I have wondered where the capacity for creating passion comes from. What inspires me to find and pursue these interests? What guides me through the dark times and rekindles my basic passion for life?

Many self-help and inspirational books do their best to illuminate the meaning of life. If I could gain such wisdom by osmosis, I would surely have it by now. But there's nothing like raising kids to show me the gap between what I "know" and how I live. When I addressed that gap deeply, I got a succinct, if not simple, message back: To teach life's lessons, I must learn to live them. It comes down to this: If I want my children to understand what it means to be creative, joyful, physically fit, engaged in their own spiritual journey, pursuing meaningful work, involved with community, connected to the earth, celebrating family

and friendships, I must model being an adult doing these things. When things don't go well—when illness or setbacks or depression come visiting, I must model facing the truth and creating a strategy to change, accept, or heal it.

Of all the challenges involved with raising and teaching kids, for me, the greatest task of all is to live my own life as fully as I can, and model to my children what I am doing. I have to learn to freely share my own stories, struggles and lessons, to remember that actions do speak louder than words. If my husband and I are silent with our own life's wisdom and history, what do our children have to go on? We spark our own motivation daily by recognizing how quickly the media could fill that void. The essence of this question is: When our children are out on their own, what will they have to refer back to? What I remember is how my parents lived day to day, how they responded to the twists and turns of life, not what they said about how life should be accomplished.

Modeling a life worth living asks me to take risks—"to show, not tell." The children witness my efforts, sometimes clumsy, to write poetry again, make a new friendship, go for a challenging job, try yoga or meditation, sing in public, formulate my own authentic spiritual truths, and give kids a hug even when they seem to asking for the opposite. My ongoing inspiration is my memories of teachers who loved kids, loved their subject, loved learning, AND SHOWED IT. Their words are long since gone. What I remember is their passion, and if today I pick up Shakespeare or history or science, it will be with the memory of their shining eyes and modeled enthusiasm.

Sometimes taking action means giving myself opportunities to enter into the stillness of life, to be quiet and conscious. I look at my cat or dog as they doze or stare off into space and think they have great lessons to teach us busy humans. Our family balances between jobs, sports, music lessons, friends, entertainment, homework, chores and community activities. We are ready for action all the time, perhaps addicted to it. A few too many quiet moments produce cries of "I'm bored." It's not just our lives, but the whole society and the times we live in. That's why it feels so difficult when we stand up against the force of the flow, and create a ritual, a moment in time, a quieting space to just be, to feel grateful and to celebrate what we've accomplished. Each week, we plan a few sit-down dinners, candles and all, despite everyone's hectic schedules. The phone is turned off. We say a blessing before the meal and share our day. Some days it works better than others, but it has become "tradition," and so we continue to re-create it every week.

I recognized recently that teenage angst is contagious to close family members. In a recent episode with it in our family, I returned to a favorite book, *Man's Search for Meaning*, by Victor Frankl, a survivor of a Nazi concentration camp. Frankl tells us clearly to stop asking about the meaning of life, rather to think of ourselves as being questioned by Life, daily and hourly. Life is asking how we will respond to each loss, each obstacle, each success. Everything else can be taken away but that fundamental freedom to choose our attitude and action to everything Life presents to us.

In the camps, Frankl lived a life where death, pain, and hunger were constant companions. He decided that if his life were to have meaning during its productive and comfortable times, it must also have meaning in times of suffering. That's an uncommon thought these days. It implies that Life's lessons are not easily mastered—and suffering can be a great teacher if we grant permission for its presence. Thinking that we can avoid suffering—for ourselves or our children—is, in itself, responsible for a lot of emotional pain. Life asks us how we will respond to the bad times. We are faced with many choices, including ignoring the pain, tranquilizing it, and facing up to its source. Sometimes finding the way in the midst of personal suffering gives great meaning to life.

Frank noted that those who had a sense of purpose developed faith in the future which served them better than physical strength. In the middle of our shared teenage/family angst, I read these chapters with sudden comprehension. The purpose of our existence changes day by day. The purpose of my existence now is to model my truths, commit fully to my life and to be the best parent I can be. I answer the meaning of my own life by surrendering to the spiritual act of loving my kids and the kids whose lives I touch. That love allows me to see their shining potential, and help them believe in it. That is what will help them survive the lures of drugs and other distractions. I hope to teach my children by example to find and articulate their truths, to recognize their talents as gifts, to treat mind, body and soul with respect and gratitude, to enjoy their relationships with friends, family and nature, to search out what gives them joy and solace, and to go to the center of their beings for wisdom and strength.

Shann Weston is a writer and founder of Positive Legacies, *an organization devoted to leaving the world a better place than we found it. With a Masters of Science in Natural Resources from the University of Alaska, she has a life-long passion for whales and marine life. She lives in the San Juan Islands and has two daughters*
.

Author's Note on Finding Passion

Dear Friends,
"To do good things in the world, first you must know who you are and what gives meaning in your life."
Paula P. Brownlee

We often don't take time to reflect on what is really important to us, to explore who we are and what we stand for. Are we doing something we really love and getting lost in it? Finding passion can give our lives fulfillment. For me, getting outdoors for a bit every day makes me feel whole, even when it is raining.

Children and parents can help each other find passion. Our children, who are naturally spontaneous, can keep us in the moment. I had a blast making a gargoyle out of clay with my son's art literacy class. On the other hand, as parents we can provide our children with opportunities to find their own passions. We can even explore with them. Sometimes your child may pick up on your passion, like my friend who shares her love of playing the guitar with her sons. However, children may not share the same passions as their parents. Your child may even explore passions shared with an adult mentor. We can encourage them to discover what "sparks the light within them" and then kindle that spark in whatever way we can.

Kathy Masarie is a pediatrician, founder of Family Empowerment Network and a Parent and Life Coach. She has a daughter and a son.

Reprinted with permission from Full Esteem Ahead, *Wings*, Winter 1999

Personal Navigation

By Molly Krupa

As A TEENAGER, finding a passion saved my life. I had been full of passions as a child: horses, soccer, gymnastics, and piano. As I entered junior high school, though, these interests were extinguished in the face of societal pressures. Through television and my peers, I "learned" that popular young women were not supposed to be active, loud, or covered in mud. The length of my fingernails and the color of my lipstick became more important than the topics I learned in my advanced classes or the score of my basketball game. My happiness also lost importance. Instead, what was "cool" dominated my existence. My guide to this coolness was soap operas, fashion magazines, and my popularity with the opposite sex. I was miserable.

When I was eighteen (and extremely difficult to get along with), my parents generously supported a dream that I had held since my childhood. I began flying. The physical separation from society's expectations gave me a much needed respite. While up in the air, I did not

have to look at pencil thin women with hair styles that I could never achieve. I did not have to behave like that actress, or look like that model. I only had to be a good pilot. Beyond that, I could begin to be me again.

Flying literally gave me the distance to see society more clearly. However, I do not believe all teens need to take up a passion as dramatic as aviation. A young person's mind only needs to be truly engaged, in a space free of commercial advertising, powerful stereotypes, and pressure from peers. For me, once my world became flying, I could see the discrepancies between my world and the world which had previously set all the rules. My new world had power, and that power began to flow towards me.

Not surprisingly, the most glaring disparity between my former and new worlds lay in the expectations of women. Before, when a joke about the fragility or incompetence of females was passed, I would giggle or act demure. For this complicit response, I was rewarded by the person who made the jest. I also internalized the comments. However, when these jokes were directed towards my ability as a pilot, I no longer thought them funny. Not only that, I knew these "jokes" (and I began to wonder, are these really jokes, or disguised attacks?) were absolutely wrong. I was an excellent pilot.

I began to see a connection between sexist remarks and societal expectations of women. When my long fingernails got caught in the cockpit controls, I cut them, and then thought, "How convenient that their desire for long fingernails matches their expectations of an incapable female pilot." I wondered how many of these connections existed, and became increasingly aware of such societal traps. Aviation gave me the power to see, and also an identity that I cared about enough to want to protect.

A passion gives a young person a purpose in life, a purpose not obscured by media and peer influence.

Moreover, when a teenager finds a passion, she finds a conduit through which her childlike fascination with life itself is rediscovered.

Aviation, which judged me by my flying skills only, liberated me from other standards. As I cast off these other, often harmful, standards, I was able to be myself. Not only did I start living again, but I gained the skills and knowledge needed to protect myself in the face of future adversities. **I believed in myself.**

At the time of this article, Molly Krupa was working as a carpenter in Southeast Portland.

Reprinted with permission from Full Esteem Ahead, *Wings*, Winter 1999

Fifteen Steps to a Simpler Life

By Victoria Moran, author of "Simplifying," excerpted from *Shelter for the Spirit*

I LOVE TO GO TO Susan's house. There's space between the furniture. You can see the wood floors. At Christmas she can put up a tree without rearranging her living room. There are empty places on the bookshelves for more books. There is room in her house for gifts and guests and possibilities. That's because Susan knows how to simplify.

Maybe she was born with the capacity to cull the inconsequential from the basic. Perhaps her mother had it, too, and her grandmother, and they passed it down like a recipe or a figure of speech. But those of us who didn't grow up with a knack for simplifying can learn how to do it later in life. We have to learn how, if we want a home and a life that nurture our spirit.

Cluttered rooms and complicated schedules interfere with our ability to treasure the moment. Ironically our houses and apartments—where some of our best moments can be—seem to attract clutter and complication like a magnet. Mail, both the welcome and the unsolicited, is delivered; purchases are unloaded; items accumulate. After several years spent in one place, it can feel as if moving would take more effort than climbing Mount Everest.

And think of the hours in the day. Are they packed so tightly they make your basement and garage look orderly by comparison? That's true for most of us. We fill hours, children of the Great Depression fill pantries: to the brim —just in case. The things the majority of people find the least time for are exercise, healthy meals, meditation, time with their spouses and children, and pursuing their dreams. Some couples even have to book appointments for making love. It's not an extra sitcom there isn't time for; it's the indispensables that are dispensed with.

You may be familiar with the sense of uneasiness, even desperation that can accompany a growing awareness of how much "stuff" is pressing down on you. There are various stopgap responses to it: a garage sale to deal with object overload, a weekend away as a break from incessant responsibilities. With the proceeds from the sale we shop again, and when we get back from our trip there's more to do than ever.

The only sure way out of the miasma of excess is to embrace simplicity, although our cultural ambivalence toward the concept can get in the way. Sometimes we like simplicity. We say, "These are great directions – really simple," and "Her dress was simple and elegant." Other times we're not so sure. "Simple living" can conjure up visions of voluntary poverty, subsistence farming, and '60s dropouts. To clear away some of the confusion, let's examine simplicity, first by looking at what it is not.

Simplicity is not poverty and lack. If you've experienced those, you know that juggling bills and chasing checks don't simplify anybody's life.

Simplicity is not self-denial. It is an indulgence, providing you with a wealth of time and space.

Simplicity is not going back to the land. Unless that's your chosen way to live and you know what you're in for, you'll end up with more complications than you ever dreamed of in Cleveland.

Simplicity is not boring. Contrary to popular belief, the alternative to incessant activity and acquisition is not vast emptiness. Instead it means experiencing life more fully than ever.

Simplicity is not giving up what you need. It is having everything you need with the bonus of being able to find it.

Now, what simplicity is:

Simplicity is discerning the essential from the unessential. Even with a commitment to living simply, you'll have lots of possessions and pastimes that aren't essential to your survival or your spiritual well-being. You just won't mistake these extras for necessities.

Simplicity is having room for the unexpected. In a simplified life an unforeseen challenge—or a sudden blessing—can be incorporated without a lot of shifting and upset.

Simplicity is savoring life. It is having a truly memorable lunch with a friend because you didn't try to cram in breakfast with another one that morning as well as tea with a third in the afternoon. It's being charmed by the ceramic bowl on your kitchen table every time you see it, rather than having so many ceramic bowls that you no longer notice any of them.

Most of all, simplicity is freedom. It's freedom to choose what you want in your life because you're not letting in everything that shows up. It's freedom to do what you want because you're not already committed to more obligations than you can handle and the maintenance of more objects than you'll ever use.

There are probably hundreds of ways to decrease the complexity of anyone's domestic domain. To keep things truly simple, though, I'll stick with five time-tested ways to simplify your space and 10 others to do the same for your time.

Five Surefire Ways to Simplify Your Space

1. Chop Up Your Credit Cards

I'm not opposed to shopping. I like it, in fact. And I like it more since I chopped up nearly all my credit cards. I did. Right down the middle and again through that corner that said "expiration date." Since then, I have sought to live by the principle of, by and large, only spending money I have. A hundred years ago, that was common sense. Today it seems wildly radical.

Since I stopped shopping with money I didn't have, my life has simplified on every level.

Operating on a pay-up-front basis, I rarely make impulse purchases and therefore don't acquire a lot of intensive-care items: bric-a-brac that demands polishing, clothes that demand dry cleaning. I am released from the culturally entrenched notion that everything I admire I should buy, and everything cheap that I remotely admire I must buy. Now I buy what I need and I buy what I love. And my house is looking more like Susan's.

Remember how good it felt when you were a kid and bought a toy or a present for Mom with your very own money? That's how it feels to pay cash, because you are shopping with your very own money. And you'll have more of it because there will be fewer bills to dog you.

However you wish to conduct your personal financial dealings, making even a minimal effort to charge less and pay cash more can guarantee you the following:

- You will end up with less junk you wish you'd never bought, and your environment will be less cluttered.
- You will look better in your clothes and feel better in your house because everything that goes on your body or in your rooms you will absolutely adore.
- With fewer bills, you'll have additional discretionary income and the satisfaction of being more fully in charge of your financial life. Your expenses will be easier to keep track of, and because cash is so tangible, money itself will become more meaningful.
- When you buy something you truly want— especially something you've "saved up for"—you'll

feel like a million bucks. And you'll greatly improve your chances for having a million bucks since you won't be shelling out a fortune in interest every month.

2. Insist on Quality

I have a crocheted vest that I bought when I was 18 and worked at a specialty store over the holi-days. The vest seem-ed expensive at the time, but it was skillfully crafted of good yarn. In the many years that have

passed since I was 18, I've sent innumerable garments to rummage sales, charity, and the rag bag. I still wear that vest, though, and it is still beautiful. Quality is never outdated.

When you're thinking of adding something new to your wardrobe or to your environment, let quality be the keynote. Quality does not necessarily mean cost, and it certainly doesn't mean the current status value of that particular item. It means only allowing into your cherished space those things that either serve a useful purpose or bring you genuine pleasure.

The highest-quality objects in my home are those made by my daughter. Her artwork, needlework, clay creations, and poems are more valuable to me than a wall full of Rembrandts. Next in quality are the heirlooms —and I don't have many—that connect me with other important people in my life or my heritage. For example, I have a quilt my great-grandmother made. It is folded on top of our piano—fitting because the quilter raised two daughters selling Steinways after she was widowed in 1910.

Also high on the quality scale for me are memorabilia of my own life and travels, books signed by their authors, gifts from people I like being reminded of, and items that by their shape, texture or color make me glad they're in my everyday world. Only you know what denotes quality to you. In general, an object made by hand touches the soul in a way something mass processed cannot. Items whose quality is determined by their practicality can come from almost anywhere, but those whose value derives from more subtle attributes are seldom found in big, barnlike discount stores. They're occasionally made of plastic, but not very often.

Look around the room where you're sitting. What things there meet the dual criteria for quality, in that they are both practical and aesthetically pleasing? Which ones have a definite purpose and are regularly used for that purpose? Which ones simply make you happy because they're in your field of vision? What else is in the room? The "what else" is what stands between you and the simplicity of space your spirit craves. Clothes you don't wear, books you don't read, little statues that don't do anything and you've never liked anyway make indirect demands that rob energy. You see them, but they don't reward your eyes. You have to shove them aside when you look for what you're really going to use. If you have too many of them, maintaining a sense of order will be impossible.

Test the contents of each room in your house or apartment with these two questions: "Is it serving a purpose?" and "Does it make me happy?" Remember, you only need a "yes" answer to one of them for the object at hand to be earning its keep. This querying can be the makings of a massive mental garage sale of "what else." Take those same questions with you when you shop. Envision your intended purchase in the place you've set aside for it. Will it be functional or genuinely promote happiness? If so, it's worthy taking on. If not, you're sabotaging your simplicity.

3. Do a Seasonal Closet Cleaning and Excess Purge
Paying cash and insisting on quality diminish the likelihood of accumulating simplicity-diminishing junk, but it creeps up on all of us. Moreover, what is useful to us changes as our lives change. An overview of your home is in order every season. Do the two-question test on each room and storage place and eliminate excess accordingly.

Closet cleaning can be like sending your soul to a spa. As you discard the worn-out, the worthless, and the size 5 jeans that haven't fit in decades, you discard ways of thinking that no long fit either. You don't have to belabor the point: "I am now cleaning out my closet and my mind." Just clean your closet. Your mind will respond.

Once you've done the major eradication that starts the process, subsequent seasonal purges will be quick

and easy. Remember: You're not giving up what adds to your life. Simplifying does not mean paring down to cold and stark. As long as what's on display or in storage serves you in any way, it can be a welcome part of your simplified lifestyle.

When you exercise discernment about everything, accepted or purchased, that stays in your house, you will find yourself in the presence of something rare and wonderful: unsaturated space. This emptiness opens the door to all those things that will enrich your life in new ways. What you want and need now is far more likely to make its way to you when you make a place for it. By eliminating the unnecessary, you create the void. Nature does her best to fill it. You decide with what and how much.

4. End the Paper Chase
The mail is here. My simplicity is at stake. There are the weekly grocery ads that come unsolicited, the pizza delivery flyers, the catalogs from every mail-order company on earth as penance for having once ordered a set of sheets and pillowcases.

I carry the entire bundle to my desk. I put the envelopes in the recycling basket; the bills go in a file until bill-paying day. I take magazines to the breakfast room since I read them in the morning with my cereal and fruit. I read the letters last when I can spend time with them. If I'm in a hurry, I put them in a special basket and read them later. If someone has taken the time to write to me, I want to give that letter more attention than I give the light bill. Everything else I either tend to immediately file or toss for recycling.

One way to get less junk mail is to answer each piece with a postcard that says, "If I have ordered from you or contributed to your organization in the past, I appreciate that association. However, I wish to have my name immediately and permanently removed from your mailing list." (I had postcards printed with this message.) It also helps to put a note with every subscription, order, or contribution asking that your name not be passed on to other companies or organizations. And you can write to the Mail Preference Service, Direct Marketing Association, P.O. Box 9008, Farmingdale, NY 11735-9008, asking that your name not be sold to lists. But you'll need to write every five years. Direct mailers are better than bloodhounds for finding and refinding potential customers.

We know our copious consumption of paper is environmentally reckless, but it has a personal price as well. All that paper goes into our homes and detracts from the beauty we should see there. Having to sort, read, and dispose of it takes away from the time we have to spend there. So deal with as little paper as necessary and set up a workable filing system for the rest.

A filing cabinet is a most useful piece of furniture. When I got mine, Frankie Grady, a self-confessed filing ace, helped me set up a very workable system. Here are her suggestions:

- Determine how you do paper-work: in one place, wherever it's sunny at the moment, whatever. Use the equipment that suits your style: a stationary cabinet, a file on wheels, or mini-files you can carry.

- Use a container equipped for hanging files. Inside each main compartment, use labeled file folders for each subcategory. The hanging files can cover broad, general headings like "house" or "finances," but avoid anything as all-inclusive as "miscellaneous." Example: Hanging file—Car. File folders within that hanging file—Repair and maintenance, Insurance, Titles and Registration.

- Clear out a file or two every season, just like your rooms and your closets. Be willing to part with unnecessary written and printed matter. The backs of used pages make fine scratch paper, fax-sending paper, kids' drawing paper.

- Put your important documents in a safe deposit box, and keep an updated list of what that box contains in your filing cabinet or computer.

- If you have a computer, file as much as you can electronically. Every once in a while clean out your hard drive, too. Excess is draining, even when it's byte-sized.

5. Organize—But Only After You've Simplified

Simplification and organization are often confused, but they're not the same. You could conceivably organize every bit of extraneous accumulation that's in your house right now. You could hang it on pegboards, stack it neatly on shelves and in cabinets, put it in drawers with those nifty little dividers, stick it on bulletin boards with matching pushpins, and place it by category in those see-through, stacking plastic boxes. In *Clutter's Last Stand*, Dan Aslett's classic on unfettered living, he calls such organizing aids "junk bunkers." If we didn't have so much junk, we wouldn't need all those places to keep it.

> Cultivating spirituality for simple living involves locating and exploring those places in our soul that ring like jubilant wind chimes to the breezes and whispers of the divine.

But be forewarned: If you organize before you simplify, things will be disorganized again in no time. This is not because you're a hopeless slob without a prayer for redemption. It is because excess cannot be organized. If it could, it wouldn't be excess.

Ask 10 friends if they think they're organized or not. Unless everybody you know is a CPA, eight out of the 10 will probably say they're dreadfully disorganized. It's a myth. We just think we're disorganized because we live in a time and place overflowing with junk.

If you practice the first four Surefire Ways to Simplify Your Space, you will find your environment becoming organized with minimal effort. When you remove from a desk drawer the broken rubber bands, dried-up pens, loose change, and year-old receipts, what remains looks pretty good. So what if there's a paper clip in with the postage stamps? That drawer is, for all intents and purposes, organized.

You can organize further if you enjoy doing it, but it isn't necessary. Too much concern over tidiness and organization can defeat your purpose of making your home friendly to human beings, starting with yourself. We all have an internal clutter/order tolerance level. Some people need houses that look like Marine barracks when the sergeant is due in for inspection. Others aren't comfortable unless there are half-read books on the tables, and open sewing basket by the big chair, and last night's Scrabble board left out.

Find your tolerance point and compromise with the tolerance points of the people you live with and the conditions of your life. If you put the well-being of living things ahead of arranging objects, you will be somewhat less organized but quite a bit happier.

The Time of Your Life

The other day I watched an attractive, professional-looking mother approaching a department store entrance at a trot, her little girl galloping behind her at two arms' length. The child was five, maybe six, one of those ages that only lasts a minute and never comes back. "Hurry up," the mother said several times. Her daughter tried to comply, while respecting the childhood conventions of studying cloud formations, running the fingers of her free hand along the turquoise railing, and of course not stepping on any cracks.

I was angry with her mother and I don't even know her. Well, in one sense I don't know her, but in another I know her intimately. She's just me in a different phase of life. I said "Hurry up" to my daughter a thousand times and she obeyed implicitly. She hurried so well that she's a teenager now, and it took her no time at all. Hurrying ourselves and those close to us is a harsher activity than we realize. We tend to be short-tempered when we are short on time. When we have the time to be patient, we usually are. When we have the time to listen, we usually do. When we have the time to help, we're glad to pitch in. Without the time, we feel pressured and annoyed.

As we add more activities to our to-do list, we become like a debtor adding creditors to the roll in an attempt to pacify those he already has. There is no bankruptcy court for people whose time account is chronically overdrawn, but you can recognize them. They're always racing. They can't sit back and enjoy themselves. They're terrified of "wasting time." They suffer from stress-related illnesses. Their relationships are strained. Their schedules are so full that even they don't know what's happening tomorrow. Misplacing a planner seems like losing a limb.

Too many physical objects to work around and care for can diminish our serenity, but too many obligations, too many activities and too many hours at the office will wipe it out completely. We've heard Ben Franklin's phrase "Time is money." In our era, time is better than money. The *American's Use of Time Project* done at the University of Maryland showed that 48 percent of Americans earning less than $20,000 a year would give up a day's pay every week for a day of free time. Seventy percent of those earning more than $30,000 a year would do the same thing. We crave more time and we're willing to pay for it. Of course, the richest person alive can't buy more than 24 hours a day. That used to be enough. Now, in spite of increased life expectancy and a bonanza of labor-saving apparatuses, the pace of life is more often than not a mad rush.

An occasional jam-packed day is exhilarating. A part of me likes the stimulation I can get from over-scheduling and arriving where I'm going, out of breath, just in time. It feels like sliding into home plate with the crowd cheering. But of course, nobody is cheering, and when I collapse at home after an overly rushed day, I bring the agitation with me. Everything is here to soothe my soul—a delightful daughter, congenial pets, art and music handpicked to suit myself—but I'm too tired to notice. A couple of things had to take place to make me want to simplify my time. The first was that I saw my incessant busyness interfering with my closest

relationships. The second was that serenity started to feel better than stimulation. It was like switching from strong coffee to herbal tea. At first it's wretched, but after a while it feels better to be naturally composed than artificially energized.

Ten Surefire Ways to Simplify Your Time

1. Say "No"

Just as you're saying "no" to gadgets you won't use and clothes you don't wear, you can say "no" to activities that aren't genuinely meaningful to you. Developing the habit of politely but consistently saying "no" when you want will give you more time at home and more peace when you're there.

When something is important to other people, they assume it should be equally so to you. The art museum docents think you should be one. The neighborhood crime watch people think you should drive patrol two hours a week. Everybody in the Save-the-Rainforest group thinks you should carry a sign this Saturday. Maybe you should. And maybe not. Our lives are multifaceted. We are workers, students, householders, losers, parents, and friends. All these identities can be part of the tapestry of our destiny. Our task is to balance the many roles we play and refrain from volunteering to understudy everybody else's. It can be tough to say "no," especially to causes we recognize as worthy. The goal is to realize that, since we can't help with everything, our time and stamina need to go into what truly speaks to your hearts.

2. Tithe Your Time

Tithing money—donating one tenth of all income to the church, to people in need or some other deserving cause —is a way of orderly giving. It not only enriches society, but those who do it believe that the practice blesses them with greater prosperity. (John D. Rockefeller's famous "Ledger A," on which he wrote his income and expenditures from boyhood, included a regular tithe.)

Time can be tithed also. You don't have to get specific—10 percent of waking hours—but you should be conscious of giving some time every week or month to something outside yourself. If lack of time is a problem, giving it away may not seem like a viable solution. But when you plan to spend a portion of the hours you've allotted in service of others, you will better organize those that are left. Be sure you tithe your time to something that genuinely moves you, and say "no" without guilt to anything that doesn't. This way it will be easy to remember that you're giving a gift, not serving a sentence.

3. Put Things With Feelings First

Balancing your checkbook is probably not as important as listening to your child. Having a romp with the dog should usually take precedence over waxing the kitchen floor. That's because bank accounts and linoleum can wait until a more convenient moment. Things with feelings can't. Because the hours in the day are finite and many of them are already taken up with sleep, meals, working, bathing, and the like, it's crucial that our discretionary time be spent where it means the most. Put things with feeling first—including yourself.

4. Allow More Time

Whatever it is you have to do, allow a little more time than you think it will take. That way, if it takes longer than you thought it would, you're covered. If it doesn't, you have some spare time, some breathing minutes. Leave for your appointment before you really need to. You can drive slower. If you get there early, you're not wasting time. Bring a book and read it. Bring your journal and write in it. Bring your spirit and meditate.

If you're expecting guests, plan for their arrival in advance of the appointed hour. That way you can rest before they're ringing your doorbell, and truly enjoy their visit once they finally get there.

5. Prioritize With the ABC Method

Priorities change from day to day, which is why the ABC method of meeting them works so well. When you make your list of what you want to accomplish each day, label every item with a letter: A – priority, it must be done today; B – important, it needs to be done soon; C – necessary, it should be done sometime.

If you only get through your A list, you've done everything you have to. The following day, a B or two is likely to rise to the A category. Eventually even the C's will be promoted—or they'll fade into insignificance.

6. Stay Well

Nothing is more time-consuming than being sick. Days and weeks can be devoted to an illness, and more are eroded by having to use them to make up for lost time. If you are a hurrier, one way to get less sick is to stop

hurrying. Colds and the like tend to pounce on hurriers mid-rush. It's as if the body and mind conspire to force a rest on those who refuse to take one otherwise.

We can't always prevent coming down with something, but if we're aware of our state of health and take care of it on a consistent basis, we can substantially hedge our bets. How are you taking care of yourself right now? How is your nutrition? How much rest do you get? Are you frequently outside to get fresh air and a little sunlight? Do you meditate daily or have another routine for stress reduction? Have you sought out health care providers you trust and with whom you can communicate freely? The time you spend preserving your health is like time invested in a savings account; you'll get it back plus interest.

7. Let the Machine Get It

Pavlov's dogs salivated at the sound of a bell, and we respond just as habitually: We answer the phone. We run in from the garden to answer the phone. We leap from the shower and track a rivulet as we dash in a towel to answer the phone. In the midst of a wonderful dinner or the part in the bedtime story where the bears just walk in on Goldilocks, we say, "Just a minute," and answer the phone.

Let the machine get it. Pick up the calls that are important, and be grateful to the callers who didn't leave messages. They just gave you something precious: time.

8. Turn Off the TV

Television can be educational, motivational, and uplifting. Families can watch quality programs together and discuss their meaning. TV can help us understand the world around us and people who are different from ourselves. Is that how you use TV? Me neither.

Regardless of what we choose from the televised menu, one thing is clear: Watching television takes time. The average American will spend one year of life just watching the commercials. If you want more time to enjoy your home, get to know your family, unleash your creativity, or ponder spiritual truths, turn off the TV. You may just want to turn it off from time to time and use that 30 or 60 minutes for something else. Or you may want to turn it off, unplug it, and give it away. Whatever choice you make, you and your television—and your VCR and your computer, for that matter—have a relationship of which you are in charge. How much time to you choose to spend with electronic companionship? Spend that much and no more. This is your life, not a pilot for an upcoming series.

9. Put Off Procrastination

My mother has lots of "do it now" phrases: "Never put off until tomorrow what you can do today." "A stitch in time saves nine." "The early bird catches the worm." The early bird also doesn't have to come up with an excuse or pay a late fee.

If you look around your life and find a great many things undone, perhaps you're trying to do too great a number of things. Procrastination can be a problem for anyone, but it usually strikes life by necessity. If you're attempting to do more than there is time to do, something has to be put off. And then something else. Before long you're lamenting that you can't finish any of it.

If this is your situation, go back over the previous Surefire Ways to Simplify Your Time. Choose the one that you think would make the most difference in the time you have, and do it for a week. That alone should give you the time you need to take care of your most pressing procrastinated issue.

Procrastination itself is a time robber. It takes time to worry about a task, plan additional ways to put it off, talk about how awful it is, and feel guilty over not having done it. If you want more time and something needs doing, do it. Then you'll have time left over.

10. Schedule In Fun

Even when time is a problem, most of us get our work done. We keep our houses reasonably clean. We care for our children. We take the car in for an oil change. We write to our parents and the friends who moved to Seattle, at least every once in a while. We do what we have to do. What we want to do, however, may never get done.

Right now put down this magazine and get out a pencil and a piece of paper. Write down everything you want to do before you die. It doesn't have to be reasonable. Just write it. Locate my best friend from sixth grade. Write it. Learn to speak Icelandic. (Why not? Lawrence of Arabia did.) Write it. When you catalogue your heart's desires, it sets in motion a chain of events that is indeed uncanny. It's as if your subconscious reads the list and sets about to make it happen.

My daughter made such a list, a poster actually, when she was seven. It had things on it like, "Go to China," "Go to Paris," "Be in a movie." These seemed fantastic at the time—it was when we were living in a cabin in the Ozarks and sharing one closet. Amazingly, a surprising number of the events she entered have come to pass for her, including China, Paris, and the movie—even though it was a nonspeaking part in a low-budget horror flick.

We were conditioned early in life to see work as more valuable than play, but play is the work of children. In school we had courses that were "solids" —math, grammar, Latin, history—and "non-solids" —art, music, poetry, sports. But what makes life worth living today, the fact that you can conjugate a verb, or that you can still recite Sara Teasdale and serve a pretty decent tennis ball?

Program your mind with this: Recreation is required. It is not optional. Look at the word: recreation. The time you give to it recreates your soul. There's no waste in that.

Bringing Simplicity Home

Eliminating the chaos from our drawers and from our days invites our spiritual self to make its presence known. In his book *Adventures in Simple Living*, Rich Heffern writes: "Cultivating spirituality for simple living involves locating and exploring those places in our soul that ring like great jubilant wind chimes to the breezes and whispers of the divine. Simplicity... frees us from clutter so that we can wake up to and hear the great chiming within us."

Because "the great chiming" is inside us, it's available to us any time and any place. Chances are, though, we'll hear it at home. At home we're in our own time and our own space—time and space we've cleared out to be amenable to chiming and such.

When the physical amenities of our homes are the necessary and the beautiful, just walking through a room can inspire us. When our calendars have substantial white space, like a well-funded advertisement, we have more time to spend in this place where we can most thoroughly be ourselves. A simplified life seems easier. And remarkable joy comes from simple things—like having work to do that matters, and having people to love who matter a lot.

Permission granted by Gideon Weil, Senior Editor, HarperOne Publishers, a division of Harper Collins. From *Shelter for the Spirit: Create Your Own Haven in a Hectic World* by Victoria Moran, Harper Perennial 1998. Moran is a certified life coach, motivational speaker, and the author of other books including *Fit from Within, Fat, Broke & Lonely No More,* and the best-selling *Creating a Charmed Life*. To learn more about her work or subscribe to her free ezine, "The Charmed Monday Minute," visit www.victoriamoran.com.

Vote With Your Life

By Janet Luhrs, author of *The Simple Living Guide, a Sourcebook for Less Stressful, More Joyful Living*

DID YOU KNOW THAT the choices you make every day are about who you are as a person? Each choice we make is like a vote. Most of us think of voting as only the action of going into a voting booth and choosing whether we want a Democrat or Republican, school levy or not, or a new city council member.

We vote every minute of every day. We vote with our time. We vote with our money. We vote with our life. How's that? Here is an example from my own life. Each time one of those new mega-discount stores opens up, I groan and moan as I pass by, complaining that our sense of community is going out the window, that life is becoming increasingly isolated and sterile, and how I miss the little Mom and Pop stores where the proprietors actually know your name and care about your day. For years, I grumbled about this, yet when I wanted to get good deals, I'd drive on over to the warehouse store, load up my cart, and cram my shelves at home with all of my good deals. I had this vague sense that it didn't feel right, but I did it anyway, rationalizing that it saved me so much money.

I stopped one day and thought about this dual life I was leading. Complaining, but still shopping. I realized I needed to start voting with my choices. I needed to decide which was more important—saving money or encouraging a sense of community and smaller stores. Was I willing to pay more for toilet paper and a jar of jam in order to keep my local store in business? Was I willing to save a little money in exchange for the incredible hassle of driving to one of those mega-stores, fighting for a parking place, wading through a vast and overwhelming maze of stuff, and standing in line for an eternity with a sea of humanity that could care less about my day?

I voted for intimacy and community. I'm not renewing my discount warehouse card. This doesn't mean I'll never again set foot in a warehouse store, because my life isn't about rigid absolutes. It does mean that I no longer will carry a card, and I will instead find another provider for the items I once bought at the warehouse store.

How can you live more in alignment with your values?

1. **Vote with your time.** If you say your family is the most important part of your life, then why are you at your office until 7:00 P.M. every night? If you say it's because you have a boss to please or you need to earn more money, then admit it and realize that you have just voted for money or your boss over your family. In my book, *The Simple Living Guide,* I wrote about a friend who owns a public relations business. He decided early on that his family was most important, and as a result, he turns down work if it means staying at his office past 5:00 P.M. or on weekends. If you say your kids are the most important to you, how often during the day do you tell them that you love them? How much time do you spend with them? If your marriage is most important, how much effort are you putting into keeping it thriving?

2. **Vote with your money.** If you love having cute little boutiques and bookstores in your neighborhood, why are you driving miles to the nearest shopping center filled with mega-stores? Decide whether money or neighborhood is more important and spend your money accordingly. Voting with your money is also about how much you spend and on what. If you are envious of people who retire early or work part-time, then why are you making car payments, TV payments, big house payments and so on? Why is your wardrobe so elaborate? You get the picture. If you want more free time, spend less money so you don't have to work as many hours.

3. **Vote with your life.** Are you leading the kind of life you've always dreamed of? If not, why not? How are you spending your money and your time that is not in alignment with who you are? Does what you do for a living fit with your values? Are you in it just for the money? If so, then money wins your vote. There is nothing wrong with money getting your vote as long as it feels like a good fit inside.

Keep this voting idea in mind as you go through your day. Take note of where your votes feel right and where they don't. And remember too, we're not perfect, and life is fluid. What may seem right this year may not fit next year. What fits for one person may not fit for another. Our job is simply to stay conscious and aware.

How to Ground Your "Helicopter" Parenting

By Kathy Masarie, MD

"Helicopter parent" is eloquently described by Wikipedia: *….a parent who pays extremely close attention to his or her child's experiences and problems. These parents rush to prevent any harm or failure from befalling their children and won't let them learn from their own mistakes, sometimes even contrary to the children's wishes. They are so named because, like helicopters, they hover closely overhead, rarely out of reach, whether their children need them or not. An extension of the term, "Black Hawk parents," has been coined for those who cross the line from a mere excess of zeal to unethical behavior, such as writing their children's college admission essays.*

Helicoptering starts out with bringing forgotten homework and lunch to school and goes on to berating the teacher for an "unfair" grade or overly helping on school projects. It evolves to calling your kid at college to be sure s/he got up for class or flying to Harvard to protest your child's biology grade or demanding the college provide more desirable plumbing for your child studying abroad in China. Colleges and now even companies are actually hiring extra staff to ward off helicopter parents.

One outcome is that parents are stressed and worried to the max. A study by the Society for Research in Child Development determined that helicopter parents reported "more sadness, crying and negative beliefs about themselves, and less joy, contentment and life satisfaction," whether the children were succeeding or failing. Helicoptering's message to the child is that "you are too ineffective to succeed on your own"; however, we all need to learn how to cope with adversity to be effective in life. How can a 22-year-old who can't address setbacks, disappointments, goals and progress at the university level, adjust to a complex job situation and an independent adult life?

Caring for our children's welfare and helping them out along the way is a fundamental part of a parent's role. But we baby boomers have made this nurturing an extreme sport. Some reasons for this parenting phenomenon are:
- Technological advances that allow 24/7 connection. This makes it easy to cross the line from involved to over-involved. The cell phone has become "the world's longest umbilical cord."
- Parent's concern for their children's safety, after school shootings, 9/11 and campus assaults.
- Rejecting the less engaged, "latch-key" parenting style today's parents were raised with.

So what are some antidotes?

1. **Consider what is the best support to enable your child to succeed toward independence**, to learn to make his or her own decisions and become self-sufficient. That answer will vary from child to child.
2. **Connect and communicate with your child.** When your kid complains about an unfair math grade, get curious about what your child sees as the problem behind it rather than storm the school. It may be s/he just wants to vent or that your child doesn't realize the value of completing an unpleasant task in realizing a long-term goal (of getting into the college he/she wants).
3. **Model healthy listening and conflict skills.** If a parent "bullies" a teacher or administrator into doing what they want, the message the kids learn is: "Might makes right." The teacher's perspective on the issue can be very insightful.
4. **Be involved in your child's education.** The Harvard Family Research Project found that teens whose parents play an active role do better in school and are more likely to enroll in college. Communicate regularly with the teacher, volunteer on projects the teacher or school needs in ways that don't stress you out.
5. **Offer support rather than rescue.** Communicate that you are not going to step in every time a child needs help. We can ask our kids, "What are you going to do to solve this problem?"
6. **Allow every opportunity for your child to practice making his/her own decisions.** Think of yourself as a life coach who provides structure, and gives suggestions. However, your child needs to "step up to the plate." Start small when they are young and gradually give them more responsibility as they grow.
7. **For every intervention ask yourself, "Is this action going to lead my child toward independence, competence and confidence or take away from it?"** In this way we give our children what they need: roots to grow and wings to fly.

Resources:
Mom Needs an "A": Hovering, hyper-involved parents the topic of landmark study by Kay Randall at www.utexas.edu/features/2007/helicopter/

You're a Helicopter Parent if you:
- Equate "love" with "success"
- Feel ashamed when your child fails
- Fight your child's battles for him/her, such as protesting an unfair grade
- Take over your child's school projects
- Start sentences about your child with "we," as in "We are applying for scholarships."
- Are preoccupied with the details of a child's activities, practices, schedules and performances
- Lurk on Facebook or MySpace to see if your child is hanging out with any bad seeds

By Erin Wade 8/15/05
Dallas Morning News

Summertime

By Peg Edera

EVERY YEAR PREPARING for summer brings us a new set of dilemmas: our work schedules are conflicting; our daughter's interests have changed; her friends are out of town every week that we are in town; we signed up for her favorite camp too late to get in, etc. Every fall, as I glance back at our summer, I see a myriad of missed opportunities, bad ideas, good ideas poorly executed (and really fun stuff.) As I look back today on my daughter's 10th summer I have decided that my goals for this year need to be clearer and simpler.

There is so much cool stuff to do and so much pressure on us all to do more that it is easy for us to forget about those long summer afternoons of our own childhoods.

I could just drift around, play with other kids, help Mom make jam, get bored and complain. What happens when we forget that those are real options—real activities that have great opportunities for learning? As a kid, I played more games of cards over tuna sandwiches than I can count. What happens when our time is so packed we don't have those simple memories of tuna and cards?

My idea is to find a balance. Last summer one practical thing we did was to schedule our daughter with a camp every other week, some of them being half-day camps. This proved to be a great balance for us all. My husband and I were lucky enough to be able to manipulate our schedules so that one of us was home during the non-camp weeks. It gave our daughter a lot of structure and experience as well as a lot of "down" time. (She also got very involved by helping to choose and schedule her camps, and clearly felt like her summer was HER summer.)

A friend of mine grew up going to three camps a summer. She could pick a one-week camp for each of the 3 A's: athletics, art and academics. Another friend of mine has made sure that her kids are involved in at least one volunteer activity each summer, helping her kids to remember that the world is filled with ways we can help and that simple acts really make a difference.

For us, summertime involves family members coming into town for a few weeks. This is a balancing act requiring great finesse in our household. We try to be available for spontaneous plans as well as organized family get-togethers. The result has frequently been frayed tempers and late nights catching up on the day-to-day obligations of life. Last year I learned how to say "No" and our lives changed. I planned only one dinner party and two special outings. These seemed less hospitable and I worried about hurt feelings, but I emerged from those weeks with several lovely memories and enough energy to weed the garden. Simplify, clarify and balance. This may be my new summer mantra.

In recent years a topic of increasing importance to me has been our spiritual lives. Going to a place of worship is, of course, a good option, but what if you are out of town most weekends? As I've grappled with this I've come up with a few small things we've included in our busy days. One is to notice the things we really love and the things that bring us a sense of wonder, and to make sure they are in balance. One small ritual we have at dinner is to say something we are thankful for in our day. Just noting what is special for each other brings a small awareness of the spirit to our table.

Another thing I have trouble balancing is trips. Our trip planning is frequently so hectic that there is a missed opportunity in it—engaging my daughter in the plan. What do we need; how do we get it; who will take care of the dog; what is our route to the destination; what does she most want to do when she's there? So often our lives are scheduled so tightly that we depart weary and worried that we have forgotten something. What would happen if we completely reframed our idea of a trip to include the preparation as part of the family fun? It sounds like a minor revolution in scheduling for us but the possibility is enticing...thrilling, even.

As I write this I am aware that our list of summer dreams has begun its morning glory-like growth.

We'll be sure to make some of these dreams into reality . . . and we'll still fit in the tuna sandwiches and the card games.

Peg Edera is a businesswoman, now a spiritual coach, facilitating labyrinth walks and workshops, writing poetry and working as a substitute teacher. She lives in Portland and has a daughter.

Reprinted with permission from Full Esteem Ahead, *Wings*, Spring, 2003.

Your Money or Your Life:
Are You Making a Dying or Making a Life?

By Joe Dominguez & Vicki Robin, authors of *Your Money or Your Life*

ONCE UPON A TIME "earning a living" was the means to an end—the means was earning, the end was living. For most employed people, work for pay now dominates their waking hours. Living is what can be fit into the remaining time. Is this really "making a living," or is it more like "making a dying"?

What is the place of work in our lives? Benjamin Franklin said that if everyone labored three hours daily, there would be no need for anyone to work more than that. Dr. Frithjof Bergmann, author of *On Being Free*, agrees: "For most of human history, people only worked for two or three hours per day."

But thanks to the Industrial Revolution, by the late 19th century, work had expanded to fill 60 hours per week. Workers began to fight for a shorter work week. Champions for the workers claimed that fewer hours on the job would decrease fatigue and increase productivity. Indeed, they said, fewer hours was the natural expression of the maturing Industrial Revolution; it would free the workers to exercise their higher faculties, and democracy would enjoy the benefit of an educated and engaged citizenry.

But along came the Depression and the work week, having fallen to 35 hours, started climbing again. Why? During the Depression, people equated free time with unemployment. In an effort to boost the economy and reduce unemployment, the New Deal established the 40-hour work week. Workers were educated to consider employment, not free time, to be their right as citizens.

During the last half century, this has created a push for full employment. There have been more people with more "disposable income," which meant increased profits, which meant business expansion, which meant more jobs, which meant more people (consumers) with yet more disposable income. Consumption has kept the wheels turning.

The fabric of family, culture and community that gave meaning to life outside the workplace has begun to unravel, and paid work has become an end in itself. At work, we now seek answers to the perennial questions of "Who am I?"; "Why am I here?"; and "What's it all for?"

We want jobs to provide the exhilaration of romance. It's as if we believe there is a Job Charming out there—like the Prince Charming in fairy tales —that will fill our needs and inspire us to greatness. We've come to expect that we can somehow have it all through our job: status, meaning, adventure, luxury, respect, power, tough challenges and fantastic rewards! Like the princess who keeps kissing toads looking for a handsome prince, we go from job to job looking for personal fulfillment.

Perhaps worst of all, we look to our jobs to provide us with a sense of identity. Remember the question we were asked in childhood, "What do you want to be when you grow up?" The very question reveals the problem. It asks what you want to "be," yet you are supposed to answer it with a "do." Is it any wonder so many of us suffer mid-life crises as we face the fact that our "doing" doesn't even come close to expressing our "being"?

Our focus on money has robbed us of the pride we can feel in who we are as people and the many ways we contribute to the well-being of others. Our task now is to retrieve our birthright of knowing ourselves as human beings rather than human earnings. As we simplify our lives, "earning a living" can take its place again as a means to the end of a whole and fulfilling life.

Editor's Note: Your Money of Your Life *has been an incredibly impactful book in prioritizing our energy toward connection, family, balance and community over paid work.*

Reprinted with permission of Health Directions, LLC. To subscribe to *Simple Living* by Janet Luhrs, visit www.simpleliving.com or call 1-888-577-6164.

Remaking a Living

By Brad Edmondson

YOUTH AND FREE TIME are both wasted on the young. Fifteen years ago, I lived on a remote desert ranch and would think nothing of climbing a hilltop to spend the afternoon watching cloud banks roll across the mountain ranges. I didn't have any "family" nearby, but I was rarely alone. I didn't have a "job" either, although there were always plenty of important things to do. I had a luxurious amount of free time and I didn't realize it.

I learned that in the desert you can see wind, hear lightning, and smell water. As I was out walking one day, a violent storm came over the pass and bore down on the ranch. Taking shelter between two boulders, I heard the blue arcs of cloud-bound lightning; smelled ozone and the essence of sage in the newly moist air; and saw small whirlwinds being pushed before the storm with sand and tumbleweeds rising within them to heights of 30 feet.

Although I didn't earn any money or make any good career moves that day, I remember it vividly. Now in the middle of a typically frantic workweek, you can stump me just by asking what I had for dinner last night.

Most people with full-time jobs must fight for every hour of free time. But even if you spend your days in a building where the windows can't be opened, the wind still blows as it always did, and the rain still falls. These simple things can offer great joy and meaning to those with time available to notice, just as men fresh out of prison have been known to cry at the taste of beer. First, however, you have to draw the line at work. You have to break loose from a life of breakfast business meetings and three-day dashes to the seashore that were supposed to be relaxing vacations.

There are several ways for people of even modest means to evade being trapped in an unrewarding career and to live more meaningful, leisurely lives. All of them involve making decisions about what is essential and what can be discarded. If the current trend heralded by Time magazine and other dedicated followers of baby-boom behavior holds true, we are likely to see a heartening upheaval in the next decade: millions of people following Thoreau's advice to "simplify, simplify." Instead of quietly battling desperation, they will quietly whittle away at their complex lives until only the heartwood is left.

There's some evidence that this trend may be more than this year's fashionable fad. According to a recent survey by the Gallup organization, most baby boomers say that they won't increase the time they spend at work in the next five years. In fact, almost half of boomer women and 37 percent of men expect to cut back on their work hours.

The problem with this retreat from work is that in most cases it hasn't been accompanied by a retreat from consumer desires. Relearning the values of frugality and thrift may not be difficult for the generation who began life during the

Depression, but it won't be nearly as easy for younger generations. Regardless of the values espoused during the '60s and '70s, baby boomers and younger adults are more oriented to the cash economy and consumer values than any other generation in American history. We still believe that we are entitled to a better life than our parents had, although we remain confused about what "a better life" really means.

Decreasing your income without decreasing your consumption is impossible for everyone except the federal government. Getting off the typical American treadmill of earning and spending will mean living by a new set of values. You won't even need to take up residence on the shore of Walden Pond or shuck everything for an organic hazelnut collective in the wilds of Oregon. Indeed, it may be possible for harried people to live much as they do now and be much happier. It all boils down to where you draw the lines.

Here are a few suggestions:

Ask your boss for a break instead of a raise. The nation's population growth rate is slowing down and so is growth in the nation's labor force. This means that highly skilled, trusted workers will become harder and harder to find as the 1990s roll on. Employers will be forced to make concessions to hold onto these kinds of workers. And unions will be in a better position to bargain for shorter and more flexible work hours. Management will give more serious consideration to a wider range of job benefits, from paid childcare leave and sabbaticals to flex-time and telecommuting.

Work part of the time at home. This delightful way to step back from your career can also be relatively painless, if your boss goes for it. If you're used to a high-pressure office environment, this option can seem almost like not working at all. You get up when you feel like it and wear what you want. When it's time to take a break, you can knead bread or watch the bird feeder instead of wandering aimlessly through beige corridors or gulping coffee.

Taking work home can actually increase the quality of your work. I find that going home to work is like escaping to a sanctuary. At the end of the day, when your housemates return, the house is clean, the work is done, supper's ready, and you're the hero.

Substitute community for cash. Most young and middle-aged Americans were raised in the suburbs and lived within the small confines of a nuclear family. When family labor couldn't provide something, the family paid cash for the extra product or service. Now, the combined efforts of economic stagnation and a pervasive desire to simplify could force a large and positive shift in values. It could teach highly individualistic people that collective behavior is often a cheaper, more satisfying way to solve a problem than cold cash.

Relying on your friends, and being there when they ask the same from you, is one of the most effective ways to reduce your dependence on paid products and services. This could mean forming a childcare cooperative instead of paying through the nose at a good day-care center, throwing potluck dinners instead of patronizing trendy restaurants, or putting up vegetables from a community garden instead of buying fresh produce flown in from South America.

Reprinted with permission of Brad Edmondson, who currently lives in Ithaca, NY. The article was originally published in *Utne Reader*, July/August 1991.

> A master in the art of living
> draws no shape distinction
> between her work and play,
> her labor and her leisure,
> her mind and her body,
> her education and her recreation.
> She hardly knows which is which.
> She simply pursues her vision
> of excellence through whatever
> she is doing and leaves
> others to determine
> whether she is working or playing.
> To herself, she always seems
> to be doing both.
>
> *Unknown*

Mindfulness

By Glenda Montgomery

Though we live unconsciously, "on automatic pilot," every one of us can learn to be awake. It just takes practice.

—Jack Kornfield, from *Buddha's Little Instruction Book*

I ARRIVED ONE DAY at my daughter's school and as I threw the car into "park," I lurched into awareness, as if suddenly awaking from deep sleep. I was there, at the school, yet how did I get there? I had no memory of the drive. I couldn't remember a single sight from the route nor whether the lights had been green or red. I had arrived safely, and so I believe that I had driven safely, but my body had been on autopilot while my mind leaped and jumped from solving anticipated problems with the class I was going to teach the next day to rehashing a conversation I'd had with my husband in the morning to launching into planning my shopping list for next week's groceries. I'd been in "monkey mind" and it had been so compelling that I had literally no awareness of my life during the moments that I had been living it.

My cavorting thoughts had caused a minor roller-coaster of anxious emotion and completely robbed me of 20 minutes of my life. The fact is that the only moment we have control of is the moment we are living right now. Jon Kabbat-Zinn of the Stress Reduction Clinic at the University of Massachusetts and author of *Coming To Our Senses*, says that much of our stress and discontent is from being caught up in analyzing and reliving our past and worrying about our futures rather than being present and fully living our "now." He extols the value of "mindfulness meditation" which includes being in silence while focusing on breath or on physical senses while letting go of thought. Mindfulness meditation focuses on deeply experiencing the present moment in its stillness and emptiness.

Kabbat-Zinn has led many research studies on the benefits of mindfulness meditation. He has found that it significantly lowers anxiety and negative emotions, reduces blood pressure and increases levels of antibodies, leaving people not only less stressed but healthier and happier. Well-known authors Wayne Dyer and Deepak Chopra, describe an experiment in the set of tapes called *Creating the World the Way You Really Want It To Be,* in which serotonin levels were measured in the brains of each of many meditators before a large group meditation session began. Serotonin is a neurotransmitter which induces feelings of calm. The higher the levels of serotonin in your brain, the greater sense of calm you experience. After the meditation session, the levels were measured again. Virtually every one of the meditators experienced a rise in their serotonin levels with a corresponding rise in their sense of peace. What is further fascinating is that people in the general vicinity of this large group meditation session ALSO experienced a rise in their serotonin levels. This supports what we already know intuitively: when we are with calm people, we too begin to feel calm.[1] Think of the positive influence your meditation practice could have not just to you but to the people around you!

Mindfulness meditation can take place anywhere. It is simple, yet its results can be profound. Some people merely focus on the in and out of their breath, saying, "In" and "Out." Others run through their senses: What am I seeing right now? What sensations am I feeling right now . . . in my toes, in my legs, in my belly, in my chest, in my shoulders, in my neck, in my face? What do I smell right now? What sounds can I hear right now? When we notice our thoughts push back, we gently let them go. We can simply say, "thoughts" and imagine them being blown by a light breeze as we resume our breath and our attention to the present moment.

You don't need a meditation cushion or quiet room or any equipment to practice; you don't even need to be sitting down. You can experience the beneficial results of mindfulness meditation just by giving your FULL attention to what you are doing at any given moment. You could wash the dishes as a practice of mindfulness, or practice while eating a meal or while taking a walk. It is a time to give your monkey mind a rest and to fully engage in the "Now." I have begun to practice mindfulness meditation as I drive. I turn the radio off, and try to be present. I focus on colors and sights and sounds. I check in with the sensations of my body and relax the tension I've accumulated by rushing through my day. I listen to my breath in and out, and any thoughts that want to crash in on my peace, I circle in an imaginary balloon, which I let float away. I find that I am calmer, more connected and I always know exactly how I got to where I am going.

Resources:

[1] *There is a Spiritual Solution to Every Problem* by Wayne Dyer, pg 99
The New Earth by Eckhart Tolle
Coming To Our Senses by Jon Kabbat-Zinn

Written for Family Empowerment Network by Glenda Montgomery, Certified Positive Disipline Instructor in Portland, Oregon at www.positiveparentingpdx.com. For reprint requests, contact www.family-empower.com.

Keeping Him Safe 8

Keeping Him Safe

"Setting an example is not the main means of influencing another, it is the only means." —Albert Einstein

"The fact that nearly one in three parents is disengaged from their adolescent's life is a clear reason to worry about the future well-being of American's young people." —Laurence Steinberg

"Children have never been very good at listening to their elders, but they have never failed to imitate them."
—James Baldwin

"That's how you grow up: experiences. The only way to get experiences is to take risks. When you're growing up you've got to find out. Well, I've heard all this stuff about sex and drugs and driving and you have to try out a little bit of everything and from that you build your own plan, your own lifestyle, and become the person you are when you become developed."
—17 yr-old answering, "What's appealing about taking risks?"
from *The Culture of Adolescent Risk-Taking*

Where citizens are activated, where local coalitions are at work, where parents are making an issue of underage and heavy drinking, where there is pressure on local police—that is where we see changes that limit these practices [adolescent binge drinking]."
—Alexander Wagenaar from *Dying to Drink*

GOALS

- To help parents understand that a goal of adolescence is for teens to form their own identity and this often involves experimenting with boundaries and risk-taking behavior

- To encourage parents to know that they can be the first line of defense between their son and common health and safety risks

- To give parents tools to communicate better with their sons about high-risk behavior and intervene earlier

- To help parents recognize signs that their sons might be in trouble

- To help parents establish support structures which encourage healthy decision-making

OVERVIEW

Protecting our children from risky behaviors is one of the most important and distressing jobs of parenthood and one that can leave parents feeling afraid and powerless. The bad news is that sexual promiscuity, depression, suicide, violence, drugs and alcohol are serious problems confronting our nation's youth, regardless of how sheltered their environment. All of our kids will be exposed to or affected by these problems well before high school graduation. Most of our teens will experiment in some ways before they graduate from high school. The good news is that there is still a lot that parents can do to instill skills in their children that are essential for successfully surviving the adolescent years. These skills include the ability to:

- Learn from one's own life experiences,
- Look at issues from multiple perspectives,
- Develop effective decision-making skills.

Our sons have tremendous ability to make good choices if they have practiced and have learned to live with the consequences of those choices. Parents can also be a great help to their teens by guiding them into "positive" risk-taking activities and by creating family and community support that provides a feeling of belonging and significance.

To some of you, this chapter on keeping your son safe may feel overwhelming; however, we believe that knowing what can happen in the world of today's youth can be used to empower you as a parent. Accurate information, combined with proactive support can move you from a feeling of powerlessness to a feeling of empowerment. You can make a difference in your son's ability to safely navigate the rough waters of adolescence. This chapter will give you both information about the dangers and difficulties inherent in the world of adolescence and specific, proven ways you can have a positive impact on the choices your son makes at this time in his life.

One critical task of adolescence is to move from making decisions based on resistance to outside authorities (parents, teachers, society, peers) to making reasoned choices that are based on values and needs. There is no more important time to use respectful, positive discipline

parenting skills than when it comes to risk-taking behaviors. Parents will want to share information with their teenagers about sex, relationships, violence, drug use and chemical dependency and to empower their teens to deal effectively with these issues. What our kids do with that information will be their choice. We can improve the chance of healthy choices if we avoid creating a family atmosphere that invites rebellion, where risky behaviors become a power struggle in which everyone loses. Sometimes our kids might even agree with what we are demanding—for example, "You will not drink"—and yet their intense desire for choice and autonomy will lead to resistance. Since our teen's world is far beyond any parent's ability to control, parents will be better off focusing on positive interactions that will help their teens develop strong self-discipline and self-knowledge skills.

Creating a strong sense of love and connection to family and community has long been proven to greatly diminish problem behaviors in teenagers. One study of 12,000 youths, summarized in our first article **"Connecting Teens and Parents: The Vital Link"** (p. 8:18), found that good connection and communication with parents was the most highly protective factor against risky behaviors. This, of course, brings us back to the Developmental Assets. A child who has at least 30 of the 40 assets is much less likely to experience problem alcohol use, drug abuse, early sexual activity or violence, as shown graphically in **"The Power of Assets to Protect"** (p. 8:19). Another proactive tool that works is to network with other adults to create a "web" of support for each other and for your children. A *Raising Our Sons* discussion group is a great place to start networking and connecting with other adults who care.

Risk-Taking and Adolescence

Discussing teens' safety issues can be very scary, especially for parents of younger children. All of us find it hard to believe OUR children will ever engage in risky behaviors. However, risk-taking is developmentally NORMAL during adolescence. Since all parents want to know what they can do now to support their children in making healthy choices later, we invite you to consider the two threads of thought in this chapter's articles. One thread addresses what parents can do now for prevention and the other thread helps identify and deal with problem behaviors once they develop. Those parents who want to know the details of risky behavior can read all the articles. Others, especially those with younger children, may find this overwhelming and will want to use them later as reference materials. We encourage all of you to participate in the group discussion of risk-taking behaviors, regardless of the amount of reading you have done before the meeting. Our goal is to get parents thinking about long-term parenting strategies that will lessen the chances that their teenagers will make risky choices that will have lifelong negative consequences. Being knowledgeable on these topics (as opposed to overreacting or jumping to conclusions) puts parents in the best possible position when their teens want to talk honestly about their lives or those of their friends.

Risk-taking in youth is normal, but the kinds of risks taken vary widely. For some teens, risky behavior might entail climbing a mountain or trying out for a school play, while for others, it entails smoking, drinking, or sexual activity. One thing to recognize is that many "risky behaviors" in youth can be considered "normal" adult behaviors. In their quest to become adults, some teenagers will take these "normal" behaviors too far, as in binge drinking, promiscuity, sniffing glue or using "club drugs" such as ecstasy at a rave (all night concert). Many would say that there is no behavior that teens do that is not modeled for them somewhere in the adult world. This creates a conundrum for parents: how are we to forbid our youth those activities that our teens see as the hallmarks of adulthood to which they aspire? Perhaps the strongest antidote to this double bind is keeping a strong line of communication, love and acceptance (with age-appropriate limits) flowing between ourselves and our teens, even if we don't always approve of their behaviors. If parents don't go out of their way to share unconditional love with their teens, it is likely that our kids will look for love and acceptance elsewhere, most likely with their peers. Parents who want to have as much influence on their teenagers as their peer culture will need to show their teens, through actions and words, that they are loved and respected, even if they choose differently than their parents would like.

We now know from brain imaging studies that our teens' brains are a work in progress. With puberty (11 to 14 years of age), the emotional part of the brain (the amygdala) gets charged up to seek rewards and stimulation. The pre-frontal cortex of the frontal lobes, which helps us with reasoning, problem-solving, considering long-term consequences, and inhibiting impulsivity, is not fully mature until 18 to 25 years of age (earlier in females than males). Most young adults continue to have cortex maturation until their late 20's. You can see that the teen brain is like a "fast car with no brakes." This means that we adults have even more proof that our teens need us. Our respectful dialog, negotiation and limit-setting, and gradual expansion of boundaries help them to learn how to put on the brakes and be more discerning. As parents we can facilitate and encourage healthy risk- taking for our teens, such as sports which push their personal limits, sharing one's poetry, handling sexual situations responsibly and safely, and speaking one's mind. These points are highlighted in the article: **"Teens and Risks"** (p. 8:20).

This chapter discusses common safety issues for today's adolescents, including body image, healthy relationships and sexuality, violence, depression, suicide, substance abuse, and motor vehicle safety. Our hope is that you can educate yourself on these issues in time to introduce preventive parenting actions—or at least to intervene with your child as early as possible—before problem behaviors turn into persistent, negative habits. We owe it to our kids to understand the myriad dangers they will face in everyday life so that we can prepare them to face these head-on and with strength of character.

If at any point you are feeling nervous or over-whelmed by what you are reading and wish you could just skip this part of parenting, join the club; you are welcome to skip over any topic for now or to go straight to the articles that share information in a gentler style with solutions on every page. Then you can come back to this Overview or to the Circle Question from a place of empowerment rather than fear.

Body Image

Men are now being affected by what used to be the domain of women: an obsession with how their bodies look. Our men and boys are bombarded by media images of muscle-bound, "perfect" male bodies in advertising, movies, TV shows, video games and even politics. The more the images of the ideal male are narrowed and pervasively extolled, the greater the probability that our boys feel as though they are substandard. The self-criticism, dissatisfaction, and depression associated with body image is no longer the sole territory of females. To achieve their goal of highly muscled and "Rambo-like" physiques, some boys take dangerous steroids or supplements. The article, **"Boy's Struggle with Body Image"** (p. 8:22) addresses these issues. Parents who spend time with their sons help counteract the negative effects our media-based society has created when they emphasize appearance over substance. Be careful not to put yourself or others down due to looks or weight. Our sons also need help learning to live healthy balanced lives with lots of physical activity, good quality foods, and a limit on junk food. Although eating disorders remain rare in males, they are on the rise in both underweight and overweight boys. As discussed in the media chapter, there is a clear link between screen time, overeating and lack of activity, which contributes to obesity and diabetes. Families who eat dinner together create an atmosphere of healthy eating and connection that has been proven to be protective against risk-taking behaviors during adolescence.

Sexual Activity/Healthy Relationships

Dealing with our kids' sexuality is probably one of the most difficult jobs for parents. After all, we want our teens to have sex … not today, but someday. This is different than many of the other behaviors in this chapter, which we would like our kids to avoid altogether. It is an extremely tricky task to help our sons develop a healthy sexual identity and a sense of healthy sexual behavior, while at the same time postponing sexual intercourse until they are "old enough" to be mature and responsible about it. This job is easier if parents acknowledge that their teenagers are sexual beings: our kids will have sex someday whether we want them to or not, and our job as parents is to prepare them as best we can for that

day. This includes giving them information on the advantages of postponing that day.

One thing is clear. Our children will get the best information from us rather than their peers. They want accurate information, even if it makes both of you uncomfortable. Accurate sexual information has been shown in multitudes of studies to be an effective tool of prevention. In the US, sex education and easy access to condoms and contraceptives have repeatedly been shown to actually delay the onset of sexual activity by an average of one to two years. European youth, exposed to bare-breasted women on the beach, good sex education in their schools and easy access to contraceptives, delay sexual intercourse about 1½ years beyond their American counterparts. There is NO EVIDENCE that education about sexuality makes a teen more likely to have sex. Our Puritan roots have allowed this rumor to flourish and deprived our nation's children of reliable, life-saving information about responsible and safe sexual behaviors. There is nothing wrong with a family value of "waiting until marriage" as long as the parents also recognize this is not a fail-proof plan. Many youth, saturated in abstinence education, are simply not prepared to use condoms and contraceptives when the "moment" suddenly arrives. This story tells it all:

> When European boys are asked if they carry condoms, they say, "Of course I do. I love and respect my girlfriend and want to be prepared if something should happen." When American boys are asked that question, they say, "Of course I don't. I love and respect my girlfriend too much to expect that it will happen."

But it does happen. Remember that European youth delay sexual intercourse 1½ years beyond their American counterparts and have much lower rates of sexually transmitted diseases and pregnancy. Teenagers are sexual beings. Parents cannot prevent the onset of sexuality in their teens, but they can promote safe and responsible sexual behaviors (something that's modeled poorly for our teens by adults and the media, unfortunately). Talking about sexuality does help, and teens need to know that there are a whole range of sexual behaviors they can engage in safely other than intercourse. It is very important to ensure that our teenagers have open access to medical care for their contraceptive and sexual health needs. Your son may want to know where to take his girlfriend, or friends that are girls, if they need birth control or the "morning after" pill. Some families may decide to keep a supply of condoms available in their homes and allow teenagers open access to them. It may be difficult for parents to accept that their children will make their own decisions about when to become sexually active. This can be easier to live with, however, if parents know they have done a good job of educating their kids about the responsibilities that must accompany this decision and about the value of "waiting."

Our culture's puritanical denial of teenagers' sexuality has had an unfortunate outcome: it has led to an epidemic of adolescent ignorance, "pregnancy by accident" and sexually transmitted diseases. Some kids think that if they have oral sex, they are not really "sexually active" and hence are not at risk for sexually transmitted diseases. They are. Other kids don't realize that it is possible to get pregnant on your very first encounter or while engaging in sexual activities other than vaginal intercourse. This lack of awareness of responsible and safe sex practices has led to a relatively new trend among some teens of "buddy sex," where friends trade sexual favors with no strings attached. Parents can provide information and a counterpoint to this casual attitude toward sexuality, as well as listening to the stresses of modern teen life.

The article "Communication Tips for Parents" (p. 8:22) offers ways to start talking with your son about his body and sexuality. A good place to start is to share information with your son about normal pubertal development. The easiest time to talk about sexuality is when situations arise that naturally lead to discussions, i.e., teachable moments. Starting these talks early in life and continuing them through puberty will desensitize the topic of sexuality in your household and will make it easier for your son to ask you for information or advice. Most teens want their parents to be honest and to share their knowledge and feelings about sexuality with them, but they are unlikely to start these conversations

themselves. Parents who can manage to overcome their own difficulties talking about sexuality with their children, and who do so in a matter-of-fact way, can greatly benefit their children's health and sexual expression. Teens need support and acceptance dealing with the struggles of growing up in a sexualized culture, as noted in the article **"Talking Back: Ten Things Teens Want their Parents to Know About Teen Pregnancy"** (p. 8:26). Also, teens who have developed a level of comfort talking about sexual issues within their own homes are much more likely to be able to talk to their potential sexual partners about these issues and much less likely to engage in casual and unsafe sex.

Healthy Relationships

Parents play a significant role in helping their sons learn to create responsible, healthy and safe relationships with others. It is important to talk with your son about healthy relationships and the respectful treatment of women. More importantly, it is essential for parents to model healthy relationships in their own lives and to raise their sons with love and respect, without the threat of violence, ridicule or shame. Healthy relationships exhibit the following qualities: self-esteem of both members, mutual respect, trust, open communication, nonviolence, personal responsibility, mutual interests/friends, shared decision making, non-controlling behavior, non-abuse of drugs, and responsiveness to the other person saying "No." As bystanders they can speak up when they see sexual harassment. **"Recipe for a Healthy Relationship"** (p. 8:27) elaborates on these ideas.

As parents, it is also our responsibility to intervene in a teenage relationship if we suspect abusive behavior, even if it is our son who is the perpetrator. Girls today may dress scantily, act provocatively, and assertively pursue their social and sexual agendas, but this is no excuse to disrespect them. Our sons need to learn what sexual harassment is and that it is against the law: someone trying (often repeatedly) to get power over another person by saying or doing something sexual that feels uncomfortable to the target. If someone tells our sons that they feel uncomfortable with what they are doing or saying, they need to stop immediately. Teach your teen sons the "Three No Rule"; if they ask someone out 3 times and they say "No," they can only say "Let me know if you change your mind" and then drop it. Hopefully they won't need the rule because they will be responsive the first time someone asks them to stop. No matter how strong a girl "comes on" to a boy, it is still the boy's responsibility to make safe, responsible and respectful sexual choices. Our culture's double standard, where "real men" are "studs" and "real women" are "virgins," tends to excuse sexual promiscuity on the part of boys. Some boys even believe it is their right to have sex or that aggression is an acceptable means to satisfy their sexual needs. They may simply be modeling behavior they see at home or in the media. However, current rape laws can put a boy in jail for nonconsensual sex, and child-support laws have made it clear that it is the fault of both parties if a woman or girl gets pregnant. Sharing with your son the information in the article **"Abuse in Teen Dating Relationships"** and **"Dater's Bill of Rights"** (pp. 8:28-8:29) will help both of you to evaluate your significant relationships for signs of healthy respect.

Violence

Boys now live in a country where around 40% of homes have guns (US Department of Justice at www.ncjrs.gov/pdfiles/165476.pdf), where popular culture glorifies violence and where the suicide and homicide rates in youth are quite high. All of our children need to know the rules around firearms regardless of whether there are any in your family. If they see a firearm that is not in a locked case, or their friend wants them to look at a gun, they need to leave the area immediately and tell you. Let them know that each year some kids die because of curiosity about firearms or because someone thought the gun "wasn't loaded." Your family rules should also clearly state that BB guns should only be used with adult supervision and goggles. In today's times, even play guns that look like real guns are not a good idea.

Prevention of violence is a prime concern for today's parents. In a study by the Family and Work Institute entitled "Youth and Violence: Students Speak Out for a More Civilized Society," 1000 youth were asked how to stop violence in America (a complete report can be found at www.coloradotrust.org). These kids suggested stopping emotional abuse (such as gossip and put

downs), embracing diversity (so kids value differences rather than "sameness"), and getting support from important people in a youth's life. From the beginning, our sons need to be taught anger control and peaceful problem-solving. Understanding that violence is largely a problem of how men are socialized can go a long way towards changing this dynamic for your son, as reviewed in the article, **"Boys, Men and Violence: Strategies for Prevention"** (p. 8:30).

One problem in our society is that to remain "manly," a boy or man must hide all of his emotions, effectively funneling them into the seemingly only socially acceptable feeling: anger. Unchecked, this anger can lead to violence. Boys can be taught to express a more full range of emotions and to deal with their anger in personally and socially healthy ways. Parents are in the best position to accomplish these lessons by teaching through example at home. The article **"Controlling the Urge to Strike Out"** (p. 8:33) discusses simple ways that parents can help their boys in this arena.

Community efforts at violence prevention can be very effective. Schools often have an anti-violence program that parents can actively support. The National Center for Injury Prevention and Control's book, *Best Practices of Youth Violence Prevention, A Sourcebook for Community Action* at www.cdc.gov/ncipc/dvp/bestpractices.htm, contains many ideas for community-wide prevention strategies. One activity that PTAs and community groups concerned about youth violence can support, is the initiation of media literacy education for kids, since violence is often glorified or romanticized in the news and entertainment media.

Depression and Suicide

Suicide is the 3rd leading cause of death for children ages 15-24. Sixty percent of these deaths were from firearms. For every completed suicide, there are many attempts. Girls attempt suicide more frequently but are less successful. When boys attempt suicide they use more lethal means, such as guns or hanging. All guns should be removed from homes with boys who have suicidal ideation. Prescription drugs should be secured and, of course, parents need to get help. Over the past 25 years, there has been a five-fold increase in the youth suicide rate, and most of these youth were clinically depressed. The key to reducing suicide is to better recognize the symptoms of depression in our youth. Depression can manifest in a variety of behaviors in our children and can include feeling sad, failing at school, engaging in violent outbursts and using drugs. Depression in boys (and men) can be especially hard to recognize, because boys tend to express their depression through anger and violence, as they have been trained since babyhood to hide their feelings and emotions. **"Depression in Boys: A Hidden Epidemic"** (p. 8:34) will help you differentiate between normal teenage moodiness and clinical depression, and when to get mental health help. It should be noted that gay youth have a higher risk of depression and suicide than other kids. Helping our teens to get constructively involved in community activities and community service, giving our kids opportunities to connect with nature, and working on a warm, open parent-teen relationship are all protective factors for our boys. Adolescence is a stressful time, and too much lonely brooding in one's room (nowadays often accompanied by video games or online activities) is not healthy for teens. We need to teach our teens how to reduce stress in healthy ways.

Substance Abuse

Although many of our adolescents are doing well and making choices that protect themselves from harm, a significant proportion of teens put their health at risk in a variety of ways. Alcohol use among teens and young adults is of particular concern, especially since binge drinking (5 or more drinks on the same occasion) has become the norm for many of our youth. We now know from brain imaging studies that large amounts of alcohol (like other drugs) can cause long-term damage to the developing brain. And research shows that young teen brains (15 and younger) are particularly susceptible to alcohol addiction. Even moderate use by teens impairs learning and memory to a much greater extent than it would for an adult user. What is a parent to do? After all, some of us tried drugs ourselves as adolescents and most of us drink some alcohol as adults, and now we don't know how to deal with our own children who are using drugs and alcohol! Take heart, you are not alone! Our kids live in a pleasure-seeking and drug-using culture,

and their choice to "use" is influenced by many factors outside the family and cannot be blamed upon parents. However, parents who want to deal constructively with their child's relationship to drugs and alcohol can help their kids in the following ways.

- Talk openly about drug dependency in the family.
- Model a healthy legal relationship to alcohol and drugs.
- Inform yourselves about common drugs and the continuum of use from abstinence to chemical dependency (see www.theantidrug.com).
- Share your own values with your children.
- Set clear rules and expectations and age-appropriate consequences.
- Teach assertiveness, delay of gratification and long term planning/goal setting skills.
- Foster emotional honesty with your kids.

Be prepared for those difficult questions your children will ask you about your own behavior. It is okay to avoid detailed answers, but it is important not to lie since you are trying to teach honesty. (You can plead the "5th Amendment"; however, that may be interpreted as a "Yes.") **"The Power of Parents"** (p. 8:37) reminds us of the important influence parents can have in raising children who are wise about alcohol.

There are known risk factors for problem substance abuse. One of the biggest risk factors is starting use in the early teen years. The Surgeon General's "Call to Action: To Prevent and Reduce Underage Drinking (2007) reports that of adults who started drinking before age 15, 40% say they have the signs of alcohol dependence. That rate is 4 times higher than adults who didn't drink until they were 21. Other serious risk factors include: a family history of substance abuse, the modeling of excessive alcohol use at home by parents or older siblings, busy parents who don't take the time to supervise or connect with their sons, affluence (resulting in too much money and free time), and access to adult alcohol. During our children's adolescence, we need to lock up, or better yet, remove alcohol from our home as well as prescription drugs such as pain-killers. The distorted view that prescription drugs are safer than street drugs has contributed to a rash of serious drug abuse, overdose, and death using drugs from medicine cabinets.

It is important to realize that many teens will experiment with alcohol and/or marijuana, and some will go toward chemical dependency. The more that our child hangs out with a "cool" crowd, the earlier experimentation may happen. Since we know that early use is a risk factor, it often pays for parents to assertively intervene when drug or alcohol use becomes apparent in our younger teens. One family discovered that their 8th-grade twins were beginning to smoke marijuana. They explained why that was against their family standards and how it might affect their ability to succeed in school, and that they would be taking the boys to have monthly UA's (urine analysis tests) until they were 15. If they had a positive test (marijuana can be detected up to one month after use), they could not get their driver's permit when they turned 15. This assertive, clear approach was very successful with their sons and the experimentation stopped. The parents also voluntarily shared this information in an 8th-grade parent meeting, which was very useful for other parents.

Nicotine, in all forms is another illegal drug of choice for our teens. If we can persuade our teens not to use nicotine until age 18 when it is legal, it is very unlikely they will be interested. Fortunately, cigarette use has been decreasing in the last few years, but nicotine comes in many forms. Since nicotine is very addictive, it is easy for our teens to become addicted if they begin smoking or chewing. What begins as an attempt to feel cool or part of the crowd easily turns into a form of self-medicating for anxiety or stress or a way to control eating. If our children become addicted they may need medical assistance to stop, as well as help handling stress and anxiety in healthier ways.

As our teens grow older than 15 or 16, our "control" over them gradually lessens and we will be more effective if we focus on what we can influence, such as the quality of our home/community environment and our relationship, so they can still receive our guidance and coaching. For older teens who are experimenting (and most teens will at some point), one effective long-term parenting goal is to help your teen honestly assess his level of drug use, so that he can avoid progressing to more serious levels of use. Above all, it is important to keep communicating with him and knowing what he is doing rather than setting down inflexible rules that will push drug use underground and out of the sphere of our influence. Parents can give their teens a safe place to learn from their mistakes and be careful not to buffer their kids from the negative consequences of their drug-using behaviors. They can continue to show their kids unconditional love and acceptance and have faith in their kids. This can be very hard for parents who were raised with rigid rules and who feel a lot of external pressure from others to exert the short-term parenting strategy of control. However, honesty is a much more effective, respectful and safe long-term approach. Kids who are exploring alcohol use in high school have the benefit of their parent's watchful eye and intervention. With this influence, the teens can learn about setting limits, using discretion and why this is important. This skill will help them for the rest of their lives, especially when they go off to college where binge drinking is rampant. Using drugs or alcohol can be an especially dangerous problem for college kids who have never discussed these issues with a parent or mentor and who do not have adequate knowledge or self-discipline to monitor their own use of chemical agents. This difficult parenting subject is covered in **"Teenagers and Drugs"** (p. 8:38).

Another area that needs to be addressed is our society's lackadaisical attitude about underage drinking. With alcohol dependency affecting at least 10% of our adults, this should come as no surprise. However, communities of people can come together to prevent underage drinking, and all of our teenagers greatly benefit. One Mom we know routinely called every party her son was invited to and just asked, "Hey, I was wondering if you needed any help with the party at your house next week? Can I help chaperone? Can I bake anything?" This was her way of making sure the parents knew there was a party at the house and that they would be there. Her son, now in college, survived this ordeal and is happy his Mom kept him out of difficult situations. Some high schools provide guidelines for parents on how to increase the likelihood that their child will stay alcohol- and drug-free, such as **"Safe Teen Parties in Your Home Guidelines"** (p. 8:44) which describes how to hold a "substance-free" party. High schools can also offer drug-free activities or parties for special events often associated with drinking, such as graduation. Parents working together can exert tremendous preventive pressure toward keeping youth activities drug- and alcohol-free.

Many of our healthy teens surround themselves with peers they can trust and look out for each other as they navigate through their adolescent world. These teens have often made advance agreements before they arrive at a party. They know that teens are vulnerable to acquaintance rape, fighting, and alcohol poisoning and they are careful to look out for their friends to make sure that everyone is safe. They may have decided not to drink. They will have a designated driver if they need one. They will leave as a group if a get-together becomes uncomfortable.

If you find your son is experimenting with alcohol or marijuana, there are several steps, in addition to keeping your connection with him that you can take to support minimum consumption:

1. Reduce access by removing all alcohol from your home and talking to his friend's parents about doing the same. Kids can often gain access easily to "locked" cabinets.
2. Do not leave your home unsupervised overnight.
3. Do not enable underage drinking. Be crystal clear with your son that you will not allow an underage youth to drink in your home. Serving alcohol to an underage youth is an incredible risk to the youth's and to your own emotional health. It may also harm your financial health since it is against the law. You can be sued even if nothing significantly negative happens to the youth you are serving alcohol to. (Some families choose to serve small amounts of alcohol to their own teens as part of special family occasions or rituals to help them experience healthy associations with alcohol. This differs significantly from including teens in adult social drinking.)
4. Let him know there will be consequences to drinking. If he gets in trouble with the authorities or drinks and drives, he will lose access to a car.
5. Connect with the parents of your son's friends to create a safety net for them. Consider meeting monthly over dinner.

One of our long-term goals for our teens is to increase the chances they are safe and grow up free from addiction. Some of our teens, however, will abuse alcohol and /or drugs to the point of addiction. Teens who are abusing and addicted to drugs/alcohol will rarely have the insights and coping skills of normal teenagers. As their parent, you are going to need outside help from community resources if you suspect your child has problem substance-abuse behaviors. If you are concerned about your son's drug or alcohol use, ask him to honestly answer to himself the questions on addiction on the last page of the article **"Teenagers and Drugs"** (p. 8:38).

Automobile Injuries and Graduated Licensing

The leading cause of death for children in the US, ages 1 to 24, is motor vehicle crashes.[2] Teenagers are known to take risks with cars. They like speed, feel invincible and are aggressive drivers with or without alcohol. They are also inexperienced, immature, over-confident, and are less able to perceive hazards. 10,000 American sixteen-year-olds die every decade from driving under the influence of immaturity and inexperience. These accidents are characterized by the following:

- When a teenage passenger dies, 1 out of 4 times, the driver is a teenager,
- The vast majority of crashes with teens have no alcohol or bad weather involved,
- Speed, immaturity, inexperience, peer pressure from other passengers and night driving are the biggest contributors to teenage car crashes,
- 16-year-olds have the most crashes, and 16- to 19-year-olds have more crashes than the elderly,
- Fatigue is a major contributor to car crashes,
- When teenagers die in car crashes, they are usually not wearing seatbelts.

The highest risk for young drivers is driving at night with other teens in the car. This sets the stage for peer pressure leading to immature and dangerous behaviors. A car is a 3000-pound weapon, and it is important for your teen to understand that driving is a privilege that will be revoked for irresponsible behavior. Also, to counteract the modeling of unsafe driving habits that are common on prime-time television, it is important for parents to model consistent use of seat belts and to exhibit law-abiding and respectful road behaviors.

Since we are unlikely to raise the driving age to 18, as in European countries, "graduated" licensing is the next best approach. Research has shown that graduated licensing successfully reduces adolescent death and injury. Within two years of implementing these laws, deaths of new drivers went down an impressive 33% in Oregon, as noted in **"Facts about Risky Driving and Graduated Licensing"** (p. 8:45).

Teenagers can also be protected against fatal mistakes by having them sign the "no questions asked" **"Contract for Life"** (p. 8:46) sponsored by SADD (Students Against Destructive Decisions). Parents realistically can't stop their children from using drugs or alcohol, but they can make sure that they don't put themselves or others in danger by driving or riding in a car under the influence. This is a healthy investment in your son's survival.

Conclusion

There are certain adolescent developmental tasks, which parents cannot derail. These include:
- Individuating and outgrowing childhood dependence on parents,
- Forming an identity in sexual, intellectual and moral realms of self-concept,
- Developing a separate identity that includes personal lifestyle preferences, and vocational/ career goals,
- Exploring risk-taking behaviors as a means of self-exploration and confidence-building.

We can help our sons to navigate safely through these developmental tasks by staying closely connected with them and talking with them about high-risk behaviors and today's tough issues. This may mean getting help for our sons who are aggressive, depressed, rageful or suicidal.

Parents can also work to build connections and assets for their sons within their own communities. Finally, there is one powerful tool for successful parenting. This is an often untapped resource and an idea that Family Empowerment Network advocates for wherever we go: NETWORK WITH OTHER PARENTS. You can bet that your son is very networked with his friends, especially if he is trying to get away with something. Talk to other parents. Confirm the plans you hear from your son. Check out the curfews and driving records of your son's friends by asking their parents. When a problem does come up, you will then have the support of invested parents to help you through it. This is especially nice to do before boys get their driver's license, which gives them incredible freedom and a strong desire to explore boundaries.

Clearly, keeping kids physically, emotionally and socially healthy is a job of great magnitude for parents in the twenty-first century. But there is hope. Skills that will help you through this difficult job include awareness, education, setting clear boundaries big enough for lots of choices, good listening, and continuous communication with your son. You will be surprised how quickly adolescence passes once you are finally through it. Then, you will know the joy of appreciating the adult your son's adolescence shaped, honed and produced.

---

[1] Mueller TE, Gavin LE, Kulkarni A. *"The association between sex education and youth's engagement in sexual intercourse, age at first intercourse, and birth control use at first sex."* Journal of Adolescent Health.2008 Jan; 42 (1)
[2] National SAFE KIDS Campaign dedicated to prevent unintentional childhood injury. www.usa.safekids

THE 40 DEVELOPMENTAL ASSETS Essential to Every Young Person's Success

There are many Developmental Assets that help a teen to be safe in her environment and resist negative influences. Notice how much the categories of Boundaries, Social Competencies and Positive Identity stand out here.

SUPPORT/ EMPOWERMENT

- Asset #3 **Other Adult Relationships:** Young people have at least 3 adults in their lives who support them.
- Asset #4 **Caring Neighborhood:** Young people have the care and support of people who live nearby.
- Asset #7 **Community Values Youth:** Young people know they are valued by the adults in their community.

BOUNDARIES

- Asset #10 **Safety:** Young person feels safe at home, school and in the neighborhood.
- Asset #11 **Family Boundaries:** Family has clear rules and monitors the young person's whereabouts.
- Asset #12 **School Boundaries:** School provides clear rules and consequences.
- Asset #13 **Neighborhood Boundaries:** Neighbors share the responsibility for monitoring youth's behavior.
- Asset #14 **Adult Role Models:** Parents and other adults set good examples for young people.

CONSTRUCTIVE USE OF TIME

- Asset #17 **Creative Activities:** Young people are involved in music, theater or other arts 3 hrs/week.
- Asset #18 **Youth Programs:** Young people are involved in sports, clubs or organizations 3 hrs/week.

POSITIVE VALUES

- Asset #31 **Restraint:** Youth believes it is important not to be sexually active or to use alcohol or drugs.

SOCIAL COMPETENCIES

- Asset #33 **Interpersonal Competence:** Young person has empathy, sensitivity, and friendship skills.
- Asset #34 **Cultural Competence:** Young people know and respect people of different racial and cultural backgrounds.
- Asset #35 **Resistance Skills:** Young person can resist negative peer pressure and dangerous situations.
- Asset #36 **Peaceful Conflict Resolution:** Young person seeks to resolve conflict nonviolently.

POSITIVE IDENTITY

- Asset #37 **Personal Power:** Young people believe that they have control over "things that happen to me."
- Asset #38 **Self-esteem:** Young people feel good about who they are.
- Asset #39 **Sense of Purpose:** Young people believe their life has a purpose.
- Asset #40 **Positive View of Personal Future:** Young people are hopeful and confident about their future.

CIRCLE QUESTION

Which safety issue is of greatest concern to you? Share the ways or situations
in which you talk to your son about these sensitive topics.

DISCUSSION QUESTIONS

1. Share what you did as a youth that was "risk-taking." How does that impact your parenting?
2. What changes in children's behavior might be a clue that they have become involved in something unhealthy or that something is disturbing them? How do you separate "moody" from the signs of serious problems such as eating disorders, depression, and drug or alcohol abuse?
3. What behaviors do you engage in that you want your child to avoid, such as anger outbursts, impulsivity, smoking, excessive drinking, or dieting? In what ways can you modify what you do in order to provide more positive modeling for your child?
4. How have you connected with neighbors? Share how you might form an agreement with them about letting you know if they see suspicious or problem behaviors with your child.
5. How have you facilitated relationships with teachers and other adults in your son's life so that they could more easily let you know if there were any problems?
6. When we see our child's friend engage in risky behavior, is our first reaction to "keep him away"? What are ways we could intervene that might be more successful?
7. What do you think about "nothing good happens between midnight and 5 am"? Do you employ curfews? If yes, what time on weeknights? Weekends?

Body Image

8. What are some things we as parents/adults can do to decrease our society's obsession with how we look?
9. How might you help your child feel comfortable about his appearance, even if it doesn't conform to popular standards?

Sexuality

10. What surprised you the most about the information on sexuality and youth?
11. Have you talked to your son about the pros of abstinence, the benefits of delaying his first sexual experience as well as where to go to get contraceptives if he needs them? If yes, share how you had this conversation, and if no, what are the barriers to having this conversation? Strategize overcoming these.

Violence

12. Does your son struggle with impulsivity and anger? Do you? What helps with this?
13. What does your son need to know to prevent acquaintance rape and sexual harassment?
14. Talk about violence concerns in your neighborhood, community or school. What could you do to help decrease some of these problems?
15. Discuss a planned reaction you could work out with your son if a friend pulled out a gun to "show-off."

Depression

16. Discuss the issues around men having difficulty sharing their feelings of being sad and vulnerable. Discuss grandiosity—the feeling that they are supposed to be everything to everybody. How can we help unmask "hidden depression" in the men/boys we love and care about?
17. How can you distinguish moodiness from depression?

18. If you have guns in your home, are they locked up with the ammunition stored separately? Is the key in the possession of the gun owner? (Kids usually know where it is "hidden.") Are there guns in the homes of houses he visits locked up?

Drugs

19. "Just Say No" and similar campaigns alone are not effective in keeping kids from trying sex, alcohol, cigarettes and drugs. What does work?

20. Imagine your son had a party while you were out of town. Role-play with each other how you would talk with him about this, keeping your anger at bay and maintaining respect and open communication.

21. What would you do if you suspected your child was taking drugs or drinking alcohol? Talk about the different reactions you might have to experimental use, social use, regular use or addiction.

PUTTING IT INTO PRACTICE

- TALK to your kids about tough issues. Start early before anyone else gives them incorrect information or explanations that lack the values you want to instill.
- Create an open environment for communication in which your children can ask any questions and share honestly—on any subject—and freely and without fear of consequence/embarrassment/ridicule.
- Use teachable moments that arise in everyday life as occasions for discussion.
- Try to be honest when you answer his questions; it will strengthen his ability to trust.
- Be patient. Let him know that he is worthy of your time.
- Communicate your values—frequently, not just once.
- Really listen → Effectiveness as a parent is more from what you hear than what you say.
- Spend time with your child.
- Network with other adults—other parents, your neighbors, relatives and friends—so he feels like there is a "conspiracy to help him turn out OK."
- Establish clear boundaries but be open and flexible so everything doesn't become a hiding game.
- If you are afraid of your son, seek help immediately.
- Avoid commenting on anyone's appearance/weight in front of your child, including his own.
- Practice healthy habits as a family.
- Review the "Dater's Bill of Rights" with your child, help make sure he knows what a safe, respectful relationship is all about.
- Find out what sex education your children are receiving in school. Use it as a discussion starter.
- If you have a depressed teen, get professional help, alert the school, and secure meds and weapons in your home. Check out www.helpguide.org/mental/depression_teen.htm to help you assess depression.
- Role-play refusal skills or assertiveness skills with your child that he can use when being pressured to engage in unhealthy behavior.
- Children "do what you do." Model good behavior regarding substance abuse (cigarettes, alcohol, or drugs) and violence (temper outburst, verbal or physical abuse). Don't drink, drive, or model "road rage."
- Remove risk factors from your home: TV and computer in the child's bedroom, guns, prescription drugs, and alcohol.
- Sign the drinking and driving "Contract for Life" with your teenager.

PUTTING IT TOGETHER—YOUR VERSION

Write down three or four ideas you have been inspired to implement in your own life after reading and discussing this chapter.

1. _____

2. _____

3. _____

4. _____

FURTHER READING

Books for Youth

Fighting Invisible Tigers: A Stress Management Guide for Teens by Earl Hipp

What's Bad about Being So Good: Perfectionism by Jan Goldberg and Caroline Price

What Are My Rights: 95 Questions and Answers about Teens and the Law? by Thomas Jacobs

Understanding the Human Volcano: What Teens Can Do About Violence by Earl Hipp

Depression Is the Pits, But I'm Getting Better: A Guide for Adolescents by E. Jane Garland, MD

Help Me, I'm Sad by David Fassler, MD and Lynne Dumas

When Nothing Matters Anymore: A Survival Guide For Teens by Bev Cobain, RNC

Highs! Over 150 Ways to Feel Really, Really Good…Without Alcohol or Other Drugs by Alex Packer

Risky Behavior

Positive Discipline for Teenagers by Jane Nelsen, EdD, and Lynn Lott, MA, MFT, see chapters: "Are Your Own Unresolved Teen Issues Getting in Your Way?" and "What To Do When Your Teen's Behavior Scares You?"

The Romance of Risk: Why Teenagers Do the Things They Do by Lynn Ponton, MD

Talking With Kids about Tough Issues: A National Campaign to Support Parents at www.talkingwithkids.org

Can We Talk? Family Activity Book and video series, great training package for families by the National Education Association Health Information Network at www.neahin.org/canwetalk/index.html

Body Image and Eating Disorders

Bully in the Mirror Up by Stephen Hall, New York Times 8/22/09

The Adonis Complex: How to Identify, Treat, Prevent Body obsession in Men/Boys by H. Pope and R. Olivardia

The National Eating Disorder Association at www.nationaleatingdisorders.org

Sexuality

The Sex Lives of Teenagers: Revealing the Secret World of Adolescent Boys and Girls by Lynn E Ponton, MD

Ten Tips for Parents to Help Their Children Avoid Teen Pregnancy at www.thenationalcampaign.org/resources/10Tips.aspx

All About Sex: a Family Resource on Sex and Sexuality by Planned Parenthood

The National Campaign to Prevent Teen and Unplanned Pregnancy at www.teenpregnancy.org

Violence

Raising Cain by Michael Thompson and Dan Kindlon

Stick Fist Knife Gun by Geoffrey Canada

Lost Boys: Why Our Sons Turn Violent and How We Can Save Them by James Garbarino
Safe at Last: A Handbook for Recovery from Abuse by David Schopick and Suzanne Burr
Ten Talks Parent Must Have with Their Children about Youth Violence by D. Capell (manageable talks for 4th–8th graders)
Helping Teens Stop Violence: A Practical Guide for Counselors, Educators and Parents by Allen Creighton and Paul Kivel
Best Practices of Youth Violence Prevention: A Sourcebook for Community Action by National Center for Injury
    Prevention Control at www.cdc.gov/ncipc/dvp/bestpractices.htm

Depression

I Don't Want to Talk About It: Overcoming the Secret Legacy of Male Depression by Terrence Real
Growing Up Sad: Childhood Depression and Its Treatment by Leon Cytryn, MD and Donald McKnew, MD
Lonely, Sad and Angry: How to Help Your Unhappy Child by Barbara Ingersoll, PhD and Sam Goldstein, PhD
Conquering the Beast Within: How I Fought Depression and Won…And How You Can, Too by Cait Irwin
Youth Suicide Prevention Pamphlets by Kirk Wolfe, MD at www.oregon.gov/DHS/ph/ipe/ysp/spubs.shtml
Youth Suicide Prevention Program at www.yspp.org
Suicide Prevention at www.yellowribbon.org/Msg-to-Teens.htm
Depression Awareness at www.psychologyinfo.com/depression/teens.htm
American Assoc. of Pediatrics at www.aap.org/advocacy/childhealthmonth/prevteensuicide.htm
American Assoc. of Suicidology at www.suicidology.org/displaycommon.cfm?an=1&subarticlenbr=25
The Nemours Foundation at www.kidshealth.org
National Mental Institute of Mental Health at www.nimh.nih.gov
American Psychological Association at www.apa.org
Center for Mental Health Services at www.mentalhealth.org

Drugs

Broken Bottles, Broken Dreams: Understanding and Helping the Children of Alcoholics by Charles Deutsch
Dying to Drink: Confronting Binge Drinking on College Campuses by Henry Wechsler, PhD and Bernice Wuethrich
"What to Do When Your Teens Behavior Scares You" chapter from *Positive Discipline for Teenagers* by Jane Nelsen
Parents. The Anti Drug at www.theantidrug.com
Partnership for a Drug Free America at www.drugfree.org
Join Together at www.jointogether.org/news/headlines/inthenews/2008/games-contribute-to-youths.html
Al-Anon and Alateen at www.al-anon.alateen.org

Automobile Injury

Not My Kid Campaign by Trauma Nurses Talk Tough at www.legacyhealth.org/body.cfm?id=1018
Teen Driving at www.teensafedriver.com or www.aigteengps.com

MEDIA EDUCATIONAL FOUNDATION: excellent videos for adults or youth at www.mediaed.org

Overall:	*Tough Guise: Violence, Media and the Crisis in Masculinity*
Sexuality:	*Teen Sexuality in a Culture of Confusion*
	Hip-Hop: Beyond Beats and Rhymes, a riveting look at manhood, sexism, homophobia
Violence:	*Date Rape Backlash: Media and the Denial of Rape*
	Dreamworlds 2: Desire, Sex and Power in the Music Video
Drug Use:	*Selling Addictions and Deadly Persuasion*, the advertising of alcohol and tobacco
	Pack of Lies, lies by tobacco industry to keep America addicted
	Spin the Bottle, about binge drinking, student deaths
	Game Over, about video and computer game addiction

Connecting Teens and Parents: The Vital Link

By Marta Mellinger

WE ALL KNOW ADOLESCENCE can be a time of great risk. As parents, we want to do all we can to help our children to move safely through the teen years and into adulthood. But what can we do? What protects teens? What empowers them to choose wisely and avoid risky behaviors?

A national scientific study was undertaken by the Adolescent Health Program at the University of Minnesota and the University of North Carolina.[1] Thirteen names are listed as co-authors, indicating the breadth of the collaboration. This research explored specific risks in adolescents' lives while seeking to identify factors within the home and school that help children avoid risky behavior. The findings of the study are profound.

Over 12,000 adolescents in grades 7 through 12 were drawn from an initial national school survey of over 19,000 around the country. Eight behaviors were considered: emotional distress, suicidal thoughts and behaviors, violence, use of cigarettes, alcohol, and/or marijuana, age of sexual debut, and pregnancy history.

The results of this comprehensive study showed that the single most important factor in helping children move safely through the teenage years is how close they feel to Mom and/or Dad.

The term "close" is defined as children perceiving they are loved, wanted and cared for by the way their  parents treat them. Secondly, children are supported most at school by feeling that teachers treat them fairly and that they are "connected" at school, and feel a part of the school and its activities. The study says the most important influence is that feeling of connectedness.

This study reinforces for professionals—counselors, teachers, educational administrators, and health professionals—what parents know intuitively. It asks all professionals to focus more attention on the relationships being built, and to help build them. And, it reinforces for parents that the absolute core of parenting adolescents is that we must take the emotional risk to stay connected.

Ever since I became a parent, I've been told that the "work" of the teenager is to establish his or her independence. I'm of a generation that embraced the motto "Do Your Own Thing," and there's an attitude about parenting teenagers that goes along with that. I've heard it said that as my kids become middle-schoolers, it's going to be "hell." People say the girls will push me away, and that by the time they reach high school, I won't see them much, if at all. We'll have fights; I won't know them or their friends. The picture is of a path leading away from me, their father, and family life.

As my own ten-year-old daughter approaches adolescence, will I let her "do her own thing"? Will I accept that this "moving away" is part of these "hell years" and allow her to emotionally distance herself from me and the family—as TV tells her to, as the movies tell her to, as much of our society tells us she should? Or do I take the risk to commit to sustaining our connection—even when she doesn't seem to want it?

Right about now, I have a choice to make. As she moves on to 11, 12 and 13, will I continue to reach out? Will I ask for her sharing by sharing myself? Will I sustain our "hokey" family rituals, enthusiastically plan family vacations she wants to skip? "Yes," I now say with more assurance. That's my job as her parent—to sustain the fragile flame of connection, even when the winds of our world are trying to blow it out.

Now, at least, I have science affirming what I've always intuitively known—in the larger scheme of things, it's our love that counts.

---

[1] "Protecting Adolescents from Harm", JAMA, Journal of American Medical Association, 278 (10):823-32, 9/10/97

Marta Mellinger, founder of The Canoe Group, a shared practice of four passionate professionals who help organizations develop new ways to succeed in rapidly changing times. With her husband of 23 years, she has two young adult daughters and is proud that they still call and come home regularly.

Reprinted with permission of Full Esteem Ahead *Wings*, Fall 1997

The Power of Assets

By Search Institute, from *The Asset Approach: Giving Kids What They Need to Succeed*

On one level, the 40 Developmental Assets represent common wisdom about the kinds of positive experiences and characteristics that young people need and deserve. But their value extends further. Surveys of almost 150,000 students in grades 6–12 (ages appoximately 11–18 years) reveal that assets are powerful influences on adolescent behavior. Regardless of gender, ethnic heritage, economic situation or geographic location, these assets both promote positive behaviors and attitudes and help protect young people from many different problem behaviors.

0–10 assets   11–20 assets   21–30 assets   31–40 assets

Promoting Positive Attitudes and Behaviors

Our research shows that the more assets students report having, the more likely they are to also report the following patterns of thriving behavior.

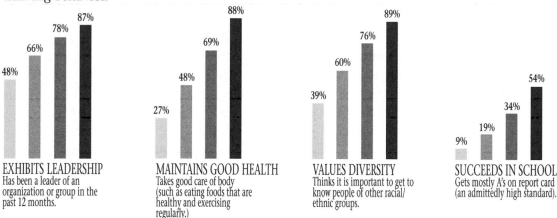

EXHIBITS LEADERSHIP
Has been a leader of an organization or group in the past 12 months.
48% 66% 78% 87%

MAINTAINS GOOD HEALTH
Takes good care of body (such as eating foods that are healthy and exercising regularly.)
27% 48% 69% 88%

VALUES DIVERSITY
Thinks it is important to get to know people of other racial/ ethnic groups.
39% 60% 76% 89%

SUCCEEDS IN SCHOOL
Gets mostly A's on report card (an admittedly high standard).
9% 19% 34% 54%

Protecting Youth from High-Risk Behaviors

Assets not only promote positive behaviors, they also protect young people: The more assets a young person reports having, the less likely he or she is to make harmful or unhealthy choices. *(Note that these definitions are set rather high, suggesting ongoing problems, not experimentation.)*

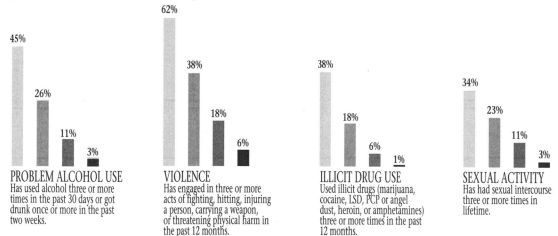

PROBLEM ALCOHOL USE
Has used alcohol three or more times in the past 30 days or got drunk once or more in the past two weeks.
45% 26% 11% 3%

VIOLENCE
Has engaged in three or more acts of fighting, hitting, injuring a person, carrying a weapon, or threatening physical harm in the past 12 months.
62% 38% 18% 6%

ILLICIT DRUG USE
Used illicit drugs (marijuana, cocaine, LSD, PCP or angel dust, heroin, or amphetamines) three or more times in the past 12 months.
38% 18% 6% 1%

SEXUAL ACTIVITY
Has had sexual intercourse three or more times in lifetime.
34% 23% 11% 3%

Teens and Risks

By Kathy Keller Jones, MA

ADOLESCENCE IS A TIME OF risk-taking. Young people experiment with life, take on new challenges, and try out how things fit together in order to define and shape both their identities and their knowledge of the world. In other words, adolescents are learning how to think and how to act. Risk-taking is actually one of the ways that teens develop their cognitive abilities. The scary part for parents, however, is that the part of the brain which drives teens to seek out exciting new experiences develops much earlier than the part of the brain which regulates risk-taking behavior. The emotional center of teens is activated by their new hormones around age 12, while the frontal cortex, which enables us to reflect about consequences, delay gratification, and plan ahead, matures between 18 and 25 years of age. The connection between the emotional and cognitive parts of the brain, however, may not fully mature until around age 30. Knowledge about youthful brains helps us to realize how important adult influence is during those teen years.

Lynn Ponton, a practicing clinical psychiatrist and psycho-analyst, has written an interesting book, *The Romance of Risk,* which can help us to understand rather than fear adolescent risk-taking.

Teens need risks in order to grow; they need parental support in order to take those risks. If the risk-taking becomes dangerous, then, of course, parents must act. But when we assume that all adolescent risk-taking is bad, we fail to recognize both the very real dangers some risks pose and the tremendous benefits that others can yield.[1]

Understanding the importance of risk to teen development helps parents to support teens in this area of their development, including encouraging healthy risk-taking of interest to their child, e.g., arranging for rock climbing lessons for a teen who wants to learn to climb. Risk-taking can promote more complex thinking, increase confidence, and help develop a young person's ability to do healthy risk-taking in the future. Even unhealthy, unsanctioned risk-taking sometimes has positive outcomes for teens. Teens who are caught breaking the rules or doing something foolish, for example, learn from the consequences of their actions that it is risky to do impulsive things and it pays to think ahead. This is particularly true, however, if parents are empathetic and also allow teens to experience the consequences of their actions. Recognizing teens' needs for adventure can help us to interact with them without blaming and fueling rebellion. Teens want to separate but they also want to be recognized by adults for the unique people they are and will become. Healthy adolescents are both connected and independent.

One of the real risks in today's times is that teens can become disconnected from their families and their friends can become more important to them than their family. Healthy teens are usually close to their friends and their family. Dr. Ron Taffel is a psychotherapist who has worked with teens and parents for over 30 years. He became curious about why children were doing worse things at earlier and earlier ages. He informally studied 250 teens, 1000 parents, teachers and counselors. What he discovered was that in many cases, the world of teens and commercial pop culture had overpowered the parents. Peers and media become a "second family"[2] to today's teens—a family which provides comfort and an attitude of live and let live. This second family, however, lacks the rules and standards that the first family used to have. Taffel also talks about how parents participate in this process by being unwilling to set and follow through on rules, i.e., they "abdicate their authority."[3] When peer culture supports children in a way that parents do not, our kids are vulnerable both to the consumerism fed to them by large corporations and to unhealthy high-risk behaviors.

Cynthia Lightfoot, in her book *The Culture of Adolescent Risk-taking,* describes adolescent risk-taking as a "transformative experience."[4] She found that youth associated risk-taking with feeling independent and mature. The youth she surveyed saw risk-taking as a challenging or novel experience with the possibility of unknown or unintended consequences. Teens mentioned the pleasure and excitement of changing the status quo, including the chance to learn about themselves and their abilities. Sometimes risk-taking also had social positives such as creating shared memories. Ten percent of the teens Lightfoot interviewed thought risks were appealing because they are an act of defiance or rebellion. The excitement of what is forbidden is a big draw to teens. A 17-year old had a party while her parents were gone but she was very careful to "leave no trace" and not allow anything "bad" to happen. Afterwards she felt proud of her ability to do this well and was glad she took the risk of being caught. Teens often take risks that help them to feel more like an adult.

How can we promote independence, growth, and risk-taking in our teens while also protecting them? Younger teens need several years of clear rules and consequences with gradually increasing freedom. Remember, their frontal cortex needs your help. Older adolescents need to be setting boundaries more collaboratively with their parents and they need room for independence while still living with the family. This also means strengthening the "first family" so the "second family" stays in its place. Teens need to feel the presence of at least one (preferably more) supportive guiding adult who is willing to listen, dialog and negotiate, while remembering to not take everything personally. Families need to have comfort time together. Parents will need to bend their own perspectives somewhat to understand and participate in the teen's world. Parents must learn to deal constructively with teenage lying, which is how teens protect their freedom. Parents can share risk assessment skills they have used in their own life. Finally, parents can encourage and support teens in finding positive ways to take risks based on their teen's interests and needs.

Some Examples of Positive Challenges and Risks:
- Sports, pushing your personal limits,
- Interpersonal risks, assertively speaking your mind,
- Pushing academic limits, trying a difficult subject,
- Auditioning for performances,
- Challenging cultural biases,
- Confronting hardships, developing resources,
- Experimenting with creativity,
- Involvement in community action projects,
- Learning new skills,
- Handling sexual situations responsibly and safely,
- Getting a job.

References:
[1] Ponton, *Teens and Risk,* p. 12
[2] Taffel, *The Second Family*
[3] Taffel, *The Second Family,* p.26
[4] Lightfoot, *The Culture of Adolescent Risk-Taking*

Boys' Struggle with Body Image

By Kathy Keller Jones, MA

DID YOU EVER THINK we'd see the day when boys and men were striving to attain unrealistic, ideal bodies portrayed in the media? Doesn't this only affect women? Aren't girls the ones who connect body image and self-esteem? Times are changing. Boys are now spending more and more time evaluating themselves in the mirror, and the messages they are sending themselves are powerful and negative, says Stephen Hall in his New York Times article *"Bully in the Mirror"* (8/22/99).

So where are these messages coming from, and who is sending them? We know that the media has contributed to this issue for decades. There are also peers inflicting their cruelty on one another. Our culture takes its toll, teaching boys to be macho, tough and cool, which prevents our boys from expressing a full range of feelings. Then there is the effect of puberty and its powerful hormones.

Harrison Pope, a psychiatrist in Belmont, Massachusetts' McLean Hospital and his colleague, Roberto Olivardia, are leaders in the studies of body image disorders. Pope and Olivardia gathered action figures from the early 1960's through today and did the mathematical calculations to place the body proportions onto a life-sized man. Their findings showed that G.I. Joe, among others, had "buffed up" over the years. Wolverine now sports measurements never attained by the most accomplished bodybuilder, and all of these figures have more defined muscles, ripples and all. (Similar information about Barbie dolls and girls has been available for quite some time now.) Understanding that these toys represent trends in our society, they conclude that our cultural expectations evolve to create these ideals. This trend contributes to body image disorders in men. Pope named this complex and his book on this topic after the Greek god Adonis,

who was the ultimate in masculine beauty for the Greeks (*The Adonis Complex: How to Identify, Treat, and Prevent Body Obsession in Men and Boys*).

Then, of course, there are all of those famous ads—Calvin Klein and Abercrombie & Fitch, to name a few. Where we used to only see images of girls and women with "perfect bodies" bombarding us from magazine pages and ad posters, the new male ideal is claiming equal space. Teenage boys are constantly viewing images of buff, bare-chested, hairless, bulked-up guys with sweat glistening on their firm, fit bodies. Couple this with the female reaction to this "media-contrived" look, and boys are suddenly feeling the pressure to live up to, or more accurately "shape up to," this new ideal. Once again, the message that "how you look is what people notice" strikes hard. The emotional toll of constantly comparing one's self to an almost impossible ideal takes its toll on the average teenage boy. Acceptance by peers is a high priority goal; this includes feeling accepted or admired by male peers and desired by females. The belief a teen boy has about having a "substandard" body that doesn't measure up leads him to territory once associated solely with girls: low self-esteem, depression and embarrassment as a result of his body image. It also may lead him to unhealthy and possibly illegal steroid use. Most teens can't effectively grasp the concept of long-term liver or kidney damage or other risks associated with steroids.

Unfortunately, this trend toward the ideal male body is gaining momentum. Boys are now equally subjected to social scrutiny and cruelty for not meeting the unrealistic standard. Our boys need support debunking our media, which is a vast industry that profits from making us feel insecure about ourselves. Our boys need to know that masculinity is not based on how they look but on who they are.

Communication Tips for Parents (Regarding Sexuality)
SIECUS Publication for Parents

Here are some tips to get parents started:

- **Parents are the primary sexuality educators of their children.** Children want to talk about sexuality with their parents and to hear their values. It is not just a parent's right, it is their responsibility. Your children need to hear your point of view. Children often want to hear about your growing up. They want to hear stories about your youth and how you dealt with issues. This can often help them with their own struggles.

- **Be an "askable parent." Reward questions.** It is never a good idea to tell your children to wait until they are older before you will answer their questions. When children ask questions, you have a chance to help them learn. Reward a question with, "I'm glad you came to me with that question." Say this before you respond to what was asked. It will teach them to come to you when they have other questions. If you don't know an answer, tell your child you will look it up and tell them later. Be sure you follow through. You might want to go to the library and look up the answer together.

- **Find "teachable moments."** Difficult situations are often "teachable moments." They offer a chance for you to teach your children what you know or believe about sexuality. You can even make use of a TV show that you believe sends the wrong message. Turn it around and say, "I think that program sends the wrong message. I want to tell you what I believe and why."

- **You don't need to wait until they ask a question.** Many children never ask questions. When our children are young, we don't wait until they ask to teach them they should look both ways before

crossing a busy street or touching a hot stove. Some things are essential for them to know. It is the job of adults—and especially of parents—to teach our children how to get along in the world. Learning about sexuality is the same. You need to decide what is important for children to know, and then tell them before a crisis arrives. Think through your own values about sexuality: What messages do you want to give your children about love, nudity, gender roles, intimacy, privacy, etc?

- **It is okay to feel uncomfortable.** Relax. Very few adults have had a formal course in sexuality, and it

is hard for many adults to talk about sexual matters. You can let your children know you are uncomfortable, but you will talk to them anyway because you love them and want to help. It is also okay for parents to set limits. You do not have to give specific answers to questions about your own sexual behavior.

- **Talk about the joys of sexuality.** This might include telling them that sexuality is natural and healthy, that loving relationships are the best part of life, and that intimacy is a wonderful part of adult life.

- **Listen, listen, listen.** When children ask questions, thank them for asking, and ask them why they want to know or what they already know. That may help you prepare your answer.

- **Facts are not enough.** In addition to sharing facts and thoughts, do share your feelings, values and beliefs. Then tell your child why you feel that way. Pre-teens and teens often seem to reject their parents' values—especially when they feel their parents want to impose their point of view with "because I say so!" Most of us have very good reasons behind our beliefs. Telling our children the why behind our values teaches them to think. Children also need help in seeing the difference between thoughts, feelings and actions. Parents can help their children understand that while it is normal to have all kinds of sexual thoughts and feelings, they are in charge of their own behavior, and they do not have to act upon their thoughts and feelings.

- **Know what is taught about sexuality in your schools, churches, temples, and youth groups.** Urge these groups to include sexuality education in their programs. While young people often joke, tease and talk about sexuality among themselves, it is more helpful when trained adults lead those talks.

- **When you talk with your children about sexuality, you are telling them that you care about their happiness and well-being.** You are also sharing your values. This is one of the real joys of parenthood.

- **Be aware of the "question behind the question."** The unspoken question, "Am I normal?" is often

hiding behind many questions about sexual development, sexual thoughts and sexual feelings. On the surface, these questions may sound like, "What is the oldest (or youngest) that a girl got her period?" or "Can a flat-chested girl

nurse a baby?" Behind each of these questions (and hundreds more) is the unspoken question, "Am I normal?" Reassure your children as often as possible.

Talking With Infants And Toddlers (0-2 Years)

Of course, infants and toddlers do not need to know the facts about sexuality. But children this age are beginning to learn about their sexuality, and you are their main teachers. Naming all the parts of their body teaches them that their entire body is natural and healthy. ("This is your arm, this is your elbow, this is your vulva/penis, this is your knee," etc.) Reacting calmly when they touch their genitals teaches them that sexual feelings are normal and healthy. Holding them, hugging them, talking with them and responding to their needs all lay the groundwork for trust and open discussions as they grow older.

Talking With Preschool Children (3-4 Years)

Children at this age are learning about their bodies. They learn about their world through play. They begin to ask questions about where babies come from and they can understand simple answers. They do not understand abstract ideas or adult sexual behaviors. They can learn simple things such as bathing, washing their hands, brushing their teeth, eating good foods and napping. They can begin to accept the need for privacy. The best thing a parent can do at this age is to create a home where children will feel free to ask questions about their bodies, health and sexuality. Children then will learn that sexuality is one of the things that can be talked about in their home.

Talking With Young Children (5-8 Years)

Children at this age are able to understand more complex issues about health, disease and sexuality. They are interested in birth, families and death. They have probably heard about sex and AIDS from TV, their friends or adults. They may have questions or fears about sex and HIV/AIDS. Children at this age can understand basic answers to their questions based on concrete examples from their lives. For example, if your child cuts his/her finger and blood appears, this is a good time to explain how germs (things that make you sick) can get into the blood system from cuts in the body. They can understand simple answers to questions about their bodies and reproduction.

Talking With Preteens (9-12 Years)

Children at this age are going through all the changes of puberty. They are concerned about their bodies, their looks, and what is "normal." For some young teens, this time marks the start of dating, early sexual experiences and trying drugs.

Because of the strong social pressures which begin at this age, it is important that you talk about sexuality, regardless of what you know about your children's sexual or drug experiences. As a concerned parent, you must make sure your children know about prevention NOW. During the changes of puberty, preteens are very curious about sex and need to be given the basic, accurate information. They need to know what is meant by sexual intercourse, homosexuality and oral, anal and vaginal sex. Preteens need to be told that sex can have consequences, including pregnancy and diseases, including HIV infection. They should be told why sexual intercourse is an adult behavior and why it is a good idea for young people to wait to have sex. They need to know how HIV is transmitted, how it is not transmitted and how to prevent transmission, including talking a bit about condoms. This may seem like a difficult task, but it will give you a chance to teach your children the values that you hope they will adopt in their lives. It is also the time to let your children know that they can come to you with any of their questions about sexuality.

Talking With Teens (13-19 Years)

Parents should share their family's values about sexual behaviors. Teenagers and preteens should be told that the best way to prevent becoming infected with STDs, HIV or becoming pregnant is by not having any type of sexual intercourse.

Many parents want to tell their children to wait to have intercourse at least until they are no longer teenagers. However, most children today are not waiting—the majority of Americans have intercourse by their twentieth birthday.

Therefore, most parents also want to make sure that their children can protect themselves. We can explain to our children that if they are going to be involved in sex, they must protect themselves against teenage pregnancy and sexually transmitted diseases, including HIV.

Parents can talk about the full range of sexual behaviors that people find pleasurable. Many of these activities are "safer sex"—they cannot transmit HIV or cause pregnancy. This means talking to your teens and preteens about kissing, hand holding, caressing, masturbation and other sexual behaviors that do not involve penetration.

Social pressure to try sex and drugs can be very strong for teens. Therefore, at this age, regardless of their personal experience with sex or drugs, all young people must know:

- Not having sexual intercourse (abstinence) is the best method for preventing sexually transmitted diseases and pregnancy.
- For teenagers who are going to have sexual intercourse, they must use condoms for each and every act of intercourse, including oral sex, anal sex and vaginal sex. Only latex (rubber) condoms should be used. Condoms are very effective at preventing pregnancy and diseases. In fact, using a condom is 10,000 times safer than not using one.
- Teenagers should avoid all drugs including alcohol. Drugs and alcohol impair good decision-making and may suppress the immune system. Sharing needles of any kind puts people at risk of HIV— that includes injection drug-use, skin-popping, injecting steroids, ear and body piercing and tattooing.

Reprinted with permission from *Communication Tips For Parents.* © SIECUS. *Now What Do I Do?* (New York: Sexuality Information Council of the United States, 1996). www.siecus.org/pubs/pubs0004.html.

Talking Back:
Ten Things Teens Want Their Parents to Know about Teen Pregnancy
Survey by the National Campaign to Prevent Teen Pregnancy

TEENS HEAR ADVICE all the time but they don't often get asked for their advice. The National Campaign to Prevent Teen Pregnancy asked teens from all over the country:

If you could give your parents and other important adults advice on how to help you and your friends prevent teen pregnancy, what would it be?

1. Show us why teen pregnancy is such a bad idea. For instance, let us hear directly from teen mothers and fathers about how hard it has been for them. Even though most of us don't want to get pregnant, sometimes we need real-life examples to help motivate us.

2. Talk to us honestly about love, sex, and relationships. Just because we're young doesn't mean that we can't fall in love or be deeply interested in sex. These feelings are very real and powerful to us. Help

> Teens are precariously balanced between the sexual values they hear at home and those they are faced with daily in our sexualized culture.

us to handle the feelings in a safe way—without getting hurt or hurting others.

3. Telling us not to have sex is not enough. Explain why you feel that way, and ask us what we think.

Tell us how you felt as a teen. Listen to us and take our opinions seriously. **And no lectures, please.**

4. Whether we're having sex or not, we need to be prepared. We need to know how to avoid pregnancy and sexually-transmitted diseases.

5. If we ask you about sex or birth control, don't assume we are already having sex. We may just be curious, or we may just want to talk with someone we trust. And don't think giving us information about sex and birth control will encourage us to have sex.

6. Pay attention to us before we get into trouble. Programs for teen moms and teen fathers are great, but we all need encouragement, attention, and support. Reward us for doing the right thing—even when it seems like no big thing. Don't shower us with attention only when there is a baby involved.

7. Sometimes, all it takes not to have sex is not to have the opportunity. If you can't be home with us after school, make sure we have something to do that we really like, where there are other kids and some adults who are comfortable with kids our age. Often we have sex because there's not much else to do. Don't leave us alone so much.

8. We really care what you think, even if we don't always act like it. When we don't end up doing exactly what you tell us to, don't think that you've failed to reach us.

9. Show us what good, responsible relationships look like. We're as influenced by what you do as by what you say. If you demonstrate sharing, communication, and responsibility in your own relationships, we will be more likely to follow your example.

10. We hate "The Talk" as much as you do. Instead, start talking with us about sex and responsibility when we're young, and keep the conversation going as we grow older.

A Recipe for Healthy Relationships

By The Raphael House, from *Take Care: A Guide to Safe Relationships*

DO YOU KNOW WHAT you're looking for in your relationships? Do you know what a healthy relationship looks like? Is it just about being physically attracted to another person or liking each other a lot? Those are certainly important things to think about, but is that all there is? Not according to the young people we talked to. According to them, the recipe for a healthy relationship would contain the following ingredients:

- **Self-Esteem**
  People who believe in themselves and their own worth are more able to believe in the worth of their intimate partner.

- **Mutual Respect**
  People in healthy relationships respect each other's opinions, feelings, goals and decisions even if they don't always agree with each other.

- **Trust**
  People in healthy relationships are honest and open with each other at all times. Trust builds over time and is based on consistent, honest behavior.

- **Open Communication**
  People in healthy relationships are not afraid to express their needs, concerns and feelings. They listen attentively while their partners do the same.

- **Nonviolence**
  People in healthy relationships do not hit, threaten, or otherwise scare each other. They do not use words to hurt each other.

- **Personal Responsibility**
  People in healthy relationships take responsibility for their own actions and feelings. They do not blame each other if they lose their temper or make a bad decision.

- **Mutual Friends & Interests**
  People in healthy relationships continue their own interests and friendships outside of their romantic relationships.

- **Shared Decision-Making**
  People in healthy relationships use communication and negotiation to make decisions about their activities. One person does not dominate the decision-making.

- **Non-Abuse of Drugs**
  People in healthy relationships do not pressure each other to use alcohol and other drugs. They do not "get high" to make the relationship better.

- **Hearing "No!"**
  People in healthy relationships don't pressure or force the other person to have sex or do things they are not comfortable doing.

- **Non-Controlling Behavior**
  People in healthy relationships are not jealous or possessive of each other.

"After several abusive relationships, I've finally learned what I want from a partner. Love, respect and honesty are the most important things to me. In past relationships, I've lost a part of myself. I found myself giving up my own interests, hobbies and even friendships to please the other person."

—Cassie, age 19

"I think that respect for each other as people is key. Stay respectful and understanding even if you're mad at each other. Don't be sexist—that's old school."

—Marcus, age 17

Reprinted with permission of the Raphael House. *Take Care: A Guide to Safe Relationships* is a Raphael House prevention project in Portland, Oregon. Contact: (503) 222-6507. www.raphael-house.com

Abuse in Teen Dating Relationships

By Jeannie La France

"When I first met him I thought he was great, but slowly things began to change. He would go with me everywhere and cause a big fight if I talked to other guys. Once he threw a glass at me at a party and it broke on the wall behind my head. Everyone just laughed. Once he threw me up against a locker at school and I slapped at him to try to get away. The security said it was just 'a slapping match between kids.' I thought no one cared. It took me two years to get out, and he still drives by my house every week; he still scares me."

—Anonymous Teen

TEEN DATING VIOLENCE is when one person in a romantic relationship uses emotional or physical or sexual abuse to gain power and keep control over the other person. Teen dating violence happens more than we think. Nearly one-third of all teenagers will have been in an abusive relationship by the time they reach their twenties. It's important to be able to tell if you or your friend's relationship is abusive so you can start taking steps to help yourself or your friend be safe. Below are some questions to help you.

Am I In an Abusive Relationship?

- Are you ever afraid of the person you are dating?
- Do they say no one else would ever go out with you?
- Do they embarrass you in public? Do they call you names or put you down?
- Does the person you're dating tell you where you can go, what to wear or who you can hang out with?
- Do you feel pushed or pressured into sexual activities? Do you feel like you will "get in trouble" if you say "no"?
- Is the person you are seeing really nice sometimes and really mean other times? (Almost like they have two different personalities?)
- Does this person ever threaten to kill themselves or hurt anyone else if you leave them?
- Does this person ever shove, grab, hit, pinch, hold you down or kick you?
- Does this person ever say it is your fault if they hurt you or yell at you?
- Does this person make frequent promises to change? Do they say you are "making it too big a deal?"

If you have answered "yes" to any of these questions, then you or your friend is in an abusive relationship. What can you do? Here are some suggestions …

If Your Friend Is In an Abusive Relationship:

- Be patient. Leaving relationships takes a long time.
- Don't spread gossip; it could put them in danger.
- Tell them the abuse is not their fault and they don't deserve it, no matter what.
- Be non-judgmental. Be a good listener.
- Don't ignore it or pretend it isn't happening.
- Support your friends in making their own choices, don't boss them around.
- Make safety plans with them about going between classes or to and from school.
- See if you can tell a supportive adult.
- Call crisis lines like National Domestic Violence Hotline at **1-800-799-SAFE.**

If You Are In an Abusive Relationship:

- You could tell people what is happening. If the first people you tell are not helpful, find other people. Try thinking of supportive adults to tell.
- You could call a crisis line. They are confidential, all ages and you can be male or female.
- You could join a support group for young women who have been abused.
- You could take a self-defense course.
- You could look into legal action. The school may have helpful policies or you could get a court restraining order to keep the abuser away from you.
- You could go to a shelter.
- Believe in yourself. Abuse is not your fault no matter what anyone says. You deserve a life without abuse.

Dating violence happens in all kinds of relationships. When it is between a boyfriend and girlfriend, 95% of the time it is the boyfriend abusing the girlfriend. Dating abuse can also happen in same-sex relationships. Abuse can happen in any relationship no matter what race the people are, how much money they have or where they live. The important thing is that no matter who the people are, dating violence hurts.

Reprinted courtesy of Jeannie La France and the Bradley-Angle House, www.bradleyangle.org. 503-232-7805 PO Box 14694, Portland, OR 97293. The National Domestic Violence Hotline is 1-800-799-SAFE.

Dater's Bill of Rights

By National Crime Prevention Council

- I have the right to refuse a date without feeling guilty.

- I can ask for a date without feeling rejected or inadequate if the answer is no.

- I do not have to act macho.

- I may choose not to act seductively.

- If I don't want physical closeness, I have the right to say so.

- I have the right to start a relationship slowly, to say, "I want to know you better before I become involved."

- I have the right to be myself without changing to suit others.

- I have the right to change a relationship when my feelings change. I can say, "We used to be close, but I want something else now."

- If I am told a relationship is changing, I have the right not to blame or change myself to keep it going.

  - I have the right to an equal relationship with my partner.

  - I have the right not to dominate or to be dominated.

  - I have the right to act one way with one person and a different way with someone else.

  - I have the right to change my goals whenever I want to.

Reprinted with permission by National Crime Prevention Council, 1000 Connecticut Avenue NW, 13th floor, Washington, DC 20036. www.ncpc.org

Boys, Men and Violence: Strategies for Prevention
By Jody Bellant Scheer, MD and Kathy Keller Jones, MA

Violence: a National Epidemic

There is a national epidemic of violence in our society, and the shocking reality is that most of it is perpetrated by males.[1] Males are also most likely to be victims of such acts.[2] This tendency is true not only for men, but for boys as well. For example, 4 times as many boys successfully commit suicide as girls, and 10 times as many boys die of homicide.[1] Culturally, this phenomenon is often attributed to the belief that violence is hardwired into males. However, the root cause of male violence cannot be shown to be innate or genetic. There is simply no biological or scientific evidence to support the myth that men are either naturally or inevitably violent.[3] In fact, most boys and men are peace-loving, caring and afraid of violence.[3] "Men's monopoly on violence is the product of a lifetime's training in how to be a real man."[4]

Masculinity is Responsible, Not Testosterone

Our society's dominant model of masculinity is really what is to blame for the link between males and violence. The current model of masculinity encourages men to be aggressive, in control, emotionally callous, tough, self-reliant, domineering and entitled to power over others.[4] One of the central images of masculinity in our culture is the murderous hero, the specialist in violence, the tough, callous hero who exacts violent revenge[4]. We live in a society awash with violent images: television, videos, computer games and songs constantly barrage our youth with images that celebrate violence, as well as glorify risk-taking behavior.[3] Traditional tough male stereotypes are constantly modeled in modern media as successful, desirable, normative and sexy. Until we can transform this distorted version of manhood, heralded in the popular bumper sticker, "I don't get mad, I get even," the terrible equation of violence and masculinity will continue to add up to high death tolls and violent behaviors for our nations' men and boys.

The Boy Code

Dr. William Pollack, author of *Real Boys: Rescuing our Boys from the Myths of Boyhood*, describes our current model of masculinity as being passed to our sons via the "Boy Code."[3] This is the code which dictates boys' behavior from the time they are born. Boys must be stoic, independent, not show weakness (or share pain or grieve openly), daring, high-energy risk takers, and they must strive to achieve status, dominance and power, act "cool," and avoid shame at all costs. Boys who express feelings or urges mistakenly seen as "feminine," such as dependence, warmth and empathy, are ridiculed.[3]

Who Creates the Boy Code? We Do!

The "Boy Code" is one way of describing the modern acculturation process of turning boys into "real men." This process is carried on almost without realizing it by many of us as we interact less with our baby boys, reward boys for ruggedness and strength, and remind them that "big boys don't cry."[3] Boys are encouraged to be daring, even to the point of ignoring their own safety. Boys are then shamed for displays of weakness or shows of emotion.[2] The act of shaming each other becomes a powerful way in which boys and men keep each other within the boundaries of established manhood.[5] Boys often take undue risks with themselves or others; war offers an extreme example.[3]

By burdening boys with a narrow band of acceptable "masculine'" emotional expressiveness, we limit their ability to express the full range of their human experience. In fact, one of the few acceptable emotions in boys tends to be anger, which can escalate to rage if a boy has been bottling up all his other feelings.[2] Boys' tendencies towards action are very different from being inherently tough or violent.[3]

Boys' Response to the Boy Code

The roots of violence begin with the "Boy Code" and with the disconnection that it demands of our boys from their emotions and from themselves and others, including their families.[3,6] To protect against their fears of inadequacy and their sense of imperfect masculinity, some boys may go on the offensive, lashing out at others.[3,7] The current model of masculinity also requires a man to always be in control: over his own emotions, over girls, over other boys.[5] Lacking other options, physical and emotional violence seem to some boys a perfect way of exercising power and control, especially since males grow up feeling entitled to having power.[5] Violence can become an expression of that sense of entitlement, as well as a form of release.

In some cases, boys also have direct experiences of violence as survivors or witnesses, which—coupled with the all-pervasive glorification of violence in the media—establishes violence as a normative and appropriate method of conflict resolution and/or stress management.[4] Acquaintance rape and domestic violence are two of the unfortunate manifestations of our code of masculinity gone awry.

The solutions to diminishing the effects of violence on our boys, then, lie in reestablishing and maintaining connection with our sons, educating them to feel empathy for others, challenging attitudes and behaviors that are supportive of violence, and giving our sons opportunities to express their true voices, their pain, and their feelings in an environment free from shame and humiliation. Our sons also deserve to grow up in homes that are safe from fear, shame, or violence, which means that as adults we must model the non-violent behaviors we wish to see in our sons.[7]

Disciplining Our Sons

Parenting is a difficult task, and so is disciplining your active, action-oriented son. Spanking (or hitting) is a common form of discipline used in America, but it increases the child's aggressiveness: research shows that these kids are up to 4 times as likely to be aggressive, are less attentive to social cues and are more likely to have delinquent behavior outside the home. As adults, they are more likely to hit their own children and spouses than peers who were not spanked.[8]

Finding a more positive form of discipline that works for your family takes a bit of thoughtful reflection. First of all, parents might want to rid themselves "of the crazy idea that in order to make children do better, first you have to make them feel worse."[9] Most adults do not feel like doing better after they feel humiliated, and neither do our children. Therefore, parents need to learn ways of discipline that teach and model kindness, firmness and mutual respect.[9] Positive time-outs for reflection and self-soothing, natural and logical consequences, encouragement and training for the behaviors that you wish to see, as well as family meetings, are all examples of methods of discipline that can empower parents to modify negative behaviors without the use of spanking.[9] "Effective parenting centers around love that is not permissive, does not tolerate disrespect, but is powerful enough to allow kids to make mistakes and live with the consequences of those mistakes....And those consequences, when accompanied by empathy —our compassionate understanding of the child's disappointment, frustration and pain—hit home with mind-changing power."[10] The thoughtful application of

non-violent forms of discipline in our own homes is well worth the effort, so that we can raise sons who are less aggressive, more attuned to social cues, and less likely to be future perpetrators of domestic violence.

Male Violence in the Form of Bullying

Our sons need to know the difference between a conflict between two equals, and bullying. Ideally, with conflict, our sons use their conflict management skills and do not need parent intervention. Bullying, however, involves inequality of power, repetition, and intent to harm, and almost always will need adult intervention. With a mild bullying incident, like name-calling, the target may try responding verbally if it is safe (try role playing this at home) and otherwise needs to report the incident to an adult. Parents may need to work closely with the school to make sure they are aware of the situation and have set up timely consequences for the aggressor(s). Encourage your son's school to implement a successful bully-proof curriculum such as *Steps to Respect,* which teaches "Recognize, Refuse, Report."

Weapons

Boys are commonly fascinated by weapons, especially with their glorification in the media and with the direct practice they get playing video games. Although it is normal for your son to draw, enact, or write about gun violence, it is important that he understand the real dangers of guns and knives and know that household firearms must always be secured in locked cabinets. It is also important to come up with a clear strategy of what he should do if he were to encounter peers with a gun or knife at their homes or school. Make sure your son knows what to do if he encounters a gun and why (don't touch it, get away from anyone handling a gun, and report the gun immediately to a responsible adult). Talking realistically about the human suffering caused by weapons can be an important antidote to the unrealistic portrayal of death and violence due to firearms on TV, movies and games.

Teaching Empathy—Reducing the Toll of Shame

Children learn far more from what they watch their parents do than from what their parents tell them; therefore, parents must model love, connection, respect, and healthy ways to deal with emotions, including rage and anger. In order to learn about alternative forms of masculinity, sons would ideally watch their fathers be empathic, emotionally expressive, active and connected to others.[3] To understand and learn about empathy, it is especially important that boys be able to express and talk about their own vulnerabilities, their fears and a full range of emotions without shame or ridicule; home must become a "shame-free zone."[3] Parents will want to be sensitive to the times when their son is willing to talk privately about his fears and vulnerable thoughts, and take advantage of these "teachable moments," such as bedtime and car time.[3] Help your son understand the feelings and viewpoints of others.

Reducing the Impact of Media Violence in Your Son's Life

Our society is awash in media violence, and this leaves parents with the challenge of determining how to manage and mitigate the negative effects. This is a formidable task for any parent, but a necessary one for anyone raising boys in our media savvy age. It is the view of Dr. Pollack, author of *Real Boys,* that boys who see a great deal of violence in the media tend to become desensitized to it, and to feel it is a "normal" part of life.[3] "This may heighten the possibility that they will tolerate violence in themselves or their friends."[3]

There are positive strategies that parents can utilize to lessen the impact of media violence on their sons. First of all, they can frequently discuss issues of violence and personal safety with their sons, as well as the content of TV programs, videos, computer games and music. Parents and sons can watch or play together, and talk about what they have seen afterwards. Computers, game consoles, and TVs should be kept in public locations within the home. Media and game selections can be made with careful regard to violent content, and hours of use limited. Although there is no way that modern parents can completely shield their children from the impact of media violence, connection to family is critical.

Staying Connected to Your Son

Boys who care about others and feel connected to them are rarely the ones who allow their anger to get out of control.[3] Boys who feel deprived of love, nurture and caring often tend to focus on their own needs over those of others and feel overly angry.[3] All these vulnerable feelings may funnel into rage, and spill over into acts of violence.[3] One of the most vital positive strategies that can prevent the link between violence and your own boy is to strengthen the power of connection in his life: with himself, with family, with friends, with a spiritual path, and with community. This strategy can take many forms.

First of all, make sure you can count some time each day for talking with your son and each week for spending special quality time with him. Make sure your actions and words are loving and supportive, so that the message of your love is always clear to him. This may be especially hard given the difficult behaviors and withdrawal that occur commonly during adolescence, but the effort to lovingly connect to the boy beneath the "mask" can be life saving. Help your son to become involved in activities that complement his interests, and help organize these if necessary. After school clubs, extracurricular activities, jobs, church groups and sports can greatly enhance your son's self esteem and feelings of connection to others. Help your son participate in some kind of community service, even if it is in the context of a family project, to enhance his connections to his local community. Tap other adults in your family or community and get them involved in activities with your son, to provide for mentoring experiences and adult connections outside of the family home. Finally, help your son with relationship-building skills, and encourage him to develop a wide range of friendships. Encourage a model of masculinity that includes nurturing and a deep respect of girls and women as equals. With parents acting as advocates in these ways to increase the web of connections a boy has to his world, it is unlikely that he will resort to violence.

Resources:
1. Kimmel, M., *"Manhood and Violence: The Deadliest Equation,"* Newsday, 3/8/01
2. Pollack, W., *"What Makes Boys Violent? We Do,"* USA Weekend Magazine, reprinted at www.usaweekend.com Pollack, W., *Real Boys: Rescuing our Sons from the Myths of Boyhood*
4. Dept. of Education, Employment, Training and Youth Affairs, "Domestic Violence, Boys, Men and Masculinity," 6/4/97, Canberra, Australia, reprinted on www.xyonline.net
5. Kaufman, M., "Positive Strategies With Boys to End Violence," UNICEF forum, 3/31/00, reprinted at www.michaelkaufmann.com
6. Goldstein, J., *War and Gender: How Gender Shapes the War System and Vice Versa,* 9/01
7. Cartwright, K., "Socializing Violence in Boys: Suggestions for Change," www.shpm.com/articles/child_behavior/changeboys.html
8. Howard, B., "Spanking: A Slap at Thoughtful Parenting," *Pediatric News,* July 2001
9. Nelsen, J., *Positive Discipline,* 2006
10. Cline, F. and Fay, J., *Parenting with Love and Logic,* 1990.
11. Kilgore, C. "One-Third of Students Involved in Bullying," *Pediatric News,* July 2001.
12. Garbarino, J. *Lost Boys: Why Our Sons Turn Violent and How We Can Save Them.*

Controlling the Urge to Strike Out:
Teaching Our Kids to Vent Anger Nonviolently
by Jody Bellant Scheer, MD

"Think of anger as a 'red light' on your dashboard....and stop and look under your 'emotional hood.'"

—Marshall Rosenberg, Nonviolent Communication

"Stop grabbing toys away from your brother!" we yell, as we grab a toy from one angry child and give it to a crying other. "Quit acting like a baby!" we implore later, when faced with a meltdown from a child angry about doing chores. What lessons are we really teaching our children, in these instances, about angry feelings and actions and our human tendency to strike out at others when we are angry? First we teach it is OK to grab if we are bigger, and second, we teach that name-calling and shaming others is OK. In both situations, our intentions were to promote justice, support, consideration, and cooperation. Our behavior, however, probably did little to promote these values. Furthermore, we did little to help our children see the feelings, thoughts or needs behind their actions, or to wonder how their behaviors might have impacted the feelings or needs of others. If we are to teach our children to vent their anger nonviolently, to control their urges to strike out, and to be empathetic, it is important to look beneath our own angry feelings and to model a course of action for them when we are angry . . . one that both resolves conflict AND is respectful to self and to others.

The secret to using anger productively is empathy, i.e., connecting with the feelings and underlying, universal values and needs behind all behaviors. Every angry behavior, no matter how ugly it looks, is an attempt to deal with the unpleasant feelings that arise when faced with a situation out of kilter in some way with a highly important value. How many times have we experienced this with ourselves, barking orders at our children; when we feel overwhelmed and need some understanding and support? We also experience this with our children, for example, our son picks fights with everyone at home and then lets you know at bedtime how lonely and left out he felt at school that day, or our daughter slams the door in our face and then tells us a week later of feeling devastated by a group of friends who excluded her. Empathizing with the feelings and needs beneath our angry feelings and behaviors helps tremendously in understanding ourselves and others, in resolving conflict

peacefully, and in controlling our human tendency to strike out in anger in ways we later regret.

How can parents help? Ask your children questions to explore three components of anger:

- **The trigger** is the behavior or action that triggered your anger. Start by describing the event as a neutral observation, as if a video camera was recording it. An example might be: "I get upset when I see the kitchen sink full of dirty dishes and lukewarm milk sitting out on the counter" rather than "The kitchen is a disaster zone!" Notice there is less triggering <u>in you</u> too.

- **The cause** is the <u>thinking</u> that occurs when you are triggered. It often has a lot of "shoulds" in it. An example might be: "The kitchen is a flipping mess! This family is just a bunch of lazy slobs! You should know better!" Such thinking almost always has elements of judgment and righteousness in it. By blaming others, we naturally feel defensive and angry and lose sight of what we can control.

- **The root** is the universal human need or value that was not being met in the situation. An example might be, "I really have a need for understanding and household support when I get home from work exhausted." When we use our unpleasant feelings, such as anger, as personal signals, we can explore where we are out of alignment with deeply held core values or universal needs. By connecting with this beautiful value, we get in touch with what really makes us tick. We are then empowered, as there are many ways to meet any one of our needs. How wonderful to have insight into core values!

Brainstorm useful strategies for self-control when triggered—such as deep breathing, counting to ten, or taking a time-out. Practice these strategies with your own children when they trigger you. Together with your children, you have an opportunity to learn, grow and deal with your anger in ways that actually enrich your life. Rollo May sums it up well: *"Real freedom is the ability to pause between stimulus and response, and in that pause, to choose."*

Depression in Boys: A Hidden Epidemic
By Jody Bellant Scheer, MD

Depression in Boys: Hidden & Hard to Diagnose

Depression in boys is a disease that is both highly under-diagnosed and unrecognized. This is because boys tend to express depression differently and more covertly than do girls. As part of our culture's masculine heritage, our boys are taught from an early age to hide their feelings of sadness and pain. Boys can learn to disconnect from their painful feelings to such a point that they are not even consciously aware of them. This disconnection then leads boys to externalize their pain, to attribute it to others, and to act it out as violence against self and others,[1] or to self-medicate with drugs and alcohol. All of these behaviors can result in diagnoses of conduct disorders, behavior problems, or addictions, instead of being correctly identified as underlying depression.[2] Finally, many boys try to deal with problems on their own and escape diagnosis (and therefore treatment) for depression because they won't actively seek out help unless forced to by family or circumstances. Depression carries a double stigma for men in this culture, as it is considered both unmanly and shameful.[3] Boys learn early that they risk shame and rejection if they admit to feelings of sadness, fear or hopelessness.[4] For all of these reasons, it is imperative that parents of boys understand the facts about boys' depression, so that they can recognize the subtle as well as the obvious signs and symptoms of this disease. Then, they will be able to get help for their sons should they fall prey to this common and sometimes life-threatening illness.

Boy's Depression: Definitions and Incidence

Depression is a mental disorder diagnosed by the presence of a persistently altered mood that impairs thinking, feeling and behavior, and which interferes with a person's capacity to be productive, to engage in pleasurable activities and to enjoy fulfilling relationships.[6] Major depression is a serious condition that is characterized by one or more overt, incapacitating and depressive episodes. Such an episode usually lasts 7 to 9 months on average in children and adolescents.[6] A less serious but more chronic form of depression is often called minor depression, or dysthymic disorder. This is where the child or adolescent experiences a chronically depressed mood for most of the day, on at least half of all days, with symptoms lasting on average for about 4 years.[6]

Population studies have shown that at any one time, between 10-15% of children and adolescents have some symptoms of depression.[6] However, by adolescence, twice as many girls as boys are diagnosed with the disease. Dr. Terrence Real, family psychotherapist and author of *I Don't Want to Talk About It: Overcoming the Secret Legacy of Male Depression*, suggests that boys DO have as much depression as girls, they just express it in covert and different ways, such as personality disorders and chemical dependencies, that are often misdiagnosed or unrecognized.[2]

According to the 2001 Surgeon General's report, the incidence of "diagnosed" depression in young children ranges between 3 and 5%, and rises to about 11.3% in adolescence.[6] These rates may underestimate the rates of true depressive disease, due to the hidden epidemic of depression in boys. By comparison, adult incidence rates are approximately 5% of the population. The rates of suicide also rise dramatically during adolescence, with suicide being the third leading cause of death for teenagers.[6] Although girls attempt suicide twice as often as boys, boys are 4 times more likely to succeed than girls.[6] This is likely due to the increased availability of firearms and increased substance abuse amongst teenage boys, according to the Surgeon General.[6] These numbers belie the common myth that children and adolescents don't need help and intervention for their depressive behaviors. As effective and loving parents, it is in our sons' best interests to recognize depression in our sons and to find help for them. Depression is a disease that is highly treatable, and appropriate treatment can lessen the pain a depressed boy is living with, greatly improve his life (and yours!) and may be life-saving.

Recognizing Hidden Depression in Boys

Depression is easier to detect in girls, who often cry, sulk, and openly express their loneliness, hopelessness and sadness. In fact, the official medical definitions of depression rely on these typically more feminine expressions of despair and may be one of the major reasons why depression is often overlooked in boys and men.[1,2,4] Boys more commonly communicate depression through behavior, in action-oriented ways.[7] Some of the earliest signs that a boy is depressed or suicidal may be acts of bravado or dangerous risk-taking,[7] or hostile or sullen, withdrawn behavior.[2] Depressed boys often have academic difficulties, low self-esteem, and are harshly self-critical.[4] They may shift towards drug or alcohol abuse and many will have sudden changes in sleep, eating, physical or sexual activity patterns.[4] Depressed boys may have increasingly rigid demands for autonomy.[4] Meantime, they often deny feelings of pain or sadness and are unable to cry.[4] All boys will exhibit these tendencies to some degree some of the time, and with moderation, these actions may be normal coping mechanisms when a boy is in pain.[4] However, when these behaviors become persistent or extreme, your son may be well on his way toward depression.[4]

Determining whether your son is just moody or really depressed is tough work. One helpful method of recognizing significant sadness or depression in your son is to look at the intensity of his behavior, how long it lasts, and whether it is persistent.[4] Teens will naturally experience moody, irritable and antisocial times, but these are normally balanced out with just as many calm, happy, and interactive periods.[7] Depressed teens will be increasingly and persistently irritable, hostile and withdrawn, and while there will be some ups and downs in their moods, happy periods won't last.[7] It is wise to talk with your son about your own observations and concerns about his mental health and happiness. Having him assessed by a mental health professional may be the only way to be reassured that he is coping safely, however. Your son will need an immediate referral to a mental health professional if he threatens suicide or harm to others, or if he exhibits cruelty towards younger children or animals.

It is helpful to remember that depression is not really just a feeling, it is a state . . . a condition of numbness and nonfeeling.[2] Depressed boys are chronically burying their feelings of pain; they are not just occasionally sad. Importantly, the cure for depression lies in learning how to tolerate and let one's painful feelings pass.[2] Dr. Real explains: "unlike states, which tend to congeal, feelings will run their own course in due time. Despite the often expressed male fear that if one were to let oneself cry, one would never stop, tears, in fact, eventually taper off if one lets them. Feelings are not endless, but our numbing attempts to avoid them can last a lifetime."[2] To understand depression in our boys and to help them avoid a lifetime of hidden depression, it is imperative to look at how we, in the name of masculinity and often with the best of intentions, poorly equip our sons with the skills of human connection and intimacy. Encouraging such skills in your own son will help shield him from the dangers of male depression.

Masculinity and Depression

Many psychologists have noticed that the societal acculturation process of gender plays a role in depression. Men and boys tend to hide their feelings of sadness and to express their feelings of despair with action and anger in part due to the way they have been socialized as men. Dr. Pollack describes this largely unconscious process of passing down the rules of manhood through the generations as the "Boy Code." This is basically a "toughening up" process that uses shame to teach boys to hide their vulnerabilities and insecurities, to disconnect from their mothers at an early age, to devalue emotions and activities that are considered "feminine," and to feel ashamed for being anything less than cocky, tough, self confident and independent.[4] The "code" teaches boys that to be a man, anger is the only acceptable emotion, otherwise you must pretend to feel nothing.[4] The high price boys pay to be men is that they must actively repress their pain, their feelings, their insecurities, and their hunger for connection in ways that are unhealthy and that can lead them to feel lonely, frightened, and very sad.[4]

Dr. Real expands our understanding of the process of masculinization by noting that the achievement of a masculine identity is not so much an acquisition as a disavowal. Boys and men, when asked to describe masculinity respond with double negatives, describing what it is not (which all boil down to, simply, I'm not a girl).[8] What men have been socialized to disavow in themselves are the attributes of dependency, expressiveness, and affiliation . . . all of the self-concepts and skills that belong to the relational, emotive world.[2] Dr. Real believes that along with whatever genetic proclivities one might inherit, it is this loss of our boys' inborn human potential for intimacy and interconnection that lays the foundation for male depression.[2] As a result of masculine disconnection, 5 times as many men in Dr. Real's practice suffer from covert or hidden depression as from overt or traditionally diagnosable depression.[3] In covert depression, what is seen are only the footprints of depression, those defenses that men use to disconnect or run from their painful feelings.[3] These defenses tend to take 3 forms: self-medication (addictions), social isolation, and lashing out.[2] For depressed men and boys, Dr. Real believes that the road to recovery is linked to reentering the world of connection and relationship.[2] Depressed men must be retrained to express a full range of emotion and to undo their masculine training to be tough, stoic, "better than," and disconnected. For parents tackling the complex task of raising happy, whole and healthy sons, it is important to teach boys a more humane sense of their masculinity. Encouraging the expression of a full range of emotions in your own home and maintaining intimate connections with your son can be both life-affirming and life-saving.

The Importance of Connection in Our Sons Lives

Dr. James Garbarino, author of *Lost Boys: Why Our Sons Turn Violent and How We Can Save Them*, emphasizes the importance of remaining connected to our sons, in spite of their sometimes difficult behaviors, and especially if they are depressed. This tendency for depressed boys to act out makes life difficult for parents and educators, and we tend to focus on punishments for problem behaviors rather than look for the underlying causes of the misbehavior. For example, is he facing disappointments or being bullied, teased or shunned? The only way to find out what is engaging him in conversation and maintaining a loving and caring connection with him in spite of

his behaviors—he is still a child who needs your love and support. You can and should set limits on his behaviors, but always reassure him that you still love him.[7] It is helpful to model the openness that you want from your son by sharing with him some of your own trials and tribulations while growing up. With time and patience, your son will open up to you if he knows he will be accepted by you, and when he trusts that he will not be shamed or discounted for revealing to you his fears, sadness or other vulnerable feelings. A national study on teen mental health found that the key factors to boys' emotional well-being were, in fact, parents who shared activities with their boys, who were physically present at key times during the day and, most important, who expressed warmth, love and caring.[4] Parents can encourage a wide circle of friendships and mentors for their sons, be alert regarding the status of their son's peer and romantic friendships, and be watchful for signs of hidden depression. Consulting with a therapist can be helpful anytime a parent feels concerned. The payoff for such care and vigilance are sons who know they are unconditionally loved and cherished.

References:
[1] *Lost Boys: Why Our Sons Turn Violent and How We Can Save Them*, by Dr. James Garbarino
[2] *I Don't Want to Talk About It: Overcoming the Secret Legacy of Male Depression*, by Dr. Terrence Real.
[3] "Men's Issues: An Interview with Terrence Real," online at www.vix.com/menmag/realivss.htm
[4] *Real Boys, Rescuing Our Sons from the Myths of Boyhood*, Chapter 12, by Dr. William Pollack,
[5] "Big Boys Do Cry," by Kim Gaines, c. 2002, online at www.imdiversity.com/villages/african
[6] "Depression and Suicide in Children and Adolescents," from Mental Health, A Report of the Surgeon General. 2001.
[7] "Depression and Violence in Teens," by Laurie Udesky, online at www.blueprintforhealth.com/topic/depteen
[8] "Men and Depression: An Interview with Terry Real," c. Men's Voices, Vol.1 #3 (Summer/Fall 1998)
[9] "Attention: Depression and Temperament," by Tom Cushman and Thomas Johnson, online at www.nasponline.org/publications/cq292Attentionpt2.html

The Power of Parents:
Teens Say Parents a Leading Influence in Helping Them Stay Alcohol-Free
By Emily Moser MPA, MA

"Peer pressure is overrated; parents are huge." —Oregon teenager who said parental influence was a major reason she chose to be alcohol-free.

THIS TEEN IS FAR FROM ALONE. A survey a few years ago by the respected Roper organization found that 76 percent of youth ages 8 to 17 said parents were a leading influence in their decision about whether to drink.

It can be easy for parents to dismiss the enormous power they have to educate and equip their kids to steer clear of alcohol. Our culture is awash in alcohol advertising that promotes the false notion that everyone drinks, with no consequences, and it can make parents feel undermined when it comes to helping their children make the healthy choice to not drink. But research underscores that parental influence is the key to keeping kids alcohol-free. Among the most important steps parents and other caregivers can take are to educate themselves about the harms of underage drinking, to share those facts with their children, to express their values on the importance of not drinking until age 21, to establish rules and clear consequences for their behavior, and to take opportunities to strengthen the connection with their kids.

It's critical that parents start talking with their kids when they are young about the harms of underage drinking because alcohol is the No. 1 drug problem among youth. About one in three eighth-graders and half of 11th-graders consumed alcohol in the past month, according to the Oregon Healthy Teens Survey. And too many teens who drink aren't just having a cocktail at the end of the day; they are drinking a lot in one sitting.

The risks associated with youth drinking are serious. Alcohol is a major cause of death among young people. The part of the brain that controls planning, delayed gratification and judgment develops last. Pouring alcohol on top of that affects a youngster's ability to make sound decisions, like whether to ride in a car with a driver who has been drinking. Beyond the sobering safety consequences, underage drinking has serious health risks. Scientific research has found that regular drinking can harm a child's brain. Studies show that tremendous brain development occurs during the adolescent and teens years, and that the brain is not fully developed until our mid-20s. For parents, helping kids make the healthy choice to stay alcohol-free falls into the same category as making sure they wear a helmet when they ride their bicycle or a seat belt when they get in a car. It is very important to emphasize that underage drinking is not an inevitable rite of passage for underage youth.

What strategies can parents apply today to protect their kids from alcohol and other drug use? A strong family bond is proven to be one of the most important factors. Here are a few suggestions to help build closeness and trust—even through everyday activities:

- Spend time doing fun things as a family, like cooking and eating dinner together, playing board games, watching a movie, shooting baskets or going to community events.
- Take advantage of everyday moments to tell your children that you love them and to share your values and expectations.
- Your child may have opinions, fears and concerns about substance use. In addition to sharing with your son or daughter the facts about alcohol and other drug use, ask them open-ended questions and listen to their perspectives.
- Help your child develop the skills to refuse offers of alcohol from their peers and others. Together, practice responses they are comfortable saying.
- Take a look at the example you're setting with your kids. What message are you sending about things such as your own alcohol use? If you do not drink, explain to your child why. If you enjoy an occasional drink, talk with your child about moderation and why the legal drinking age is 21 (studies show the law has saved lives on the road and prevented injuries, and it has kept countless adolescents and teens from drinking at early ages). And let your son or daughter see you say "no" to a drink from time to time, too.
- Remember that parenting doesn't have to be done in isolation. You'll find other parents share many of the same concerns and challenges about raising kids. Together, you can establish standards of behavior, explore ways to build your parenting skills through classes and seminars, and become an even better parent.

Written for Family Empowerment Network by Emily Moser, MPA, MA, Director of Parenting Program at Oregon Partnership. Reprinted with permission from Emily Moser at emoser@orpartnership.org. 503-224-5211, or www.orpartnership.org.

Teenagers and Drugs

By Kathy Masarie, MD

Serenity Prayer: "God grant me the serenity to accept the things I cannot change, the courage to change the things I can, and the wisdom to know the difference."

THE SERENITY PRAYER says it all when it comes to intervening in teen drug use. (We consider alcohol a "drug" in this article.) When a parent is clear about what they do and don't have control over, they can be extremely effective in reducing teen substance abuse. What a community of caring adults do have control over is a support structure that encourages healthy choices. What we don't have control over is the moment when our teen is faced with the choice of taking drugs or alcohol. That moment lays 100% in his or her hands. Our teens know this. What we as parents can do to focus our energy on what we do have control over: empowering our teens to make healthy decisions and fostering an environment that makes it difficult for them to drink. At the same time, we can work to help create a cultural norm that glamorizes a healthy life-style rather than a life-style of drinking and drugs.

Connection with Your Teen Is Key

Connectivity with parents is a vital element in reducing alcohol and drug use. Parents who have good communication with their teens can share all of the information listed below. Their teens hear it and trust the information because they know their parents are honest, open and have their well-being in mind. Teens with a trusting connection with their parents know their parents are not trying to control them or take away their autonomy and are sharing this information to help them stay alive, stay healthy and stay safe. Even though our teens might not always make the choice we hope for, we have done our job as competent parents to support a good decision. If our teens choose to use drugs or alcohol, we want to know so we can help them. Teens with a good relationship with their parents will tell their parents when they are struggling with a serious problem; they trust their parents will actually help them and not over-react with anger and consequences. One of the best sources of information on long-term parenting strategies comes from Jane Nelsen's book, *Positive Discipline for Teenagers*.[1]

Be Aware of Family Patterns That Invite Chemical Dependency

Genetics and family patterns are very influential in whether a teen will become addicted. Parents who hide the embarrassing stories about alcoholism in the extended family are setting their kids up. Our kids need to know these stories and they need to hear them early.

Alcoholism is a disease that develops when alcohol reacts with a person's particular body chemistry. Depending on a person's physical make-up, it may take a lot of drinking to trigger alcoholism or it may take just a little. Each person is born with a certain level of risk for developing this disease. Teenagers can become alcoholics in 6-18 months while it usually takes older people several years, partially because a young person's liver metabolizes alcohol more rapidly than an adult's does.[2] A teen who feels "like she has come home" when she drinks can be an addict even if it's her first time. Teens may build up a tolerance to the drug, requiring more and more alcohol to achieve the same affect. A teen who "holds his liquor" can be genetically predisposed to alcoholism.

Creating a home environment that is free of chemical dependency is an important first step to protecting our teens from drugs. One in four US children, sometime before the age of 18, lives with a family member who abuses alcohol.[3] Children model what they learn at home; parents who look at their own relationship with drugs and alcohol can evaluate whether they are modeling unhealthy behaviors. Households with problem drug or alcohol users teach kids to use chemical agents to numb their feelings, emotions and fears. Wanting a healthy lifestyle for your teen can be a great motivator for healing dysfunctional family patterns.

Talk to Kids Early to Influence "Alcohol Expectancy"

Our brains store information in memory so we are prepared for similar situations (otherwise every moment would be an overwhelming new experience). This stored automatic information is called "expectancies." Researchers are now finding that expectancies play an important role in alcohol use. Children acquire their alcohol expectancies very early—even as young as 3 or 4 years old. Young children often have negative expectancies that alcohol makes one sick or mean. Over time they are exposed to the community norms that make drinking seem "cool": ads everywhere marketing alcohol to teens, movies where there are rarely negative consequences to drinking, MTV spring break promotion of binge drinking, and so on. By 5th-6th grade, children's expectancies may shift to the positive effects of alcohol to be socially successful, happy, sexy, etc. Individuals who have strong positive alcohol expectancies drink more and are at risk for abuse.[4]

Inform Yourself about Your Community Norms

Even though parents are fearful of drug and alcohol abuse, there is a tendency to think "not my kid" when in comes to alcohol and drugs. Just to give you a general idea, nationally norms from 2005[5] are:

Age	% of Teens who Have Used Alcohol	
	Males	Females
12	10%	9%
14	32%	33%
16	60%	62%
18	73%	76%

Nearly 50% of college-aged men and nearly 40% of college-aged women binge drink (5+ drinks in a row) monthly.[6] Find information about the rates of alcohol use among teens in your community, the severity of use, the rates of deaths and complications from drugs and alcohol, how they get the alcohol, and strategies high schools, police and community are doing to curtail the problem.

Why Do Kids Do Drugs and Alcohol?

Ask yourself why you drink and teen's reasons are similar: it is fun, it feels good, it makes one feel more comfortable socially (part of the group, less shy or boring, happier). Teens are hormonally charged for risk, and they see alcohol as exciting, cool and sexy. They like the escape from boredom and their life of school and chores. They want to be like the "cool" guy who sold them the drugs or their music and movie idols who glorify drugs. Some girls take speed to lose weight. Boys may associate alcohol with sex. Kids who are over-controlled or over-protected may use drugs to rebel against their parents (even when they don't really want to). Using drugs and alcohol fits into the norm of the culture they live in. Again, like some of the adults in the culture, kids are looking for "quick fixes" to feel good, especially if they are feeling lonely or depressed and want to numb out painful problems or feelings.

One thing very different about teens is that they drink to get drunk. Although they may use less frequently than adults, when they do drink they consume on average 5 drinks on a single occasion. This is binge drinking and can have serious consequences.[7] There is now a "coming of age" ritual to drink 21 shots on your 21st birthday, which of course can be lethal.

Sex, Lies and Alcohol, a Media Education Foundation video[6] discusses several other causes of drinking that come from cultural norms. For men, there is a bravado pressure to "hold your liquor." Boys will consciously work to raise their alcohol tolerance to avoid being called "girl" or "wuss." They also have drinking competitions to see who can drink the most. Girls are socialized on one hand to be good (get good grades, be a virgin, be nice), yet on the other hand, the media airs messages that being "bad" is attractive, sexy and "cool." Alcohol is the perfect solution: be "good" by day and "bad" by night. It is a way to experiment with sex and still be "innocent" by saying, "It was not my fault. The alcohol made me do it."

Share Information with Your Teen

Parents who can share what they know about the many facets of drug abuse and dependency, and who do so in a non-threatening manner can help provide their kids with the information they need to make good decisions for themselves. We now know that

- Kids who start drinking under 15 are 4 times more likely to become addicted. Every day the first drink is delayed is a plus. Age of first use is also associated with a variety of other problems, including early and unwanted pregnancy, depression and suicide. [8]

- Alcohol-dependent teens have impaired memory, altered perception of spatial relationships, and verbal skill deficiency even when not actually drinking.[9]
- Alcohol poisoning can look similar to being drunk. Knowing the difference can save their friends' lives. Signs are confusion, stupor, coma, not responding to pinching of the skin, vomiting or urinating while sleeping, breathing slowly 8 times/minute or breathing irregularly with 10 seconds between breaths, and low body temperature where the skin is cool, clammy and looks pale or somewhat blue. Do not put a friend to bed in this state. Stay with them, protect them from vomiting, and call 911.
- Acquaintance rape is now such a common occurrence that colleges encourage their new students to have buddies who watch out for each other at a party. Teach this system to your teen, even if they aren't planning on drinking. Some girls get so drunk (or are drugged) that they are not even sure what happened when they wake up the next morning.

Understand That Drug Use Exists Along a Continuum from Benign to Crippling

The drug use continuum stretches from abstinence, experimental use, social use, regular use, and problem use to chemical dependency. It is important for anyone who wishes to monitor the results of their own drug use to understand where they lie within the continuum of use. Although most parents would like their kids to choose abstinence, it is unlikely that most kids will choose this path (again look at the rates of use in your community and high schools). Parents can have conversations with their kids about the progressive nature of chemical dependency and about the responsibility of each person to monitor their own drug-using behaviors. Teens can learn that it's OK to get help before they hit bottom. They can choose to learn from their mistakes, change to a different level of drug use, or get into treatment for problem drug behaviors. This is more likely to happen if parents are willing to keep a door open for honest, non-punitive discussions, even if they don't agree with the choices their children have made.

Beautiful Boy: A Father's Journey Through his Son's Addiction gives insight into teen drug abuse. David Sheff recounts how he first found his son using pot at 13 and thought things were OK until he discovered he had lost his son to meth at 18. He shares the long, agonizing struggle to get him back. His 25 year-old son, clean for 2 years, shares his version of the experience in *Tweak,*

including the sordid details of turning to prostitution for drugs and serious infections from dirty needles.

Share Your Values

It is important to be honest about your own values when it comes to drugs. However, sharing values is not the same as imposing them on your children, and "imposing" your values on your kids is impossible anyway. Most importantly, it is critical to model the responsible behaviors you want your child to have with regard to drugs, and to think about long-term strategies that will protect your child. Having a plan to pick up a child who is intoxicated without fear of punishment or reprisals, for example, can save lives. Teaching kids to be responsible with their behaviors must take precedence over controlling their behaviors. Denial creates an environment where kids can be ignorant of the dangers of alcohol and drug use and can be fatal.

Give Teens a Safe Place to Learn from Their Mistakes

The only true way to protect kids from chemical dependency is to allow them a safe place to work out on their own how they feel about using drugs. Kids will either be open about their drug use or they will hide it; much will depend on the relationship they have with their parents. Supporters of connected parenting believe that parents are much more likely to be able to influence their teenagers if they have a respectful, honest, and open relationship with their teen. This includes not over-reacting to a mistake about drug use, respecting the dignity of their teen and having faith in the ability of their teen to learn from their experiences and use what they have learned to help them to make healthy choices.

Foster Emotional Honesty

Emotional honesty helps parents to achieve connection with their teen without trying to control or abandon them. This skill must be learned and practiced. Putting an arm around a teen, admitting your own fears, and asking them to help you understand what is going on for them is not the same as condoning negative behaviors. But it does let the teen know that you love them and are curious about them, and that you respect their ability to process how their behaviors are affecting their own lives. Listening to your teen's point of view does not mean that you agree with them. It DOES mean that you show them that you are interested in understanding their world.

Use Long-Term Parenting Strategies

Parents who are clear about their long-term parenting goals can more easily enact strategies that may be difficult for parents in the short term. Empowerment is a long-term parenting strategy that helps kids develop self-discipline and responsibility. Supporting kids in their strengths and refusing to support them in their weaknesses is the key to empowering teens, especially when it comes to chemical abuse. Another long-term parenting strategy is to decide what YOU will do, discuss this with your child in a kind, firm and non-punitive way, and be especially careful to carry through on your own commitments. This teaches children to be accountable, trustworthy and in charge of their own behaviors, since you are not trying to control theirs.

When it comes to substance abuse, we can parent a bit differently for younger (under 16) versus older (16 and up) teens. Because drugs can be so devastating on a young teen brain, we can use more clear boundaries to delay use every day we can. When our teens are older and autonomy is even more important, clarity, connection and good "coaching" questions to help them think through situations will be more effective tools. Kids appreciate and value your full honesty. Honesty about "Our family rules and values are for health and not doing drugs or alcohol. We also know we can't stop you if you decide to drink or do drugs. That will be your decision. What we can share with you is that every day you wait is better for your brain."

Long-term parenting strategies are not easy, and come only with study, contemplation and practice. The reward is a child who possesses the internal skills to make good choices for themselves when faced by the myriad of bad choices available to them in a free, democratic society.

Don't Rescue or Buffer Children from the Consequences of Their Behaviors

Learning to have faith in teenagers to make their own decisions also means you have to learn not to rescue or buffer them from the negative results of their own choices. Letting children start this learning process early in their lives will mean that they have lots of experience with good decision-making skills before they have easy access to drugs and alcohol. This also means not abandoning them if they do get into trouble. Being a supportive presence while they figure out how to extricate themselves from the mess they have made teaches kids self-discipline and responsibility. Loving kids in spite of their mistakes and not taking their behaviors personally will help kids to navigate the world successfully.

Allow for Differences

It is highly unlikely that your kids will feel just like you do when it comes to drugs and alcohol, primarily because you have had a lifetime of experiences upon which to base your opinions. Your kids also will need life experiences upon which to base their own opinions. Respecting differences will go a long way towards keeping communication open and honest between you.

Show Love and Unconditional Acceptance

The message of love and unconditional acceptance in spite of behaviors or differences can go a long way towards minimizing the effects of drugs and alcohol in the lives of children. Appreciating your child's uniqueness and place in the family can take many forms, but does take some conscious thought.

Some Specific Ideas Helpful to Reduce Substance Abuse and Dangerous Behavior:

- Have your child sign a Contract for Life before they get a driver's license—see last article of this chapter.
- Never let other people's underage kids drink in your home (even at 20). Not only are you potentially encouraging alcohol dependency and damage, you might lose all financial security from a civil lawsuit if something happens to that kid.
- Remove alcohol from your home: Since up to 70% of alcohol comes from kids' homes, remove it from yours (and encourage other families to do the same).
- Let your kid know if there are any incidents with drugs or alcohol there will be a delay of their driver's permit/license.

Create a network of support with other parents, since given our kids' brain development, some might not be able to make sound decisions, even when good information is shared with them. The frontal lobe that gives people the ability to have good judgment and make long-term plans is poorly developed in teens until they are 18-25 years of age. Consider connecting with people with "mature frontal lobes," parents, especially parents of your child's friends. Meet monthly with parents of your child's friends to discuss timely topics. Then if there is "an incident," you have already established trusted relationships. Start this as early as you can, even when kids are in 5th grade.

Host talks through the local high school PTA to share information with other parents. A great panel to present to both parents and kids 6th grade and up is: trauma nurse or doctor[10], lawyer, policeman and representative from your state Liquor Control Commission. One mom found that having her 15-year-old son and his friends attend this panel discussion helped her enforce the "We will not have kids underage drinking in our home" even into the college years. Her son understood the threat of a lawsuit better than the threat to a friend's health.

Community Support to Address Substance Abuse

If "nothing else to do" is a cause of teen drinking, help your community to create safe spaces and teen-friendly activities, like teen-run coffee shops with weekend entertainment by high school performers.

The message teens receive when alcohol advertising is pervasive throughout the community landscape is that drinking is central to a desirable life. Not only is it acceptable, it is expected. The linking of community events to alcohol through sponsorship also sends teens the message that alcohol is integral to fun and community. You can work with others in your town or city to reduce the impact of the alcohol industry on local teens by educating the community and lobbying local government officials to restrict location, content and pervasiveness of outdoor advertising as well as minimizing or eliminating alcohol industry sponsorship of events.

Know When to Get Help

Getting help is a wise investment in a family's health. Few sport teams can thrive without a coach, and there are times when any family may need coaching to learn new skills, see new perspectives and learn from its mistakes. When drug or alcohol use enters into routine, problem or addictive use, families will benefit from help that is available in many forms in the community. Accepting help does not mean failure; it means that a family is dedicated to optimum health for everyone.

Look for the Signs of Addiction, and Get Help

The attitude of an adolescent who is chemically dependent is very different from that of normal teenagers, who have periods of moodiness and unhappiness interspersed with equally long periods of time when they are engaging and happy.

Chemically dependent persons also have difficulty expressing feelings, look for external rather than internal positive strokes, and are willing to continue doing what doesn't work over and over and over. A pattern of thinking and acting in these ways leads to a desire to numb feelings, and drugs and alcohol are often the treatment of choice for such teens. Seeking professional help for chemically dependent teens can be life-saving. Although it would be nice to believe that parents could send kids off for a miracle "cure," it is more likely that the whole family will benefit from family counseling. Chemical dependence develops within a web of relationships at home and in the community; helping your child may entail learning some new ways of relating with each other at home. It is also helpful to have support from a professional with expertise in teen substance abuse and to enlist his or her advice so that you can create a home environment that will facilitate your child's return to sobriety.

If you are concerned about your teen's drug or alcohol use, you can tell your son that you are worried and you want him to give himself honest answers about the following questions that indicate a chemical dependency. It is important to remember that a very common symptom of alcoholism is denial, sometimes lasting decades.

- Do you find yourself lying about your use to friends, family and yourself?
- Are others concerned about your use?
- Do you plan your days around your "next high," at the expense of other things you want to do (schoolwork, friends, and/or sports)?
- Do you use in the morning?
- Can you "handle your liquor" better than your friends?
- Have you had a "run in" with the police?
- Have you continued to use in spite of past problems like fights, lost items, arguments?
- Are you getting drunk/high on a regular basis and experiencing hangovers or "blackouts"—forgetting what you did while using?
- For you, are drugs necessary to have fun?

- Are you feeling run-down and depressed?
- Is alcohol interfering with your life in any way?

If you answered "Yes" to 3 or more of these questions, it is time to get an evaluation from an addiction specialist.

Have Faith

It is important for parents to remember that they themselves are successful survivors of adolescence. Indeed, most teenagers grow up and do not remain as adults who they are as teenagers. Growing up in an empowering and loving environment can make the adolescent journey less harrowing. Parents who have faith in their teens can increase the chances that their teen will avoid a pattern of drug abuse, because they are communicating to their teen faith in their ability to make choices, to learn from their own experiences and to function successfully in this world of many temptations. Trust does not mean sticking your head in the sand. Parents who are able to "let go," not only keep open communication and continue to check in with their teens, but also trust that their teen can handle challenging situations and learn from the mistakes he or she makes. These parents trust that their teen is constantly evolving, growing up into a wonderful person.

Resources:
[1] *Positive Discipline for Teenagers: Resolving Conflict with your Teenage Son or Daughter* (1st Ed), and *Positive Discipline for Teenagers: Empowering your Teen and Yourself Through Kind and Firm Parenting*, 2000 by Jane Nelsen & Lynn Lott.
[2] *Reality Matters: Under the Influence,* Discovery Education, 2005
[3] Grant, BF, *Estimates of US Children exposed to alcohol abuse/dependency in families.* Am J Public Health 90 (1): 112-115.
[4] Dunn ME, Goldman MS, 1998. *Age and drinking related differences in the memory organization of alcohol expectancies in 3rd, 6th, 9th, 12th graders.* Consult Clin Psychol 66 (3): 579-85.
[5] Substance Abuse and Mental Health Services Administration, *2005 National Survey on Drug and Health*
[6] *Sex, Lies and Alcohol* from Media Education Foundation video. See www.mediaed.org for discussion guides.
[7] *The Surgeon General's Call to Action: To Prevent and Reduce Underage Drinking: What It Means to You.* www.surgeongeneral.gov/topics/underagedrinking/FamilyGuide.pdf
[8] Grant, BF, Dawson DA, 1997, *Age of onset of alcohol use and its association with DSM-IV alcohol abuse and dependence:* Results from the National Longitudinal Alcohol Epidemiologic Survey. J Subst Abuse 9: 103-110.
[9] Brown, SA, Tapert SF, Granholm E, Delis, DC, 2000, *Neurocognitive functioning of adolescence: Effect of protracted alcohol use.* Alcohol Clin Exp Res 24 (2): 164-171.
[10] *Not My Kid* Presentation by Legacy's Trauma Nurses Who Talk Tough, www.legacyhealth.org/tntt.

FOR PARENTS TO LOOK AT THEIR OWN USE

Alcoholics Anonymous

Alcoholics Anonymous, Families Anonymous, Al-anon and Alateen are all fantastic support structures for anyone who is struggling with alcohol themselves or alcoholics in their lives.

www.aa.org   www.alanon.org.
www.familiesanonymous.org
www.al-alon.alateen.org/questions.html

Twenty Questions to Evaluate if you're an Alcoholic

www.step12.com/alcoholic-20-questions.html

Take this 20-question test to help you decide whether or not you are an alcoholic.

1. Do you lose time from work due to drinking?
2. Is drinking making your home life unhappy?
3. Do you drink because you are shy with other people?
4. Is your drinking affecting your reputation?
5. Have you ever felt remorse after drinking?
6. Have you ever got into financial difficulties as a result of drinking?
7. Do you turn to lower companions and an inferior environment when drinking?
8. Does your drinking make you careless of your family's welfare?
9. Has your ambition decreased since drinking?
10. Do you crave a drink at a definite time?
11. Do you want a drink the next morning?
12. Does drinking cause you to have difficulty in sleeping?
13. Has your efficiency decreased since drinking?
14. Is drinking jeopardizing your job or business?
15. Do you drink to escape from worries or trouble?
16. Do you drink alone?
17. Have you ever had a complete loss of memory as a result of drinking?
18. Has your physician ever treated you for drinking?
19. Do you drink to build up your self-confidence?
20. Have you ever been to a hospital or institution because of drinking?

What's your score?

- If you have answered YES to any one of the questions, there is a definite warning that you may be an alcoholic.
- If you have answered YES to any two, the chances are that you are an alcoholic.
- If you answered YES to three or more, you are definitely an alcoholic.

Dear Parenting Guide Participant,
You can make an impact in your community! Here is a letter you can encourage to be inserted into your high school's "Back to School" package. It is an effective way to share information and network your high school community to reduce teen drug and alcohol use.

Safe Teen Parties in Your Home: *"It takes a village to raise a child."*

Dear Parents: This note is a vehicle to network our community to work together to reduce the impact of drug and alcohol use in our teens. This sheet addresses common pitfalls. By coming together, we can create a community where substance access and places to have unsupervised parties are reduced. After signing this form, an asterisk will be placed by your teen's name in the student directory to distinguish you as a family who will do your best to keep your home safe from teenage drug/alcohol use.

Thank you,   HS principal _____ and PTA president or HS Safety Committee: _____

- Model respectful use of alcohol and prescription drugs in your home.
- Ideally, remove the alcohol and prescription drugs from your house (up to 70% of alcohol teens use comes from their own home).
- Don't leave teens home alone without adult supervision, especially over the weekend. A party of 80 can happen in 1-2 hours with cell phones.
- If you do go away for the weekend, be sure to ask all of your direct neighbors to keep an eye on the house. Also ask an adult friend your teen likes or a neighbor, if they would support your teen in a dangerous or difficult situation.
- Be aware of where your child is when he/she goes out. Call parents where parties are held.
- Know your teen's friends and his/her parents. Make a point of keeping in touch with these parents. Communicating and connecting with each other is ESSENTIAL. Our kids will benefit if we network as effectively as they do.
- Hold your child accountable for his/her behavior. Many parents remove car privileges when their child abuses alcohol or drugs.
- Do not serve alcohol to other teens in your home. It is not "safer." Teens brains are more susceptible to damage and addiction than adults at all ages up to 21 years-old (especially if <15). Also, if something happens to that teen, you are libel and can lose your assets in a civil lawsuit.

Tips for parents whose teen is planning a party
- Make a guest list and stick to it (uninvited guest are not allowed to attend the party).
- Restrict entry and exit areas to deter guests from bringing in contraband or drinking out in their parked car or from a bottle hidden in the yard.
- Establish one area for coats and bags and monitor it.
- Set a beginning and end time to the party.
- Make it clear to your teen and all the guests that alcohol and other drugs are not allowed. Put away your alcohol, valuables, weapons, and breakables.
- Define an area for the party; do not allow party-goers in other areas (bedrooms, garages, etc.).
- Have sufficient chaperones to monitor the areas and the partygoers. Frequently monitor the party area as well as areas that are off-limits to guests.
- Establish a signal that your child may use if he/she needs help. For example, when your child says, "Sorry I forgot to take out the garbage" on the phone, it can be code for, "Come pick me up right now." Another example is: pulling at his/her ear when asking to spend the night is code for you to say, "No."
- Be prepared to call a guest's parents if he/she appears to be "under the influence" or brings alcohol or drugs to the party.

-------------------------------------Cut here-------------------------------------
PLEASE SIGN HERE AND YOUR FAMILY HOME WILL BE DESIGNATED AS A "SAFE HOME"
I have read the Safe Home guidelines and will do my best to prevent teenage drug and alcohol use in my home. Please put an asterisk by my family's name in the student directory so others will be aware of our commitment.

Name _____ Date _____

Facts about Risky Driving and Graduated Licensing

- The best, most well-intentioned teenager can makes poor decisions and exhibit inappropriate behavior, especially when under the influence of alcohol and other drugs.

- 10,000 sixteen-year-olds die every decade because of driving under the influence of immaturity & inexperience.
- One American teenager dies every three hours in an alcohol- or drug-related crash.
- Approximately 450,000 teens/year are arrested for driving under the influence of intoxicants.
- 67% of fatal teenage crashes had another teen driving.
- Teens can be sued and a 20-year judgment filed.
- Every weeknight from 1 pm-1 am, 1 of 13 drivers are drunk.
- On weekends from 1 am-6 am, 1 of 7 drivers are drunk.
- Remember the highest risk for young drivers is at night or with other teens in their car. This is when peer pressure can lead to immature, dangerous behavior.

Graduated Licensing: Insurance Institute for Highway Safety Recommends:

- 200 hours or 6000 miles to be logged by the teen before they are granted privilege as principle driver.
- Graduated licensing: Systematic & progressive, it limits opportunities for immature behavior. Peer pressure can lead ANY teenager to ignore rules set by adults. The highest risks for young drivers are: driving at night or with other teens in the car. This is when peer pressure is most likely to lead to immature and dangerous behavior. Oregon has a good model for graduated licensing which parents can use with their own family.
- Teach teen passengers to remain awake to help the driver stay alert. Fatigue is a major contributor to car crashes.

Graduated Licensing in Oregon: A Good Example for Everyone

To get this started in your state, contact your state's Department of Motor Vehicles or government officials.

The Law	Beyond the Law
LAW: Six months of driving with a permit.	Parents may want to extend this time frame.
LAW: At least 50 hours of adult-supervised (older than 21) training plus a safety course, or an additional 50 hours of adult-supervised training. Keep a driver's log to document this.	Parents riding with a young driver after 50-100 hours who find they still need to caution the young driver about speed, signals, tailgating, traffic conditions, weather conditions, etc., may want to increase the hours of supervised driving.
LAW: In the first six months, a teen can carry no one younger than 20-years-old, except immediate family.	It might be safer without siblings as they may be the hardest to control of ALL. Reminder: Licensing a teen to make life more convenient for parents is not advisable.
LAW: In the second six months, a teen can carry no more than three passengers younger than 20, except family.	When adding passengers, parents can expand beyond the law to allow ONLY ONE passenger for three months and add additional passengers SLOWLY.
LAW: Curfew between midnight and 5:00 am unless it is work-related, to or from a school event, or with a licensed driver 25 or older.	47% of crashes involving teenage drivers occur between 9:00 pm and 6:00 am.

Reprinted with permission from the *"NOT MY KID"* Campaign Parent Handbook. Materials and Program made possible through funds from ODOT, TSD and NSTSA Section 410 Grant, and "Trauma Nurses Talk Tough: Family Education." www.legacyhealth.org/tntt

Contract for Life

A Foundation for Trust and Caring
This Contract is designed to facilitate communication between young people and their parents about potentially destructive decisions related to alcohol, drugs, peer pressure, and behavior. The issues facing young people today are often too difficult for them to address alone. SADD believes that effective parent-child communication is critically important in helping young adults to make healthy decisions.

Young Person
I recognize that there are many potentially destructive decisions I face every day and commit to you that I will do everything in my power to avoid making decisions that will jeopardize my health, my safety and overall well-being, or your trust in me. I understand the dangers associated with the use of alcohol and drugs and the destructive behaviors often associated with impairment.

By signing below, I pledge my best effort to remain free from alcohol and drugs; I agree that I will never drive under the influence; I agree that I will never ride with an impaired driver; and I agree that I will always wear a seat belt in a moving car.

Finally, I agree to call you if I am ever in a situation that threatens my safety and to communicate with you regularly about issues of importance to both of us.

_____

Young Person

Parent (or Caring Adult)
I am committed to you and to your health and safety. By signing below, I pledge to do everything in my power to understand and communicate with you about the many difficult and potentially destructive decisions you face.

Further, I agree to provide for you safe, sober transportation home if you are ever in a situation that threatens your safety and to defer discussions about that situation until a time when we can both have a discussion in a calm and caring manner.*

I also pledge to you that I will not drive under the influence of alcohol or drugs, I will always seek safe, sober transportation home, and I will always wear a seat belt.

_____

Parent/Caring Adult

Editors Note: We have permission to use the contract as it is written above. Consider altering it to offer your teen an "unconditional" ride home. Perhaps even make an arrangement with a cab company or a caring neighbor to drive him or her home. If safety is your top priority, do not put up any barriers that would decrease the chance of your teens taking you up on your offer to get home safely.

Reprinted with permission of SADD, Inc. SADD–Students Against Destructive Decisions is "students helping students make positive decisions about challenges in their everyday life" with many great resources at www.sadd.org.

Supporting Him 9

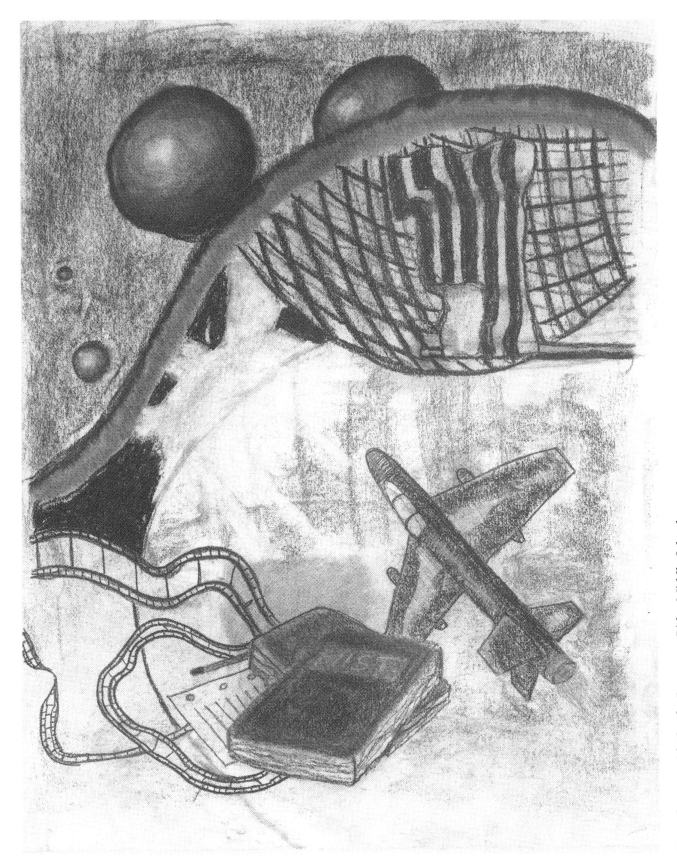

Tom Flannery, 6th Grade, Rosemont Ridge Middle School

Supporting Him

> "To the world you may be one person, but to one person you may be the world." —Heather Cortez
>
> "I love you not only for what you are, but for what I am when I am with you. I love you not only for what you have made of yourself, but for what you are making of me. I love you for the part of me that you bring out."
> —Elizabeth Barrett Browning
>
> "Physical fitness is not only one of the most important keys to a healthy body;
> it is the basis of dynamic and creative intellectual challenge." —John F. Kennedy
>
> "Sports are a double-edged sword. They can do our children a lot of good or a lot of harm. They can give them a sense of belonging, character, self-esteem, and good health. Or they can cripple them in body, warp them in mind, teach them bad values, and lead to a crushing sense of failure."
> —Steve Biddulph, author of *Raising Boys*

GOALS

- To understand the value of "safe havens" where your son can be his authentic self and be accepted

- To appreciate the value of including other adults in life of your son's life and the benefits of rites of passage celebrations

- To see sports activities and exercise as a way to achieve physical fitness, mental and emotional well-being, and to encourage all boys to do some form of exercise

- To encourage trainings where coaches and parents can learn about developmentally appropriate expectations, making sports fun, and the importance of encouraging all athletes equally

- To encourage team sports where team work, discipline, and sense of fair play are more important than winning

OVERVIEW

Connected, engaged, and committed communities and families are more likely to raise kids who are resilient and successful at transitioning from adolescence to adulthood. Strengthening the connections and commitments between children and adults within a community supports the healthy development of all our children and is the cornerstone of the Search Institute's Developmental Asset program. One way that parents can build assets in their son's life is to make sure that he becomes involved in supportive community activities that involve cooperation, build on his strengths, and expose him to a diversity of people of all ages, races, abilities and genders. By encouraging honest and healthy relationships with others, parents can help their sons build positive visions of themselves, their capabilities and their futures as valued members of a caring community.

This chapter focuses on supporting our sons within their community by involving them in support groups, mentoring relationships, coming of age rituals, fitness and sports. These activities share in common an opportunity for your son to develop genuine, caring and honest relationships with himself, as well as with others in his community. A boy can feel both acceptance and a strong sense of belonging when he becomes an essential part of a team effort, a community ritual, a special relationship, or a group that meets regularly to share some kind of mutual hobby or interest. This strengthens his ability to know and trust himself and to be honest, genuine and comfortable in his relationships with others. This really pays off during adolescence, when a child's ability to make good choices depends upon having a strong sense of self, a positive view of his place in the world, and a safety net of valued, involved mentors who can help him set a course of moderation through stormy adolescent waters.

Support Groups

Support groups for boys take many forms and can be created by anyone with a sincere desire to engage boys in enjoyable and enriching activities. Such support groups provide a safe haven for boys to bond, interact and have fun together, while encouraging positive values and healthy relationships. Group activities geared specifically for boys can be found within child advocacy organizations such as the Boy Scouts of America, Camp Fire, and the YMCA. Younger boys especially seem to like the activities and camps offered by these organizations. However, since children often lose interest as they mature, it may be up to you to find or create an appropriate support group for your son.

William Pollack, author of *Real Boys,* reminds us that boys open up and talk more freely when they are doing something active. Groups that incorporate physical activities within their format will likely be more successful than those that focus just on talking; building trust and revealing feelings can go slowly for boys. Here are some good activity ideas for boys:

- Blindfold sundaes: one partner directs their blindfolded partner to build an ice cream sundae.
- Trust walk: each partner leads his blindfolded partner through an obstacle course.
- Self-portrait: they build a collage about what they like about themselves.
- Friend collage: an outline of a boy is drawn on a large sheet of paper. The boys work in groups of 3 to fill in the "body" with magazine pictures that represent characteristics of a good friend.

Any group that meets regularly over time can become an important source of support, acceptance and enrichment for your son.

What we have noticed is that many women—from teen to elderly—have stepped up to run Girls' Empowerment Groups over the last fifteen years. People are seeing the benefit to the girls and wanting the same support for our boys. Our boys are struggling with the "boy code," sharing emotions, anger outbursts, and poor school performance. There is clearly a need for "safe havens" for boys where they can be themselves. However, right now there seems to be more need than availability. One problem is that boys don't overtly show us that they want to talk, with their "tough guise" bravado. Another is that men who may be the ideal leaders are uncomfortable sharing their own feelings, let alone being able to lead action-oriented boys to share their feelings. Another is that we adults are not even sure we can get boys to talk with us. In the article **"Listening to Boys"** (p. 9: 14) Howard Hiton, a therapist who specializes in boys issues, had to get over his preconceived notion that the boys probably would NOT talk to him. The boys were "bribed" into the group with pizza (always a good idea) and then he was pleasantly surprised when these high-risk boys were not only open about some very difficult topics, but they wanted more.

Howard Hiton went on to write a curriculum on how to support boys in school (see Chapter 6). He and co-authors Peter Mortola and Stephen Grant then created a fabulous model for boys' empowerment groups that honors their need for movement, as described in **"BAM! Boys Advocacy and Mentoring: A Strengths-Based Support Group for Boys"** (p. 9:15). Their book, *BAM! Advocacy and Mentoring Leader's Guide to Facilitating Strengths-Based Groups for Boys: Helping Boys Make Better Contact by Making Better Contact with Them,* provides fantastic support for facilitators. They also provide trainings at www.BAM.com.

The Boys Council (www.boyscouncil.org) is also a wonderful source of ideas for running boys' groups. For 9- to 14-year-old boys' groups, they offer:
- Growing Healthy, Going Strong
- Standing Together: A Boys Council Journey into Respect.

For 13-18 year old boys' groups, they offer:
- Living a Legacy: A Boys Council Rite of Passage.

We expect to see more books and programs as this idea of supporting boys to be themselves spreads.

Mother-son groups can be particularly fun and provide mothers with a means to connect to their sons: for example, hiking, biking, or swimming together, having a cookout, going to movies and discussing them, or going to watch a sporting event as a group. Mother-son book clubs are a great way to stay connected to your son and provide community for him and for yourself, as described in **"Sense of Belonging: Mother-Son Book Club"** (p. 9:16). Reading some of the book aloud with your family might ease the task for sons who are not in the habit of reading for pleasure. *Great Books for Boys* has a wonderful list of books to choose from.

Parents or adults who are willing to commit to an activity with a group of boys over time can have an enormously positive impact on the lives of these boys by simply caring about them and sharing life's lessons. Such groups also offer adults a way to get to know their sons and neighborhood youth better. For example, discussions that occur at a parent-child activity can be a great tool for parents to better understand how their son and his friends view the world. Hiking, biking or sports clubs that meet after school or on the weekends can be very popular with boys, and are a fun way to share physical activity. Churches and synagogues often have youth groups and activities already in place and they generally welcome kids from their community regardless of religious denomination. You can get a feel for the flavor of any established program by talking to the leaders and with the families already involved in the program. **"Safe Havens: Support Groups for Youth"** (p. 9:17) reviews many ways that we can help our boys get involved in groups in the community where they feel accepted for who they are.

School remains another arena where boys benefit from additional support, especially if they are in an environment where bullying or aggression is a problem. Lunchtime activities, clubs, intramural sports and after-school activities sponsored by the school or by interested parents can be an exceptional way to give kids a place to feel at home and to bond to school and to other teens. Since bonding to school is a critical protective factor for teens, it is wise for parents to encourage their children to take advantage of extracurricular activities at school. Finding or creating supportive group activities within your community in which your son can participate may take some creativity and time, but the rewards of giving your son a sense of belonging far outweigh the effort.

Mentoring
The Search Institute has shown that young people do better if they have 3 or more non-parent adults in their lives from whom they receive support, care, guidance and advocacy. Other organizations have demonstrated similar findings. The Big Brothers/Big Sisters of America found that young people with mentors are about one-half as likely to use illegal drugs or skip school and about

one-quarter as likely to use alcohol. Unfortunately, few of our culture's youth benefit from adult mentoring. A 1997 Multnomah County, Oregon survey of 10,000 youth found that only one-quarter of kids surveyed could identify an adult they looked up to as a role model, and 6 in 10 had no adults other than parents involved in their lives. These results correlate closely with the Search Institute's national findings in their Developmental Asset research.

A mentor can be any caring adult who makes an active, positive contribution to the life of a child who is not his or her own. A mentor can be anyone who has experienced life and who cares enough to pass their own lessons along to a young person in a supportive way. A mentor is a friend, a guide, a coach. He or she may be a grandma, an uncle, a neighbor, a co-worker, a sport coach, a family friend, or someone down the street who shares an interest with your child. Sometimes mentoring relationships develop naturally, other times, not. Parents may need to actively seek out an appropriate adult and set up a formal mentoring relationship for their son. This may feel awkward at first, but the rewards are manifold.

Stan Crow trains people all over the US on mentoring and rites of passage programs and helps run the Rites of Passage Journeys program in Washington. He has written the following two articles on the importance of mentoring adolescents: **"The Role of a Mentor"** and **"The Stance of a Mentor"** (pp. 9:19-20). Mr. Crow eloquently defines a mentor is a "journey master, one who takes a measure of responsibility for this other person." **"Teenagers Can Be Mentors, Too"** (p. 9:21) reminds us that teenagers can feel the same sense of competence, generosity, and meaning that we feel when they mentor younger children. Mentoring also helps teens escape from social and academic pressures and remember how to play. Finding a way to become personally involved with youth and parents within your community as a mentor will enrich your own life and your teen's life, as well as the lives of others in your community.

Coming of Age Rituals

Parents may wonder why coming of age rituals are presented here as a way to support your son's development.

"Cherishing Teens Reconnects Communities: The Power of Coming of Age Celebrations" (p. 9:22) reviews the historical and modern-day importance of these rituals. Most indigenous societies from around the globe mark the passage of their members from the world of childhood into the benefits, freedoms, restrictions and responsibilities of adulthood with some sort of community ritual. Traditionally a coming of age ritual has been an important milestone for youth. In the process, young people understand that they are an important member of a larger community and experience within themselves a newfound capacity for increased decision-making, responsibility, and accountability for their own actions. Our American melting pot has resulted in the loss of any common ritual that marks the beginning of a boy's journey towards manhood and that establishes him as an important member of our society. Boys, however, yearn for proof of their manhood. As a result, young men have largely replaced community coming of age rituals with ones of their own creation: rituals that tend to be harmful and/or dangerous. Activities such as smoking, using drugs, getting drunk, sexually exploiting women, using firearms, driving unsafely and more tend to be used as proof of manhood. Unfortunately, these behaviors are often carried out without community sanction and without any thought as to the impact on self or others. Wouldn't it be better to acknowledge the milestone of emerging manhood in our sons by creating a ritual that surrounds our boys with caring men and family members and by helping our sons to see themselves as capable, compassionate and responsible?

One of the few examples of a coming of age ritual that has survived through the ages in America is the Jewish faith's practice of Bar Mitzvah. This ceremony initiates boys into their faith as full-fledged members at age 13, requiring a period of study, reflection and instruction prior to the ceremony. Parents of other faiths may have to create their own coming of age rituals to mark one of their son's special birthdays or milestones. Two families describe their unique ways to welcome their son into young adulthood in the articles **"Bar Gaia"** (p. 9:24), which is about climbing a challenging mountain, and **"Building Community for Our Sons: A Coming of Age Celebration"** (p. 9:25) about a coming of age book written by relatives and family friends. Some extended families have used annual father-son-uncle-cousin camping trips to initiate their boys as they turn 13. During the course of the trip, the older men and teens welcome youth by sharing on topics such as intimacy, power, heroes, fears, dreams, work and women and by bestowing blessings. **"Boy Psychology/Man Psychology"** (p. 9:27) introduces a definition for mature masculinity and four forms of mature masculine energy we can share with our sons: King, Warrior, Magician, and Lover.

There are many ways in which teens can experience this transition; other examples include a special gathering of mentors who pledge to support a boy in his passage to adulthood. This could involve a father/son wilderness adventure, a year-long study and support group, a church-sponsored program, or a specially designed experience offered by an organization which specializes in rites of passage for youth, as described in the articles **"Finding a New Skin: Rites of Passage from Child to Youth"** and **"Collective Work"** (p. 9:28-29). **"Lessons from Nature"** (p. 9:31) explores how rites of passage and life milestones can be enhanced by learning lessons from the natural world.

Finding a coming of age ritual that fits within your own family circumstances and is reflective of your son's personality is a work of creativity and love. Your son may not understand or fully appreciate the significance of such a ritual in the moment, but in the long run, it will become a valuable memory and a reminder, not only of the caring community of support that surrounds him, but of the strength and goodness of his own special place in the world.

Fitness

Healthy boys are physically active boys. However, in this period in history, we have seen drastic reductions in physical education programs nationwide and the cutting of P.E. out of school curriculums altogether. Our modeling and encouragement of fitness in our families is especially crucial. We can support our sons by cultivating their interest in living an active life. Families, communities, and schools all play a role in teaching our

sons that their bodies were made to move. Families are in the best position to cultivate their son's athletic interest by being active together (e.g., tossing a ball, swimming, biking, playing tennis, roller blading), spending lots of time outdoors, giving him equipment of his own, taking him to sporting events, limiting screen time, and promoting an active life for fun and fitness rather than competition. Remember that the experiences our sons have in the first 12 years of their lives become part of their self-identification: "I enjoy doing ... I am good at ..." This section will discuss the importance of fitness to boys' self-esteem and health, life lessons that sports convey to our sons, using sports as a vehicle for good communication, getting the most out of organized sports while avoiding the pitfalls, and tips for coaches.

The article **"Family Fitness"** (p. 9:32) reminds us that there are many avenues to experience the growth, health, and transformation that can come from physical activities. Families can guide their children in various ways to be physically active: active lifestyle, outside play, fitness programs, individual sports and team sports, to name a few. The article **"Growing Back into Our Bodies"** (p. 9: 33) describes the way that sports, organized or individual, can help our sons to deepen their mind-body connection and sometimes their connection to nature as well. One way to help our boys to keep fit is to enroll them in organized sports. These adult-run teams and leagues can offer a myriad of benefits to our boys. However, there are many other options other than organized, competitive team sports. They include encouraging the development of sports that tend to be "life-long" fitness activities such as running, golf, swimming, tennis and biking. Parents can find out what kinds of non-competitive sports are available in their community. Club sports, intramural leagues, recreational leagues, the YWCA, and parent- or student-led activity groups are a few alternatives to more organized sports. **"What Tae Kwan Do Can Do"** (p. 9: 34) encourages us to examine all the great alternative exercise programs our community offers. One way to find the kinds of fitness or sports activities that would be right for your son is to really listen to his thoughts about what inspires and motivates him. In fact, talking about his sports can be a wonderful vehicle to improve your communication with your son. **"Tell Me More:**

Connecting through Sport Talk" (p. 9:35) gives parents specific ways to enhance communication with their children that will work with any topic of discussion.

Organized sports have largely displaced the more informal neighborhood "pick up games" of the past, where young kids spent hours playing, making up and enforcing their own rules, and generally spending time together learning about each other and fair play. Informal games organized by the boys who played them required and encouraged the development of leadership, collaboration, compromise and sportsmanship. Today when sports are not organized by adults, most boys don't even seem to consider the possibility that they can organize their own informal games. However, some children will take this on. Be grateful if your child is one who does, and encourage any steps towards this peer-generated play, as the skills that are developed and practiced will be beneficial through life. In one neighborhood, a 10-year-old boy created an informal weekly neighborhood hockey game. The kids got to make up and negotiate their own rules and settle conflicts with peer mediation, which reminds us that the benefits of the pick up games of the past need not be lost in contemporary culture. Because organized sports are recruiting and attracting children at younger ages, it is becoming more difficult to find children being active of their own accord in a spirit of joyful, active play among peers. "Sports Clubs Can Lead to Lifelong Enjoyment" (p. 9:37) is about a mom who did not want to spend family time at long baseball games and practices, so she started a baseball sports club after school one day a week. This reminds us that we parents can support our kids to create their own sports clubs that are truly family-friendly and fun.

Organized Sports

Organized sports are, by far, today's most utilized method of keeping boys fit. Participation in organized sports has potential to be a vehicle for healthy child development. At their best, sports programs promote:

• better overall fitness
• responsible social behavior
• greater academic success
• confidence in one's physical abilities
• appreciation of personal health and fitness

• strong social bonds between individuals and with institutions.

The discipline and work ethic that sports require can be of benefit throughout one's life. Sports provide a venue for helping young people work toward an ethical understanding of fair play, sportsmanship, integrity and compassion. In fact, the arena of sports offers boys a place where they can experience and express a full spectrum of emotions, from exhilaration and joy to frustration, anger and disappointment within a context where it is socially acceptable. This is very liberating for boys who feel that anger is the only socially acceptable emotion to express. Sports programs can create positive life learning environments so that children grow to understand that benefits can be derived from losing, including resilience, reflection and creating new goals. Athletes can come to understand that effort is a key component to any competition, and the outcome is less important than how one reacts in response to a win or a loss. Social bonding between boys on a team can be a life-changing experience and the sense of self confidence earned through sports can positively influence how a boy feels about himself in all other areas of his life.

Honor the Athlete/Honor the Game

Though the benefits of gaining life skills, physical fitness, athletic skills and social skills make organized sports seem ideal, sports can be double-edged swords for our boys. There is much in the world of organized sport which is less than ideal.

Now that organized sports begin at such a young age there tends to be a trend towards earlier attrition due to "burn out." This quitting of organized team play is well underway by age 10 and peaks at ages 14-15, such that 50% of all sports participants will drop out by the time they reach early adolescence. The number one reason that kids leave sports is that "it isn't fun anymore." Elementary school-aged children are developing a cognitive understanding of complex concepts such as the difference between ability, task difficulty and effort, offensive and defensive strategies, teamwork, and the fact that losing does not mean failure. Children whose parents and coaches focus on skill development, rather than strictly on "winning", during the childhood years attain the positive social, emotional and physical outcomes that we all want to see. Therefore, early childhood involvement in sports should emphasize instruction more than competition and should be based on fostering a love of physical fitness and enjoyment of "the game."

Professional sports organizations often promote youth sports. This allows kids to have uniforms and increases the number of kids able to participate. Yet parents need to consider the motivation behind this support. Professional sport organizations, including college sports, are largely commercial, profit-making enterprises concerned with the bottom line. As such, they are constantly concerned with creating the next generation of sports consumers. It is well known in the sports industry that the best method of creating fans is to hook young athletes through participation in youth sports, most of which are played in childhood, but only "watched" as adults. Parents need to recognize that their young athletes may be considered consumers by these professional organizations.

It is easy to get caught up in teams which are overzealous and overstress the need to win. Experiences on teams or in leagues like this can be especially harmful to youth. Sanctioned brutality and aggression, being coerced to play despite injuries, shaming and humiliating by coaches, tolerance for treating officials with disrespect, vilifying the opposing team, mandatory, demanding schedules that ignore the child's need for family time, homework time and "down time" can be devastatingly detrimental to our boys. No child benefits from feeling that their parents' or their friends' approval is tied to success in sports. On the contrary, our children benefit from playing the game for its own sake. Parents who have a talented child at the elite level are particularly susceptible to getting caught up in the craziness of the demands of a coach, team or league. Part of the rationale to "push" their son is sometimes the possibility of earning scholarships. Yet, prolonged training seasons and high intensity training to produce optimal performance outcomes often has an opposite effect. The data on burnout and attrition support the contention that for almost all young athletes, such periods of intensive training have no justifiable physiological, psychological or educational benefits.

The article "Teaching Independence and Responsibility versus Compliance and Conformity" (p. 9:38) comes from "The Role of Sports in Youth Development," a fantastic collection of articles published from a meeting convened by the Carnegie Corporation of NY. It echoes concerns about organized sports placing too much emphasis on winning and not enough on the physical and psychological development of the players. It pays to look carefully at your son's sports programs to be sure they are teaching the values that are important to you. Parents, coaches and the media can help decrease socially unacceptable aggressive behaviors in athletes by promoting commendable behaviors in athletes, by refusing to glorify violent athletes and their behaviors, and by resisting the promotion of hostility between teams. Holding student athletes personally accountable for their actions is another especially important tenant of a healthy sports program. High school athletes are often required to sign contracts saying they will not use drugs or alcohol during the season, which supports them in making good choices. Parents can enhance the quality of sports programs by actively insisting that these positive qualities be incorporated into the structure of their sons' team-sport programs.

Tips for a Positive Coaching Experience

Another index of the quality of a child's experience in youth sports is determined by the competence of the coach. Unfortunately, the vast majority of youth sport coaches do not have the essential skills that are prerequisites for coaching young athletes. Coaching youth requires not only knowledge of specific skill development for the sport in question, but also an awareness of how to effectively work with children in order to inspire and motivate them while keeping the "big picture" of fun, movement and improvement toward mastery in mind. Most coaches are volunteers with little formal training. This, coupled with a turnover rate estimated at 50% per year, leads to many problems with coaches and coaching every year. Despite this, excellent coaches do exist. In the article "Learning Life Lessons through Sports" (p. 9:41), we hear from one dad coach who recognizes that sports and fitness activities can be used as tools for learning lifelong lessons. He talks about learning that team-building, working effectively with others, encouraging one another, and "winning is just a byproduct of success" are all lessons that can be learned through team experience. There are organizations that help to train coaches to work effectively and appropriately with young athletes. Organizations such as the **"Positive Coaching Alliance"** (p. 9:42) have been developed to help coaches and parents "create a positive culture around youth sports." Workshops are carried out by this organization in many cities around the nation for both coaches and parents to help adults create programs where kids will experience practices and games as fun and where kids can tap into a joy of playing that will last a lifetime. You are encouraged to use **"Asset-Building Ideas for Coaches"** (p. 9:44) as a handout to share with your child's coaches and coaching association in order to inspire the development of this kind of awareness among the coaches in your community.

Parents have a powerful role in establishing a healthy lifestyle of fitness and sport in their son's life. Through modeling a lifelong commitment to exercise and physical wellbeing, parents do much of the work to ensure that their son will follow suit. Cultivating the spirit of play, age-appropriate skill building, and healthy attitudes toward winning allows our boys to utilize sports as a positive avenue of growth, learning and well-being. Whether your son is involved in an organized competitive sports program or not, a critical message for him to receive early in life is that moving his body vigorously and often will allow him to thrive. Being fit will inspire a joyful life in which he will be able to fully offer his gifts to the world.

THE 40 DEVELOPMENTAL ASSETS Essential to Every Young Person's Success

The 40 Developmental Assets are research proven building blocks that support the healthy development of our youth and help them to grow up to be caring and responsible. The topics in Supporting Him—support groups, coming of age rituals, mentoring, and sports—relate directly to over half of the assets, both internal and external. What you can do is focus on supporting him with external assets that can lead to the blossoming of internal assets.

- Asset #1 **Family support:** Family life provides high levels of love and support.
- Asset #3 **Other adult relationships:** Young person receives support from three or more nonparent adults.
- Asset #5 **Caring school climate:** School provides a caring, encouraging environment.
- Asset #7 **Community values youth:** Young person perceives that adults in the community value youth.
- Asset #10 **Safety:** Young person feels safe at home, school, and in the neighborhood.
- Asset #14 **Adult role models:** Parent(s) and other adults model positive, responsible behavior.
- Asset #15 **Positive peer influence:** Young person's best friends model responsible behavior.
- Asset #18 **Youth programs:** Young person spends three or more hours per week in sports, clubs, or organizations at school and/or in the community.
- Asset #28 **Integrity:** Young person acts on convictions and stands up for her or his beliefs.
- Asset #29 **Honesty:** Young person "tells the truth even when it is not easy."
- Asset #30 **Responsibility:** Young person accepts and takes personal responsibility.
- Asset #33 **Interpersonal competence:** Young person has empathy, sensitivity, and friendship skills.
- Asset #35 **Resistance skills:** Young person can resist negative peer pressure and dangerous situations.
- Asset #36 **Peaceful conflict resolution:** Young person seeks to resolve conflict nonviolently.
- Asset #37 **Personal power:** Young person feels he or she has control over "things that happen to me."
- Asset #38 **Self-esteem:** Young person reports having a high self-esteem.
- Asset #39 **Sense of purpose:** Young person reports that "my life has a purpose."

CIRCLE QUESTION

Is there a group your son belongs to where he can be his authentic self?
Are there other groups you know about that might be valuable for him?

POSSIBLE DISCUSSION QUESTIONS

1. Would you consider starting a BAM group, Boy's Council or a parent-son group?
2. Who are the adults your son can talk to about important issues and questions? How can you create a sense of extended family that brings many other adults into your children's lives?
3. Share activities in your community that you think are powerful for supporting our youth?
4. Describe important adults in your life when you were growing up and their influence on you.
5. Does your son have Developmental Asset *#3 Other Adults Relationships: Young person receives support from three or more nonparent adults* (53% of 150,000 surveyed) or *#4 Caring Neighborhood: Young person experiences caring neighbors* (37% of 150,000 surveyed)?
6. How can your son benefit from having other adults in his life? Does this idea bring up hesitations or resistance for you?
7. Did you have a coming of age experience? How might a coming of age event benefit your son? How do think you might organize a ceremony or event for your son?
8. How do you model fitness for son?
9. What can you do to maximize family activities for bonding and fitness? Share what you do now. Does your family spend more time watching sports (including watching your child) or actively participating in sports?
10. What physical activities is your son involved in?
11. Are his activities teaching him teamwork, sportsmanship, integrity, compassion, and sense of fair play, as well as skill development.
12. Discuss examples of adult conduct you have seen before, during, and after a youth sporting event.
13. Are you consistently modeling the moral and ethical behavior you want your son to exhibit? Do you help your son see the positive values to both winning and losing?
14. Are there coaching clinics available in your area? Does your league use these services? What will you do to promote healthy coach-parent-youth athlete relationships on the next team your son is on?
15. Discuss the way the media covers athletics in your area. Are there changes you would like to see?
16. Do you make a point to attend field trips, academic events, and school social gatherings as well as your child's athletic events? How does your support for athletic and academic success differ?

PUTTING IT INTO PRACTICE

- Show boys—your own and others you know—you care about them:
  - Look at and greet every boy you see.
  - Talk with boys about their interests.
  - Give boys your time.
  - Invite a young person to an activity you think they might enjoy.
  - Welcome neighborhood kids and your son's friends into your home.
- Make a point of getting to know the people in your neighborhood.
- Plan events with neighborhood families: games, picnics, camping trips, bike rides, and hikes.

- Start a boy's group with your son and some of his friends.
- Take part in youth-serving programs through schools, community organizations and churches.
- Invite caring adults into your son's life.
- Imagine and create a coming of age ceremony for your son and enact it.
- Model healthy exercise habits and eat a balanced diet. Have healthy, easy snack foods available.
- Help your son start a low-key sport club in your neighborhood.
- Attend your son's academic, music and art interests with the same vigor you attend his sporting events.
- Find alternative exercise/sports activities if your son does not excel at the traditional ball sports, such as dance, yoga, rock-climbing, kayaking, martial arts. Make daily physical activity a family priority and exercise or play a sport with your son often.
- Plan a meeting of parents and coaches to discuss expectations that the coach has of the parents and the players and what the players and parents expect of the coaches (e.g., subjects can include playing time, parent behavior, rules, sportsmanship, etc.).
- Talk to other parents or coaches who are yelling inappropriately to the referees or players.
- Deal with problems with your son's team or coaching experience EARLY.
- Find out what kinds of coaching clinics are available in your area and find ways to have your son's coaches attend.
- Evaluate your values concerning pro sports and help keep them in proper perspective for your son.
- If you have limited time, show him he is important by interacting directly with him off the field, rather than watching from the sidelines. Remember it is OK to not attend every game, especially if you need time alone or need to exercise yourself.

PUTTING IT TOGETHER—YOUR VERSION

Write down three or four ideas you have been inspired to implement in your own life after reading and discussing this chapter.

1. _____

2. _____

3. _____

4. _____

FURTHER READING

Empowerment Groups

BAM! Boy's Mentoring and Advocacy by Howard Hiton, Stephen Grant and Peter Mortolla at www.BAM.com

The Boy's Council at www.boyscouncil.org

Great Books for Boys: More than 600 Books for Boys 2-14 by Kathleen Odean

Parent-Son Book Clubs

Challenges: A Young Man's Journal for Self-Awareness and Personal Planning by Mindy Bingham, Judy Edmondson, and Sandy Stryker.

Mentoring

Connect 5: Finding the Caring Adults You May Not Realize Your Teen Needs by Kathleen Kimball-Baker

Big Brothers/Big Sisters of America: Little Moments, Big Magic. Contact (215) 567-7000 or www.bbbsa.org
Mentor promotes, advocates and is a resource for mentors and mentoring initiatives worldwide at www.mentoring.org

Rites of Passage
Boy Into Man: A Father's Guide to Initiation of Teenage Sons by Bernard Weiner
Crossroads: The Quest for Contemporary Rites of Passage by Louise Carus Mahdi, Nancy Christopher, and Michael Meade
Nature and the Human Soul: Cultivating Wholeness and Community in a Fragmented World by Bill Plotkin
Betwixt and Between: Patterns of Masculine and Feminine Initiations by Louise Carus Mahdi, Steven Foster, and Meredith Little
Rites of Passage Journeys at www.ritesofpassagejourneys.org
Prairie Star Coming of Age Program. Contact Beth Brownfield at bethbrown@aol.com
Coming of Age: Deepening Ties within Your Congregation at uucoa@mac.com

Fitness and Sports
Dr. Rob's Guide to Raising Fit Kids: A Family-Centered Approach to Achieving Optimal Health by Robert Gotlin, DO
Your Active Child: How to Boost Physical, Emotional, and Cognitive Development Through Age-Appropriate Activity by Rae Pica
The Role of Sports in Youth Development, a fantastic collection of articles published from a meeting convened by the Carnegie Corporation of NY (including one in this book "Teaching Independence and Responsibility versus Compliance and Conformity")
The Double Goal Coach: Positive Coaching Tools for Honoring the Game and Developing Winners in Sports and Life by Jim Thompson, Positive Coaching Alliance at www.positivecoach.org
Learning To Play, and Playing To Learn by Charlie Steffens and Spencer Gorin
Whose Game Is It, Anyway?: A Guide to Helping Your Child Get the Most from Sports, Organized by Age and Stage by Richard Ginsburg, Stephen Durant, and Amy Baltzell
Sports Without Pressure by E. Margenau
Why Johnny Hates Sports by Fred Engh

Books and Movies for Boys
Rites of Passage
Author! Author! by Susan Terris
Borderlands by Peter Carter

Fitness
Into Thin Air by Jon Krakauer (mountain climbing)
It's Not About the Bike by Lance Armstrong (bike racing)

Movies
"Finding Forester"	"Jerry Maguire"
"Remember the Titans"	"Cutting Edge"
"Rudy"	"Chariots of Fire"
"Hoosiers"	"Bad News Bears"
"Hoop Dreams"	"Breaking Away"
"Basketball Diaries"	"Field of Dreams"
"Coach Carter"	"Karate Kid"

Listening to Boys: An Interview with Howard Hiton

By Julie Salmon

PUT A GROUP OF adolescent boys in a room with one male adult. Ask them a bunch of serious questions about girls, sexual behavior, dating and teen pregnancy. Think you'll get any serious answers? No way, you say?

Think again.

A local County Health Department gave Howard Hiton, a Licensed Professional Counselor, exactly this assignment over the past year. In an effort to update a video on male sexual health, they contacted Hiton to do a series of focus groups with at-risk teenage boys, to get boys more concerned about teenage pregnancy prevention. As the boys started talking, however, they revealed much more.

The questions they were asked—"Where do you get your information on sexuality, dating, and relationships with girls? Who do you perceive as credible sources? How can we get boys better involved? We started to get information that was broader and deeper than expected, yet equally important and interesting."

Hiton first discovered that among the boys "mistrust of girls was a pervasive theme." The boys said things like, "Girls dress older than they are, so don't trust them. If a girl tells you she's on birth control, don't trust her. If she tells you she's pregnant and it's your child, don't believe it. Get a paternity test." Hiton said he thinks this mistrust and misunderstanding of girls demonstrates the need for more cross-gender dialogue. Boys and girls need to be able to talk to each other in a structured way so that boys can better understand girls. Continued mistrust will hinder developing trusting relationships, as well as allow boys to abdicate responsible sexual behavior.

Next, Hiton found these kids focused almost exclusively on the short-term consequences of their sexual behavior. Instead of concern about pregnancy, they admitted to feeling more worried about "getting caught" by their mother, or their girlfriend's mother, when engaging in sex. Only after the fact does concern about long-range consequences—like pregnancy or sexually-transmitted diseases—come into play. Most of the boys, moreover, wanted to know the "real deal" concerning long-term consequences. "They want to talk to other boys who have become fathers. They want to see pictures of STDs (sexually transmitted diseases). That's what they want, and anything less than that just doesn't speak to them."

Hiton's most compelling discovery was that these boys really wanted to talk. When first approached with this assignment, Hiton thought, "I'll do this, but I don't think a group of boys sitting in a group are going to talk about this. That was the big learning point for me because here I am this advocate for boys, and a man myself, yet I still have these assumptions. We don't give boys a chance."

Despite his misgivings, Hiton interviewed an assortment of kids from alternative and traditional schools, mostly from high-risk situations, and every one of them willingly and enthusiastically shared their views on sexual behavior. In fact, most of them wanted to talk more. In every single focus group, the boys said, "Will you come back again? Can we talk about this some more? Why haven't we been asked to do this before?"

Hiton said he thinks the boys particularly appreciated having a man to talk to. Again and again the boys said they wouldn't be able to talk about sexual matters if a woman led the discussion. As a whole, they appreciated Hiton's willingness to just listen to them. "They really liked that I just listened. I didn't preach. I was just there to keep it from getting too goofy. They valued the chance to be real with each other."

Hiton said we need to provide boys with more opportunities to talk with each other, especially with a respected adult male around. "We can't assume that because they are boys, they won't be honest and don't want to share with each other," said Hiton. They will and they do, if we give them the chance.

Julia Salmon is a freelance writer/editor and mother of three.

Reprinted with permission from Full Esteem Ahead, *Wings*, Winter 2000.

BAM! Boys Advocacy and Mentoring
A Strengths-Based Support Groups for Boys
Helping Boys Make Better Contact by Making Better Contact with Them
By Howard Hiton, MS, LPC

BAM! POW! KABOOM! ZOOM! Boys burst forth into the world, into their families, schools, and social arenas with unique energy and needs. Understanding these needs and supporting boys' growth has been the focus of our work for many years. We are three Portland, Oregon professionals who advocate for and provide support to boys in various settings. Over our years of closely working with boys, we have witnessed the challenges that they face in our schools and communities. We have found that many of their difficulties arise out of their limited relational abilities in an increasingly relational world.

Boys support groups can draw boys into conversations about what it means to be a healthy and connected man. BAM! uses methods that reflect an understanding and respect of boys' communication styles and activities that honor boys' need for movement. Each BAM! group begins with a facilitator telling a story of their childhood. Sharing stories allows us as adult leaders to make good contact with the boys in our groups because the stories we tell allow the boys to see us as interesting, willing to be vulnerable, and as having been young once, too. As we tell stories we make contact with the boys by sharing our experience. Imagine the storyteller animated and present while an eager listener leans forward, silent and focused on the speaker's words. This is the very contact boys often lack and the type of contact we want them to have in these groups.

Following the facilitator story, each BAM! group session contains a group physical challenge. In addition to creating outlets for boys' energy and opportunities to guide their physicality, the activities used in BAM! groups create cohesion among group members, make abstract ideas more concrete, and build a playful learning atmosphere. By doing activities with each other, boys build a sense of connection and belonging. In BAM! groups, participants must work cooperatively and supportively to complete the physical challenges, helping make the group environment inclusive and safe.

BAM! groups offer boys an opportunity to develop and practice the skills they need to become more relationally competent. We believe with these new abilities boys will be able to better manage their own behavior, engage more in school, and ultimately find more success in life. Our hope for boys who participate in BAM! groups is an experience that plants the seeds in them to be healthier, more relationally skilled men.

Howard Hiton is a therapist who has worked with boys and their families, school districts and non-profits to foster boys' healthy well-being. He lives in Portland, OR with his wife and two sons. He and his colleagues have written a book, BAM! Boys Advocacy and Mentoring: A Strengths-Based Support Groups for Boys *on how to run boys' support groups. You can learn more about BAM! groups and trainings by visiting www.BAMgroups.com.*

Written for Family Empowerment Network by Howard Hiton, co-author with Peter Mortola, Stephen Grant of *BAM! Boys Advocacy and Mentoring* at www.hitonassociates.net. For reprint requests, contact www.family-empower.com.

Sense of Belonging: Mother-Son Book Club

By Rebecca Manning Ryan

HOW DO YOU GET 13- and 14-year-old boys to turn off the TV or computer and read? One group of moms came up with an answer . . . form a Mother-Son book group.

It all began a year ago when Suzi Merz, the mother of a 7th grader, was trying to find a way not only to get her son to read more but also to spend more time doing things with him. Her son was spending more and more time with friends and less with his parents. She acknowledged this was normal but didn't want to lose the connection that she had with him. After reading about other mother/son reading groups that had been successful, she came up with the idea.

Suzi started by inviting the boys in their small classroom and their mothers to a meeting to discuss the idea. As it turned out only five of the fifteen boys in the class could commit to a once a month book read and meeting. They then invited a few boys and mothers from a nearby school and the group got started.

That was a year ago and it has been quite successful. Once a month one of the boys chooses the book and the meeting place (with a little help from his mother-- she has to read the book, too). The evening meetings start with the boys grabbing a few snacks and something to drink and the discussion begins.

Each boy and mother comes prepared to ask a question about the book and to learn something about the author. Here are some of the books from last year:
- We started out with a classic, *Huckleberry Finn*
- A *Harry Potter* book, of course
- For December, *The Best Christmas Pageant Ever*
- For winter it was *Animal Farm*
- For the last one it was, *It's Not About the Bike* by Lance Armstrong

At times, the book club has watched movies of the books we've read and contrasted the book and the movie. This was a treat for the boys.

The book club might not be a success if the boys did not enjoy reading. This group truly enjoys it. The discussions are usually quite in-depth and since the mother's feel this is the boys club they try not to dominate any of the discussions. It has formed some good friendships, especially with boys and mothers from another school. Hopefully it will encourage them to continue to read the rest of their lives.

For information on how to start a book club, see:

Great Books for Boys by Kathleen Odean
The Mother-Daughter Book Club by Shireen Dobson (see chapter on how to start a club)

Rebecca Manning Ryan is mother to a son and daughter and works for Providence Health System. Some of the moms are planning to start another book club now for the younger brothers, who are just entering middle school. They have been anxiously waiting for when it would be their turn to have their own book club.

Reprinted with permission from Full Esteem Ahead, *Wings*, Spring, 2001.

Creating "Safe Havens" for Youth

By Kathy Masarie, MD

ALL OF US LONG TO be part of a group where we feel accepted for who we are. This group can be hard to find in school unless you are a jock or popular. As ironic as it seems, being a good student may not be enough in a culture that models "nerd bashing" as a sport in movies. Providing interest groups outside of sports and academia can foster comfortable settings for kids to be themselves, especially for teens who are shy, loners or outcasts. When funding for schools dwindles as it has in some states, we see fewer and fewer of these interest groups, such as art, band and foreign language, being provided by schools.

As parents, we are in a powerful position to create these "safe havens" for our children, whether in our homes or at school during lunch, after school or in the evening. One of the most important things a parent can do for their youth is to start to understand the world their child is living in. Being part of a support group of adult and youth interacting with each other is an excellent way to accomplish this. All interactions—youth-to-youth, youth-to-adult and adult-to-adult—are valuable. As an adult facilitator, it is important to work toward empowering the youth to take charge of and choose activities for the meetings.

We can't expect the kids to be immediately open. Initially, the youth may not share that much with the group. As they get more comfortable they open up. One mother-daughter hiking club found that it took about a year of just being together before the girls started opening up to the other adults in the group (it might take boys longer). Eventually there were very strong bonds that developed between the adults and the youth.

General Structure

One or two adults and group of youth. This can work with a parent facilitator who understands youth. Sometimes a teen will open up to a non-related facilitator in ways they feel too inhibited to do when someone's parent is there. Young adults, religious educators and school counselors are especially effective at facilitating discussions among teens about their life struggles and issues. If teachers are involved in after-school or lunch clubs, they should be reimbursed generously.

One parent/one child (mother-daughter, mother-son, father-daughter, father-son) groups. This is an excellent way for parents and youth to understand each other better, especially the intergenerational interactions between unrelated pairs. This sets up a natural buffer for your children even outside the group, as the other youth and adults who get to know and love your child will be looking for him/her when there is trouble or need.

Gathering with families regularly. When our kids are little we naturally socialize with other families with children of similar ages. When we keep meeting for holidays, regular potlucks or outings, our children grow up together and feel at home with the other children and adults.

Age to Start

It is ideal to start a group while your child is in grade school or the first part of sixth grade. It is difficult to start a group when your child becomes "cool" and you become an embarrassment, as often happens during the middle school and early high school years. However, if you started a group earlier they will often ride right through these tough years. They don't want to quit something they are enjoying. It is never too late; my daughter was happy to start a mother-daughter book club in 10th grade when someone else's mom suggested it.

Meeting Times

Regular: weekly, monthly or yearly

Irregular: "when you have time" but if you don't have some structure/leadership you may never get around to meeting.

After-school clubs: This is a great place for schools to offer programs they wish were part of the curriculum (language, art, music, theater, book club).

Lunch clubs: For those kids who don't fit into the social scene, lunch can be an excruciatingly long time to be exposed to loneliness or harassment.

General Activities

Any common interest the youth and adults share can bring a group together. It could be an outdoor adventure, craft activity or even meeting at a restaurant together.

The list below is by no means a complete list but is designed to expose you to some different styles and formats that have worked. Don't let yourself be limited by these choices.

- *"Name Your Group"*—playful activities such as pizza parties, swimming, baseball game, art projects. Let the kids' interest drive the activities. One group we know meets every other month for mom-daughter activities of the girls choosing. Every other month the moms meet alone for a discussion on parenting.
- *Youth Groups*—in religious settings can provide the safest havens for kids who don't fit-in in traditional settings, especially since the theme is centered on acceptance of our differences and loving one another.
- *Coming of Age programs*—in religious settings can be a fantastic experience. They can challenge teens to think for themselves and to start to take more responsibility, while formally recognizing the important transition from childhood to adolescence. Otherwise our teens are more likely to do their own rituals of smoking, drinking, drugs or sexual promiscuity to "prove" that they are older.

Empowerment Groups

Empowerment groups are run by non-related adults to discuss issues which concern youth: for example, self-esteem, gossip, exclusion, friendships, risky teen behavior, media, over-focus on athleticism and other burning issues. These groups are particularly effective at helping children deal with interpersonal interactions and relationships.

- *The Girls Circle*—www.girlscircle.com
- *Girl's Empowerment Circles*—Girls Inc. at www.girlsincnw.org
- *BAM! Boys Advocacy and Mentoring*—at www.BAMgroups.com
- *Boys Councils*—at www.boyscouncil.com

Fitness and Sports Groups

It is very important for youth to learn to move their body while they are young and to get in the habit of exercise before they are 10 years old. For girls, the added bonus is that they see their body functionally rather than as an ornament. For boys, the added bonus is "action talk"; they will open up more easily while moving their body. For both, it can be a place where cooperation is more important than competition. Examples:

- *"Sports Clubs"*—around any activity. An alternative to long baseball practices and games is to have a baseball club that meets once a week. Think of any sport you can and there could be sport club around it.
- *Girl's Sport Clubs*—a weekly after-school club that meets to play and do alternative sports such as yoga, self-defense, kick boxing, and hip-hop dance
- *Action Club*—meet weekly to go for a hike, bike riding, roller-blading or different adventures.

Adult and Child Groups

- *Mother-Daughter Project*—empowerment group for moms and daughters (www.motherdaughterproject.com)
- *Book Club*—read and discuss a book monthly
- *Movie Club*—watch and then discuss movies
- *Campfire, 4-H and Scouts*—programs from kindergarten to high school. They have great curriculum, leadership training and support.
- *Science Club*—after-school science club run by moms, such as MAD Scientist or AWSEM: Advocates for Women in Science, Engineering and Math at www.saturdayacademy.org
- *Choices or Challenges*—for middle-schoolers and their parents

Family Gatherings

- Monthly potlucks or block dinners; holidays
- Yearly outdoor adventures: camping, backpacking, rafting, fishing, to name a few
- Family camps offered by local camps or churches

Lunch Clubs: "Safe havens" during lunch breaks

- *Library Fun*—nearly all schools have their libraries open during lunch, but not all quiet kids like to read. Some libraries set up a puzzles area with a 1000-piece puzzle to work on over time.
- *Game room*—this is a room full of board games and a couple foosball tables for active kids who don't want to go on the playground.
- *Support groups*—this is a great time for counselors (or outside facilitators) to work with kids who are in conflict: a group of girls who seem to attack each other, a group of kids who need to learn social skills or a group of boys who don't communicate well.

The Role of the Mentor

By Stan Crow

A MAJOR PRESUMPTION I use for mentoring is, "My role is to provide an experience which takes this person beyond their comfort level." Physical activity, honest dialogue, initiative games, rituals, and councils in which real issues are raised and dealt with are all discomforting. I often find myself uncomfortable as a mentor, wondering if I am on track with some of what I do. Then, I think, if I'm not uncomfortable, I'm probably not taking my role as a mentor seriously enough. There is no script, no set of tactics that will always work. In fact, one of the risks is that you will fail to connect. When this becomes evident, a good mentor will yield to another mentor.

One can be a mentor or be a friend, but not both. Friendship is developed as people go through trials together. A real trust and ability to be honest with each other must be nurtured. The mentor's role is to be a journey master, a "sensei"—one who takes a measure of responsibility for this other person. As arrogant as this sounds—to take responsibility for the life journey of another human—this awareness must be present.

In many traditional societies, the parents were not allowed to initiate their own children. Today, some parent groups organize rites of passage for their own children. Yet, someone else must do the mentoring, because for a parent to mentor is a conflict of roles. A parent cannot be a mentor and that is not bad! A parent's role is to protect and nurture. A mentor's role is to push and challenge. One of the major functions a mentor plays is to introduce a different adult voice, a differing world view for the young person to relate to, perhaps even in the devil's advocate role. A mentor offers the initiate an opportunity to try out ideas or ask questions in an accepting environment. The mentor's task is to give the young person permission to quest beyond his or her customary borders and to help process the journey.

Mentors have the possibility of being more objective than parents because they don't have the full experience (or baggage) of parenthood. I have seen young people who "heard" something a mentor said and made some life changes, even though the parents had been saying the same thing for years.

Recently, a person I had mentored told me, "You know why I changed? Because you told me what I needed to hear. Other people may have been thinking it, but no one else said it. And you let me know that you cared about me and wanted to see me change so people wouldn't treat me like a child anymore." I know this person's parents had done a good job, and had said similar things, but I had a chance to help him hear.

As mentors who are on journeys of investigation and discovery ourselves, our role is to assist the initiate to discover their own answers, to teach by question and by encouraging the initiates to risk in situations which drive them to reflect on meaning and relationships. We must ask, "How can we assist them to have an experience that pushes them beyond their comfort level and into recognition of their personal power?"

Stan Crow has been teaching, training and leading mentoring and rites of passage programs for decades, including a Coming of Age Program at Woodinville Unitarian Universalist Church. He has shared his programs in trainings offered all over the US. He now works with Rite of Passage Journeys, established in 1968, which fosters self-discovery, community and connection with the natural world for children, teens, and adults.

Stan writes that the role of the mentor is to set up situations to challenge the initiate:

I know a mentor who was trying to help a group of young people whom he considered selfish and unaware of how well-off they were. Their only contact with suffering people was on TV. In discussions with them, he saw they weren't seeing the pain which many people in their community were experiencing. He arranged a "sleep-over," and about 11 PM got everyone into cars and headed for the charity hospital. They sat in the emergency room waiting area, watching victims of heart attacks, drug overdoses, knifings, shootings and auto accidents being rolled in on a busy, icy Friday night.

The next day, after a little sleep, the youth had a chance to talk about the difficult experience. They had encountered real suffering, and their reflection was no longer theoretical. Several years later, I met one of the young men who told me it was a life-changing event for him.

Reprinted with permission from *Rites of Passage Journeys*. Rites of Passage Journeys offers rites of passage programs and several kinds of backpacking and camping adventures for kids (and for adults)—all in the state of Washington. To find out more, go to www.ritesofpassagejourneys.org.

Stance of a Mentor

By Stan Crow

IN A RECENT SEMINAR, someone said, "You have said several times that a good mentor challenges the mentee to meet various goals, do their best, etc." That sounds combative to me; is that what you mean?

I had to admit it could sound that way, and, I guess at times it could even look that way, but it certainly isn't my stance.

My basic intent as a mentor is to do whatever is necessary to convince the mentees to live their lives as the great human beings they are. Now I'm sure there are those who will respond, "Yea? How do you call some of these young people we deal with 'great'? Many of the youth we see are lacking self-confidence, have a history of failure and don't trust adults, let alone themselves."

My response was, "Right! That's what makes being a mentor so darn hard. There is no one guideline. Each situation is different, and what works once is seldom a reusable tool. The mentor will find him or herself as challenged as the mentee."

However, I do operate from a basic stance toward the mentee that grows out of my earlier intent statement and a deep-seated commitment to how we treat each other. At present, my draft of this stance toward the mentee is:

- I believe that you are a capable human being.
- Let's not waste time while you try to convince me that you are incapable. Rather, let's spend time identifying the challenges you face and how you might overcome them.
- I am not here to fix you, but to help you see the gifts you have and ones that are within your reach.
- When I challenge you to do something, it will be because I believe you have what it takes to do it, no matter how difficult or scary it is.
- I trust that somewhere within you there is a desire to have others see you as capable.
- Nervousness and fear are OK, as long as they don't paralyze you. They are a reminder that you really want to succeed.
- I will promise not to set you up for failure, but I will not bail you out either (unless you are physically in danger).
- We all have failures, and they are a part of the Life School. Our task is to learn from them, to turn our failures into ideas for how we'll succeed next time.

- I believe that a major part of my task as mentor is to help you reflect on and learn from both your wins and your losses.
- In the long term, what you learn may be more important than whether you completed a task.
- I will not engage in shame or blame and ask that you don't either.

This is not a covenant I make all at once with the mentee; it is rather a series of mini-covenants, which get promised along the journey as appropriate. I can envision some situations in which a gift of such a covenant might be profitable, my experience is that once I have identified what I believe my stance is, and then when it is appropriate, it will be available for a conversation with the mentee.

This reflection leads me to ask, "What is your stance as a mentor?" I invite your reflections.

Stan Crow has been teaching, training and leading mentoring and rites of passage programs for decades, and has shared his programs in trainings offered all over the US. He now works with Rite of Passage Journeys, established in 1968, which fosters self-discovery, community and connection with the natural world for children, teens, and adults.

Reprinted with permission from Rites of Passage Journeys. Rites of Passage Journeys offers rites of passage programs and several kinds of backpacking and camping adventures for kids (and for adults)—all in the state of Washington. To find out more, go to www.ritesofpassagejourneys.org.

Teenagers Can Be Mentors, Too!

By Susan Hopkins

As BOTH TEACHER AND parent, I am heartened by the expanding chorus of voices promoting parent involvement. I hear a renewed sense of mission in the messages that caring adults are delivering: TALK to your daughter about her self-image, VOLUNTEER in her classroom, MAKE TIME for a family meal, and so forth.

The media are joining in, with activities and strategies to help families prepare their teenagers for a successful transition into adulthood. Wisely, teachers and others who care about adolescents are sharing the stage with parents. Parents are realizing that kids are watching the adults in their lives, tuning in to examples of wisdom and self-esteem. Indeed, a theme in these discussion guides has been modeling a life worth celebrating; modeling our own efforts as adults—toward good health, good sportsmanship, and self-respect.

As strongly as I endorse this approach, it appears to flow in only one direction, adults as leaders; youth as followers. No matter how inspiring the leadership, however, teenagers can more easily embrace healthy adulthood after they themselves have had an opportunity to lead, and serving as a positive role model for a child is a priceless opportunity to do so. Leadership is another step on the path toward adulthood that I feel is too valuable to ignore.

My children spend their days in multi-grade classrooms. We who support mixed-age classrooms recognize that children best explore what they know when called upon to teach it. Children can proudly claim their own knowledge and expertise as they patiently pass it along to someone else. Teaching in small, everyday interactions helps them to feel both competent and generous toward those who are coming up from behind.

For most teenagers, the adults closest to them—teachers and parents and coaches—appear to have the right answers and to see through any mistakes. No matter how patient and respectful their approach may be, adults are more experienced and appear to be more knowledgeable. With such "together" adults all around, a teenager may be reluctant to risk the failure of trying new ideas, new hobbies, or new ways of connecting. But when a teenager mentors, tutors, or coaches, s/he becomes the expert in the eyes of the young followers.

This can result in the confidence boost to take intellectual risks and explore ideas.

Paradoxically, mentoring children serves another important purpose for teenagers. As with anyone, a teen occasionally needs a break from striving toward self-control and competence. Destructive ways of "taking a break" are all too obvious today, as adolescents abruptly turn away and establish their own contrasting identities. Mentoring children allows teens a healthier choice for escaping from social and academic pressure. They can re-visit childhood. I watch as my friends' teenagers eagerly play with my small children. For these teenagers, "helping me with the kids" is a dignified opportunity to have a really good time in the fort-building, secret-sharing world of childhood, which was their own refuge not so long ago. The challenge for teenagers is to gain inspiration by emulating worthy adults, while honoring their own desire to hang on to childhood. Being with children gives a teenager a respectable excuse to relax and linger awhile, to make the most of, well, playtime. Now that's a skill worthy of passing along to adults!

For an adolescent, serving as a mentor to a younger child can contribute to self-esteem, add to a sense of belonging in the community, and help bridge the passage from childhood to adulthood. When we encourage our teens to mentor others, we send a powerful message: "We believe you are someone to look up to, just as we hope you look up to us."

Susan Hopkins is a teacher, writer, and mother to a girl and a boy. She hopes to combine teaching with her former career as a city planner to develop programs to guide youth in creating livable communities.

Reprinted with permission from Full Esteem Ahead, *Wings*, Spring 1999

Cherishing Teens Reconnects Communities:
The Power of Coming of Age Celebrations
By Glenda Montgomery

THROUGHOUT THE WORLD, ritual and community-based celebration have marked the transition between the life of a child and the life of a young adult. Guided by elders and others who have been taught and tested before them, youth have learned necessary adult skills, been challenged, taken risks and have been acknowledged and embraced by their societies. The time and attention given towards these endeavors benefited not only the youths but their communities as a whole. Unfortunately, our modern western culture is a great exception in the diverse history of humankind because of our lack of established Rites of Passage. By failing to jump in and actively engage with our youth in this vital time of their lives, our culture alienates and confuses them. As a society, we tend to fear teenagers and their worlds. We end up collectively shunning youth at a time when they are driven developmentally toward pushing at the edges of their known world, taking risks and demanding new roles. Instead, we could be training them and skillfully guiding their energy within the embrace of the larger community, as they do where Rites of Passage are an integral part of community life. Not only do our youth miss out, our whole communities suffer from this void.

Today, in land-based, season-focused cultures (most of the world!), vibrant rituals and rites are practiced to mark Coming of Age. There is common structure in virtually all of these; they tend to have three phases:

- The first marks the leaving behind of childhood and of the day-to-day life of a child. It often is literally a "leaving behind." Hair is sometimes cut and the youth may leave his or her childhood home to spend time with other youth and elders.

- The next phase is one of "grounding down to be fashioned anew." It is a time of intense acquisition of skill-based knowledge and of ordeal, when youths learn what they are made of and are tested emotionally, physically and spiritually.

- The final phase is reintroduction back into the community. This is a time of celebration and reunification, when the society acknowledges that the youth is no longer a child and now carries different rights and responsibilities.

The recognition ceremony often provides a sense of renewal for the entire community. In fact, Rites of Passage are an integral part of community life. Not only do our youth miss out, our whole community suffers.

In our society we idolize the individual and individu-

alism. As a result, the skills of collaboration, mediation, compromise, group problem-solving, listening and personal contribution are not given the status as those of being a leader, a rebel, or a star. We do not actively support or recognize the skills that are so crucial for the continued surviving and thriving of any community. In fact, we don't know what skills we *should* help children to pursue nor how to teach them. Youth end up being confused by our culture's mixed messages and our inaction.

Furthermore, today when there is great competition in the labor market, young people are required often to depend on their parents for a much longer period of time than what was traditionally the case. Because of attending higher education and/or requiring financial support, sometimes youth do not leave behind their childhood home, childhood domestic responsibilities, patterns and expectations until their mid-twenties.

While transition from childhood to adulthood is no longer clear, our culture makes it clear that transition from adult to elder results in marginalization. Elders who in other places are honored for their life experience and entrusted with the guidance of the youth, in our culture are relegated to insignificant or indulgent roles in children's lives.

In this world of unsure transition, contradictory messages of what is important, fear and shunning from the greater community and a developmental drive to individuation and risk-taking, teens are taking initiation into their own hands. High risk behavior, hazing, gang activity, drinking and drugs, tattoos, and even random acts of violence and denigration against the larger community can be parts of these self-imposed initiations. This separation from childhood and community is not guided and overseen by elders towards positive goals as it is in cultures where the rites of passage are integral to growing up and it often does not culminate in the ritualized and celebratory reintegration with the society at large, which is so important. Instead, this separation isolates and breeds mistrust.

The book, *Crossroads: The Quest for Contemporary Rites of Passage*, states:

> One reason for the great demand of psychiatric services for adolescents today may be the absence of socially sanctioned rites of passage. Throughout human history these rites have served humanity well. The desire for some rites and rituals at puberty as well as at the end of the teen years is natural, even today. Young people seem to want the real thing ... There is truly a hunger for initiation ... Together with the culture, the community and the individual elders offering nurturing guidance and support, whole villages are needed to help raise our children, to help them survive.

Not only do socially sanctioned programs of rites of initiation help *youth* survive and thrive, they are equally important for the survival of a thriving, healthy community.

What do we do then, given the absence of most universally accepted rites of passage in this culture, its ambivalence to youth, the largeness of the task and its importance? There are three ways you might provide your child with a profound Coming of Age experience. You

might want to send your adolescent to one of the many excellent Rites of Passage camps; you might want to start or become involved in a local community or church-based program, or you may want to create a Coming of Age celebration just for your own child at your home.

There are many companies that specialize in taking youth into the natural world and guiding them in groups through Coming of Age rites of passage. Many incorporate all of the three stages: leaving behind, learning/testing and reuniting. Research some on the web and see what might be right for your teen:

- www.theritejourney.com
- www.ritesofpassagejourneys.org
- www.outwardbound.org

All of these are excellent choices to research and utilize.

If you have a school community, religious community or neighborhood that is interested in a program to do at the community level "in house" to guide a group of teens or preteens through a period of initiation and coming of age, there are a few excellent choices that you can explore. Usually the program arrives as a book or manual with "how to" instructions to help you with your community effort. Two excellent resources are:

Prairie Star Coming of Age Program: by Beth Brownfield
Order a copy at Bethbrown@aol.com
Coming of Age: Deepening Ties within Your Congregation
Order a copy at uucoa@mac.com

Finally, you can create your own homespun Coming of Age celebration to honor your son or daughter. Bring together "elders" to teach skills and act as guides in these transition years; honor the path your son or daughter has walked as a child so far and celebrate the adult they are evolving into. With a gathering of family and friends, celebrate your adolescent and reaffirm the importance of their unique qualities, skills and knowledge. Reassure them that they have the support of the group and of individuals within the group as they are tested and challenged on the journey to adulthood.

It is time for us to build anew the rites and rituals of passage that mark the transition from child to emerging womanhood and manhood. Youth hunger for them; our communities suffer from lack of them. It is time for us to remind our youth that they are valued and are part of a place where they are both needed and cherished.

Written for Family Empowerment Network by Glenda Montgomery, parent coach and Certified positive Discipline Instructor in Portland, OR and mother of a girl and a boy, www.positiveparentingpdx.com. For reprint requests, contact www.family-empower.com.

© 2009 Family Empowerment Network™ All Rights Reserved.

Raising Our Sons

Bar Gaia

By David Sweet

HOW DOES A BOY become a man? Does it come at a certain age—13, 18, 21? When he passes certain cultural milestones—driver's license, high school graduation, draft registration, voting age, drinking age? When I was 13, I became a Bar Mitzvah, or "Son of the Commandments," and was welcomed into the Jewish community. My family is not now associated with the Jewish community. When my son Jacob turned 13, I looked for something different; a way to welcome him into the community of life.

Jacob and I brainstormed how we wanted to mark his passage to manhood. The answer finally came to us the winter Jacob turned 13, as we discussed possible summer camping trips. "Could we go to Jerry Lakes?" Jacob asked. I was surprised he thought of it. A remote destination in the North Cascades, Jerry Lakes is an arduous, two-day hike, most of it steeply uphill and off trail. He had never attempted anything so difficult. We agreed that we would make the trip in late summer, and spend the intervening months preparing for it.

Our prep became a rich extended ritual, starting with finding sturdy hiking boots, water-proofing them and breaking them in. In February, we began a series of increasingly difficult hikes. Physical stamina was only part of the program. More important was the mental discipline needed to cope with the discomfort of long climbs. Gradually, Jacob began to discover the rewards of great effort. With one climb he said, "That was really hard, but the view is worth it, and I feel really good about myself for doing it."

Our training hikes gave us unhurried time. We began to find a new ease and intimacy in our companionship. We spoke more about the things that matter to us. I was able to share with Jacob the simple joy that fills my heart in wild mountain places. Also, because it was part of the experience, we talked about pain. We spoke of its place in our lives; how a man's response to pain differs from a boy's; how our experience of life can be broader and richer if we don't fear pain.

Jacob had several chances to test the limits of his physical and emotional reserves. One afternoon in July, we lost the trail in the snow coming. We wandered for two hours before finally finding the trail. Although exhausted and worried, Jacob never once complained or slowed down. We both learned something important that day about Jacob's response to hardship.

The trip to Jerry Lakes was all we had hoped for. Carrying a heavy pack on that steep and rugged route was the hardest thing Jacob had ever done. The destination was glorious. With no other humans within miles we feasted on trout and blueberries, sharing the place with bear, bobcat, osprey, peregrine, and marmot. Since we couldn't assemble a council of elders in that remote spot, I had asked a dozen men to contribute their written thoughts about manhood. These we shared in the evenings around the fire. Bringing the wisdom of others into our ritual helped to make this a community undertaking, rather than a private one.

Returning to our community, we gathered friends and family to honor Jacob on becoming a Bar Gaia—a "Son of the Earth." (Gaia is the ancient Greek goddess of the earth.) Jacob spoke movingly of his experience, and the lessons he would take from it. "Going to Jerry Lakes," he said, "was THE hardest thing I have ever done. I learned a lot about my dad and I learned even more about myself and what I am capable of." He recalled the wisdom in the letters. He appreciated several that advised him to be willing to take risks and make mistakes as a path to growth and understanding. He also remembered the advice of his grandfather, a retired logger, about keeping things in perspective. "A scratch on your car—that's not important. Two Kenworth trucks colliding head on—now that's important!"

As I looked around the circle of those who had come to acknowledge Jacob's passage, I saw the power of our ritual. We had marked a transition. Not only had Jacob changed—a quieter confidence that bespoke a growing understanding of his worth—but Jacob's role in his community had changed. From this point on, his friends and family would have different expectations of him, and he would have different expectations of himself. He had accepted greater responsibility for himself and for the well-being of his family, his community and the earth.

That is what a man does.

David Sweet was the National Outreach Coordinator for the Northwest Earth Institute. He lives in a small co-housing group and loves gardening and sustainable living.

Reprinted with permission of Full Esteem Ahead, *Wings*, Fall 2000.

Building Community for our Sons: A Coming of Age Celebration

By Chip Masarie, MD

We wanted to do something for our son, Jon, to mark his "coming of age" as a thirteen-year-old. He was into basketball, hanging out with his friends, and Nintendo, so I was a bit hesitant as to how he would react to some "woo-woo" ceremony with a bunch of adults. He agreed to participate (thank you very much) so the planning began.

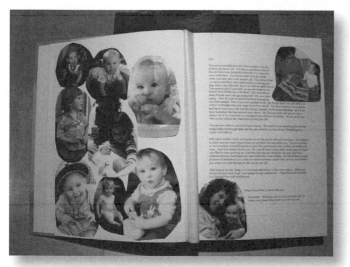

We invited adults who have been influential or involved in Jon's life. This included grandparents, aunts and uncles, teachers, coaches, parents of his friends, and family friends. Following the lead of a friend of ours, we asked each of the people that we invited to send us something to be included in a Coming of Age scrapbook—pictures, poems, words of wisdom, what they would have liked to have known at 13, what is was like for them at 13, etc. We asked them to get the material to us ahead of time so that the scrapbook could be shared at the ceremony.

We asked Jon to be gone until a certain time. By that time, all the participants had arrived and taken their places. Since Jon did not know exactly who was invited, we used a Trust Walk as a way for every participant to say "hello" to Jon without giving his or her name. A Trust Walk involves one person leading another person (who is blindfolded) on a walk. Jon was blindfolded and led to the first person in the chain. People were spread out throughout our house and each person knew who and where they were to carefully walk Jon, saying whatever

they wanted to him along the way. It was a very gentle way for him to be "introduced" to the folks who were going to share in the ceremony with him. We believe that having him walk into a big group of adults would have been a bit intimidating. While Jon was doing the Trust Walk, my father (his grandpa) and I had our faces painted. More on this later.

The participants sat in a big semi-circle around the room. Jon sat in the front with Kathy and me. Kathy began the ceremony with some context setting, talking about the importance of coming of age ceremonies in the lives of our kids. We then had a Nerf introduction. Jon stood in the center with a Nerf ball. He was instructed to throw the Nerf ball to each person in the room. When they caught (or picked up) the ball,

they gave their name and a short account of how they know Jon. We instructed the participants to keep it to 30 seconds or so and asked them to speak directly to Jon. The purpose of this event was to make contact with Jon

and let the others in the room see the connection. Thirteen-year-old boys like action and the Nerf ball trick really worked. He enjoyed being involved in determining who would speak next.

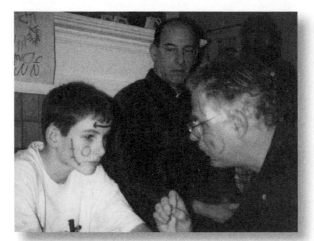

The next part of the ceremony was the candle lighting. We had set out 13 candles on a board, one representing each year of his life. Kathy, Kaitlin (his 15 year-old sister), and I each took turns lighting a candle, pausing at each "year" to recount milestones in Jon's life—usually one or two sentences. This was very powerful and gave perspective to his life. We saved the 13th candle for later.

The Sharing of Stories followed. This was a chance for each celebrant to share a short story about when they were 13 OR an experience they would like to share that they had with Jon. Everyone did not have to participate. They were instructed to keep stories to 2 minutes or less. We used the Nerf ball as a talking stick. When they were finished with their story, they threw the Nerf ball to the next individual who indicated a desire to speak. We encouraged them to not to give it to the person next to them, but rather throw it across to someone: more excitement and action that way.

Next we had a small urn in which we burned something from his childhood to signify the transition

which was followed by a face painting ritual in which his dad and his grandpa (whose faces were already painted) painted Jon's face. Jon then lit the 13th candle. We all then gathered in the kitchen for some ice cream and goodies. I will be forever reminded of how hard it is for us adults to stay connected with kids. As we gathered in the kitchen, the adults started their adult chit-chat, leaving Jon not sure what he was supposed to do. He knew that he should be there, so he brought his homework up and worked on it in the kitchen.

I have included the closing remarks from the ceremony as I believe they sum up the experience:

Coming of age is a transition. For Jon, it has been starting out the day as a boy and being led by each of us, with trust and caring, to his beginning as a young man. Jon, I hope you have seen today, that there are many people who love and care about you. They have shared their joys, their insecurities, and their experiences today and through their contributions to your coming of age book.

To all of you: Thank you for participating in this ceremony with us today and for your beautiful contributions to Jon's coming of age book. The book is overflowing with love and wisdom and beauty. Wouldn't if be nice if we could all hold in our hands such a book as we move through our next life passage.

Chip Masarie, Kathy's husband, is a consultant in medical informatics. He is a lifelong learner, passionate about community, personal growth, family, and speaking foreign languages.

Boy Psychology/Man Psychology

All of these have something in common:
- the chronically "crabby" boss
- the indifferent graduate school adviser
- the "hot shot" junior executive
- the coach who ridicules his star athlete
- the unfaithful husband
- the father who can never find the time to attend his son's school programs
- the company "yes man"
- the yuppie
- the gang member
- the wife beater
- the drug dealer

They are all boys pretending to be men. They got that way honestly, because nobody showed them what a mature man is like. They were told things like "big boys don't cry," "be a stud"—a macho man who doesn't need to acknowledge his feelings or be sensitive to others. We are continually mistaking a man's controlling, threatening and hostile behavior for strength. In reality, he is showing an underlying extreme vulnerability and weakness, the vulnerability of the wounded boy.

Mature masculine power is a masculine personality that is marked by calm compassion, creativity, has clarity of vision, openness, being real with his emotions and who he is, and is self-accepting. The key to maturity is humility and honesty.

There are four forms of mature masculine energies, all need to be kept in balance:

The King:
- Positive energy is calmness, making a safe place, knowing there is power greater than himself.
- Negative energy is seeking personal power and glory.

The Warrior:
- Positive energy is carrying through, completing any task, focused stamina, self-discipline.
- Negative energy is impotent, workaholic or sadistic.

The Magician:
- Positive energy is understanding, knowledge, therapist, cool, detached, wants to interpret everything.
- Negative energy is manipulation.

The Lover:
- Positive energy is passion, aliveness, interested in play and display, brimming with vitality and sensitivity.
- Negative energy is problems with boundaries and depression.

Resources: to explore these ideas further

King, Warrior, Magician, Lover: Rediscovering the Archetypes of the Mature Masculine by Robert Moore and Douglas Gillette. To help males become more nurturing and mature, Moore and Gillette identify four archetypes of masculine energies from myth and literature: Lover, Magician, King, and Warrior, whose energies often go awry in destructive activity. Dream analysis, meditation, and ritual processes are among the tools set forth in a clear, concise map to territories of masculine selfhood.

Fire in the Belly: On Being a Man by Sam Keen: The new male that Keen envisions is neither devoted careerist nor self-absorbed New Age guy, nor cool, detached "post-modern man." He is husbandman and steward of the earth—strong, vulnerable, with a capacity for moral outrage, empathy and wonder—whose right livelihood is consonant with ecological awareness.

Finding a New Skin: Rites of Passage from Child to Youth

By John Burbidge

"I WISH I'D BEEN able to go through this when I was their age. It helped me reinterpret many of my adolescent experiences, it affirmed that I can endure a lot and that I can relate to total strangers. All kids need this kind of experience."

This was how staff counselor Suzanne West summed up her experience in the Rite of Passage program conducted last summer by the Institute of Cultural Affairs (ICA). Suzanne, a communications disorders specialist with the North Shore School District, was one of four adult guides and sixteen children who participated in this three-week journey, marking the transition from child to youth.

The Rite of Passage Program is based on the stages of Joseph Campbell's *"The Hero/Heroine's Journey."* Participants experience the Call to Adventure and the Refusal to the Call, cross the Threshold of Ogres, navigate the Road of Trials, embark on Magic Flights, and cross the Return Threshold to come back as Master of Two Worlds.

The program melds together rites from Native American, Celtic, and other traditions with a ropes course, hiking, camping, and numerous opportunities for group and individual reflection. During the early stages of the program, children are "cared for" by adults, but in the remainder of their time together the tables are turned. Said 13-year-old Maurice Tyson: "This rite of passage taught me that people are not always going to be there for me … I'm going to have to depend on myself to do things and believe in myself more."

A pivotal moment for the whole group came early in the program during the ropes course. The task was to have everyone scale a fourteen-foot wall. The challenge was having only themselves to do it. Several were ready to give up before they started, but others were more determined. They finally settled on a plan of hoisting themselves up on one another's shoulders, with those at the top pulling the others up.

A turning point of the three weeks was the 24-hour vigil held in the awesome solitude of the Lake Ozette on the Pacific coast. During this time, participants went without food and sleep, tended their fires, and wrote reflections in their journals. Even though the counselors checked on each child at intervals throughout the night, silently and from a distance, the vigil was a solitary experience. Several children acknowledged that this was the hardest thing they'd ever done.

A precursor of the vigil was the sweat lodge. Led by local guide Walt Hoesel, children and adults alike participated in this Native American cleansing and purification ritual. Hoesel's carefully prepared context included storytelling, sharing about the medicine wheel, astrology, and animal totems. "This sweat lodge is to prepare you for your vigil and to be cleansed. What happens here I have very little to do with. What you put into this, you get back, so put a lot into it. Push yourself 10% further than where you want to go. And pray for good intent on the part of all of us."

Two powerful events brought closure to the journey. One was making a video to rehearse and celebrate the completion of the journey. The other was the Council of Elders, where each youth came before the staff and individually reflected on the experience and its significance for his or her life.

In the course of the three weeks, a number of issues cropped up that demanded to be dealt with. Sometimes, these were personal matters but more often, they affected the whole group. A key element in handling these issues was the circle gatherings–everyone had a chance to be heard and to listen to one another. A sense of "all being in the same boat" soon developed. People relaxed and bonding increased.

To many, the three-week duration of the program was quite intimidating, but as counselor Jason Paulsen of Shelton, WA pointed out, this length of time was most beneficial. "The three weeks made it impossible for the kids to bury their feelings. Some tried to do this but their feelings soon surfaced. For many of them, it was the first chance they'd had to come to terms with what was happening to them."

From the beginning to the end of the three weeks, the change in the participants' behavior was dramatic. Thrown together as a group, they exhibited the usual signs of nervous anticipation—either attention-craving exhibitionism or quiet withdrawal. When it came time to go home, it was a different story. "There was the same amount of energy present but it was transformed into group energy," noted Jason. "They wanted to do things together. They weren't necessarily best friends but they were much more supportive of one another."

Why should parents send their children on a Rite of Passage program? Arlene Albright, herself a mother of a seventh grader, [says] "So much is going on in children's lives at this time. They need to step off the merry-go-round once in a while to digest what is happening to them. The Rite of Passage gives them this opportunity."

Or as another staff member put it, it's the time in a person's life to try on a new skin—a new skin of the time in-between.

Reprinted with permission from *Rites of Passage Journeys,* who offer rites of passage programs for all ages. Check out www.ritesof-passagejourneys.org. Originally published in *ICA Rites of Passage Journeys,* No. 1, 1997.

Collective Work

By Kevin Riley

WE WERE HALF WAY through the second backpacking trip on our Coming of Age Journey and near the completion of the entire 21-day adventure. The three mentors were enjoying a fragile respite on the beach. The sun was tucking itself into the Pacific Ocean and painting the clouds a deep orange. We had just finished off a pot of sturdy macaroni and cheese for 3 and were starting to sip our hot chocolate when Jeremy, one of the young people on the trip, walked up reluctantly. He carried a large bag of rice and a disappointed scowl.

"The fire won't start," he said accusingly, "and we can't find the beans and Stan and David won't help and me and Leif are doing all the work."

The mentors looked at one another but together we fought off the urge to jump in and fix the situation. Instead, Edan looked at this young man confidently in the eye and said, "It sounds like you guys need to work together."

On the Coming of Age Journey, the second hiking trip is designed as an opportunity for the initiates to put into action what they have learned in the previous weeks. The mentors take a step back and let the young people make the decisions and carry them out. They decide how far we hike and in which direction. They plan the meals, cook, clean, and hang the bear bags.

> Each young person enters the woods knowing that if they stumble on the trail physically, emotionally, or mentally, there is a circle of people there to help.

The last few nights, the mentors will even set up camp 30 yards down the beach, ready to step in with any safety concerns but otherwise letting the group fend for itself. This period is like a final exam for one of the most important learning tasks on the trip: working together in a group.

In the previous weeks, the three of us had played the traditional role of youth leaders. We often found ourselves prodding and haranguing these guys to wake up in the morning, pack their bags, and get along with one another. Such is to be expected with a group of 13-year-old kids. At this stage of the journey, however, the expectations are different. Each participant has gone through his or her initiation and is now considered a young adult. Moreover, they have hopefully learned how to operate collectively. It is now up to the group whether or not the group eats.

For much of the year, these young people live in a society that places competition and individual goals above all else. In school, they are graded by how well they learn compared to other students. Tests scored on a curve put them in direct competition with their classmates. On the playing fields, the emphasis is on outperforming and conquering. Even in team sports, many young people take their cues from their professional idols and keep a watchful eye on their own "stats." And, of course, the cutthroat high school social scene is a dog-eat-dog affair. In that environment, there is little room for teaching young people how to work together toward a mutual goal. There are few lessons about listening to the suggestions of others and hearing a diversity of voices.

This missing element is readily apparent in adult life. Leaders in business and other organizations will tell you one of the hardest things to teach employees is how to work effectively with others in a cooperative environment. It is no surprise that expensive corporate consultants are needed to teach "team building."

Teaching young people how to work together in a group is an example of the mentored learning that is an integral component of the Coming of Age Journey. During the trip, much of the emphasis of mentoring is related to respect for the environment, wilderness camping skills, and conscious self-reflection. The most consuming topic, however, and the one on which the entire journey depends is how the group will come to a consensus and work as a team.

The young people start learning how to work collectively from the first day of the journey. All the members of the trip sit together and write up a "Full Value Contract." This document is a set of mutually agreed upon expectations from each participant. They decide for themselves the rules within which each group will operate.

Soon afterwards, the group challenges itself on a ropes course. Using elements of the course like the 40-foot high *Giants Ladder* or the (lower to the ground) *floating tent poles,* the group meets its first real frustrations. Tempers fly and blame gets tossed around as everyone fights for the reins. There are dozens of good ideas but no one left to carry them out. Slowly, the mentors and the course facilitator help the group slow down and listen to one another. They start to try one idea at a time and take turns at leadership. The course is a valuable learning experience where we can identify some of the difficulties that this group will have in working together and figure out ways to get through them. Later in the trip, when the group is having a hard time hanging a bear bag or tying up the shelters, we can look back on this struggle and use its lessons. Much of the Coming of Age Journey is an individual challenge. Each young person signs the full value contract holding him or herself accountable for his or her individual actions. On the hikes, each participant must carry his or her own gear. And, of course, each person spends 24 hours alone fasting in the woods on their vigil. However, these individual challenges can only be met because of the support of the community. Sometimes that support is tangible. Along with their own gear, each participant must carry a portion of the food and equipment for the group. The group must work together to cook the meals and hang the tarps.

Sometimes the support comes in other ways. Just before stepping on the trail at the beginning of each hike, the group forms a circle. Each young person states the following: "My name is ____ and I choose to do this hike willingly. Will you support me?" Everyone answers with a hearty "Yes!" or "Haho!" This type of ritual symbolizes both types of responsibility expected of every participant. It demonstrates that each member is present of their own accord and will be responsible for their own actions. At the same time, it commits each of the other members to support him or her when needed. Each young person enters the woods knowing that if they stumble on the trail physically, emotionally, or mentally, there is a circle of people there to help.

The expectation is that initiates will bring back to their communities an increased ability to work together in a group along with the willingness to offer and receive support from others.

Reprinted with permission from Rites of Passage Journeys. Rites of Passage Journeys offers rites of passage programs and several kinds of backpacking and camping adventures for kids (and for adults)—all in the state of Washington. To find out more, go to www.ritesofpassagejourneys.org. Originally published in *ICA Rites of Passage Journeys*, No. 1, 1997. Photos courtesy of ICA Journeys.

Lessons from Nature
By Marta Mellinger

RITES OF PASSAGE OFTEN draw on lessons from the natural world. It is in nature that we may be still enough to know our true selves. Teens will learn merely by spending time surrounded by nature and paying close attention, but adults can use the outdoors to guide and deepen a teen's experience. Asking thought-provoking questions and using the natural world as an analogy for "life" are two ways that an adult can enrich a teen's learning from an experience of nature. Here are some "rules" and questions compiled from an exercise where a Coming of Age group, after much discussion and preparation, separates from one another for a solo experience in the woods, where they took a journal and spent a number of hours in silent contemplation.

The Six Rules of a Milestone Solo Experience in the Woods

1. NUMBER ONE RULE FOR LIFE: PAY ATTENTION TO WHERE YOU ARE.
2. Don't be afraid to ask for help. Blow your whistle loud if you get lost, injured or have a real emergency. If you hear someone else blow their whistle, head back home and check in before rushing off into the woods to the rescue.
3. If you lose your way, return to the last milestone. If you lose your milestone, stop immediately, see where you are and use your whistle.
4. You need to see your last milestone to stay on path.
5. You can "come home" any time.
6. Life's about learning to learn, and learning what is needed to trust yourself and your choices.

If you think about these rules as "rules for life" what do they tell you that you need to remember? How do you think about each one as it applies to your life right now? How might you think about each one as it might apply to your life at age 21?

Milestone Questions

Moving through the land is the same as moving through life. If done well, it requires looking for answers, finding solutions, asking and being willing to receive gifts, noticing details (which way is the sun, that rock is in my right hand), envisioning your future and discovering your purpose. You may have lots and lots to think about without these questions. That's great. But here are some things you might want to consider now while sitting in the woods—or later on.

- Write a note to yourself at age 21. What do you want to be sure to remember about this time in your life? What do you want to remember to ask yourself about your life when you reach 21?
- Make a list of all the living beings you have seen on your milestone walk. Close your eyes for a while and imagine an animal coming to you and offering words of counsel and encouragement. What animals do you imagine? What did your animal guide say?
  - What are you searching for in life and how will you know when you have found it?
  - How will you recognize the need to slow down, use your senses to tune in and find your path, the paths that have heart (meaning) for your life?

  - Will you be able to accept that you will make

mistakes along this journey; can you become comfortable not knowing the answers? In what ways do you want to be treated differently when you return home? Are there any specific privileges you would choose to ask for that you believe would help you grow in your independence? In what ways would these privileges help you grow.

Marta Mellinger founded Canoe Group to help organizations succeed in rapidly changing times. She has two young adult daughters.

Family Fitness

By Kathy Keller Jones, MA

IT IS IMPOSSIBLE TO read the news nowadays without being reminded about the abysmal state of our children's fitness. We have an epidemic of overweight citizens and the number of obese and overweight children has more than doubled since 1970. Obese children are beginning to have the same problems adults' experience, such as diabetes and heart disease. We are inadvertently creating a culture that is unhealthy for many of our youth. We know many of the elements that have contributed to this, so how do we create healthy communities for our children where making healthy choices comes more naturally?

The family teaches and models physical health in so many ways. It is natural that we teach our children to brush their teeth, bathe, and sleep well, and it is equally important that we teach them to be active every day and to eat well. That all sounds straightforward, but it turns out it is not. Powerful forces, such as the many screens

in our homes, our own fears of letting kids go outside, our busy lives, commercialism, the plethora of junk food, and the fact that we drive everywhere, are interfering with what was natural for previous generations. Kids went out every day and played actively, they ate homemade dinners with their families, had much less screen time, more imaginative play and more freedom to roam the neighborhood. In today's world it takes a conscious and concerted effort to maintain a healthy lifestyle for our families.

We can make a commitment to duplicate some of the positive conditions of a healthier past and to teach our children the joys of movement and the outdoors, as well as the satisfaction of doing activities together. Parents will need to encourage healthy eating habits and active play, while at the same time limiting the unhealthy influences. That means, in part, having

systems and limits that work for all sorts of electronic devices, making sure that computers and TVs are in "public" home spaces, eating dinner together whenever possible, and making time for free play, family play and active family fun. In this way family food preparation and fitness become family priorities.

As we know, fitness can take many forms, all of which involve movement and reasonably healthy food intake. Our younger children are fit, for example, when they play actively everyday, walk to school with their family and go swimming once a week. Free play improves motor skills, provides an outlet for energy, and encourages kids to use their imagination. Elementary-aged children also need free play, and they grow in confidence when they develop skills and try out new activities. Kids need a balance between being in their bodies in their own authentic way, responding to their own inner rhythm, and learning new physical skills through enjoyable physical activity. Teens can be involved in individual or group sports, or commit to working out several times a week. One girl ran with her father in the early morning hours from middle-school on, and even though they ran in silence she felt very bonded to her father through their common fitness goal.

The family acts powerfully when they change their behavior in the direction of fitness. For example, they decide to walk or ride bikes to school rather than drive. They plan healthy meals, cook together, and stock the house with healthy snacks. They have a common understanding about why they spend less time on screens and more time having fun together: biking, playing catch, hiking, playing active games such as tag, exploring local parks, playing touch football, swimming at family swim, roller-blading, shooting baskets, you name it. The family can save money toward buying equipment that encourages active play, visit secondhand stores and stock the garage with balls and other fun equipment. Some families organize fun neighborhood games such as softball, volleyball, or badminton. When our family commits to outdoor activities like fishing, camping, and cabin trips, we are committing to a healthy active lifestyle. Fitness is a priority and a lifelong commitment and families have a golden opportunity to start their children on the right track.

Growing Back Into Our Body

By Cathy Gwin

HAVE YOU EVER SEEN a toddler streaking through the house after a bath? I fondly recall my two-year-old son, John, running like the wind, with freedom and confidence. At that moment, he was so alive—experiencing his inner core of strength, his body-mind-spirit connection. He was comfortable with his body and his body was there for him. Of course that wonderful experience would come to an abrupt halt when he stumbled and fell, but for a fleeting moment, the connection was made. That mind-body-spirit connection was real for him then and has remained so. It is the foundation of his growth and change.

A child grows by accumulating these experiences. Each experience of "being just right with one's body" deepens and strengthens the mind-body connection and allows the child to build greater physical competence. For instance, my son reconnected with his seat of strength and aliveness through the physical activity of sports. At the age of six, he took up fishing. In the beginning, he focused on how many fish he could catch. Over a period of a few years, however, he became more in touch with the experience of fishing. He would become animated and alive when he described how he fooled a large mouth bass into biting a specific lure or how he moved his float tube across the lake to a rather inaccessible spot.

Over and over he experienced his body doing what he wanted it to do which strengthened his experience of competence. In time he no longer focused on the fish brought home. He caught and released them and took home the "connection" he made. Only a few months ago I went fishing with him. Though he is now a 29-year-old man, I could still feel his intense childlike aliveness as he tried to help me lure a trout onto my line.

However, as with most adolescents, he moved through the stressful stage of development and change and this constant within him became less available.

Lately, the experience of organized sports has become a mixed bag. Narrowly focused organization prevents widely varying individuals from fulfilling their multiple needs and expectations. A child can engage in a physical activity and be totally disconnected from his body-mind-soul connection. He can never find himself when the experience is felt as a win-loss, or a criticized-praised experience.

I found this so painfully true with my son as he played soccer. From the age of 10 to 15, he developed into a very "successful" player who at that time was defined by amount of time played, the number of goals scored, and the number of games won. When he was fifteen, we moved to California, were he spent the first two months of the long soccer season sitting on the bench. This shook his confidence. Both of us were at a loss as to how to deal with this experience.

We needed to help each other find John again. We worked hard to consciously make that mind-body connection again. We began to remember in detail specific experiences where he felt his strength and that connection with himself. We went deeper than just describing it as a game where he scored. We focused on the time when he felt his body responding, as he wanted it to. We began to talk about his experience of soccer and relating it to his experiences fishing. This was an important turning point. John was able then to find more of himself while playing. Reconnecting with these core experiences began the change that allowed him to go on to play successfully at the college level and beyond. His experiences of body-mind-spirit connection helped sustain him through the stresses of competitive life.

Cathy Gwin is a psychologist in private practice in Portland, Oregon. She works with children, youth, families and adults.

Reprinted with permission from Full Esteem Ahead, *Wings,* Spring 1998.

What Tae Kwon Do Can Do

By Karen Costello

BOY SCOUT MOM? Soccer mom? Piano mom? No, call me a Tae Kwon Do mom. That's right, I'd rather hang my name on Tae Kwon Do than any other sport or activity my children have participated in. Tae Kwon Do is one sport that is well deserving of the time, effort, money and energy that families put into pursuing sports and activities.

Initially I struggled with Tae Kwon Do. On the surface, it seemed to encourage many of the behaviors I'd spent years trying to discourage —punching, kicking and well, violence. Could this really be a good sport for my boys?

During the first lesson, I was impressed when I heard the children reciting the "Tenets of Tae Kwon Do," courtesy, modesty, self-control, perseverance, and indomitable spirit. Wow, these were exactly the types of skills I wanted my children to learn from participating in sports. Skills that would help them through out life, skills I hadn't necessarily seen displayed on the soccer field! Then there was the Tae Kwon Do Oath—I shall observe the tenets of Tae Kwon Do; I shall respect my instructors and seniors; I shall never misuse Tae Kwon Do; I shall be a champion of freedom and justice; I shall build a more peaceful world. Wow again! I was starting to like this sport! It seemed like the perfect marriage of physical fitness and spiritual fitness. Now that was something I was sure I hadn't seen in other sports.

But, there was still the issue of punching and kicking to deal with. Did this sport promote fighting and violence? Thankfully, I discovered the answer to that question was—no. Tae Kwon Do is considered an art of self-defense. Self-defense includes the ability to prevent injury to oneself, fall safely, communicate with aggressors and escape from violent situations. Students are taught not to "attack" unless they are being attacked. Self-defense is not just about physically dealing with violence. It's about avoiding becoming a victim of violence. I was beginning to feel that my children were going to think differently the next time they felt the need to hit or kick one another. Now they would both be armed with defensive skills and a deeper understanding of the reason to avoid fighting in the first place.

There really are many benefits to studying Tae Kwon Do aside from the physical and spiritual ones already mentioned. It is a sport open to people of all body types, coordination and skill levels. This makes it is a great sport for the entire family and particularly for children who don't think they are athletic. The self-confidence children gain by participating in Tae Kwon Do comes from knowing that they are personally responsible for their own achievements as they master different moves and advance in belt color. There are no "free" trophies given out in Tae Kwon Do. It is said that Tae Kwon Do is a psychological leveler—students with quick, hot tempers learn to control their emotions, students who are meek and mild learn to be more assertive. Students learn a small amount of Korean history, culture and language. Children at more advanced belt levels are asked to help train the less advanced students. In Tae Kwon Do it is a privilege to help those who are not as good as you, not an inconvenience to have them "on your team." Tae Kwon Do is taught visually, audibly and by physically positioning the body. This makes it a good sport for all types of learners. Most Tae Kwon Do instructors have dedicated their lives to studying and teaching the sport. They practice what they preach and tend to make excellent coaches and role models.

Tae Kwon Do is a sport with lofty goals. It is a discipline of the mind and body. It strives not only to develop the physical being, but the moral and spiritual being as well. Tae Kwon Do is not just a method of self-defense; it is a philosophical approach to life. Many children can benefit from what it has to offer.

Karen Costello is the mother of two sons. She helped develop the Raising our Sons curriculum and organized the start of many "Raising Our Sons" groups, including a couple's group she was in.

Reprinted with permission from Full Esteem Ahead, *Wings*, Spring 2001

Tell Me More and Other Great Tips on Connecting with Your Kid

By Positive Coach Alliance at www.positivecoach.com

Empowering Conversations with Your Child

When we think about what makes people friends with each other, a number of things come to mind. For example, our friends like us and enjoy spending time with us, as we enjoy them. And what is it we mostly do when we are together with our friends? Mostly we talk and listen to each other.

Conversations are the glue between people, the essential element in a strong relationship. Relationships wither without communication, and the very best form of communication is the conversation. Many parents fall into the trap of thinking that it is their job to talk and their child's to listen. Actually that's only half-right. It is also our job to listen and the child's job to talk. It's a wonderful thing when a parent and child can really talk to and hear each other.

It is important that parents intentionally seek out conversations about sports with their athletes. Here are some suggestions for how to engage your child in a conversation about sports.

1. Establish Your Goal—A Conversation Among Equals: A conversation is something between equals. Kings didn't have conversations with their subjects. They told them what to do. Prepare yourself for a conversation with your child by reminding yourself that sports is her thing, not yours. Remember that you want to support her, to let her know that you are on her side. Your goal is not to give advice on how to become a better athlete. It should be to engage your child in a conversation among equals, one of whom (you!) is on the side of the other (her!).

2. Adopt a Tell-Me-More Attitude: Brenda Ueland penned one of the most important essays on relationships ever written, "Tell Me More": "When we are listened to, it creates us, makes us unfold and expand. Ideas actually begin to grow within us and come to life." Adopt the attitude that you want your child to tell-you-more ("I really want to hear what you have to say."), and then listen to what he has to say—even if you don't agree with it or like it—and you will begin to tap into what Ueland calls the "little creative fountain" in your child.

If you are very tired, strained … this little fountain is muddied over and covered with a lot of debris … it is when people really listen to us, with quiet fascinated attention, that the little foun-tain begins to work again, to accelerate in the most surprising way.

Think of your conversation with your child as an Olympic event with judges. A conversation that rates a 9 or a 10 is one in which the child does more talking and the parent more listening. Set your goal before you start, and go for it.

3. Listen! In many instances you may know exactly what your child can do to improve. However, this is a conversation, remember? Your goal is to get your child to talk about her sports experience, so ask rather than tell. Save your tellings for another time.

4. Use Open-Ended Questions: Some questions lend themselves to one-word responses. "How was school today?" "Fine." Your goal is to get your child to talk at length, so ask questions that will tend to elicit longer, more thoughtful responses.
- "What was the most enjoyable part of today's practice/game?"
- "What worked well?"
- "What didn't turn out so well?"
- "What did you learn that can help you in the future?"
- "Any thoughts on what you'd like to work on before the next game?"

5. Also ask about life-lesson and character issues: "Any thoughts on what you've learned in practice this week that might help you with other parts of your life?" Even if you saw the entire game, the goal is to get your child to talk about the game the way she saw it, not for you to tell her what she could have done better.

6. Show You Are Listening: Make it obvious to your child that you are paying attention through use of nonverbal actions such as making eye contact as he talks, nodding your head and making "listening noises" ("uh-huh," "hmmm," "interesting," etc.).
Listening is one of the greatest gifts you can give your child! Ueland again:

> *Who are the people, for example, to whom you go for advice? Not to the hard, practical ones who can tell you exactly what to do, but to the listeners; that is, the kindest, least censorious, least bossy people that you know. It is because by pouring out your problem to them, you then know what to do about it yourself.*

7. Let Your Child Set the Terms: William Pollack, MD, author of *Real Boys: Rescuing Our Sons from the Myths of Boyhood,* notes that children have different "emotional schedules" that determine when they are ready to talk about an experience. Forcing a conversation right after a competition (when there may be a lot of emotion) is often less successful than waiting until the child gives an indication that he is ready to talk. Boys may take longer than girls to talk about an experience, so look for prompts that a child is ready. And conversations don't have to be lengthy to be effective. If your child wants a brief discussion, defer to his wishes. If he feels like every discussion about sports is going to be long, he'll likely begin to avoid them. And don't be afraid of silence. Stick with it and your child will open up to you.

8. Connect through activity: Sometimes the best way to spark a conversation is through an activity that your child enjoys. Playing a board game or putting a puzzle together can allow space for a child to volunteer thoughts and feelings about the game and how he performed. This is especially important for boys, who often resist a direct adult-style of conversation.

9. Enjoy: The most important reason why you should listen to your child with a tell-me-more attitude: Because then she will want to talk to you, and as she (and you) get older, you will find there is no greater gift than a child who enjoys conversations with you.

Guidelines for Honoring the Game
The key to preventing adult misbehavior in youth sports is a youth sports culture in which all involved "Honor the Game." Honoring the Game gets to the ROOTS of the matter and involves respect for the Rules, Opponents, Officials, Teammates and one's Self. You don't bend the rules to win. You understand that a worthy opponent is a gift that forces you to play to your highest potential. You show respect for officials even when you disagree. You refuse to do anything that embarrasses your team. You live up to your own standards even if others don't. Here are ways that parents can create a positive youth sports culture so that children will have fun and learn positive character traits to last a lifetime.

- **Before the Game:**
  1. Make a commitment to Honor the Game in action and language no matter what others may do.
  2. Tell your child before each game that you're proud of him or her regardless of how well he or she plays.

- **During the Game:**
  1. Fill your children's "Emotional Tank" through praise and positive recognition so they can play their very best.
  2. Don't give instructions to your child during the game. Let the coach correct player mistakes.
  3. Cheer good plays by both teams (this is advanced behavior!)
  4. Mention good calls by the official to other parents.
  5. If an official makes a "bad" call against your team? Honor the Game—BE SILENT!
  6. If another parent on your team yells at an official? Gently remind him or her to Honor the Game.
  7. Don't do anything in the heat of the moment that you will regret after the game. Ask yourself, "Will this embarrass my child or the team?"
  8. Remember to have fun! Enjoy the game.

- **After the Game:**
  1. Thank the officials for doing a difficult job for little or no pay.
  2. Thank the coaches for their commitment and effort.
  3. Don't give advice. Instead ask your child what he or she thought about the game and then LISTEN. Listening fills Emotional Tanks.
  4. Tell your child again that you are proud of him or her, whether the team won or lost.

Reprinted with permission from Positive Coaching Alliance. Check out more great resources on healthy coaching at: www. positivecoachingalliance.org.

Sports Clubs Can Lead to Lifelong Enjoyment

By Kathy Masarie, MD

DO YOU WANT TO get away from the hassles of car-pooling, weekend games, dinner-hour practices, and over-zealous competition, and still have your child enjoy a sport? A sports club may be the answer. This is what I call a group of kids and an adult mentor who get together once or twice a week to enjoy their sport. It attempts to mimic what we grew up with: backyard sports where kids just gathered Saturdays on the grade school field for a pickup game. Today most of us live far apart and we are uncomfortable letting our kids just go off for hours at a time. Sports clubs can help kids build skills in a sport while providing low-key, low-cost fun. A sport that we love can provide us with lifelong thrills and benefits.

My sports club experience involved my son Jon when he was in the third grade. We had finished T-ball where everyone got to play equally. On the other hand, we had heard horror stories about baseball leagues —cut-throat competition, frequent practices, three-hour games, over-involved parents and intense coaches who focused only on winning. We decided regular baseball would take too big a bite out of family time with only questionable benefits. So, we organized all the kids who weren't participating in baseball to meet at our local grade school field right after school at 3:00 PM. Since most coaches didn't finish work until after 4:00 PM, the fields were free until then.

About 10 players met every Friday afternoon for eight weeks. We had matching baseball caps and snacks and drinks at practice. We did drills and played "work-up" (a scrimmage game). Occasionally, kids from a regular team joined us for an actual game. Everyone's skills improved, and we were all home by 4:30 PM for real family time.

Here's another example. Ann Garrett, a Physical Education teacher at a local elementary school, started a running club. Passionate about kids being active, she disliked the intensity she saw in organized sports. She wanted kids to have fun and get fit at the same time. She thinks kids naturally want to move their bodies and find something they enjoy. Her goal was for club members to be fit enough to compete in a local 5K run. About two months before the race she sent a flyer home with the fourth and fifth graders. The response was about 35 kids who then worked out for an hour twice a week as a group, and a third time on their own. They did warm-ups and relay games and then ran through the neighborhood, rewarded with Popsicle's at the end of practice. Parents sometimes joined them. All kept logs of their mileage. The day of the race everyone wore matching hats, used the buddy system, and had parent supervisors.

If a sports club is not for you, there are other choices. Some children are more suited to a non-traditional sport. My favorite story concerns a mom who took up rock climbing for fun. Her son, Bryan, joined her and now is a successful, national competitor. And best of all, they spend time together. If you focus on family fitness, everyone benefits. Too many families exercise separately. Personally, I'd rather do sports with my kids than sit on the sidelines watching. Remember—"the family that plays together, stays together." Getting your child into a sport he or she enjoys can lead to competence and enhance mental and physical health. Success in a sport builds confidence and carries over into the rest of our lives.

Reprinted with permission from Full Esteem Ahead, *Wings*, Spring 1998.

Aerobics • Archery • Backpacking • Badminton • Ballet • Baseball • Basketball • Bike racing • BMX bike riding • Bowling • Boxing • Canoeing • Capoeira • Cricket • Croquet • Cross-country skiing • Curling • Dancing • Diving • Downhill ski • Dragon boat racing • Fencing • Fishing • Folk-dancing • Footbag • Frisbee • Frisbee Golf • Gymnastics • Hackey sack • Hiking • Horse riding • Ice hockey • Ice-skating • Jogging • Karate • Kayaking • Lacrosse • Martial Arts • Mountain biking • Mountain climbing • Orienteering • Parachuting • Poekoelon • Pull-pull-pedal (ski, canoe, bike) • Racquetball • Recumbent bikes • Rock-climbing • Rodeo • Roller-blade hockey • Roller-blading • Rowing • Rugby • Rythmics • Sailing • Scuba diving • Skateboarding • Sculling • Snowboarding • Snow shoe • Snow shoeing • Softball • Special Olympics • Squash • Surfing • Swimming • Soccer • Synchronized swimming • Table tennis • Tae Kwan Do • Tai chi • Taiko (drumming) • Tennis • Track and Field • Triathlons (swim, bike, run) • Ultimate Frisbee

Teaching Independence and Responsibility versus Compliance and Conformity

By Carnegie Corporation

THE ISSUE OF TEACHING interdependence and responsibility versus compliance and conformity is a very controversial issue in the environments of sport and work. Shield and Bredemeier articulated the controversy as follows: "Sport functions as an instrument of ideological manipulation by helping to manufacture a social consensus about such values as hard work, corporate loyalty, and belief in hierarchical organization, specialization, meritocracy, and patriarchy.[1] These values and beliefs are necessary to maintain a compliant and productive work force in the modern capitalist state, a set of social arrangements that, in turn, tremendously benefit a few but disadvantage and disempower many." In support of this assertion, Berlage asked fathers of youth soccer and hockey players to identify three attributes that sports develop that they considered valuable.[2] The values selected were those most essential to a bureaucratic and corporate structure, i.e., authoritarianism, team loyalty, and excellence in performance.

Coakley stated that there is too much emphasis placed on winning and not enough on the physical and psychological development of the participants.[3] As the organized youth sport programs became more prevalent in the post-World War II era, youth sport experiences shifted from the schools and backyards and playgrounds to adult-centered events. Adults hoped that sports, especially team sports, would teach boys from lower-class backgrounds how to cooperate and work together peacefully. In the case of middle-class boys, it was hoped that strenuous sport activities would turn boys into strong, assertive, competitive men by providing them with an alternative to home lives dominated by women.[3] The vast majority of sport programs emphasized competition as a means of building the achievement orientation that would hopefully lead to personal success and community growth.

The adult-organized approach to teaching youth the skills and values necessary for success in a capitalist society may be counterproductive. Leonard Koppett, a sports writer and columnist, wrote, "The most important part of play is learning how to set up the game, choose sides, agree with your peers, make compromises, figure out answers, and submit to self-directed rulings so that the game can continue. These important civilizing functions are bypassed by adult-run leagues."[4] Koppett raised an interesting issue as to whether participation in sport does prepare our youth for our everyday work life. Coakley detailed how organized, com-

petitive sports are different from our everyday lives.[3] These differences are presented in the table below.

The purpose of this comparison is not to say that participation in organized sports is a worthless source of learning. Coakley contended that it is when the differences between sport and everyday life are recognized that people are able to open up themselves to new experiences in sports.[3]

One of these differences is the fact that success and failure in sport is unrelated to careers, family life, and friendships. In other words, playing a tennis match after school or work can be a valuable experience simply because the outcome of the game does not have any impact on grades in class, job evaluations, the love of family members, and the quality of friendships. When one's identity is tied up in sport outcomes, i.e., winning or losing, people form a very limited definition of success in life.

Teaching compliance and conformity is counterproductive to developing leadership qualities and the willingness to try something different, i.e., take risks. Leadership has been defined as "the behavioral process of influencing individuals and groups toward set goals."[6] The qualities of effective leaders include intelligence, assertion (NOT compliance), empathy, intrinsic motivation, and self-confidence."[5]

Compliance and conformity have not been valued by persons living in a democratic culture. Leadership that is based on compliance and conformity has been labeled as a dictatorship, where persons are taught their role and are limited in what they can aspire to contribute to society. Within the adult-organized youth sport arena, compliance with rules and expectations of coaches and parents is extremely valued. During children's formative years, it is critical that they be taught skills that are more closely aligned with everyday life, i.e., to value cooperation and caring about others, and to be allowed to take risks in a "safe" environment where they can learn from their successes and failures, gain confidence in their abilities to meet a challenge, and to develop leadership skills that will foster growth in a culture where the power is in the hands of a few. Teaching responsibility and independence may be a better way to prepare youth for life.

Organized, Competitive Sports versus Everyday Life: A Comparison

Organized, Competitive Sports	Everyday Life
Sports have artificial boundaries in time and space, and participation is not universal.	Life encompasses much more than competitive games and its boundaries are natural and universal (birth and death).
Competition is part of sport experiences; it is often taken for granted.	Competition is incidental in everyday life experiences; it is often avoided.
Sports are simplistic and intentionally clear-cut.	Life is complex and essentially ambiguous.
Meanings are predefined and explicit.	Meanings are emergent and open to question.
Events are distinctly delimited in time and space and have definite beginnings and ends.	Events occur in a continuous series, each growing out of the past and leading into the future.
Evaluation is based on objective scores, and outcomes are clear-cut and easy to understand.	Evaluation is generally subjective, and outcomes are often difficult to define and understand.
Opponents are known and confronted directly; their goals are explicit and their progress toward goals is observable.	Opponents may be unknown or confronted only indirectly; their goals and progress toward achieving goals may be indeterminable or intentionally hidden.
Rules are clear-cut and formally agreed upon; they are enforced by formal agents of control (referees, umpires, etc.) who directly observe the actions of those involved.	Rules are often ambiguous and may not be based on consensus; enforcement usually depends on self-control, since formal agents of control have little or no opportunity to make direct observations.
Success depends primarily on physical skills; only a minimum of interpersonal skills is required for participation.	Success depends primarily on interpersonal skills and is generally unrelated to physical skill.
Individuals usually seek out competitors who will test their abilities.	Individuals try to avoid or eliminate the influence of competitors.
Events are organized so all participants face standardized sets of conditions; everyone starts out as equals within the competitive structure of sports.	Events are not organized, and everyone faces different conditions; some people have advantages over others because of inequalities.
Action involves ethical choices related to immediate issues that seldom have significance beyond the event itself.	Action involves ethical choices related to ultimate issues and these ethical choices sometimes have pervasive implications.

If people wish that life could be more like sports, they are expecting too much from sports. A former NFL player noted, "[Athletes are] in one of the most highly stressed jobs in the country, and there's no assistance, so it's gonna continue to turn out guys who are mentally unstable, bankrupt, divorced, alcohol and substance abusers. Athletes are set up to be very high-risk people in terms of being abusers of things—money, substances, everything. These problems have to be dealt with by attacking the problem, and not just the symptom. And the problem is being ill-prepared for life."[3] Coakley observed from his experience in football that, "the athlete doesn't have to grow up because the coach lives his life for him … the sad thing is [that] it actually benefits the team to keep the player naïve and dependent."[3] Similarly, Dorcas Butt, a former top-ranked tennis player in Canada agreed, "social behavior expected of an athlete resembles in many ways that expected of a young, ill, or irresponsible person.[7] The unquestioned adherence to rules deprives athletes of the very experiences needed to become responsible and mature people.

Sport can provide the experience necessary to teach our youth to be independent and responsible. To do this, however, some changes will need to be made in the adult-centered programs. These changes should be made with the physical, social, and psychological needs of the children placed ahead of the organizational needs of the programs and ahead of the adult. Additionally, changing rules to increase the amount of action in a game would allow more opportunities for children to learn skills and to experience both success and failure. Limited action enhances the significance associated with every error or mistake that a child makes. Through overcoming errors, children gain confidence and become more independent in assessing their own performances. Coaches need to use challenging or difficult situations as a way to teach youth responsible decision-making. Youth athletes need to understand that there are consequences associated with each decision they make. This process increases the understanding of being responsible.

In addition to rule changes, using equipment that is more appropriate for youth's physical capabilities would allow for more action and increase the confidence of the children. For example,

the use of a "reduced injury factor" baseball reduces the fear that youth have of being hit with a ball that is thrown or struck. This means that softball and baseball players will not be afraid to try to make a play because they know they will not be hurt. Other changes could include creating equitable playing opportunities for all the children on a team. This means that all of the children would be starters as well as substitutes and children could learn to play all of the positions on a team and not be specialized simply by their physical presence. Teach sportsmanship and interpersonal skills that reflect those valued by society. Coaches should be models of these behaviors if they are to work with our youth. Because most of our youth sport coaches and majority of our high school coaches are volunteers or non-faculty, respectively, coaches' education appears to be essential to help these well-intentioned individuals understand the needs of the youth they are teaching, as well as develop the skills to teach sports skills and ethics.

The value of sport as a social environment for preparing youth for adult roles has been limited, unfortunately, to boys. As society has changed and women are seeking and assuming more leadership roles, the valuing of the benefits and lessons learned from sport must be provided for girls. It is also possible that these benefits and lessons are more valued for European American males than for minority males.

References

1. Sheild, D.L. and Bredemeier, B.J. (1995). Character development and physical activity, Champaign, IL: Human Kinetics
2. Berlage, G.I. (1982). Children's sports and the family. ARENA Review, 6 (1), 43-47
3. Coakley, J.J. (1994) Sport in Society: Issues and Controversies (5th ed.) St. Louis, MO: Mosby—Year Book
4. Koppett, L. (1981) Sports Illusion, Sport Reality. Boston, MA: Houghton Mifflin Co.
5. Weinberg, R.S. and Gould D. (1995) Foundation of sports and exercise psychology, Champaign, IL: Human Kinetics.
6. Barrow, J. (1977) "The Variables of Leadership: A Review of Conceptual Framework," Academy of Management Review, 2, 231-251.
7. Butt, D.S. (1976) Psychology of Sport. New York: Van Nostrand Reinhold Co.

Learning Life Lessons through Sports

By Kathy Masarie, MD and Coach John Child

Positive Self-Critique

John Child's coaching style started with his management role at work. When he started a review with "you are doing 'this' wrong," people would shut down and get defensive. So he started asking, "Tell me what you're proud of," and then asked, "What's sub-par?" He found people to be surprisingly honest. It was easy for John to just "coach" them along to figure out solutions for improvement.

When John started coaching his child's team, the same thing happened. Kids shut down when told what they were doing wrong, not unlike the adults. Over time he developed a routine. Early in the season, after the first game, he starts the practice with what he thinks the team did well, then poorly as a team. Then he asks the kids to share something they were proud of and something they want to work on. He picks the kids with naturally out-going personalities first. Without fail, they pick something accurate in their self-critique. There are always 3-4 shy, non-athletic kids who find this process very painful, but John helps them through it. Every 2-3 games he repeats this, and gradually the shy ones have their hands up in the air as fast as the others. In addition, they start to critique themselves as a team and to see what the other team didn't do as a team. This leads them to think for themselves on the field.

> Team sports are a great place to learn life lessons.

Team Building: Start Early

Team sports are a great place to learn life lessons.

1. We belong. In addition to their team name, the team develops a song and a banner. Each game the kid who tried especially hard takes the banner home (John starts this at age 9. Every kid gets picked by the end of the season).
2. Empowerment—everyone counts: If you show up to practice you get equal playing time.
3. Everyone does something well and even the "best" have their weak points. We want the kids to be proud of themselves and to be proud to be on the team. We want them to learn to critique themselves.
4. Life is not fair. There will always be bad referees, people make mistakes. It is no big deal. (John deliberately makes bad calls in practice so they get used to it. "Bad calls" occur many times in life, too.)

5. Winning is just a by-product; success is something more. John likes to start with his soccer teams early at the kindergarten coed level and stay with them until they enter classics or high school. His "average" caliber kids have a lot of fun and also win most of their games.

Parents

"The best way to deal with problems is to avoid them," says John. "At the first team meeting, our parents sign pledges: 'At games I will yell for the team—I will not yell at a particular kid—I will not give specific directives—I will be on time.' However, I tell them kids are responsible for getting ready and getting their parents there on time."

"Most important way to deal with parents is to not single anyone out." If some kids have been late, the entire group hears, "Some of you have been getting to practice late. That's not fair to everyone else." If there is a serious issue, he recommends talking to the parent in private. No confrontation on the field. If the parent is psyched out by a bad call, let them "know you noticed it too and that you will deal with it. It's not helping anybody to be screaming."

> **ATTENTION ADULTS:**
> 50% of kids drop out of youth sports by age 13.
> Number one reason: "It's not fun anymore."
> **LIFE LESSON HAVE FUN!**

Two new tips:

1. "Let parents know what skills you are having the kids concentrate on—passing or trapping the ball. This helps the parents focus on those goals, rather than just on scoring."
2. "Don't coddle your girls." From the girls' moms he's hearing, "Do they have to practice for 1.5 hrs? Do they really need to practice two times a week?" He coached boy's teams for years and never once did a mom worry that their boys were working too hard.

John Child is the father of a son and a daughter.

Reprinted with permission from Full Esteem Ahead, *Wings*, Spring 2002

Positive Coaching Alliance:
Transforming Youth Sports so Sports Can Transform Youth

By Harmony Barrett

It's another afternoon of watching your son and his baseball team play their cross-town rivals. The coaches have been preparing the boys all week to crush the other team—the enemy. You chat with the other parents, but as a group, you are careful to keep your distance from the other teams' parents. No making friends with the enemy! One dad sitting near to you yells orders at his son, criticizing his every move. You hear the Head Coach tell the players to run over anyone who gets in their way.

Suddenly, your son hits a ball into right field, the right fielder picks it up and throws it to first base, just as your son's foot hits the bag—the referee calls him "Out!" The coaches

jump up from the bench and charge towards the official, parents start yelling out insults, and the players join in on the barrage of objections. In the middle of the commotion, your son turns around and looks directly at you for guidance. Your next move will send him a myriad of messages, from how to handle conflict and what respect means, to the values you hold for him and the importance of healthy competition.

As we find ourselves in an increasingly problematic youth sports culture, a movement is emerging to curtail the growing aggression among youth, parents, coaches, and officials at youth sporting events, as well as belittling and negative coaching techniques.

The Positive Coaching Alliance (PCA), a national organization out of Stanford University, reports that in any given year, more than 4 million coaches work with more than 40 million young athletes in the US. Ideally, this experience "provides opportunities for children to learn important lessons about determination, commitment, hard work, teamwork, and empathy while acquiring increased self-confidence and positive character traits" (www.positivecoach.org). Sounds great, doesn't it? Isn't this exactly the experience we want for our kids? The question remains, how did we get so far away from this ideal vision of youth sports?

That is exactly the question the PCA is trying to answer; but, more importantly, they are trying to create a culture where kids love to play the game while maintaining a healthy sense of competition.

"Positive coaching is very difficult because of the arena we are in," said Rob Baarts, a former professional soccer player who now coaches for a Soccer Club in Portland, Oregon. Baarts noted that, while professional sports have positive effects on youth sports, the influence from the inflated importance put on professional teams and players has trickled down to younger players. Sometimes parents and coaches have inflated expectations of kids.

Furthermore, the PCA provides an arena for parents, coaches, and leadership members to feel empowered to make changes in their local areas. Primarily, they achieve this by promoting the Positive Coaching Mental Model, defined by three main themes:

1) Redefining what it means to be a winner: "The problem in sports right now is the 'win at all costs' mentality. What we're trying to do is change that to the Positive Coaching Mental Model. A Positive Coach is a 'Double-Goal Coach' who wants to win and also helps players develop character, so they can be successful in life. Winning is important, but the second goal, helping players learn 'life lessons,' is more important," explained Baarts.

He suggests that coaches work to develop character by making it clear to their players that effort and learning are more important than not making mistakes. This reduces anxiety and raises confidence.

Some coaches have developed a mistake ritual with their players to let the person who made the blunder know that it is okay to forget about it. One such ritual is called "the flush," where everyone on the court or field mimics flushing a toilet when someone makes a mistake, as if they are flushing it away ... to "let it go."

2) Honoring the Game: Honoring the Game is getting to the ROOTS of the matter and involves respect for the Rules, Opponents, Officials, Teammates and one's Self. Don't bend the rules to win. Understand that a worthy opponent is a gift that forces you to play to your highest potential. Show respect for officials even when you disagree. Refuse to do anything that embarrasses your team. Live up to your own standards even if others don't.

It is important that coaches model behavior that they expect of their players, such as respecting the officials. If the coach doesn't agree with the official, but does not speak up, it is their responsibility to explain why they didn't argue the call and to validate the kids' frustrations. This will promote healthy responses in the future by the kids and help them to focus on the game while moving past the officials' calls.

3) Filling the Emotional Tank: A Positive Coach is a positive motivator who refuses to motivate through fear, intimidation, or shame. Baarts compared this technique to filling the tank of a car: filling kids up with positive feedback keeps them going and keeps their energy up, which makes them more coachable and more apt to listen. On the contrary, negative criticism drains them so they run "out of gas."

A positive way to build team unity is to hold a "Winners Circle," where each player says one thing they were proud of in the game and one thing they think they need to work on. Or, each player says something positive that they saw someone else do.

Youth Tell What Coaches Need to Know

YMCA coach Nick Firchau has heard kids say::

When coaches yell at us, it makes me feel bad. We're trying to do something good. I think couches should encourage us.

—Jessica, 11, 5th grade, plays softball

Coaches make you practice and that's good. If they're really bossy, or if they're pushing too hard, then it is not fun. But if they push you hard but not too hard, then it makes you do something. And usually you are not doing it. Parents shouldn't be competitive at my age. It depends on what they yell, but I think if they are booing the other team then it's not good.

—Jon, 10, 4th grade, plays soccer, baseball, basketball

When coaches yell, you get discouraged. They should make you want to do the sport instead of not wanting to do it. Coaches shouldn't order you around like they're your mother or father.
—Selena, 9, 4th grade, ice skating

Coaches shouldn't yell at us, because we already know what we're trying to do. When coaches yell at me, it makes me feel like an idiot. —Michael 8, 2nd grade, plays baseball

Positive Coach Alliance offers workshops to educate coaches, parents, and youth sports leaders (including Board of Directors, the registrar, officials' representatives, field administrators, and head referees) about positive coaching and positive interactions between these entities. These workshops are delivered through partnerships with cities, schools and local and national youth sports organizations. Check out www. positivecoach.org to find out how to start a positive sports environment for the kids in your community.

Harmony Barrett was the Program Manager for Full Esteem Ahead and now lives in Boulder, CO.

Reprinted with permission from Full Esteem Ahead, *Wings,* Spring 2002.

Healthy Coach-Parent Partnership
1. Recognize the commitment the coach has made.
2. Make early, positive contact with the coach.
3. Fill the coach's emotional tank with positive feedback.
4. Don't put the player in the middle by talking with the coach directly when you don't like something.
5. Don't give instructions during a game or practice
6. Fill your child's emotional tank.
7. Fill the emotional tank of the entire team.
8. Encourage other parents to "Honor the Game."

Reprinted with permission of the Positive Coach Alliance.

Family Empowerment Network Recommended Handout for Coaches and Parents

A healthy experience on a sport team can be an incredible way to build assets in a child's life. Potential Developmental Assets include: #3 *Other adult relationships*; #7 *Community values youth*; #8 *Youth as resources*; #14 *Adult role models*; #16 *High expectations*; #18 *Youth programs*; #26 *Caring*; #30 *Responsibility*; #31 *Restraint*; #32 *Planning and decision-making*; #33 *Interpersonal competence*; #36 *Peaceful conflict resolution* and #38 *Self-esteem*. Coaches can be powerful, important mentors in your child's life. Have Fun!

For information on 40 Developmental Assets, check: www.search-institute.org
For information on discussion guides to support parents, check: www.family-empower.com

Asset Building Ideas for Coaches:

Coaches teach young people not only the rules and strategy of games but important lessons about life as well. You can help young people develop confidence and self-esteem, help them learn to resolve conflicts peacefully, teach them ways to take care of their health and well-being, and help them develop skills for communicating with others. Here are a few ways coaches can be asset builders:

- **Learn the names of all the players on your team** and call them by name. Make a point to talk at least once with each player each time your practice or play.
- **Create and maintain a positive atmosphere.** Two top reasons young people participate in sports are to have fun and to spend time with their friends. Winning is not one of their top reasons.
- **Focus on helping players get better, not be the best.** It will reduce players' fear of failure and give them permission to try new things and stretch their skills (asset #16: High expectations).
- **Know that highly competitive sports can often cause a great deal of stress for young people.** The intense pressure that goes along with trying to be the best can sometimes lead to unhealthy outcomes such as substance abuse and/or disorders. Be careful not to push young people too hard and learn about the warning signs of possible problems.
- **Care about your athletes' lives outside of the sport** and show them that they are valuable people as well as team members.
- **Adapt your teaching style and language to the players' age level.** Young children do not always know sports terms. Use words and concepts they understand. On the other hand, older youth may be more successful when they understand the big picture of what they are trying to accomplish as well as the specific skills or strategies needed.
- **Set goals both for individuals and for the team.** Include young people in setting these goals.
- **Catch kids doing things right.** Be quick to praise a player's efforts. The best feedback in immediate and positive.
- **Use the sandwich method of correcting a player's mistake.** First praise, then constructively criticize, then praise again.
- **Always preserve players' dignity.** Sarcasm does not work well with young people. They may not always remember what you say, but they always remember how you said it.
- **Insist that all team members treat one another with respect.** Then model, monitor, and encourage respect. Have a zero-tolerance policy for teasing that hurts someone's feelings.
- **Be specific about a code of conduct and expectations** for athletes, parents, spectators, and team personnel.
- **Encourage athletes to do well in school** and to be motivated to achieve.
- **Respect other activities and priorities in athletes' lives.** Avoid conflicts with their other commitments and respect their need for time with their families.
- **Find ways each child can participate,** even if he or she is not particularly skilled in the sport.
- **Listen to and encourage your athletes' dreams,** concerns, and desires—sports-related or otherwise.
- **Develop leadership skills in young athletes** by giving them opportunities to lead practice drills and develop a team code of conduct.
- **Take time at the end of practice to have the group offer positive comments about each player's performance that day.** Make sure no one is left out.
- **Split up cliques on the team by mixing up groups for drills and scrimmages.**
- **Plan a community service project for the team.** It teaches players to give something back to the community.
- **If you have an end-of-season gathering, take time to say a few positive things about each player.** Avoid Most Valuable Player awards and other "rankings." Focus on the relationships, the improvements of the team, and the unique contributions of each player.

Reprinted with permission from *Pass It On! Ready to Use Handouts for Asset Builders*. Handout [#37]. Copyright © 1999, 2006 Search Institute®. Minneapolis, MN; www.search-institute.org. All rights reserved.

Creating Community 10

Amanda Russel, 7th Grade, Rosemount Ridge Middle School

Creating Community:
Building a Culture that Cares about Kids

"It is in the shelter of each other that the people live."
—Irish Proverb

"Do not pray for an easy life, pray to be a strong person."
—Anonymous

"Thousands of candles can be lighted from a single candle and the candle of life will not be shortened. Happiness never decreases by being shared."
—Buddha

"Whatever you can do or imagine, begin it; boldness has beauty, magic and power in it."
—Goethe

"You can create the life you dream about—the family life you long for. Just decide you want a 'connected, thriving family', vision it, and then commit to it. The rest will follow."
—Kathy Masarie

GOALS

- To solidify a vision for yourself, your son and your family and to plan what next steps you will take to create a nurturing, supportive, and connected family and community.

- To use the Developmental Assets to build on what is strong and positive in your family and community.

- To integrate regular volunteering into your family activities, as well as actively contributing to a strong, inclusive community.

- To establish a personal plan for staying connected to other parents and their sons.

OVERVIEW

In our first chapter, we asked parents to make a list of positive visions and wishes for your family and your son. This is a good time to look at that vision again, as your discussion group reads this last chapter and you start to think of next steps to nurture your son's mental, social, and emotional development. Over the past nine sessions, you have discussed and shared some difficult issues that families and boys may face in today's world. Remembering a positive vision for your son will help empower you to network within your own family, with other parents, and with your community to create a positive and supportive environment for your son and for all children. It is our hope that you will bring these visions to fruition.

Family Empowerment Network believes that parents are the best resource for helping their children thrive in the transition from childhood to adulthood. Parents can foster an environment at home and within their community that supports their children's emerging competence, caring and responsibility. We sincerely hope that you will take the information you have learned from *Raising Our Sons Parenting Guide* and apply it constructively within your lives. A group of committed individuals like yourselves, choosing to take the time and effort to make a difference, can truly turn positive visions for our youth into realities.

Families Making a Difference

Changing your son's world for the better starts at home. Families are the most important source of encouragement, caring, support, and unconditional love for our children. Connection to family is one of your son's greatest protective factors. Families are more important than ever now that we are living in a time when our outside culture is often discouraging and even harmful to the healthy development of our children. Dr. Stephen Covey, in his book *The Seven Habits of Highly Effective Families,* encourages parents to clearly understand the power they have to create the kind of nurturing family life that will inspire and protect their children. He states:

One of the best parts of being a family is that you can encourage one another. You can put courage into one another. You can believe in one another. You can affirm one another. You can assure one another that you are never going to give up, that you see the potential, and that you are acting in faith based on that potential rather than on any particular behavior or circumstance. You can be bold and strengthen one another's hearts and minds. You can weave a strong and secure safety net of encouraging circumstances in the home so that family members can cultivate those kinds of internal resiliencies and strengths that will enable them to deal with the discouraging, anti-family circumstances outside.

Mary Pipher, in her book, *The Shelter of Each Other: Rebuilding our Families,* echoes these same sentiments. She reminds us that much of what ails families today is related to our toxic culture. When our kids have problems with sexuality, addictions, or school failure, for example, it is simply not helpful to shift the blame to parents or teens. Our popular culture significantly endangers the healthy development of our children.

Pipher suggests that modern American families think of themselves as immigrants within their own culture. Immigrants, like families in modern America, must find ways to straddle two different cultures, the family culture and the outside one, each with its own set of values and behaviors.

We are all immigrants today living in a culture whose stories are not our stories and whose values are not our values. Families are stronger when they acknowledge this and unite to resist the messages and influences that would harm them.

To survive, the immigrant family must use discretion to pick the best values and behaviors, while rejecting negative or harmful outside forces. Faced with these difficulties, families who unite together will flourish, while those who attack each other from within will flounder. Likewise, families can embrace the wonders and joys of modern living, while limiting the impact of and exposure to harmful technologies, influences and behaviors. In this way, families can successfully learn to work together, to enrich their relationships and to create healthy communities in spite of the difficulties encountered in the outside world.

More than any single factor that parents can control, studies have repeatedly shown that "feeling cared about and connected" during one's youth is the key to a safer adolescence and a happy adult life. In Chapter 8: "Keeping Him Safe" (p. 8:19), we shared the National Longitudinal Study of Adolescent Health, a survey of over 90,000 youth, which found that there were two factors (out of more than one hundred) that most protected children from negative outcomes during adolescence. The first protective factor was a feeling of connectedness at home, defined as closeness to parent(s), perceived caring by parent(s), and feeling understood, loved, wanted and paid attention to by family members. The second protective factor was a feeling of connectedness at school, defined as being treated fairly by teachers, feeling close to and having good relationships with students and teachers. Again, we can see the supreme importance of relationships to the healthy development of our children. In a fascinating sociological study of 8 teens living in a well-off suburb, Patricia Hersch, author of *A Tribe Apart,* helps us to understand from the inside out how much teens need parents, teachers and other adults to be involved in their lives and how overwhelming their lives can be without enough adult presence. The good news is that creating connected relationships costs very little. It does, however, require giving our children a significant investment of our time and energy, learning ways of relating to our children that are loving, empowering and supportive, and setting limits on screen time. In **"Slow Down: You're Movin' Too Fast … For Real Connection"** (p. 10:14), Marta Mellinger shares some sage advice for families from Simon and Garfunkel:

> Slow down, you move too fast. Gotta make the morning last. Just kickin' down the cobblestones— lookin' for fun, and feelin' groovy.

Taking the Time to Build Assets

Taking the time to build deeper connections in our families and communities is what this last chapter of *Raising Our Sons* is about. This is called community building: creating the world of connection that we want for all our children. If our intention is to build a healthy, supportive family and community for our children, regardless of where we live, how are we to do this? One answer brings us full circle back to the Developmental Assets. Increasing the assets in your son's life is a research-proven way to enrich his relationships, to protect him from risky behaviors and to help him feel more connected with his family and community. Asset building can be summarized in three words all of us can remember: CONNECT WITH KIDS. Kids grow and develop best when surrounded by caring, nurturing adults who are actively involved in their lives. The authors of the book *What Young Children Need to Succeed* state that making Developmental Asset building a part of your everyday life is easy:

> All you need is the belief that children are important and that people need to be there to support them, guide them, and cheer them on. Building Assets in children helps you bring out the best in them—and in you. You can begin to build children's Assets in 3 simple steps: believe that children deserve your attention and care, make a commitment, and act… Asset-building can be as simple or complex as you'd like. It can use a little of your time or a lot of it. It all depends on what you want to do. Many people prefer to start small. If this is true for you, follow the ABC's of Asset-building and do easy, quick things to build Assets in children. If you want to have a greater impact, use the XYZ's of Asset–building as a guide to building Assets in deeper, long-term ways. Building Assets can take only a few minutes of your time—or years of your life, depending on what you choose to do. You can choose to build Assets in 3 major ways: as an individual, as part of an organization, or as part of a community. It doesn't matter which way (or ways) you choose. All that matters is that you start.

There is a saying that a vision without action is just a dream. Likewise, building connection and healthy relationships in your family and community requires positive intention coupled with action. Peter Benson, the

ABC's of Asset Building	XYZ's of Asset Building
• Quick	• Slower
• Offer immediate results	• Lead to long-term results
• Don't take long	• Take more time
• Need little preparation	• Require preparation
• Simple	• More complex
• Spontaneous	• Intentional
• Easy commitment	• Greater commitment
• Requires little energy	• Requires more energy

From the book *What Young Children Need to Succeed*, by Jolene Roehlkepartain and Nancy Leffert.

founder of the Search Institute, explains the core asset-building principles in **"Adding Up Assets"** (p. 10:15):

- The 40 Developmental Assets provide a common language.
- Assets are contagious.
- Assets protect and enhance.
- Assets are fragile.
- Community capacity is enormous and unlimited.
- Unleashing capacity requires a critical mass.
- Youth can be asset builders.
- Asset building is a movement.

"Listen up, Adult Advocates: How Can Adults Be More Supportive of Young People?" (p. 10:16) reminds us that if we want to build assets for youth we need to remember to be present, reach out, be consistent, listen, be clear, be willing to share power, be engaged and be sincere. This chapter will help you to picture clearly what you want for your children and design a plan for increasing assets in your son's life.

Building Assets One-on-One

Asset building can be simple, as easy as a smile, and can take myriad forms. It takes only one person at any one time to make changes that benefit one's own child or a whole community. It could be as simple, yet challenging, as being home every day to welcome our teens when they arrive home. Sometimes we build assets through unique family rituals that provide a lifelong sense of bonding to family and nature, such as an annual camping trip. In other situations, the attempts of one individual can change the life of a

young person. "Making a Difference One by One" and "Asset-Building Stories About the Power of Individual Action" (pp. 10:17-10:18) will give you ideas about how you can create community for your son and how one simple step can lead to a rich future. **"Brewing Up Assets: A Friendly Adult Stirs in Some Support"** (p. 10:19) is a great reminder to all of us that in our everyday lives we either leave time to connect or we don't.

Building Assets with Neighbors and Friends

Families, parents, and sons thrive when they feel part of a greater community of neighbors and friends. These overlapping communities involve people of all ages who feel cared for and secure and support each other. We don't always get to choose the makeup of our neighborhood, but an asset-building perspective helps us to take initiative in creating community within our neighborhood (as shared in **"Asset-Building Ideas for Neighbors and Neighborhood Groups"** (p. 10:20)). Some neighborhoods have a focal point such as a park, a pool, a community garden, a basketball net, or a sledding hill, which can be used to enhance everyone's connection to the neighborhood. One of the authors was fortunate enough to grow up in a community where an elderly couple opened their pool to the neighborhood in the mornings. Neighbors set up a complete swim instruction program for all ages, and neighborhood teens helped out; the summer culminated in an evening water show complete with homemade costumes. Although this example required a pool with very generous owners, most neighborhood bonding activities—from badminton tournaments to 4th of July bike parades to weekly pizza nights—do not. **"May Day Basket Celebration"** (p. 10:21) shares a delightful neighborhood-based activity that enhances community while building assets for all of the neighborhood's children. In addition to being lots of fun, the annual May Day photo collage of the neighborhood children enables every neighbor to recognize every child. This makes it easier, especially for elderly neighbors, to engage with the children.

In addition to creating community in our neighbor-hoods, asset-building parents can organize with other adults to create family magic. Some family magic is created with our own extended families of cousins, aunts and uncles and grandparents. Sons who can spend time with loving grandparents, aunts and uncles are lucky indeed. However, for those of us who are not close to family, or may only see them once or twice a year, creating a sense of family with friends becomes increasingly important. Some families with younger children band together to form babysitting co-ops where families take care of each other's children, moms meet monthly for "Mom's Night Out" and the families get together for holidays and even weekend getaways. Even though the families don't live in the same neighborhood, the children grow up feeling like they are part of a community of people who know them well, welcome them into their homes, and care deeply for them. **"Asset-Building Stories about the Power of Neighbors and Friends," "Get-Away Weekend,"** and **"Family Magic"** (pp.10:22-10:24) will give you many ideas for bonding with other families. Finally **"Why Aren't There More Dads' Groups?"** (p. 10:25) addresses the isolation dads can feel because men do not bond via groups as readily as women. As we know, parents who feel supported—moms or dads—are better able to parent wisely.

Building Assets Through Schools

As we wrote in detail in Chapter 6, schools are an important milieu for asset building, from teachers reaching out to students and families, to parents volunteering and being involved in learning.

Furthermore, feeling bonded to school is one of the top protective factors for teens. Stephen Covey's book, *The Leader in Me,* shows how schools can develop internal assets in our kids by directly teaching leadership, communication, and initiative skills, as well as getting business and civic leaders involved in the process. School is also such an excellent opportunity for parents to meet other parents and children. Walking and riding bikes to school, carpooling, volunteering, attending school events, and staying after school while children play on the playground and parents talk are all great ways to connect. When our schools are "community" schools where the doors are always open to meet community needs, the possibilities for building assets

grow exponentially. **"Asset-Building Stories about School Connection"** (p. 10:26) will give you ideas for building community at your schools. **"SUN—Schools Uniting Neighborhoods"** (p. 10:27) is an excellent example of how to create a community-responsive school. SUN schools open their doors to the whole neighborhood for afternoon, evening and weekend classes and events, essentially becoming a neighborhood community center.

Asset Building Through Volunteering

Volunteering or service learning is one of the most powerful of asset builders, since you can build several assets at once. **"Virtues of Volunteering"** (p. 10:28) shares the many ways volunteering can support your son. He will:

- Feel useful and valued by the community,
- Learn that he has something to offer and can make a difference,
- Build skills and develop a sense of personal competence,
- Enhance his self-esteem,
- Create a supportive network of relationships with other adults and with healthy peers.

Research shows that people who volunteer are happier. Kids in service to others learn there are interesting people out in the world if they make the effort to get to know them. Volunteering enhances boys' engagement with the community and feelings of social responsibility towards others. Adults who volunteer with kids are often amazed by how much kids know and how skillful they can be. Some projects can also provide a parent and child with one-on-one time, working together with a common purpose. Volunteering as a family adds significantly to a feeling of family cohesion.

In our culture, boys (and men) particularly need to be encouraged to volunteer, as described in **"Let's Get Girls and Boys Equally Involved in Volunteering"** (p. 10:30). **"Volunteering—The Youth Perspective"** (p. 10: 31) gives us insight into how satisfying volunteering can be from a teen's point of view. The article describes four teen service projects: painting a house, helping students learn English, raising money to help others, and volunteering to help adults with their computers.

How do we help our kids and ourselves to get involved? **"Connect with Kids by Helping Them to Help Others"** (p. 10:33) takes us step-by-step through the process of coming up with community service ideas. Finally, **"Hands On Portland: Volunteering Made Easy"** (p. 10:34) describes a model organization that connects volunteers with needs in Portland, Oregon. This website connects volunteers with opportunities at scores of organizations in the metro area, making it incredibly easy for busy people to volunteer. Your community can duplicate this wonderful non-profit idea, which is win-win for everyone These articles show that volunteering is not limited by gender, age, occupation or working full-time. Taking an interest in children and improving our communities can happen at all levels of our society.

Building Assets in the Greater Community

Asset building can also affect the community at large for parents who have the motivation to work on this level. For example, the entire community can learn about the 40 Developmental Assets if the local newspaper dedicates a weekly column to spreading the word about asset-building ideas. Local businesses can also get connected with schools and develop assets in a variety of ways from encouraging employees to volunteer at schools to developing a school-to-work program where students participate in business activities **"Asset Building Stories about Businesses and the Greater Community"** (p. 10:35) shares several asset-building projects instigated by parents that affect whole communities. Parents in some states have created **"Stand for Children"** (p. 10:37) groups, a grassroots advocacy movement that lobbies to improve children's lives from educational needs to health needs and rights. They have demonstrated that banding together can transform political policies.

How would our communities look if many of our local businesses became family-friendly workplaces and encouraged their employees to volunteer with children in the community as tutors, mentors and classroom resources? **"Businesses—Join Up and Volunteer To-day"** (p. 10:38) shows how one community's businesses give back to the community. **"Take Your Kids to Work Day"** (p. 10:39) is another excellent way to forge a connection between families and business. As in all school-to-work

programs, kids learn about careers, and adults learn from and become bonded to kids and teens.

In many other industrialized nations, the importance of parenting is acknowledged and supported by both government and industry. In modern America it receives much less support than it deserves. Sylvia Hewlett and Cornel West, professors at Harvard, created a task force that networked parents around the country to create a blueprint for parents' rights, as described in their book *The War on Parents: What We Can Do for America's Beleaguered Moms and Dads*. The Bill of Rights is a vision for how our country could improve the assets of parents and families. This approach and Internet advocacy groups such as MomsRising.org, attempt to change the structure of our society in order to support and nurture families.

A Parent's Bill Of Rights
Mothers and Fathers are Entitled to:
1. Time for their children
   - Paid parenting leave
   - Family-friendly workplaces
   - A safety net
2. Economic security
   - A living wage
   - Job opportunities
   - Tax relief
   - Help with housing
3. A pro-family electoral system
   - Incentives to vote
   - Votes for children
4. A pro-family legal structure
   - Stronger marriage
   - Support for fathers
   - Adoption assistance
5. A supportive external environment
   - Violence-free neighborhoods
   - Quality schooling
   - Extended school day and year
   - Child care
   - Family health coverage
   - Drug-free communities
6. Honor and dignity
   - An index of parent well-being
   - National Parents' day
   - Parent privileges

What would it look like if we had a culture that actually honored these family rights at all levels of our society, from schools to businesses to government? What if we all knew and operated from the idea that the health and well-being of our children reflects the health and well-being of all of us, like "canaries in the mines"? What if we greeted each other every day with the question the Masai greet each other with, "How are the children?"

Your Action Plan

Congratulations! You have completed reading and discussing the many chapters of *Raising our Sons*, and it is time to take action. Read **"Family Empowerment Network: Final Session of Raising our Sons"** (p. 10:40) and think about how you would like to continue nurturing your new awareness and connections. To help prepare yourself to take action and actively increase the assets in your son's life, take out (or recreate) your list of positive visions and wishes for your son from Chapter 1, your list of 40 Developmental Assets that is posted on your refrigerator, and your nine lists of "Putting It Together" ideas from each of the previous chapters. Using these ideas, fill out the form **"Next Steps: A Tool for Creating a Vision and Taking Action"** (p. 10:41). Now you have a list of ideas that will keep you on track towards actively building the world you want for your son. This form can be used again and again, whenever you have specific or general goals that you want to achieve within your family or your community. It helps to keep your vision and intention clearly in mind, and to recognize honestly where you are along the way. Delineating these two things clearly will make it easy to plan your action steps to accomplish your vision.

To enhance the success of your goals and action steps, here are some coaching tips from life coach, Kathy Masarie:
* Write your goals in the present tense as if they already happened.
* Focus on what you have control over.
* List concrete actions that are doable and can be measured in some way. That way, you will be able to know when you have accomplished each task.
* Put a timeline on each action step and post the form where you will see it often.
* Keep in touch with your discussion group and support each other. Share how and what you are doing and consider working together to build assets.

Creating a Culture That Cares

In the end, creating a new culture of acceptance and connectedness for our sons begins with one person at a time. However, there are cultures in the world that place a priority on connecting with and celebrating their youth, which is illustrated in this vivid example from author Barbara Kingsolver (from *High Tide in Tucson: Essays from Now or Never*):

As I walked out the street entrance to my newly rented apartment, a guy in maroon high-tops and a skateboard haircut approached, making kissing noises and saying, 'Hi, gorgeous!' Three weeks earlier, I would have assessed the degree of malice and made ready to run or tell him to bug off, depending. But now, instead, I smiled, and so did my four-year old daughter, because after dozens of similar encounters I understood he didn't mean me, but her.

This is not the United States.

For most of the year my daughter was four we lived in Spain, in the warm southern province of the Canary Islands.

I struggled with dinner at midnight and the subjunctive tense, but my only genuine culture shock reverberated from this earthquake of a fact: people here like kids. They don't just say so, they do. Widows in black stop on the street to have little chats with my daughter. Routinely, taxi drivers leaned out the window and shouted 'Hola, guapa!' My daughter, who must have felt my conditioned flinch, would look up at me wide-eyed and explain patiently, 'I like it that people think I'm pretty.' With a mother's keen myopia I would tell you, absolutely, my daughter is beautiful enough to stop traffic. But in the city of Santa Cruz, I have to confess, so was every other person under the height of one meter. Not just those who conceded to be seen and not heard. Whenever Camille grew cranky in a restaurant (and really, what do you expect at midnight?), the waiters flirted and brought her little presents, and nearby diners looked on with that sweet, wistful gleam of eye that I'd thought diners reserved for the dessert tray. What I discovered in Spain was a culture that held children to be its meringues and éclairs.

Isn't this the culture we all crave for all of our children? We can make a difference. Nothing has ever changed in this world without the thoughtful, committed work of a creative group of individuals. Family Empowerment Network's mission is to create families and communities where children are truly valued, supported and cared for,

as described in **"Our Dream for our Sons: Authenticity, Self Love, and Self Acceptance"** (p. 10:42). How would our lives change if we loved our children and ourselves unconditionally? We hope that you will take stock of your own family and community, and then take action toward making this vision a reality in your own life.

"Never doubt that a small group of thoughtful, committed citizens can change the world. Indeed, it's the only thing that ever has."

—Margaret Mead

THE 40 DEVELOPMENTAL ASSETS Essential to Every Young Person's Success

The Search Institute's "40 Assets" inventory and survey was introduced in Session 1. The following are the assets that can be built through community building and creating "safe havens" of support for youth.

- Asset #3   **Other Adult Relationships:** Young people have at least three other adults in their lives giving them support in addition to parents.
- Asset #4   **Caring Neighborhood:** Young people have the care and support of people who live nearby.
- Asset #7   **Community Values Youth:** Young people know they are valued by the adults in their community.
- Asset #8   **Youth as Resources:** Young people serve useful roles in their school, family and community.
- Asset #9   **Service to Others:** Young people volunteer one hour or more per week to help others.
- Asset #13   **Neighborhood Boundaries:** Neighbors share with parents the responsibility for monitoring young people's behavior.
- Asset #14   **Adult Role Models:** Parents and other adults set good examples for young people.
- Asset #15   **Positive Peer Pressure:** Youth's best friends model responsible behavior.
- Asset #17   **Creative Activities:** Young people are involved in music, theater or other arts three hours per week.
- Asset #18   **Youth Programs:** Young people are involved in sports, clubs or organizations at least three hours per week.
- Asset #19   **Religious Community:** Young people are involved in spiritual growth.
- Asset #26   **Caring:** Young people feel that it is important to help others make the world a better place.
- Asset #27   **Equality and Justice:** Young people believe in fairness and equity and are committed to social justice.
- Asset #34   **Cultural Competence:** Young people know and respect people of different racial and cultural backgrounds.
- Asset #37   **Personal Power:** Young people believe that they have control over the direction of their life.
- Asset #38   **Self-esteem:** Young people feel good about who they are.
- Asset #39   **Sense of Purpose:** Young people believe their life has a purpose.

Circle Activity

This last week, you will have a group activity instead of a circle question.

- Take your individual Next Steps Action Plans and share with each other.
- Copy the outline of the "Next Steps: Making a Vision and Taking Action" on a large piece of paper.
- Brainstorm as a group and decide on one project that you would like to accomplish together, and place this in the Vision Box. This could be a group celebration with your sons, a group picnic, a school or community project, or any other service activity that you could work on together to increase the feeling of connectedness within your community.
- Fill in the current reality box describing where you are now.
- Brainstorm the action steps needed to make your vision happen.
- Brainstorm how you will continue meeting.

This process is a great way to honor yourselves and each other for successfully completing *Raising Our Sons*.

DISCUSSION QUESTIONS
1. How has this *Raising Our Sons* discussion group impacted your life and your parenting?
2. If you have had a positive experience with *Raising Our Sons,* how might you create other ROD groups within your child's school or community?
3. Where can you find support in your own life for your challenging job as a parent?
4. What kinds of community support exists for children and families in your community that you could be a part of?
5. How do you build assets in your neighborhood or greater community?
6. How can you build volunteering into your own life and that of your child?

PUTTING IT INTO PRACTICE
- Go through all your "Putting It Together—Your Version" lists from the previous 10 chapters. Mark three of your favorites, put them on your calendar and do them.
- Show girls—your own and those you come into contact with—that you care about them:
  - Give them your time.
  - Look at and greet every girl you see.
  - Talk with girls about their interests.
  - Invite a young person to an activity you think they might enjoy.
  - Welcome neighborhood kids into your home.
- Make a point of getting to know the people in your neighborhood. Host a community event—like a neighborhood potluck, the porch cookie campaign, or making May Day Baskets.
- Get involved in your neighborhood organization, a Mom's or Dad's support group, or organizations within your kid's school.
- Plan an event with extended family and friends like a bike trip, softball game, summer BBQ, or a camping trip.
- Educate your community on Developmental Assets: put out flyers in the library or schools, and start an asset-building column in your local newspaper or school newsletter.

- Fill out the asset checklist—both you and your child—(p. 1-33) and compare the differences and similarities.
- Encourage your son to build relationships through service projects, volunteering, or mentoring. Choose a family volunteering project and do it.
- Take part in youth-serving programs through schools, community organizations and congregations.
- Invite caring adults into your daughter's life.

PUTTING IT TOGETHER—YOUR VERSION

Collect your top ten favorite ideas from all the previous overviews.

1. _____

2. _____

3. _____

4. _____

5. _____

6. _____

7. _____

8. _____

9. _____

10. _____

FURTHER READING

What Teen's Need to Succeed by Peter Benson, PhD

All Kids Are Our Kids: What Communities Must Do to Raise Caring and Responsible Children and Adolescents by Peter Benson PhD, President of the Search Institute.

A Tribe Apart by Patricia Hersch

The Leader in Me: How Schools and Parents Around the World Are Inspiring Greatness, One Child at a Time by S. Covey

The War on Parents: What We Can Do for American's Beleaguered Moms and Dads by Sylvia Ann Hewlett

DVDs

At the Table: Youth Voices in Decision Making from Community Partnerships with Youth, 6319 Constitution Dr., Fort Wayne, IN 46804 (219-436-4402). 15-minute video features youth leaders and adults who have successfully incorporated meaningful youth involvement into their organizations.

Books for Teens

The Kid's Volunteering Book by Arlene Erlbach

Kids with Courage: True Stories about Young People Making a Difference by Barbara Lewis

The Kid's Guide to Service Projects by Barbara Lewis

160 Ways to Help the World: Community Service Projects for Young People by Linda Duper

The Kid's Guide to Social Action: How to Solve the Social Problems You Choose and Turn Creative Thinking into Positive Action by Barbara Lewis

What Do You Stand For? A Kid's Guide to Building Character by Barbara Lewis

Other Resources

Working mother's rights at www.momsrising.org

The Best of Everything Social Action Resource: A collection of successful social action and social justice projects for children and teens. Contains lists of resources, such as books, DVDs, and programs, poems, stories, and quotations. Detailed information on a "Random Act of Kindness" program, and quilt–making with children. Contact Beth Brownfield at (360-738-8899) or bethbrownf@aol.com.

Search Institute (Developmental Asset Building): 1-800-888-7828 at www.search-institute.org

Big Brothers/Big Sisters of America at www.bbbsa.org

Youth Volunteer Corps and the Youth Involvement Network: Provides resources for youth volunteers to find and conduct community service projects in their area. 1-888-828-9822 at www.yvca.org

Activism 2000 Project: Youth-led initiatives at www.youthactivism.com

Smart: Volunteer coaches help early school-aged children become confident readers at www.getsmartoregon.org.

Hands on Portland: Connects volunteers with community needs at www.handsonportland.org

Friends of Trees: Brings people together to plant city trees and restore urban natural areas at www.friendsoftrees.org

Friends of the Children: Professional mentors serve high-risk children at www.friendsofthechildren.org

Americorps Community Service Program at www.americorps.org

Green Corps at wwwgreencorps.org

Service and Conservation Corps at www.corpsnetwork.org

LeapNow: Alternative international service-oriented college program at www.leapnow.org

Slow Down: You're Movin' Too Fast For Real Connection
By Marta Mellinger

Slow down, you move too fast.
You gotta make the morning last.
Just kickin' down the cobblestones
Lookin' for fun, and feelin' groovy ...
—Simon and Garfunkel song

Slow down

We bemoan our fast-paced, information age world. Listening, really listening, requires that we truly slow down. To listen, first we must be in one place long enough for our teen to sit down beside us. Driving carpool is not such a bad thing. Doing dishes side-by-side isn't either. But do sit down together as often as possible. Slow down long enough to sit down.

You move too fast

If you quiet your mind, you can open your heart. Inside each of us is a personal voice. Some of us have judging voices, or idea-generating voices. Some are always thinking about what to do next. Many of us are busy thinking about what we want to do or say next, instead of concentrating on what our teen is saying to us right now. Concentrate on each word and each pause and each nuance, instead of thinking about what to say next. Watch body language.

You gotta make the morning last

"Make the morning last" is a way to remember to be "in the moment" with our teens. That's where they live. THEIR reality is that they will be a teenager forever; what happened yesterday is monumental. And that WE cannot POSSIBLY understand. Forget trying to "understand." Let them know that you just want to listen. Then, just listen. Listen as if their life depends on your understanding of their life and their perceptions. (And . . . forget trying to tell them your own.)

Just kickin' down the cobblestones

The absolutely best time to listen may be when teens are hanging out. Talking to parents can feel risky because teens both want and don't want to care about what we think. When they are with their friends, or watching TV, or on vacation, we can listen. Talking together becomes less of a big deal, when we're all just hanging out together. Choose the easy times to "practice your listening skills."

Lookin' for fun

Knowing, really knowing, your teen is fun. Trying to change your teen is NOT fun. (And that is another article: If a teen is in trouble, or really needs "saving," this article is not for you.) Look for fun in listening, the fun of knowing who they are turning out to be.

And feelin' groovy

Feel—and notice—your feelings while you're listening to your teen. But ALWAYS remember you don't have to tell THEM how you feel. If they say, "My best friend got a tattoo," you may notice that you feel anxious. Anxiety can lead even the most listening parent to say something like, "Tattoos might affect Nick's future career options." But if instead we notice anxiety, we may zip our judging parental lips and listen long enough to hear what our teen thinks about tattoos. This may actually be MORE interesting than their response to our anxiety. Feel your feelings, own your emotions, and (most of the time) choose to listen instead.

Marta Mellinger is the founder of The Canoe Group—a shared practice of four passionate professionals who help organizations develop new ways to succeed in rapidly changing times. With her husband, she parents their two college-aged daughters and is proud that they still call and come home.

Reprinted with permission of Full Esteem Ahead, *Wings*, Spring 2001.

Adding Up Assets

By Peter Benson, author of *Sparks: How Parents Can Help Ignite the Hidden Strengths of Teenagers*

Both for the novice and the old hand, Search Institute® president Peter Benson offered these core Asset-building principles in his keynote address at a Healthy Communities – Healthy Youth Conference in Denver.

- **The 40 Developmental Assets provide a common language.** Language is consciousness and consciousness has so much to do with dictating action. The Assets create a language of possibility that breaks change into small molecules and suggests we all have capacity. With the asset language, we can begin to reframe the human imagination about responsibility, capacity, and change.

- **Assets are additive.** More is better. Remember, this is a culture always looking for the quick fix, the panacea, the one thing we can do that will make everything worthwhile and healthy for our kids. There isn't one thing. It's about weaving a fabric.

- **Assets protect and enhance.** There are over 25 years of scientific research that continue to demonstrate again and again how the Developmental Assets help "inoculate" young people from some of the dangers of the world and help to enhance many forms of thriving—like school success, like showing up as a leader, like the affirmation of diversity.

- **Assets are fragile.** In every community that has done the assessment of Developmental Assets— and that's many, many communities now—one of the things that we discover is a rupture in the developmental infrastructure. Most American young people are now living in towns and cities with huge capacity, but where that capacity is dormant.

- **Community capacity is enormous and unlimited.** The question is: Can we awaken community power? Recently, at the Jimmy Carter Presidential Library in Atlanta, I saw a quote from Carter that said, "The only position in America more important than president is citizen." The President cannot build community for you. CEOs aren't going to build your community. Your superintendent and legislators aren't going to build your community. I think what Carter is telling us is that it's about neighbor and parent and bus driver and parishioner. It is about peer influence. It is about the people of community knitting the fabric of community.

- **Unleashing capacity requires a critical mass of human beings.** This is hard work. This requires communication and engagement with adults of all walks, with kids of all walks, so that they get it deeply, so it becomes a heart work. This is about taking advantage of the moment and the opportunities before us to connect, to engage, to know, to look deeply inside, to pay attention.

- **Youth are asset builders.** Young people, think about your power with your peers. You know how important peer influence is. You have such important credibility and integrity with the kids you hang around with. Imagine your power to build assets in your peers. Imagine your own power for building your own assets. Don't wait for adults to build them. In many communities, what I see is that teenagers don't want to have a whole lot to do with smaller kids. Get over it. Use your power.

- **Asset building is a movement.** By placing ourselves in the context of a movement, rather than simply implementing programs, we can learn from the history of sustainable movements. One of the things we know is that sustainable movements trigger acts of symbolic power. Rosa Parks comes to mind. The Boston Tea Party comes to mind. What in your communities are the symbolic acts that touch the imagination and the heart?

Listen Up, Adult Advocates
Ideas that Work, Opinions that Matter, Research that Illuminates
Written and compiled by Kalisha Davis

How CAN PARENTS and other adults improve how they support young people? We attended Assets for Colorado Youth's State Youth Summit in August to get the inside scoop. Youth sharing their honest opinions, ideas, and solutions included Katrina Harris, 14, of Denver; Mary Hottenroth, 15, of Steamboat Springs; Katrina Robertson, 18, of Denver; Lucia Sanchez, 17, of Greeley; and Kendra Youngren, 16, of Greeley.

How can adults be more supportive of young people?

Be present

There are a lot of youth I know who are in bad situations. They have adults in their household who aren't positive role models. They need to heal. They need adults to support them who are willing to spend the time. You have to be willing to walk with them.

Reach out

Adults need to make more time for youth because, more likely than not, youth are not going to be the ones to come forward. Adults have to seek them out.

Be consistent

If you start mentoring once a week, it's usually better to keep that. If you say, "I'm more busy than I was before, so I think I'll take away some of my time," that kid is going to feel rejected.

Listen

When kids have problems, they have to be able to talk to their parents without consequence. If parents say, "I'm never going to let you do this again," kids won't feel comfortable talking. You have to work through it together.

What can adults do in meetings to make youth involvement more meaningful?

Be clear

You need to speak English. We don't want every single detail. Give us a general outline. Let us know what's going on.

Be willing to share power

I don't see why we have to classify each other as youth or adult. Why can't we just call each other coworkers? We're working together, aren't we?

Be engaged

A lot of times adults meet and it's boring. The adults don't even seem to be into what they're doing, but when youth come in with new ideas, all of a sudden things just start rolling again.

Be sincere

Adults ask what we want and they're not sincere. You have to want to do it. We can see through the fakeness.

Making a Difference One by One

By Peter Benson, PhD, author of *All Kids Are Our Kids*

MOBILIZING INDIVIDUALS FOR action may seem inefficient and time-consuming. It is harder to show progress on a grand scale. But, one by one, individuals can have a tremendous impact. In every community that begins this work, we hear the stories of one person who has made a difference. It took one person to turn around Deon Richardson of St. Louis Park, the first community to embrace asset building as a framework for community action.

Ninth grade wasn't a good year for Richardson. Every day he would skip class. He would write graffiti on the walls and the school lockers. He got into fights. By the end of the school year, he had only earned half of an academic credit.

One of his teachers, Tom Bardal —a health and driver's education teacher— noticed. He often sought out Richardson and would talk with him. He noticed that when Richardson skipped class, he often headed to the gym to shoot baskets with his peers who were also skipping class.

"I could see how basketball was very important to him," Bardal says. "He had potential not only as an athlete but as a student as well." Bardal also happened to be the varsity basketball coach, and he often encouraged Richardson to try out for the team. But Richardson kept turning him down.

"I never had time for it," Richardson says. "I never wanted to play [on a team]."

Bardal didn't give up, however. "He would talk to me during my freshman year, and I would just push that all to the side," Richardson says. "But then my sophomore year came around . . . and he said I could be one of the best if I would really try."

Despite Richardson's skepticism, he decided to try out for the team. He made it. "I never had anybody tell me I was good," Richardson says. "He was the first coach who told me I could be somebody. He was the first one. And that's why I think I will thank him right now for being there. Otherwise, I would have still been on that wrong path."

Not only did Bardal take an interest in Richardson's playing ability, but also in his schoolwork. He checked on Richardson every day to see if he was attending class. He talked to Richardson's other teachers. When he found out that Richardson was skipping study hall, he brought Richardson into his room to help him with his homework. "I saw a kid with potential and that's what teachers are all about," Bardal says. "We can talk about curriculum and teach it day in and day out, but sometimes that's not as important as turning a kid's life around."

Still, Bardal credits Richardson for making most of the changes. By his junior year, Richardson had caught up on all his academic credits by going to summer school and attending after-school classes. Today his favorite subjects are English, math, and chemistry, and he's getting A's and B's. He's now comparing colleges. "I want to go into business," Richardson says. "I want my own business. I think it would be cool to have your own business. And basketball is something I can fall back on."

Where does Richardson think he would be now if he hadn't changed? He figures he would be in jail. Or he would have seriously hurt someone by now.

"When he was a ninth grader, I thought, this kid isn't going to make it," says John Headlee, assistant principal of St. Louis Park High School. "Now he is one of the leaders on the basketball team. All the kids respect him. He's a success story."

The respect is far-reaching. When the junior class voted to choose two to three peers to be on the Natural Helpers Committee (a program that provides peer support for students), Richardson was chosen.

"Kids now say, 'Hey, if Deon can do it, anybody can do it,'" Richardson says. "There's good stuff in everybody. And I tell them, instead of going out looking for trouble, go home and read a book. And they look up to me. They admire me for that."

Reprinted with permission from John Wiley and Sons, Inc. From *All Kids are Our Kids: What Communities Must Do to Raise Respectful and Caring Children & Adolescents* by Peter Benson (1997).

Asset-Building Stories about the Power of Individual Action

Parent Networking Diffuses a Tough Situation (from Mike Roach, owner of Paloma Clothing)

Through participation in a *Raising Our Daughters* parent group, I learned how to handle a situation like an invitation to a coed sleepover, something that happens in high schools these days. I now understand why saying, "NO WAY!" to my daughter doesn't work or foster our relationship. (And, of course, "Yes" isn't an option either!) I learned instead to connect with the parents of the other girls invited so my daughter wasn't the only one excluded and arrange for an alternate activity that was less likely to lead to risky behavior —like an all-girl sleepover at our house on the same night complete with pizza and videos. It's so affirming as a parent to have the tools to diffuse these potentially dangerous situations without alienating my daughter. And this is only one of the tools I learned!

Dusty's Garden

Dustin Hill, a 12-year old middle-schooler, wanted to build a garden to grow fresh vegetables for Sisters of the Road Café, a nonprofit public lunch café that serves low cost, basic comfort foods in exchange for cash, food stamps or labor at the restaurant. Dustin learned about community service when he was little; his family would gather apples and mittens at Christmas time for the homeless. He applied for a mini-grant for the lumber for raised beds, soil and seeds. He persuaded eight other students and some neighbors to help him. When a cancerous tumor on Dusty's leg was diagnosed and successfully removed, the other youth tended the garden. He pitched in on crutches.

Raising our Daughter's Parent Group Blossoms and Grows (from Diana Zapata)

I was inspired to form a parenting group when my ten-year-old daughter had several teary nights in a row. I could tell how frustrated she was with the budding relational aggression happening around her and I didn't really feel equipped with the tools to help her through. I was determined begin the Raising Our Daughter's (ROD) curriculum with other interested parents. This group was a great way to start the process, and we began to bond as a community of concerned parents. Both Moms and Dads attended the first year. We were not afraid to open up. This created a recipe for trust that we still have today. Our group has evolved over the years, but we are still thriving.

- First we had Moms and Dads with the ROD curriculum. It was a little advanced for fourth-grade parenting—but this got us going!
- The second year we evolved into an all Mom's group, discussing our own challenges as Moms, wives, daughters and professionals.
- The third year we formed a mother/daughter support group with our sixth-graders and studied the Choices curriculum, that teaches girls about making good choices during the middle and high school years and how their choices, good and bad, will affect them. This was an excellent activity for us.
- The fourth year, we had our seventh-grade girls decide which direction we would take. They decided to have book discussions every other month and activities such as cooking classes or printmaking the other months. It was a great community gathering each time. The biggest disappointment was when not everyone could make it (which always happens).

I think it works for us because we trust that our conversations/meetings are confidential. I always feel supported, knowing that my daughter's situation is not so unusual and we are not the only ones going through this stage of the game! We also try to support each other's children, as a "go to" person, besides the parent. Not many have really done this yet—but the choice is there. So what started out as a simple *Raising Our Daughters* group four years ago has turned into a great group of supportive families who love to get together on a regular basis. I have enjoyed this community so much and hope it continues well into the high school years—so we'll see!"

Brewing Up Assets: A Friendly Adult Stirs in Some Support

By Kay Hong, Asset Magazine, Search Institute

THE OTHER DAY, I decided to treat myself to a really good cup of coffee on the way home from a hard day's work. Feeling tense, I walked into my favorite coffeehouse with my briefcase on my shoulder. "Hello, Jeremy," I said and watched as the face of the boy at the counter lit up. "Hey, where've you been?!" he asked. I pleaded a busy work schedule then we chatted a little about what books we'd been reading. I had to go, but he made my day by calling out, "You should come in more often!"

One my way out, I saw Carly rise out of her chair with a gangly teenage grace and move toward me with an intense expression. We hugged and I whispered in her ear, "Is something going on?" She said yes, and began to tell me about a new boyfriend who wanted her to have sex with him, and what did I think? We spoke about safety and respect, about being good to yourself, and being careful. We laughed a little and hugged again, then I picked up my coffee and headed home with an unexpected feeling of warmth and satisfaction. A few short weeks ago, such scenarios were simply not a part of my daily life.

How did the change happen? When I first started working at Search Institute, I felt a need to balance out big-picture thinking about community change with my own closer look at the realities of young people's lives. I have no children of my own, but as I learned more about the Developmental Assets, I became fascinated with the broader possibilities of informal asset building and I wanted to extend my reach. I decided to concentrate in an intentional way on asset #3, other adult relationships, and to take to heart the admonitions we often put in our publications—to say hello to the community's young people, to call them by name, to form relationships with them—and see if such gestures really work.

I started with a small experiment. At the grocery store one day, when a teenage clerk with numerous earrings and an unusual hairstyle rang up my purchases in a moody silence. I gave myself a little internal push and complimented him on his hair, asking him what he did to make it look that way. He looked up at me in surprise, smiled a little, and revealed his combination gel-and-finger-combing technique while we finished the transaction. He thanked me, and as I walked away, I heard him greet the next customer in line. Encouraged, I made a simple remark about the weather to the girl who was wheeling out my groceries—a comment that led to a friendly discussion of the future outdoor jobs she might consider.

Given those successes, I've continued with my experiments, and now enjoy several warm, fun-filled relationships with teens at the coffeehouse I frequent. What has meant the most to me, and what I hadn't expected, has been the great gift of their trust. Their confidences bring opportunities for everyday asset building in their wake, and I feel a deep responsibility for responding as wisely and lovingly as I can.

We joke together over cappuccino and Rice Krispy bars and talk about boyfriends and girlfriends. Jeremy asks what it's like to be a writer and editor, and Carly asks how to know when you're really in love, and Tom asks me how to break up responsibly with a girl he's been dating. Jon tells me his dad yelled at him for not disabling his mom's car the night before, so she drove drunk and was arrested, and I assure him it's not his fault. I tell them all that their lives are just beginning, and that they'll keep making mistakes and learning new things and changing and growing all through their time on this earth. And I tell them that talking with them and listening to them helps me keep learning things too.

Kay Hong has been an editor at the Search Institute for three years.

Asset-Building Ideas for Neighbors and Neighborhood Groups

From Pass It On! Ready-to-Use Handouts for Asset Builders

A NEIGHBORHOOD IS MORE than a place where people sleep or grab a bite to eat. A neighborhood can and should be an important community in which people of all ages feel cared for and secure. This kind of neighborhood isn't the norm in most communities, but with a focus on asset building it could be. Two of the 40 Developmental Assets, #4: caring neighborhood; and #13: neighborhood boundaries, focus specifically on the important role neighbors have in building assets. Here are ideas on how neighbors can build these and other assets:

Individuals

- **Learn the names of kids who live around you.** Find out what interests them.
- **Treat neighbors of all ages with respect and courtesy;** expect them to treat you with respect and courtesy too.
- **If you live in an apartment or condominium,** spend time in gathering places, such as front steps, courtyards, meeting rooms, pools, laundry rooms, and lobbies. Greet and talk with others there. If you have a front yard, hang out there.
- **Take personal responsibility for building Asset #13: neighborhood boundaries.** When you see someone in the neighborhood doing something you think is inappropriate, talk with her or him about why it bothers you.
- **Find other neighbors who want to make a long-term commitment to Asset-building.** Begin developing strategies for working together to build assets in your neighborhood.
- **Take time to play or just be with the young people on your block and or in your building.** Encourage them to talk and then listen to what they have to say.
- **Invite neighbors (especially those with children and teenagers) to your home.** Get to know each other and find out what you have in common.
- **Once in a while, leave a message** (with chalk on sidewalks or by hanging notes on doors) saying how much you appreciate a certain neighbor. Do this for neighbors of all ages.
- **If you have children, talk to other parents about the boundaries and expectations they have for their children.** Discuss how you can support one another in areas where you agree.
- **Figure out what you can provide for young people in your neighborhood.** Can you set up a basketball hoop? Can you offer some space for a neighborhood garden? Can you give one hour of your time on weekends to play softball with young people who live near you?
- **If you have concerns about your neighborhood, talk with other neighbors about your feelings.** If others share your concerns, gather a group to work on addressing them. Even if you don't solve all of the problems, you'll strengthen your neighborhood in the process.
- **Attend a game, play, or event** that a neighborhood child or teenager is involved in. Congratulate the young person after the event.
- **Be aware of graduations and other major events** in the lives of children.
- **Once you know your neighbors, find out more about their extended family and friends.** Some elderly people have grandchildren who visit. Or parents may have custody of their children on certain days of the week. Get to know these young people who periodically visit.
- **Pay attention whenever you see a young person.** Take time to smile and say hello. If you have a few moments, ask a few questions and express your interest in her or him. Do this while you're walking, waiting for a bus, or waiting in line somewhere.

Groups

- **Start a neighborhood group. Focus on safety,** neighborhood improvement, or just having fun.
- **Organize a neighborhood book swap.** Ask neighbors to donate books they've already read and have everyone come to find new books.
- **Meet with neighborhood parents and other concerned adults to find out how neighbors can help children and teenagers with homework.** Consider finding adult "study buddies" for kids.
- **Start a neighborhood check-in program.** Form small clusters and check in with each other on a regular basis. If someone needs help or support, gather a group to pitch in and help out.
- **If you have problems with crime or safety in your neighborhood, regularly talk with your local police department** to find out what is being done to address the issues. Ask them what you and other neighbors can do to make a difference.

May Day Basket Celebration

By Lori Delman and Carolyn Quatier

Do you want the kids in your neighborhood to help build closer community? Do you want your neighbors to know your kids and build stronger relationships? Do you want your kids to feel they are doing something really worthwhile and valuable, to connect with parents and other adults—young and old in your neighborhood—and to have fun doing it?

If yes, then we've got a great neighborhood project for you… delivering flower baskets on the first of May. Celebrating May Day in this way brings neighbors out of their homes, after being cooped up all winter and is a wonderful "springtime ritual." Here are two May Day Celebration stories.

Lori's Story

For the past five years, I have invited over the "street kids"—what my six-year-old daughter calls the children on our suburban block. Our project each May 1st is to make flower baskets for each of the block's households. "It's fun at the May Day Party because we get to work on a project together," says thirteen-year-old Lucy.

In addition to the beautiful little baskets that all the kids help make, we created a photo collage of all the neighbor children and included a copy with each basket. This collage turned out to be a hit not only with the children—who love to be on "display"—but also with households that don't have children but want to feel more connected and to know who the kids are. This gives their parents the benefit of an extra set of "eyes and ears" watching over them. Even more important, it makes it easier to talk with a kid whose name you know. The best is the empowerment felt by some of the preteen girls on the block who now want to be in charge of the photo collage layout.

In small ways this tradition has helped build community and to know the value of being a connected neighbor. The first year of this project, a neighbor called to thank us for bringing back the warm, cohesive atmosphere she felt the block had when she was raising her children 30 years ago. Older generations are nostalgic about the days when all neighborhood children attended the same school, making block friendships much easier. Our neighborhood is reflective of the current period of diverse school choices—we have five grade schools, three middle schools, and two high schools represented. Our kids love this chance to connect with the kids from all the schools.

Carolyn's Story

Eight years ago, Kathy Masarie and I introduced our neighborhood to this May Day tradition. We have streamlined the process by getting several parents involved: bringing snacks, buying flowers, building the cones, making May Day tags, collecting photos, making the photo collage, updating our neighborhood phone and email directory. With our larger suburban lots, we are spread out and tend to spend time isolated in our backyards. Almost every May Day, we also become a "Welcome to the Neighborhood" party for new families. Sue Gregoire said, "We were new to the neighborhood, so it was nice for our children to see so many other kids their age. It was a creative activity and a great way to connect with every person in the neighborhood." Emily captures the essence of the appeal, "It was fun because I got to leave the flowers on the doorstep, ring the doorbell, and run away. I also met my new neighbors and now we carpool together."

May Day baskets are simple, fun, and resonate with every generation's hearts. Consider opening up your children's experience to this wonderful, connecting ritual.

Lori Delman is a part-time pharmacist, enjoys her book club and garden and is mother to twin girls. Carolyn Quatier loves gardening and teaching sewing to children and is mother to three girls and a boy.

Reprinted with permission from Full Esteem Ahead, *Wings*, Winter 2001.

Asset-Building Stories about the Power of Neighbors and Friends

Building Community—One Porch at Time (from *Assets Magazine, The Neighborhood Porch Cookie Campaign, Findlay, OH)*
"I had fond memories of sitting on the porch sharing with family and friends while growing up," says Brahm, a Hancock County (Ohio) extension agent. After hearing a talk about the importance of assets in building youth and family resiliency, she decided to do more than just share her own porch cookies and lemonade.

Brahm brought her Porch Cookie Campaign idea to several community leaders from the United Way, youth and religious groups, the police department, and the media. Together they developed a plan that included plenty of print and broadcast promotion. People who send in pictures or favorite stories of their porch parties are eligible for prizes. Now in its second year, the campaign runs from May through Labor Day.

The possibilities for porch parties are endless. Here are a few examples: a homeless shelter invited previous residents for a porch party, a retirement center had a porch party with a daycare center, a city councilman invited residents of his ward to two parties through newspaper ads, children had porch parties with their dolls, the block watch program adopted the campaign as a project, United Way invited staff from neighboring offices for cookies and lemonade.

Why has the campaign been successful? Says one mother of two boys: "It was fun, didn't cost much, and took little time. You didn't even have to clean your house!"

Reprinted with permission from "Building Community—One Porch at a Time," *Assets: The Magazine of Ideas for Healthy Communities and Healthy Youth.* Copyright © Autumn, 1998 Search Institute®, Minneapolis, MN; www.search-institute.org. All rights reserved.

Camaraderie and Networking at Work (from Adrienne Greene) We started a *Raising Our Daughters* discussion group at work with about 8 members nearly 5 years ago. Since then, 4 of us continue to meet over lunch and seek out each other when we have parenting issues that need another perspective. Raising teens is challenging work, and it has been extremely rewarding to have a confidential support network of co-workers to rely on. I know it's provided me with a sense of confidence and friendship.

A Safe Network of Friends for My Daughter (from Nellie Nix) Our *Raising our Daughter's* group means

knowing that there are nearly a dozen moms—and dads, too—that I trust. I trust their opinions, though they're varied and sometimes different from mine. And since my daughter is close friends with many of their girls, it's so nice to know that I can trust that she'll be safe when she's with them.

Men's Bike Group Unites Families (from Glenda Montgomery) When my husband found out that some men in the neighborhood were getting together to ride bikes on Sunday mornings, he pulled out his 20-year-old bike from a forgotten corner of the garage. It got dusted off and cleaned up and carried him along to join the group, providing an opportunity for my husband to connect with other men and, in turn, to connect all the men's families to one another. He's now been riding for nine years. During these years, the bike group has become the core of our neighborhood experience. The kids feel like cousins, and the couples enjoy hanging out. We've gone camping and have an annual Christmas progressive dinner. When the weather is not rainy and cold, the men ride as often as they can. The high point of their year is the "Reach the Beach," an organized ride in May when the men ride 100 miles from our neighborhood in Portland to Pacific City on the Coast. The families pack up food, clothes, and supplies and caravan down to the beach in time to cheer on their Dads and husbands as they cross the finish line. The rest of the weekend is about free flow fun. The kids are a happy gang, representing a span of almost a decade, from 9 to 18 years old. For them, this weekend is like their Christmas. It is full of laughter and freedom, friendship and tradition and layer upon layer of fun memories. They truly can't remember their lives before we began making this annual pilgrimage and they look forward to it passionately every year.

Iron Mountain Day Camp (from Kathy Keller Jones) After 3 neighborhood girlfriends had their first week at overnight summer camp at ages 11 and 12, they decided that they could earn money and have fun by organizing the neighborhood children in a week-long half-day camp. After all, they already knew all the songs, crafts, and skits they would need. Thus began the Iron Mountain Day Camp in our large yard. In addition to developing many skills in the teens, the day camp brought together all of the younger children in the neighborhood and their families into one happy group and developed a tremendous sense of cohesion in our neighborhood.

A Getaway Weekend for Parents and Kids or
How to Let your Hair Down Instead of Pulling it Out!

By Jane Blackman

AS A SINGLE MOM for 15 years, I've had plenty of one-on-one time with my daughter, Holly. We've done lots of day trips and weekend excursions together. One special trip that we took last fall added a new dimension to our time together that proved very rewarding—a Seaside weekend getaway with three other moms and their daughters. For the girls, it was a chance to be with their buddies doing something different and fun. For us moms, it provided an opportunity to share mutual concerns, issues and questions about raising our daughters. For both, it was a time of discovery about who we were and how others perceived us. We packed enough food and games for a month in the Outback and had a ball. The weather was sunny and mild enough to allow for lots of walks and even a two-hour surrey ride for the girls. Our rental house was a bit musty and the beds we shared had seen better days, but no one minded. This is how it worked. None of the moms knew each other except in passing. The common denominator was our sophomore daughters, who had known each other since middle school. One mom found a house to rent in Seaside just a few blocks from the beach and issued the invitation. She picked a weekend when the kids had Friday off so we were able to get an early start that morning. Each mom/daughter team brought whatever snacks they wanted plus the food to prepare one of the main meals for the weekend. We divided meal chores ahead of time so we'd know who was fixing what. There were no rules about time for bed or getting up and that worked just great. The girls had a separate bunkroom off the porch that allowed for privacy and "girl talk." We moms enjoyed tea and conversation in the breakfast nook before the girls appeared for the day and the hubbub began. We planned indoor activities for

nighttime, including a scavenger hunt with prizes. The last evening together ended with a circle share. Each person gave a one-word description of everyone else in the circle. I don't know which I enjoyed hearing more, what the girls had to say or what the moms had to say. It was a very moving experience. Weekend getaways are an ideal way to spend time with your children. And the presence of other parents and kids adds texture and insight that is invaluable. In Holly's words, "I think it's important for kids to spend time with their friends' parents. You get a whole new perspective from them and it helps develop a great support system." All of us voted to make the getaway an annual event. My only regret is that we didn't start it years ago. I can't wait for our next adventure!

Some suggestions for or-ganizing your own getaway:

•   Keep it simple. Plan easy menus, bring one change of clothes. Limit everyone to one set of towels. Consider bringing a sleeping bag instead of doing linens.

• Look for bargains. Our lodging cost only $25 a night per person. Take advantage of off-season rates and shop the Internet for values (www.cabins.com is one example).

• Be flexible. One of the moms couldn't come so we ended up with an extra girl. We "adopted" her for the weekend and she had a great time. One mom snored and one needed a firmer mattress so we designed extra sleeping quarters in the living room the second night.

Jane Blackman is mother of a young adult daughter. She is the founder of A Festive Heart (www.festiveheart.com), teaches wellness workshops and has a private energy healing practice in Portland, OR.

Reprinted with permission from Full Esteem Ahead, *Wings*, Spring 2003.

Creating Family Magic

By Jody Bellant Scheer, MD

I AM HOPELESSLY nostalgic for the long weeks of summer when my kids were young. My kids, our neighbors and I spent hours swimming off our houseboat decks, building rafts and forts, reading books, working on projects, and exploring our nearby waterways in a variety of small watercraft. While the kids in my neighborhood lived in a rich and inviting natural environment that encouraged activity and creativity, one of their greatest assets was the way they became part of a community of adults and children who interacted often and cared about one another. Our houseboat community consists of 29 homes and 60 to 70 people, including about a dozen kids, who for years ran in a pack together. Some of the advantages of this arrangement were that our children experienced a variety of family styles and rules; they interacted with kids of a mixture of ages; they developed on-going relationships with adults other than their own parents; and they benefited from the collective creativity of a group of adults who worked together to enrich their lives during the long summer months.

For parents who don't live in such a ready-made community, finding other families who wish to share in some group activities can be a great way to build

community and offer similar advantages to your own children. Networking with neighbors, churches, schools, community centers, as well as your children's friends, can help parents find other families willing to embark on some group adventures. The possibilities for shared activities are endless and need not take a lot of time, money or effort to create. When I asked my own children about their favorite childhood memories, they did not mention the more exotic and expensive trips we made together. Instead, they remembered contests amongst the neighborhood kids to see who could run the farthest down the hot, black moorage walkways before

having to jump into the water to cool off, floating in big herds of inner tubes down the length of our moorage, and playing in the mud, clay and sun on the shores of our slough. They remembered with relish the spontaneous picnics where we invited anyone home on the moorage, young to old, to join us for a collective meal on our deck or at a nearby beach. In today's society, it may seem odd to ask an older housewife or elderly neighbor to join in some family fun, but for us, it worked to the advantage of all parties involved.

Other group projects can be more intensive. My kids, husband, neighbors and I planned activities that included neighborhood camping trips, group hikes, museum visits, road trips, community gardens and varied explorations of the kids' interests. Our neighborhood built a tree house and playground when our children were little and a basketball court when they grew older.

Several summers, moorage families hosted Asian exchange students and enjoyed sharing the Pacific Northwest with them and each other. One spring, a neighbor invested in a variety of wood supplies and their boys created a multitude of forts, vehicles and projects over the course of the whole summer with their buddies. Weeks of entertainment were provided for my nieces and their friends, who organized a family theater production about pioneers, complete with vintage clothes and props they made themselves. Weekly projects, such as a book club, sewing circle or game night, can regularly bring kids and parents together to share over the course of a summer. Any project where adults and kids can work together, where kids can exercise creativity and independence, and where the outcome is less important than having fun in the process is worth the effort to create and will greatly enrich all of your lives. Creating such family magic will give you years of memories to cherish, and it will entice your children to come home for more once they've left the nest!

Jody Bellant Scheer, a pediatrician, lives on a houseboat and has three young adult children.

Reprinted with permission of Full Esteem Ahead, *Wings,* Spring 2003.

Why Aren't There More Dads' Groups?

By Joe Kelly, author of *Dads and Daughters*

feel ready to start talking to each other about our kids. A jog, a card game, a yard project, a round of golf, or any number of other "guy" activities can serve as safe places for us to jump in, or at least stick our toes in to test the water. For others of us, a more formal, organized setting dedicated specifically to talking about raising daughters works best.

Whenever I mention men's groups, there's at least one guy in the audience who rolls his eyes or makes a wisecrack. Men's groups have a bad reputation with many men; they're considered weird, bizarre, creepy, or just plain ridiculous. There are probably men's groups that are all of these things, but that doesn't mean that every men's group is. It doesn't mean that we can't start up groups with our own rules; and it's also no excuse for staying silent about our fathering.

A big part of the problem is that there simply aren't enough men's or fathering groups out there. The smaller number of groups, the smaller the variety, and thus the fewer chances for a dad to find a group in which he'll feel comfortable. Somebody must be responsible for this shortage, and that somebody is me and you. It looks like we've been too afraid to take the risks and do the work to get what we need from one another.

I think we haven't formed or sustained groups because we're afraid. It takes courage to admit we don't know everything and to ask other fathers for help. It takes leadership to keep the conversation going even when other fathers say they are too busy to participate.

I'm part of a loosely organized book group made up of a half dozen men who I don't know all that well. There's a business consultant, a city planner, a naturalist/teacher, a psychiatrist, and a man who manages his wife's chiropractic office.

We've discussed novels, a collection of environmental essays, a memoir about sailing to Greenland, and even a volume of poetry. These are all pretty safe topics and while no one has revealed any deep, dark secrets, we really enjoy each other's company. Recently I tried to push the envelope a bit by picking Will Glennon's *The Collected Wisdom of Fathering* (Conari Press, 2002), my favorite fathering book.

> I have to set aside my expectations when I talk fathering with another dad.

I thought the conversation got off to a slow start. It seemed as if there was more off-the-topic small talk than usual, and a couple of the guys didn't seem as enthusiastic about the book as I am. We only talked about our kids a little, and only after prodding each other with plenty of questions.

When the group broke up for the evening, I was disappointed, for I'd hoped we might be ready to use our father experience to jump into a deeper level of conversation. I didn't feel as if that hope had been fulfilled.

The next day, however, I got a phone call and two e-mails from the guys thanking me for the topic and saying it was the best meeting we'd had yet. They were excited and stimulated by a conversation that I had considered halting and uncertain. They've mentioned several times since how much they enjoyed the discussion. And I learned something important here.

I have to set aside my expectations when sitting down to talk with another dad. What I think is irrelevant might be central for him; a conversation I find stumbling and disjointed might be the first time he's ever spoken to another father about being a dad—and those words might amount to great eloquence for him. It turns out that our book group's halting discussion of fathering had laid a foundation for more interesting and personal talk down the road. It's slow going, but it's progress.

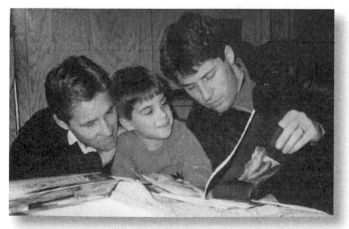

Asset-Building Stories about School Connection

Roach, Paloma Clothing, Portland) I have always known that the most valuable gift I could give my daughter was time. I invested a lot in those early years and was starting to think about slowing down. Adolescence is just on the edge of the radar screen in 4th grade when I took the *Raising Our Daughters* class and realized I needed to "ramp up," not slow down. One activity I learned about that I wanted for all the kids as they entered middle school, was a Girls/Boys Night Out—spending the night together at the school, having lots of fun, but also talking about importance of healthy friendships and treating others with respect. So when Isabel was in 5th grade I started volunteering at the middle school and made that happen for all the 6th graders the next year. Just learning the importance of "knowing a name," helped me memorize the names of the 60 other kids in her 5th grade I didn't already know. When I saw them in middle school, a big smile would beam across their face as I "high-fived" them by name. I think they think, "I must be important if someone else's dad went out of his way to learn my name." I was also inspired to create a coming of age book for Isabel when she turned 13 and distribute a letter on asset-building ideas to her coaches. I also helped foster a $500 grant for *Raising Our Sons'* and *Raising Our Daughters'* groups for anyone who wanted to take them in our middle school to broaden the base of parents who understand that being involved in helping other people's children also helps your own child.

Dads and Doughnuts

When one middle school received a $500 mini-grant, they decided to use it in a way that would bring dads and other male role models together with kids. The 5th and 6th grade students each sent their special male figure a personal invitation to come to their school one morning on the way to work. The mini-grant funded doughnuts, muffins, juice and coffee. The students explained their educational program and provided their guests with information on how to enhance children's ability to survive and thrive by getting more involved and building assets in children's lives.

Dragon's Breath Café

In addition to raising reading levels, Janet Muller, a third-grade teacher, wanted to instill in her students an enthusiasm and love of reading. With funds from a small grant, she transformed her classroom into a small, cozy café with hot chocolate, warm, fresh cookies, black and white checkered tablecloths, and little tagboard dragons. Students and their parents came together one evening a month to share thoughts and lessons learned from their book-of-the-month. Questions encouraged critical thinking.

Bike Club

Tom Bright, a middle school teacher, wanted to teach practical skills as well as science in his classroom. He received a $500 mini-grant and used it to fund bike repair and pay for bike maintenance equipment. His repair shop opens up twice a week during lunch. As the weather improves, he hopes to involve parents and other community members and to assist with organizing bike rides after school and on weekends.

Walking to School Builds Community (from Glenda Montgomery)

While visiting Toronto I helped walk my friend's kids to school. I was curious because in suburban America we tend to drive our kids to school. I was delighted by the scene that unfolded before me. My friend's kids were bundled in their snow gear. As we spilled out onto the front porch the same scene was being enacted on all of the other front porches. Parents followed brightly-hued little bundles down the front steps and onto the street. On both sidewalks people made their way in happy clusters towards Queen's Street, the main thoroughfare. There, we met up with a steady stream of more parents holding hands with yet more kids. People called out to one another, smiled and waved happily as each side street stream of school-bound groups joined and headed east together. Across from the urban elementary school, a crossing guard greeted both children and parents alike and we crossed Queens to join the cheerful throng of dads, moms, nannies and children building snow men, making snow forts and milling about on the school grounds. It was like the scene of some idyllic winter movie from the past. When a bell rang, I thought that the moment would be over, kids would disappear and we'd turn around and head home. But instead, the kids ran to hug their kneeling parents in a chaotic jumble of snowsuits and mittens and scarves, then moved up to the building and stood in their classroom lines. My friend and I joined the rest of the adults, who hung out behind the lines of children and chatted. When a second bell sounded, the kids turned around and waved goodbye to their parents who smiled and waved back. The ritual of another day's beginning was finished. What a joyful way to begin the day! Why can't we, in the US, take the time to enact this lovely community-building ritual instead of the one we overwhelmingly choose: a stressed rushing to school, isolated in our own greenhouse, gas-emitting vehicles, to drop our kids at the curb?

SUN—Schools Uniting Neighborhoods

By Julie Salmon

of eight and three. But when the bell rings and the kids go home, not much else happens—the occasional after-school activity, maybe a parent/teacher conference or two, sports on the weekends, or a few yearly fundraising events for families. Otherwise, you're driving elsewhere to seek services and activities for your family—unless your child goes to a SUN school.

SUN, or Schools Uniting Neighborhoods, is a collaboration of city, county, state and schools in Portland, Oregon. Its purpose? To open the school building every day late on school days, over weekends, and during the summer to respond to the needs of children, their parents and the community. SUN schools are busy schools. Their doors are almost always open, and people in their community use their facilities to fill a myriad of needs.

SUN Schools have five basic goals:
- To provide enrichment activities for families that tie into student success, healthy development and good behavior
- To increase family involvement in the schools
- To increase community and business involvement in the schools
- To improve the collaboration among school districts and community-based groups and businesses
- To use schools as a public resource.

WHAT IF....?
*There was a way to help all kids succeed?
*There was a way to involve all families in their child's education?
*There was a way that the whole community would feel connected to your school?
*There was a way that schools were open from 7 a.m. to 9 p.m.? On weekends? In the summer?

Diane Meisenhelter, coordinator of the SUN school at Buckman Elementary in southeast Portland, explains that Buckman became a SUN school in 1999 after first extensively surveying the community to assess its needs. Parent volunteers, operating under the assumption that people don't always respond to just one way of communicating, took a multiple approach in surveying. They put out questionnaires in school newspapers. They asked parents, staff and students to respond to surveys. They went out into the neighborhood and talked to people on the street, in shopping areas, and door-to-door. They sat with kids at lunch tables and got their "laundry lists" of ideas. They met with student advisory groups and the PTA. They did in-depth family assessments with a cross-section of families. All in all, Meisenhelter says they spoke to more than 1,000 people to figure out what kinds of activities might work best for their community.

Next they applied to Multnomah County and the City of Portland to become an official SUN school.

There are currently 13 SUN sites in the Portland area. All SUN schools receive grant money from Multnomah County to administrate the program. After qualifying as a SUN school, Buckman volunteers went to work meeting their primary purpose: filling vacant classrooms with people. After only one year, Buckman "extracurricular" activities include:
- 30 after-school classes serving over 200 kids
- An expanded summer school program.
- "Themed" learning days for kids who need an extra boost during teacher planning days
- After-school homework and reading clubs
- Family fun nights at least once a month
- Health fairs for families
- Healthy heart club to promote exercise and fitness for families
- Working with the local Food Bank, offering classes that teach cooking and nutritional information for families who could use this extra boost
- Translations for ESL families
- Support groups for new families
- Families and Schools Together, or FAST, classes which promote family empowerment and community-building.

Student and parent evaluations revealed that children got very excited about what their classes were doing and this seemed to bolster confidence and self-esteem. The teachers agree. "We saw a few students blossom and gain confidence in areas they had shied away from."

Why not use your local school building as a centerpiece of your neighborhood, using it to enhance the lives of the community during the hours that it usually has locked doors? If you'd like to open up your local school's doors to your community, check out the SUN web site at www.sunschools.org.

Julie Salmon is the mother of three children and is a freelance writer/editor and lifelong volunteer.

Virtues of Volunteering

By Julie Salmon

THE SUMMER LOOMS before us, not exactly those lazy, hazy days of our own youth, because it's our children we're talking about. In an effort to avoid taxiing to the mall or movies and patrolling TV, we flip through camp catalogues and class schedules, looking for just the right activity to fill their time. But the price tags are so high, the rewards hazy, the choices confusing. What to do? Consider volunteer service!

"Youth gain basic skills, a sense of community, and a sense of power through volunteering," says Sabrina Burke, coordinator of Youth Involvement Network, a Camp Fire-sponsored program designed to help youth, ages 11 to 17, become more involved in their community. Volunteering "gives natural, tangible benefits back to your son or daughter" and it doesn't cost a cent.

Volunteering can also help instill in your child certain personal assets necessary for growing up healthy, caring and competent. A decade of research conducted by the Search Institute and undertaken by the Multnomah Commission on Children and Families has identified at least forty assets that kids need to succeed. Their research shows that on the average, youth have only nineteen of the forty, leaving them vulnerable to many negative influences. Getting involved in their community as a volunteer, however, provides several important assets. Some are:

- Learning that the community values them
- Developing relationships with adults
- Developing a sense of purpose
- Allowing them to be valuable resources
- Service to others, at least one hour per week

- Bringing adult role models into their lives
- Positive peer influence—having friends who set good examples
- Developing a sense of caring, empathy, and sensitivity

The Commission and the research behind the Take the Time program have found that the more assets a person has, the less likely she or he will get involved in dangerous or self-destructive activities. Volunteer service is a rich resource for counteracting some of those negative influences.

It has never been easier to find the right service job for your child. Camp Fire's Youth Volunteer Corp works to connect young people with community organizations that can use their help. It provides training and technical assistance to both the youth and the organizations. It has even created a website to help kids plug into just the right service opportunity. Finding the right spot for the right kid is an important part of YVC and its technical arm, Youth Involvement Network.

"A huge part of the Youth Volunteer Corp," says Vanessa Diamond, the AmeriCorp Team Leader at the YVC, "is to make people realize that service isn't just service. It has to be meaningful. It has to be rewarding. I think that's what sells the youth on it. They actually do make a difference."

Kids can sign up for two-week stints throughout the summer. They can work with the elderly, repair houses, plant trees, learn to landscape, work with disabled kids —you name it. The opportunities are boundless, and each one can give your child tangible benefits. There are also several other opportunities throughout the year.

Volunteering is not only about giving, which is reward in itself, it is also about learning. Every project teaches skills, from empathy, compassion, and knowledge of how other people struggle, to life skills, such as painting, construction, and knowing what it really costs to raise a family. These are topics that schools don't usually include in their curriculum.

Volunteering gives kids an important role in our community. It allows them to realize some of their potential right now, rather than existing simply as people in waiting. "In my opinion, people under eighteen are one of the last really disenfranchised groups of folks," says Burke. "They are treated like 'future beings'."

Volunteering gives them a role in the here and now. They can be empowered by the feeling "I can effect change," and by a sense of belonging.

OK, the benefits are clear, but how do you motivate your child to get involved? Burke feels that younger kids, ages 11 or 12, don't usually require a lot of motivation. Older teens are harder to motivate. Burke encourages talking to them about how a volunteer experience can help a teen get a better job than flipping burgers. For example, she's seen many young people gain experience for landscaping jobs by working in community gardens or volunteering with the park department. Real work experience and letters of recommendation are invaluable when applying for work.

Volunteering with a friend, or being invited to volunteer by a friend, can also be motivating. "If they go with someone else and they have fun, they'll do it again," says Burke. It might be necessary to get two friends together and strong-arm them into trying it the first time. After the first few days, though, they'll want to come back.

Even better is being invited by a friend who already volunteers. Diamond believes it places young people in the "I am important to society" category. The volunteer is telling her friend "Hey, it's really fun, but we need your help." In addition, volunteering with a friend helps to build initial confidence. To show up somewhere to volunteer and not know anyone can be really scary.

Burke has one more piece of advice for parents. She encourages parents to emphasize the positive aspects of the volunteer work. For example, if your child went to the Multiple Sclerosis Society and stuffed envelopes, instead of saying "Oh, that's boring," say, "That's how organizations spread the word about their cause."

Once your child is volunteering, success is almost assured. Volunteering may be especially beneficial to those kids who don't particularly shine in other aspects of their lives; for example, academics or sports. "Anybody can be a successful volunteer," says Diamond. "All they need to do is have compassion and the motivation to do it. There is no failure in volunteering if you stick with what you're going to do, and you do it with a good heart."

Julia Salmon is a freelance writer/editor and lifelong volunteer. She spends most of her time and effort, however, raising her three children.

Reprinted with permission from Full Esteem Ahead, *Wings,* Spring 1999.

Research Shows Connection between Volunteering and Emotional Well-Being
By Kathy Masarie, MD

Happy people invest more hours in volunteer service[1] and volunteer at higher levels for charity and community service groups, including religious, political, educational and health-related organizations[2] than do unhappy people. So, does this show that it takes a happy person to volunteer or does it mean that when you volunteer, you become happy? According to research, people may in fact feel a rush of happiness when they help others.[3,4] Reward centers in the brain are activated when people help a charity—even when they do it through paying taxes.[5] There is evidence, though, that as distance comes between a donor and the person receiving help, the benefits are not as great. For instance, giving money may distance the donor from the recipient, whereas volunteering time has social, identity and connection implications that are highly beneficial to creating happiness. [6,7,8]

Much in our lives adds to our feelings of subjective happiness; close friends, pets, a satisfying love life, physical health and laughter, to name a few; however, one avenue to happiness is often overlooked, and that is the blossoming of happiness as a result of giving of yourself to others … through volunteering. [9]

[1] Thoits, Peggy A. and Lyndi N. Hewitt (2001), "Volunteer Work and Well-Being," *Journal of Health and Social Behavior,* 42 (June), 115-131.
[2] Krueger, Hicks and McGue (2001), "Altruism and Antisocial Behavior: Independent Tendencies, Unique Personality Correlates, Distinct Etiologies," *Psychological Science, 12* (Sept), 397-402.
[3] Gilbert, Daniel (2006), *Stumbling on Happiness,* New York, NY: Vintage Press.
[4] Williams, Tonya P. and Angela Y. Lee (2007), "Me and Benjamin: Transaction versus Relationship Wealth in Subjective Well-being," Under review at *Journal of Personality and Social Psychology.*
[5] Harbaugh, William T., Ulrich Mayr, and Daniel R. Burghart (2007), "Neural Responses to Taxation and Voluntary Giving Reveal Motives for Charitable Donations," *Science,* 316 (June), 1622.
[6] Reed, Americus II, Karl Aquino and Eric Levy (2007a), "Moral Identity and Judgments of Charitable Behaviors," *Journal of Marketing,* in press.
[7] Vohs, Kathleen D., Nicole L. Mead and Miranda R. Goode (2006), "The Psychological Consequences of Money," *Science, 314,* 1154-1156.
[8] Vohs, Kathleen D., Nicole L. Mead and Miranda R. Goode (2007), "Money Changes Personal and Interpersonal Behavior: The Self-Sufficiency Hypothesis," University of Minnesota Working Paper.
[9] Liu, Wendy and Aaker, Jennifer, "The Happiness of Giving: The Time-Ask Effect," J. of Consumer Research. Oct 2008

Let's Get Boys and Girls Equally Involved in Volunteering

By Nancy Huppertz

MANY PEOPLE HAVE the perception that volunteerism is something that only women do. That belief recalls a time when women did not comprise nearly half of the paid work force and when larger numbers of women than today were not employed outside the home.

The notion of volunteerism being a female responsibility began at an early age. While boys were mowing lawns, shoveling snow and delivering papers, most often for pay, girls were volunteering in hospitals as candy stripers. Later, it was, for the most part, women who attended PTA meetings and provided other adult volunteer services. The perception persists, even though female and male roles have undergone dramatic change.

> Just as all occupations are now open and available to females and males, it is important that all volunteer opportunities be similarly open to all.

Today, with nearly equal numbers of women and men in the workforce, it would seem to follow that equal numbers of women and men should be available and willing to do volunteer work in the community. And just as all occupations are now open and available to females and males, so should all volunteer opportunities be similarly open to all.

Youth volunteerism serves a number of purposes. Perhaps the most important is instilling a sense of altruism, of giving something back to the community, of helping others just because it is the right thing to do. Second, it is an opportunity to learn a variety of life skills that might not be offered in school. The National Service-Learning Cooperative has issued a document called "Essential Elements of Service-Learning." It sees service learning, an organized form of volunteerism, as among the methods that "tries to create thoughtful and meaningful contexts in which students can be motivated to not only acquire new knowledge, but to retain and creatively transfer what they have learned throughout their lifetime as successful citizens and workers." The range of skills is wide, from care-providing at a nursing home or day care center, to carpentry on a Habitat for Humanity project. Altruism and meaningful contexts are valuable for character development and intellectual growth for all young people ... male and female.

Finally, volunteerism provides an opportunity to learn at an early age how to interact and work with a variety of people. "Communication with diverse individuals" is one of the Essential Elements in the National Service Learning document, as is "participation by diverse groups." Given a choice, most people will choose to associate with others similar to themselves ... such as by sex, race or some other characteristic. The opportunity to meet and work with others who are different will serve students well when they go on to function in a diverse society.

Parents and those in charge of volunteer or service learning programs must be vigilant about not limiting young people's opportunities according to their own preconceived, gender-based notions about appropriate kinds of activities. They must also be alert to attempts by the volunteer sites to stereotype work according to sex or to exclude students by race. The days of "Send me three strong boys ..." are over, happily replaced by, "Send me three people who can do ..." Within the guidelines of safe, honest, and non-exploitative work, students should have the freedom to choose what they want to do.

Recently, a team of high school students, including both males and females, was sent to the home of an elderly man to help him with home maintenance and repair. All of the students expected to be working outside, but when they arrived he gave the boys jobs outside and asked the girls to do the inside housework. All the students would have benefited from doing both kinds of work.

The many benefits of service learning and volunteerism should be open and available to all.

Nancy Huppertz is a gender equity specialist who runs Apogee Training and Consulting, a firm that does consulting in gender equity issues for organizations and schools throughout the United States.

Volunteering—The Youth Perspective

Gal Pals Go Painting

By Molly Krupa, a college graduate

Justine, 13, and Kaitlin, 15, volunteered last summer through the Youth Volunteer Corps. Their two-week project involved painting a house. The location of the project was significant for Kaitlin and Justine. It was the first time they had really paid attention to a neighborhood different from their own. In fact, when I asked what they had learned from the experience, the people and the neighborhood seemed to have had more of an impact on them than any of the work skills they had learned. Both girls enjoyed the exposure to the people they met; in particular, the stories one neighbor shared with them while they painted. The opportunity to experience life in a different setting, coupled with the reward of helping others, is what made the Youth Volunteer Corps most worthwhile for these girls.

Justine and Kaitlin had some advice for others who have thought about becoming involved:

- If possible, sign up with a friend. Meeting others is often easier if you are already with at least one familiar person.
- Examine the projects well, and pick one that really interests you.
- Be prepared to do hard work!

Justine, Kaitlin, and I also talked about requiring volunteering for high school graduation. To my surprise, both favored mandatory volunteering. Though kids might at first be disgruntled about yet another requirement, "Once they experience volunteerism, they'll like it!"

Molly Krupa is applying to medical school.

Sharing a Love of Words

By Clara Settle, a high school senior

"Since I couldn't speak English, I felt like I didn't know anything." That's what 13-year-old William said when I asked him what it was like to come to the United States a year-and-a-half ago, after spending most of his life in Guatemala. In exchange for helping William learn English, he gave me something valuable in return—a new perspective.

What began as a community service project has turned into one of my favorite parts of the week. Every Tuesday I go over to my former middle school and help tutor ESL (English as a Second Language) students. In that classroom, the common language is not English or Spanish. Instead, the most important and universal sign is a smile, or a laugh, and the students I work with have plenty to go around. What I do is fairly simple, but is no doubt very important to the kids I help. I give them an hour of my time and share with them my love for my language, something that is easy for me to give. I might help them work on spelling, go over reading questions, or finish up homework. However, I think one of the best things I can do is talk to them.

When I am talking to William, he seems shy, and almost afraid. I try to smile a lot, and maybe that helps. I can understand that confidence is a little hard to come by when you aren't sure how to express yourself in a new language. For William, neither of his parents speaks English, and his friends speak "English a little bit ... but more Spanish." He says that the only person that he can speak English with is his sister and even she isn't fluent. "My sister is 16. She is in high school." He says with pride. I smile and say that I'm in high school, too. His eyes light up. While our conversations might not have much to do with the book they're reading, or the spelling test they're studying for, I know that he has to challenge himself to talk to me and to understand me.

Another boy I look forward to seeing is Max, who, like William, came from Guatemala. He is open and talks to me, even though he might not say it exactly how he wants. He just talks, and I listen. He is not entirely fluent in English, but I've noticed that what he says often comes through crystal clear. His attitude itself would be inspirational, but what impressed me even more was to learn about what he had gone through. He left his family in Guatemala four years ago to come to the US, a country where he did not speak the local language at all. Then, he was transferred to school after school, never staying in any place for very long. I try to imagine what this must be like. In the end, I can't begin to possibly understand how it is that, after all of it, Max is sitting in front of me laughing and smiling.

The Big Help
An Interview with
Mia (11) and Maggie (13)
By Lisa Sloan

WHAT IS THE Big Help?
It's a way we make money that we can give away to help others.

How do you make the money?
We do jobs for money: things like babysitting, yard work, house cleaning, car washing and pet care. We will also type for you or draw a portrait—basically anything people will pay us money for. We did a lemonade stand, too, and sold things we didn't need anymore at a garage sale.

What made you think to start it?
We read a section in American Girl Magazine about girls who were helping people and we wanted to do that. They also talk a lot at school about charity work. We thought it would be pretty cool.

How did you decide what to do?
Well, we fought a lot in the beginning. Then we just made a list of things we were good at and made prices for each thing. We put up signs and handed out our flyers to our neighbors and we got lots of work.

Has it been successful?
Oh, yes! The first year we made $38. (Another friend helped that year too) and we donated it to the People's Bank. It was really cool to get a letter from them saying they used the money to buy mattress for someone. The second year we made $102 and the third year we made $200. Both of those times we gave the money to the Neighborhood House. They gave us a tour and thanked us for what we did.

What has been the best part of the Big Help?
We really like doing the jobs we offer, especially babysitting! It also feels really good to be helping someone else.

Will you to it again?
Definitely! We will do this or something like it forever!

Teens Triumph over Techno-Tribulations
From *Assets* Magazine

YOUR COMPUTER'S NOT working. You live in a small community, and help could be days coming. Who are you going to call? If you live in the Dassel-Cokato area of Minnesota, you can contact a techno-savvy high school student who will fix your problems at no charge, thanks to the Computer Service Club (CSC).

The CSC grew out of an effort to meaningfully engage youth who were idle after school. "A Search Institute survey and local data indicated that nearly half of our youth did not participate in any extra-curricular activities anywhere," says Gary Herman, coordinator of Dassel-Cokato Area Character Counts Initiative. The club answered an important need for many of the nonparticipants—and the community.

Flo Osness had difficulty using e-mail and called the Computer Service Club. "I had just gotten my computer," says the senior citizen. "Everything was new to me." CSC sent out Ryan, age 17, to guide her through the new computer woes. "Oh, he gets a good report from me," says Osness. CSC not only provides a real service to the community, it helps students develop a wide range of assets.

Connect with Kids by Helping Them to Help Others

By Harmony Barrett and Jennifer McCoy

IN A TIME WHEN MANY children are receiving brand new TVs and expensive clothing in place of parental involvement in their lives, other parents are developing productive and fun ways to connect with their kids. One such parent, Jennifer McCoy, felt that many of the activities in kids' lives, such as sports and school, fostered competition and a "me" attitude rather than compassion for others. So she developed an avenue to show, rather than tell, them what values she holds important.

In 1999, with the help of her children, Katie and Riley, she started *Kids That Care,* a group of 2nd to 6th graders who gather donations to help nurture children moving into foster care. So far 500 backpacks filled with toiletries, toys, and comfort items have accompanied foster children to their new homes, providing them with things of their own during this difficult transition. The group deals directly with the local county Department of Human Services.

In addition to getting supplies donated, the students have raised money through activities such as baby-sitting at a local church for a parents' night out and selling fresh flowers in vases they painted.

Jennifer said she could have found an established group in the community with the values she was looking for, but "I don't like just dropping my kids off," she said. "I guess … I felt I needed to be part of the community, too." Together, by creating an activity to share, she and her daughter have been brought closer together during the middle school years, when parents and their children often drift apart.

They hope other parents might try to form community service groups of their own, maintaining that the commitment can involve just a few hours a month if well organized. The children don't have to meet often. They also are considering changing it to an after-school enrichment class to involve more children.

This idea is just one of many for community service projects that parents and kids could start or be involved in together. Jennifer has generated the following tips for parents who are interested in starting a community service project of their own:

1. Come up with an idea: Inspiration can come from a book, newspaper article, something mentioned by a family member or friend, or a need identified by a social service group.
2. Research: Contact a local social service agency or organization to find out more about the community needs, programs already in place, and what help would be welcomed.
3. Remain flexible: An agency or organization might refer you to another, more suitable one or make suggestions on how to modify the project.
4. Spread the word: Tap existing networks such as classmates, sports teams and neighbors to find children and parents interested in joining the effort.
5. Get help: Approach local businesses and schools for help with supplies or meeting places. Recruit other parents to assist in the work and supervision.

Kids That Care represents a positive movement in our culture—parents and kids rising as equals to social challenges and finding new ways to share important experiences and values together. As always, actions speak louder than words. *Kids That Care* has demonstrated that the gift of involvement and giving extends far beyond any toy. You (and kids you know) can do it, too.

Harmony Barrett lives in Boulder, Colorado. She is always interested in finding new ways to stay involved in kids' lives and help inspire them. In addition to Kids That Care, Jennifer McCoy volunteers in many arenas, her childrens' schools and community. She is the mother of two.

Reprinted with Permission from Full Esteem Ahead, *Wings,* Winter 2002.

Hands on Portland: Volunteering Made Easy

To build community and enrich lives by providing a gateway to service and empowering volunteers

By Kathy Masarie, MD

HANDS ON PORTLAND IS a treasure in Portland, Oregon. It is a one-stop-shop for done-in-a-day volunteer projects and it can be mimicked in any community. Through this website you can explore what really grabs you as a volunteer—from working in gardens, tearing up ivy, painting, serving meals, shopping, washing cats ... who knows until you've tried it. A family can sign up for an activity once and move on to a new one. Eventually the hope is that you will get "hooked" and stick with a

certain activity. Take Michael who washed cats for the Humane Society one Saturday afternoon when he was in middle school. When his service-learning requirement came up in high school a few years later, he knew where to go. He went beyond just filling up his hours. He liked the work and knew he was committed to the cause.

Hands on Portland breaks down a lot of the barriers that make volunteering difficult—it does the research for us by finding and listing meaningful work; it breaks down the commitment to "doable" proportions and makes the process of signing up online really easy. All

you have to do is go on their website, www. handsonportland.org, each month and pick the opportunities that await you. Here is a sampling of opportunities:

- Care for cats as they await adoption
- Repair bikes for low-income youth at the Community Cycling Center
- Play soccer with Ugandan refugees
- Get involved with the Transportation Alliance Bike Safety Program
- Serve a meal at a homeless shelter.
- Shop or deliver groceries for house-bound folks for Store to Door (a personal favorite)
- Do yard work for elderly with Project Linkage
- Play and do crafts with children at low-income apartment for Human Solutions
- Make cards for juvenile residents of Good Neighbor Center
- Organize school supplies or clothes at the PTA Clothing Center
- Paint Friends of the Children headquarters
- Beautify our world with Friends of Tryon Creek, Portland Community Garden, and Metro-Oxbow Park.

It was Fran Loosen, a committed volunteer in Portland, who decided that her city needed a central "clearing house" to connect willing volunteers with projects that required volunteer help. The result of her work has been extraordinary. The ease with which a person or family can volunteer for meaningful work has inspired the community to volunteer even more. What Fran did for her community by creating Hands on Portland can be replicated anywhere.

Contact www.handsonportland.org to see how you might get started in your community.

Asset-Building Stories from Our Greater Community and Businesses

Community (from Ann Lider, Co-Founder of LO-ABC Coalition) I was in one of the first *Raising Our Daughters* classes. I was really struck by how powerful the assets are and how many people come back to the assets as the "glue" to support kids in a healthy way. I met with my neighbor, Jann Lane, to brainstorm about asset building in Lake Oswego, OR, and we came up with the LO-ABC coalition. Jann helped bring together the mayor, our schools, and local businesses, including the town newspaper. This became way bigger than I ever thought it would be but we grew step-by-step. Our passion helped keep things going when we got overwhelmed or discouraged by funding struggles.

County-Sponsored Mini-Grants

"Take the Time" was a successful program of the Multnomah County Commission. For several years mini-grants of up to $500 were given to creative projects that helped build the 40 Developmental Assets in the lives of young people. Individual proposals for how the money could be spent were reviewed by volunteer adults and youth from the Portland, OR community. It is astounding how far a small amount of money can go, when combined with passion, determination and support of others. People were very creative, coming up with ideas that connected youth and adults, empowering kids with learning skills that they could use now and as adults and working to strengthen communities and schools. Any community can bring groups together into a coalition that funds and finds grants that can be given out to people who are willing to organize projects for the well-being of our youth. The results of many small projects can be powerful and influential.

Community Centers Build Community (from Glenda Montgomery)

Things have changed in Albuquerque, New Mexico. I'm glad they have. As a young professional couple, my husband and I had a blast starting out our married lives in Albuquerque; there was plenty for us to do to keep active and happy. But, when we had our kids, we noticed what Albuquerque didn't have many of at the time: community centers. There was one run-down YMCA near us, and we couldn't find any sign of a vital community center. As a young mom at home, I felt isolated and alone. I took my kids to the park every day, and because we could afford it, I took them to a private athletic club to learn how to swim. That was it. When I moved to Portland, Oregon, I couldn't believe the difference: a thriving community-center system linked my kids and me into feeling a sense of community and offered classes such as art, clay, woodworking, dance, cooking and swimming; and all of these were just a selection of classes offered to kids from 2 to 4 years old! It seems in Portland that every neighborhood has its own heart and this tends to be its Parks and Recreation Center. As a new mom in Portland, my days were easily filled with indoor park, "Tots and Moms" classes, yoga, aerobics, and a variety of other recreation center activities that allowed me to meet other at-home moms while my

kids met friends who shared common passions. Daddy-daughter dances, teen nights and basketball and volleyball drop-in leagues brought whole families together and connected them to other families. Through our move, we realized how crucial a community center system is to the building and nurturing of community feeling and to the quality of the lives of kids and families.

Company Sponsors School Programs and Provides Adult Volunteers. Tony Arnerich of AM&A, an investment firm, gets his employees involved with young people. The firm divides its employees up between three schools. There, 35 employees volunteer on company time to the tune of 1-2 hours per week. Activities range from reading tutors to a girls' club focusing on leadership skills, math and science clubs, and a study hall program. AM&A also hired a full-time coordinator to keep the programs running smoothly.

What motivates this business? The desire to show kids that they are important and so is their education. And Americh adds, "There is a huge but subtle business advantage in what we are doing. When you hire people who are willing to give back to the community, you get great people."

Church Youth Groups Provide Opportunities for Kids to Be Welcomed and Appreciated 15-year-old Sam seemed pretty introverted. He wasn't doing very well in school and hadn't committed to any kind of activity outside of class. Frankly, his mother was worried about him. He stayed home, watched movies and played guitar. He had no interest in sports. He had a couple of friends he hung out with, but he wasn't a part of anything … he didn't have a group. That changed when his best friend Karl took him to his church youth group. Sam wasn't sure to begin with, but with Karl as a buddy who was already a part of the community, Sam didn't have to work hard to become integrated. Where Karl was welcomed, Sam was too. Eventually, Sam found his niche. The kids in youth group were friendly and open. The leaders were excellent, providing Sam with a strong male role model that he didn't have in his single-mom household. They organized fun activities and outings that Sam began to take part in regularly, even if Karl was

unable to attend. He was going out and experiencing things that he would not have experienced otherwise. He began to feel comfortable and accepted and began to join in when the youth group went to services in the church. Sam and Karl played guitar for the congregation and were acknowledged and appreciated for their talent and their willingness to share that talent. Sam became known and welcomed by the larger group. When the

youth group became counselors for the children's summer camp, Sam realized that he was good working with kids and they showed their appreciation by looking up to him and using him as a role model. Now Sam's mother reports that her son is much more self-confident. He has come out of his shell and is aware of his talents and strengths and has a place to use them where they are acknowledged and are meaningful. He knows he can be himself and be appreciated for who he is by both adults and kids, for his wacky sense of humor and for his talents, and even just for his presence. What a gift! Church youth group allowed Sam to create a world for himself where he could be himself and where he enjoyed being. It took a vital high school youth group with strong adult leadership, a welcoming community, and the invitation of a friend.

What About Boys? National Resources for Boys AND Girls. The Ophelia Project was created to take up the cause of girls in our society. When it provided excellent resources to enhance the safety, health, self-esteem, competence and well-being of girls, people began to ask, "What about boys?" Relational aggression, bullying, health and well-being issues all exist for boys as well, but weren't being given the same attention. That was when the Boys Initiative was born. Instead of reinventing the wheel, The Boys Initiative was spawned from the Ophelia Project and brought together the same resources, though gender-specific to boys and their specific gender needs. They also tapped into resources for boys in the community that already existed. Speaker's bureaus, teacher-leader trainings and workshops for kids were set up, following the organizational pattern already in use by the successful Ophelia project, and using many of the same workshop ideas and trainings. Just like the Ophelia project, Boys Initiative offers programs at schools, community centers and libraries. It is committed to violence prevention, leadership development and peer support. Like the Ophelia Project, it functions as a resource to help create a world where kids can safely grow up to become competent, capable, compassionate members of society. The Boys Initiative stresses that "With the addition of a gender-specific perspective and accurate information about social and emotional development, youth and teen programs can be much more applicable, effective, and long-lasting." Both the Ophelia Project and The Boys Initiative are incredible resources. Check out: www.theopheliaproject.org and www.boysinitiative.org.

Stand for Children:
Grassroots Group Influences Government Decision-Making
By Glenda Montgomery

JONAH EDELMAN, THE Executive Director of Stand for Children, believes passionately in the power of grassroots movements to enact real change in our society. He also believes passionately in our responsibility to America's children: "To me, children are the most oppressed group in our society and our ill-treatment of them is a litmus test of where and who we are." Edelman explains that many caring Americans support advocacy groups that provide our politicians with information about our failure to support the health and well-being of children; yet he says, "I think that (having) good information is a necessary condition, but it is not a sufficient condition for change. The average politician knows that kids don't have health insurance and that schools don't have enough funding, and they choose not to address it because there's limited funding and competing priorities that are supported by more influential interests."[1] We parents need to become the influential interest that makes politicians pay attention. We can do that, he says, by banding together to build a powerful and persuasive force, able to push forward transformation at the very top ... on a political level.

Jonah Edelman's two passions converged as he helped to organize "Stand for Children Day" in Washington DC on June 1, 1996. More than 300,000 people showed up to make it the largest rally for the well-being of children in American history.[2] In 1998, he co-founded "Stand for Children" in Oregon, a grassroots organization of parents and other adults interested in the health, education and well-being of children, who work together to gain the political clout necessary to affect electoral and legislative change. Stand for Children focuses on supporting political candidates who demonstrate their commitment to the welfare of children. It builds effective local and statewide networks of advocates to convince elected officials and voters to invest in programs and public education to help children to become successful, productive citizens who thrive. Local chapters and teams of volunteers research key concerns, decide together on a focus issue, set specific goals for change and work in coalition with other organizations to produce significant results. Stand for Children has now grown to 2000 members and seven chapters.

Stand for Children has had great success in Oregon:
- ✓ **Helped elect a 60% pro-schools supermajority to the Oregon House of Representatives in 2008** by playing a key role in the successful campaigns of Brent Barton and Greg Matthews, who replaced incumbents with weak records on children's and education issues.
- ✓ **Helped secure $242 million to make urgent health and safety repairs to 48 Salem-Keizer schools, and build a middle school and three elementary schools** to relieve overcrowding by playing a key role in passing the largest bond measure for schools in the state's history.
- ✓ **Played a key role in renewing the Portland Children's Investment Fund,** which supports more than 60 cost-effective, proven programs delivering before- and after-school mentorship, early childhood education, child abuse prevention and intervention, and support for foster children (programs serve 16,000 Portland kids each year).
- ✓ **Prevented the loss of 160 teachers in Eugene** by helping renew the 4-J School District Local Option Levy, generating about $15 million per year—10% of the District's funding.
- ✓ **Enabled most school districts to begin to reduce class sizes and restore essential programs** by helping secure a K-12 appropriation of $6.245 billion for 2007-2009—the first reinvestment in more than a decade.
- ✓ **Increased teacher quality and retention** by designing and winning legislative approval for the Oregon New Educator Mentor Program, providing mentors for nearly 1,000 new K-12 teachers.
- ✓ **Confronted the epidemic of childhood obesity** by helping craft and pass statewide legislation requiring the removal of unhealthy snacks and drinks from school vending machines, student stores, and a là carte lines, thereby improving Oregon's national school nutrition rating from an F to an A-.[3]

Since 1998, other successful Stand for Children organizations have come together in Tennessee, Massachusetts, and Washington State. If you are interested in becoming involved in Stand for Children in any of these states or if you are interested in beginning a Stand for Children in your state, visit www.standforchildren.org.

---

[1] www.aecf.org/MajorInitiatives/RelatedInitiative/ProgramProfiles
[2] www.huntalternatives.org
[3] www.standforchildren.org

Businesses—Join Up and Volunteer Today

By Kathy Masarie, MD

At a time when it is so clear that involvement in the schools and in the community is critical to healthy youth, many companies are reaching out to help. They are setting up company-wide projects, making it convenient for everyone to get involved. Some are even giving employees paid time off to volunteer. Only 20% of US families consistently attend school programs and 40% never do. A study conducted by the Mattel Foundation discovered that lack of time was noted as a particular problem for many employees, particularly low-income parents. Employees said they need the support of their employers to provide them the flexibility to visit schools during working hours. Here are a few of the stories of employer support we have heard about.

> Lack of time is a major barrier keeping parents, especially low-income parents, from attending school programs.

There is a program that is reaching out to get adults involved in the schools. It is called "8 for Kids" sponsored by The Greater Hand-in-Hand Coalition and Children First for Oregon. It encourages businesses to provide employees with 8 hours of paid leave (or more) per year to be specifically used for school visits. This could include parent-teacher conferences, volunteering in the schools or mentoring a student. LSI Logic allows employees up to 40 paid hours to participate in children's school activities. The City of Portland is encouraging their employees to get involved as "a caring adult in the life of a child" through the school volunteer programs.

Small companies can be successful with employee volunteer programs too. S and J Heating and Air Conditioning gives their 12 employees eight hours of paid volunteer time per year, allowing these fathers to get involved in their child's education. Sheri Renhard, the former owner, said it was a win-win situation. Since they adopted the "8 for Kids" contract (available from Children First for Oregon), they have seen less sick leave, a higher retention rate and have actually come out ahead financially.

Morgan Anderson at Intel's Human Resources Department says they encourage volunteering by giving matching grants—for every hour their employee volunteers, the place where they are volunteering

> Employer flexibility is essential for allowing parents the opportunity to visit their children's schools during working hours.

receives $5, which at 15,000 hours added up to $74,000 donated last year. Intel even provides their own volunteer opportunities, such as Smart Reading, Boys and Girls Club, and Adopt-A-Family at Christmas.

Hanna Anderson gives back to the community in many ways. The company supports its workers by providing excellent benefits, including paying for almost half of employees' childcare costs and allowing for a flexible work week so that parents can go to children's doctor appointments, attend teacher conferences, run errands, or even volunteer. This company organizes volunteer opportunities and allows up to 16 paid hours annually for volunteer time. In addition, Hanna Anderson donates $100 to the classroom of each employee's child. The children are encouraged to decide how the money should be used in the classroom. This teaches them that their parent's employer cares about their education and future, as well as giving them a taste of altruism themselves.

Portland General Electric has supported its employee's efforts to enrich their communities for many years. Most of PGE's employees this year have already committed at least 16 hours of volunteer service through PGE-sponsored volunteer activities or by volunteering in their own neighborhoods or schools. Power Generation is the volunteer program of the employee's children. PGE puts money, people, and power into the communities where its employees live and work. Their success can even be seen with their retiree's commitment to community. They become very active volunteers after leaving their paid work. "It's just in us," a PGE retiree reports.

How about asking your employer to join in and begin creating a family-friendly workplace? If you own a business, use the stories above as examples to follow. How can we expect our kids to give back to the community and care for one another if we adults don't model it?

Reprinted with permission from Full Esteem Ahead, *Wings*, Spring 1999.

Take Your Kids to Work Day: Building Community in Business
By Sue Strater

Having been involved with the "Take Our Daughters to Work" Day at a previous employer, I was interested in starting it with my new company. This national program helps pre- and early-adolescent girls stay strong and confident by having them explore what contributions they can bring to the workplace. Being the mother of two boys, I wanted to expand the program to give girls and boys (ages 6 to 15) exposure to working adults, career choices, and our work environment. So, in 1998 at our company, Medicalogic, we started Kids Day, held on the national day for "Take Our Daughters to Work" (the fourth Thursday in April). Our first year, we had 45 children—belonging to 150 employees—participate. Three years later, we had 70 kids turn out, many for the third year in a row. My son, Zack, an 8-year-old, liked the idea of meeting new friends and seeing old friends each year at this event.

Planning
I set up a core team with volunteers from different departments—representatives from Software Development, Customer Support, Marketing, and Human Resources. A diverse team representing different careers met weekly at lunch for 5-6 weeks prior to the event. Our objectives were:
- Have the kids learn about our company and how we develop products.
- Have the kids learn about different careers.
- Have the employees learn from the kids.
- Make it fun for everyone.

The first meeting, we brainstormed potential activities in four categories—product-related, community-based, career-oriented, and fun. The other meetings covered areas like identifying trinkets for the kids, e.g. T-shirts, ordering food, registering kids so we knew the number and ages, identifying and getting materials, and finding rooms for the day. We divided the children into groups of about 12 for many events, and mixed boys and girls of all ages together—older kids helping the younger ones. Jenny, a 13-year old, said she "learned how to work well with younger kids" from being at Kids Day.

The Day
The day started with a few minutes together to cover rules and expectations, followed by a 15-minute talk by one of the executives. One year, the CEO gave a slide show about his personal and career choices while growing up. Another talk by our Product Development V.P. showed how the company started and grew. The kids were together for pizza lunch with parents and at the end for fun time—games, face painting, and more food. Each year, the kids created an art project that became part of Medicalogic's work environment. The first year, they created a mural on a lunchroom wall—putting paint on their hands or feet and leaving their mark. Another year, kids drew pictures of themselves in a career in which they were interested. We framed these to hang in conference rooms for employees to enjoy. To learn about our company, its products and customers, the kids role-played doctor, nurse or patient and created a medical chart on a computer. Another year, they simulated a surgical operation. To help the kids learn about different careers, employees played 20 questions with the kids who, in turn, tried to figure out what the employees did. One year, the Audubon Society came and the kids built birdhouses to take home. We placed some of the birdhouses on the wetlands next to our offices.

Lessons Learned
Make the activities hands-on and fun, get money budgeted for it, and include a member from Human Resources in your planning so they integrate the day's result into the company's culture. Take initiative and organize your own Kids Day! It's a tremendous learning experience for kids and employees. The kids might also learn one more thing: their parent's company cares about them.

Sue Strater works in Quality Assurance for a software organization and is the mother of two boys.

Reprinted with permission from Full Esteem Ahead, *Wings*, Winter 2001.

Final Session of Raising Our Sons
By Family Empowerment Network

CONGRATULATIONS! You have completed Family Empowerment Network's *Raising Our Daughters Parenting Guide*. We hope you have found strength in reading and collaborating with others, and it is our sincerest hope that you will remain connected as the next few critical years pass. It could be a quick chat in the halls, keeping an eye out for each other's kids or a more regular monthly or quarterly gathering. Talk with each other about how this might happen.

If you enjoyed the book, please encourage others to participate, purchase books of their own, and start a discussion group. This will foster the building of a community of people committed to our children. Consider becoming a mentor to help new groups to form in your community. It can be as simple as setting up a meeting to share your experience with others interested.

WHERE TO GO FROM HERE . . .
Individual Readers
If you have read this book on your own and liked it, we recommend that you start a group now. After reading the book, you now realize what a great difference it could make for you to create a support group for yourself. Get a group of friends or the parents of your daughter's friends together and discuss one chapter at each meeting. This will help make what you read come alive with possibility and will add richness and depth to your experience.

Discussion Group Readers
Many people find the continued connection and support from other parents invaluable, as their children move through adolescence. Many groups that end up staying together have a project or shared vision. This direction may have come up in the discussions as you went along, or may come up now as you pool all your ideas and see where you want to go. Here are just a few of many ideas:

Continued Regular Gatherings
Support Group
- You have shared for many sessions now—don't stop. Meet monthly over topics, books, videos, events, lunch or community activity. Some groups have even repeated this curriculum.
- Attend local lectures or conferences together.

Parenting Book Club
- Continue to learn by reading one parenting book a month and discussing it. Pick from our TOP TEN (p. 1: 10)

Parent-Child Book Club
- This is an awesome way for a group of kids and parents to bond, no matter what age you start

Mother-Daughter Group or Father-Daughter Group
- Start a mother-daughter or father-daughter group for fun, play, volunteering and learning together.

Parent-Child Gathering
- Bring both Mom and Dad and kids together. Let the kids plan the agenda.
- Consider a self-defense class together—everyone deserves that extra safety information.
- Volunteer together! Choose a project and jump in!

Parent Education and Networking
Seminars - bring a parent seminar to your school, community group or business

***Build Community by Fostering more* Raising Our Sons *or* Raising Our Daughters *Discussion Groups**
- If you have a son, consider starting a *Raising Our Sons* Discussion Group.
- Be a Parenting Group Organizer: set up a meeting via school newsletter/emails for parents interested in ways to support their sons and daughters proactively. Share experiences from your parenting group.
- Share your experience with the school counselor, or other staff member who might be interested in a group.

Project-Based Activities
- Get youth involved in leadership: start school-based volunteer activities or a Student Advisory Board.
- Start a *Parent Resource Committee* on your PTA to offer more resources and get more parents involved in the school.
- Bring *Girls' Night Out* or *Boys' Night Out* to your middle school—kids help plan it with teen mentors, who help run it.
- Bring *Turnoff* Week to your school with a parent-education program sent home.

Even if you don't start another formal activity, just keep talking to one another. Wave to your neighbors; say hello to kids as you pass them; go to PTA meetings; get involved in your community. You've taken a giant first step—just keep going!

Next Steps: A Tool for Creating a Vision and Taking Action

Step #1 Think of an inspirational vision or goal for you, your son and/or your family.
Don't limit yourself by thinking about how it will happen. Tap into what you really long for. Write it out in the present tense (as if you already had it). Is it something you have 100% control over? For example, rather than "I have a healthy relationship with my son" which reqires cooperation on his part, say "I prioritze connection and good communication with my son," which you have control over.

Step #2 Describe your present reality, where you are now. Include what interferes with achieving your goals. How do you support yourself now and how do you get support from others?

Step #3 List the action steps you will take to achieve your goal with a timeline attached. Include how to support yourself and what support would be helpful from others in achieving your goals.

	ACTION STEP	DUE DATE
1		
2		
3		
4		
5		
6		
7		
8		
9		
10		

CELEBRATION: Plan how you will celebrate when you have achieved your goal(s).

My Dream for All of Us: Authenticity, Self-Love and Self-Acceptance

By Kathy Masarie, MD, founder of Family Empowerment Network™

YOU SEE THIS PHOTO of my daughter when she was about 18 months. I remember this day. You can see the aliveness and sureness in her stride. She is confident, open, and most importantly, loving and accepting herself unconditionally. She was clear about herself then, where she fit in the world. She knew she was loved and that she mattered. When was the last time you loved yourselves unconditionally? When you felt "worthy" and "enough?" When was the last time your daughter loved herself unconditionally or your son loved himself unconditionally?

This is the dream I have for all of us—not only for our daughters and sons—but for parents, professionals, and all caring adults.

It is not about being perfect. Who is perfect anyway? If we were, it would be boring. What makes each and every one of us completely fascinating and lovable are our quirky differences, for better AND for worse.

When each of us can accept and love ourselves unconditionally, we can take on the world. When we are aware and accept what pulls us down, we can change it. When we share honestly what gets in our way, it empowers others to do the same. Together, with all of us open and authentic, we can direct our energy outward and contribute in a way the world has never seen.

Your daughters and sons are already part of a fantastic generation who have the loyalty of their traditionalist grandparents, the optimism of the boomer generation, tempered with the caution of the Gen X generation. With this rock-solid base, these realists can do the work needed to shift our direction from destruction and greed toward a life-sustaining society. What can you do to foster this?

You are now at a pivotal point. You have completed the *Raising Our Daughters* or *Raising Our Sons Parenting Guide*. We so hope your journey has been fruitful. What will you do with these new-found connections with other parents? In what ways will you commit to stretching yourself as a parent and caring adult? Knowing the importance of connection, how will you find more ways to connect with your own daughters and sons and with the other children in your neighborhood? How will you sustain the energy and keep this momentum going? Use the love, support, and empowerment you feel now to focus on what makes a real difference for your family. Have faith that when you start extending yourself, others will too, and watch the magic as the connected neighborhood you helped create starts to overlap with other connected communities. Together we will all contribute, one small step at a time, to building a culture that cares for our children and our children's children, and we will build a world in which every one of us will be accepted, supported and able to thrive.

> *If not now, when?*
> *If not us, who?*
> —Attributed to J.F.K.

Wishing you the best on your life-long journey as a parent.
Have fun and enjoy the ride.

Love,
Kathy

ACKNOWLEDGMENTS

Session 2: What Influences Him?

ROS 2:9   Excerpt from TV Timer - Bob: The Latest in Electronics and TV Time Management at
www.familysafemedia.com/tv_timer_hopscotch_bob.html

ROS 2:10   Excerpt reprinted with the permission of William Pollack, who is the author of *Real Boys:
Rescuing Our Sons from the Myths of Boyhood, Real Boys' Voices,* and *Real Boys' Workbook: The
Definitive Guide to Understanding and Interacting with Boys of All Ages.*

Session 4: Nourishing Healthy Masculinity

ROS 4:5   Excerpt from Thompson, Michael, PhD. *Raising Cain: Protecting the Emotional Life of Boys,*
2000. Pp. 11-12. Reprinted with permission from Random House.

ROS 4:5   Excerpt from Gurian, Michael. *The Wonder of Boys.* New York: Tarcher/Putnam, 1997.
Page 16.

ROS 4:31   Excerpt from Pollack, William. *Real Boys: Rescuing Our Sons from the Myths of Boyhood,* 1998.
Pp. 195 and 198. Reprinted with permission from Random House.

Session 5: Nurturing Emotions and Compassion

ROS 5:4   Excerpt reprinted with the permission of Scribner, A Division of Simon & Schuster, Inc.
from *I Don't Want to Talk About It: Overcoming the Secret Legacy of Male Depression* by Terry
Real. Copyright © 1997 by Terry Real. All rights reserved. Pp. 133-4.

Session 6: Teaching Him

ROS 6:6   Excerpt from Sobel, David. *Place-Based Education: Connecting Classrooms and Communities.*
Orion Society, 2004. Page 7.

ROS 6:41   Brief quotes from pp. xvi, 5, 13, 20 from *The Bully, The Bullied, and the Bystander* by Barbara
Coloroso. Copyright © 2003 by Barbara Coloroso. Reprinted by permission of
HarperCollins Publishers.

Session 7: Making Time for Him

ROS 7:7   Excerpt from Tolle, Eckhart. *The New Earth: Awakening to Your Life's Purpose.* New York:
Plume, 2006. Page 204.

Session 7: Cont'd

ROS 7:23   Excerpt from "Helicopter Parent." <u>Wikipedia, The Free Encyclopedia,</u> Wikimedia Foundation, Inc. <u>http://en.wikipedia.org/wiki/Helicopter_parent</u>.

ROS 7:23   Excerpt from Wade, Erin. 'You're a Helicopter Parent if you' from "8 Ways to Avoid Helicopter Parenting," The Dallas Morning News, August 15, 2005. Reprinted with permission of The Dallas Morning News.

Session 8: Keeping Him Safe

ROS 8:20   Excerpt from Ponton, Lynn. *The Romance of Risk*. New York: Harper Collins Publishers, 1997. Page 12.

Session 10: Creating Community for Him

ROS 10:4   Excerpt from Covey, Stephen. *The 7 Habits of Highly Effective Families*. New York: St Martin Press, Franklin Covey Company, 1997. Page 358. Reprinted with permission of Simon Schuster.

ROS 10:4   Excerpt from Pipher, Mary. *Shelter of Each Other*. New York: GP Putnam Sons, 1996. Page 81.

ROS 10:5   Excerpt used with permission of the authors of *What Young Children Need to Succeed* by Jolene L. Roehlkepartain and Nancy Leffert, Ph.D. (Minneapolis: Free Spirit Publishing, 2000). Pp. 287-288.

ROS 10:9   Excerpt from pp. 99-100 (303 words) from *High Tide in Tucson: Essays from Now or Never* by Barbara Kingsolver. Copyright © 1995 by Barbara Kingsolver. Reprinted by permission of HarperCollins Publishers.

Permissions

All material in this list is copyright protected. Please contact authors directly for reprint requests.
For permission of material not listed here, please contact www.family-empower.com.

Session 1: What's Happening to My Son?

The 40 Developmental Assets® framework, articles, handouts, data and statistics included in this publication have been reprinted with permission from Search Institute, 615 First Avenue NE, Suite 125, Minneapolis, MN 55413; 1-800-888-7828, www.search-institute.org. All rights reserved. The following are trademarks of Search Institute: Search Institute®, Developmental Assets®, MVParents℠, and Healthy Communities • Healthy Youth®.

The list of **40 Developmental Assets®** is reprinted with permission. Copyright © 1997, 2006 Search Institute®. All rights reserved. No other use is permitted without prior permission from Search Institute, 615 First Avenue NE, Minneapolis, MN 55413; www.search-institute.org.

"What I Want for My Sons" by Mark Amendola. Reprinted with permission from The Ophelia Project ® All rights reserved. Visit www.opheliaproject.org for more information or call 1-888-256-5437.

"Fast Facts About Developmental Assets for Youth" Reprinted with permission from *Pass It On! Ready to Use Handouts for Asset Builders* Handout [#3]. Copyright © 1999, 2006 Search Institute®, Minneapolis, MN; www.search-institute.org. All rights reserved.

"The Challenges Facing Communities" Reprinted with permission from *The Asset Approach: Giving Kids What They Need to Succeed.* Copyright © 1997 Search Institute®, 615 First Avenue NE, Minneapolis, MN 55413; www.search-institute.org. All rights reserved.

"The Power of Assets" Reprinted with permission from *The Asset Approach: 40 Elements of Healthy Development.* Copyright ©2002, 2006 Search Institute®, 615 First Avenue, NE, Minneapolis, MN 55413; www.search-institute.org. All rights reserved.

"How You Can Build Assets" Reprinted with permission from *The Asset Approach: Giving Kids What They Need to Succeed.* Copyright © 1997 Search Institute®, 615 First Avenue NE, Minneapolis, MN 55413; www.search-institute.org. All rights reserved.

"Asset Building Difference" Reprinted with permission from *Pass It On! Ready to Use Handouts for Asset Builders* Handout [#6]. Copyright © 1999, 2006 Search Institute®, Minneapolis, MN; www.search-institute.org. All rights reserved.

"Are Americans Afraid of Youth" Reprinted with permission from Kathleen Kimball-Baker, "Are Americans Afraid of Youth," *Assets: The Magazine of Ideas for Healthy Communities and Healthy Youth.* Copyright © Summer 1999 by Search Institute®, Minneapolis, MN; www.search-institute.org. All rights reserved.

"Connecting with Boys Closing the Asset Gap" Reprinted with permission from Eugene Roehlkepartain, "Connecting with Boys Closing the Asset Gap," *Assets: The Magazine of Ideas for Healthy Communities and Healthy Youth.* Copyright © Summer 2001 by Search Institute℠, Minneapolis, MN; www.search-institute.org. All rights reserved.

"Raising Better Boys" Reprinted with permission of Geoffrey Canada, Harlem Children's Zone, 2770 Broadway, New York, NY, 10025. Originally published in the *Educational Leadership Journal,* December 1999/January 2000, by Association for Supervision and Curriculum Development © 1999.

"The Asset Checklist" Reprinted with permission from *The Asset Approach: Giving Kids What They Need to Succeed.* Copyright © 1997 Search Institute®, 615 First Avenue NE, Minneapolis, MN 55413; www.search-institute.org. All rights reserved.

Session 2: What Influences Him?

"Some Media Facts to Get Us Started" Reprinted with permission of Carol Ann McKay and Dr. Riva Sharples. Carol Anne McKay has worked as a nurse and an attorney and is currently teaching law in upstate New York. Dr. Riva Sharples is an Associate Professor with the Contemporary Media and Journalism Department, University of South Dakota.

"Our Children and Consumerism" Reprinted with permission of Carol Ann McKay and Dr. Riva Sharples (see above). Originally published in *The Ophelia Project Newsletter*, Aug 2003, www.opheliaproject.org.

"Fear Sells: Is No News Good News?" Reprinted with permission of Carol Ann McKay (see above).

"Internet Literacy: Safe Surfing in the Online World" Reprinted with the permission of Media Think: committed to strengthening critical thinking skills for understanding media, and empowering people to shape media that better serves the needs of individuals and communities (formerly Northwest Media Literacy Center) at www.MediaThink.org.

"CyberbullyingNOT: Stopping Online Social Aggression" Reprinted with permission of Nancy Willard, author of *Cyberkids and Cyber Savvy Teens* at www.cyberbulling.org.

"TV-Free Families: Why—and How—They Unplug" by Nelle Nix. Reprinted with permission from Nelle Nix and *Metro Parent: Serving the Families of the Portland Metropolitan Area*, April, 2004, © *Metro Parent* at www.metro-parent.com. All rights reserved.

"12 Tips to Tame the Tube" Reprinted with permission of National Institute on Media and the Family: Building Healthy Families through the Wise Use of the Media. For reports on media research, latest recommendations, and more media tips see www.mediawise.org or contact 612-672-5437.

"Media Literacy in Action" Reprinted with the permission of Media Think (see above).

Session 3: Parenting Him

"Positive Discipline Guidelines" Reprinted with permission from Jane Nelsen, EdD, MFT, author of "Positive Discipline Guidelines", www.positivediscipline.com. For information on Jane Nelsen's seminars, please contact jane@positivediscipline.com.

"Taking Charge: Basic Concepts of JoAnne Nording's Caring Discipline" Written for Family Empowerment Network by JoAnne Nordling, author of *Taking Charge: Caring Discipline That Works, at Home and at School* and director of Parent Support Center at www.parentsupportcenter.org. For reprint information, please contact JoAnne Nordling at 503-796-9665 or info@parentsupportcenter.org.

"Your Emotions as Tools" Written for Family Empowerment Network by Glenda Montgomery, parent coach and Certified Positive Discipline Instructor in Portland, Oregon at www.positiveparentingpdx.com. For reprint information, please contact Glenda Montgomery at www.positiveparentingpdx.com.

"Parent's Job: Set Aside and Let the Kids Become Heroes" Reprinted with permission of Lionel Fisher. Originally from the Oregonian 9/25/04. Lionel Fisher is the author of several personal growth self-help books, including *Celebrating Time Alone: Stories of Splendid Solitude* (Beyond Words Publishing, 2001).

"Peaceful Parenting: How to Turn Parent-Child Conflict into Cooperation" from *Greater Good Magazine* Volume 4, Issue 3, Winter, 07-08. Reprinted with permission of Sura Hart and Victoria Kindle Hodson, MA. Sura and Victoria are co-authors of three books: *The Compassionate Classroom: Relationship Based Teaching and Learning; Respectful Parents, Respectful Kids: 7 Keys to Turn Family Conflict into Cooperation;* and *The No-Fault Classroom: Tools to Resolve Conflict and Foster Relationship Intelligence* (2008). They also offer consultation and workshops based off their website at www.k-hcommunication.com.

"Healthy Men, Strong Families: Thoughts on Being a Strategic Father Figure" Reprinted with permission of Howard Hiton, author of *BAM! Boys Advocacy and Mentoring* and *Helping Boys Succeed in Portland Public Schools*. For more information see www.BAMgroups.com and www.hitonassociates.net.

"Tips on Running a Successful Family Meeting" Written for Family Empowerment Network by JoAnne Nordling (see above). For reprint information, please contact JoAnne Nordling at 503-796-9665 or info@parentsupportcenter.org.

"Nine Steps to Raising Money Smart Kids" Reprinted with permission of MFS Fund Distributors, Inc.: Helping Yourself, Helping Your Parents, Helping Your Children. Check www.mfs.com for more financial information. All rights reserved.

Session 4: Nourishing Healthy Masculinity

"Men, Masculinities, and Media: Some Introductory Notes of the Tough Guise" Reprinted with permission by Jackson Katz. Jackson Katz, lecturer, anti-violence educator, anti-sexism, narrator of *Tough Guise*" video from National Media Education. Check outwww.jacksonkatz.com.

"Relationships with Family, Friends, Self, and Others" by Barbara A. Lewis. Excerpted from *What Do You Stand For? A Kid's Guide to Building Character* by Barbara A. Lewis, copyright © 2005. Used with permission of Free Spirit Publishing Inc., Minneapolis, MN; 1-800-735-7323, www.freespirit.com. All rights reserved.

"When Our Kids Fight with Friends" Written for Family Empowerment Network by Glenda Montgomery, parent coach and Certified Positive Discipline Instructor in Portland, Oregon at www.positiveparentingpdx.com. For reprint information, please contact Glenda Montgomery at www.positiveparentingpdx.com.

"Fun Things To Do When You're Alone" by Barbara A. Lewis (see above).

Session 5: Nurturing Healthy Emotions

"Passionate Parenting" Written for Family Empowerment Network by Kris King, owner of Wings Seminars/Innovative Learning Group. Wings is a Personal Development Centre that offers experiential seminars in personal development and communication skills. Please contact Kris King at www.wings-seminars for reprint permission.

"Parent as Coach" Written for Family Empowerment Network by Diana Sterling, CEO of New Generations and author of *The Parent as Coach Approach: The Seven Ways to Coach your Teen in the Game of Life*. Visit www.parentascoach.com for more information. Please contact New Generations International at support@parentascoach.com for reprint permission.

"Staying Connected to Boys" Reprinted with permission of Howard Hiton, author of *BAM! Boys Advocacy and Mentoring*. Check out www.hitonassociates.net for a complimentary copy of "Connecting with Boys."

"Compassionate Connection: Attachment Parenting and Nonviolent Communication" and **"The Steps of NVC"** by Inbal Kashtan. Reprinted with permission of the author. Excerpted from her book, *Parenting From Your Heart: Sharing the Gifts of Compassion, Connection and Choice,* and also published in Mothering, Jan/Feb 2002. For copies of Inbal Kashtan's booklet, go to www.cnvc.org. For her CD, *Connected Parenting: Nonviolent Communication in Family Life,* and for workshop information, go to www.baynvc.org. All rights reserved.

"Parenting for Peace" by Inbal Kashtan. Reprinted with permission of the author. Excerpted from her book, *Parenting From Your Heart: Sharing the Gifts of Compassion, Connection and Choice* and also published in Paths of Learning (Spring 2003) and California HomeSchooler (Oct 2002). All rights reserved.

"Transforming Children's Anger" by Inbal Kashtan. Reprinted with permission of the author. From PuddleDancer Press Quick Connect, October 2006. All rights reserved.

"Ten Tips to Building Resilience" by American Psychological Association. Reprinted with permission from the American Psychological Association. Check out www.apahelpcenter.org/featuredtopics. All rights reserved.

"Building Moral Intelligence: 10 Tips for Raising Moral Kids" Reprinted with permission of Michele Borba, EdD, author of *Building Moral Intelligence: The Seven Essential Virtues that Teach Kids to Do the Right Thing* and 21 other wonderful books. For more information go to www.micheleborba.com.

"Developing Capable People" Reprinted with permission of Stephen Glenn and Jane Nelsen, authors of *Raising Self-Reliant Children in a Self-Indulgent World* at www.empoweringpeople.com. Jane Nelsen, EdD, MFT, is also the author of *Positive Discipline* and *Positive Discipline for Teenagers*; www.positivediscipline.com. For information on Jane Nelsen's seminars, please contact jane@positivediscipline.com.

Session 6: Teaching Him

"Every Student a Star: School Staff Reach Out To The Forgotten Half" Reprinted with permission from "Every Student a Star: : School Staff Reach Out To The Forgotten Half," *Assets: The Magazine for Ideas for Healthy Communities and Healthy Youth.* Copyright © Spring 2000 Search Institute®, Minneapolis, MN; www.search-institute.org. All rights reserved.

"Great Places to Learn: How Asset-Building Schools Help Students Succeed" Reprinted with permission from Neal Starkman PhD, Peter C. Scales PhD, and Clay Roberts MS, "Great Places to Learn," *Assets: The Magazine for Ideas for Healthy Communities and Healthy Youth.* Copyright © Autumn 1999 by Search Institute®, Minneapolis, MN; www.search-institute.org. All rights reserved.

"Asset Building Ideas for Teachers" Reprinted with permission from *Pass It On! Ready to Use Handouts for Asset Builders* Handout [#28]. Copyright © 1999, 2006 Search Institute®, Minneapolis, MN; www.search-institute.org. All rights reserved.

"At Home in Our Schools: A Guide to School-Wide Activities That Build Community" Reprinted with permission of Developmental Studies Center, 2000 Embarcadero, #305; Oakland, CA 94606, 1-800-666-7270, www.devstu.org. Copyright 1994. All rights reserved.

"Summary of Strategies to Help Boys Learn" Reprinted with permission of Howard Hiton, author of *Helping Boys Succeed in Portland Public Schools* and *BAM! Boys Advocacy and Mentoring.* For a free download of *Helping Boys Succeed in Portland Public Schools* check out www.hitonassociates.net.

Session 7: Making Time for Him

"Fifteen Steps to a Simpler Life" Reprinted with permission of Victoria Moran, author of *Shelter for the Spirit: Create Your Own Haven in a Hectic World.* Moran is a certified life coach, motivational speaker, and the author of other books including *Fit from Within, Fat, Broke & Lonely No More,* and the best-selling *Creating a Charmed Life.* To learn more about her work or subscribe to her free E-zine, "The Charmed Monday Minute," visit www.victoriamoran.com.

"Vote With Your Life" by Janet Luhrs from *Simple Living.* Reprinted with permission of Healthy Directions, LLC. To subscribe to *Simple Living* by Janet Luhrs visit www.simpleliving.com or call 1-888-577-6164.

"Your Money or Your Life: Are You Making A Dying or Making a Life" by Joe Dominguez and Vicki Robin authors of *Your Money or Your Life.* Reprinted with permission of Healthy Directions, LLC. To subscribe to *Simple Living* by Janet Luhrs visit www.simpleliving.com or call 1-888-577-6164.

"Remaking a Living" Reprinted with permission of Brad Edmondson, who currently lives in Ithaca, NY. The article was originally published in *Utne Reader,* July/August 1991.

Session 8: Keeping Him Safe

"The Power of Assets" Reprinted with permission from *The Asset Approach: 40 Elements of Healthy Development.* Copyright ©2002, 2006 Search Institute®, 615 First Avenue, NE, Minneapolis, MN 55413; www.search-institute.org. All rights reserved.

"Communication Tips for Parents" Reprinted with permission of © SIECUS. From *What Do I Do?* (New York: Sexuality Information Council of the United States, 1996). www.siecus.org/pubs/pubs0004.html.

"Talking Back: Ten Things Teens Want Parents To Know About Teen Pregnancy" Reprinted with permission of National Campaign to Prevent Teen Pregnancy, © 2001. Contact www.teenpregnancy.org/tip.

"A Recipe for Healthy Relationships" Reprinted with permission of the Raphael House from *Take Care: A Guide to Safe Relationships. Take Care* is a Raphael House prevention project in Portland, Oregon. Contact: (503) 222-6507 or www.raphaelhouse.com.

"Abuse in Teen Dating Relationships" by Jeannie LaFrance. Reprinted courtesy of Jeannie LaFrance and Bradley-Angle House, www.bradlegangle.org, 503-232-7805. The National Domestic Violence Hotline is 1-800-799-SAFE.

"Dater's Bill of Rights" National Crime Prevention Council © 1997. Reprinted with permission from National Crime Prevention Council, 1000 Connecticut Avenue, NW, 13th floor, Washington, DC 20036. For more information check out www.ncpc.org.

"Power of Parents – Teen Drinking" Written for *Family Empowerment Network* by Emily Moser, MPA, MA, Director of Parenting Programs at Oregon Partnership. For reprint permission contact Emily Moser at emoser@orpartnership.org, 503 244-5211, or www.orpartnership.org.

"Did You Know: Facts about Risky Driving" and **"Graduated Licensing in Oregon"** by Cathy Bowles, Trauma Nurses Talk Tough Not My Kid. Reprinted with permission from the *"NOT MY KID" Campaign Parent Handbook*. Materials and Program made possible through funds from ODOT, TSD and NSTSA. Section 410 Grant and "Trauma Nurses Talk Tough: Family Education" at www.legacyhealth.org/tntt.

"Contract for Life" Reprinted with permission from SADD, Inc. SADD– Students Against Destructive Decisions is "students helping students make positive decisions about challenges in their everyday life" with many great resources at www.sadd.org..

Session 9: Supporting Him

"The Role of a Mentor" and **"The Stance of a Mentor"** by Stan Crow. Reprinted with permission of Rites of Passage Journeys, who offer rites of passage programs and several kinds of backpacking and camping adventures for kids and for adults—all in the state of Washington. To find out more, go to www.ritesofpassagejourneys.com.

"Collective Work" by Kevin Riley from *ICA Rite of Passage Journeys*, No 1, 1997. Reprinted with permission of Rites of Passage Journeys (see above).

"Finding a New Skin: Rites of Passage from Child to Youth" by John Burbidge from *ICA Rite of Passage Journeys*, No. 1, 1997. Reprinted with permission of Rites of Passage Journeys (see above).

"Tell Me More and Other Great Tips on Connecting with Your Kids" Reprinted courtesy of Positive Coaching Alliance. Check out more great resources on healthy coaching at www.positivecoach.org.

"Teaching Independence and Responsibility versus Compliance and Conformity" and **"Organized, Competitive Sports versus Everyday Life: A Comparison"** Reprinted with permission by Carnegie Corporation of New York.

"Asset Building Ideas for Coaches" Reprinted with permission from *Pass It On! Ready to Use Handouts for Asset Builders* Handout [#37]. Copyright © 1999, 2006 Search Institute®, Minneapolis, MN; www.search-institute.org. All rights reserved.

Session 10: Creating Community

"Adding Up Assets" Reprinted with permission from Peter Benson, "Asseteria: Adding Up Assets," *Assets: The Magazine of Ideas for Healthy Communities and Healthy Youth*. Copyright © Autumn 1999. Search Institute ®, Minneapolis, MN; www.search-institute.org. All rights reserved.

"Listen Up Adult Advocates" Reprinted with permission from Kalisha Davis, "Asseteria: Listen Up Adult Advocates," *Assets: The Magazine of Ideas for Healthy Communities and Healthy Youth*. Copyright ©, Summer 2000. Search Institute ®, Minneapolis, MN; www.search-institute.org. All rights reserved.

"Making A Difference One by One" by Peter L. Benson from *All Kids Are Our Kids*. Reprinted with permission of John Wiley and Sons Inc.

"Brewing Up Assets" Reprinted with permission from Kay Hong, "Brewing Up Assets: A Friendly Adult Stirs in Some Support," *Assets: The Magazine of Ideas for Healthy Communities and Healthy Youth*. Copyright © Spring 2000 Search Institute ®, Minneapolis, MN; www.search-institute.org. All rights reserved.

● ●

"Asset Building Ideas for Neighborhood Groups" Reprinted with permission from *Pass It On! Ready to Use Handouts for Asset Builders* Handout [#27]. Copyright © 1999, 2006 Search Institute®, Minneapolis, MN; www.search-institute.org. All rights reserved.

"Building Community—One Porch at a Time" Reprinted with permission from "Building Community—One Porch at a Time," *Assets: The Magazine of Ideas for Healthy Communities and Healthy Youth.* Copyright © Autumn, 1998 Search Institute℠, Minneapolis, MN; www.search-institute.org. All rights reserved.

"Why Aren't There More Dad's Groups?" by Joe Kelly. © New Moon Girl Media, all rights reserved. Reprinted from www.daughters.com with permission of New Moon Girl Media www.newmoon.com and Joe Kelly www.TheDadMan.com.

"Teens Triumph over Techno-Tribulations" Reprinted with permission from "Asseteria: Teens Triumph over Techno-Tribulations," *Assets: The Magazine of Ideas for Healthy Communities and Healthy Youth.* Copyright © Autumn, 1998 by Search Institute®, Minneapolis, MN; www.search-institute.org. All rights reserved.

Index

About the Authors

KATHY MASARIE, MD is generous in heart and in spirit. Her caring commitment to the well-being of families touches all facets of her life. As a pediatrician, she spent extra time to get to know each family. As the founder of Full Esteem Ahead, a non-profit to support families, she worked with thousands of caring adults to help kids stay healthy and thrive. As a parent and life coach, she proactively improves family dynamics for connection and success. Through all of this, her focus has always been on prevention and early action. She wants to share with caring adults everywhere what she has learned from her life's work with children and families. These two books, *Raising our Sons* and *Raising our Daughters Parenting Guides,* are the realization of that dream. She lives in Oregon with her husband, and considers her son and daughter to be her greatest teachers and inspiration in life. They are now two strong, authentic young adults. Her other passions in life include biking, a commitment to life-long learning and connection with family and friends.

JODY BELLANT SCHEER, MD is a pediatrician whose dream is creating healthy relationships and peaceful co-existence within all families, institutions and communities of the world. She has worked for over 27 years with sick newborns, premature infants and their families in Portland, OR. She is co-founder of Medical and Educational Relief International Association (MERIA), Inc, a nonprofit working to provide essential medical and educational services worldwide. As well, she regularly volunteers as a physician in developing countries, serves as a volunteer and Board member of numerous non-profit organizations, is a foster parent, and teaches compassionate communication skills to medical, parent and community groups. She loves spending time in nature through hiking, kayaking, and traveling to diverse corners of the world. She lives with her husband on a houseboat in Oregon, where they enjoy frequent visits from their three adult children and large extended family.

KATHY KELLER JONES, MA is a developmental psychologist and licensed school counselor. For nearly 25 years she has supported elementary and middle schools by teaching social-emotional skills to students, conducting group and individual therapy, consulting with staff and parents, and creating school-community connections. She currently teaches parenting classes and consults with parents on the many challenges of doing their job well. In addition to working with children and families, Kathy has worked as a writer and a research psychologist. She is interested in the individual's search for meaning and the importance of one's connection to nature. She has an MA from Ohio State University, and post-graduate training in her areas of special interest—Jungian/archetypal psychology and play therapy. She and her husband live in Oregon and share the joys of nature with their adult children and their partners, two dogs, a cat and two chickens.